On This Day
in
Tudor
History

MadeGlobal
Publishing

ON THIS DAY
IN
TUDOR HISTORY

ISBN-13: 978-84-943721-9-3

M MadeGlobal Publishing

For more information on
MadeGlobal Publishing, visit our website:
www.madeglobal.com

First published in 2012 by CreateSpace
Second Edition 2015 by MadeGlobal Publishing

To Tim, Christian, Verity & Joel,
Always and forever
xxxx

In memory of Suzanne Crossley (1971-2015),
The best friend ever
x

Acknowledgements

This book is the result of over three years of hard work and the support and encouragement of many people. Apologies if I miss anyone out.

Nasim Tadghighi and Paul Wiltshire for reminding me of "on this day in history" events I'd missed in my research via their tweets.

The Anne Boleyn Files visitors and Anne Boleyn Fellowship members for their ongoing encouragement.

Authors and historians Leanda de Lisle, Suzannah Lipscomb, John Guy and Julia Fox for all their encouragement over the past few years.

George Skipwith and his team at Rosslare Arts International for their editing skills.

My family for putting up with me researching and writing at all hours of the day and night – sorry!

Clare Cherry for being there to bounce ideas off and for keeping me grounded.

Sarah Bryson of the blog Anne Boleyn from Queen to History, Emma Fuery and Darren Wilkins of the Tudor Roses, and author J Thorn for all your support. Thank you!

INTRODUCTION

The Tudor period ran from the accession of Henry VII, after the *Battle of Bosworth* on 22nd August 1485, to the death of Elizabeth I, the last Tudor monarch, and Henry VII's granddaughter, on 24th March 1603. In those 118 years, six monarchs ruled England – albeit one who was quickly removed – and two were iconic monarchs whose images are still recognised throughout the world today: the tyrannical Henry VIII and Elizabeth I, the Virgin Queen.

The Tudor period is a fascinating period for history lovers. The Reformation was sweeping through Europe, there were challenges to the throne, bloody executions, brutal persecutions, the plague, disease, poverty and superstition. And, of course, it was the time in which England broke with Rome, the Church of England was formed and two queens were executed on the orders of their husband, the King. England would never be the same. It wasn't all bad, though. There were also the Renaissance and Elizabeth I's Golden Age, with the births of poets and playwrights like William Shakespeare, Christopher Marlowe and Philip Sidney.

This book will take you through the year, giving details of key events that happened on those days in Tudor history - births, deaths, marriages, baptisms, executions, annulments, battles, treaties and more – as well as information on feast days and Tudor traditions. You will notice that there are many more deaths than births in this book, and that is because many people's births were not recorded; parish records, unfortunately, do not go that far back.

My thanks go to visitors to The Anne Boleyn Files website and Facebook page for encouraging me to continue my research and to expand my little daily "on this day in history" posts into a full length book. I hope you enjoy it as much as I have enjoyed researching it.

A NOTE ON THE 2ND EDITION

When I first published this book in 2012, writing and publishing was a completely new experience for me. I didn't know if people would be interested in a work that was this long, and whether anyone would consider buying it. I'm pleased to say that this book has been an incredible success and people have been using it as a reference guide for more than three years.

The second edition of "On This Day in Tudor History" contains the same information as the first edition, so please don't buy this one if you're looking for something different.

The main reason for re-publishing the book is that the original version was not available for purchase from a wide range of bookstores. This one is available in book stores as well as online and in e-book format.

I have also made some additions - some more "on this day in history"s for you

Thank you for buying this book and I wish you an exciting adventure through Tudor History.

CLAIRE RIDGWAY

Using this Book

On this Day in Tudor History is laid out as a modern diary or calendar, from 1st January to 31st December, even though the Tudor *New Year* began on 25th March, "Lady Day". This makes it easy to find the date you're looking for. You will also find sections on Lent, Easter and Christmas.

As well as reading this book from cover to cover, to learn more about the Tudor period, you can also use *On this Day in Tudor History* for:

- *Educational purposes* – It's an excellent resource for teachers and children studying a Tudor topic.

- *Competitions and quizzes* – The perfect resource for pub quizzes and trivia nights.

- *Birthdays* – If your friend is a Tudor history lover, then why not add a Tudor fact to their birthday card?

- *Annoying* (sorry, I mean educating) friends, family and work colleagues on a daily basis with your Tudor trivia. *Wow* them with your knowledge!

- *Dipping into* – over your morning coffee you can expand your mind.

There are many quotations from primary sources, such as chronicles and letters from the Tudor period, and the old English may baffle you at first and look like nonsense because there was no standardized spelling. Simply read aloud and remember that "u"s and "v"s tend to be interchangeable, all will become clear!

Note: The House of Stuart is spelled as both "Stuart" and "Stewart", and both are correct. Apparently the "Stuart" spelling came from the French version of the name because there was no letter "w" in the French language.

THE TUDOR DYNASTY

Henry VII (1457-1509)

Ruled from 22nd August 1485 to his death on 21st April 1509.

Henry VIII (1491-1547)

Son of Henry VII. Ruled from 21st April 1509 to his death on 28th January 1547.

Edward VI (1537-1553)

Son of Henry VIII. Ruled from 28th January 1547 to 6th July 1553.

Lady Jane Grey (1537-1554)

Granddaughter of Mary Tudor, Queen of France, great-granddaughter of Henry VII. Ruled from 6th July 1553 to 19th July 1553, when Mary I was proclaimed Queen. She was executed on 12th February 1554 for treason.

Mary I (1516-1558)

Eldest daughter of Henry VIII, and his first wife, Catherine of Aragon. Ruled from 19th July 1553 to her death on 17th November 1558.

Elizabeth I (1533-1603)

Daughter of Henry VIII and his second wife, Anne Boleyn. Ruled from 17th November 1558 to her death on 24th March 1603. She died childless, and James VI of Scotland ascended to the throne, becoming James I and starting the Stuart period.

House of Stuart
The Scottish Monarchy
during the Tudor Period

James III of Scotland (1451-1488)

Ruled from 3rd August 1460 to his death on 11th June 1488. He was the son of James II.

James IV of Scotland (1473-1513)

Ruled from 11th June 1488 to his death on 9th September 1513 at the *Battle of Flodden*. He was the son of James III.

James V of Scotland (1512-1542)

Ruled from 9th September 1513 to his death on 14th December 1542. He was the son of James IV.

Mary, Queen of Scots, or Mary I of Scotland (1542-1587)

Ruled from 14th December 1542 to 24th July 1567, when she was forced to abdicate. She was the daughter of James V.

James VI of Scotland/James I of England (1566-1625)

Ruled Scotland alone from 1567 to 1603 and then ruled England, Scotland and Ireland as James I from 24th March 1603 until his death on 27th March 1625. He was the son of Mary, Queen of Scots.

The Tudor Calendar
Feast Days and Special Days

Note: The calendar starts on 25th March, because that's when the Tudor *New Year* began.

March

25th "Lady Day", or the *Feast of the Annunciation of the Blessed Virgin* - This feast day commemorated the day that Mary was first told she was carrying Jesus. It was the first day of the Tudor Calendar.

April

23rd – *St George's Day* – The feast day of the patron saint of England and also the day for announcing new appointments to the Order of the Garter, the highest order of chivalry in England. Some towns held special St George's Day processions, complete with replica dragons and statues of St George, and pageants depicting George killing the dragon.

25th – *St Mark's Day*

May

1st – *May Day* – The main spring celebration. Traditions included going to local woods to "make the may", i.e. collect greenery and make garlands, the singing of bawdy songs, and decorating and dancing around the maypole. The royals celebrated with jousting and pageants.

June

2nd – *St Elmo's Day* – The traditional day for sheep shearing.

24th – *Midsummer and the Feast of St John the Baptist* – Traditions included bonfires in the streets, midsummer 'watches', which consisted of processions and pageants, and a lit cartwheel being rolled down a hill. It was said that if the fiery wheel got to the bottom without the fire being extinguished, there would be a good harvest.

29th – *Feast of St Peter and St Paul*

Rushbearing Ceremonies – These ceremonies took place in the summer, and consisted of villagers replacing the old rushes that covered the earth floors of the church with fresh, sweet-smelling rushes. Each village had its particular day for this tradition.

Church ales – Fund-raising events, which consisted of feasting and drinking, held in the summer months.

July

2nd – *Feast of the Visitation of the Blessed Virgin Mary*
15th – *Feast of St Swithin*
22nd – *Feast of St Mary Magdalen*

August

1st – *Lammastide*, or *Lammas Day* – The festival of the wheat harvest. It was celebrated with games like apple bobbing, processions of candles and decorating the home with harvest garlands.

15th – *Feast of the Assumption of the Virgin Mary*
24th – *Feast of St Bartholomew*

September

Harvest Home – A festival to celebrate the last corn sheaf being harvested. Traditions included crowning the last of the harvest with a crown of flowers and feasting at the harvest home supper.

29th – *Michaelmas*, or the *Feast of St Michael* – A traditional feast of goose or chicken was enjoyed.

October

First Sunday - Wakes were held at the end of the summer to celebrate the dedication of the local parish church, and in Henry VIII's reign, the date became fixed as the first Sunday in October.

18th – *Feast of St Luke*

25th – *Feast of St Crispin and St Crispinian* – Celebrations included bonfires, revelry and the crowning of a King Crispin. The day also marked the anniversary of Henry V's victory at the *Battle of Agincourt*.

31st – *All Hallows Eve – The Feast of the Dead*, a night to mark the passage of souls through purgatory. It was believed that the souls walked the earth on *All Hallows Eve*, so masks were worn and bonfires lit to protect people from evil spirits.

November

1st – *All Saints* – With the *Reformation*, this went from a day of remembering the dead and helping them move through purgatory through prayer, to commemorating the Saints.

11th – *Feast of St Martin*

17th – *Crownation Day* – This was a feast day in Elizabethan England because it was the anniversary of Elizabeth I's accession to the throne.

30th – *Feast of St Andrew*

December - Advent and Christmas

Advent, the four weeks leading up to Christmas, was a time of fasting which did not end until Christmas Day. Alison Sim, in "Pleasures and Pastimes in Tudor England", writes of how Christmas Eve was particularly strict, and Tudor people were not allowed to eat eggs, cheese or meat.

On Christmas Day, the festive celebrations began early with a mass before dawn and two further masses later in the day. Church congregations held lighted tapers as the genealogy of Christ was sung, and then they went home to enjoy a well-deserved Christmas Day feast.

For details on the *Twelve Days of Christmas* see the December section.

26th – *Feast of St Stephen*
28th – *Holy Innocents' Day* or *Childermas*
29th – *Feast of St Thomas of Canterbury*

January

1st – New Year's gifts were given to the monarch. Although the Tudor New Year began on 25th March, this gift-giving came from the Roman tradition of New Year.

6th – *Twelfth Night* (Epiphany) - *Epiphany* was the most important feast day of the year, and was celebrated with a church service, feasting and entertainment, such as masques.

Plough Monday – *Plough Monday* was the official end of the *Twelve Days of Christmas*, and was the time when work on the land began again. Most farmers took turns using a communal plough, which was often kept in the church during the *Twelve Days of Christmas*. Often, a plough light would be kept burning before the Sacrament or Rood until *Plough Monday*, when the younger men of the parish would collect the plough, harness themselves to it and drag it around demanding money from people, and ploughing up the ground in front of their door if they didn't give them any. In 1538, Henry VIII banned the plough light in churches, and ten years later Edward VI banned the *Plough Monday* festivities completely.

13th – *Feast of St Hilary*

25th – *Feast of the Conversion of Saint Paul the Apostle*

February

2nd – *Purification of the Virgin*, or *Candlemas* – This feast day commemorated the purification of the Virgin Mary after the birth of Christ, but was also seen as the start of spring. It was marked by a special *Candlemas* service in which the people processed with candles lit by the priest when he blessed them.

14th – *St Valentine's Day* – Historian Alison Sim writes of how "valentines were chosen by lot from among a group of friends, who then had to buy their valentine a gift."

24th – *Feast of St Matthias the Apostle*

Moveable Feasts

Lent - See section between February and March

Easter - See section between March and April

Rogation Sunday – The fifth Sunday after Easter. The local people and clergy processed around the fields carrying the church's cross and banners to bless the fields and pray for a good harvest.

Whitsun/Pentecost – This took place fifty days after *Easter*. It commemorated the coming of the Holy Spirit to the first Christians at *Pentecost*, and was marked by processions in some towns.

Trinity Sunday – The eighth Sunday after *Easter*.

Corpus Christi – This was celebrated on the Thursday after *Trinity Sunday*, and was a popular summer festival of processions and plays with a biblical theme.

NEW YEAR

Although the Tudor *New Year* did not begin until 25ᵗʰ March, upper classes exchanged *New Year's* gifts on 1ˢᵗ January. Tudor poet Thomas Tusser wrote about gift giving, saying:

"At Christmas of Christ many Carols we sing, and give many gifts in the joy of that King."

Historian Alison Sim writes of how gift giving was treated very seriously at the Tudor court, and that gifts had major political significance. There are still records today outlining the instructions for the reception of gifts at the court of Henry VIII. After the King dressed in his chamber, one of the Queen's servants would bring him a gift from the Queen, and then he would receive gifts from other courtiers. While he was doing that, the Queen would receive gifts in her chamber.

The way that a monarch responded to a person's gift was very telling of who was in royal favour. In 1532, Henry VIII refused Catherine of Aragon's gift, while accepting the one from Anne Boleyn, and Elizabeth I famously refused the Duke of Norfolk's gift of a beautiful jewel in 1571, because he was in the Tower of London for being involved in a revolt against the crown. A monarch was meant to respond to gifts by giving the giver something in return, and it was expected that they would give them something more expensive than the item that had been given to them.

1ST JANUARY

On *New Year's Day* 1511, Queen Catherine of Aragon gave birth to a son, Henry, Duke of Cornwall. His birth was met with celebrations throughout England - bonfires, wine flowing through the streets of London, cannons firing, pageants, banqueting and jousts - he was, after all, King Henry VIII's only son and heir.

A few days after his birth, little Henry was christened at the Chapel of Observant Friars at Richmond. The French King, Louis XII, had been chosen to be one of his godfathers, and so sent a golden cup and salt as christening gifts. William Warham, Archbishop of Canterbury, was the other godfather, and Margaret of Austria was his godmother, although she did not attend.

The prince was then put under the care of Elizabeth Poyntz and a staff, who included four "rockers" to rock his cradle and help him sleep, yeomen and grooms, and a physician. All the care in the world could not prevent his death shortly after the celebration pageants at Westminster, on 22nd February 1511, just fifty-two days after his birth. It is not known what caused his death, but infant mortality was high in Tudor England. Henry VIII and Catherine of Aragon were devastated. They had lost their baby, their "little Prince Hal", and the heir to the throne. Little did Henry know that it would be another twenty-six years until he had a surviving, legitimate son and heir.

1463 – Probable birthdate of Silvestro Gigli, diplomat and Bishop of Worcester, at Lucca in Italy. Gigli was nominated as Bishop of Worcester in December 1498, and enthroned in April 1499.

1540 – Henry VIII met his bride-to-be, Anne of Cleves, at Rochester. Following the great chivalric tradition, Henry disguised himself and attempted to kiss her, but a shocked Anne did not recognise him as King. It was a disastrous first meeting, and Henry was sorely disappointed that she could not recognise him as her true love.

1514 – Death of Louis XII of France, less than three months after his marriage to Mary Tudor, the sister of Henry VIII. He did not have a son, and so was succeeded by Francis I, his cousin's son and the husband of Louis' daughter, Claude. Louis was buried in Saint Denis Basilica.

1537 – Marriage of James V of Scotland and Madeleine de Valois, daughter of Francis I, at Notre Dame in Paris.

1556 – Nicholas Heath, Archbishop of York, became Mary I's Lord Chancellor.

2ND JANUARY

In 1539, Geoffrey Pole, son of Sir Richard Pole and Margaret Pole, Countess of Salisbury, was pardoned after attempting suicide for the third time.

Pole had been imprisoned in the Tower of London on 29th August 1538 after being banned from court, due to his brother Reginald's promotion as Cardinal. He was interrogated regarding letters he and his family had received from his brother, and words which he had uttered showing his support for the Cardinal, who had denounced the King and the royal supremacy in his treatise *Pro ecclesiasticae unitatis defensione* (*De unitate*). As a result of information gleaned from Geoffrey Pole, his brother, Henry Pole, 1st Baron Montagu, was arrested for treason along with his brother-in-law, Sir Edward Neville, and Henry Courtenay, Marquis of Exeter, and his family (wife Gertrude Blount and son Edward Courtenay). The three men were accused of conspiring against the King, seeking to deprive the King of his title of supreme head of the church and plotting with Cardinal Reginald Pole. Pole's mother, Margaret, was also arrested and imprisoned in the Tower of London.

Neville, Montagu, Exeter and Margaret were all executed for treason. Only Geoffrey survived, thanks to his broken spirit and his testimony against his family.

<hr>

1492 – King Boabdil surrendered Granada to the forces of King Ferdinand II of Aragon and Queen Isabella I of Castile.

1525 – Death of Sir William Uvedale. Uvedale had been created a Knight of the Bath and Knight of the Royal Body by Henry VII, and served Arthur, Prince of Wales, as his counsellor.

1536 – Eustace Chapuys, the Imperial Ambassador, arrived at the dying Catherine of Aragon's bedside in Kimbolton Castle.

1550 (2nd or 4th) – Death of Sir Christopher Barker, Richmond Herald, Norroy King of Arms and Garter Principal King of Arms, at Paternoster Row in London. He was buried in St Faith's under St Paul's.

1554 – Sir Thomas Wyatt the Younger and Sir Peter Carew were summoned to appear before Mary I's Privy Council. They ignored the summons and continued plotting what was to be *Wyatt's Rebellion*.

1598 – Death of Maurice Kyffin, soldier and author. He served Elizabeth I as Comptroller of the Musters to the army in Ireland from 1596, and is known for his *Deffynniad Ffydd Eglwys Loegr*, a Welsh translation of Bishop John Jewel's *Apologia*.

3RD JANUARY

On 3rd January 1521, Pope Leo X issued the papal bull *Decet Romanum Pontificem* excommunicating reformer, German priest and professor of theology Martin Luther from the Catholic Church.

The Pope had asked Luther to retract his "Ninety-Five Theses" (full name: "The Ninety-Five Theses on the Power and Efficacy of Indulgences or *Disputatio pro declaratione virtutis indulgentiarum*"), which Luther had published in 1517, but Luther refused. Luther was then called by Charles V, Holy Roman Emperor, to renounce or defend his religious stance at the Diet of Worms. He did not back down, and Charles V issued the *Edict of Worms* on 25th May 1521, declaring Luther an outlaw and heretic.

In his "Ninety-Five Theses", Luther had, amongst other things, attacked the sale of indulgences, emphasised that salvation was free through Christ by faith and repentance, explained the limiting power of the Pope, emphasised that true repentance should be a way of life and not earned by confession, and declared that it was blasphemous to consider the cross with papal arms on it as of equal worth of Christ's cross.

Luther is known for his doctrine of "Justification by Faith", the idea that salvation and redemption were only attainable through faith in Christ and by God's grace. Luther said "This one and firm rock, which we call the doctrine of justification, is the chief article of the whole Christian doctrine, which comprehends the understanding of all godliness."

◇◇

1540 – Official reception of Anne of Cleves at Greenwich Palace.

1541 – Anne of Cleves visited Hampton Court Palace to greet her former husband, Henry VIII, and his new wife, Catherine Howard, and to exchange *New Year's* gifts.

1541 – Death of John Clerk, Bishop of Bath and Wells, and diplomat to Henry VIII and Cardinal Wolsey. His final embassy was to the Duke of Cleves in 1540 to try and obtain an annulment of Henry VIII's marriage to Anne of Cleves. He died in Aldgate, London, and was buried at St Botolph's Church.

1590 – Death of Robert Boyd, Scottish nobleman, courtier and Protestant, at Kilmarnock. He was buried there in the Laigh Church. Boyd supported Mary, Queen of Scots, but could not support her marriage to the Catholic Lord Darnley, and so joined the Earl of Moray's faction, involving himself in the *Chaseabout Raid* of summer 1565. He managed to escape punishment by reconciling with Darnley. Boyd was also a member of the jury who acquitted the Earl of Bothwell for Darnley's murder in 1567, and supported his marriage to Mary.

4TH JANUARY

On the 4th January 1578, William Roper, author of "The lyfe of Sir Thomas Moore, knighte", died. Although he had expressed his wish to be buried with his wife, Margaret, in the More Chapel of Chelsea parish church, he was buried in the Roper chapel of St Dunstan's, Canterbury, and his wife's body was exhumed and re-interred next to him. Margaret had been buried with her father's head, which she had rescued from Tower Bridge after his execution in 1535.

William Roper was born in the late 1490s and was the eldest son of Henry VIII's Attorney-General, John Roper, and his wife, Jane. He resided in Sir Thomas More's house while studying law, and it was there that he met More's eldest daughter, Margaret, the apple of his eye and a highly educated woman. They married in 1521.

Roper caused controversy when he was charged with heresy after preaching Lutheran doctrines, but fortunately was discharged by Cardinal Wolsey with a warning, due to his connection with More. More tried to reason with him, but was unsuccessful; however, prayer was more successful and Roper gave up his Lutheran views.

In Mary I's reign, in 1557, More's nephew, William Rastell, More's friend, John Clement, and Nicholas Harpsfield published a volume of Thomas More's English works, and Harpsfield was also working on a biography of More, based on information gathered from Roper. The biography was never published due to Elizabeth I coming to the throne. Harpsfield was imprisoned and Rastell and Clement went into exile. Roper was able to remain in England and narrowly escaped imprisonment when he was accused of financially supporting those in exile.

Roper's recollections of More were published as a biography of More in 1626 by the English Jesuits of St Omer. It was given the title "The Mirrour of Vertue in Worldly Greatnes", or, "The Life of Syr Thomas More Knight, sometime Lo. Chancellour of England".

◇◇

1493 – Christopher Columbus left the New World on return from his first voyage.

1519 – Martin Luther met with Karl von Miltitz, the Papal Nuncio, at Altenburg in Saxony.

1568 – Burial of Roger Ascham, author, scholar and royal tutor, in St Stephen's Chapel at St Sepulchre-without-Newgate, London.

1575 – Death of Sir William Pickering, courtier and diplomat, in London. He was buried in the chancel of St Helen's, Bishopsgate. Pickering had escaped execution for his part in *Wyatt's Rebellion* in 1554 by fleeing to France and then providing the English government with information on other conspirators. He was pardoned in December 1554.

5TH JANUARY

On this day in history, 5th January 1531, Pope Clement VII wrote to Henry VIII forbidding him to remarry, and threatening him with excommunication if he took matters into his own hands and disobeyed Rome:-

"At the request of the Queen, forbids Henry to remarry until the decision of the case, and declares that if he does all issue will be illegitimate. Forbids any one in England, of ecclesiastical or secular dignity, universities, parliaments, courts of law, &c., to make any decision in an affair the judgment of which is reserved for the Holy See. The whole under pain of excommunication. As Henry would not receive a former citation, this is to be affixed to the church gates of Bruges, Tournay, and other towns in the Low Countries, which will be sufficient promulgation. Rome, 5 Jan. 1531." (LP v.27)

Henry VIII sought an annulment of his marriage to Catherine of Aragon so that he could marry his new love, Anne Boleyn. He applied for a dispensation to marry again back in August 1527, never dreaming that it would take nearly six years to get the marriage annulled. A seemingly simple request for a dispensation turned into "The King's Great Matter", and resulted in the fall of Cardinal Wolsey, England breaking with Rome, Henry declaring himself to be "sole protector and supreme head of the English church and clergy", and the executions of men like Thomas More, John Fisher and the Carthusian monks, who would not swear the oath of supremacy.

Henry VIII finally married Anne Boleyn in a secret ceremony on 25ᵗʰ January 1533, and their marriage was declared valid on 28ᵗʰ May 1533, just days before Anne's coronation on the 1ˢᵗ June.

◇◇◇◇◇◇◇◇◇◇◇◇◇◇◇◇◇◇◇◇◇◇◇◇◇◇◇◇◇◇◇◇◇◇◇◇◇◇

1511 – Baptism of Henry, Duke of Cornwall, son of Henry VIII and Catherine of Aragon, at the Chapel of the Observant Friars, Richmond.

1546 – Birth of Richard Willes, geographer and poet. His published works included *Poematum liber* (1573) and "History of Travayle" (1577).

1551 – Death of Sir Anthony Cope, courtier, author and landowner, probably at his home, Hanwell Hall, near Banbury. He was buried in the chancel of Hanwell Hall. Cope had served Henry VIII in the *Northern Uprisings* of 1537, was Chamberlain of Queen Catherine Parr's household and was knighted in the reign of Edward VI. Cope was also a published author, having published "The Historie of Two of the Moste Noble Capitaines of the Worlde" in 1544, and "A Godly Meditacion upon XX Select and chosen Psalmes of the Prophet David" in 1547.

1589 – Death of Catherine de' Medici. She was buried at Blois, then moved to the Cathedral Basilica of Saint-Denis. Catherine had been Queen Consort of France as wife of Henry II, and then Queen Mother when her sons, Francis II, Charles IX and Henry III reigned.

6TH JANUARY

On 6ᵗʰ January 1540, Henry VIII married Anne of Cleves, or Anna von Jülich-Kleve-Berg.

The bride was completely unaware of the fact that her groom had been trying his utmost to get out of the marriage, and that was why the wedding had been postponed from 4th January - Henry had been desperately searching for a way out. By the evening of 5th January, Henry realised that he had no other option but to go ahead with the proposed marriage. If he cancelled the wedding, it might "dryve her brother into the hands of the emperowre", and he could not risk that.

On Epiphany, Tuesday 6th January 1540, a reluctant Henry VIII married Anne of Cleves in the Queen's Closet at Greenwich Palace. The chronicler Edward Hall describes Anne:-

"Then the Lordes went to fetche the Ladye Anne, whiche was apparelled in a gowne of ryche cloth of gold set full of large flowers of great & Orient Pearle, made after the Dutche fassion rownde, her here hangyng downe, whych was fayre, yelowe and long: On her head a Coronall of gold replenished with great stone, and set about full of braunches of Rosemary, about her necke and middle, luelles of great valew & estirnacion."

The King was wearing "a gowne of ryche Tyssue [cloth of gold] lyned with Crymosyn".

Hall records that Anne curtsied to the King three times and then the couple were married by Thomas Cranmer, the Archbishop of Canterbury. Anne's wedding ring was engraved with the words "GOD SEND ME WEL TO KEPE".

After the ceremony, the bride, groom and guests enjoyed the usual wine and spices, followed by "Bankettes, Maskes, and dyuerse dvsportes, tyll the tyme came that it pleased the Kyng and her to take their rest". It was time for the all-important consummation of the marriage, something which seems to have been a complete disaster. The next morning, when Thomas Cromwell asked a rather bad-tempered Henry what he thought of his queen, Henry replied:-

"Surely, as ye know, I liked her before not well, but now I like her much worse. For I have felt her belly and her breast, and thereby, as I can judge, she should be no maid... [The] which struck me so to the heart when I felt them that I had neither will nor courage to proceed any further in other matters… I have left her as good a maid as I found her."

Henry discussed the matter with his physicians, telling them that "he found her body in such sort disordered and indisposed to excite and provoke any lust in him". Henry was unable to consummate the marriage and blamed it on Anne's appearances, for he "thought himself able to do the act with other, but not with her".

It seems that Anne did not have any sexual knowledge at all, and Lady Rochford had to break it to her that it took more than just sleeping beside the King to be with child. Anne replied, saying, "when he comes to bed, he kisses me and taketh me by the hand and biddeth me, "Goodnight sweetheart"; and in the morning kisses me and biddeth me, "Farewell, darling". Is that not enough?" The Countess of Rutland replied, "Madam, there must be more than this, or it will be long ere we have a Duke of York", but Anne said that she was content with the status quo and did not know what more was needed.

Things never improved between the couple, and it wasn't long before Henry's head was turned by the young Catherine Howard, whom he married on 28th July 1540. Fortunately for Anne, she kept her head and walked out of the marriage with the title of the King's Sister, property including Hever Castle, jewels, plate and an annual payment of £4000 per year.

⸙⸙⸙⸙⸙⸙⸙⸙⸙⸙⸙⸙⸙⸙⸙⸙⸙⸙⸙⸙⸙⸙⸙

1538 – Birth of Jane Suárez de Figueroa (née Dormer) at Eythrope, Buckinghamshire. Jane was the daughter of Sir William Dormer and his first wife, Mary Sidney. She was a favourite of Queen Mary I, and was the one Mary trusted on her deathbed to deliver her jewels to Elizabeth I. Jane married Gómez Suarez de Figueroa, Count then Duke of Feria, in December 1558.

1587 – Baptism of Elizabeth Hastings (née Stanley), Countess of Huntingdon, at Knowlsey, Lancashire. She was the daughter of Ferdinando Stanley, 5th Earl of Derby, and Alice Spencer. Elizabeth married Henry Hastings, the future 5th Earl of Huntingdon, in 1601.

1591 – Burial of George Puttenham, author and literary critic, at St Bride's, Fleet Street, London. He is thought to be the author of the 1588 "The Arte of English Poesie". Puttenham is also known for his messy divorce from Lady Windsor and his short imprisonment at Fleet prison in 1570 for high treason, after being accused of slandering the Queen and inciting Julio Mantuano to kill the Bishop of London.

1616 – Death of Philip Henslowe, theatre financier, in London. He was buried in the chancel of St Saviour's Church. Henslowe had financed the building of the Rose and Fortune playhouses.

The 6th January was also *Epiphany*. It would be celebrated with a church service, feasting and entertainment.

7TH JANUARY

On 7th January 1536, at two o'clock in the afternoon, Catherine of Aragon died at Kimbolton Castle. She had been ill for a few months, but felt worse after drinking a draught of Welsh beer in December 1535. This, combined with the embalmer's report that all of her organs were healthy apart from her heart, "which was quite black and hideous to look at", gave rise to rumours that Catherine had been poisoned. However, the embalmer, who was a chandler and not a medical expert, also found a black body attached to Catherine's heart, and it is likely that this was a tumour.

On the 29th December 1535, Catherine's doctor had sent for Eustace Chapuys, Imperial Ambassador and a friend of Catherine - she had taken a turn for the worse. Chapuys sought permission from the King to visit Catherine, and it was granted. Mary, Catherine's daughter, was not so lucky. Henry refused to let her see her mother in her last days, something which must have broken the hearts of both women. As Chapuys travelled to Kimbolton, Catherine received a surprise visitor, her former lady-in-waiting and confidante, María de Salinas, now Lady Willoughby, on *New Year's Day*. She rushed up from London on hearing the news of Catherine's illness, and managed to gain entry to the castle by claiming that she had been thrown from her horse, was in need of shelter, and that a letter giving permission for her to see Catherine was on its way. The Catherine that María saw on that day must have been a far cry from the woman she had once known. Catherine was weak and in constant pain.

Chapuys arrived the next day, and although the former queen was weak, she was still lucid enough to know that she needed witnesses in the room when she first spoke to him, so that she could not be accused of plotting against the King - later conversations, however, were held in private. Chapuys visited Catherine every afternoon for two hours over four days, and he reported that she was worried about her daughter, Mary, and was concerned that the Pope and Emperor were not acting on her behalf. Catherine was also worried that she might be to blame for the "heresies" and "scandals" that England was now suffering because of the battle over the divorce. She was haunted by the deaths that had resulted from Henry's "Great Matter," and the fact that it led to England breaking with Rome – were they down to her stubbornness, her refusal to go quietly? These were the questions preying on her mind during her last days.

Catherine's health seemed to rally in the first few days of January. She ate some meals without becoming sick, she was sleeping well and was chatting and laughing with visitors, so Chapuys was dispatched back to London. However, on the night of 6th January, Catherine became fidgety, and in the early hours of the 7th, she asked to take communion. It was unlawful for communion to be taken before daylight, but Jorge de Athequa, Catherine's confessor and the Bishop of Llandaff, could see that his mistress did not have long to live, and so administered communion and listened to her confession. Catherine settled her affairs, giving instructions on what she wanted done with her worldly goods and her burial – she wanted to be buried in a chapel of Observant Friars (Franciscans). It is also said that she wrote a letter to her former husband, Henry VIII, although this letter is now thought to have been a fake:

"My most dear lord, king and husband,

The hour of my death now drawing on, the tender love I owe you forceth me, my case being such, to commend myself to you, and to put you in remembrance with a few words of the health and safeguard of your soul which you ought to prefer before all worldly matters, and before the care and pampering of your body, for the which you have cast me into many calamities and yourself into many troubles. For my part I pardon you everything and I wish to devoutly pray to God that He will pardon you also. For the rest, I commend unto you our daughter Mary, beseeching you to be a good father unto her, as I have heretofore desired. I entreat you also, on behalf of my maids, to give them marriage portions, which is not much, they being but three. For all my other servants, I solicit the wages due to them, and a year or more, lest they be unprovided for. Lastly, I make this vow, that mine eyes desire you above all things."

Catherine continued praying until the end. Catalina de Aragón, daughter of the great Catholic Reyes, Isabella I of Castile and Ferdinand II of Aragon, had not died in some sumptuous palace surrounded by her loved ones, but in a small, dark, cold castle with her faithful staff in attendance. A sad end to a woman who had once been Queen of England, and who defeated the Scots as Regent.

On the 29th January 1536, Catherine of Aragon was laid to rest at Peterborough Abbey, now Peterborough Cathedral.

She was, of course, buried as the Dowager Princess of Wales, not as Queen, but her grave is now marked with the words "Katharine Queen of England".

1557 – England lost Calais. Thomas Wentworth, the Lord Deputy of Calais, was forced to surrender when French troops led by the Duke of Guise stormed the castle. It was a huge blow for Mary I and England, and it is said that Mary exclaimed to one of her attendants, "When I am dead and opened, you shall find 'Philip' and 'Calais' lying in my heart".

1557 – Death of Balthasar Guercy, surgeon and physician. He was buried at St Helen's, Bishopsgate. He had been physician to Anne Boleyn in 1532, and had been imprisoned briefly in the Tower of London in 1543 for supporting papal authority.

1581 – Death of Giulio Borgarucci, Dr Julio, in London. He was buried at St Botolph without Bishopsgate. Borgarucci had come to England as a Protestant refugee and, after treating the Dudley and Sidney families, was made Physician to the Royal Household in 1573.

1619 – Burial of Nicholas Hilliard, goldsmith and miniaturist, at the parish church of St Martin-in-the-Fields, London. Hilliard is known for his beautiful portrait miniatures of the English court in the reigns of Elizabeth I and James I, and his paintings of Elizabeth I: the "Pelican" portrait and the "Phoenix" portrait.

8TH JANUARY

According to the Imperial Ambassador, Eustace Chapuys, on the 8th January 1536, Henry VIII celebrated Catherine of Aragon's death by dressing in "yellow, from top to toe, except the white feather he had in his bonnet". He then paraded to mass with his two year-old daughter, Elizabeth, "with trumpets and other great triumphs". The chronicler Edward Hall, however, puts Anne Boleyn in yellow, writing that "Quene Anne ware yelowe for the mournyng" and making no mention of the King's attire.

When a messenger arrived at Greenwich Palace with the news of his first wife's death, Henry VIII cried out, "God be praised that we are free from all suspicion of war!". Catherine's death meant that Henry no longer had any quarrel with the Emperor, Catherine's nephew, and that the French would be forced to keep him happy or risk England siding with the Empire. War had been averted and Anne Boleyn was pregnant - it was something to celebrate.

1499 – Marriage of Louis XII and Anne of Brittany, widow of Charles VIII of France and the Queen Dowager. The couple had two surviving children: Claude, Queen of France, and Renée, Duchess of Ferrara.

1543 – Burial of King James V of Scotland at Holyrood Abbey, Edinburgh.

1570 – Death of Henry Clifford, 2nd Earl of Cumberland, at Brougham Castle. He was buried at Holy Trinity Church, Skipton. Clifford's career included serving Henry Fitzroy, Duke of Richmond, at Pontefract Castle, being made Knight of the Bath at the coronation of Anne Boleyn, serving as Carver to Henry VIII in 1540, and being appointed to the Council of the Borders and the Council of the North. He was married to Henry VIII's niece, Eleanor Brandon.

1571 – Burial of Mary Shelton (married names: Heveningham and Appleyard) at Heveningham Church, Suffolk. Mary was the daughter of Sir John Shelton and his wife Anne (née Boleyn), and wife of Sir Anthony Heveningham, then Philip Appleyard. Mary served Queen Anne Boleyn as one of her ladies.

1586 – Death of Sir George Seton, 5th Lord Seton, politician, Scottish nobleman and loyal supporter of Mary, Queen of Scots. He was a member of Mary's Privy Council. Seton was buried in Seton Church, East Lothian.

1594 – Death of Sir Wolstan Dixie, merchant and Lord Mayor of London, in London. He was buried at the parish church of St Michael Bassishaw. Dixie served as Lord Mayor of London in 1585-1586.

9TH JANUARY

On this day in 1514, Anne of Brittany, wife of Louis XII of France, died at the Chateau of Blois. She was buried in the Cathedral Basilica of Saint Denis.

Anne had been married three times. In 1490, she was married by proxy to Maximilian I of Austria, but was then forced to put this marriage aside and marry Charles VIII of France in 1491. When he died in 1498, Anne found herself being pushed into marrying the new French king, Louis XII. The couple married in 1499 after the annulment of his previous marriage.

1522 – Adriaan Florenszoon Boeyens was elected as Pope, becoming Pope Adrian VI.

1554 – Birth of Pope Gregory XV, born as Alessandro Ludovisi, in Bologna, Italy.

1539 – Executions of Henry Pole, 1st Baron Montagu, and Henry Courtenay, Marquis of Exeter, on Tower Hill. They were found guilty of high treason in December 1538 for denying the King's supremacy, desiring the King's death and favouring and promoting Cardinal Reginald Pole, Montagu's brother, "in his traitorous proceedings".

1587 – Death of Clement Adams, schoolmaster and map engraver. He was buried at St Alfege, Greenwich. Adams is known for his re-engraving and re-working of Sebastian Cabot's "World Chart" 1544, which he did in 1549. Adams' chart was responsible for England focusing on the Northeast passage, rather than the Northwest passage. In 1552, Adams was given a life appointment as schoolmaster to the King's henchmen.

10TH JANUARY

On 10th January 1480, Margaret of Austria (Princess of Asturias and Duchess of Savoy) was born to her parents, Maximilian of Austria and Mary of Burgundy. Margaret was their second child and was named after her maternal stepgrandmother, Margaret of York, Duchess of Burgundy and third wife of Charles the Bold (Duke of Burgundy).

When she was just two years old, Margaret was promised in marriage to Louis XI's son, Charles the Dauphin, and so was sent to France to be educated and prepared for her role as Queen Consort. However, Charles ended up marrying Anne of Brittany and Margaret married John, Prince of Asturias, the only son of Isabella I of Castile and Ferdinand II of Aragon, and brother of Catherine of Aragon, in 1497. Margaret quickly became pregnant, but sadly, John died six months into the marriage and Margaret suffered a stillbirth two months after his death. Margaret married again in 1501, but her husband, Philibert II, Duke of Savoy, died three years into the marriage, causing Margaret to vow that she would never marry again, and that she would spend the rest of her life in mourning.

Margaret's father, Maximilian, appointed her as Governor of the Habsburg Netherlands in 1507 as regent for her nephew, Charles, the man we know as the future Charles V, Holy Roman Emperor. When Charles came of age in 1515, he took her title away, but then settled it on her again in 1519. Acting as Governor of the Netherlands made Margaret an immensely powerful woman, in fact, the most powerful woman in Europe. Her court at the Palace of Mechelen became famous for its culture, its courtly love tradition, education, vast library and Margaret's collections of paintings, illuminated manuscripts and music books. This was the court where the young Anne Boleyn stayed between 1513 and 1514.

In 1529, Margaret and Louise of Savoy, mother of Francis I of France, and his regent when he was away, negotiated the *Treaty of Cambrai*, also known as the *Paix des Dames* (*The Ladies' Peace*), between Charles V and Francis I.

Margaret of Austria died at her home of Mechelen on the 1st December 1530, and was laid to rest with her second husband in their mausoleum at Bourg-en-Bresse. Her nephew, Charles V, was chosen as her heir.

1514 – Completion and printing of the first section of the "Complutensian New Testament" in Hebrew, Aramaic, Greek and Latin at Alcala, Spain.

1532 – Probable date of the burning of Thomas Dusgate, Protestant martyr, at Liverydole in Heavitree, near Exeter.

1603 – Probable date of death of Arthur Dent, religious writer and Church of England clergyman, from a fever. Dent's works included his "Sermon of Repentance", "The Plaine-Mans Pathway to Heaven" and "The Ruine of Rome, or, An Exposition upon the Whole Revelation".

11TH JANUARY

On 11th January 1569, the first recorded lottery, "a verie rich Lotterie Generall", was drawn at the west door of St Paul's Cathedral. Its purpose was to raise funds for the "reparation of the havens and strength of the Realme, and towardes such other publique good workes". Tickets began to be sold in 1566, so Elizabeth I's government was able to borrow the proceeds until 1569, when the lottery was drawn and the money raised went on prizes. It was a far more popular policy than raising funds by taxing the people.

A contemporary record of this lottery, kept at Loseley House in Surrey, tells us that it consisted of 400,000 lots costing "tenne shillings sterling onely". There were many thousands of prizes, but the main winner of the lottery was to receive a mixture of money, plate, tapestries and cloth: "the value of five thousande poundes sterling, that is to say, three thousande pounds in ready money, seven hundred poundes in plate gilte and white, and the rest in good tapisserie meete for hangings, and other covertures, and certain sortes of good linen cloth".

***

1503 – Birth of painter Francesco Mazzuoli Parmigiano in Parma, Italy.

1564 – Death of Sir Richard Southwell, the Tudor administrator who had served Henry VIII, Edward VI and Mary I. He was buried in the chancel of Woodrising Church, Norfolk.

1579 – Burial of George Ferrers, courtier, member of Parliament, Lord of Misrule and poet, at Flamstead, Hertfordshire. Ferrers is known for the *Ferrer's Case*, when Ferrers was arrested for debt and fought with the arresting officers. Ferrers contributed works to "A Mirror for Magistrates".

1584 – The Execution of William Carter, printer. He was hanged, drawn and quartered at Tyburn after being found guilty of treason, for printing a book which allegedly contained a passage inciting the assassination of Elizabeth I.

1591 – Birth of Robert Devereux, 3rd Earl of Essex, son of Elizabeth I's favourite, Robert Devereux, 2nd Earl of Essex. His maternal grandfather was Sir Francis Walsingham. Devereux was Captain-General of the parliamentary forces in 1642, and Lord-General in 1643.

12TH JANUARY

On 12th January 1510, Henry VIII jousted for the first time as King. The joust was a private one, and took place at Richmond Park. Henry and his friend William Compton attended in disguise, and there was panic when Compton was seriously injured by Edward Neville. Nobody knew whether it was Compton or the King, and it was only when his visor was raised that people knew, and someone cried out "God save the King!". Then the King took off his disguise to reassure worried spectators.

William Compton survived the accident and served the King as his Groom of the Stool until Wolsey's "Eltham Ordinances" forced his resignation. He died in June 1528 after contracting sweating sickness.

Jousting was a popular sport in Tudor times, but actually dated back to the Middle Ages when it was used to prepare knights for warfare. It kept them fit, and was good practice of weapon skills. As time went on, jousting became rooted in the chivalric tradition, and ladies would offer favours (a ribbon or a handkerchief) to knights to wear on their clothing during the joust.

The sport involved two knights, in armour and equipped with lances, riding towards each other at speed. By Tudor times, a barrier or "tilt", separated the knights' courses to prevent collisions, and lances had been made blunt. A herald would start the joust, and the knights would charge at each other and attempt to strike or unseat their opponent. It was a dangerous sport, and was actually discontinued in France after the death of the French king, Henry II, when his eye was pierced by a splinter from a lance while jousting in 1559.

1519 – Death of Maximilian I, Holy Roman Emperor, in Wels, Upper Austria. He was buried in the Castle Chapel at Wiener Neustadt, but visitors to the Hofkirche Court Church in Innsbruck can see a cenotaph tomb for Maximilian there because the church was built in memory of Maximilian by his grandson, Ferdinand I.

1539 – Francis I of France and Charles V, Holy Roman Emperor, signed the *Peace of Toledo*, agreeing to make no other alliances without the consent of the other.

1547 – Thomas Howard, 3rd Duke of Norfolk, who was imprisoned in the Tower of London, tried to save himself from execution by signing a confession.

1559 – Elizabeth I travelled to the Tower of London to prepare for her coronation, which was scheduled for the 15th January.

1560 – Death of John White, Bishop of Winchester, in South Warnborough. He was buried in Winchester Cathedral. White was a Catholic, was imprisoned in the Tower of London and deprived of his bishopric after the accession of Elizabeth I.

1573 – Death of William Howard, 1st Baron Howard of Effingham, soldier and naval commander, at Hampton Court. He was buried at Reigate Church. Howard was the fourth son of Thomas Howard, 2nd Duke of Norfolk, and his second wife, Agnes Tilney.

1577 – Death of Thomas Fisher (also known as Hawkins), landowner and member of Parliament. The first record of Fisher shows him serving John Dudley, who was then Viscount Lisle, but by 1544 he was working for Edward Seymour, Earl of Hertford. In Mary I's reign, he served as a Justice of the Peace and member of Parliament. He was buried in St Mary's Church, Warwick, in a tomb with his first wife, Winifred.

1587 – Death of Matthew Godwin, Organist and Choirmaster at the Cathedral Churches of Canterbury, then Exeter.

13TH JANUARY

On 13th January 1547, Henry Howard, Earl of Surrey, poet and soldier, was sentenced to death. He was tried in front of a common inquest at Guildhall, and despite pleading 'not guilty' and defending himself vigorously, he was found guilty. It was alleged that "he had on 7 October 1546 at Kenninghall displayed in his own heraldry the royal arms and insignia, with three labels silver, thereby threatening the king's title to the throne and the prince's inheritance". His trial lasted a day and he gave a spirited defence, but it was no good. He was found guilty and sentenced to death.

1563 – Birth of Mark Alexander Boyd, poet and humanist scholar, in Ayrshire, Scotland. His works included the collections *Epistolae quindecim and Epistolae heroides et hymni*, and his famous Scots sonnet "Fra banc to banc".

1584- Death of Thomas Wentworth, 2nd Baron Wentworth and de jure 7th Baron Le Despenser, soldier and administrator, at Stepney. Wentworth served Mary I as Lord Deputy of Calais, and was the one in charge when Calais fell to the French in January 1558.

1592 – Death of Sir Henry Brooke, courtier and diplomat, at Sutton-at-Hone. Although he was not Baron Cobham himself - that title belonged to his father then brother - he used Cobham as his surname. He served Elizabeth I as an ambassador in Spain, the Low Countries and France, and was the resident ambassador in France from October 1579 to September 1583.

1593 – Death of Sir Henry Neville, Groom of Henry VIII's Privy Chamber. He was buried at Waltham St Lawrence in Berkshire.

1599 – Death of Edmund Spenser, poet and administrator in Ireland. He died in Westminster and was buried in Westminster Abbey. Spenser is best known for his allegorical poem "The Faerie Queene", which was dedicated to Elizabeth I.

1602 – Death of Sir John Forster, soldier and Warden of the Middle Marches, at Spindlestone, Northumberland. He was buried at Bamburgh parish church.

1612 – Death of Jane Suárez de Figueroa (née Dormer), Duchess of Feria. She was buried in the monastery of Santa Clara at Zafra, Spain.

1613 – Death of Edward Gresham, astrologer, astronomer, mathematician, magician and writer of the treatise "Astrostereon". He died in London and was buried at All Saints-the-Less.

1628 – Death of Sir Anthony Ashley, Baronet, translator and politician, at Holborn House. He was buried at Wimborne St Giles in Dorset. Ashley published an English edition of Lucas Waghenaer's nautical charts, which he adapted and added to with accounts of Sir Francis Drake's 1587 raid on Cadiz and, of course, the 1588 *Spanish Armada*. It was published as "The Mariners Mirrour".

14TH JANUARY

Elizabeth left the Tower for her eve of coronation procession at 3pm on the 14th January 1559 in a cloth of gold covered litter carried by two mules. As she passed the Tower of London menagerie, Elizabeth prayed to God, thanking him for her deliverance, like that of Daniel from the lion's den.

Elizabeth was a natural. She charmed the crowd, smiling warmly at people, joking and replying to their good wishes. It was usual for pageants to be part of a coronation procession, and Elizabeth had five:

Gracechurch Street – This pageant referred to Elizabeth's genealogy, her Tudor roots and the history of the House of Tudor. The people were reminded that her name sake and grandmother Elizabeth of York had brought peace to the land by marrying Henry Tudor and uniting the warring Houses of York and Lancaster. Elizabeth, too, would bring peace and unity to the land.

Cornhill – This pageant referred to Elizabeth's new government as being upheld by four virtues: True Religion, Love of Subjects, Wisdom and Justice.

- *Soper's Lane* – This pageant was based on the New Testament Beatitudes and, as Starkey explains, applied them to Elizabeth's sufferings at the hands of her sister.

- *Little Conduit, Cheapside* – This pageant with its subject of "Time" attacked Mary's reign, contrasting "a decayed commonwealth" to "a flourishing commonwealth" in two tableaux. Time's daughter, Truth, carried an English Bible labelled the "Word of Truth", which Elizabeth's government was said to possess. When Elizabeth saw this pageant, she asked for the Bible and "kissed it, and with both her hands held up the same, and so laid it on her breast, with great thanks to the City therefore."

- *Fleet Street* – This pageant depicted Elizabeth as the prophetess Deborah who had rescued Israel from Jabin, King of Canaan. Like Deborah, Elizabeth would reign over her people for over forty years.

The procession ended at Westminster in readiness for her coronation ceremony the next day in Westminster Abbey.

***

1478 – Birth of Henry Algernon Percy, 5th Earl of Northumberland. He was the eldest son of Henry Percy, 4th Earl of Northumberland, and Maud Herbert, daughter of William Herbert, 1st Earl of Pembroke.

1515 – Charles Brandon, Duke of Suffolk, was sent to France to bring back Henry VIII's sister, Mary Tudor, Queen of France.

1526 – Francis I and Charles V signed the *Treaty of Madrid*. Francis I had been captured at the *Battle of Pavia*, and was held until this treaty was concluded. By the terms of the treaty, Francis renounced his claims to lands in Italy, Flanders, Artois and Tournai. Once he was released and back in France, Francis refused to ratify the treaty.

1589 – Francis Kett, physician, was burned for heresy near Norwich Castle. He had claimed that "Christ is not God, but a good man as others be". Kett was dragged to the stake "clothed in sackecloth" and went to his death "leaping and dauncing" and "clapping his hands".

15TH JANUARY

On 15th January 1559, a date chosen by her astrologer Dr John Dee, a triumphant Elizabeth Tudor, daughter of Henry VIII and Anne Boleyn, processed from Westminster Hall into Westminster Abbey to be crowned queen. She was just twenty -five years old, was the third child of Henry VIII to become monarch, and was the longest reigning of them, ruling England for over 44 years.

Elizabeth's coronation day began in Westminster Hall, which had been decorated with her father's sumptuous tapestries and his collection of gold and gilt plate. Blue cloth had been laid from the Hall to the Abbey, and Elizabeth, wearing her crimson parliament robes, processed along this cloth, which was then torn to shreds by people as souvenirs.

Elizabeth processed to the crossing in the Abbey and withdrew to a curtained enclosure to change. She was then led by Owen Oglethorpe, Bishop of Carlisle, up onto the stage, where he proclaimed her queen in each of the four corners, asking the congregation if they would have her for their queen and listening for their enthusiastic replies of "Yea! Yea!". Elizabeth then made the traditional offerings at the altar and sat in the throne of estate to listen to the sermon. After the sermon, Elizabeth knelt for the Lord's Prayer, took the oath, then withdrew to the traverse to change for the anointing part of the service. Wearing a kirtle of gold and silver and leaning on cloth of gold cushions, which had been placed before the altar, Elizabeth was anointed on the shoulder blades, breast, arms, hands and head. She was then dressed in white gloves, a white coif and the white dalmatic (tunic) of a deacon. Now that she had sworn the oath and been anointed, she could sit in St Edward's Chair and receive the sword, armils, mantle, ring and sceptre, and be crowned. She was crowned with three different crowns, one after the other, with fanfares marking each crowning.

Elizabeth was then dressed in gold right down to her shoes, and with the sceptre in one hand and orb in the other, she processed onto the stage where she sat in the throne. There, her people greeted her and Oglethorpe, and the Lords Spiritual and Temporal paid homage to their new queen by kneeling at her feet and kissing her cheek. The coronation pardon was read, and this was followed by the coronation mass, which included the Epistle and the Gospel being read out in both Latin and English. Elizabeth then kissed the Bible. Oglethorpe, defied his new queen by elevating the host, at which point Elizabeth withdrew to change into her purple robes. The Queen then processed from the Abbey, through Old Palace Yard and back to Westminster Hall to enjoy her coronation banquet. Elizabeth was now the official queen, and her coronation and accession had been a huge success.

1522 – Death of Richard Fitzjames, Bishop of London, in London. He was buried in the nave of St Paul's.

1522 – Death of Sir John Heron, Treasurer of the Chamber to Henry VII and General Receiver to Henry VIII. He was buried at the Whitefriars, London.

1535 – Henry VIII declared himself head of the Church in England.

1555 – Death of Jane Dudley, Duchess of Northumberland and wife of John Dudley, Duke of Northumberland. Jane died in Chelsea, London, and was buried there. She outlived her husband, who was executed in 1553 after Mary seized the throne from his daughter-in-law, Lady Jane Grey.

1569 – Death of Katherine Knollys (née Carey), wife of Sir Francis Knollys and daughter of Sir William Carey and Mary Boleyn. Queen Elizabeth I was grief-stricken at the death of her cousin and friend, and gave her a lavish funeral at Westminster Abbey. Some believe Katherine to have been the illegitimate daughter of Henry VIII.

16TH JANUARY

On 16th January 1549, Edward VI's uncle, Thomas Seymour, was alleged to have broken into the King's apartments at Hampton Court Palace to kidnap the young King. As he entered the royal residence, it is said that he disturbed the King's beloved spaniel who started barking at him. In a panic, Seymour is said to have shot the dog, a noise which alerted one of the guards, who then apprehended Seymour. Seymour was arrested and taken to the Tower of London.

Thomas Seymour was not only accused of trying to kidnap his nephew. He was also accused of plotting to marry the teenage Elizabeth, daughter of the late Henry VIII, and put her on the throne. As her husband, he would then have been made Lord Protector, just like his brother was for Edward VI.

Seymour was interrogated in the Tower and examined before the Privy Council. On 25th February a bill of attainder was introduced into Parliament, and lawyers argued that Seymour's offences 'were in the compasse of High Treason'. The bill was passed on 5th March, and Thomas Seymour was executed on Tower Hill on 20th March 1549.

1486 – The Bishop of Imola, the papal legate, authorised the marriage of Henry VII and Elizabeth of York, which was due to take place on 18th January.

1501 – Birth of Sir Anthony Denny, courtier and close friend of Henry VIII, at Cheshunt. He was the second son of Sir Edmund Denny and his wife, Mary.

1558 – Death of Thomas Alsop, Chief Apothecary to Henry VIII and Serjeant of the Royal 'Confectionary' to Edward VI. He was buried in St Mary Woolchurch.

1572 – Thomas Howard, 4th Duke of Norfolk, was tried and found guilty of treason at Westminster Hall.

1585 – Death of Edward Fiennes Clinton, 1st Earl of Lincoln, military commander, in London. He was buried in St George's Chapel, Windsor Castle. Clinton served Elizabeth I as a Privy Councillor and Lord Admiral until his death.

1606 – Death of Matthew Hutton, Archbishop of York, at Bishopthorpe. He was buried at York Minster.

17TH JANUARY

On 17th January 1569, Agnes Bowker of Market Harborough, Leicestershire, allegedly gave birth to a cat.

According to the midwife, Elizabeth Harrison, Agnes had told her of how "the likeness of a bear, sometimes like a dog, sometimes like a man" had carnal knowledge of her in its various guises.

Harrison went on to describe how Agnes gave birth to the cat, "the hinder part coming first". The other six women who were present at the birth were questioned, but none seemed very sure of what had happened. One Margaret Harrison said "that she was at the birth of the monster with her child in her arms, and the wives willed her to fetch a candle for they had not light… and when she came in with the candle she saw the monster lie on the earth and she thinketh it came out of Agnes Bowker's womb." Another woman spoke of seeing the monster, but none of them were present when it was actually born.

Testimonies from the local men were also taken. They had examined the cat and even dissected it, finding bacon in its digestive system. This convinced them that the "monster" was nothing but a real cat who had been enjoying a piece of bacon in the last few hours, rather than being carried in the womb of young Agnes. They also spoke of how Agnes had recently tried to borrow a cat and that a neighbour's cat had gone missing. Their testimonies, and those of the women present at the birth, were heard at a special ecclesiastical court in front of the Archdeacon of Leicester. A secular hearing was also set up to examine the evidence and to see if a crime, such as infanticide, had been committed.

Agnes herself was obviously examined, and she told some rather tall tales involving being seduced by a schoolmaster who gave her "falling sickness" (epilepsy), and who told her that she could be cured by having a child. According to Agnes, Mr Brady, the schoolmaster, sent "a thing" to her "in the likeness of a man", and she slept with him. When questioned about her pregnancy and its outcome, she went from saying that she had given birth to a child who was being nursed at Guilsborough, to saying that she had given birth before Christmas to a dead child, which was buried in Little Bowden. Then she changed her mind and said she didn't know what had happened when she gave birth in January, but that the midwife told her that the monster had come out of her body.

The case was referred to Henry Hastings, the Earl of Huntingdon, on 18th February 1569 and Anthony Anderson, the Archdeacon's Commissary, passed on a drawing of the cat, the results of the examination of the cat and another cat as comparison, and full transcripts of testimonies. This package of information was then passed to William Cecil, Elizabeth I's Secretary of State, who shared it with Edmund Grindal, Bishop of London in August 1569. Grindal concluded "for the monster, it appeareth plainly to be a counterfeit matter; but yet we cannot extort confessions of the manner of doings". In other words, he could not establish what exactly had happened. The case had to be investigated, though, because people were seeing it as a portent, and news of Agnes Bowker's cat had spread quickly via a pamphlet.

***

1504 – Birth of Pope Pius V, at Bosco in the Duchy of Milan, Italy. He was born Antonio Ghislieri.

1517 – Birth of Henry Grey, Duke of Suffolk and father of Lady Jane Grey, at Bradgate, Leicestershire. He was the son of Thomas Grey, 2nd Marquis of Dorset, and Margaret Wotton. Suffolk was executed at the Tower of London on 23rd February 1554 for his part in *Wyatt's Rebellion*.

1541 – Sir Thomas Wyatt the Elder, courtier, diplomat and poet, was arrested and sent to the Tower of London after being accused of corresponding with Cardinal Pole, and referring to the prospect of Henry VIII's death.

1562 – *Edict of Saint-Germain*, or *Edict of January*. This edict, issued by the regent of France, Catherine de' Medici, aimed at ending the persecution of the Huguenots by allowing them freedom of belief and private worship.

1587 – Death of Bartholomew Newsam, famous clockmaker and sundial maker. He was buried in St Mary-le-Strand. Examples of his work can still be seen in the British Museum.

18TH JANUARY

On 18th January 1486, the twenty-nine year-old Henry VII married the twenty year-old Elizabeth of York.

They made a striking couple. Elizabeth of York had classic English Rose looks – blonde hair, blue eyes and fair skin – and Henry was tall, slim, dark haired and handsome. They were the perfect couple, and their marriage brought hope to the country. It reconciled the warring Houses of Lancaster and York, and began a new royal house and era: the Tudor dynasty.

The bride, Elizabeth of York, had been born on 11th February 1466, and was the daughter and eldest child of Edward IV and Elizabeth Woodville. Her father had managed to capture and imprison Henry VI in 1461, dethroning him and taking the crown for himself, starting the royal House of York. In 1464, he secretly married Elizabeth Woodville, a young widow. It was a love match, not a diplomatic one, and caused trouble when Elizabeth alienated powerful Yorkist supporters, causing them to side with Lancastrians and challenge Edward. The result was that Edward was driven into exile and the throne became Henry VI's once more in October 1470. Henry's reign was short-lived, though, as Edward overthrew him once again in April 1471. It was a brutal coup. Ex-Yorkists and Lancastrians were defeated in battle, and Henry VI was killed in the Tower. Edward had stamped out his enemies.

Unfortunately, tragedy struck the House of York at *Easter* 1483 when Edward caught a chill on a fishing trip. He died on 9th April, and his thirteen year-old son, Edward, became Edward V. Edward V was too young to reign in his own right, so his uncle, Richard, Duke of Gloucester, became the Protector. However, to cut a rather long story short, this was not enough for Richard. With Edward and his younger brother, Richard, Duke of York, 'residing' in the Tower of London, Richard was crowned King Richard III on 6th July

1483, and the boys disappeared, going down in history as 'The Princes in the Tower'.

Elizabeth of York mourned the loss of her brothers, but her mother decided on revenge, and this is when she decided to approach Lady Margaret Beaufort. Although the two ladies were supposed to be on different sides, Elizabeth being from the House of York and Margaret being a Lancastrian, neither lady was happy with Richard on the throne, and decided that a union between their children could bring about Richard's downfall.

The bridegroom, Henry VII, was born at Pembroke Castle on 28th January 1457. His parents were the thirteen year-old Lady Margaret Beaufort and Edmund Tudor, 1st Earl of Richmond, who, unfortunately, had died of the plague three months before Henry's birth. Both Margaret and Edmund were linked to the House of Lancaster. Edmund was the son of Owen Tudor and Catherine Valois (Catherine of France), the widow of Henry V and mother of Henry VI. Margaret Beaufort was descended from John of Gaunt, Duke of Lancaster (third son of King Edward III) and his mistress and eventual wife, Katherine Swynford. Neither of Henry's parents had a strong claim to the throne, with Edmund having no English royal blood and Margaret being descended from a line which was deliberately excluded from the succession. This, however, did not stop Henry VII from claiming the throne after his Lancastrian forces defeated Richard III's Yorkist forces at the *Battle of Bosworth Field* on 22nd August 1485, where Richard was killed.

On 27th August 1485, Henry entered London as King Henry VII, and he was crowned on 30th October. On the 10th December, Parliament petitioned him to marry Elizabeth of York, the Speaker declaring "Which marriage, they hoped God would bless with a progeny of the race of kings, to the great satisfaction of the whole realm". Henry agreed, and the marriage took place five weeks later.

1510 - The King and twelve of his men disguised themselves as outlaws, or Robin Hood and his men, and surprised Queen Catherine and her ladies in the Queen's chamber. After "certain daunces, and pastime made", the King and his men departed.

1543 – Baptism of Alfonso Ferrabosco, composer and court musician at the court of Elizabeth I, at the Cathedral of San Petronio, Bologna, Italy.

1616 – Burial of John Bettes the Younger, portrait painter, at St Gregory by St Paul's.

19TH JANUARY

On 19th January 1547, the poet, courtier and soldier Henry Howard, Earl of Surrey and son of Thomas Howard, 3rd Duke of Norfolk, was executed by beheading on Tower Hill. He was laid to rest at All Hallows-by-the-Tower (All Hallows Barking), but was moved in 1614 by his son Henry, Earl of Northampton, to a beautiful tomb in the family church, St Michael's at Framlingham.

Surrey had been found guilty of treason on 13th January 1547 at a common inquest at Guildhall. It was alleged that he had displayed the royal arms in his own heraldry, and that he planned to usurp the throne on Henry VIII's death. He was sentenced to death.

According to historian Susan Brigden, Surrey spent his last days paraphrasing Psalms 55, 73 and 88. The themes of these psalms were abandonment and betrayal, which Surrey could obviously identify with because he was the victim of an increasingly paranoid king.

Surrey was executed on Tower Hill on 19th January 1547. His father, the Duke of Norfolk, who had also been sentenced to death for treason, escaped a brutal death because

Henry VIII died before his scheduled execution. Norfolk was released and pardoned by Mary I in 1553, and died naturally on 25th August 1554.

Surrey is best known for his poetry, and is referred to as the "Father of the English Sonnet".

⬦⬦⬦⬦⬦⬦⬦⬦⬦⬦⬦⬦⬦⬦⬦⬦⬦⬦⬦⬦⬦⬦⬦⬦⬦⬦⬦

1561 – Death of Sir Edward Carne, administrator and diplomat, in Rome. Carne carried out diplomatic missions for Henry VIII, was a Royal Commissioner during the dissolution of the monasteries, negotiated the marriage of Henry VIII and Anne of Cleves, and was Mary I's English ambassador to Rome.

1601 – Death of Henry Herbert, 2nd Earl of Pembroke, at Wilton, near Salisbury. Herbert was the son of William Herbert, 1st Earl of Pembroke, and Anne Parr, sister of Queen Catherine Parr. He was a friend of Robert Dudley, Earl of Leicester, and patron of the theatre company, Pembroke's Men.

1636 – Death of Marcus Gheeraerts, painter, in London. He is known for his "Ditchley" portrait of Elizabeth I.

20TH JANUARY

On 20th January 1569, Bible translator and Bishop of Exeter, Miles Coverdale died. He was buried in the chancel of St Bartholomew by the Exchange, London, on 22nd January.

It is thought that Coverdale was born in the North Riding of Yorkshire in 1488, although nothing is known of his family or early life. He became an Augustinian friar and studied at Cambridge, where he was influenced by the reformist views of Robert Barnes. His whereabouts in the late 1520s and early 1530s are not known, but he was in Antwerp by 1534 with John Rogers and William Tyndale. That year, an English translation of Campensis' Latin work on the psalms was published in Antwerp, and it is believed that this was written by Tyndale, who had already started his translation of the Bible. His translation was completed in October 1535, and was the first English translation of the whole Bible.

He returned to England in late 1535 and published his translation of German hymns, "Goostly Psalmes and Spirituall Songs Drawen out of the Holy Scripture", in London. This was followed by translations of other German religious texts. In 1537, Thomas Cromwell asked Coverdale to revise the "Matthew Bible", a Bible which combined the work of Tyndale and Coverdale, and print it in Paris. However, there was trouble when one of those overseeing the printing was accused of heresy, and around 2500 finished copies were confiscated by the Inquisition and eventually burned. Fortunately, the publishers, Richard Grafton and Edward Whitchurch, managed to flee Paris with some unbound copies. In April 1539, 3000 copies of the "Great Bible" were printed, followed by another 3000 copies in spring 1540. This meant that a copy could be put into every church in England.

The "Act of the Six Articles" of June 1539 led to many reformers, Coverdale included, going into exile to escape persecution. Coverdale's former mentor, Robert Barnes, was executed for heresy in July 1540, as was Thomas Cromwell. England was not safe for Coverdale. He fled to Strasbourg, where he stayed for three years, translating and writing tracts. He returned to England in 1548, during the reign of Edward VI, and became Almoner to Catherine Parr, the Dowager Queen. After her death in September 1548, he became a Royal Chaplain and then Bishop of Exeter in 1551. The death of the Protestant Edward VI saw Coverdale put under house arrest when Mary I came to the throne, and losing his bishopric. The King of Denmark intervened to have Coverdale released, and in 1555 he went into exile, spending a few weeks in Denmark before heading to Bergzaben, then Aarau in Switzerland and finally Geneva.

Coverdale returned to England in 1559, in Elizabeth I's reign, and began preaching. In 1564 he accepted the living of St Magnus the Martyr by London Bridge, but resigned in the summer of 1566. He carried on preaching, though, and died immediately after standing in for a preacher at the church of St Magnus the Martyr in London. Although he was buried in St Bartholomew by the Exchange, his remains were moved to St Magnus the Martyr when St Bartholomew's was pulled down in 1840.

1525 – Death of Richard Bere, Abbot of Glastonbury. He was buried in the south aisle of the nave of the abbey church.

1557 – "The Queen's Grace's pensioners did muster in bright harness" before Mary I.

1558 – The state opening of the fifth Parliament of Mary I's reign. This is one of the only mentions of a public appearance by Mary after the second departure of her husband, Philip of Spain, in July 1557.

1607 – Death of Jacob Verzelini, glassmaker, in Crutched Friars, London. He was buried at Downe Chapel. His work, which includes a cylindrical crystal tankard with silver-gilt lid and base and goblets, can be found in the British Museum and in the Victoria and Albert Museum.

1618 – Death of Ferdinando Putlon, legal researcher and writer, at Bourton, near Buckingham. He was buried in the parish church at Desborough.

21ST JANUARY

On the night of 21st January 1543, there was trouble in London. A group of half a dozen young men, including ringleader Henry Howard, Earl of Surrey, went on a five hour rampage smashing windows, shooting prostitutes using *stonebows* and shouting obscenities. The trouble lasted until 2am. The next day, a rather repentant Surrey commented to his friend, George Blagge, that he was very sorry for his actions and wished "it were undone", but that "we will have a madding time in our youth."

∞∞∞∞∞∞∞∞∞∞∞∞∞∞∞∞∞∞∞∞∞∞∞∞

1510 – Henry VIII opened the first Parliament of his reign.

1542 – Bill of Attainder passed against Catherine Howard, Henry VIII's fifth wife.

1556 – Death of Eustace Chapuys, Imperial Ambassador at the English court from 1529-1545, at Louvain. He was laid to rest in the Chapel of Louvain College, the college he had founded.

1571 – Death of Walter Haddon, civil lawyer, reformer, MP and college head, in London. He was buried at Christ Church Greyfriars. As well as his work in colleges, Haddon is known for his polemical exchange with Portuguese priest Jerome Osorio da Fonseca who, in 1563, published an epistle calling for Elizabeth I to return to Catholicism, and Haddon was ordered by the government to reply.

1608 – Death of Sir Richard Lowther, soldier and landowner, at Lowther Hall. He was buried at the church in Lowther. His offices included Sheriff of Cumberland and Lord Warden of the West March.

22ND JANUARY

Between 8 o'clock and 9 o'clock on the morning of the 22nd January 1552, former Lord Protector of England, Edward Seymour, Duke of Somerset, was executed by beheading on Tower Hill in London.

The famous Tudor chronicler, Charles Wriothesley, recorded his execution:-

"Fryday, the 22 of January 1552, Edward Seimer, Duke of Somersett, was beheaded at Tower Hill, afore ix of the clocke in the forenone, which tooke his death very patiently, but there was such a feare and disturbance amonge the people sodainely before he suffred, that some tombled downe the ditch, and some ranne toward the houses thereby and fell, that it was marveile to see and hear; but howe the cause was, God knoweth."

There is a note on that page of "The Chronicle" explaining that "Edward VI appears to have been perfectly convinced of his uncle's guilt, and in that conviction to have given himself no further concern about the duke, only noting in his diary that 'the Duke of Somerset had his head cut off upon Tower Hill between eight and nine o'clock in the morning.' " Edward VI had now lost both of his uncles, Edward and Thomas Seymour, to the executioner for alleged treason.

Edward Seymour was laid to rest in the Chapel of St Peter ad Vincula at the Tower of London, and records show that he was buried next to Anne Boleyn in the chancel area.

◇◇

1528 – Henry VIII and Francis I declared war on Charles V, Holy Roman Emperor.

1554 - Thomas Wyatt the Younger met with fellow conspirators at his home of Allington Castle in Kent to make final plans for their uprising (Wyatt's Rebellion) against Mary I and her decision to marry Philip of Spain.

1561 – Birth of Francis Bacon, Viscount St Alban, the Elizabethan Lord Chancellor, politician, philosopher, author and scientist, at York House in the Strand, London. Bacon is known as "the Father of the Scientific method" and developed an investigative method, the Baconian method, which he put forward in his book *Novum Organum* in 1620. Some people (Baconians) believe that Francis Bacon was the true author of William Shakespeare's plays.

1575 – Death of James Hamilton, 2nd Earl of Arran and Duke of Châtelherault, at Kinneil. Arran was appointed Regent for the infant Mary, Queen of Scots after James V's death in 1542, but surrendered the regency to Mary's mother, Mary of Guise in 1554.

1613 – Death of Sir David Williams, Serjeant-at-Law in Elizabeth I's reign and Puisne Justice of the King's Bench in James I's reign, from a fever at Kingston House, Kingston Bagpuize, Berkshire. His body was buried at St John's Chapel, Brecon, and his entrails were buried at Kingston.

23RD JANUARY

1516 – Death of Ferdinand II of Aragon in Madrigalejo, Extremadura. He was laid to rest in la Capilla Real, the Royal Chapel of Granada. Ferdinand was the husband of Isabella I of Castile and the father of Catherine of Aragon, Henry VIII's first wife. Ferdinand was succeeded by his daughter, Juana (Joanna), who ruled jointly with her son, Charles, who became King Charles I of Spain.

1540 – Birth of Thomas Egerton, 1st Viscount Brackley and Lord Chancellor to James I. Egerton was the illegitimate son of Sir Richard Egerton, a landowner from Cheshire, by a servant girl.

1571 – Official opening of the Royal Exchange in London by Queen Elizabeth I. It had been founded in 1565 by mercer and merchant, Sir Thomas Gresham.

1552 – Parliament met to discuss the revision of the 1549 "Book of Common Prayer".

1554 – Baptism of Richard Edes, Dean of Worcester, at Newport on the Isle of Wight. He became Dean of Worcester in June 1597. Edes was also Chaplain and Court Preacher to Elizabeth I and James I.

1570 – Assassination of James Stewart, 1ˢᵗ Earl of Moray, illegitimate son of James V and Regent for James VI between 1567 and 1570. He was shot in Linlithgow by assassin James Hamilton of Bothwellhaugh. The hit was ordered by the Hamilton family, supporters of Mary, Queen of Scots.

1576 – Death of James Pilkington, Bishop of Durham. He was buried at the church of St Andrew, Bishop Aucklan, but then moved later that year to Durham Cathedral.

1584 – Death of John Watson, Bishop of Winchester, in Winchester. He was buried in Winchester Cathedral.

1600 – Death of John Case, writer and philosopher. He was buried in the chapel of St John's College, Oxford. Case is known for his commentaries on the works of Aristotle.

1620 – Death of Sir John Croke, judge and Speaker of the House of Commons, in Holborn, London. He was buried at Chilton, Buckinghamshire. He was elected as Speaker of the House of Commons in October 1601.

24TH JANUARY

On the 24th January 1536, the forty-four year-old King Henry VIII had a serious jousting accident at Greenwich Palace. Eustace Chapuys, the Imperial Ambassador, reported it in his dispatches, writing:-

"On the eve of the Conversion of St. Paul, the King being mounted on a great horse to run at the lists, both fell so heavily that every one thought it a miracle he was not killed, but he sustained no injury. Thinks he might ask of fortune for what greater misfortune he is reserved, like the other tyrant who escaped from the fall of the house, in which all the rest were smothered, and soon after died."

Dr Ortiz recorded the accident in a letter to the Empress:-

"The French king said that the king of England had fallen from his horse, and been for two hours without speaking. "La Ana" was so upset that she miscarried of a son."

As historian Suzannah Lipscomb points out in her book "1536: The Year that Changed Henry VIII", the combination of speed, the weight of Henry's armour and possibly the horse, and the blow to his head made it a serious accident, and it is amazing that Henry survived.

<hr />

1502 – Henry VII ratified a peace treaty, the *Treaty of Perpetual Peace*, with James IV of Scotland. Part of this treaty was the agreement of a marriage between Henry VII's daughter, Margaret, and James.

1503 – The foundation stone of King Henry VII's chapel was laid at Westminster Abbey.

1555 – A great joust was held at Westminster between English and the Spanish knights – "grett ronnying at the tylt at Westmynster, with spayrer, boyth Englys men and Spaneards".

1566 – Death of Rowland Meyrick, Bishop of Bangor. He was buried at Bangor Cathedral.

1597 – Death of Thomas Molyneux, Elizabeth I's Chancellor of the Court of Exchequer, and Receiver of Customs and Imposts on Wines, in Dublin. He was buried in Dublin's Christ Church Cathedral.

1634 – Death of Nathaniel Giles, composer, Organist and Choir master at St George's Chapel, Windsor and the Chapel Royal. He was Choir Master at Windsor for forty-nine years. A memorial tablet to him can be found on the floor of Rutland Chapel in St George's Chapel.

25TH JANUARY

According to Thomas Cranmer, Henry VIII married Anne Boleyn on *St Paul's Day*, the 25th January 1533. In a letter to Archdeacon Hawkyns, written in June 1533 and recording Anne Boleyn's coronation, Cranmer wrote:-

"But now, sir, you may not imagine that this coronation was before her marriage; for she was married much about St Paul's Day last, as the condition thereof doth well appear, by reason she is now somewhat big with child."

Cranmer went on to challenge the rumours that he had performed the ceremony:-

"Notwithstanding it hath been reported throughout a great part of the realm that I married her; which was plainly false, for I myself knew not thereof a fortnight after it was done."

So secret was the marriage ceremony that even Cranmer had been kept in the dark until weeks afterwards, and Eustace Chapuys, the Imperial Ambassador, was still writing to the Emperor at the end of March about rumours of a wedding being planned before *Easter*. Little did he know that Anne and Henry were already married! Of course, the reason why it was kept secret was because Henry VIII was still married to Catherine of Aragon.

The Catholic apologist, Nicholas Harpsfield gave more details of the wedding in his "A Treatise on the Pretended Divorce between Henry VIII and Catharine of Aragon" written in Mary I's reign:

"The first whereof was that the King was married to [the] Lady Anne Bulleyne long ere there was any divorce made by the said Archbishop [of Canterbury]. The which marriage was secretly made at Whitehall very early before day, none being present but Mr Norris and Mr Henage of the Privy Chamber and the Lady Barkeley, with Mr. Rowland the King's chaplain, that was afterward made Bishop of Coventry and Lichfield.

To whom the King told that now he had gotten of the Pope a lycence to marry another wife, and yet to avoid business and tumult the thing must be done (quoth the King) very secretly; and thereupon a time and place was appointed to the said Master Rowland to solemnize the said marriage."

Harpsfield goes on to describe how when a troubled Lee asked to see the licence so that it could be read to all present "or else we run all and I more deep than any other into excommunication in marrying your grace without any baynes asking, and in a place unhallowed, and no divorce as yet promulged of the first matrimony", the King replied, "I have truly a lycence, but it is reposed in another sure[r] place whereto no man resorteth but myself, which, if it were seen, should discharge us all. But if I should, now that it waxeth towards day, fetch it, and be seen so early abroad, there would rise a rumour and talk thereof other than were convenient. Goe forth in God's name, and do that which appertaineth to you. I will take upon me all other danger." Lee had two choices: ask for the licence, showing that he did not trust his King, or get on with the ceremony, and I don't think he can be blamed for going ahead with the marriage!

Some sources actually give *St Erkenwald's Day* 1532, 14th November, as Anne Boleyn and Henry VIII's wedding date. The chronicler Edward Hall wrote:

"The kyng, after his returne [from Calais] maried priuily[privily] the lady Anne Bulleyn on sainet Erkenwaldes daie, whiche mariage was kept so secrete, that very fewe knewe it, til she was greate with child, at Easter after."

This was straight after their return from Calais, from a trip where Anne Boleyn had played the part of Henry VIII's consort, and where she had been accepted by Francis I. We know that they started co-habiting after this trip, and that Anne was pregnant by the time of the ceremony in January 1533, so a marriage or a betrothal in November 1532 does make sense.

1540 – Birth of Edmund Campion, Jesuit and martyr St Edmund Campion, in London. He was hanged, drawn and quartered on 1st December 1581 for treasonable conspiracy. Campion was beatified in 1886 by Pope Leo XIII and canonized in 1970 by Pope Paul VI.

1554 – Thomas Wyatt the Younger raised his standard in Maidstone, and other rebels in Kent made simultaneous proclamations in Rochester, Tonbridge, Malling, and Milton.

1559 – Elizabeth I's first Parliament was inaugurated.

1567 – Death of Sir William Hewett, Lord Mayor of London from 1st September 1559.

1586 – Robert Dudley accepted the title of Governor-General of the Netherlands.

26TH JANUARY

1528 – Death of Sir Francis Poyntz, courtier and diplomat, in London. He died of the plague. He was made an Esquire of the Body to Henry VIII in 1516, and then a Carver in 1521. Poyntz carried out a diplomatic mission in 1527, when Henry VIII sent him to the Holy Roman Emperor, Charles V, to help negotiate peace between Charles and Francis I of France.

1533 – Henry VIII appointed Thomas Audley as Lord Chancellor to replace Sir Thomas More, who had resigned the previous year. Audley had actually been carrying out the duties of Lord Chancellor since May 1532.

1546 – Death of Sir John Spelman, Judge of Assize and Law Reporter. He was buried at Narborough, Norfolk. He is known for his reports of cases from 1502 to 1540, which included the proceedings against Cardinal Wolsey, Bishop Fisher, Sir Thomas More and Anne Boleyn.

1554 – Mary I wrote to Elizabeth I summoning her to court and warning her about *Wyatt's Rebellion*. Elizabeth did not obey the summons, pleading illness as an excuse.

1567 – Death of Nicholas Wotton, diplomat, Secretary of State and Dean of Canterbury and York. He died in London and was buried in Canterbury Cathedral.

1612 – Burial of Jane Suárez de Figueroa (née Dormer), Duchess of Feria, at Zafra, in the monastery of Santa Clara.

27TH JANUARY

On the 27th January 1596, Sir Francis Drake, explorer, sea captain and pirate, died of dysentery in Portobelo harbour, Panama. When he realised that death was near, he asked to be dressed in his armour. Although he requested burial on land, Drake was buried at sea in a lead coffin, along with his second cousin, Admiral Sir John Hawkins.

Drake made his first voyage to the New World at the age of around twenty-three, with Hawkins, whose family owned a fleet of ships based in Plymouth. Another voyage saw the fleet trapped by Spaniards in the Mexican port of San Juan de Ulua in 1568. Fortunately, the two men managed to escape, but they lost all but two of their fleet. In 1570 and 1571, Drake undertook two trading voyages to the West Indies, and in 1572 took two ships on a marauding campaign against the Caribbean's Spanish ports. Drake was able to capture the port of Nombre de Dios and return to England, his ships laden with Spanish booty. In 1573 Drake attacked a mule train with the help of Guillaume Le Testu, the French buccaneer, capturing around 20 tons of gold and silver.

In 1577, Elizabeth I secretly commissioned Drake to lead an expedition to the American Pacific coast where there were Spanish colonies. Drake left Plymouth on the 15th November 1577, but only one of his fleet made it to the Pacific Ocean, his flagship the *Pelican*, which arrived there in October 1578. The ship was renamed the *Golden Hind* (after Sir Christopher Hatton's coat of arms), and Drake became the first English sailor to navigate his way through the Straits of Magellan. The *Golden Hind* made its way north, along South America's Pacific coast, plundering towns and Spanish ports as it went, and capturing Spanish ships laden with gold, silver and jewels. In June 1579, Drake landed just north of Point Loma (present day San Diego, California), which was Spain's northernmost holding in the Americas. He claimed it for England in the name of the Holy Trinity and called it *Nova Albion*, "New Britain". He then turned south and made his way back home, arriving in England in September 1580. He was the first Englishman to circumnavigate the globe.

His achievements and his rich cargo of treasure and spices led to Elizabeth I knighting him on board his flagship on 4th April 1581. Drake presented Elizabeth with a jewel to commemorate his successful circumnavigation. It was from Mexico and was made of enamelled gold decorated with an African diamond, and a ship with an ebony hull. In return, Elizabeth presented Drake with a jewel and a portrait of herself.

In 1585, Drake set sail for the West Indies and the Florida coastline where he did what came naturally to him - plundering. He captured the Spanish port of San Augustín and returned home with some unsuccessful English colonists from Roanoke Island. His actions made Philip of Spain furious and war was imminent, but worse was to come for the Spanish king: in 1587, Drake sailed to Cadiz and Corunna, in Spain, where he destroyed 37 ships with which Spain was preparing to attack England.

In 1588, Drake was Vice Admiral of the English fleet under Lord Howard of Effingham, the fleet which defeated the Spanish Armada. On 29th July 1588, Drake and Howard organised fire ships to send into the Spanish fleet at Calais to break their formation and to force them out to sea. The next day, Drake was present at the famous *Battle of Gravelines*.

In 1589, Sir Francis Drake and Sir John Norreys were given orders to 1) Seek out and destroy any remaining Spanish ships, 2) Help the rebels in Lisbon, Portugal and 3) Take the Azores for England. Unfortunately, 12,000 lives and 20 ships were lost off the Spanish coast.

Drake's final voyage to the West Indies and South America was a bit of a disaster. He failed to take the port of Las Palmas, and also San Juan in Puerto Rico. He managed to survive a Spanish attack which saw a cannonball shot through the cabin of his ship, but he died of dysentery in 1596.

1501 – Death of Thomas Langton, Bishop of Winchester and Archbishop-elect of Canterbury, from the plague. He had been elected Archbishop on 22nd January, but died before his consecration. He was buried at Winchester Cathedral, in the chantry chapel.

1510 – Death of Sir Thomas Brandon, soldier, courtier and diplomat. He was buried at the London Blackfriars on 29th January. Brandon served Henry VII as Master of the Horse and Henry VIII as Warden and Chief Justice of the Royal Forests to the south of Trent.

1541 – The parsonage, lands and right to appoint clergy in Haverhill, Suffolk, were granted to Anne of Cleves. Her marriage to Henry VIII had been annulled in the previous July.

1548 – Archbishop Thomas Cranmer wrote to Bishop Bonner informing him that the Lord Protector had decided "that no candles should be borne upon *Candlemas Day*, nor also from henceforth ashes or palms used any longer."

1550 – Execution of Humphrey Arundell, rebel, at Tyburn. He was hanged as a traitor after leading the rebel forces in the Cornish *Prayer Book Rebellion* of 1549.

1556 – Execution of Bartholomew Green, Protestant martyr, at Smithfield, with six other Protestants. Green was a zealous evangelical and also appears to have been behind the circulation of a bill denouncing Philip of Spain and Mary I, and supporting Elizabeth.

1606 – The Trial of the eight surviving conspirators of the *Gunpowder Plot*, including Guy Fawkes, began in Westminster Hall. They were found guilty of treason and sentenced to be hanged, drawn and quartered. Some were executed on 30th January, but Guy Fawkes met his end on the 31st.

28TH JANUARY

On this day in history, 28th January 1457, Henry VII, or Henry Tudor, was born at Pembroke Castle in Wales. His parents were Edmund Tudor, 1st Earl of Richmond and son of Owen Tudor and Catherine of Valois, and his thirteen year-old wife, Margaret Beaufort, great-granddaughter of John of Gaunt, 1st Duke of Lancaster, and his mistress (and later wife) Katherine Swynford. It was through this Beaufort side going back to John of Gaunt that Henry VII derived his claim to the throne of England, and he became King after defeating Richard III and his troops at the *Battle of Bosworth* on 22nd August 1485. He ruled for over 23 years.

Also, on this day in history, 90 years later, in the early hours of 28th January 1547, Henry VII's son and successor, Henry VIII, died at Whitehall Palace. He had been ill for some time and had made amendments to his will at the end of December. In early January, De Selve and La Garde, the French ambassadors reported to Francis I that Henry was ill, but that he was well enough to meet with ambassadors on 16th January. However, on 27th January, the King was too ill to attend the commission which agreed on the Duke of Norfolk's attainder, and it became clear that he was dying. His doctors were afraid to tell the King that the end was near, for fear that they'd be accused of treason, so Henry's good friend Sir Anthony Denny broke the news to the King. Henry asked for Archbishop Cranmer and then slept for a few hours. By the time Cranmer arrived, the King was unable to speak, but when the Archbishop asked him to give a sign that he trusted in God, the King was able to squeeze his hand. He lapsed into unconsciousness and died in the early hours. He had been King for over thirty-seven years, and his iconic portrait is recognised by people all over the world, who either love him or hate him.

Henry VIII's nine year-old son, Edward, inherited the throne and became King Edward VI.

⸱⸱⸱⸱⸱⸱⸱⸱⸱⸱⸱⸱⸱⸱⸱⸱⸱⸱⸱⸱⸱⸱⸱⸱⸱⸱⸱⸱⸱⸱⸱⸱⸱⸱⸱

1501 – Death of John Dynham, 1st Baron Dynham, politician and administrator, at Lambeth. He was buried at the London Greyfriars on 30th January. His offices included Lord High Treasurer of England, Lord Chancellor of Ireland, Lieutenant of Calais and High Sheriff of Devon.

1521 – Opening of the *Diet of Worms*, which ran from 28th January to 25th May 1521 with Charles V, Holy Roman Emperor, presiding over it. Reformist Martin Luther was summoned to the Imperial diet to renounce or reaffirm his beliefs, and he appeared there on 16th April. On 25th May 1521, the *Edict of Worms* was issued by the Emperor denouncing Luther and calling for him to be punished as a heretic. It offered a reward to anyone who could capture him.

1598 – Death of Edward Barton, diplomat and Elizabeth I's ambassador to the Ottoman Empire, of dysentery on the island of Heybeli Ada, in the Sea of Marmara, off the coast of Istanbul. He was buried on the island in the Christian cemetery.

29TH JANUARY

On this day in history, 29th January 1536, Catherine of Aragon was laid to rest in Peterborough Abbey, now Peterborough Cathedral. She had requested that she should be buried in a Chapel of her beloved order, The Observant Friars, but Henry's dissolution of the monasteries meant that there were none left. The Spanish princess, who had left her homeland nearly thirty-five years ago to become Queen of England, was buried as Princess Dowager, not queen. To make matters worse, the Bishop of Rochester spoke in his sermon of how "in the hour of death she acknowledged she had not been Queen of England". It is no wonder that her great friend Eustace Chapuys, the Imperial Ambassador, decided to miss the service, and remember her in his own way in London.

On the same day that her predecessor, Catherine of Aragon, was laid to rest, Anne Boleyn miscarried. The Imperial Ambassador reported the miscarriage to his master, Charles V:-

"On the day of the interment [Catherine of Aragon's funeral] the Concubine had an abortion which seemed to be a male child which she had not borne 3½ months, at which the King has shown great distress. The said concubine wished to lay the blame on the duke of Norfolk, whom she hates, saying he frightened her by bringing the news of the fall the King had six days before. But it is well known that is not the cause, for it was told her in a way that she should not be alarmed or attach much importance to it. Some think it was owing to her own incapacity to bear children, others to a fear that the King would treat her like the late Queen, especially considering the treatment shown to a lady of the Court, named Mistress Semel, to whom, as many say, he has lately made great presents."

On 25th February, Chapuys mentioned miscarriage again:-

"I learn from several persons of this Court that for more than three months this King has not spoken ten times to the Concubine, and that when she miscarried he scarcely said anything to her, except that he saw clearly that God did not wish to give him male children; and in leaving her he told her, as if for spite, that he would speak to her after she was "releuize." The said Concubine attributed the misfortune to two causes: first, the King's fall; and, secondly, that the love she bore him was far greater than that of the late Queen, so that her heart broke when she saw that he loved others. At which remark the King was much grieved, and has shown his feeling by the fact that during these festive days he is here, and has left the other at Greenwich, when formerly he could not leave her for an hour."

Catholic recusant, Nicholas Sander, who was in exile during Elizabeth I's reign, wrote of how Anne Boleyn blamed her miscarriage on catching the King with Jane Seymour on his lap, and Jane Dormer (Duchess of Feria and lady-in-waiting to Mary I) also wrote of this and reported that "there was often much scratching and bye-blows between the queen and her maid."

1547 – Edward Seymour and Anthony Denny informed the young Edward VI that his father, Henry VIII, had died the day before.

1559 – Death of Sir Thomas Pope, founder of Trinity College, Oxford, member of Parliament and Privy Councillor in Mary I's reign, at Clerkenwell. He was buried at St Stephen's Church, Walbrook. In 1556, Pope acted as a guardian for Princess Elizabeth at Hatfield House, and handled the correspondence when Eric of Sweden was interested in marrying Elizabeth.

1577 – Death of Richard Harpur, Law Reporter and Judge of the Common Pleas. He was buried at Swarkestone Church in Derbyshire.

1613 – Death of Sir Thomas Bodley, scholar, diplomat and founder of Oxford's Bodleian Library at his house next to St Bartholomew's Hospital in London. He was buried in Merton College chapel on 29th March.

30TH JANUARY

On the 30th January 1554, rebel Thomas Wyatt the Younger and his men besieged Cooling Castle, owned by George Brooke, 9th Baron Cobham, who had withdrawn to his castle after the Duke of Norfolk's forces had mutinied and dispersed. According to his biographer, C. S Knighton, Cobham claimed that he had fought valiantly against the rebels for seven hours before surrendering to them, but Knighton points out that his resistance was most probably a "pretence". Things were looking good for Wyatt who then marched on to London. Unfortunately, on 6th February Wyatt was forced to surrender, and the rebellion was over.

1520 – Birth of Sir William More, member of Parliament, Protestant and son of Sir Christopher More, a powerful administrator in Henry VII's reign. More served Elizabeth I as Constable of Farnham Castle, Treasurer of the Lottery, Commissioner for Ecclesiastical Causes, Collector of the Loan, Chamberlain of the Exchequer, Master of Swans and Deputy Custos Rotulorum. He was also a commissioner on various commissions of oyer and terminer during her reign.

1531 – Death of Sir Robert Brudenell, judge. He served Henry VII as King's Serjeant and Henry VIII as Chief Justice of the Common Pleas. He was buried at Deene church, Northamptonshire.

1593 – Ippolito Aldobrandini was elected as Pope Clement VIII.

1606 – Execution of Robert Winter and three of his fellow conspirators, at St Paul's. He was hanged, drawn and quartered for his part in the *Gunpowder Plot*. His brother, Thomas, was executed the next day.

31ST JANUARY

On this day in history, 31st January 1510, Queen Catherine of Aragon gave birth to a still-born daughter. Her confessor, Fray Diego, reported that the miscarriage occurred "without any other pain except that one knee pained her the night before."

Henry VIII and Catherine had married on 11th June 1509, and were crowned together on 24th June. The months following these events were like one big honeymoon as the couple celebrated Henry's accession and their marriage by holding jousts, banquets and going hunting. They also went on a *royal progress* in the August and September of that year, and it seems that this was when Catherine became pregnant. Henry VIII was ecstatic that his wife had become pregnant so quickly, and wrote to his father-in-law, Ferdinand of Aragon:-

"Your daughter, her Serene Highness the Queen, our dearest consort has conceived in her womb a living child and is right therewith."

The news was also announced to the general public who rejoiced at the news. Unfortunately, on 31st January 1510, Catherine went into premature labour and gave birth to a still-born baby girl. Although she had lost her baby, Catherine's abdomen stayed rounded and actually began to increase in size, leading her physician to conclude that "the Queen remained pregnant of another child and it was believed". It appeared that Catherine had lost one of a pair of twins. The couple, who had obviously been saddened at the loss of their little girl, clung onto this diagnosis even when Catherine began to menstruate again. At the end of February 1510, Henry ordered the refurbishment of the royal nursery and Elizabeth Denton, the former Lady Mistress of Henry's own nursery, was brought out of retirement in anticipation of the birth. In March 1510, Catherine entered her confinement and waited for her labour to begin. It never did. Eventually Fray Diego reported that the swelling had decreased and that Catherine was not pregnant after all. It seems to have been a phantom pregnancy.

A shaken and embarrassed Catherine finally wrote to her father on 27th May 1510 telling him that she had just miscarried, a blatant lie but understandable considering what she had been through. Rumours began to circulate that Catherine was barren and that she would never conceive, but Catherine proved these wrong. As she was writing to her father about the miscarriage, she was actually pregnant, and on New Year's Day 1511, Catherine gave birth to a son, Prince Henry. However, the celebrations were short-lived as the little prince lived just fifty-two days, dying on 22nd February 1511.

1540 – Henry VIII met his bride-to-be, Anne of Cleves, at Rochester. Following the great chivalric tradition, Henry disguised himself and attempted to kiss her, but a shocked Anne did not recognise him as King. It was a disastrous first meeting, and Henry was sorely disappointed that she could not recognise him as her true love.

1547 – Thomas Wriothesley announced the death of Henry VIII to Parliament and Edward VI was proclaimed King.

1597 – Burial of Sir Hugh Cholmondeley, soldier, member of Parliament and Vice-President of the Council in the Marches of Wales, at Malpas Parish Church.

1606 – Executions of *Gunpowder Plot* conspirators Thomas Winter, Ambrose Rookwood, Robert Keyes, and Guy Fawkes at the Old Palace Yard, Westminster. All eight plotters had been found guilty of high treason in a trial at Westminster Hall on 27th January, and four of them had been executed on 30th January at St Paul's.

EDWARD VI (1537-1553)

1ST FEBRUARY

On this day in 1554, Queen Mary I gave a rousing speech at the Guildhall to rally Londoners to her cause and to oppose *Wyatt's rebellion*. Contemporary John Proctor recorded that Mary "did so wonderfully enamour the hearts of the hearers as it was world to hear with what shouts they exalted the honour and magnanimity of Queen Mary".

Mary denounced Wyatt and his rebels, defended her plan to marry Philip of Spain as being beneficial to England and affirmed:

"For I am already married to this Common Weal and the faithful members of the same; the spousal ring whereof I have on my finger: which never hitherto was, nor hereafter shall be, left off. Protesting unto you nothing to more acceptable to my heart, nor more answerable to my will, then your advancement in wealth and welfare, with the furtherance of GOD'S glory."

John Foxe recorded his version of Mary's speech in his book "Actes and Monuments" and, again after denouncing the rebels, he has Mary saying:

"I am your Queen, to whom at my coronation, when I was wedded to the realm and laws of the same (the spousal ring whereof I have on my finger, which never hitherto was, not hereafter shall be, left off), you promised your allegiance and obedience to me. And that I am the right and true inheritor of the Crown of this Realm of England, I take all Christendom to witness. My Father, as you all know, possessed the same regal state, which now rightly is descended unto me; and to him always you showed yourselves most faithful and loving subjects, and therefore I doubt not, but you will show yourselves likewise to me, and that you will not suffer a vile traitor to have the order and governance of our person, and to occupy our estate, especially being so vile a traitor as Wyatt is. Who most certainly as he hath abused my ignorant subjects, which be on his side, so doth he intend and purpose the destruction of you, and spoil of your goods. And I say to you, on the word of a Prince, I cannot tell how naturally the mother loveth the child, for I was never the mother of any; but certainly, if a Prince and Governor may as naturally and earnestly love her subjects as the mother doth love the child, then assure yourselves that I, being your lady and mistress, do as earnestly and tenderly love and favour you. And I, thus loving you, cannot but think that ye as heartily and faithfully love me; and then I doubt not but we shall give these rebels a short and speedy overthrow."

***

1506 – Birth of George Buchanan, Scottish historian, poet, playwright, humanist scholar and administrator, at Moss Farm in Killearn, Stirling, Scotland. Buchanan's works included two tragedies: "Baptistes" and "Jephthes", his satire "Chamaeleon", poems and books of verses, the treatise *De jure Regni apud Scotos* and his *Rerum Scoticarum Historia*, a history of Scotland.

1514 – Henry VIII granted the Dukedom of Suffolk to Charles Brandon, his future brother-in-law. He also granted the dukedom of Norfolk to Thomas Howard, making him 2nd Duke of Norfolk, and Howard's son Thomas became Earl of Surrey.

1552 – Birth of Roger Cooke, alchemist and former assistant of Dr John Dee. He also appears to have been employed by Henry Percy, 9th Earl of Northumberland and a man known as the "Wizard Earl" to set up and run a still house in the Tower of London.

1555 – Burial of Jane Dudley, Duchess of Northumberland and wife of John Dudley, Duke of Northumberland, at Chelsea.

1562 – Death of Sir Richard Edgcumbe, courtier and politician. He was buried at Maker Church in Cornwall. Edgcumb served as a member of Parliament for Cornwall, High Sheriff of Devon (1543 and 1552), High Sheriff of Cornwall (1556) and Commissioner of Muster in Cornwall in 1557. In 1559, he was appointed as a commissioner for the Royal Visitation of the Diocese of Exeter.

1587 – Elizabeth I called her secretary, William Davison, to her and asked him to bring her Mary, Queen of Scots's death warrant. She then signed it.

2ND FEBRUARY

On this day in 1550, Sir Francis Bryan, courtier, diplomat, poet and a man nicknamed "the Vicar of Hell", died suddenly at Clonmel in Ireland. He had settled in Ireland after marrying Joan Butler, Dowager Countess of Ormond, and had travelled to Tipperary as Lord Justice "to check the incursions of the O'Carrolls". His last words were allegedly "I pray you, let me be buried amongst the good fellows of Waterford (which were good drinkers)".

Bryan had only one eye. He lost an eye jousting in 1526 and historian Susan Brigden writes of how he joked about it, saying of *Pilgrimage of Grace* rebel Robert Aske, who also had only one eye, "I know him not, nor he me … yet we have but two eyes".

Bryan had served Henry VIII as a diplomat during the King's *Great Matter*, as Ambassador to Francis I in 1538, as Vice-Admiral in 1543 and as Ambassador to Charles V in 1543. He was made Knight-Banneret in 1547 for his role in the expedition against the Scots as commander of the horse and then appointed Lord Marshal in January 1549, leading Edward VI's forces in Ireland. In December of that year, he was appointed Lord Justice, but died less than two months later.

1508 – Death of John Argentine, physician and Provost of King's College, Cambridge. He died at King's College and was buried there in the Chantry Chapel. Argentine was physician to Prince Arthur, son of Henry VII, and was also said to be the last man to attend on the Princes in the Tower.

1575 – Death of John Parkhurst, Bishop of Norwich, probably at Ludham, Norfolk. He was buried in the nave of Norwich Cathedral. He had become Bishop of Norwich in 1560, after his return to England from exile in Mary I's reign. Parkhurst was Chaplain to Queen Catherine Parr, and also to Charles Brandon, Duke of Suffolk, and his wife, Katherine (née Willoughby).

1597 – Burial of James Burbage, joiner, actor and theatre builder, in Holywell Street, Shoreditch. Burbage acted in Leicester's Men and built "The Theatre", a playhouse in Shoreditch, with his brother, Robert.

1597 – Death of James Morice, lawyer and member of Parliament. He hoped to be made Attorney-General, but he angered Elizabeth I in 1593 by causing a heated debate in Parliament when he claimed that church courts were acting against the "Magna Carta". He was temporarily put under house arrest.

3RD FEBRUARY

On this day in 1587, the Privy Council met in William Cecil, Lord Burghley's chambers at Greenwich and agreed to send Mary, Queen of Scots' signed death warrant to Fotheringhay. Burghley appointed the Earls of Shrewsbury and Kent to direct the execution, and the council agreed to keep Elizabeth in the dark until the deed was done.

Elizabeth I had called her secretary, William Davison, to her on 1st February 1587, asking him to bring Mary's execution warrant for her to sign. She signed it and later claimed that she had instructed him to not let the warrant out of his hands until he had permission from her. Davison's story differed. He claimed that Elizabeth told him that she wished the execution to take place in the Great Hall of Fotheringhay Castle without delay, for she was disturbed by reports of an attempt to rescue Mary. As instructed, Davison asked Sir Christopher Hatton, the acting Lord Chancellor, to seal the warrant with the Great Seal of England to validate it. Hatton and Davison had then taken the warrant to Lord Burghley, fearing that Elizabeth would change her mind.

The warrant was sent to Fotheringhay on 4th February.

1478 – Birth of Edward Stafford, 3rd Duke of Buckingham at Brecon Castle. He was the eldest son of rebel Henry Stafford, 2nd Duke of Buckingham, and his wife, Katherine Woodville. His father had been executed in 1483 after rebelling against Richard III, but his attainder was posthumously reversed, allowing Edward to become Duke of Buckingham. Unfortunately, Edward was also executed in 1521 after being found guilty of treason.

1537 – Execution of Thomas Fitzgerald, 10th Earl of Kildare (known as Silken Thomas), his five uncles and Sir John Burnell, at Tyburn. Thomas was hanged and beheaded, but his uncles and Burnell were hanged, drawn and quartered. He had renounced his allegiance to King Henry VIII back in June 1534, at St Mary's Abbey, Dublin, after his father's execution in London.

1554 – Thomas Wyatt the Younger and his rebels reached Southwark, London. By this time, however, Mary I had rallied her troops, and Wyatt found the city guarded and barricaded. He had to move on to Kingston, where he managed to enter London on 6th February.

1576 – Henry of Navarre, future Henry IV of France, escaped from Paris after being forced to live at the French court and convert to Catholicism, following the *St Bartholomew's Day Massacre* of August 1572.

4TH FEBRUARY

On this day in 1520, Mary Boleyn, sister of Anne Boleyn, married William Carey, an Esquire of the Body and a relative and close friend of Henry VIII, in the Chapel Royal at Greenwich. The King attended the wedding.

Carey was descended from Edward III, and his maternal grandmother was cousin to Henry VIII's maternal grandmother, Margaret Beaufort. He was a suitable husband for a Boleyn/Howard girl, particularly as he was a member of the King's Privy Chamber. The couple would have lodged at court after their wedding, allowing Carey to continue his duties serving the King. They both attended the Field of Cloth of Gold in June 1520, serving the King and Queen there.

At some point, Mary began a relationship with the King, a relationship which is still causing controversy today as historians argue over the paternity of her children: Henry and Catherine Carey, the meaning behind the grants which were given to her husband in the 1520s, the King's real feelings for Mary and even the length of their relationship. Some historians suggest that their affair began sometime around *Shrovetide* 1522 when the King rode out to the traditional joust with the motto "Elle mon Coeur a navera", she has wounded my heart. Mary may have rebuffed the King's advances at first, but there is no evidence that the King forced himself on her or pursued her relentlessly.

Mary's husband was rewarded a series of royal grants between 1522 and 1526, and it is all too easy to see these as payments for the use of his wife, but the King was in the habit of rewarding those who served him, and Carey was an up and coming courtier. Mary gave birth to two children in the 1520s: Catherine in 1524 and Henry in 1526. The King did not acknowledge either child as his, and although historians and authors argue over their paternity, it is impossible to say when we don't even know when Mary was involved with the King.

Mary was widowed in June 1528 when Carey died of sweating sickness.

***

1495 – Anne of York, daughter of Edward IV and Elizabeth Woodville, married Thomas Howard, Earl of Surrey and the future 3rd Duke of Norfolk at Westminster Abbey.

1521 – Death of William Atwater, Bishop of Lincoln, at Wooburn in Buckinghamshire. Atwater also served as Vice-Chancellor of Oxford University, Dean of the Chapel Royal and Chancellor of Lincoln. He was buried in the Cathedral church of Lincoln, in the nave.

1523 – Death of Thomas Ruthall, Bishop of Durham, at Durham Place in London. He was buried at Westminster Abbey, in the St John's Chapel.

1541 – Burial of Sir William Brereton, Lord Justice of Ireland, at St Canice's Cathedral, Kilkenny, in the choir.

1555 – Burning of Protestant martyr, clergyman and Biblical editor, John Rogers, at Smithfield. Rogers was the first England Protestant burned in Mary I's reign after being condemned as a heretic. Rogers refused the chance of a last minute pardon if he recanted, and died bravely. His wife and eleven children, one being newborn and at the breast, attended his burning. Martyrologist John Foxe recorded that Rogers "constantly and cheerfully took his death with wonderful patience, in the defence and quarrel of the Gospel of Christ."

1593 – Death of Sir Gilbert Gerard, member of Parliament and judge. He was buried in Ashley Parish Church in Staffordshire. Gerard's offices included Attorney-General and Master of the Rolls. Gerard was involved in trying Elizabeth I's secretary William Davison, in 1587 after he had presented the death warrant of Mary, Queen of Scots before the Queen's Council, and also the Earl of Arundel in 1589.

5TH FEBRUARY

1537 – Birth of diplomat Sir Henry Brooke, son of George Brooke, 9th Baron Cobham, and his wife Anne Bray. Anne Bray was a lady in waiting to Anne Boleyn, and there is controversy over whether she was the "Nan Cobham" who was one of the Queen's accusers in 1536. In Elizabeth I's reign, Brooke was made a gentleman pensioner and carried out embassies to Spain, the Low Countries and France for her. In October 1579, Elizabeth appointed him as her resident ambassador in France, until he was replaced by Sir Edward Stafford in 1583.

1556 – *Treaty of Vaucelles* between Philip II of Spain and Henry II of France. By the terms of this treaty, Henry II had to relinquish Franche-Comté to Philip, but the treaty was quickly broken.

1557 – Death of Sir William Portman, judge and Lord Chief Justice of England and Wales from 1555. He was buried at St Dunstan-in-the-West, Fleet Street, London.

1576 – Henry of Navarre, the future Henry IV of France, abjured Catholicism at Tours, rejoining the Protestant forces, following his escape from Paris on 3rd February.

1605 – Death of Sir Edward Stafford, son of Sir William Stafford (Mary Boleyn's second husband) and his second wife Dorothy Stafford. Edward was an member of Parliament and diplomat, and there is controversy over his "spying" activities during the Armada and exactly how much information he passed to Mendoza. He was buried in St Margaret's, Westminster.

6TH FEBRUARY

On Saturday 6th February 1557, the remains of reformers Martin Bucer and Paul Fagius were exhumed and publicly burned, after being posthumously found guilty of heresy. They were burned, along with their books, on Market Hill in Cambridge. Fagius had died from the plague in 1549 and Bucer had died of tuberculosis in 1551.

After the burnings, Thomas Watson, Bishop of Lincoln, preached a sermon against Bucer, Fagius and their heresies. Their former burial places, St Mary's Church and St Michael's Church, were then reconsecrated to purify them, and the Blessed Sacrament was paraded through the city's streets. It seemed that Cambridge needed to be cleansed of the 'evil' these men had brought to the city.

Both men's condemnations were overturned in 1560, in Elizabeth I's reign, and a ceremony held to restore their honour.

1561 – Baptism of Tailboys Dymoke (pseudonym Thomas Cutwode) at Kyme in Lincolnshire. He was the son of Sir Robert Dymoke, and his wife, Bridget (née Clinton). Dymoke is known for his allegorical poem, *Caltha poetarum*, or, "The Bumble Bee", which he published under the name of Thomas Cutwode.

1585 – Death of Edmund Plowden, lawyer, legal scholar and law reporter, in London. He was laid to rest in the Middle Temple Church. Cambridge University libraries and the British Library contain manuscripts of his commentaries and opinions, and he is known for his 1571 "Les comentaries ou les reportes de Edmunde Plowden" volume of law reports covering cases during the reigns of Edward VI, Mary I and Elizabeth I.

7TH FEBRUARY

This day in 1477 or 1478 is the traditional birthdate of Sir Thomas More in Milk Street, London. He was the son of Sir John More, lawyer and judge on the King's Bench, and Agnes Graunger, daughter of Thomas Graunger, a Merchant of the Staple of Calais and an Alderman of London.

More joined the household of John Morton, Archbishop of Canterbury, before studying Latin and logic at the University of Oxford. He then studied law in London. It was while he was a student that he met and became friends with men like William Lilye, John Colet and Erasmus.

Between 1499 and 1503, More stayed at the Carthusian priory, London Charterhouse, while he considered joining the order. He also considered becoming a Franciscan monk, but decided to devote himself to the law after he realised that a life of celibacy did not suit him. More became a Member of Parliament in 1504, an Undersheriff of the City of London in 1510, a Master of Requests in 1514, one of the King's counsellors in 1517 and then a Privy Councillor in 1518.

In 1521, Thomas More was knighted and made Under-treasurer after proving himself by carrying out a diplomatic mission to Charles V with Cardinal Wolsey. He rose in influence as the King's personal secretary and adviser, became Speaker of the House of Commons in 1523, and then the High Steward of the Universities of Oxford and Cambridge. He was appointed the Chancellor of the Duchy of Lancaster in 1525. In 1529, More was made Lord Chancellor after the fall of Cardinal Thomas Wolsey.

More supported the Catholic Church, which he saw as the true faith, and campaigned against the *Reformation* and heresy. His actions against the *Reformation* included helping Cardinal Wolsey to prevent the importation of Lutheran books into England, producing scholarly works against

Luther's writings and persecuting people whom he perceived as heretics. His non-religious scholarly work included "History of King Richard III" and "Utopia".

He was a loyal servant of King Henry VIII, but ended up being executed as a traitor on 6th July 1535 after refusing to take the Oath of Succession. He believed that "no temporal man may be the head of spirituality", even his beloved King.

More is famous as St Thomas More, after being beatified in 1886 and canonised in 1935. His feast day is celebrated on 22nd June in the Roman Catholic Church and 6th July in the Anglican Church.

1531 - Convocation ordered to recognise Henry as "sole protector and supreme head of the English church and clergy". The resulting "haggling" results in Thomas Cromwell adding the phrase "so far as the law of Christ allows".

1587 – Sir Amyas Paulet read out Mary, Queen of Scots' death warrant to her, and informed her that she would be executed the following day.

1591 – Burial of Sir Nicholas Bagenal (Bagnal), soldier and Marshal of the army in Ireland in the reigns of Edward VI and Elizabeth I. He was buried at Newry.

1594 – Death of Barnabe Googe, pastoral poet and translator. He was buried at Cockerington church, near Alvingham. Googe's works included a dedicatory poem in Thomas Gressop's translation of Nicolaus Cabasilas, "A briefe treatise, conteynynge a playne and fruitfull declaration of the popes usurped primacye", a translation of *Zodiacus vitae* by Marcellus Palingenius, and his "Eglogs, Epytaphes, and Sonettes".

1623 – Death of Thomas Cecil, 1st Earl of Exeter, courtier, soldier and eldest son of William Cecil, 1st Baron Burghley, probably at Wimbledon. He was buried in the St John the Baptist Chapel, Westminster Abbey. His offices under Elizabeth I included High Sheriff of Northamptonshire, Lord

Lieutenant of Yorkshire, Lord President of the Council of the North and Knight of the Garter.

8TH FEBRUARY

On Wednesday 8th February 1587, Mary, Queen of Scots was executed at Fotheringhay Castle. The warrant for her death had arrived the day before, and Sir Amyas Paulet, Mary's gaoler, wasted no time in arranging Mary's execution. Paulet, his assistant Sir Drue Dury, and the Earls of Shrewsbury and Kent, barged into Mary's room. Paulet tore down her cloth of state, and then the warrant for Mary's execution was read out to her. A worried Mary was reassured by Drury that she would not be quietly murdered like Richard II, saying, "Madam, you need not fear it, for that you are in the charge of a Christian Queen." Historian John Guy points out that Mary would not have been so reassured if she had known that Elizabeth had intended for Mary to be assassinated.

Mary thanked the men for their news, crossing herself and saying "I am quite ready and very happy to die, and to shed my blood for Almighty God, my Saviour and my Creator, and for the Catholic Church, and to maintain its rights in this country", obviously seeing herself as a martyr. She then asked for her chaplain, a request which was denied her, and then set about preparing herself for her death. She prayed, made her will, distributed her belongings between her ladies and servants, and then wrote some letters of farewell. Her final letter was to her brother-in-law, Henry III of France:

"Today, after dinner, I was advised of my sentence. I am to be executed like a criminal at eight o'clock in the morning. I haven't had enough time to give you a full account of what has happened, but if you will listen to my physician and my other sorrowful servants you will know the truth, and how, thanks be to God, I scorn death and faithfully protest that I face it innocent of any crime...

The Catholic faith and the defence of my God-given right to the English throne are the two reasons for which I am condemned, and yet they will not allow me to say that it is for the Catholic faith that I die...

I beg you as most Christian Majesty, my brother-in-law and old friend, who have always protested your love for me, to give proof now of your kindness on all these points: both by paying charitably my unfortunate servants their arrears of wages (this is a burden on my conscience that you alone can relieve) and also by having prayers offered to God for a Queen who has herself been called Most Christian, and who dies a Catholic, stripped of all her possessions...

Concerning my son, I commend him to you inasmuch as he deserves it, as I cannot answer for him...

I venture to send you two precious stones, amulets against illness, trusting that you will enjoy good health and a long and happy life."

It is a moving letter, written by a woman who was ready to face her death with courage and a strong faith, but who was clearly worried about her servants. She was obviously a loving woman.

At 6am on the 8th February, Mary rose, after spending most of the night writing letters, and her will was read out to her household. She then said her farewells to her staff and began to pray, her prayer being interrupted by the Earls of Shrewsbury and Kent, and Thomas Andrews, Sheriff of Northamptonshire. They had come to escort her to the great hall. Mary grabbed her prayer book and her ivory crucifix and made her way to the place of her death, a hall filled with around three hundred spectators.

According to a contemporary report, Mary was wearing a black satin gown "set with buttons of jet and trimmed with pearl, and short sleeves of satin, cut with a pair of sleeves of purple velvet", a caul with a lawn veil, a pomander on a chain, "an Agnus Dei" and a crucifix of gold around her neck. She was also carrying a bone crucifix.

Mary approached the straw covered scaffold, turned to her loyal ladies and said "Thou hast cause rather to joy than to mourn, for now shalt thou see Mary Stuart's troubles receive their long-expected end." As the Dean of Peterborough prayed aloud in English, Mary read her Catholic Latin prayers louder, and then refusing the help of the executioner, took off her black gown to reveal a scarlet bodice and petticoat. The vivid scarlet of her clothes proclaimed that she was considered herself a martyr to the Catholic faith.

The executioner knelt before the Queen of the Scots, begging her forgiveness, and then Mary knelt, laying her head on the block ready, repeating "*In manuas tuas, Domine, confide spiritum meum*", "Into Thy hands, O Lord, I commend my spirit." The executioner then did the deed, although it took him two blows to kill Mary. When the executioner picked up Mary's head to show the crowd, her cap and wig fell off, revealing cropped grey hair, and when he went to remove the clothes from the body "he found her little dog under her coat, which, being put from thence, went and laid himself down betwixt her head and body, and being besmeared with her blood, was caused to be washed..."

***

1545 – Death of Sir John Arundell of Lanherne at the home of his nephew, Richard Roscarrock of Roscarrock, in St Endellion in Devon. He was buried at St Columb Major. Arundell had fought against the Cornish rebels in 1497 and served Henry VII and Henry VIII as receiver of the Duchy of Cornwall from 1508 until 1533.

1601 – Robert Devereux, 2ⁿᵈ Earl of Essex, his supporters and two hundred soldiers gathered at Essex House. Essex then marched into the city crying "For the Queen! For the Queen!

The crown of England is sold to the Spaniard! A plot is laid for my life!". However, the people ignored him and stayed indoors. Essex was forced to give up after his supporters deserted him, and he surrendered after Lord Admiral Nottingham threatened to blow up his house if he did not give himself up.

1608 – Death of Nicholas Bond, clergyman and President of Magdalen College, Oxford, from 1590. He was buried in the college chapel.

1614 – Burial of John Bracegirdle, poet, at St Mary's Church, Rye, in Sussex. He is known for his 1602 "Psychopharmacon, the mindes medicine, or, The phisicke of philosophie", a translation of the work of *Anicius Manlius Torquatus Severinus Boethius* into English blank verse.

9TH FEBRUARY

1554 – Original date set for the execution of Lady Jane Grey and Lord Guildford Dudley. Extra time was given for Dr John Feckenham, Mary I's Chaplain and Confessor, to try and save Jane's soul by persuading her to recant her Protestant faith and return to the Catholic fold.

1555 – Protestant martyr John Hooper, Bishop of Gloucester and Worcester was burned at the stake in Gloucester. He had been deprived of his bishopric in March 1554, due to his marriage, and was executed for heresy as part of Mary I's persecution of Protestants.

1555 – Burning of Rowland Taylor, Protestant martyr, Rector of Hadleigh in Suffolk, Canon of Rochester Cathedral, Archdeacon of Bury St Edmunds, Archdeacon of Cornwall and former chaplain to Thomas Cranmer. He was burned for heresy on Aldham Common, near Hadleigh.

1604 – Death of Anne Dudley (née Russell), former maid-of-honour to Elizabeth I, Countess of Warwick and third wife of Ambrose Dudley, Earl of Warwick. She died at North Hall in Northaw, Hertfordshire, the property left to her by her husband on his death in 1590. Anne served Elizabeth I as an extraordinary Gentlewoman of the Privy Chamber until Elizabeth's death. Anne chose to be buried with her family, the Russells, at Chenies in Buckinghamshire, rather than with her husband at Warwick.

10TH FEBRUARY

On this day in 1567, Henry Stuart, Lord Darnley, was murdered at Kirk o' Field, Edinburgh, in the Royal Mile, just a few hundred yards from Holyrood House where his wife, Mary, Queen of Scots, and baby son, the future James VI/I, were staying.

Henry, Lord Darnley, had been lodging at Kirk o' Field while convalescing after contracting either syphilis or smallpox. What he didn't know was that while he had been recovering, his enemies had been filling the cellars of the house with gunpowder.

At 2 o'clock in the morning of 10th February 1567, Kirk o' Field was blown to pieces by a huge explosion which was said to have been heard throughout Edinburgh. The house was reduced to rubble and Darnley's body was found in a neighbouring garden, by a pear tree, beside that of his groom, with a dagger lying on the ground between them.

Historian Magnus Magnusson wrote of how his nightgown clad body showed signs of strangulation and concluded that Darnley had been strangled to death before the explosion. Perhaps something had awoken Darnley and he had attempted to flee the house, with his groom, using the chair and rope, which were also found in the garden, to escape from a first floor window. It appears that both men were intercepted and murdered. Perhaps the explosion was an attempt to cover up their murders, but the men had got out of the house before meeting their murderer.

Mary, Queen of Scots observed forty days of mourning for her husband, but there were rumours that she was insincere, and rumours of murder. It was not long before the Earl of Bothwell's name (James Hepburn, 4th Earl of Bothwell) was linked to Darnley's murder because the shoes of Archibald Douglas (Parson of Douglas), a supporter of Bothwell, were found at the scene of the crime, and it was alleged that Bothwell had supplied the gunpowder.

On the 24th April 1567, Bothwell and 800 men met Mary on the road between Linlithgow Palace and Edinburgh, and Bothwell warned Mary that there was danger waiting for her in Edinburgh. He then insisted that she go with him to Dunbar, to his castle, so that he could protect her. On arrival at Dunbar at midnight, Bothwell took Mary hostage and allegedly subjected her to a violent rape so that she would marry him. On 12th May, Mary made Bothwell Duke of Orkney and then married him on the 15th May at Holyrood, just over a week after his divorce from Jean Gordon, Countess of Bothwell, came through. On reporting the events to London, Sir William Drury noted that although it looked as if Mary had been forced into the marriage by Bothwell, things were not as they appeared. There was evidence that Mary had shown an interest in Bothwell in October 1566, when she travelled four hours by horseback to visit him at Hermitage Castle when he was ill. It was all very suspicious.

It is thought that Lord Darnley's murder and Mary's links with Bothwell were factors in her eventual trial and execution. The famous "Casket Letters", which were produced at the York Conference in 1568, were said to implicate Mary in Darnley's murder, but many historians now believe that these letters were forgeries. It looks like we will never know whether Mary, Queen of Scots played a part in the murder of her husband, Lord Darnley, father of James I of England.

1542 – Catherine Howard, fifth wife of Henry VIII, was taken to the Tower of London by barge.

1550 – Death of Sir Edmund Walsingham, soldier and Lieutenant of the Tower of London. He was buried at Chislehurst. Walsingham was Lieutenant of the Tower when Anne Boleyn and Catherine Howard were imprisoned there.

1554 – Death of Sir William Sidney, courtier and former Steward to Prince Edward (future Edward VI), at Penshurst. He was buried at Penshurst parish church.

1557 – Death of Sir Edward Montagu, lawyer and judge, at his manor of Boughton, Northamptonshire, and buried in the church of St Mary, Weekley. Montagu served Henry VIII as Lord Chief Justice of the Court of the King's Bench from 1539 to 1545 when he became Lord Chief Justice of the Common Pleas. He was also a Privy Councillor and acted as one of the executors of the King's will in 1547.

1564 – Death of Henry Neville, 5th Earl of Westmorland, at Kelvedon, Essex. He was buried at Staindrop. The teenage Neville was taken hostage during the 1536 *Pilgrimage of Grace* to ensure his father's co-operation with the rebels. He served Henry VIII as Privy Councillor and, when Edward VI was dying, signed the letters patent naming Lady Jane Grey as his successor. He swapped sides shortly after Edward's death, declaring for Mary I and bore the Second Sword and Cap of Maintenance at her coronation in October 1553.

1612 – Death of Jodocus Hondius (Joost de Hondt), artist, engraver and cartographer, at Amsterdam. Hondius worked with De Bry and Augustin Ryther in 1589 on engravings for the English version of "The Mariner's Mirror", and was also responsible for a world map. Other works included portraits of Elizabeth I, illustrations for the voyages of Sir Francis Drake, a celestial globe and terrestrial globe.

11TH FEBRUARY

Elizabeth of York was born on the 11th February 1466, and was the daughter and eldest child of Edward IV and Elizabeth Woodville. Her father had managed to capture and imprison Henry VI in 1461, dethroning him and taking the crown for himself, starting the royal House of York. In 1464, he secretly married Elizabeth Woodville, a young widow. It was a love match, not a diplomatic one, was controversial and caused trouble when Elizabeth alienated powerful Yorkist supporters, causing them to side with Lancastrians and challenge Edward. The result was that Edward was driven into exile and the throne became Henry VI's once more in October 1470.

Henry's reign was short-lived, as Edward overthrew him once again in April 1471. Ex-Yorkists and Lancastrians were defeated in battle, and Henry VI was killed in the Tower. Edward had stamped out his enemies.

Unfortunately, tragedy struck the House of York at *Easter* 1483 when Edward caught a chill on a fishing trip. He died on 9th April, and his thirteen year-old son Edward became Edward V. Edward V was too young to reign in his own right, so his uncle, Richard, Duke of Gloucester, became the Protector. However, to cut a rather long story short, this was not enough for Richard. With Edward and his younger brother, Richard, Duke of York, 'residing' in the Tower of London, Richard was crowned King Richard III on the 6th July 1483 and the boys disappeared, going down in history as 'The Princes in the Tower'. It is not clear what happened to them.

Elizabeth of York mourned the loss of her brothers, but her mother decided on revenge, and this is when she decided to approach Lady Margaret Beaufort. Although the two ladies were supposed to be on different sides, Elizabeth being from the House of York and Margaret being a Lancastrian, neither lady was happy with Richard on the throne, and decided that a union between their children could bring about Richard's downfall. Henry Tudor defeated Richard III on 22nd August 1485 at the *Battle of Bosworth Field*, becoming King Henry VII, and went on to marry Elizabeth on 18th January 1486. The couple had four children who survived infancy: Arthur, Prince of Wales, Margaret, Henry (future Henry VIII) and Mary. Elizabeth's final pregnancy ended in tragedy in February 1503 with the death of the premature baby, a little girl named Katherine, on the 2nd February, and Elizabeth's death on the 11th February from a post-partum infection. Elizabeth was buried at Westminster Abbey.

1503 – Death of Elizabeth of York, wife of Henry VII, from a post-partum infection.

1531 – Convocation granted Henry VIII the title of "singular protector, supreme lord, and even, so far as the law of Christ allows, supreme head of the English church and clergy".

12TH FEBRUARY

On this day in 1554, Lady Jane Grey and her husband, Guildford Dudley, were executed for treason.

At 10am on the 12th February, Guildford Dudley, brother of Robert Dudley and son of the late John Dudley, Duke of Northumberland, was led out of the Tower of London and up to the scaffold site on Tower Hill. No priest accompanied him onto the scaffold because Guildford was a reformer. On the scaffold, Guildford addressed the crowd briefly and then got down on his knees and prayed. After asking the crowd to pray for him, he put his neck on the block and the executioner beheaded him with a single blow of the axe.

Although his wife, Lady Jane Grey, had allegedly refused to see Guildford, she insisted on watching the execution from a window and the chronicler, Raphael Holinshed, writes of how, as she was being led out of the Tower to be executed, Jane met the cart carrying Guildford's body.

Although her husband had been executed on Tower Hill, Lady Jane Grey was executed inside the Tower of London, on Tower Green. Once the executioner had time to make his way back from Tower Hill, Jane was led out to the scaffold. Although her ladies "wonderfully wept", Jane, who was dressed all in black, managed to maintain her composure. She addressed the waiting crowd:-

"Good people, I am come hither to die, and by a law I am condemned to the same; the fact indeed against the Queen's Highness was unlawful and the consenting thereunto by me: but touching the procurement and desire thereof by me or on my behalf, I do wash my hands thereof in innocency before the face of God and the face of you good Christian people this day.

I pray you all good Christian people to bear me witness that I die a true Christian woman and that I do look to be saved by no other mean, but only by the mercy of God, in the merits of the blood of his only son Jesus Christ. I confess when I did know the word of God I neglected the same and loved myself and the world, and therefore this plague or punishment is happily and worthily [deservedly] happened unto me for my sins. I thank God of his goodness that he has given me a time and respite to repent.

Now good people, I pray you to assist me with your prayers."

After her speech, Jane knelt and said Psalm 51, the Miserere, in English, "Have mercy upon me O God, after they great goodness: according to the multitude of thy mercies, do away mine offences". She then embraced John Feckenham, Mary I's chaplain and confessor, the man who had been sent to Jane to prepare her for her death, and said to him "Go and may God satisfy every wish of yours". Jane then gave her handkerchief and gloves to Elizabeth Tilney, and her prayer book to Thomas Brydges, Deputy Lieutenant of the Tower, who had been charged with passing it on to her father. She then removed her gown, headdress and collar, refusing the help of the executioner. After forgiving the executioner and begging him "despatch me quickly", Jane knelt at the block, tossing her hair forward and out of the way, and putting on the blindfold. It was then that she lost her composure and panicked, "What shall I do? Where is it?". A bystander took pity on the floundering girl and guided her to the block where she lay her neck, praying "Lord, into thy hands I commend my spirit." The executioner took her head off with one blow.

The bodies of Guildford and Jane were then taken to the Chapel of St Peter ad Vincula for burial.

1567 – Death of Sir Thomas White, founder of St John's College, Oxford, and former Lord Mayor of London, at his property in Size Lane, London. He was buried in St John's College Chapel.

1584 – Executions of five Catholic priests, including James Fenn. They were hanged, drawn and quartered at Tyburn. Fenn was beatified by Pope Pius XI in 1929.

1590 – Death of Blanche Parry, chief Gentlewoman of the Privy Chamber, at the age of eighty-two. She was buried in St Margaret's, Westminster, with funeral rites which were usually reserved for a baroness. She has a monument in St Margaret's and also one in Bacton Church, her home village in Herefordshire, which bears an inscription of twenty-eight lines of verse recording Blanche's service to her beloved Queen.

1611 – Probable date of death of Sir Henry Lee, Queen's Champion from c.1580 to November 1590. He was buried at Quarrendon in Buckinghamshire.

13TH FEBRUARY

On this day in history, the 13th February 1542, Catherine Howard and Lady Jane Rochford were executed at the Tower of London.

Eustace Chapuys, the Imperial Ambassador, wrote of how Catherine prepared herself for her execution:-

"On Sunday the 12th, towards evening, she was told to prepare for death, for she was to die next day. That evening she asked to have the block brought in to her, that she might know how to place herself; which was done, and she made trial of it."

Chapuys goes on to say that at 7am the next morning, the 13th, members of the King's Council (Suffolk and Norfolk were absent) and other dignitaries arrived at the Tower to serve as witnesses to Catherine's execution. Charles de Marillac, the French ambassador, reported to his master, Francis I, that the Queen was executed at around 9am, followed by Lady Rochford. Marillac recorded that "The Queen was so weak that she could hardly speak, but confessed in few words that she had merited a hundred deaths for so offending the King who had so graciously treated her". Marillac, however, was not an eye-witness.

Merchant Ottwell Johnson witnessed the executions and recorded:-

"And for news from hence, know ye, that, even according to my writing on Sunday last, I see the Queen and the lady Retcheford suffer within the Tower, the day following; whose souls (I doubt not) be with God, for they made the most godly and Christians' end that ever was heard tell of (I think) since the world's creation, uttering their lively faith in the blood of Christ only, with wonderful patience and constancy to the death, and, with goodly words and steadfast countenance, they desired all Christian people to take regard unto their worthy and just punishment with death, for their offences against

God heinously from their youth upward, in breaking of all his commandments, and also against the King's royal majesty very dangerously; wherefor they, being justly condemned (as they said), by the laws of the realm and Parliament, to die, required the people (I say) to take example at them for amendment of their ungodly lives, and gladly obey the King in all things, for whose preservation they did heartily pray, and willed all people so to do, commending their souls to God and earnestly calling for mercy upon Him, whom I beseech to give us grace with such faith, hope, and charity, at our departing out of this miserable world, to come to the fruition of his Godhead in joy everlasting. Amen."

So it appears that, contrary to a report in "The Spanish Chronicle", which seems to have been the Tudor equivalent of tabloid newspapers, and "The Tudors" TV series, Catherine did not utter the words "I die a Queen, but I would rather die the wife of Culpeper".

Next was the turn of Jane Boleyn, Lady Rochford, wife of the late George Boleyn, and the woman who was accused of committing high treason by helping Catherine commit adultery. Chapuys says of Lady Rochford's execution:-

"Then Lady Rochford was brought, who had shown symptoms of madness till they told her she must die. Neither she nor the Queen spoke much on the scaffold; they only confessed their guilt and prayed for the King's welfare."

And Marillac reported:-

"The lady of Rochefort said as much in a long discourse of several faults which she had committed in her life."

It is a myth that Lady Rochford confessed to giving false testimony against her husband and her sister-in-law, Anne Boleyn; she did nothing of the sort. Neither Chapuys nor Ottwell Johnson make any mention of such a confession. It appears that Jane's execution confession was the work of Gregorio Leti, a man known for making up stories and inventing sources.

After her short address, Lady Rochford knelt, laying her neck on the block, and her head was taken off with one blow of the axe. The bodies and heads of Catherine Howard and Lady Rochford were then taken to the Chapel of St Peter ad Vincula for burial. Visitors to the Chapel at the Tower of London can pay their respects to these two women at their memorial floor tiles, which lie underneath the altar table.

◇◇◇

1564 – Baptism of John Harvey, astrologer and physician, at Saffron Walden in Essex. Harvey was the third son of John Harvey, farmer and rope-maker, and his wife, Alice. His published works included "An Astrologicall Addition" (1583), a series of almanacs and "A Discoursive Probleme Concerning Prophesies" (1588).

1579 – Death of John Fowler, the English Catholic printer and publisher, in Namur, during his exile in the reign of Elizabeth I. He was buried there in the church of St John the Evangelist. He is known as one of the most important English Catholic publishers of the 1560s and 70s.

1585 – Death of Nicholas Robinson, Bishop of Bangor. He was buried in Bangor Cathedral with a memorial brass marking his resting place.

1608 – Death of Elizabeth Talbot, Countess of Shrewsbury, known as Bess of Hardwick, at Hardwick. Her body lay in state at Hardwick until her funeral at All Hallows, Derby (now All Saints' Cathedral), on 4th May 1608. Bess was married four times - Robert Barlow (c. 1543), Sir William Cavendish (1547), Sir William St Loe (c. 1557/8) and finally to George Talbot, 6th Earl of Shrewsbury (1567). Bess is known for her building projects, which included Chatsworth and Hardwick Hall, her beautiful needlework and the fact that she and Shrewsbury were guardians of the captive Mary, Queen of Scots between 1569 and 1584.

14TH FEBRUARY

On this day in 1547, Henry VIII's coffin was taken to Windsor for burial after resting overnight at Syon Abbey. Apparently, some liquid leaked out of it on to the floor at Syon, and this was thought to fulfil the prophecy made by Franciscan friar William Peto in 1532. He had preached in front of the King at Greenwich that "God's judgements were ready to fall upon his head and that dogs would lick his blood, as they had done to Ahab."

1492 – Death of William Berkeley, Marquis of Berkeley and a man known as "William Waste-all". He was buried in the Augustinian friary in London with his second wife, Joan.

1539 – Trial of Sr Nicholas Carew. He was found guilty of treason, after being implicated in the *Exeter Conspiracy*, and sentenced to death. Carew was executed on 3rd March 1539 at Tyburn.

1556 – Thomas Cranmer was degraded from his office of Archbishop of Canterbury for heresy.

1601 – Execution of Thomas Lee, soldier, at Tyburn. He was hanged, drawn and quartered after being implicated in the failed rebellion of Robert Devereux, Earl of Essex.

15TH FEBRUARY

Thomas Arden, businessman and inspiration for the 1592 Elizabethan play, "The Tragedie of Arden of Feversham and Blackwill", was murdered on this day in 1551. Arden was murdered by his wife, Alice, her lover, Thomas Morsby, and other conspirators after a series of botched attempts.

Raphael Holinshed gives an account of the murder in his chronicle, recording the various attempts on Arden's life:

- Attempted poisoning.

- A man known as "Black Will" was meant to accost Arden at St Paul's churchyard, but couldn't, because there were too many people there.

- Black Will was meant to gain entry to the Arden's house by the back door, which was meant to be left open by the servant, but he locked it again for fear that Black Will would murder him, too.

- The plot for Black Will to attack Arden at "Reinam Downe" (Rainham Down) but Arden was not alone on his journey.

- A plan for Black Will to lie in wait for Arden in Broom Close, between Faversham and the ferry, but Black Will waited in the wrong place!

- The attempt to bait Arden and cause a fight, but Arden would not fight.

- The final successful attempt when Black Will hid in Arden's house. Black Will strangled Arden with a towel, Morsby struck him with a "pressing iron of fourteene pounds weight", Black Will slashed him on his face and then Mrs Arden "with a knife gave him seven or eight pricks into the brest".

Alice was burned in Canterbury. Morsby and his sister were hanged at Smithfield, one servant was burned and another was hanged, drawn and quartered. A man Alice accused of procuring Black Will was hanged in chains at Canterbury, another man was hanged at Faversham, and Black Will, who had fled to Flanders, was burned to death at Flushing in 1553.

1499 – Death of James Goldwell, Bishop of Norwich, at the bishop's palace in Hoxne, Suffolk. He was buried in Norwich Cathedral, in the chantry chapel.

1503 – Death of Henry Deane, administrator and Archbishop of Canterbury. As well as serving Henry VII as Archbishop, Deane also served as Chancellor of Ireland, Deputy Governor for Prince Henry and Keeper of the Great Seal. He died at Lambeth Palace and was buried at Canterbury Cathedral at a lavish funeral.

1536 – Death of Richard Rawlins, Bishop of St David's and former warden of Merton College.

1564 – Birth of Galileo Galilei, the Italian physicist, mathematician, astronomer, and philosopher, in Pisa, Italy. He was one of the central figures of the Scientific Revolution and supported Copernicanism (the heliocentric model). He has been referred to as "the Father of Modern Science", "the Father of Modern Physics" and "the father of modern observational astronomy". He is also known for his discovery of the Galilean Moons (Jupiter's satellites), his improved military compass and his work on the telescope.

1571 – Death of Sir Adrian Poynings, soldier. He served as a soldier in Boulogne from 1546 to 1550, when he was made Lieutenant of Calais Castle, then in the St Quentin campaign of 1557 and in Le Havre in 1562.

1598 – Death of John May, Bishop of Carlisle, at Rose Castle, his episcopal residence. He was buried in Carlisle Cathedral.

1616 – Death of Sir George Carey, Lord Deputy of Ireland. He was buried at Cockington, Devon.

16TH FEBRUARY

On the 16th February 1547, Henry VIII's body was interred in a vault in St George's Chapel Windsor, alongside that of his third wife, Jane Seymour. Here is an eye witness account of the proceedings:-

"16 strong Yeomen of the Guard took the coffin and with four strong linen towels, which they had for their fees, let it into the vault near unto the body of Queen Jane Seymour, his third wife. Then the Lord Chamberlain, the Lord Great Master, Mr Treasurer, Mr Comptroller and the Sergeant Porter, breaking their white staves upon their heads in three parts, as did likewise all the Gentleman Ushers, threw them into the grave. Thus the funeral ended, the trumpets sounded in the Rood loft and the company dispersed."

Today, there is a memorial slab marking his resting place under the Quire of St George's Chapel. As well as containing Henry and Jane, this vault also contains the remains of Charles I and an infant child of Queen Anne, the Stuart queen.

1495 – Execution of Sir William Stanley by beheading on Tower Hill. He had been found guilty of treason for allegedly supporting the pretender Perkin Warbeck. Stanley is known for his change of sides at the *Battle of Bosworth*, when he decided to fight with Henry Tudor against Richard III.

1497 – Birth of Philipp Melancthon, German reformer, scholar and friend and colleague of Martin Luther, at Bretten, near Karlsruhe.

1560 – Death of Jean du Bellay, diplomat and Bishop of Paris, in Rome. He was buried in the church of Trinità dei Monti.

1587 – Funeral of Sir Philip Sidney, courtier and author, at St Paul's Cathedral.

1595 – Probable date of the death of Adam Hill, Church of England clergyman and religious writer. He was buried in Salisbury Cathedral on 19th February. His published works included "The Crie of England" and "The Defence of the Article".

17TH FEBRUARY

On this day in 1547, Edward Seymour, uncle of King Edward VI, was made Duke of Somerset. Somerset became Lord Protector of England in February 1547, shortly after Henry VIII's death. Henry VIII's will had named sixteen executors who were to form a regency council, along with twelve other advisers, until Edward VI came of age, so Edward Seymour (then Earl of Hertford) had not been appointed Lord Protector by Henry VIII. The plan was that the council would rule collectively with every member having equal power and rights. However, the will also allowed the executors to grant themselves lands and honours, so Somerset took advantage of this and made himself Duke of Somerset and Lord Protector of his nephew's council, with the agreement of 13 out of the 16 executors. Somerset then went on to rule by proclamation, making all of the decisions himself.

1557 – Death of Henry Radcliffe, 2nd Earl of Essex, at Cannon Row, Westminster. He was buried firstly at St Laurence Pountney and then moved to Boreham in Essex.

1584 – Burial of John Watson, Bishop of Winchester, at Winchester. He was buried in the cathedral.

1590 – Death of Edward Leeds (Lydes), Rector of Croxton and Master of Clare College, Cambridge from 1560 to 1571. He died at his manor at Croxton in Cambridgeshire, and was buried at Croxton Church. Leeds had served Archbishop Matthew Parker as one of his chaplains.

18TH FEBRUARY

In the early hours of the 18th February 1516, a healthy baby girl was born at the Palace of Placentia in Greenwich (Greenwich Palace). Her name was Mary, and she was the daughter of King Henry VIII and Catherine of Aragon.

The little girl had been named Mary after her father's favourite sister, Mary Tudor, and Mary's biographer, historian Linda Porter, writes of how the baby princess was "small but pretty" and "already showed signs that she had inherited the red-gold hair of both her parents and the clear Tudor complexion." She had also inherited her parents' pride, intelligence and strength of character. As her parents gazed at their daughter, breathing sighs of relief that she seemed fit and healthy, they would have had no idea that this tiny girl would one day be Queen of England, that she would face many challenges with courage and would fight for her throne and win. Whatever we think of Mary I, the "Bloody Mary" of myth and legend or the damaged daughter of a tyrant, she should be admired for her achievements, and she certainly paved the way for her half-sister, Elizabeth I. In an excellent article on Mary, in BBC History magazine, historian David Loades listed some of Mary's achievements:-

- She preserved the Tudor succession.
- She strengthened the position of Parliament by using it for her religious settlement.
- Mary established the "gender free" authority of the English crown.
- She restored and strengthened the administrative structure of the Church.
- Mary maintained the navy and reformed the militia.

1503 – Henry Tudor, the future Henry VIII, was created Prince of Wales.

1558 – Death of Sir George Barne, former Alderman and Lord Mayor of London. He was buried at St Bartholomew by the Exchange, London.

1561 – Death of Sir Thomas Denys, administrator. His offices included Comptroller to Princess Mary, Chancellor of Anne of Cleves' household, member of Parliament for Devon, Sheriff of Devon and Deputy Lieutenant of Devon and Cornwall.

1563 – Francis, Duke of Guise, was wounded by a Huguenot assassin. He died six days later.

1612 – Death of Roberto di Ridolfi, the merchant and conspirator famed for the *Ridolfi Plot* to assassinate Elizabeth I. He died in Florence, Italy.

19TH FEBRUARY

On this day in history, 19th February 1592, the Rose Theatre, an Elizabethan play house, was opened in London on Bankside.

In 1585 Philip Henslowe, a London businessman and property developer, leased a tenement and gardens known as the *Little Rose*. In 1587, with the help of grocer John Cholmley and carpenter John Griggs, Henslowe built The Rose Theatre, which opened in 1592. The Rose Theatre website tells of how not much is known about the theatre between 1587 and 1592, but we have records from 1592 when Henslowe started to keep an account book, "Henslowe's Diary". In that same year, Henslowe's step-daughter married Edward Alleyn, a well-known actor, who moved his group of actors made up from the Admiral's Men and Lord Strange's Men acting groups to the Rose Theatre. The theatre was then enlarged for this troupe of actors, and the extra spectators who would come to see them.

"Henslowe's Diary" and Edward Alleyn's papers from the College of God's Gift (Dulwich College), which he founded in 1619, record not only the expenditure involved in extending the Rose Theatre and its upkeep, but also the plays that were staged there, the number of spectators and also the props and costumes used. From these records, we know that the Rose Theatre's repertory included Shakespeare's "Henry VI Part 1" and "Titus Andronicus", Kyd's "Spanish Tragedy", and Marlowe's "Doctor Faustus", "The Jew of Malta" and "Tamburlaine the Great".

In 1594-1596 the Swan Theatre was built, followed by the Globe Theatre in 1599. These rival theatres adversely affected the popularity of the Rose. When in June 1600, the Privy Council decreed that only two theatres would be allowed to stage plays – the Globe Theatre and the Fortune Theatre (also built by Henslowe and Alleyn) – the Rose Theatre began its decline and was abandoned by 1605, if not earlier.

In 1988, the demolition of a 1950s office block meant that the site of the Rose Theatre could be investigated, and in 1989 a campaign to "Save the Rose" was launched by Lord Olivier (actor Laurence Olivier). In May 1989, archaeologists from the Museum of London were successful in uncovering two thirds of the Rose Theatre's ground plan. As well as giving vital information on how the Rose Theatre was built and how it would have looked, the site gave up over 700 precious Elizabethan artefacts: coins, fragments of the money boxes used to collect entrance money, tokens, hazelnut shells from the nuts eaten by the Elizabethan audiences, and jewellery. The articles found are now kept at the Museum of London.

1473 – Birth of Nicholas Copernicus, the Renaissance mathematician and astronomer, in Thorn, in the province of Royal Prussia, Poland. Copernicus is known for his theory of heliocentric cosmology, or the idea that the sun was stationary in the centre of the universe and that the earth revolved around it.

1546 – William Cavendish was appointed Treasurer of the Privy Chamber. He later claimed that he had paid £1000 for the position.

1567 – The imprisoned Margaret Douglas, Countess of Lennox, was informed of the murder of her son, Henry Stewart, Lord Darnley, by William Cecil's wife, Mildred, and Lady William Howard. The Spanish ambassador recorded that Margaret's grief was such "that it was necessary for the Queen to send her doctors to her".

1598 – Death of Jasper Heywood, Jesuit and poet, in Naples. Heywood had been deported to France in January 1585, after being imprisoned in the Tower of London for treason, and was then summoned to Rome. He never returned to England.

1601 – Death of Thomas Fanshawe, at Warwick Lane. He was buried in the south aisle of Ware church in Hertfordshire. Fanshawe was an Exchequer official during Elizabeth I's reign.

20TH FEBRUARY

On this day in history, 20th February 1547, King Edward VI was crowned King at Westminster Abbey. However, the celebrations had begun the day before…

On the afternoon of Saturday 19th February, the boy King processed out of the Tower of London. He was dressed in white velvet, which was embroidered with silver thread and decorated with lovers' knots made from pearls, along with diamonds and rubies. He also had a gown of gold mesh and a sable cape, and the horse upon which he rode had been dressed in crimson satin decorated with pearls.

The procession consisted of the King's messengers, the King's gentlemen, his trumpeters, his chaplains and esquires of the body, all walking. Then came the nobility on horseback and members of the council paired with foreign diplomats. After them processed the gentlemen ushers and Henry Grey, the Marquis of Dorset and Constable of England, bearing the sword of state. Finally, there was the nine year-old king, Edward VI, escorted by the Duke of Somerset (his uncle, Edward Seymour) and the Earl of Warwick (John Dudley). They were followed by the Sir Anthony Browne (the King's Master of the Horse), the henchmen, the Gentlemen of the Privy Chamber, the pensioners and the guard.

Edward VI's biographer, Chris Skidmore, writes of how Cheapside was richly decorated with cloth of silver and gold, but that some of the pageants arranged for the day, at very short notice, "turned into shambles". One pageant drew on the coronation of Henry VI as King of France in 1432, another boy king, and another made use of Jane Seymour's phoenix, Henry VIII's lion and the roses and hawthorn bush devices of the Tudor dynasty. Skidmore describes how the phoenix descended from the heavens to land on a mount decorated by red and white roses and hawthorn bushes. A crowned lion then approached, followed by a young cub. At the cub's appearance, two angels descended and crowned him with an Imperial crown. The phoenix and lion then departed, leaving the crowned cub alone.

Other displays along the route included depictions of Edward the Confessor, St George and "Truth", a child representing the New Religion. Skidmore writes of how the young king particularly enjoyed watching a tightrope walker, who balanced along a cable as he descended to kiss the King's foot.

The next day, at 9am, King Edward VI travelled to Whitehall by barge. He was met by the guard and pensioners and then he walked to the chamber of the Court of Augmentations, where he put on his Parliament robes of ermine-trimmed crimson velvet. The King then processed to Westminster Abbey for the coronation ceremony under a canopy carried by the barons of the Cinque Ports. He was flanked by the Earl of Shrewsbury and the Bishop of Durham, and followed by John Dudley, William Parr and Thomas Seymour, who all bore his train.

Behind them processed the Gentlemen of the Privy Chamber, the nobility, the pensioners, the guard and the court servants.

A dais had been erected in the richly decorated Abbey. On it was a throne decorated in damask and gold, with two cushions to help raise the small King. The traditional coronation ceremony, used since 1375, had been adapted for the boy King. Instead of twelve hours, it would be seven. Thomas Cranmer, Archbishop of Canterbury, had also changed the coronation oath so that "reformation of the Church could now be enabled by royal prerogative, the king as lawmaker". The changes were explained in a sermon by Cranmer, who also likened Edward to the Biblical Josiah, and then the young king was anointed and crowned with the St Edward's crown, the Imperial crown and a custom-made lighter crown. Edward then held the orb, the sceptre, St Edward's staff and the spurs. He was King, and the nobility now came before him one by one to kiss his left cheek.

The coronation ceremony was followed by a banquet in Westminster's Great Hall, more feasting and entertainment at Whitehall, and then two days of jousting and feasting.

Trivia: Edward VI was the first monarch to be anointed as Supreme Head of the English Church.

1516 – Baptism of Princess Mary, the future Mary I, in the Church of the Observant Friars at Greenwich. The princess was carried to the font by the Countess of Surrey, and her godparents were Catherine Courtenay, Countess of Devon and daughter of Edward IV; Margaret Pole, Countess of Salisbury and daughter of George, Duke of Clarence; the Duchess of Norfolk and Cardinal Thomas Wolsey.

1523 – Hanging of Agnes Hungerford, Lady Hungerford, at Tyburn. Agnes was hanged, with her servant William Mathewe, after they were found guilty of murdering Agnes's first husband, John Cotell. It was said that Agnes arranged for her servants, William Mathewe and William Ignes, to strangle Cotell in 1518. Mathewe and Ignes were found guilty of murder 'by the procurement and abetting of Agnes Hungerford', and Agnes was found guilty of inciting and abetting the murder. Ignes was hanged at a later date. Agnes was buried at Grey Friars, London.

1552 – Death of Anne Herbert, sister of Catherine Parr and wife of William Herbert, 1st Earl of Pembroke. Anne died at Baynard's Castle and was buried in St Paul's. Anne was a maid of honour to Jane Seymour, keeper of the jewels to Catherine Howard and was serving the Lady Mary (future Mary I) at the time of her death.

1579 – Death of Sir Nicholas Bacon, lawyer, administrator, Lord Keeper of the Great Seal and father of Sir Francis Bacon at Old Gorhambury House, the house he had built in Hertfordshire. He lay in state for nearly two weeks at York Place before being buried in St Paul's Cathedral.

21ST FEBRUARY

On this day in 1590, Ambrose Dudley, 3ʳᵈ Earl of Warwick, Master of the Ordnance, Privy Councillor and fourth son of John Dudley, Duke of Northumberland, died at Bedford House on the Strand. He was laid to rest in the Beauchamp Chapel of the Collegiate Church of St Mary, Warwick.

Ambrose was born around 1530 and, like his father and brother, Robert Dudley, Earl of Leicester, was an influential Tudor man. He was attainted for treason after the short and unsuccessful reign of his sister-in-law, Lady Jane Grey, in July 1553, but was subsequently pardoned and released. When Elizabeth I came to the throne in November 1558, Ambrose was restored to royal favour and was appointed to the office of Master of the Ordnance. In 1561, he was created Baron Lisle and Earl of Warwick, and in 1562 Ambrose led a disastrous expedition to Le Havre, which had to be abandoned due to an outbreak of the plague. Ambrose came home with a nasty leg wound. In 1571, he was made Chief Butler of England and in 1573 he was appointed to Elizabeth I's Privy Council.

In early 1590, one of his legs, the one he had injured at Le Havre, had to be amputated due to gangrene. Ambrose did not recover and died on 21st February 1590.

He was married three times: Anne Whorwood, Elizabeth Tailboys and Anne Russell.

1498 – Birth of Ralph Neville, 4th Earl of Westmorland. He was the second son of Ralph, Baron Neville, and his wife, Edith, daughter of Sir William Sandys of the Vyne. Westmorland served Henry VIII in the North, and was a member of the jury at the trials of George and Anne Boleyn in 1536.

1513 – Death of Pope Julius II from a fever. He was buried in St Peter's in the Vatican.

1549 – Death of Sir Richard Gresham, Mayor of London, mercer and merchant adventurer, at Bethnal Green. He was buried in the church of St Lawrence Jewry in London.

1568 – Burial of Katherine Seymour (née Grey), Countess of Hertford, at Yoxford. Her remains were later re-interred, by her grandson, in the Seymour family tomb at Salisbury Cathedral.

1579 – Death of Thomas Bentham, Bishop of Coventry and Lichfield, at Eccleshall, Staffordshire. He was buried in the chapel of the Episcopal Palace at Eccleshall.

1589 – Death of William Somerset, 3rd Earl of Worcester, in Clerkenwell, Middlesex. He was buried in Raglan parish church.

1595 – The execution of Robert Southwell, Jesuit priest and writer, at Tyburn. He was hanged, drawn and quartered. Southwell was canonized in 1970.

22ND FEBRUARY

Tragedy struck Catherine of Aragon and Henry VIII on this day in history, 22nd February 1511, when their fifty-two day-old baby boy, Henry, Duke of Cornwall, died. We do not know what caused his death, but it was unexpected. Perhaps it was SIDS (Sudden Infant Death Syndrome or Cot Death). It was a tragedy, and little did Catherine of Aragon realise that this loss would ultimately lead to the end of her marriage, and little did Henry VIII realise that he would not have another living son and heir until October 1537 – a long wait!

1540 – Marie de Guise, consort of James V of Scotland and mother of Mary, Queen of Scots, was crowned in Holyrood Abbey.

1571 – Death of John Bury, translator. He had never recovered from a fall from his horse in August 1570, which had resulted in him breaking a leg. He is known for his "The Godly Advertisement or Good Counsell of the Famous Orator Isocrates", an English translation of Isocrates' Greek speech *Ad demonicum*.

23RD FEBRUARY

On the 23rd February 1554, Henry Grey, Duke of Suffolk, was executed on Tower Hill, just 11 days after his daughter, Lady Jane Grey, and less than a month after the beginning of *Wyatt's Rebellion*.

Suffolk had been imprisoned for just a few days after Mary I had taken the throne from Jane, but rather unwisely joined Sir Thomas Wyatt, Sir Peter Carew, and others who were unhappy with Mary's decision to marry Philip of Spain, in a rebellion in January 1554. Suffolk's involvement was rather half-hearted, with him fleeing to the Midlands to denounce the marriage there after he realised that he had been found out by the Queen's Privy Council. Suffolk failed to gather any support for the rebellion in the Midlands, and so attempted to flee the country, in disguise. He was arrested before he could escape and was condemned to death for high treason at a trial at Westminster Hall. He had been charged with inciting war in the county of Leicester, posting proclamations against the Spanish marriage, and plotting the death of the Queen.

He was escorted to Tower Hill at 9am on 23rd February and, according to John Foxe's account, as he climbed the scaffold Mary I's Chaplain, Hugh Weston, attempted to follow him. Suffolk pushed him back down the stairs and a scuffle ensued, but Weston told Suffolk that it was the Queen's orders that he speak to the crowd. Weston went ahead and preached a sermon attacking Suffolk's Protestant beliefs. Suffolk then addressed the crowd, saying:

"Masters, I have offended the queen and her laws, and thereby am justly condemned to die, and am willing to die, desiring all men to be obedient. And I pray God that this my death may be an en-sample to all men, beseeching you all to bear me witness, that I die in the faith of Christ, trusting to be saved by his blood only, and by no other trumpery, the which died for me, and for all them that truly repent, and stedfastly trust in him. And I do repent, desiring you all to pray to God for me; and that when you see my breath depart from me, you will pray to God that he may receive my soul."

Then he asked for forgiveness and knelt down, holding up his hands and looking up to heaven, saying the psalm, *Miserere mei Deus*. He ended by saying "*In manes tuus, Domine, commendo spiritum meum*" (Into thy hands, O Lord, I commend my spirit) and then stood up, took off his cap and scarf, and gave them to the executioner. The executioner asked for Suffolk's forgiveness, but the proceedings were interrupted by a member of the crowd, a man who was owed money by Suffolk, asking how he should go about getting the money. Suffolk replied, "Alas, good fellow! I pray thee trouble me not now; but go thy way to my officers." Then he tied a handkerchief over his eyes and knelt down once more, praying the Lord's Prayer followed by the words "Christ have mercy upon me". He laid his head on the block and his head was struck off with one blow. His remains were buried in the chancel area of St Peter ad Vincula, the Tower chapel.

1503 – Burial of Elizabeth of York, Queen Consort of Henry VII and mother of Henry VIII, at Westminster Abbey.

1512 – Birth of William Framyngham, scholar and author, at Norwich, Norfolk. Unfortunately, his works are lost, but his friend, Dr John Caius listed seven of his works, which included heroic verse, a poem in pentameters and hexameters, a poem on idolatry and two books of prose.

1525 – Start of the *Battle of Pavia* during the *Italian Wars* of 1521-1526. The Imperial troops of Charles V defeated those of Francis I and Francis I was captured, imprisoned and forced into signing the *Treaty of Madrid*.

1533 – Death of James Denton, Archdeacon of Cleveland and Dean of Lichfield, at Ludlow. He was buried in St Lawrence's Church, Ludlow. Denton had also been Chancellor to the Council of Princess Mary.

1574 – France began the fifth *Holy War* against the Huguenots.

1601 – Burial of Job Throckmorton, religious pamphleteer and Member of Parliament, at Haseley in Warwickshire. It is believed that he was one of the men responsible for the "Martin Marprelate tracts". In his article on Throckmorton, Patrick Collinson, writes that a comparison of Throckmorton's "The Defence of Job Throkmorton Against the Slaunders of Maister Sutcliffe" (1594) with the Marprelate satires "has persuaded modern critical opinion that if these satires had a single author, that author was Throckmorton", although Throckmorton denied it.

1628 – Burial of John Guy, politician, colonist and Governor of Newfoundland. It is said that he was buried in St. Stephen's Church, in his home-town of Bristol, but there is no record of his burial there.

24TH FEBRUARY

Charles V, Holy Roman Emperor, was born in Ghent on this day in 1500. He was the son of Joanna of Castile, who has gone down in history as Juana La Loca (Joanna the Crazy), and Philip I of Castile. Here are some facts about Charles:

- His grandparents were the Catholic Reyes, Isabella I of Castile and Ferdinand II of Aragon, and Maximilian I, Holy Roman Emperor, and Mary of Burgundy.

- Charles was the heir of three powerful dynasties: The House of Habsburg, the House of Valois-Burgundy and the House of Trastámara.

- Charles was the nephew of Henry VIII's first wife, Catherine of Aragon.

- In 1521 Charles became betrothed to five year-old Princess Mary, daughter of Henry VIII and Catherine of Aragon, but married Isabella of Portugal in 1525.

- Charles and Isabella had seven children: Philip II of Spain, Maria of Spain, Isabella, Ferdinand, Joan of Spain, John and Ferdinand. Charles also had children with his mistresses: Margaret of Parma by Johanna Maria van der Gheynst, and John of Austria by Barbara Blomberg.

- He was King of Spain (Charles I) from 1516-1556 and Holy Roman Emperor from 1519-1556.

- He was also Duke of Burgundy, Lord of the Netherlands and Count Palatine of Burgundy.

- He abdicated from ruling the Holy Roman Empire and Spain in 1556 – His brother, Ferdinand I, became Holy Roman Emperor, and his son, Philip II, became King of Spain.

- Charles V suffered from an enlarged jaw, and this pronounced jawline became known as the Habsburg Jaw. He was also epileptic and suffered from gout, which led to him being carried around on a special chair in later life.

- Charles V's vast empire is shown by his titulature: Charles, by the grace of God, Holy Roman Emperor, forever August, King of Germany, King of Italy, King of all Spains, of Castile, Aragon, León, Navarra, Grenada, Toledo, Valencia, Galicia, Majorca, Sevilla, Cordova, Murcia, Jaén, Algarves, Algeciras, Gibraltar, the Canary Islands, King of Two Sicilies, of Sardinia, Corsica, King of Jerusalem, King of the Western and Eastern Indies, Lord of the Islands and Main Ocean Sea, Archduke of Austria, Duke of Burgundy, Brabant, Lorraine, Styria, Carinthia, Carniola, Limburg, Luxembourg, Gelderland, Neopatria, Württemberg, Landgrave of Alsace, Prince of Swabia, Asturia and Catalonia, Count of Flanders, Habsburg, Tyrol, Gorizia, Barcelona, Artois, Burgundy Palatine, Hainaut, Holland, Seeland, Ferrette, Kyburg, Namur, Roussillon, Cerdagne, Zutphen, Margrave of the Holy Roman Empire, Burgau, Oristano and Gociano, Lord of Frisia, the Wendish March, Pordenone, Biscay, Molin, Salins, Tripoli and Mechelen.

***

1525 – *Battle of Pavia.* The French were defeated by Imperial troops and Francis I was taken prisoner. Richard de la Pole, son of John de la Pole, 2nd Duke of Suffolk, and a claimant to the English throne, was killed in the battle.

1540 – Birth of Henry Howard, Earl of Northampton, courtier, author and administrator, at Shottesham in Norfolk.

He was the second son of courtier and poet Henry Howard, Earl of Surrey, and his wife, Lady Frances de Vere. After his father's execution in 1547, Howard was put into the care of his aunt, Mary Howard, Duchess of Richmond, who appointed John Foxe, the martyrologist, and scholar Hadrianus Junius to educate him and his brothers. Between 1553 and 1558, Howard served Bishop John Whitgift as a page, and in 1559 he went to King's College, Cambridge, to study. He went through periods of disfavour in Elizabeth I's reign due to his links with Catholics, but he rose in favour in the late 1590s due to his friendship with the Earl of Essex and then his links with the Cecil faction at court. He served James I as a Privy Councillor, constable of Dover Castle and lord warden of the Cinque Ports, and Lord Privy Seal. He was created Baron of Marnhull, Dorset, and Earl of Northampton in 1604.

1580 – Death of Henry Fitzalan, 12th Earl of Arundel, at Arundel House. He was buried in the collegiate chapel at Arundel. Fitzalan was a member of the jury at the trials of George and Anne Boleyn and served Henry VIII as Deputy of Calais, Privy Councillor and Lord Chamberlain. He was High Constable at Edward VI's coronation, and was among the men who signed Edward VI's letters patent naming Lady Jane Grey as his successor. He swapped sides after Edward's death and joined those supporting Mary I, acting as High Constable at her coronation and serving her as Lord Steward of the Household. He was not favoured in Elizabeth's reign, and was actually put under house arrest at times.

1603 – Death of Katherine Howard (née Carey), Countess of Nottingham, at Arundel House. She was buried at All Saints, Chelsea (Chelsea Old Church). Katherine was the eldest daughter of Henry Carey, 1st Baron Hundson, and his wife, Anne, making her granddaughter of Mary Boleyn. Katherine was appointed a Gentlewoman of Elizabeth I's Privy Chamber in 1560 and married Charles Howard, 2nd Baron Howard of Effingham and 1st Earl of Nottingham, in 1563. Katherine was close to Elizabeth I, and the Queen was devastated by her death and died just a month later.

25TH FEBRUARY

At just before 8am on the 25th February 1601, Robert Devereux, 2nd Earl of Essex was brought out of the Tower of London and walked to the scaffold. He was wearing a black velvet gown, black satin doublet and breeches and a black hat, which he took off as he climbed up onto the scaffold so that he could bow to the people gathered. He then made a speech acknowledging "with thankfulness to God, that he was justly spewed out of the realm", and said:-

"My sins are more in number than the hairs on my head. I have bestowed my youth in wantonness, lust and uncleanness; I have been puffed up with pride, vanity and love of this wicked world's pleasures. For all which, I humbly beseech my Saviour Christ to be a mediator to the eternal Majesty for my pardon, especially for this my last sin, this great, this bloody, this crying, this infectious sin, whereby so many for love of me have been drawn to offend God, to offend their sovereign, to offend the world. I beseech God to forgive it me – most wretched of all."

After praying that God would preserve the Queen and asking the crowd to join him in prayer, he begged God to forgive his enemies. He then removed his gown and ruff and knelt at the block, looking up at the sky and saying the Lord's Prayer. After forgiving the executioner, who knelt in front of him, Essex repeated the Creed and then took off his doublet, as it was covering his neck, to display a waistcoat of scarlet, the colour of martyrs. He laid himself on the block, stretched out his arms and prayed, "Lord be merciful to Thy prostrate servant... Lord, into Thy hands I commend my spirit." After repeating two verses of Psalm 51, he could take no more and cried out, "Executioner, strike home!". The executioner swung his axe to behead Essex, but, unfortunately, it took three blows to sever his neck. When the deed was finally done, the executioner held the head aloft, shouting, "God save the Queen!"

It was the end of a man who had given Elizabeth I much joy, but also much anger during her later years.

Doyne C Bell, author of "Notices of the Historic Persons Buried in the Chapel of St Peter ad Vincula in the Tower of London", writes of how the body and head of Essex were put into a coffin and buried in the chancel of the Chapel to the right of the resting places of the Earl of Arundel and the Duke of Norfolk.

Trivia: Essex's executioner was Thomas Derrick, a man whom Essex had pardoned for rape on the condition that he become an executioner.

1567 (24th or 25th) – Burial of Sir Thomas White, founder of St John's College, Oxford, in St John's College Chapel. The famous Roman Catholic martyr and Jesuit priest, Edmund Campion, gave his Latin funeral oration.

1570 – Excommunication of Queen Elizabeth I by Pope Pius V.

1618 (24th or 25th) – Death of Elizabeth Carey (née Spencer, other married name Eure), Lady Hunsdon, literary patron and wife of Sir George Carey, 2nd Baron Hunsdon, from "a palsie". She was buried at Westminster, in the Hunsdon family vault. Hunsdon died in 1603, and Elizabeth married Ralph Eure, 3rd Baron Eure, in late 1612 or early 1613. She is known for being a literary patron and had works by Edmund Spenser, Thomas Nashe, Thomas Churchyard, Thomas Playfere and Henry Lok dedicated to her.

26TH FEBRUARY

On this day in 1564 Christopher Marlowe, poet, translator and playwright, was baptised at St George's Canterbury. Marlowe was the second child of John Marlowe, shoemaker, and his wife, Katherine. Marlowe's works included "Tamburlaine", "Dr Faustus", "The Jew of Malta" and "The Passionate Shepherd to his Love". Marlovians believe that Marlowe was responsible for the works attributed to William Shakespeare.

Here is Marlowe's "The Passionate Shepherd to his Love":

"Come live with me, and be my love;
And we will all the pleasures prove
That hills and valleys, dales and fields,
Woods, or steepy mountain yields.

And we will sit upon the rocks,
Seeing the shepherds feed their flocks
By shallow rivers, to whose falls
Melodious birds sing madrigals.

And I will make thee beds of roses
And a thousand fragrant posies;
A cap of flowers, and a kirtle
Embroidered all with leaves of myrtle;

A gown made of the finest wool
Which from our pretty lambs we pull;
Fair-lined slippers for the cold,
With buckles of the purest gold;

A belt of straw and ivy-buds,
With coral clasps and amber-studs:
And if these pleasures may thee move,
Come live with me, and be my love.

The shepherd-swains shall dance and sing
For thy delight each May-morning:
If these delights thy mind may move,
Then live with me and be my love."

<hr />

1548 – Birth of courtier George Carey, 2nd Baron Hunsdon, son of Henry Carey, 1st Baron Hunsdon, and his wife, Anne. George was the grandson of Mary Boleyn, sister of Anne Boleyn.

1552 – Executions of conspirators Sir Thomas Arundell, Sir Michael Stanhope, Sir Miles Partridge and Sir Ralph Fane. Arundell and Stanhope were beheaded on Tower Hill, while Partridge and Fane were hanged. They were condemned as traitors after being accused of conspiring with Edward Seymour, Duke of Somerset, against John Dudley, Duke of Northumberland.

1608 – Death of John Still, Bishop of Bath and Wells, in the palace at Wells. He was buried in Wells Cathedral.

1619 – Death of Edmund Bunny, clergyman, preacher and theological writer, at Cawood, Yorkshire. He was buried in York Minster. His works included "The Whole Summe of Christian Religion" (1576), "A Book of Christian Exercise, Appertaining to Resolution" (1584) and "A Briefe Answer, unto those Idle and Frivolous Quarrels of R.P." (1589), a response to Jesuit Robert Person.

27TH FEBRUARY

On 27th February 1545, the English forces were defeated by the Scots at the *Battle of Ancrum Moor*, near Jedburgh in Scotland.

The battle was part of the 1543-1550 *War of the Rough Wooing*, a war attempting to put pressure on the Scots to agree to a marriage match between the infant Mary, Queen of Scots and Henry VIII's son, Edward (the future Edward VI).

The Scottish chronicler Robert Lindsay of Pitscottie recorded that "the Scottismen's speares war longer then the Inglismen's be fyve quareteris, or an elne, quhilk, when they joyned with the Inglishmen, they had thame all rivin doune before evir the Inglishmenis speares might touch thame", showing that the Scots used their pikes effectively during the battle. The English forces scattered and around 800 were killed, while another 100 were taken prisoner. This brought about a temporary lull in the war.

1531 – Birth of Roger North, 2nd Baron North, politician, diplomat and administrator at the court of Elizabeth I. North served as a Member of Parliament, Privy Councillor and Treasurer of the Household.

1555 – Death of Sir William Babthorpe, member of Parliament and a man who was created Knight of the Bath at the coronation of Edward VI in 1547. Babthorpe had originally been on the rebel side in the *Pilgrimage of Grace* in 1536, but fortunately swapped sides.

1574 – Death of Sir William Harper, Lord Mayor of London, in London. He was buried in St Paul's, Bedford, in the chancel. He was Lord Mayor from September 1561 to his death.

1583 – Death of Richard Madox, diarist and Church of England clergyman, near Espirito Santo harbour, near Vitória, Brazil. He was Chaplain and Secretary to Captain Edward Fenton on his 1582 voyage to the Moluccas and China. Madox's last diary entry was 31 December 1582. It is thought that he was buried at sea.

1601 – Execution of Mark Barkworth (also known by the alias Lambert), Benedictine monk and martyr, at Tyburn. He was hanged, drawn and quartered dressed in the habit of the Benedictine order. He was beatified in 1929. Two others died that day: Roger Filcock, Jesuit, and Anne Line, a widow who had harboured Filcock. Line was canonised in 1970 and Filcock was beatified in 1987.

28TH FEBRUARY

On this day in 1525, Gerald Fitzgerald, 11th Earl of Kildare, was born. He was the eldest son of Gerald Fitzgerald, 9th Earl of Kildare, Lord Deputy of Ireland, and his second wife, Elizabeth Grey. Fitzgerald became a fugitive in 1534 after a failed rebellion led by his half-brother, known as Silken Thomas. Thomas and five of Gerald's uncles were executed as traitors and Gerald went on the run. He was pardoned by Edward Seymour, Duke of Somerset and Lord Protector, in 1549, and restored to favour. In 1554, he was created Earl of Kildare and Baron of Offaly after helping Mary I's forces to suppress *Wyatt's Rebellion*. He got into trouble twice in Elizabeth I's reign, when his enemies attempted to make him a scapegoat for rebellion in the Irish Pale. He was arrested and imprisoned in the Tower of London both times, but subsequently cleared and released. He died on 16 November 1585 in London, but was buried at Kildare.

1540 – Execution of Thomas Forret, Protestant martyr. He was burned at the stake in Castle Hill in Edinburgh in front of King James V after being condemned as a heretic. John Knox and David Calderwood record the year of his execution as 1539, but John Foxe and George Buchanan, who had actually spent time with Forret, recorded it as 1540.

1551 – Death of theologian and Protestant reformer Martin Bucer during the night of 28th February/1st March in Cambridge. He was buried in Great St Mary's Church at a funeral attended by around 3,000 people.

1555 – Death of Sir Robert Bowes, lawyer, Master of the Rolls and Warden of the East and Middle Marches, at Berwick while organising the defences there. Bowes was a member of Edward VI's Privy Council, and was appointed Master of the Rolls in 1552. He was also a member of Lady Jane Grey's council.

1556 – Burial of Stephen Gardiner, Bishop of Winchester, in a chantry tomb in Winchester Cathedral.

1577 – Death of Edmund Guest, Bishop of Salisbury, at Salisbury. He was buried in the cathedral choir.

1594 – Death of William Fleetwood, lawyer, antiquary and Queen's Serjeant, at his home in Aldersgate, London. He was buried on his estate in Great Missenden, Buckinghamshire. Fleetwood was a Member of Parliament in the reigns of Mary I and Elizabeth I, Recorder of London from 1571-1591 and Queen's Serjeant from 1592 until his death.

29TH FEBRUARY

The burning of Patrick Hamilton, theologian and Scotland's first 'Protestant' martyr, took place on this day in 1528 outside St Salvator's College, St Andrews. It was an horrific death, with it taking around six hours for Hamilton to die. Alexander Alesius wrote of how Hamilton was roasted, rather than burned. Hamilton was condemned as a heretic after being found guilty of thirteen charges, seven of which were to do with doctrines from Philipp Melancthon's *Loci communes rerum theologicarum seu hypotyposes theologicae*. John Knox recorded Hamilton's awful death:

"The innocent servant of God being bound to the stake in the midst of coals, some timber and other matter appointed for the fire. A train of powder was made and set alight, but although it scorched his left hand and that side of his face, it neither kindled the wood nor yet the coals. And so remained the appointed to death in torment til men ran to the castle again for more powder and more wood for the fire, which being at last kindled, with a loud voice he cried "Lord Jesus, receive my spirit! How long shall darkness overwhelm this realm? And how long will thou suffer this tyranny of men?". The fire was slow and therefore was his torment the more. But most of all was he grieved by certain wicked men, amongst them Campbell the Black Friar, who continually cried "Convert, heretic. Call upon our Lady; say salve regina" etc. To whom he answered "Depart, and trouble me not, ye messengers of Satan."But will that the foresaid Friar still roared one thing with great vehemence, he said unto him, "Wicked man, thou knowest the contrary and the contrary to me thou hast confessed. I appeal thee before the tribunal seat of Jesus Christ!" After which, and other words which could not be understood or marked, both for the tumult and vehemence of the fire, the witness of Jesus Christ gained victory after long suffereance, the last of February in the year of God 1528."

1604 – Death of John Whitgift, Archbishop of Canterbury, at Lambeth Palace. He was the last Archbishop of Canterbury in Elizabeth I's reign, and had been in office since 1583.

LENT

Lent was, and is, the lead-up to Holy Week, and it lasted six and a half weeks. In Tudor times, it was a period of fasting, a time in which meat, eggs and cheese were forbidden. Prior to this, fasting was a time of celebration, Shrovetide, which began on the seventh Sunday before *Easter*, a day known as *Shrove Sunday*.

The three days of *Shrovetide* – *Shrove Sunday*, *Collup Monday* (a 'collup' being a piece of fried or roasted meat) and *Shrove Tuesday* – were the last opportunities to use up those forbidden foods and to have some fun. *Shrove Tuesday*, the last day before *Lent*, was marked with court celebrations and entertainment such as jousting, plays, music and masques. Alison Sim, in "Pleasures and Pastimes in Tudor England" describes one Shrovetide entertainment, "threshing the cock", which consisted of tethering a cock and having people trying to kill it by throwing things at it. A prize was given to the person who killed it. Sim also writes of how "sometimes the cock was buried with just its head sticking out of the ground and then blindfolded people would try to kill it with a flail."

Lent was not just a time of fasting, it was also a time of self-denial, and couples were forbidden to have sexual relations.

In churches during *Lent*, a *Lent* veil would hide the chancel from the nave and cloths would cover the lectern and altars. These cloths and veils symbolised the hiding of the way to salvation. The *Lent* veil would remain in place until the Wednesday of Holy Week when the priest would read out the passage from the Bible concerning the veil in the Temple in Jerusalem.

Pancakes were a way of using up eggs before *Lent*, so eating pancakes became a custom in many countries. In England, pancake races became a way of using up the rich food forbidden during *Lent*, and also of having fun. The traditional pancake race of Olney in Buckinghamshire dates back to 1445. The story behind the tradition is that a housewife was busy making pancakes when the churchbells rang for the service. The lady was in such a rush to get to the service that she allegedly ran to church with her frying pan and pancake, tossing the pancake as she went!

MARY I (1516-1558)

1ST MARCH

On the evening of *Shrove Tuesday*, 1st March 1522, Anne Boleyn played the part of Perseverance at the pageant of "The Château Vert", her first recorded public appearance at court since her return from France.

Edward Hall, in his "Chronicle", describes how on the evening of *Shrove Tuesday* at York Place, Cardinal Wolsey, the King and ambassadors enjoyed a supper followed by a pageant in the great chamber, which was richly decorated with arras and torches. At the end of the chamber was a castle with towers decorated with banners, one showing three "rent hartes" (torn hearts), another showing "a ladies hand gripyng a mans harte" and the third showing "a ladies hand turnyng a mannes hart" upside down. One of the towers had a cresset burning and in the castle were musicians, hidden from sight, and eight ladies visible in the towers. These ladies, dressed in white satin, were Beauty, Honour, Perseverance, Kindness, Constance, Bounty, Mercy and Pity, the virtues held high in chivalric tradition. The King's sister, Mary Tudor Queen of France, played Beauty, the Countess of Devonshire played Honour, Jane Parker (later Boleyn) played Constancy, Mary Boleyn played Kindness and Anne Boleyn played Perseverance. Hall describes how each lady had her name (or virtue) embroidered on her dress in gold, and how they wore cauls and gold Milan bonnets decorated with jewels.

Hall goes on to describe how these women, or virtues or graces, were guarded by eight women dressed as Indian women who were named "Danger, Disdain, Gelousie, Vnkyndenes, Scorne, Malebouche, Straitngenes" or Danger, Disdain, Jealousy, Unkindness, Scorn, Malebouche (evil tongue/mouth or Sharp Tongue) and Strangeness, which Eric Ives takes to mean "Off-handedness". Suddenly, eight lords dressed in cloth of gold caps and blue satin cloaks entered the chamber "led by one all in crimosin sattin with burnyng flames of gold, called

Ardent Desire". These men were named "Amorus, Noblenes, Youth, Attendance, Loyaltie, Pleasure, Gentlenes, and Libertie" and the kyng was chief of this compaignie". Ardent Desire then asked the ladies, the virtues, to come down from their towers, but Scorn and Disdain told him that "they would holde the place", so the men attacked the castle throwing dates, oranges "and other fruites made for pleasure" at it. The ladies defended the castle with rose water and "comfittes" or sweetmeats and although Lady Scorn and her company tried to defend themselves with "boows and balles", they were forced to flee and the lords took the "ladies of honor as prisoners by the handes" and led them out of the castle to dance.

The lords and ladies then unmasked themselves and went on to enjoy a rich banquet with those who had watched the Château Vert pageant.

───────────────

1546 – Hanging and burning of George Wishart, Scottish evangelical preacher and martyr, at St Andrews, Scotland. In his preaching. Wishart had denounced the Pope and had continued preaching contrary to Cardinal Beaton's orders. He was tried on 1ˢᵗ March 1546, eighteen charges being levelled against him, and was condemned to death. He went to his death with courage, asking Christ's forgiveness for those who had condemned him to death "ignorantly".

1553 – Edward VI opened Parliament. The King was ill at the time, so it was a much more low key ceremony than usual.

1554 – Birth of William Stafford, son of Sir William Stafford (husband of the late Mary Boleyn) and his second wife Dorothy Stafford. William is known as a conspirator, having concocted a plot, *The Stafford Plot*, probably on the instructions of William Cecil. This plot was supposedly against Elizabeth I, but its purpose is likely to have been to show Elizabeth that her life was in danger from Mary, Queen of Scots and her followers.

1559 – Death of Sir Thomas Tresham, Catholic politician and Grand Prior of England in the Order of Knights Hospitallers of St John of Jerusalem, at Rushton in Northamptonshire. He was buried at St Peter's Church, Rushton. When Edward VI died in 1553, Tresham had supported Princess Mary's claim, and proclaimed her Queen in Northampton.

1562 – *The Massacre of Vassy*. Sixty-three Huguenot worshippers were killed, and over a hundred injured, when Francis, Duke of Guise, ordered his troops to set fire to the barn being used as a church in Vassy (Wassy), France. Trouble had started when some of his men had barged their way into the barn, and the Duke was hit by a stone being thrown.

1568 – Death of Sir Thomas Throckmorton, son of William Throckmorton. He was buried at Tortworth in Gloucestershire. In the reigns of Edward VI and Mary I, Throckmorton was a Justice of the Peace, and in Elizabeth I's reign he was a Sheriff, also serving on the Council in the Marches.

1587 – Death of Welsh landowner, lawyer and antiquary Rice Merrick at Cotrel. He was buried at St Nicholas' Church. Merrick was the author of *Morganiae archaiographia* ("A Book of Glamorganshire's Antiquities").

1602 – Death of Herbert Westfaling, Bishop of Hereford, at Hereford. He was buried in the cathedral there.

1620 – Death and burial of physician, poet and musician Thomas Campion. He was laid to rest at St Dunstan-in-the-West, Fleet Street. His works included "Poemata, a collection of Latin panegyrics, elegies and epigrams" (1595), the 1601 songbook "A Booke of Ayres" and the 1602 "Observations in the Art of English Poesie".

2ND MARCH

1535 – Death of Sir Robert Drury, lawyer, Privy Councillor and Speaker of the House of Commons.

1545 – Birth of Sir Thomas Bodley, scholar, diplomat and founder of the Bodleian Library, in Exeter. He was the son of John Bodley, a Protestant merchant who took his family into exile to Germany during Mary I's reign. The family returned to England in Elizabeth I's reign, and Bodley was able to study at Magdalen College, Oxford. He then lectured at Merton College before serving Elizabeth as a Gentleman Usher and then diplomat. He re-founded the Oxford University library in 1598, and it was re-opened in 1602 as Bodley's Library, or the Bodleian Library.

1618 – Burial of Elizabeth Carey, Lady Hunsdon, wife of Sir George Carey (Mary Boleyn's grandson). She was buried in the Hunsdon vault in Westminster Abbey.

1619 – Death of Anne of Denmark, consort of James VI and I, of dropsy and consumption. She was buried in Henry VII's Chapel in Westminster Abbey. According to her biographers Maureen M. Meikle and Helen Payne, her entrails were buried at the Abbey on 5th March and her body lay in state at Denmark House from 9th March to 13th May, when she was laid to rest at the Abbey. Her funeral was "in form and scale comparable to that of Queen Elizabeth."

3RD MARCH

3rd March 1500 is the traditional date given for birth of Cardinal Reginald Pole, Mary I's Archbishop of Canterbury, at Stourton Castle in Staffordshire. He was the third son of Sir Richard Pole and Margaret Pole (née Plantagenet), Countess of Salisbury. His mother was the daughter of George, Duke of Clarence, brother of Edward IV and Richard III.

Pole was created a Cardinal in 1537, then papal legate, after being Prebendary of Salisbury, Dean of Exeter, Canon of York and studying at Padua. Although he initially supported Henry VIII's quest for an annulment of his marriage to Catherine of Aragon, being sent to Paris to secure support from theologians at the Sorbonne, he is actually known for his opposition to it, and the treatise he sent the King, *Pro ecclesiasticae unitatis defensione*. He wrote the treatise while abroad in self-imposed exile. His family suffered for his opposition as the King wreaked revenge on them, executing his brother and mother.

He returned to England in 1554, when Mary I came to the throne, and he helped Mary return England to Catholicism. He became her Archbishop of Canterbury in 1556.

───────────────────────────

1528 – Marriage of Margaret Tudor, sister of Henry VIII and widow of James IV, and her third husband, Henry Stuart (Stewart), 1st Lord Methven. She had divorced her second husband, Archibald Douglas, 6th Earl of Angus, in 1527. Margaret's marriage to Methven was not happy for long, though. Margaret had managed to pick another unfaithful husband, so she fought for a divorce, as she had with her second husband, but was not supported by her son, King James V. Margaret was later able to reconcile with Methven.

1542 – Death of Arthur Plantagenet, Lord Lisle, courtier, soldier, diplomat, administrator and illegitimate son of Edward IV. He had been arrested in May 1540 for alleged treasonable communications with Cardinal Pole, and, according to John Foxe, suffered a heart attack on 3rd March 1542 when told the news of his release from the Tower.

1551 – Death of Thomas Wentworth, 1st Baron Wentworth and Lord Chamberlain in the reign of Edward VI. He was a member of the jury at the trials of Anne Boleyn and George Boleyn, Lord Rochford, as well as those of Henry Pole, Baron

Montagu, and Henry Courtenay, Marquis of Exeter. He was buried in the St John the Baptist Chapel, Westminster Abbey.

1551 – Burial of Martin Bucer, theologian and reformer, in Great St Mary's Church, Cambridge. He died 28th February.

1582 – Birth of Edward Herbert, 1st Baron Herbert of Cherbury, soldier, diplomat, philosopher, poet and author of "The Life and Raigne of King Henry the Eighth". Although his career was in the Stuart period, Tudor historians make use of his work on Henry VIII.

4TH MARCH

On this day in 1526, Henry Carey, 1st Baron Hunsdon, courtier and administrator, was born. He was the only son of William Carey, courtier and favourite of Henry VIII, and his wife, Mary (née Boleyn). There is controversy over his paternity due to Mary Boleyn having a sexual relationship with Henry VIII at some point, but the majority of historians believe that Henry was fathered by Carey.

In 1528, the two year old Henry Carey became Anne Boleyn's ward after the death of his father, William Carey, from sweating sickness. It was his aunt, Anne Boleyn, who ensured that the boy received a top notch education under the famous French poet, Nicholas Bourbon. This education helped Henry become an important and influential courtier.

In 1547, he became a Member of Parliament, and when his cousin came to the throne in November 1558, he was knighted. He was one of Elizabeth I's favourites, and his offices and titles included: 1st Baron Hunsdon, Master of the Queen's Hawks, Knight of the Garter, Lieutenant General, Warden of the East Marches, Keeper of Somerset House, Privy Counsellor, Captain General, Lord Chamberlain of the Household, Lord Chamberlain Lieutenant, Principal Captain and Governor of the Army, Chief

Justice in Eyre, High Steward of Ipswich and Doncaster, Chief Justice of the Royal Forces and High Steward of Oxford.

Henry Carey died on 23rd July 1596 at Somerset House, and it is said that Elizabeth I offered him the title of Earl of Wiltshire on his deathbed, but he refused, saying "Madam, as you did not count me worthy of this honour in life, then I shall account myself not worthy of it in death." Like his sister, Catherine, he was laid to rest in Westminster Abbey.

1584 – Death of Bernard Gilpin, reformer, theologian, Church of England clergyman and preacher. He was known as the "Apostle of the North" due to him carrying out preaching tours in Northern England. Some say he died in 1583.

1590 – Execution of Christopher Bales, Catholic Priest, in Fleet Street, London. He was found guilty of treason under the "Acts against Jesuits and Seminarists" (1585), 27 Elizabeth, Cap. 2.

1606 – Death of Sir Edward Fitton, member of Parliament and administrator, in London. He was buried in Gawsworth Church in Cheshire. Fitton served Elizabeth I as Receiver-General for Ireland, and was involved in the plantation of Ireland.

1607 – Death of George Coryate, clergyman and Latin poet, at Odcombe in Somerset. He was Rector there and died in his parsonage. He was buried in the chancel of his church. His son, Thomas, published some of George's work, *Posthuma fragmenta poematum Georgii Coryati Sarisburiensis*, in his own book, "Crudities".

1609 – Death of William Bullokar at Chichester. Bullokar was a spelling reformer and grammarian. His works included the 1580 book "A Short Introduction or Guiding to Print, Write, and Reade Inglish Speech", "The Booke at Large", a translation of Aesop's Fables and the "Pamphlet for Grammar". He also reformed the alphabet.

5TH MARCH

On 5th March 1496, King Henry VII of England issued letters patent to John Cabot (Giovanni Caboto), the Italian navigator and explorer, giving him

"...free authority, faculty and power to sail to all parts, regions and coasts of the eastern, western and northern sea, under our banners, flags and ensigns, with five ships or vessels of whatsoever burden and quality they may be, and with so many and with such mariners and men as they may wish to take with them in the said ships, at their own proper costs and charges, to find, discover and investigate whatsoever islands, countries, regions or provinces of heathens and infidels, in whatsoever part of the world placed, which before this time were unknown to all Christians."

Under this commission, Cabot set off to find Asia and instead discovered parts of North America, including an island he named "new found land", although it's not clear that it was in fact present day Newfoundland.

1549 – A bill of attainder was passed against Thomas Seymour, Baron Sudeley, after it was argued that his offences "were in the compasse of treason". Seymour had been accused of attempting to kidnap his nephew, Edward VI, and also of plotting to marry the teenaged Elizabeth and put her on the throne.

1558 – Smoking tobacco was introduced in Europe by Francisco Fernandes.

1563 – Birth of Sir John Coke, politician and influential administrator during Charles I's reign.

1572 – Death of Edward Hastings, Baron Hastings of Loughborough, nobleman and soldier. In July 1553, when Lady Jane Grey became queen, he was involved in assembling supporters of Princess Mary in the Thames Valley and became one of Mary's trusted confidants. In the reign of Elizabeth I he was imprisoned in the Tower for hearing mass, but was released after taking the oath of supremacy.

1575 – Birth and baptism of William Oughtred, the mathematician responsible for developing a straight slide-rule, a gauging rod and various sundials. He also introduced the "×" symbol for multiplication and the abbreviations "sin" and "cos" for the sine and cosine functions.

1618 – Burial of Robert Abbot, Bishop of Salisbury, in Salisbury Cathedral.

6TH MARCH

On this day in 1492, Juan Luis Vives was born in Valencia, Spain. Vives was a scholar and humanist, and is known for being the friend and adviser of Catherine of Aragon and the tutor of Mary I. Catherine of Aragon commissioned him to write the treatise "Education of a Christian Woman" and he created the *"Satellitium animi,* or Escort of the Soul", a study plan for the Princess Mary, which also included "spiritual mottoes and devices". It was the forerunner of the 16th and 17th century emblem books, books which contained a number of emblematic images with an accompanying explanatory text.

As well as tutoring Princess Mary, Vives also lectured in philosophy at Corpus Christi College, Oxford, and produced a number of educational, religious and philosophical works, including the *De disciplinis, De anima et vita* and *De veritate fidei Christianae.* He died at Bruges on 6th May 1540 and, was buried at the St Donatian Church.

◇◇

1536 – Introduction into Parliament of the "Act for the Suppression (or Dissolution) of the Lesser Monasteries". The act affected the "lesser monasteries"; those with fewer than twelve members and those worth less than £200 per year. They were to be dissolved, their heads pensioned off and their members to become secularized or moved to larger monasteries "where they may be compelled to live religiously for reformation of their lives".

1547 – Thomas Wriothesley lost the Great Seal of his Lord Chancellorship and was confined to his home at Ely Place for abusing his authority. He was found guilty of issuing a commission without the knowledge or permission of the other executors of Henry VIII's will, but it was probably more to do with his opposition to Edward Seymour, Duke of Somerset, becoming Lord Protector. He was later re-admitted to the Privy Council, a position he'd also lost at his fall.

1597 – Death of William Brooke, 10th Baron Cobham, courtier and diplomat, from an ague. He died at Blackfriars and was buried at St Mary Magdalene Church, Cobham. Brooke was the son of George Brooke, 9th Baron Cobham, and his wife, Anne (née Bray), an attendant horsewoman at Anne Boleyn's coronation. In Elizabeth I's reign, Cobham served as Lord Warden of the Cinque Ports, Constable of Dover Castle, Lord Lieutenant and Vice Admiral of Kent, and Privy Councillor.

7TH MARCH

On this day in 1530, Pope Clement VII wrote to Henry VIII forbidding him to marry again, and threatening him with excommunication if he did.

Here is the record from Letters and Papers:

"Bull, notifying that on the appeal of queen Katharine from the judgment of the Legates, who had declared her contumacious for refusing their jurisdiction as being not impartial, the Pope had committed the cause, at her request, to Master Paul Capisucio, the Pope's chaplain, and auditor of the Apostolic palace, with power to cite the King and others; that the said Auditor, ascertaining that access was not safe, caused the said citation, with an inhibition under censures, and a penalty of 10,000 ducats, to be posted on the doors of the churches in Rome, at Bruges, Tournay, and Dunkirk, and the towns of the diocese of Terouenne (Morinensis). The Queen, however, having complained that the King had boasted, notwithstanding the inhibition and mandate against him, that he would proceed to a second marriage, the Pope issues this inhibition, to be fixed on the doors of the churches as before, under the penalty of the greater excommunication, and interdict to be laid upon the kingdom. Bologna, 7 March 1530, 7 Clement VII."

1544 – Executions of Germaine Gardiner, nephew of Stephen Gardiner, and John Larke for denying the royal supremacy. They were hanged, drawn and quartered at Tyburn. Germaine had already been in trouble in 1543 when he was implicated in the *Prebendaries' Plot* against Archbishop Thomas Cranmer.

1544 – Execution of Robert Singleton, clergyman, for treason at Tyburn. Singleton served Thomas Cromwell as a Preacher and Anne Boleyn as a Chaplain before becoming Arch-priest of St Martin's-le-Grand in Dover. It appears that his execution was down to his heretical writings.

1556 – One of the days on which the *Great Comet*, or the Comet of Charles V, was seen and recorded by Paul Fabricius, mathematician and physician at Charles V's court.

1574 – Baptism of John Wilbye, composer and musician, at Diss in Norfolk. He composed and published two sets of madrigals, and also contributed "The Lady Oriana", to a collection in praise of Elizabeth I in 1601, and two madrigals to William Leighton's 1614 collection.

1594 – Death of Sir John Burgh, soldier, from a rapier wound suffered in a duel with John Gilbert, stepbrother of Sir Walter Ralegh. This duel happened during Burgh's second voyage to the West Indies. He was buried in Westminster Abbey, in St Andrew's Chapel.

8TH MARCH

In 1539, Sir Nicholas Carew was beheaded on Tower Hill for treason. Apparently, a letter was found at the Marchioness of Exeter's home, which was evidence of Carew being involved in a conspiracy with the Marquis of Exeter and Baron Montagu, and plotting with Cardinal Pole, Montagu's exiled brother.

Sir Nicholas Carew was born c.1496, and was the eldest son of Sir Richard Carew of Beddington, Surrey, and of Maline Oxenbridge. Carew was brought up at court and was serving the King as a Groom of the Privy Chamber by 1511. In 1515 he became an Esquire of the Body, and in 1518 he became a Gentleman of the Privy Chamber. His wife, Elizabeth, was the daughter of Sir Thomas Bryan, Vice Chamberlain of Catherine of Aragon, and of Lady Margaret Bryan who was governess to the Princess Mary and then to Princess Elizabeth.

Carew was best friends with his brother-in-law, Sir Francis Bryan. In 1535 he sheltered the King's fool, who had angered the King by calling Anne Boleyn "a ribald" and the Princess Elizabeth "a bastard". He thus showed his clear sympathy with the Catholic conservatives, Catherine of Aragon and the Lady Mary. He is also said to have coached Jane Seymour in how to appeal to Henry VIII when the King was married to Anne Boleyn.

Carew was chosen to be in charge of the font at Edward VI's baptism in October 1537, and his wife was one of the ladies at Jane Seymour's funeral in November 1537. He was a royal favourite until his arrest 31st December 1538.

***

1495 – Birth of John of God (João Cidade) in Montemor-o-Novo, Portugal. He was one of Spain's leading religious figures and the order he created, the Brothers Hospitallers of St John of God, still has bases around the world today.

1542 – Burial of Geoffrey Blythe, clergyman, Treasurer of Lichfield, former Warden of King's Hall, Cambridge and former Archdeacon of Stafford. Blythe was one of the divines recorded by martyrologist John Foxe as preaching against Hugh Latimer at Cambridge. Blythe was buried at All Saints' Church in Cambridge.

1569 – Death of Richard Tracy, evangelical reformer and cousin of Protestant martyr James Bainham, at his manor in Stanway, Gloucestershire. Tracy's works included "Profe and Declaration of thys Proposition: Fayth only iustifieth", which was dedicated to Henry VIII, "'A Supplycation to our most Soueraigne Lorde, Kynge Henry the Eyght" and "A Bryef and short Declaracyon made wherebye euery Chrysten Man may knowe what is a Sacrament". In Elizabeth I's reign, he served as a Commissioner of the Peace and Sheriff in Gloucestershire.

9TH MARCH

In 1566, David Rizzio, the private secretary of Mary, Queen of Scots was assassinated in front of Mary, who was heavily pregnant.

Rizzio was born around 1533 near Turin, Italy, and is first recorded as David Riccio di Pancalieri in Piemonte. He is known as David Rizzio, David Riccio or David Rizzo. He came to Scotland in the employ of the ambassador of the Duke of Savoy as a musician, but in late 1564, Mary chose him to replace her Confidential Secretary and Decipherer, Augustine Raulet.

At 8pm on the night of Saturday 9th March 1566, Mary's husband, Lord Darnley, and a large group of conspirators (around 80 men) made their way through the Palace of Holyroodhouse to the Queen's supper chamber where she was enjoying a meal with Rizzio and some other friends. Darnley entered first, to reassure his heavily pregnant wife, and then Lord Ruthven, in full armour, entered the room informing

Mary that Rizzio had offended her honour. Mary asked him to leave, saying that any offence committed by Rizzio would be dealt with by the Lords of Parliament, but she was ignored, and Ruthven ordered Darnley to hold her. Mary got up angrily, and the terrified Rizzio hid behind her as Mary's friends tried to grab Ruthven, who drew his dagger. Ruthven and another man then proceeded to stab Rizzio who was then hauled out of the room. Mary could not do anything to help him, as she had a pistol pointed at her.

Rizzio was then stabbed multiple times, with the final blow being delivered by Lord Darnley's dagger, although he was not the one brandishing it. Mary reported that her secretary was stabbed fifty-six times before the gang of assassins fled. When she confronted Darnley, wanting to know why he had been a part of such "a wicked deed", he replied that she had cuckolded him with Rizzio and that Rizzio was to blame for the problems in their marriage. After this argument between the King and Queen, Rizzio's lifeless body was thrown down the stairs and Mary was kept guarded, a sentry put at her door. However, the wily Queen wasted no time planning her escape. She managed to see Darnley by himself, offering to make love to him, and soothing him. Mary was able to persuade her husband to escape with her, which they did, escaping to the home of the sister of the Earl of Bothwell. On 18th March, Mary entered Edinburgh with her troops, which numbered three to five thousand, and after a few days, moved into the castle to prepare for the birth of her baby. Her enemies fled to England – she had won.

○○

1528 – Death of Sir Ralph Egerton, courtier, administrator and a favourite during the early reign of Henry VIII. In 1513, he was a Standard Bearer in France, keeping that office until 1524, and was knighted after the capture of Tournai. He also served as a Knight of the Body and Treasurer of the Council in the Marches of Wales. He was buried in his chantry chapel at Bunbury.

1571 – Death of Sir Clement Heigham, judge, Speaker of the House of Commons and Chief Baron of the Exchequer in Elizabeth I's reign. He was buried at Barrow Church in Suffolk.

1578 – Death of Lady Margaret Douglas, Countess of Lennox, daughter of Margaret Tudor and Archibald Douglas, 6th Earl of Angus. She was buried at Westminster Abbey, in the Henry VII Chapel.

1579 – Burial of Sir Nicholas Bacon, lawyer, administrator and poetry lover, in St Paul's Cathedral. He had died on 20th February.

1589 – Death of Lady Frances Radcliffe (née Sidney), wife of Sir Thomas Radcliffe, Lord Fitzwalter, and one of Elizabeth I's Ladies of the Bedchamber. She lost the Queen's favour in 1583 due to her husband's enemies turning the Queen against her. Frances died at her home in Bermondsey, and was buried at Westminster Abbey in the Chapel of St Paul. She is known for being the benefactor of Sidney Sussex College at Cambridge.

10TH MARCH

On this day in 1524, King Henry VIII suffered a jousting accident after he forgot to lower his visor in a joust against Charles Brandon, Duke of Suffolk.

Tudor chronicler, Edward Hall, gives the following account of the accident:

"The 10th day of March, the king having a new harness [armour] made of his own design and fashion, such as no armourer before that time had seen, thought to test the same at the tilt and appointed a joust to serve this purpose.

On foot were appointed the Lord Marquis of Dorset and the Earl of Surrey; the King came to one end of the tilt and the Duke of Suffolk to the other. Then a gentleman said to the Duke, "Sir, the King is come to the tilt's end." "I see him not," said the Duke, "on my faith, for my headpiece takes from me my sight." With these words, God knoweth by what chance, the King had his spear delivered to him by the Lord Marquis, the visor of his headpiece being up and not down nor fastened, so that his face was clean naked. Then the gentleman said to the Duke, "Sir, the King cometh".

Then the Duke set forward and charged his spear, and the King likewise inadvisedly set off towards the Duke. The people, perceiving the King's face bare, cried "Hold! Hold!", but the Duke neither saw nor heard, and whether the King remembered that his visor was up or not few could tell. Alas, what sorrow was it to the people when they saw the splinters of the Duke's spear strike on the King's headpiece. For most certainly, the Duke struck the King on the brow, right under the defence of the headpiece, on the very skull cap or basinet piece where unto the barbette is hinged for power and defence, to which skull cap or basinet no armourer takes heed of, for it is evermore covered with the visor, barbet and volant piece, and so that piece is so defended that it forceth of no charge. But when the spear landed on that place, it was great jeopardy of death, in so much that the face was bare, for the Duke's spear broke all to splinters and pushed the King's visor or barbet so far back by the counter blow that all the King's headpiece was full of splinters. The armourers for this matter were much blamed and so was the Lord Marquis for delivering the spear when his face was open, but the King said that no-one was to blame but himself, for he intended to have saved himself and his sight.

The Duke immediately disarmed himself and came to the King, showing him the closeness of his sight, and swore that he would never run against the King again. But if the King had been even a little hurt, the King's servants would have put the Duke in jeopardy. Then the King called his armourers and put all his pieces together and then took a spear and ran six courses very well, by which all men might perceive that he had no hurt, which was a great joy and comfort to all his subjects there present."

This jousting accident was not as serious as the one Henry suffered on 24th January 1536. That one gave Henry a severe blow to the head and, according to Chapuys, he went "two hours without speaking".

◇◇

1513 – Death of John de Vere, 13th Earl of Oxford, magnate and one of the main commanders on the Lancastrian side during the *Wars of the Roses*. At the 1485 *Battle of Bosworth*, Oxford commanded Henry Tudor's archers. Henry VII rewarded his loyalty and his offices included Lord Admiral, Constable of the Tower of London, Captain of the Yeoman Guard and Lord Great Chamberlain of England.

1526 – Marriage of Charles V, Holy Roman Emperor, and Isabella of Portugal. Their children included Philip II of Spain, who went on to marry Mary I.

1538 – Birth of Thomas Howard, 4th Duke of Norfolk, eldest son of Henry Howard, Earl of Surrey, and Frances de Vere, at Kenninghall Palace in Norfolk. Like his father before him, Howard was executed as a traitor, being beheaded on 2nd June 1572 for plotting to marry Mary, Queen of Scots.

1572 – Death of William Paulet, 1st Marquis of Winchester, nobleman and administrator. His offices under Henry VIII included Lord Treasurer, Great Master of the Household and Lord Great Chamberlain, and he served under Edward VI, Mary I and Elizabeth I.

11TH MARCH

On 11th March 1611, Giles Fletcher the Elder, poet, diplomat and member of Parliament during Elizabeth I's reign, died in London. His last words to his son, Phineas, were:

"Had I followed the course of this World, and would either have given, or taken bribes, I might (happily) have made you rich, but now must leave you nothing but your education ... But know certainly, that I your weak, and dying Father leave you to an everliving, and All-sufficient Father, and in him a never fading inheritance; who will not suffer you to want any good thing, who hath been my God, and will be the God of my seed."

Fletcher started his career lecturing at King's College, Cambridge, in 1572. By 1580, he was Dean of Arts. In 1586, he accompanied Sir Thomas Randolph on a diplomatic mission to Scotland and then in June 1588 he went to Moscow as special ambassador, recording his travels in his 1591 "Of the Russe Common Wealth, or, the Maner of gouernement of the Russe emperour, (commonly called the Emperour of Moskouia) with the manners, and fashions of the people of that countrey".

Fletcher's literary works include the sonnet "Licia" and "The Rising to the Crown of Richard III".

1513 – Giovanni di Lorenzo de' Medici was proclaimed Pope Leo X after being elected on 9th March. He was Pope until December 1521.

1521 – Death of Andrew Forman, diplomat and Archbishop of St Andrews, at Dunfermline. He was buried at St Andrews Cathedral.

1563 – Death of Antoine de Noailles, soldier, Admiral of France and French ambassador to the English court during the reign of Mary I, at Bordeaux. He was also Chevalier of the order of St Michel. His body was buried at Noailles, but his heart was buried in Bordeaux Cathedral. It was rumoured that Noailles was poisoned.

1609 – Burial of William Warner, poet and lawyer, at Great Amwell in Hertfordshire. He was buried there at the church of St John the Baptist. His works included "Albion's England" and "Pan his Syrinx, or Pipe, Compact of Seven Reedes".

12TH MARCH

On 12th March 1539, Thomas Boleyn, Earl of Wiltshire and Earl of Ormond, and father of Queen Anne Boleyn, died at Hever Castle, aged around sixty-two. His servant, Robert Cranwell, wrote to Thomas Cromwell the next day to inform him of his death:-

"My good lord and master is dead. He made the end of a good Christian man. Hever, 13 March."

Henry VIII ordered masses to be said for his soul, a clear sign that Thomas was back in favour at his death, and Thomas was laid to rest in the family church, St Peter's Church at Hever. You can still see his tomb there today. It is decorated by a magnificent brass which shows him dressed as a Knight of the Garter, and above his right shoulder sits his daughter Anne's falcon crest. At his feet there is a griffin. His son, Henry Boleyn, is buried nearby, his tomb marked with a small cross on the stone floor.

Thomas Boleyn was an important ambassador in Henry VIII's reign, and served the King as Privy Councillor, Treasurer of the Household and Lord Privy Seal.

⬦⬦⬦⬦⬦⬦⬦⬦⬦⬦⬦⬦⬦⬦⬦⬦⬦⬦⬦⬦⬦⬦⬦⬦⬦⬦⬦⬦⬦⬦

1537 – Execution of William Haydock, Cistercian monk. He was hanged for his involvement in the *Pilgrimage of Grace*. Interestingly, his remains were discovered in the family's home, Cottam Hall, in the early 19th century because his nephew had saved his body and hidden it there.

1564 – Baptism of Christopher Bales, Roman Catholic priest and martyr. Bales was executed by hanging on 4th March 1590 in Fleet Street. Two others, Nicholas Horner and Alexander Blake, were executed at Smithfield and Grays Inn Lane for harbouring him.

1573 (11th or 12th) – Death of Edmund Brydges, 2nd Baron Chandos, soldier, politician, Lord Lieutenant of Gloucestershire and Vice-Admiral of Gloucestershire. He was laid to rest at Sudeley.

1628 – Death of John Bull, composer, musician and organ builder, at Antwerp.

13TH MARCH

1540 – Death of Henry Bourchier, Earl of Essex. He died after falling off a horse, and his title was given to Thomas Cromwell. His daughter, Anne, married Sir William Parr, brother of Queen Catherine Parr.

1543 – Death of Sebastian Giustinian, the Venetian diplomat. He died in Venice at the age of eighty-three. Giustinian served as the Venetian ambassador to England from 1514 to 1519, and wrote 226 letters during his embassy there. He became ambassador to France in 1526 and procurator of St Mark in 1540.

1594 – Death of John Woolton, Bishop of Exeter, from asthma at the bishop's palace in Exeter. He was buried in the cathedral choir.

1601 – Execution of Welshman Sir Gelly Meyrick at Tyburn. He was hanged, drawn and quartered for his part in the rebellion led by Robert Devereux, 2nd Earl of Essex. Meyrick attended Essex as Steward of his household and Receiver-General of his rents and revenues. He was executed with Sir Henry Cuffe, author, politician and fellow rebel.

1619 – Death of Richard Burbage, actor and star of Shakespeare's Lord Chamberlain's Men and the King's Men. He was named in Shakespeare's will of 1616 as a "fellow", meaning a close friend or colleague.

14TH MARCH

1471 – Death of Sir Thomas Malory, known for his work "Le Morte d'Arthur", which he wrote in prison. He was laid to rest in St Francis's Chapel, Greyfriars, Newgate.

1540 – Death of Sir John Port, judge. He is known for mumbling in 1535 in Lord Dacre's case and being counted on the wrong side, giving the Crown a majority. He was taken ill at Worcester during the *Lent* assize and died at Bewdley.

1553 – Death of Arthur Bulkeley, Bishop of Bangor, at his home in Bangor. He was buried in the cathedral choir.

1555 – Death of Sir John Russell, 1st Earl of Bedford, courtier, envoy and landowner, at his home on the Strand in London. Russell served Henry VIII as Lord High Admiral and Lord Privy Seal, following the fall of Thomas Cromwell. He was an executor of Henry VIII's will, and carried on as Lord Privy Seal in the reigns of Edward VI and Mary I.

15TH MARCH

On this day in 1551, the Lady Mary, sister of Edward VI and the future Mary I, rode through London causing a stir. Here is diarist Henry Machyn's record of the event:

"The xv day the Lady Mary rode through London unto St John's, her place, with fifty knights and gentlemen in velvet coats and chains of gold afore her, and after her iiij score gentlemen and ladies every one havyng a peyre of bedes of black. She rode through Chepe-syde and thrugh Smythfeld."

A note in the diary by historian John Strype notes that the carrying of beads was "to make an open profession, no doubt, of their devotion for the mass" and the carrying of rosaries during Edward's Protestant reign was definitely a statement.

1493 – Arrival of Christopher Columbus, explorer and navigator, at Palos in Spain after his 1492 voyage to the New World.

1504 – Death of John Arundell, Bishop of Exeter, at Exeter House in the Strand, London. He was buried at St Clement Danes Church in London.

1532 – William Warham, Archbishop of Canterbury, criticised Henry VIII in the House of Lords when Parliament was discussing the annulment. The King responded with what historian G. W. Bernard describes as "foul language".

1554 – Marian martyr John Hooper was deprived of the bishopric of Gloucester while imprisoned in Fleet Prison. He had been charged with owing over five hundred pounds in unpaid first fruits, a charge he denied.

1628 – Burial of composer John Bull in the Groenplats cemetery near Antwerp Cathedral.

16TH MARCH

1485 – Death of Anne (née Neville), Queen Consort of Richard III, in London. She was buried on the south side of the high altar at Westminster Abbey. Anne was the daughter of Richard Neville, 16th Earl of Warwick and a man known as the "Kingmaker", and his wife, Anne (née Beauchamp). She married Edward, Prince of Wales and son of Henry VI, in 1470 but he was killed in 1471 at the *Battle of Tewkesbury*. Anne went on to marry Richard, Duke of Gloucester sometime before July 1473, and the couple became King and Queen on 26th June 1483 when Richard usurped the throne, putting aside his nephew, Edward V.

Anne and Richard had one child, Edward of Middleham, Prince of Wales, but he died in 1484 at the age of ten, which was a huge blow to his parents. Anne did not have any more children, and it was rumoured that Richard was going to set her aside and marry his niece, Elizabeth of York. Richard formally denied this on 30th March 1485, after Anne's death.

Richard III's enemies spread rumours that the King had poisoned his wife, but she had been in ill health for some time, and there is no evidence that he murdered her.

1503 – Death of Edward Story, Bishop of Chichester. He was buried at the cathedral, on the north side of the altar.

1523 – Birth of Anthony Rudolph Chevallier, French Protestant Hebraist, at Montchamps, Normandy, France. It appears that Chevallier tutored Princess Elizabeth, the future Elizabeth I, in French and Hebrew in the early 1550s. During Mary I's reign, he taught Hebrew in Strasbourg and Geneva, and in Elizabeth I's reign he taught Hebrew at Cambridge. He went back to France in 1572, but the *St Bartholomew's Day Massacre* caused him to flee to Guernsey, and he died there in October 1572.

1533 – Death of John Bourchier, 2nd Baron Berners, soldier, translator and diplomat, at Calais, while serving Henry VIII as Deputy of Calais. He was succeeded by Arthur Plantagenet, Viscount Lisle. Berners' translations included "Froissart's Chronicles", "Golden Book of Marcus Aurelius", "The History of Arthur of Lytell Brytaine" and "Huon of Bordeaux".

1553 – Death of Sir Richard Lyster, judge and Chief Justice of the King's Bench. He was buried at St Michael's Church in Southampton.

1559 – Death of Sir Anthony St Leger, Lord Deputy of Ireland, at Ulcombe, Kent. He was appointed Lord Deputy in 1540 and served in the position until his death, although he was being investigated for keeping false accounts at his death. He was buried at Ulcombe Parish Church.

1561 – The body of Marie de Guise (Mary of Guise), mother of Mary, Queen of Scots, was put on a ship heading to France to be buried at Rheims.

1589 (15th or 16th) – Executions of priests Robert Dalby and John Amias at York as traitors, due to their Catholic faith.

1590 (15th or 16th) – Death of Bartholomew Clerke, civil lawyer, politician and diplomat, at Clapham. Clerke served Elizabeth I as a member of Parliament, as an ambassador to the French court and to Flanders, and Archdeacon of Wells. He was buried in the old church at Clapham, where he was Lord of the Manor.

1593 – Death of Thomas Snagge, lawyer, Serjeant-at-Law and Speaker of the House of Commons in Elizabeth I's reign, in his chambers at Serjeants' Inn. He was laid to rest in St Mary's Church, Marston Moretaine, in Bedfordshire.

1619 – Burial of actor Richard Burbage at St Leonard's Church, Shoreditch.

17TH MARCH

On this day in 1565, Alexander Ales (Alesius, Aless), theologian and reformer, died in Edinburgh.

Ales became friends with theologian Philip Melancthon in 1532 when Ales began studying at Wittenberg University, and he began to be concerned with making the Bible available in the vernacular. He published an open letter to James V of Scotland in 1533, *Alexandri Alesii epistola contra decretum quoddam episcoporum in Scotia*, appealing for him to annul recent legislation making it illegal to own or distribute the New Testament in the vernacular. When the Catholic Johannes Cochlaeus, countered this with a letter to James accusing Ales of translating the New testament and sending it to Scotland, and claiming that it would cause unrest, Ales answered with

Alexandri Alesii Scotti responsio ad Cochlei calumnias. In this letter, Ales emphasised how Continental reformers were simply trying to lead people back to the Bible and the teaching of the Early Church.

In August 1535, Ales travelled to England with copies of *Loci Communes* by Melancthon for Henry VIII and Thomas Cromwell, and when he travelled there again in October, he was appointed King's Scholar at Cambridge University. Spring 1536 was a time of worry for Ales, with the fall of Anne Boleyn, a keen reformer, and resistance to reformist ideas, coupled with the fact that Cromwell hadn't paid his stipend, forced him to leave the university and train as a physician in London. This enabled him to keep in contact with friends such as Archbishop Thomas Cranmer, and contacts like Thomas Cromwell, Henry VIII's Vicar-General.

In summer 1537, Ales was involved in a public row with John Stokesley, Bishop of London, who protested against the view that Ales put forward, as King's Scholar, regarding there being only two sacraments. This debate was published by Ales in 1542 in his *De authoritate verbi Dei.*

Ales left England suddenly in June 1539 after being warned, by Cranmer, of the dangers of being a married reformer when the "Act of Six Articles" was about to be made law. This act demanded a vow of celibacy, but Ales was married. Ales travelled back to Wittenberg and then became a professor of theology at Frankfurt an der Oder. After trouble there in 1542, he was forced to leave and take up a position at Leipzig. There, in 1547 during the siege of Leipzig, his house and library were destroyed, but it was the place where Ales chose to end his days, visiting England during Edward VI's reign and translating for Cranmer Latin versions of the "Order of Communion" and the "First Prayer Book".

Ales's works include *Cohortatio ad Concordiam Pietatis, missa in Patriam suam* (1544), *Ad duos et brevis triginta articulos ... aeditos a theologis Lovaniensibus brevis & moderata responsio* (1545) *Expositio Libri Psalmorum Davidis* (1550), *Ad libellum Ludovici Nogarolae ... de traditionibus apostolicis & earum necessitate responsio* (1556) and *Cohortatio ad Pietatis Concordiam ineundam* (1559).

∞∞∞∞∞∞∞∞∞∞∞∞∞∞∞∞∞∞∞∞∞∞∞∞∞∞

1473 – Birth of James IV, King of Scots, at Stirling in Scotland. He was the eldest son of James III and Margaret of Denmark, the husband of Margaret Tudor and the father of King James V. James' reign lasted from June 1488 to 9th September 1513 when he was killed at the *Battle of Flodden*.

1570 – Death of William Herbert, 1st Earl of Pembroke, soldier, courtier and landowner, at Hampton Court, aged sixty-three. Herbert was married to Anne Parr, sister of Catherine Parr. Herbert served Henry VIII as an Esquire of the Body, a 'gentleman spear' and a Gentleman of the King's Privy Chamber. When his sister-in-law Catherine Parr became queen, he was even more favoured, was awarded various grants and offices, and was promoted to be Joint Chief Gentleman of the Privy Chamber. He was also named as an executor of the King's will. Herbert was made a Knight of the Garter in Edward VI's reign and won favour with Mary I by helping to put down *Wyatt's Rebellion* in 1554. He continued to be in favour in Elizabeth's reign.

1612 – Death of Thomas Holland, Calvinist scholar and theologian, at Exeter College, Oxford. He was buried in the University Church of St Mary the Virgin, in the chancel. Holland, with six other scholars, helped to translate the prophetic books of the "Old Testament" for the "Authorised Version of the Bible", and held the positions of Rector of Exeter College and Regius Professor of Divinity.

18TH MARCH

On this day in 1496, Henry VIII's beloved sister, Princess Mary Tudor, was born at Richmond Palace. She was the youngest of Henry VII's and Elizabeth of York's children to survive infancy, and was sister to Prince Arthur, Princess Margaret and Prince Henry.

Mary was renowned for her beauty, being described as "a Paradise - tall, slender, grey-eyed, possessing an extreme pallor" by the Venetian ambassador, and her motto was "La volenté de Dieu me suffit" (The will of God is sufficient for me).

In 1507, Mary was betrothed to Charles of Castile (the future Charles V Holy Roman Emperor), and their wedding was planned for 1514. However, the betrothal was cancelled due to Henry VIII's diplomatic dealings and, much to Mary's horror, she was betrothed instead to the fifty-two year-old King Louis XII of France, a man thirty-four years her senior, as part of Cardinal Wolsey's peace treaty with France.

Mary married King Louis XII of France in Abbeville on 9th October 1514 when she was just eighteen, but the marriage was short-lived, with the King dying just a few months later, on 1st January 1515. Mary had been in love with Charles Brandon, Duke of Suffolk and a great friend of Henry VIII, and before her marriage to Louis XII she had made her brother promise that if she married the French King and outlived him, that she could choose her next husband.

Mary was kept isolated from men for six weeks at the Palais de Cluny to see if she was carrying the heir to the French throne, but then her real love, Charles Brandon, was sent to France to escort her home. Mary and Charles Brandon took a huge risk by secretly marrying in France on 3rd March 1515, without the King's permission, something which could be classed as treason. Henry VIII was furious but his love for his favourite sister and his friendship with Brandon led to him forgiving the couple, and they were officially married at Greenwich Palace, 13th May 1515. Although she was now the Duchess of Suffolk, Mary was still referred to as the "French Queen".

Mary had four children by Charles Brandon, the Duke of Suffolk, but only two daughters, Frances and Eleanor, survived childhood. Frances married Henry Grey, Marquis of Dorset, and was the mother of Lady Jane Grey. Eleanor married Henry Clifford, the 2nd Earl of Cumberland.

Mary became ill in 1533, and died on 25th June (some sources say 24th) at Westhorpe, Suffolk. She was laid to rest in the abbey at Bury St Edmunds, Suffolk, and then moved to St Mary's Church in Bury St Edmunds during the *Dissolution of the Monasteries*.

1496 – Death of Thomas Burgh, Baron Burgh, soldier and administrator. He was buried in the chantry chapel he had built in Gainsborough Parish Church. Burgh had served as an Esquire of the Body, Master of the Horse and Privy Councillor to Edward IV, and also served Henry VII as Knight of the Body and Privy Councillor.

1539 – Death of Sir Robert Wingfield, diplomat, probably in Calais. He was laid to rest in St Nicholas Church, Calais. Wingfield served both Henry VII and Henry VIII as a diplomat, and was appointed Lord Deputy of Calais in 1526.

1601 – Execution of Sir Christopher Blount, soldier, secret agent and rebel, after his involvement in the rebellion of Robert Devereux, Earl of Essex. He was executed at the Tower of London for high treason and buried there. Blount corresponded with Thomas Morgan, an exiled agent of Mary, Queen of Scots, in Paris, but as he was the Earl of Leicester's Master of the Horse at the time, it appears that he was working as an agent for Leicester and Sir Francis Walsingham. Blount married Leicester's widow, Lettice (née Knollys) in the spring of 1589.

19TH MARCH

Translator and poet Arthur Brooke died on this day in 1563 in the shipwreck of the *Greyhound* off the coast of Rye in East Sussex, while travelling to LeHavre. Brooke is known for producing the first version of the "Romeo and Juliet" legend in English, "The tragicall historye of Romeus and Juliet, written first in Italian by Bandell, and nowe in Englishe by Ar. Br." which was printed in 1562. It not only served William Shakespeare as the main source for his famous "Romeo and Juliet", but was also used by Bernard Garter and William Painter.

George Turberville, in his "Epitaph on the death of Maister Arthur Brooke drownde in passing to New Haven", refers to Brooke's authorship of "Romeus and Juliet":

"In proof that he for myter did excell,
As may be judge by Julyet and her Mate:
For ther he shewde his cunning passing well
When he the tale to English did translate."

Brooke also produced the 1563 "The agreemente of sondry places of scripture, seeming in shew to jarre, serving in stead of commentaryes, not onely for these, but others lyke", a translation of a Huguenot work.

Sir Thomas Finch, who had just been appointed knight-marshal by Elizabeth I, was also killed when the *Greyhound* sank.

* * *

1563 – *Peace (Edict) of Amboise* signed at the Château of Amboise by Catherine de' Medici, as regent for her son, Charles

IX. Catherine initiated this truce after the assassination of Francis, Duke of Guise, at the *Siege of Orléans*. The *Edict* ended the first phase of the *French Wars of Religion* and guaranteed the Huguenots religious privileges and freedoms. Peace did not last long, however.

1577 – Death of Edmund Harman, former barber of Henry VIII, at Burford in Oxfordshire. He had retired there after Henry VIII's death. Harman was buried at Taynton Church.

1590 – Baptism of William Bradford, separatist and founder of the Plymouth Colony, Massachusetts, at Austerfield in Yorkshire. Bradford was Governor of the colony for over thirty years.

20TH MARCH

On this day in 1549, Thomas Seymour, 1st Baron of Sudeley and Lord High Admiral, husband of the late Dowager Queen Catherine Parr and brother of Queen Jane Seymour and Protector Somerset, was executed after being charged with thirty-three counts of treason.

He caused the King's Council concern for some time, but it was the alleged plot to kidnap the young King Edward VI, his nephew, in January 1549 which led to his execution. On the night of 16th January 1549, Seymour had broken into the King's apartments at Hampton Court Palace and had shot the King's beloved pet Spaniel after it barked at him. He was arrested, charged with treason and executed on 20th March 1549, after the King signed his death warrant.

During his imprisonment in the Tower of London, Seymour wrote the following poem:-

"Forgetting God
to love a king
Hath been my rod
Or else nothing:
In this frail life
being a blast
of care and strife
till in be past.
Yet God did call
me in my pride
lest I should fall
and from him slide
for whom loves he
and not correct
that they may be
of his elect.

The death haste thee
thou shalt me gain
Immortally
with him to reign
Who send the king
Like years as noye
In governing
His realm in joy
And after this
frail life such grace
As in his bliss
he may have place."

Seymour's execution was highly unpopular, and the King's
Council had to take steps to calm the situation by blackening
Seymour's name. The Council spread it around that Seymour
had written letters to Mary and Elizabeth encouraging them to
rise up against their brother's government, and Hugh Latimer,
the cleric who had been friends with Seymour, and who had

had Seymour as his patron, preached a sermon vilifying him, and accusing him of being an atheist, traitor and debaucher of women:-

"He was, I heard say, a covetous man:...I would there were no more in England. He was, I heard say, an ambitious man: I would there were no more in England. He was, I heard say, a seditious man, a contemner of common prayer: I would there were no more in England. Well he is gone. I would he had left none behind him."

As touching the kind of his death, whether he be saved or no, I refer that to God only... And when a man hath two strokes of the axe who can tell but that between two strokes he doth repent? It is very hard to judge. Well, I will not go so nigh to work; but this I will say if they ask me what I think of his death, that he died very dangerously, irksomely, horribly... He was a man the farthest from the fear of God that I knew of or heard of in England... surely he was a wicked man and the realm is well rid of him."

Nicholas Throckmorton said of Seymour's end:-

"Off went his head, they made a quick despatch,
But ever since I thought him sure a beast
Who causeless laboured to defile his nest
Though guiltless, he, through malice, went to pot
Not answering for himself nor knowing cause."

John Harington, Seymour's servant and friend, wrote of Seymour:-

"Friend to God's truth, and foe to Rome's deceit...
Yet against nature, reason and just laws
His blood was spilt, guiltless, without just cause."

It is alleged that the fifteen year-old Elizabeth, on hearing of Seymour's death, said: "This day died a man of much wit and very little judgement".

1469 – Birth of Cecily, Viscountess Welles and princess, also known as Cecily of York, third daughter of Edward IV and Elizabeth Woodville. She was born at Westminster Palace. A marriage alliance with Scotland was made in 1473 promising Cecily to James, the infant son of James III, but Cecily was still unmarried at her father's death in 1483. Her uncle, Richard III, arranged Cecily's marriage to Ralph Scrope of Upsall, but Henry VII dissolved the marriage in 1486 and she married John Welles, Viscount Welles, the King's half-uncle. After Welles' death in 1499, Cecily went on to marry Thomas Kyme of Friskney. Cecily died in 1507.

1544 – Baptism of Cuthbert Mayne, Roman Catholic priest and martyr. He was hanged, drawn and quartered at Launceston on 30th November 1577 after being charged with traitorously getting hold of a papal bull and publishing it at Golden Manor, defending the authority of the Pope, purchasing a number of Agnus Dei and giving them to people, and celebrating the Catholic mass.

1555 – Burial of John Russell, Earl of Bedford, courtier and magnate, at Chenies, following his death 14th March. It was a lavish funeral with three hundred horses, all in black trappings.

1560 – Birth of Sir Edward Hoby, scholar, theologian, politician and diplomat, at Bisham in Berkshire. He was the eldest son of Sir Thomas Hoby and Elizabeth (née Cooke), daughter of Sir Anthony Cooke. Elizabeth I favoured Hoby, and used him on a number of secret missions.

1572 – Death of Mary Bassett (née Roper), translator and granddaughter of Sir Thomas More. Her education was praised by Roger Ascham and Nicholas Harpsfield, and she presented Mary I with a copy of five books of Eusebius's "Ecclesiastical History" which she had translated from Greek into English.

21ST MARCH

On 21st March 1556, Archbishop Thomas Cranmer was burned at the stake in Oxford for heresy. His execution was a despicable act, in that it was unlawful because Cranmer had actually recanted five times. He should have been absolved, but he wasn't.

On the day of his execution, Cranmer was ordered to make a final public recantation at the University Church Oxford. He agreed, but after praying and exhorting the people to obey the King and Queen, he renounced his recantations and professed his true faith:-

"And now I come to the great thing which so much troubleth my conscience, more than any thing that ever I did or said in my whole life, and that is the setting abroad of a writing contrary to the truth, which now here I renounce and refuse, as things written with my hand contrary to the truth which I thought in my heart, and written for fear of death, and to save my life, if it might be; and that is, all such bills or papers which I have written or signed with my hand since my degradation, wherein I have written many things untrue. And forasmuch as my hand hath offended, writing contrary to my heart, therefore my hand shall first be punished; for when I come to the fire, it shall first be burned.

And as for the Pope, I refuse him as Christ's enemy, and antichrist, with all his false doctrine. And as for the sacrament, I believe as I have taught in my book against the bishop of Winchester, which my book teacheth so true a doctrine of the sacrament that it shall stand in the last day before the judgment of God, where the papistical doctrines contrary thereto shall be ashamed to show their face."

He was quickly dragged out of the pulpit and taken to the stake. Martyrologist John Foxe describes what happened next:-

"With thoughts intent upon a far higher object than the empty threats of man, he reached the spot dyed with the blood of Ridley and Latimer. There he knelt for a short time in earnest devotion, and then arose, that he might undress and prepare for the fire. Two friars who had been parties in prevailing upon him to abjure, now endeavoured to draw him off again from the truth, but he was steadfast and immoveable in what he had just professed, and before publicly taught. A chain was provided to bind him to the stake, and after it had tightly encircled him, fire was put to the fuel, and the flames began soon to ascend. Then were the glorious sentiments of the martyr made manifest;—then it was, that stretching out his right hand, he held it unshrinkingly in the fire till it was burnt to a cinder, even before his body was injured, frequently exclaiming, "This unworthy right hand!" Apparently insensible of pain, with a countenance of venerable resignation, and eyes directed to Him for whose cause he suffered, he continued, like St Stephen, to say, "Lord Jesus receive my spirit!" till the fury of the flames terminated his powers of utterance and existence. He closed a life of high sublunary elevation, of constant uneasiness, and of glorious martyrdom, on March 21, 1556."

1522 – Death of Christopher Urswick, courtier, diplomat, former confessor and chaplain to Lady Margaret Beaufort, and almoner to Henry VII. His ecclesiastical offices included Dean of York, Canon and Prebendary of St George's Chapel, Windsor and Dean of Windsor. He was also registrar of the Order of the Garter. He died at the rectory of St Augustine's in Hackney, and was buried there.

1540 – Death of John de Vere, 15th Earl of Oxford. He died at Earls Colne in Essex, and was buried at Castle Hedingham on the 12th April. Oxford served Henry VIII as an Esquire of the

Body, Lord Great Chamberlain and royal councillor. He was also a Knight of the Garter.

1555 – Birth of Sir John Leveson, Kent landowner and Deputy Lieutenant of Kent. In 1601, Leveson helped put down the Earl of Essex's rebellion by commanding men on Ludgate Hill and giving no ground to Essex and his rebels. Essex and his men were forced to withdraw.

1565 – Death of John Warner, Dean of Winchester and physician, at his home in Warwick Lane, London. He was buried at Great Stanmore in Middlesex.

1591 – Death of Edmund Freake, Bishop of Norwich and then of Worcester. He was buried in Worcester Cathedral. In 1579, he tried Matthew Hamont, a Norfolk playwright, for heresy. Hamont was found guilty and burned at Norwich Castle.

1617 – Burial of Pocahontas, the Algonquian Indian princess. Pocahontas was the daughter of Chief Powhatan (Wahunsonacock) of the Virginia Algonquian nation. She was renamed Rebecca in 1614 when she was baptised, and she married John Rolfe in Jamestown in April 1614. The couple, and their son Thomas, went to England in 1616. She was ill, probably from pneumonia or tuberculosis, when the family set sail for Virginia in March 1617 and had to be put ashore, where she died. She was buried at St George's in Gravesend, Kent.

22ND MARCH

1459 – Birth of Maximilian I, Holy Roman Emperor, at Wiener Neustadt. He was the son of Frederick III, Holy Roman Emperor, and Eleanor of Portugal, and became Holy Roman Emperor in 1493. He was married to Mary of Burgundy, and was the father of Margaret of Austria and Philip I of Castile (Philip the Handsome).

1515 – Death of James Stanley, Bishop of Ely and son of Thomas Stanley, 1ˢᵗ Earl of Derby, at Manchester. He was buried in the Ely Chapel of the collegiate church, which is now Manchester Cathedral. Stanley owed his rise in the Church to his father and his stepmother, Lady Margaret Beaufort, mother of Henry VII.

1519 – Date given for the birth of Katherine Willoughby (married names Brandon and Bertie), Duchess of Suffolk and leading patroness of Reform. She was the daughter of William Willoughby, 11ᵗʰ Baron Willoughby de Eresby, and Lady Maria de Salinas, lady-in-waiting to Catherine of Aragon. She became Charles Brandon's ward in 1529 and married him in 1533.

1580 – Burial of Henry Fitzalan, 12ᵗʰ Earl of Arundel, at Arundel's collegiate chapel.

1582 – Burial of William Bourne, gunner, mathematician and writer, at Gravesend. His works included "Almanacke and Prognostication for iii Yeres", "A Regiment for the Sea", "Treasure for Traveilers", "The Arte of Shooting in Great Ordnance" and "Inventions, or, Devises".

1599 – Birth of Sir Anthony Van Dyck, painter and etcher, in Antwerp.

23rd March

This day in 1534, was an important day for King Henry VIII and Queen Anne Boleyn, because it was on this day that Parliament passed the "First Act of Succession" declaring the validity of Henry VIII and Anne Boleyn's marriage, and recognising the rights of their issue to inherit the throne.

The main points of the act were:

- Parliament's declaration that the marriage between "the Lady Katherine" and the King was "void and annulled", judged to be against God's laws and that "the said Lady Katherine shall be from henceforth called and reputed only dowager to Prince Arthur, and not queen of this realm".

- Parliament's Declaration that the marriage between Henry VIII and Anne Boleyn was valid – "that the lawful matrimony had and solemnized between your highness and your most dear and entirely beloved wife Queen Anne, shall be established, and taken for undoubtful, true, sincere, and perfect ever hereafter, according to the just judgment of the 1534."

- Parliament's ruling on marriages "within the prohibited degrees" which had been allowed to take place due to papal dispensations and its declaration that "no man, of what estate, degree, or condition soever he be, has power to dispense with God's laws".

- Parliament's declaration on the children of these unlawful marriages – "and that the children proceeding and procreated under such unlawful marriage, shall not be lawful nor legitimate; any foreign laws, licences, dispensations, or other thing or things to the contrary thereof notwithstanding."

- Parliament's declaration that the succession would pass through the heirs of Henry VIII and Anne Boleyn.

- Parliament's declaration that in the absence of sons, the succession would pass to "the issue female" of Henry VIII and Anne Boleyn".

The Act was to be proclaimed throughout England on the 1st May 1534, and the penalty for not accepting the Act was for the offender to be judged as a "high traitor". There was also a penalty for publishing or speaking "slander or prejudice of the said matrimony", which was deemed to be "misprision of treason". Nobles of the realm, "spiritual or temporal", were to make "a corporal oath" that they "constantly, without fraud or guile, observe, fulfil, maintain, defend, and keep, to their cunning, wit, and uttermost of their powers, the whole effects and contents of this present Act". Refusal to take the oath would be deemed as "misprision of high treason".

<hr>

1540 – The Dissolution of Waltham Abbey, the last abbey to be dissolved by Henry VIII.

1596 – Death of Sir Henry Unton (Umpton), soldier, member of Parliament and diplomat in the reign of Elizabeth I. He died after being taken ill with "a violent, burning fever" after accompanying Henry IV of France to the siege at La Fère. His body was returned to England, and he was buried in Faringdon, at All Saints' Church.

1628 – Death of Robert Daborne, playwright. In his later years he took up holy orders and was Dean of Lismore, where he died in 1628. His works included "A Christian Turn'd Turk" and "The Poor Man's Comfort".

24TH MARCH

On this day in history, 24th March 1603, Queen Elizabeth I, daughter of Anne Boleyn and Henry VIII, died at Richmond Palace at the age of sixty-nine. She was the third of Henry's children to be monarch but reigned for far longer than her siblings, ruling for 44 years and 127 days.

Sir Robert Carey, Earl of Monmouth, and grandson of Mary Boleyn, recorded Elizabeth's last days:

"On Wednesday 23rd of March, she grew speechless. That afternoon, by signs, she called for her council, and by putting her hand to her head, when the king of Scots was named to succeed her, they all knew he was the man she desired should reign after her. About six at night she made signs for Archbishop Whitgift and her chaplains to come to her, at which time I went in with them, and sat upon my knees full of tears to see that heavy sight. Her Majesty lay upon her back, with one hand in the bed, and the other without. The bishop kneeled down by her, and examined her first of her faith; and she so punctually answered all his several questions, by lifting up her eyes, and holding up her hand, as it was a comfort to all the beholders. Then the good man told her plainly what she was, and what she was to come to; and though she had been long a great Queen here upon earth, yet shortly she was to yield an account of her stewardship to the King of kings. After this he began to pray, and all that were by did answer him. After he had continued long in prayer, till the old man's knees were weary, he blessed her, and meant to rise and leave her. The Queen made a sign with her hand. My sister Scroop knowing her meaning, told the bishop the Queen desired he would pray still. He did so for a long half hour more, with earnest cries to God for her soul's health, which he uttered with that fervency of spirit, as the Queen, to all our sight, much rejoiced thereat, and gave testimony to us all of her Christian and comfortable end. By this time it grew late, and every one departed, all but her women that attended her.

This that I heard with my ears, and did see with my eyes, I thought it my duty to set down, and to affirm it for a truth, upon the faith of a Christian; because I know there have been many false lies reported of the end and death of that good lady."

...and diarist John Manningham recorded the moment of her death:-

"This morning, about three o'clock her Majesty departed from this life, mildly like a lamb, easily like a ripe apple from a tree... Dr Parry told me he was present, and sent his prayers before her soul; and I doubt not but she is amongst the royal saints in heaven in eternal joys."

Although some historians question whether her reign was really "The Golden Age", there is no denying that it made a huge impact on English history. Elizabeth I – Gloriana, the Virgin Queen and Good Queen Bess – daughter of the infamous Anne Boleyn and the iconic Henry VIII, was one of England's greatest monarchs.

Elizabeth I's death was the end of an era in so many ways: the end of England's "Golden Age", the end of a long reign and the end of the Tudor dynasty. The Tudor line died with the Virgin Queen and it was the son of Mary, Queen of Scots, James VI of Scotland, who became James I of England, and who established the House of Stuart in English history.

1582 – Death of Sir James Dyer, judge, law reporter and Speaker of the House of Commons during the reign of Edward VI. His other offices included King's Sergeant-at-Law, Judge of the Common Pleas and Chief Justice of the Common Pleas. He was buried at Great Staughton Church in Huntingdonshire, next to his wife.

1619 – Death of Robert Rich, 1st Earl of Warwick, nobleman and politician, at Warwick House in Holborn. He was buried at Felsted Church. Rich was married to Penelope Devereux, daughter of Walter Devereux, 1st Earl of Essex, and Lettice Knollys, and sister of Robert Devereux, 2nd Earl of Essex. It was not a happy marriage, and the couple separated in 1590 after the birth of their second son, and divorced in 1605. Penelope began a relationship with Charles Blount, the future Lord Mountjoy, in 1590 and went on to have children by him.

25TH MARCH

In Tudor England, the *New Year* began 25th March, a day known as *Lady Day* or the *Feast of the Annunciation of the Blessed Virgin*. This feast day commemorated the day that Mary was first told that she was carrying Jesus.

Although the year officially started on this day, *New Year's* gifts were still given on 1st January, which came from the Roman tradition of *New Year.*

On *Lady Day* in 1555, during Mary I's reign, diarist Henry Machyn recorded jousting at Westminster:

"The xxv day of Marche, the wyche was owre lade [day,] ther was as gret justes as youe have sene at the tylt at Vestmynster; the chalyngers was a Spaneard and ser Gorge Haward; and all ther men, and ther horsses trymmyd in whyt, and then cam the Kyng and a gret mene [menée or retinue] all in bluw, and trymmyd with yelow, and ther elmets with gret tuyffes [tufts or plumes] of blue and yelow fether, and all ther veffelers [whifflers or forerunners] and ther fotemen, and ther armorers, and a compene lyke Turkes red [rode] in cremesun saten gownes and capes, and with fachyons [falchions] and gret targets; and sum in gren, and mony of clyvers colers; and ther was broken ij hondred stayffes and a-boyff [above]."

The only knight named is Sir George Howard, but the knights were both English and Spanish, and a record two hundred staffs were broken.

◇◇◇◇◇◇◇◇◇◇◇◇◇◇◇◇◇◇◇◇◇◇◇◇◇◇◇◇◇◇◇◇◇◇◇◇◇◇

1571 – Roberto di Ridolfi left England with a commission to open negotiations to end the trade war, but also with authorisation from Mary, Queen of Scots and the Duke of Norfolk to get Spanish aid for their plot against Elizabeth I.

1584 – Letters patent granted to Walter Ralegh to "discover, search for, fynde out and view... landes, countries and territories", for the benefit of himself, "his heyres and assignes forever."

1586 – Catholic martyr Margaret Clitherow (née Middleton), known as "the Pearl of York", was pressed to death at the tollbooth on Ouse Bridge in York, under 7 or 8 hundredweight. She was executed for harbouring Catholic priests.

26TH MARCH

On this day in 1556, the Archbishop of Canterbury, Matthew Parker, and Bishop of London, Edmund Grindal, summoned one hundred and ten ministers to Lambeth Palace to get them to pledge their willingness to wear vestments, as worn by the man in front of them: Robert Cole, a former non-conformist who now complied. The outfit consisted of a square cap, gown, tippet, and surplice. They were also asked "to inviolably observe the rubric of the Book of Common Prayer, and the queen's majesty's injunctions, and the Book of Convocation" and to commit to these orders on the spot, by writing "volo" or "no volo".

Thirty-seven ministers refused and were suspended. This sparked off a pamphlet war between Parker and non-conformists like Robert Crowley, Vicar of St Giles-without-Cripplegate, who published "A Briefe Discourse Against the Outwarde Apparel of the Popishe Church".

1533 – Convocation was asked to pronounce on the validity of a papal dispensation allowing a man to marry his brother's widow, the man and widow in question being Henry VIII and Catherine of Aragon.

1546 – Death of Sir Thomas Elyot, humanist scholar and diplomat. He was buried at Carleton Parish Church in Cambridgeshire. Elyot's offices included Clerk of the Privy Council, High Sheriff of Oxfordshire and Berkshire, High Sheriff of Cambridgeshire and Huntingdonshire, and a commissioner in the inquiry into the monasteries before their dissolution. He also acted as a diplomat, visiting the court of Charles V in 1531, and was one of the men chosen to receive Anne of Cleves in 1540. Elyot's works include the 1531 treatise "The Boke named the Governour", the 1536 medical treatise

"The Castell of Helth", his 1538 "Latin Dictionary" and a number of translations.

1609 – Date of death for John Dee, astrologer, mathematician, alchemist, antiquary, spy, philosopher, geographer and adviser to Elizabeth I, given by John Pontois, a merchant who inherited some of Dee's books. This date was backed up by Anthony Wood, who told Elias Ashmole that Dee had died at Pontois' house in Bishopsgate Street. Dee was buried in Mortlake Church. The traditional date for Dee's death is December 1608.

1618 – Death of John Bridges, Dean of Salisbury in Elizabeth I's reign and Bishop of Oxford in James I's reign, at Marsh Baldon, Oxfordshire. He was buried there.

27TH MARCH

On this day in 1489, the *Treaty of Medina del Campo* was signed between England and Spain. One part of it was the arrangement of the marriage between Arthur, Prince of Wales, and Catherine (or Catalina) of Aragon. It was signed by Spain on this day and ratified in 1490 by Henry VII.

According to the terms of the treaty, Catherine's parents, Ferdinand II of Aragon and Isabella I of Castile, agreed to pay Henry VII a marriage portion or dowry of 200,000 (about £40,000), split into two instalments, and Henry agreed to settled a third of the Prince of Wales' lands on Catherine so that she would have an income if Arthur died. Other terms included clauses regarding military support and each country coming to the aid of the other.

Catherine of Aragon and Arthur, Prince of Wales, married in November 1501, over twelve years after the treaty had been made.

1539 – Burial of George Talbot, 4th Earl of Shrewsbury, at St Peter's Church, Sheffield. He is known for his loyalty to the King during the *Pilgrimage of Grace* uprisings, which was seen as crucial to the failure of the rebellion. His offices under Henry VIII included Chamberlain of the Exchequer, Lieutenant of the Vanguard in the 1513 French campaign and Lieutenant-General in 1522 in the Scottish borders.

1555 – Burning of William Hunter, Protestant martyr. Nineteen year-old Hunter got into trouble when he was found reading the Bible in Brentwood Chapel. The plaque at the spot where he was burned reads:

> "WILLIAM HUNTER. MARTYR. Committed to the Flames March 26th MDLV.
> Christian Reader, learn from his example to value the privilege of an open Bible. And be careful to maintain it."

1563 – Death of Richard Pallady, member of Parliament and member of the household of Edward Seymour, Duke of Somerset and Lord Protector.

1599 – Robert Devereux, 2nd Earl of Essex, left London for Ireland as Lieutenant General.

1604 – Funeral of John Whitgift, Archbishop of Canterbury, at St Nicholas Chapel, Croydon Minster.

1620 – Death of Edward Lister, Physician-in-Ordinary to Elizabeth I and James I, in Aldermanbury in London. He was buried at St Mary's Church in Aldermanbury.

1625 – Death of James I at Theobalds, Hertfordshire. He was laid to rest in the Henry VII Chapel, Westminster Abbey on 5th May. John Donne gave the funeral sermon. James had been suffering with ill health for a few months, having kidney problems and attacks of arthritis and gout, followed by tertian ague and a stroke. It seems that he died during a severe attack of dysentery. He was succeeded by his son, Charles I.

28TH MARCH

28th March 1483 is one of the birthdates given for Raffaello Sanzio da Urbino, or Raphael as he is known, the Italian Renaissance artist and architect. The other date is 6th April. He was born in Urbino in the Marche region of Italy, and was the son of Giovanni Santo, poet and court painter to Federico da Montefeltro, the Duke of Urbino.

Raphael is known for his Madonnas and the famous four Stanze di Raffaello, or Raphael Rooms, in the Vatican Palace, with their frescoes painted by Raphael, including "The School of Athens". As well as these beautiful frescoes, Raphael also painted portraits, including those of Popes Julius II and Leo X, and was an architect working on the new St Peter's and palaces, like the now lost Palazzo Branconio dell'Aquila.

Raphael died on Good Friday (6th April) 1520, allegedly after a passionate night with his mistress Margherita Luti, or "La Fornarina". He was buried in the Pantheon.

1489 – Death of Thomas Kemp (Kempe), Bishop of London and nephew of John Kemp, Archbishop of Canterbury, in Fulham. He was buried in the chantry chapel of St Paul's.

1552 – Death of John Skip, Bishop of Hereford, in London. Skip is known for being the chaplain and almoner of Queen Anne Boleyn, and preaching his controversial Passion Sunday sermon in April 1536. He survived the fall of Anne Boleyn and became Bishop of Hereford in 1539, when Edmund Bonner became Bishop of London. He was buried at St Mary Mounthaw, London.

1579 – Death of Sir Thomas Gargrave, administrator and Speaker of the House of Commons. He was elected as Speaker at Elizabeth I's first Parliament in 1559.

1591 – Birth of William Cecil, 2nd Earl of Salisbury and politician, son of Robert Cecil, 1st Earl of Salisbury, and grandson of William Cecil, 1st Baron Burghley.

29TH MARCH

On this day in 1555, former Dominican priest and Protestant martyr, John Laurence, was burned at the stake in Colchester. The martyrologist John Foxe wrote of his death:

"The next day being the 29. day of this moneth, the sayd Iohn Laurence was brought to Colchester, and there being not able to go, (for that as wel his legges were sore worne with heauie irons in the prison, as also hys bodye weakened with euill keeping) was borne to the fire in a chayre, and so sitting, was in hys constant faith consumed with fire.

At the burning of this Laurence, hee sitting in the fire the young children came about the fire, and cryed, (as wel as young children could speake) saying: Lorde strengthen thy seruaunt, and keepe thy promise, Lord strengthen they seruaunt, and keepe thy promise."

1551 – The marriage of Mary Dudley, eldest daughter of John Dudley, Duke of Northumberland, and Henry Sidney. Mary became a Gentlewoman of Elizabeth I's Privy Chamber in 1559, and is known for nursing the Queen through smallpox in 1562. Mary caught the disease and was badly disfigured as a result.

1564 – Death of Sir Edmund Peckham, Privy Councillor in Mary I's reign, and High Treasurer of all the mints from 1544. He was buried at Denham Church in Buckinghamshire.

1591 – Burial of William Wager, playwright and Church of England clergyman, at the church where he was Rector, St Benet Gracechurch. His plays included "Enough is as Good as a Feast" and "The Longer thou Livest the More Fool thou art", both polemical Protestant interludes.

1613 – Burial of Sir Thomas Bodley, scholar, diplomat, and founder of the Bodleian Library, Oxford. He was laid to rest in Merton College Chapel, Oxford.

1628 – Death of Tobie Matthew, Archbishop of York, at Cawood. He was buried in York Minster. Matthew had become Bishop of Durham in 1595, and then Archbishop of York in 1606.

30TH MARCH

On this day in history, Passion Sunday 30th March 1533, Thomas Cranmer, Archdeacon of Taunton, was consecrated as Archbishop of Canterbury in St Stephen's College, Westminster Palace.

Cranmer's first duty as Archbishop was to preside over the convocation meeting to discuss the validity of the Henry VIII's marriage to Catherine of Aragon, his brother's widow. On 5th April 1533, Convocation determined "1, that the Pope has no power of dispensing in case of a marriage where the brother's widow has been cognita. The house consisted of 66 theologians. The proxies were 197; the negatives 19. The second question was, whether Katharine was cognita. The numbers present, 44; one holding the proxies of three bishops. Decided in the affirmative against five or six negatives."

On 11th April, Cranmer wrote to the King, "Beseeching the King very humbly to allow him to determine his great cause of matrimony, as belongs to the Archbishop's spiritual office, as much bruit exists among the common people on the subject", and the King replied the next day:-

"Received on the 12th April his letters dated Lambeth, 11th April, desiring leave to determine his great cause of matrimony. Cannot be displeased with Cranmer's zeal for justice and for the quieting of the kingdom; and although Henry is his King, and recognises no superior on earth, yet as Cranmer is the principal minister "of our spiritual jurisdiction," and is so in the fear of God, cannot refuse his request. Gives him licence accordingly by these letters under the sign manual, sealed with the King's seal."

This gave Cranmer the official permission he needed to open a special trial into the annulment proceedings, which he did at Dunstable Priory, Bedfordshire. On 23rd May 1533, the court gave their sentence regarding the King's "great and weighty cause" and Archbishop Cranmer sent the King notification of the sentence, which dissolved the marriage between Henry and Catherine.

On 28th May 1533, Cranmer declared the marriage between Henry VIII and Anne Boleyn valid, and on 29th May the coronation pageantry began, culminating with the crowning of Anne Boleyn as Queen at Westminster Abbey on the 1st June 1533.

〰〰〰〰〰〰〰〰〰〰〰〰〰〰〰〰〰〰〰

1555 – Burning of Protestant martyr, Robert Ferrar, Bishop of St David's, at Carmarthen. He had already been deprived of his bishopric because he violated the vow of chastity by marrying and was condemned after refusing to agree to articles presented to him, articles which he saw as having been drawn up by man and not by God. He went to his death with courage.

1558 – Queen Mary I made her will, believing that she would soon give birth, and childbirth was a risky process. One of her desires expressed in the will was for her mother's remains to be moved from Peterborough to Westminster Abbey. This, of course, never happened. The will also made her unborn child her heir, with her husband, Philip of Spain, as regent. It was actually a false pregnancy, so Mary never went into labour.

1587 – Death of Sir Ralph Sadler, at the age of nearly eighty. Sadler was a diplomat and administrator who worked as Cromwell's Secretary before being noticed by Henry VIII. At his death, he was one of the richest men in England.

31ST MARCH

On Easter Sunday 1532, 31st March, Princess Mary's confessor, Friar William Peto, preached a rather controversial sermon in the King's presence at Greenwich's Franciscan chapel.

Instead of focusing on the *Easter* story and Christ's resurrection, Peto, who supported Catherine of Aragon, spoke on 1 Kings 22, in which Micaiah shares his prophecies with King Ahab, but Ahab ignores them and imprisons Micaiah. Ahab then died from wounds inflicted during the battle:

"So the King died and was brought to Samaria, and they buried him there. They washed the chariot at a pool in Samaria (where the prostitutes bathed), and the dogs licked up his blood, as the word of the Lord had declared."

Peto compared Henry VIII to Ahab, drawing comparisons between Anne Boleyn and Jezebel, Ahab's wife, who had replaced God's prophets with pagan priests, as Anne was promoting men of the New Religion. Peto concluded by warning the King that if he carried on the way he was, he would end up like Ahab, and dogs would lick up his blood, too.

Peto wanted to set Henry VIII on the right path. He wanted him to abandon Anne Boleyn, with her heretical views, and return to Catherine of Aragon. Henry, however, believed his marriage to Catherine to be invalid, and tried to persuade Peto of that. Although Peto had preached a dangerous sermon, he escaped with his life and was just imprisoned for a few months. He left England and went into exile.

When Henry VIII's coffin rested at Syon, on its way to Windsor for burial in February 1547, it is said that some liquid leaked out of it. Of course, this was seen as the fulfilment of Peto's prophecy.

1499 – Birth of Pope Pius IV, born Giovanni Angelo Medici, in Milan. He was Pope from 1559 to 1565.

1509 – The dying Henry VII made his last will and testament at Richmond Palace, three weeks before his death. It was based on an earlier draft, with some new provisions added, for example, the addition of Sir Richard Empson and Edmund Dudley to the list of executors.

1519 – Birth of Henry II of France, at Château de Saint-Germain-en-Laye, near Paris, Henry was the son of Francis I and Queen Claude, and he was King of France from 1547 to his death in 1559. His consort was Catherine de' Medici.

1547 – Death of Francis I of France, at the Château de Rambouillet in the Île-de-France, and accession of Henry II on his 28th birthday.

1553 – Edward VI dissolved Parliament, after having opened it 1st March. It was his last Parliament.

1596 – Birth of René Descartes, French philosopher, mathematician, and writer, the "Father of Modern Philosophy", at La Haye en Touraine in France. He is known for his dictum "I think, therefore I am".

1631 – Death of John Donne, metaphysical poet, satirist, lawyer and clergyman. He was laid to rest in St Paul's Cathedral on 3rd April. Donne served as a member of Parliament, Royal Chaplain and Dean of St Paul's, but is best known for his poems, sonnets and epigrams, which included "For whom the bell tolls" and "The Flea".

EASTER

HOLY WEEK

On the first day of Holy Week, *Palm Sunday*, the priest read out the story of Christ's triumphant entry into Jerusalem, and branches of greenery were blessed by the priest so that they could be used in processions. In many countries today, we celebrate *Palm Sunday* with palm leaves or crosses made out of palm leaves, but these leaves were hard to come by in Tudor England, so they would use local greenery to make crosses.

A special shrine would also be prepared for *Palm Sunday*. This shrine contained the blessed Sacrament to represent Jesus Christ, and the church's own relics. The clergy carried this special shrine around the outside of the church as the laity processed around the church in the opposite direction, with the two processions meeting at the church door. The *Lent* veil (a veil hiding the chancel from the nave during *Lent*) was drawn up and then dropped down again as they passed.

On the Wednesday of Holy Week, the priest read out the passage from the Bible concerning the veil in the Temple in Jerusalem. As this passage was read aloud, the *Lent* veil separating the chancel and the nave was dropped and put away until next year's *Lent*.

On *Maundy Thursday*, the church was prepared for *Easter* with water and wine being used to wash the altars. It was also traditional for people to go to confession on this day.

Good Friday

On *Good Friday* in Tudor times, people attended the ceremony known as "Creeping to the Cross". Christ's suffering and crucifixion and what it meant were commemorated by the clergy creeping up to a crucifix held up before the altar on their hands and knees. When they got to the crucifix, they would kiss the feet of Christ. The crucifix was then taken down into the church for the congregation to do the same.

Good Friday was also the day for the preparation of the *Easter* Sepulchre. The sepulchre consisted of a stone or wooden niche, to represent Christ's sealed tomb, which was filled with the consecrated host and an image of Christ. Once this was "sealed" by covering it with a cloth, candles were lit around it, and members of the church would guard it just as the Roman soldiers had done when the body of Christ was sealed in the cave.

Easter Sunday

On *Easter Sunday*, the candles in the church and around the sepulchre were extinguished, and then the church lights were re-lit by the priest, from a fire. The sepulchre was opened, and Christ's resurrection was celebrated with a special mass.

The *Easter Sunday* mass marked the end of *Lent*, a period where people's diets were restricted, so it was only natural to celebrate it with good food. Dairy products and meat were back on the menu, and people enjoyed roasted meats like chicken, lamb and veal.

Easter and the Reformation

The *English Reformation* led to many of the *Easter* rituals and celebrations being banned. The blessing of the greenery on *Palm Sunday*, the "Creeping to the Cross" ceremony and the *Easter* Sepulchre tradition are all rituals that did not survive the *Reformation*.

1ST APRIL

On this day in 1536, Eustace Chapuys wrote a very long and detailed letter to his master, Emperor Charles V, in which he mentioned an incident concerning King Henry VIII and his alleged new flame, Jane Seymour.

Chapuys wrote of how he'd heard that the King had sent Jane "a purse full of sovereigns" and that on receiving the purse, Jane had kissed the letter and begged the messenger to tell the King that she could not take the purse because "she was a gentlewoman of good and honorable parents, without reproach, and that she had no greater riches in the world than her honor, which she would not injure for a thousand deaths, and that if he wished to make her some present in money, she begged it might be when God enabled her to make some honorable match."

According to Chapuys, Jane was being coached by Sir Nicholas Carew and the Catholic faction in how to appeal to the King, and also to tell him how much the people of England "detested" his marriage to Anne Boleyn. Was Jane's behaviour all part of an act, or was she simply being a virtuous woman who was concerned about her reputation? It's hard to know. Whatever the truth behind Jane's actions, Henry was warming to the thrill of the chase and had moved Edward Seymour and his wife, Anne Stanhope, into Cromwell's chamber to make it easier for him to see Jane.

Henry was married to Anne Boleyn at the time, but she was executed on 19th May 1536, and he went on to marry Jane Seymour on 30th May 1536.

<hr />

1538 – Death of Sir Amyas (Amias) Paulet, soldier and landowner, at Hinton St George. In Henry VIII's reign, he served as a Sheriff, Justice of the Peace and steward of the estates of the Bishop of Bath and Wells. Henry VII chose him to meet Catherine of Aragon as she travelled to London to marry his son, Arthur.

1570 – Death of William Alley, Bishop of Exeter. He was buried in Exeter Cathedral.

1571 – Death of Sir Thomas Cusack, Anglo-Irish judge, Master of the Rolls in Ireland, Keeper of the Great Seal, Chancellor of the Exchequer in Ireland, Lord Chancellor and Lord Justice. He was buried in Trevet, county Meath.

1572 – Death of John Cawood, Queen's Printer to Mary I, in London.

1577 – Death of Anthony Rush, Dean of Chichester. He was buried in St George's Chapel, Windsor.

1578 – Birth of William Harvey, English physician and the man who discovered the circulation of blood.

1578 – Death of Sir Arthur Champernowne, soldier, naval commander, member of Parliament and Vice-Admiral of the West. Edward VI knighted him for his service in France, and he was also involved in putting down the *Prayer Book Rebellion*.

1604 – Death of Thomas Churchyard, author and soldier, in Westminster, London. He was buried in St Margaret's Church, Westminster. Churchyard started writing in the reign of Edward VI and some of his poems were published in "Tottel's Miscellany". His literary works include "The Firste Parte of Churchyardes Chippes", "A Generall Rehearsall of Warres", "Churchyardes Chance", "Churchyardes Charitie" and "Churchyardes Charge". Churchyard was also an active soldier, serving with the Duke of Somerset in Scotland and fighting as a mercenary for Protestants in Europe.

2ND APRIL

On this day in 1502, Arthur, Prince of Wales, son and heir of King Henry VII and Elizabeth of York, died at Ludlow Castle in the Welsh Marches. He was just fifteen years old, and had only been married to the Spanish princess Catherine of Aragon for four and a half months.

It is not known exactly what killed the young prince. The theories include consumption, diabetes, sweating sickness, testicular cancer and pneumonia. Catherine also became ill, but fortunately recovered and went on to marry Arthur's younger brother, Henry, when he became King in 1509. Arthur was laid to rest in Worcester Cathedral, in Prince Arthur's Chantry.

***

1536 – Anne Boleyn's almoner, John Skip, preached a rather controversial sermon in front of the King. Skip spoke on the Old Testament story of King Ahasuerus "who was moved by a wicked minister to destroy the Jews" but Queen Esther stepped in with different advice and saved the Jews. In Skip's sermon, Henry VIII was Ahasuerus, Anne Boleyn was Queen Esther and Thomas Cromwell, who had just introduced the "Act of Suppression of the Lesser Monasteries" into Parliament, was Haman, the "wicked minister". The sermon was an attack on what had been debated in Parliament and it was a statement on Anne's stance and her beliefs.

1552 – The fourteen year-old Edward VI fell ill with measles and smallpox. Fortunately, he survived. His biographer, Chris Skidmore, believes that it was this bout of illness which suppressed the King's immune system and which led to him dying of consumption (tuberculosis) on the 6th July 1553.

1559 – *The Peace of Cateau-Cambrésis*, ending the *Italian Wars*, was signed between Henry II of France and Elizabeth I of England.

1568 – Death of Sir Ambrose Cave, member of Parliament, Chancellor of the Duchy of Lancaster and Knight of the Hospital of St John of Jerusalem, at the Savoy. He was buried at Stanford after a funeral at the Savoy Chapel.

1571 – Death of Richard Onslow, lawyer, Solicitor-General and Speaker of the House of Commons. He caught a fever in Shrewsbury, while visiting his uncle there.

3RD APRIL

1559 – The second session of Parliament, in Elizabeth I's reign, met after the *Easter* break. Its purpose was to obtain parliamentary sanction for royal supremacy and Protestant settlement.

1559 – *The Peace of Cateau-Cambrésis*, ending the *Italian Wars*, was signed between Henry II and Philip II of Spain.

1578 – Burial of Lady Margaret Douglas, Countess of Lennox and daughter of Margaret Tudor and Archibald Douglas, 6th Earl of Angus. She was buried in Henry VII's Chapel of Westminster Abbey.

1585 – Death of Thomas Goldwell, Bishop of St Asaph, in Rome. He had travelled to Rome at the beginning of the Protestant Elizabeth I's reign. He was buried in the convent of San Silvestro.

1606 – Burial of Sir Edward Fitton, member of Parliament and Elizabeth I's Receiver-General, in Gawsworth Church in Cheshire.

4TH APRIL

1483 – Death of Henry Bourchier, 1ˢᵗ Earl of Essex, great-grandson of Edward III and Lord High Treasurer. He was buried in Beeleigh Abbey.

1506 – Birth of Sir Edward Saunders, Chief Justice of the Queen's Bench in Elizabeth I's reign.

1572 – Birth of William Strachey, writer and historian of Virginia. William Shakespeare used Strachey's account of the 1609 shipwreck of the *Sea Venture* for his play "The Tempest".

1581 – Francis Drake was awarded a knighthood by Elizabeth I. He was dubbed by Monsieur de Marchaumont on board the *Golden Hind* at Deptford.

1589 – Death of Mildred Cecil (née Cooke), Lady Burghley, noblewoman, scholar and second wife of William Cecil, 1st Baron Burghley. Mildred was known for her standard of education and the library she built up.

5TH APRIL

On this day in 1531, Richard Roose (or Rouse), Bishop John Fisher's cook, was boiled to death after confessing to poisoning the soup (or porridge) that was served to the Bishop and his guests. Fisher, the Bishop of Rochester, survived, but some of his guests, who'd eaten more of the soup, died.

People were quick to blame Anne Boleyn, saying that she and her family had bribed Roose to poison the soup to get rid of Fisher, and that her father had even provided Roose with the poison, but Henry VIII did not believe this to be the case, and there is no evidence that the Boleyns or their supporters were involved.

The primary source evidence is the preamble of the 1531 "Acte for Poysoning" (22 Henry VIII c.9), which stated:-

"On the Eighteenth day of February, 1531, one Richard Roose, of Rochester, Cook, also called Richard Cooke, did cast poison into a vessel of yeast to baum, standing in the kitchen of the Bishop of Rochester's Palace, at Lambeth March, by means of which two persons who happened to eat of the pottage made with such yeast died".

Roose allegedly claimed that he had just put purgatives into the food as a joke, and that he meant no harm, but two poor people, Bennett Curwen and Alice Tryppytt, died from eating the food. Roose was "attainted of high treason" and "boiled to death without benefit of clergy". He was taken to Smithfield and boiled to death.

<hr>

1478 – Death of John Booth, Bishop of Exeter, at East Horsley. He was buried in the parish church there.

1513 – *Treaty of Mechlin* signed by Henry VIII, Maximilian I, Holy Roman Emperor, Ferdinand II of Aragon and Pope Leo X against France.

1532 – Death of William Bolton, royal administrator and Prior of St Bartholomew's, West Smithfield, London. In Henry VIII's reign, Bolton oversaw works in Henry VII's Chapel in Westminster Abbey, Hampton Court Palace and the rebuilding of New Hall. He died in London and was buried in his priory church, before the altar.

1533 – Convocation ruled on the case of Henry VIII's annulment, ruling that the Pope had no power to dispense in the case of a man marrying his brother's widow, and that it was contrary to God's law.

1559 – Funeral of Sir Anthony St Leger, Lord Deputy of Ireland, at the parish church in Ulcombe in Kent.

1588 – Birth of Thomas Hobbes, philosopher and author of the famous philosophical work, "Leviathan", in Westport, Malmesbury, Wiltshire.

1605 – Death of Adam Loftus, Church of Ireland Archbishop of Dublin, in Dublin at the archbishop's palace of St Sepulchre. He was buried at St Patrick's Cathedral.

6TH APRIL

On this day in history, 6th April 1590, Elizabeth I's Principal Secretary, Sir Francis Walsingham, died at around the age of fifty-eight. Although he had served the Queen for many years, he died in debt, as he had underwritten the debts of Sir Philip Sidney, his son-in-law.

Walsingham was an incredibly important man during Elizabeth I's reign, being a statesman, private secretary, adviser, diplomat and spymaster, and he probably saved the Queen's life many times by uncovering various plots against her. Elizabeth called him her "Moor".

He was born c.1532 (some say 1530) at Scadbury Park, Chislehurst, Kent, and was the son of William Walsingham and Joyce Denny. His father died when he was an infant, and his mother married Sir John Carey, a relation of Mary Boleyn, Anne Boleyn's sister. Walsingham's father was Common Sergeant of London, his mother was related to Sir Anthony Denny, a member of Henry VIII's Privy Council, and his uncle, Sir Edmund, was Lieutenant of the Tower of London.

Walsingham studied at King's College, Cambridge, and then, in 1550, he went abroad to continue his education. In 1552, he returned to England and enrolled at Gray's Inn (The Honourable Society of Gray's Inn, an Inn of Court). When Mary I came to the throne, Walsingham, who was a staunch Protestant, fled abroad and continued his law studies at the University of Padua, and then lived in Switzerland between 1556 and 1558.

Elizabeth I's accession to the throne in 1558 meant that Walsingham could return to England. In 1559, his friendship with Sir William Cecil helped him to become a member of Parliament for Banbury, and then for Lyme Regis in 1563. In 1569, Walsingham was asked by William Cecil to investigate the *Ridolfi Plot*, and in 1570 Elizabeth I asked Walsingham to help the Huguenots in France negotiate with Charles IX, because he had built up a good relationship with them. In the same year, he became the ambassador to France, and it was to his house that Protestant refugees fled during the time of the *St Bartholomew's Massacre* and other troubles.

Walsingham returned to England in 1573, and was rewarded for his hard work by being made the Queen's principal secretary, a position he shared with Sir Thomas Smith until 1576 when Smith retired. In 1577, he was rewarded again with a knighthood and was trusted with special embassies in 1578 and 1581 to the Dutch and French courts. In the late 1570s, Walsingham was known for his opposition to the plans to encourage Elizabeth I to marry the Duke of Anjou, and for his encouragement of military intervention in the Low Countries. In the mid to late 1580s, he and William Cecil worked on preparing England for war with Spain.

Although Walsingham was an important diplomat and the Queen's principal secretary for a time, he is best known as Elizabeth I's spymaster, and for his successful work uncovering plots against the Queen. He worked on uncovering the *Ridolfi Plot*, and put a stop to the Throckmorton (Throgmorton) and *Babington Plots*. It was the *Babington Plot* which convinced Elizabeth I of the need to execute Mary, Queen of Scots, and Walsingham was one of the advisers who encouraged her to take this course of action.

1523 – Death of Henry Stafford, Earl of Wiltshire. Stafford had served Henry VII and was made a Knight of the Garter in his reign, and although he was imprisoned for a time due to his brother's plotting, he was a favourite of Henry VIII.

1523 – Death of Edward Stanley, 1st Baron Monteagle, soldier, peer and Knight of the Garter, at Hornby Castle.

1582 – Hanging of Nicholas Nugent, Solicitor General for Ireland, Baron of the Irish Court of Exchequer, and Chief Justice of the Irish Common Pleas, for treason after being implicated in the rebellion of his nephew, William Nugent.

1593 – Hanging of Henry Barrow and John Greenwood, religious separatists, after being condemned to death on 23rd March, for writing and publishing seditious literature.

1605 (5th or 6th) – Death of John Stow, historian and antiquary, in London at the age of eighty. He was buried in St Andrew Undershaft Church. Stow's works included his 1561 "The woorkes of Geffrey Chaucer, newly printed with divers additions whiche were never in printe before", the 1565 "Summarie of Englyshe Chronicles" and his famous "Annales, or a Generale Chronicle of England from Brute until the present yeare of Christ 1580".

1621 – Death of Edward Seymour, 1st Earl of Hertford, son of Edward Seymour, Duke of Somerset, and Anne Stanhope, and husband of Lady Katherine Grey (Lady Jane Grey's sister). He was aged eighty-one at his death, and had been married three times. His other wives were Frances Howard, gentlewoman of Elizabeth I's Privy Chamber, and widow Frances Prannell, who was the daughter of Thomas Howard, 1st Viscount Howard of Bindon. All three of his marriages were secret ones.

7TH APRIL

On this day in 1538, Elizabeth Boleyn, Lady Wiltshire, wife of Thomas Boleyn and mother of the late Queen Anne

Boleyn, was buried in the Howard Chapel of St Mary's Church, Lambeth.

She had died a few days earlier, on 3rd April, at Baynard's Castle, home of the Abbot of Reading, an event which Thomas Warley reported to Lady Lisle in Calais on 7th April 1538:-

"My lady of Wiltshire died on Wednesday last beside Baynard's castle."

Elizabeth's funeral was also reported to Lady Lisle, this time by John Hussey on 9th April:-

"My lady Wiltshire was buried at Lamehithe on the 7th… She was conveyed from a house beside Baynard's Castle by barge to Lambeth with torches burning and four baneys [banners] set out of all quarters of the barge, which was covered with black and a white cross."

Sir John Russell, Lord Comptroller, was the chief male mourner and Elizabeth's half-sister, Katherine Howard, Lady Daubenay, was the chief female mourner.

St Mary's Church, Lambeth, is now a garden museum and Elizabeth's tomb is not visible because it lies underneath the wooden floor of the museum café. Although some people have commented on how awful this is, the museum actually saved the church, and so saved the Howard tombs.

Many people wonder if the fact that Elizabeth is not buried next to her husband at Hever is evidence of some kind of separation between them, but as Linda Saether points out in her wonderful article about her search for Elizabeth's tomb on "The Anne Boleyn Files" website, there are many Howard women buried at Lambeth, and she wondered if "Howard women expected to be 'brought home' for burial in the Howard Chapel, regardless of whom they married." We also know that Elizabeth died at Baynard's Castle in London, so perhaps it made sense for her to be buried in London rather than to be taken back to Hever in Kent.

It is not known what Elizabeth Boleyn died of, but she was reported as being "sore diseased with the cough which grieves her sore" in April 1536, and Anne Boleyn, when arrested and taken to the Tower in May 1536, had commented "O, my mother, [thou wilt die with] sorow". Perhaps Elizabeth had been fighting tuberculosis.

<hr>

1498 – Death of Charles VIII of France and accession of Louis XII.

1537 – Robert Aske and Thomas Darcy, 1st Baron Darcy, were sent to the Tower of London. Aske was one of the rebel leaders in the 1536 *Pilgrimage of Grace rebellion*, and Darcy became involved with the rebels after yielding Pontefract Castle to them. Darcy was beheaded 30th June 1537, and Aske was hanged in chains on 12th July 1537.

1571 – Burial of Richard Onslow, lawyer and Speaker of the House of Commons, in St Chad's Church, Shrewsbury.

1589 – Death of Sir Henry Gates, member of Parliament, Gentleman of Edward VI's Privy Chamber, Controller of the Petty Custom at the port of London, Receiver-General of the Duchy of Cornwall and member of the Council of the North.

1590 – Burial of Sir Francis Walsingham, Elizabeth I's principal secretary, at St Paul's at 10pm in the same tomb as Sir Philip Sidney. He had died the previous day.

1619 – Burial of Robert Rich, 1st Earl of Warwick, at Felsted.

8TH APRIL

On this day in 1554, a cat dressed as a priest, a symbol of Catholicism, was found hanged on the gallows in Cheapside. Chronicler John Stow describes how the cat's head was shorn, it was dressed in vestments, and a "singing cake" (consecrated wafer) had been placed between its tied feet.

1580 – Birth of William Herbert, 3rd Earl of Pembroke, courtier, patron of the arts and son of Henry Herbert, 2nd Earl of Pembroke, and Mary Sidney, sister of Sir Philip Sidney.

1586 – Death of Martin Chemnitz, Lutheran theologian and a man known as "Alter Martinus" or the "Second Martin" after Martin Luther.

1608 – Death of Magdalen Browne (née Dacre), Viscountess Montagu and patron of Roman Catholics, at Battle following a stroke in January 1608. She was buried at Midhurst. Magdalen was the daughter of William Dacre, 3rd Baron Dacre of Gilsland and the second wife of Anthony Browne, 1st Viscount Montagu. She served as Maid of Honour at Mary I's wedding and was a staunch Catholic. Even though she was Catholic, she had a good relationship with Elizabeth I, following her and her husband's declaration that they would be loyal to the Queen if the Pope invaded or caused trouble. When the Queen visited the Montagus in 1591, they kept their priests hidden.

9TH APRIL

On the 9th April 1533, a delegation of the King's councillors, headed by the Duke of Norfolk, visited Catherine of Aragon and informed her that Henry VIII was now married to Anne Boleyn. After they left, Catherine's Chamberlain, Sir William Blount, 4th Baron Mountjoy, had to tell her that she had been demoted from Queen to Dowager Princess of Wales.

Imperial ambassador, Eustace Chapuys, reported all of this to his master, Emperor Charles V, on 10th April:-

"But there is no chance that the King will listen that the affair be determined otherwise than by the Archbishop, of whom he is perfectly assured, as he has performed the office of espousal (de l'esposement), as I have formerly written to you; and he is fully resolved, as he has told many, and those of his Council publish, that immediately after Easter he will solemnize his marriage and the coronation of the Lady. The better to prepare the way, he sent yesterday the dukes of Norfolk and Suffolk, the marquis and the earl of Ausburg to the Queen, to tell her that she must not trouble herself any more, nor attempt to return to him, seeing that he is married, and that henceforth she abstain from the title of Queen, and assume the title of duchess (princess), leaving her the entire enjoyment of the goods she formerly had, and offering her more, if she needed more. The Queen would not fail to advertise me of the interview. I know not whether they are in any doubt as to the Queen's willingness to dislodge or not; but about eight days ago, the King's council commanded my lord Mountjoy to rejoin her with all diligence, and keep watch upon her, and not leave her."

1483 – Death of Edward IV at the Palace of Westminster. He was laid to rest in St George's Chapel, Windsor Castle, on 20th April. His cause of death is unknown. It may have been caused by a chill, but he was known for overindulging in food and drink, and that would not have helped his health.

1557 – Cardinal Reginald Pole's legatine powers were revoked by Pope Paul IV.

1582 – Death of Richard Bertie, evangelical, member of Parliament and second husband of Katherine Willoughby (other married name Brandon), Duchess of Suffolk, at Bourne. He had met Katherine when he became her Gentleman Usher. He was buried with Katherine, who died in 1580, at Spilsby.

1590 – Funeral of Ambrose Dudley, Earl of Warwick. He was laid to rest in the Beauchamp Chapel of St Mary's Church, Warwick.

1626 – Death of Francis Bacon, Viscount St Alban, Lord Chancellor, politician and philosopher. It appears that Bacon died from inhaling nitre or opiates in a botched experiment.

10TH APRIL

On this day in 1512, James V, King of Scotland, was born at Linlithgow Palace. He was the fourth child of James IV and Margaret Tudor, sister of Henry VIII. He was the only one of James and Margaret's children to survive childhood, and so inherited the crown of Scotland when his father was killed at the *Battle of Flodden*, 9th September 1513.

James was just seventeen months old when he was crowned King at Stirling on 21st September 1513, so Scotland was ruled by regents: his mother, Margaret, then John Stewart, 2nd Earl of Albany and Robert Maxwell, 5th Lord Maxwell. In 1525, his stepfather, Archibald Douglas, 6th Earl of Angus, took custody of James and so acted as regent for him for the next three years until James escaped and decided to reign over Scotland in his own right.

James was married twice. His first wife was Madeleine of Valois, daughter of Francis I, whom he married on 1st January 1537. Unfortunately, Madeleine died in July 1573, shortly after her arrival in Scotland. James's second wife was Mary of Guise, daughter of Claude, Duke of Guise, who he married by proxy on 12th June 1538. Mary had three children by James, but only their daughter Mary, who was born on 8th December1542, survived childhood. It was this infant daughter who became Mary, Queen of Scots when James V died on 14th December 1542.

◇◇

1550 – Edward Seymour, Duke of Somerset, was re-admitted into Edward VI's council.

1559 – Death of Sir Rice Mansel, soldier and administrator, at his home in Clerkenwell. He served Henry VIII as Vice-Admiral in 1542, in France and Scotland, and in 1544 as Knight-Marshal. He was also Chamberlain of Chester.

1585 – Death of Pope Gregory XIII, the Pope known for his introduction of the Gregorian Calendar, in Rome. He was succeeded by Pope Sixtus V.

1586 – Death of Sir Bernard Drake, sea captain, in Crediton, Devon, from probable typhus. It appears that he caught the disease from Portuguese prisoners whose ships he had captured, which were laden with Brazilian sugar, on his voyage to the West Indies.

1588 – Death of Robert Glover, herald, genealogist and antiquary in Elizabeth I's reign. He was buried in St Giles-without-Cripplegate.

1605 – Death of John Young, Bishop of Rochester and Vice-Chancellor of the University of Cambridge, at Bromley Palace. He was seventy-one, and was buried at Bromley Church.

1635 – Death of Lady Helena Gorges (née Snakenborg), previous married name Parr. Helena was Swedish but came to England in 1564 with her mistress, Princess Cecilia, Margravine of Baden, daughter of Gustav Vasa. She fell in love with William Parr, Marquis of Northampton and brother of Catherine Parr, and so remained in England and joined Elizabeth I's household. Helena married Parr in 1571 after the death of his first wife, Lady Anne Bourchier (Parr had actually been divorced from her since 1551). After Parr died, she married courtier Thomas Gorges and had eight children with him. She was laid to rest in Salisbury Cathedral.

11TH APRIL

On the 11th April 1554, Sir Thomas Wyatt the Younger was beheaded and then his body quartered for treason, for leading *Wyatt's Rebellion* against Queen Mary I.

Wyatt had already shown his opposition to Mary when he supported Lady Jane Grey's claim to the throne after the death of Edward VI – he escaped punishment that time – but he felt compelled to act when he found out about Mary I's plans to marry King Philip II of Spain.

The plan was to have a series of uprisings in the South, Southwest, Welsh Marches and Midlands, and then a march on London to overthrow the government, block the Spanish marriage, dethrone Mary and replace her with her Protestant half-sister, Elizabeth, who would marry Edward Courtenay. Unfortunately for Wyatt, other rebel leaders like the Duke of Suffolk (Lady Jane Grey's father) and the ill-fated Lady Jane Grey (who had nothing to do with the revolt), the plan failed.

The government was alerted to the plots when Sir Peter Carew refused a summons to court and Ambassador Renard heard that a French fleet was assembling off Normandy. Courtenay was interviewed by his mentor Stephen Gardiner, and divulged everything. When the rebels learned that Mary knew of their plans, they did not give up, instead deciding to spring into action, with three out of the four planned provincial revolts going ahead. They were a failure due to the lack of organisation. However, Sir Thomas Wyatt did manage to raise a considerable "army" in Kent, but his delay in marching on London gave Mary a chance to rally her troops.

On the 1st February 1554, Mary gave a speech to the City government in the Guildhall, reminding them that she was England's queen, that she was "wedded to the realm and the laws", that she was the true heir to the throne, her father's daughter, and that she loved her people. She said:-

"On the word of a prince, I cannot tell how naturally the mother loveth the child, for I was never mother of any. But certainly, if a prince and governor may as naturally and earnestly love her subjects, as the mother doth the child, then assure yourselves, that I being your lady and mistress, do as earnestly and tenderly love and favour you."

According to diarist Henry Machyn, Mary ended the speech by saying that:-

"She never intended to marry out of the realm, but by her council's consent and advice. And that she would never marry but all her true subjects shall be content."

This rousing speech of half lies worked their magic and won over the people. When Wyatt arrived at Southwark on 3rd of February, he found it barricaded and guarded. A few days later, he tried entering the City from Kingston, and was successful. As they entered the City, the rebels split, and although they were now at a disadvantage, having split into groups, a group of them still managed to scare off the Queen's Guards near the Holbein Gate. However, by the time Wyatt and his troops reached Ludgate, Mary's force had gathered their wits and closed the gates. Mary's troops far outnumbered the rebels and, with his men surrendering around him and no hope of winning, Sir Thomas Wyatt the Younger surrendered and was captured. Wyatt was taken to the Tower of London.

Not only did *Wyatt's Rebellion* lead to his execution and the shadow of the axe hanging over Elizabeth's neck for many months, but it sealed the fate of Lady Jane Grey who had been kept in the Tower since Mary seized the throne from her in July 1553. On 12th February 1554, Lady Jane Grey and her husband Guildford Dudley were executed, a tragic end to Lady Jane's short life and a frightening event for Elizabeth who knew she would be implicated in *Wyatt's Rebellion*, and who had a very shaky relationship with her half-sister, Mary.

Sir Thomas Wyatt was tried at Westminster Hall on 15th March. He denied plotting the Queen's death and would only admit to sending Elizabeth a letter to which she replied (though not in writing) "that she did thank him much for his good will, and she would do as she should see cause." He did not implicate her in any other way.

Wyatt was found guilty and sentenced to death, but his execution was delayed for a time – it is thought that the Queen's advisers hoped that Wyatt would still implicate Elizabeth in an attempt to escape execution.

On 11th April 1554, Sir Thomas Wyatt was led out to the scaffold, making the following speech before being beheaded, his body quartered and his innards and genitals burned:

"And whereas it is said and whistled abroad that I should accuse my lady Elizabeth's grace and my lord Courtenay; it is not so, good people. For I assure you neither they nor any other now in yonder hold or durance was privy of my rising or commotion before I began. As I have declared no less to the queen's council. And this is most true."

His head and the quarters of his body were then taken to Newgate where they were parboiled, nailed up and the head placed on a gibbet at St James's. It is not known what happened to his head, as it disappeared from the gibbet.

1492 – Birth of Marguerite de Navarre (also known as Marguerite of Angoulême and Marguerite de France), sister of Francis I of France, daughter of Louise of Savoy and Charles, Count of Angoulême, and author of "Miroir de l'âme pécheresse".

1533 – The Royal Council was ordered by Henry VIII to recognise Anne Boleyn as Queen.

1548 – Death of Sir John Welsbourne, Gentleman of the Privy Chamber to Henry VIII and Justice of the Peace.

1609 – Death of John Lumley, 1st Baron Lumley, conspirator (*Ridolfi Plot*), patron and collector. His library was said to be one of the largest in England, and he collected manuscripts, books, paintings, sculptures, marble busts and furniture. Lumley was buried at night, probably so that he could be buried with a Catholic service, in the Lumley Chapel of St Dunstan's in Cheam.

12TH APRIL

Following on from Henry VIII's announcement to his council the day before, that Anne Boleyn should be recognised as his Queen, Anne attended mass on 12th April 1533, *Easter* Saturday, "with all the pomp of a Queen, clad in cloth of gold, and loaded (carga) with the richest jewels". It was her first public appearance as Queen, and it was time to make a statement that she was Henry VIII's rightful wife and Queen.

The Imperial Ambassador, Eustace Chapuys, reported this event to Emperor Charles V, and his description shows how big a statement Anne was making:-

"On Saturday, Easter Eve, dame Anne went to mass in Royal state, loaded with jewels, clothed in a robe of cloth of gold friese. The daughter of the duke of Norfolk, who is affianced to the duke of Richmond, carried her train; and she had in her suite 60 young ladies, and was brought to church, and brought back with the solemnities, or even more, which were used to the Queen. She has changed her name from Marchioness to Queen, and the preachers offered prayers for her by name. All the world is astonished at it, for it looks like a dream, and even those who take her part know not whether to laugh or to cry. The King is very watchful of the countenance of the people, and begs the lords to go and visit and make their court to the new Queen, whom he intends to have solemnly crowned after Easter, when he will have feastings and tournaments; and some think that Clarencieux went four days ago to France to invite gentlemen at arms to the tourney, after the example of Francis, who did so at his nuptials. I know not whether this will be before or after, but the King has secretly appointed with the archbishop of Canterbury that of his office, without any other pressure, he shall cite the King as having two wives; and upon this, without summoning the Queen, he will declare that he was at liberty to marry as he has done without waiting for a dispensation or sentence of any kind."

1533 – Thomas Cromwell became Chancellor of the Exchequer.

1535 – Death of Giles Duwes (Dewes), musician, royal librarian and French tutor to Henry VII's children: Arthur, Henry, Margaret and Mary, and to Henry VIII's daughter, the future Mary I. He also taught Mary I music. He was buried in the church of St Olave Upwell in London.

1550 – Birth of Edward de Vere, 17th Earl of Oxford, courtier and poet. The Oxfordian theory of Shakespearean authorship proposes that de Vere wrote Shakespeare's works and some believe that he was the illegitimate son of Elizabeth I.

1587 – Death of Sir Thomas Bromley, Lord Chancellor to Elizabeth I, at York House in London. He was buried in Westminster Abbey. It was Bromley who had presented Elizabeth I with Parliament's petition for the execution of Mary, Queen of Scots, and it was he who applied the Great Seal on her execution warrant in 1587.

1639 – Death of courtier Robert Carey, 1st Earl of Monmouth, youngest son of Henry Carey, 1st Baron Hunsdon, and grandson of Mary Boleyn.

13TH APRIL

1534 – Sir Thomas More was summoned to Lambeth to swear his allegiance to the "Act of Succession".

1557 – Death of John Brydges, 1st Baron Chandos of Sudeley, landowner, soldier and Lieutenant of the Tower of London. He died at Sudeley Castle. When Lady Jane Grey was in the Tower, she gave him her English prayer book in which she wrote a homily for him, and when Elizabeth was in the Tower, he was accused of being too lenient with her.

1598 – Henry IV of France issued the *Edict of Nantes* granting the Huguenots freedom of religion in France.

1606 – Death of Richard Day, Church of England clergyman, printer and son of the famous printer John Day, who had printed John Foxe's "Actes and Monuments". In 1578 Richard printed his own translation of "Christ Jesus Triumphant" by Foxe, and then got into trouble with his father when he started printing his works without his permission. His father had his printing equipment and stock seized, and Richard was forced to become a clergyman, becoming Vicar of Mundon, Essex.

1630 – Death of Anne Howard (née Dacre), Countess of Arundel, at Shifnal. She was laid to rest in the Fitzalan Chapel of Arundel Castle. Anne was the eldest daughter of Thomas Dacre, 4th Lord Dacre of Gilsand, and wife of Philip Howard, 13th Earl of Arundel. Anne was a staunch Catholic and harboured priests.

14TH APRIL

On this day in 1578, James Hepburn, 1st Duke of Orkney and 4th Earl of Bothwell, died aged forty-four at Dragsholm Castle after being imprisoned and held in appalling conditions by Frederick, King of Denmark. It is said that the imprisonment caused Bothwell to go insane.

Bothwell was the son of Patrick Hepburn, 3rd Earl of Bothwell and Lord High Admiral, known as the "Fair Earl", and his wife Agnes Sinclair, daughter of Henry Sinclair, 3rd Lord Sinclair. In 1556, on his father's death, James became 4th Earl of Bothwell and Lord High Admiral of Scotland.

In 1559/1560 Bothwell visited Denmark on the way to France and met Anna Throndsen (Anne Thorssen). He is alleged to have seduced and even married Anne, but deserted her. In 1566, he married Jean Gordon, second eldest daughter of George Gordon, Earl of Huntly, but the marriage was not a happy one, as Jean accused Bothwell of adultery with her maid and seamstress, Bessie Crawford. The marriage was annulled in May 1567 on the grounds of consanguinity. Eight days after the divorce, Bothwell married Mary, Queen of Scots.

Bothwell was one of the men implicated in the murder of Mary, Queen of Scots's second husband, Henry Stuart (Stewart), Lord Darnley, on 10th February 1567. Bothwell was tried and acquitted. On 24th April 1567, Mary was riding to Linlithgow Palace when she was intercepted by Bothwell, who warned her that it would be dangerous for her to carry on to Edinburgh. He offered to take her to safety to his castle at Dunbar, and it was there that he took her prisoner and allegedly raped her. On the 12th May, Mary made Bothwell the Duke of Orkney, and the couple were married at Holyrood on 15th May 1567.

The Scottish Lords did not approve of the marriage, and rose up against Mary and Bothwell. Mary was captured and imprisoned in Lochleven Castle, where she miscarried twins fathered by Bothwell, in July 1567. On 24th July 1567, Mary was forced to abdicate, and her son, James, became James VI of Scotland, with James Stewart, Earl of Moray and Mary's illegitimate half-brother acting as regent. Bothwell escaped capture, but all of his titles and estates were forfeited by an act of Parliament.

Bothwell fled to Scandinavia, but it was there that his past caught up with him. He was captured off the coast of Norway, which at that time was a Danish territory, and taken to Bergen, the home of his former love, Anna Throndsen, who then sued him for abandonment. Bothwell was able to settle the case with Anna out of court, giving her one of his ships and promising her an annuity.

Although he managed at first to gain the Danish King's goodwill by offering to help him recapture the Orkneys and Shetland Isles, his luck ran out after the fall of Mary, Queen of Scots, and he was imprisoned in Dragsholm Castle, in

Zealand. Solitary confinement there led to Bothwell going insane. He died on 14th April 1578, and was buried at the church of Fårevejle (Faareveille).

~~~~~~

1556 – Death of Sir Anthony Kingston, former Constable of the Tower of London, at Cirencester while on his way to be tried in London. He was accused of conspiring to rob the Exchequer for money to support Henry Dudley and his plot against Mary I. Dudley appears to have been planning an invasion of English exiles from France to topple Mary and replace her with Elizabeth.

1565 – Birth of Edward Gresham, astrologer, astronomer and magician, in Stainsford, Yorkshire. He is known for his treatise "Astrostereon" and his astrological almanacs, published between 1603 and 1607.

1587 – Death of Edward Manners, 3rd Earl of Rutland, at Greenwich. He'd been taken ill earlier that month. He was buried on 15th May at Bottesford, Leicestershire.

1599 – Death of Sir Henry Wallop, member of Parliament and administrator, in Dublin while serving there as Treasurer-at-War. He was buried in St Patrick's Cathedral, Dublin.

15TH APRIL

1530 – Death of Gilbert Tailboys, 1st Baron Tailboys and first husband of Elizabeth (Bessie Blount), mistress of Henry VIII. He was laid to rest in South Kyme Church.

1545 – Death of Sir Robert Dymoke, champion at the coronations of Henry VII and Henry VIII. He also served in the households of Catherine of Aragon and Anne Boleyn.

1589 – Burial of Frances Radcliffe (née Sidney), Countess of Sussex and founder of Sidney Sussex College, Cambridge. She was buried in Westminster Abbey, in the Chapel of St Paul.

1599 – Robert Devereux, 2nd Earl of Essex, was sworn in as Lord Lieutenant of Ireland.

1624 – Burial of Sir John Scudamore, husband of Mary Shelton, who served in Elizabeth I's Privy Chamber, at Holme Lacy. It was alleged that Elizabeth I broke one of Mary's fingers in a temper.

16TH APRIL

It is not known exactly what date Guy Fawkes was born, possibly 13th April 1570, but he was baptised on 16th April 1570 at the Church of St Michael le Belfrey in York.

Guy Fawkes, or Guido Fawkes (the name he used when fighting in the Low Countries on the side of Spain), is obviously famous for being involved in *The Gunpowder Plot*, the plot to blow up the Palace of Westminster on the opening session of Parliament. It was Fawkes who was caught red-handed in the cellars beneath Westminster on the night of the 4th/5th November with 36 barrels of gunpowder.

On 31st January 1606, Guy Fawkes and three of his fellow conspirators were dragged from the Tower of London to the Old Palace Yard at Westminster, where they were to be hanged, drawn and quartered. Fawkes managed to cheat the executioner and crowd of the full horror of his sentence by jumping from the gallows and breaking his neck. His body was still quartered but he was already dead.

⁘⁘⁘⁘⁘⁘⁘⁘⁘⁘⁘⁘⁘⁘⁘⁘⁘⁘⁘⁘⁘⁘⁘⁘⁘⁘⁘⁘⁘⁘

1512 – The *Mary Rose* began her first tour of duty in the English Channel on the hunt for French warships.

1521 – German Protestant reformer, Martin Luther, appeared in front of Emperor Charles V at the *Diet of Worms*. He had been summoned to the diet to either recant or reaffirm his religious views.

1550 – Birth of Francis Anthony, alchemist, apothecary and physician. He was probably born in London and was the son of Derrick Anthony, a goldsmith. Anthony was imprisoned twice for practising as a physician without a licence, and is known for his *aurum potabile* (drinkable gold), made from gold and mercury, which he claimed had amazing curative powers. His works included *Medicinae chymicae et veri potabilis auri assertio* (1610).

1578 – Burial of Thomas Drant, Church of England clergyman and poet. He was part of the "Areopagus" intellectual circle at court, but also had an ecclesiastical career and was chaplain to Edmund Grindal, Bishop of London. He is known for his work on prosody (metre), and actually drew up some rules concerning it, which were mentioned by Edmund Spenser, Gabriel Harvey, Philip Sidney, Edward Dyer and Fulke Greville.

1587 – Death of Anne Seymour (née Stanhope), Duchess of Somerset and wife of Edward Seymour, Duke of Somerset and Lord Protector during part of Edward VI's reign. Anne was a reformer and a literary patron. She died at Hanworth Place and was buried at Westminster Abbey.

1595 – Death of Ferdinando Stanley, 5th Earl of Derby and literary patron. His sudden death caused rumours of poisoning and witchcraft, but nothing was ever proved. Stanley was patron of the Strange's Men company of players, which probably included William Shakespeare, and he was also a patron of poets. It is thought that he also was a poet.

17TH APRIL

On this day in 1534, Sir Thomas More, Henry VIII's Lord Chancellor, was sent to the Tower of London after refusing to swear the "Oath of Succession". On arriving at the Tower, he wrote a letter to his eldest daughter, Margaret Roper, to inform her of events, explaining:

"When I was before the Lords at Lambeth, I was the first that was called in, albeit Master Doctor the Vicar of Croydon was come before me, and divers others. After the cause of my sending for, declared unto me (whereof I somewhat marveled in my mind, considering that they sent for no more temporal men but me), I desired the sight of the oath, which they showed me under the great seal. Then desired I the sight of the Act of the Succession, which was delivered me in a printed roll. After which read secretly by myself, and the oath considered with the act, I showed unto them that my purpose was not to put any fault either in the act or any man that made it, or in the oath or any man that sware it, nor to condemn the conscience of any other man. But as for myself in good faith my conscience so moved me in the matter that though I would not deny to swear to the succession, yet unto the oath that there was offered me I could not swear, without the iubarding [jeopardising] of my soul to perpetual damnation. And that if they doubted whether I did refuse the oath only for the grudge of my conscience, or for any other fantasy, I was ready therein to satisfy them by mine oath. Which if they trusted not, what should they be the better to give me any oath? And if they trusted that I would therein swear true, then trusted I that of their goodness they would not move me to swear the oath that they offered me, perceiving that for to swear it was against my conscience."

He concluded by saying:

"Surely as to swear to the succession I see no peril, but I thought and think it reason that to mine own oath I look well myself, and be of counsel also in the fashion, and never intended to swear for a pece, and set my hand to the whole oath. Howbeit (as help me God), as touching the whole oath, I never withdrew any man from it, nor never advised any to refuse it, nor never put, nor will, any scruple in any man's head, but leave every man to his own conscience. And methinketh in good faith that so were it good reason that every man should leave me to mine."

Unfortunately, More's refusal to swear the oath led to him being accused of treason and being executed on 6th July 1535.

◇◇◇◇◇◇◇◇◇◇◇◇◇◇◇◇◇◇◇◇◇◇◇◇◇◇◇◇◇◇◇◇

1554 – Sir Nicholas Throckmorton was acquitted of treason for being involved in *Wyatt's Rebellion*. The jurors were arrested straight after the trial and Throckmorton remained in prison until January 1555.

1554 – Thomas Wyatt the Younger's head was stolen in the rejoicing after Throckmorton's acquittal.

1554 – Birth of Stephen Gosson, Church of England clergyman, satirist and anti-theatrical polemicist. In 1579 he published his "Schoole of Abuse, containing a pleasant invective against Poets, Pipers, Plaiers, Jesters and such like Caterpillars of the Commonwealth".

1568 – Birth of George Brooke, conspirator, son of William Brooke, 10th Baron Cobham and his wife Frances (née Newton). Brooke conspired with Sir Griffin Markham and William Watson to kidnap King James I and end the persecution of Catholics. The plot was called the *Bye Plot*, and never took place because the authorities found out about their plans. Brooke was arrested, tried at Winchester 15th November 1603 and executed on Winchester Castle green 5th December 1603.

1595 – Execution of Henry Walpole (St Henry Walpole), Jesuit martyr, in York. He was hanged, drawn and quartered. He was accused of treason on three counts "Walpole had abjured the realm without licence; that he had received holy orders overseas; and that he had returned to England as a Jesuit priest to exercise his priestly functions".

18TH APRIL

On this day in 1587, John Foxe, the English historian, reformer and martyrologist, died aged around seventy. He is known for his book "Actes and Monuments", commonly known as "Foxe's Book of Martyrs", an account of Christian martyrs throughout history, with particular emphasis on the Protestant martyrs who died during the reign of Mary I.

Foxe was also a lecturer of logic at Oxford University, and was a tutor to Thomas Lucy's children and the orphaned children of Henry Howard, Earl of Surrey.

He was ordained as a deacon in 1550, but had to go into exile during Mary I's reign, preaching in Frankfurt and then proofreading in Basel. He wrote his religious drama *Christus Triumphans* while in exile. Foxe returned to England in Elizabeth I's reign, began work on "Actes and Monuments" and was also ordained as a priest. The first edition of "Actes and Monuments" was published by John Day 20th March 1563, and was around 1800 pages in length. It was hugely popular, and a second edition was published in 1570. Convocation, in 1571, ordered that a copy of it should be placed in every cathedral church, along with the "Bishop's Bible".

Foxe died while working on a Latin commentary of Revelation with his son, Samuel Foxe.

1536 – Eustace Chapuys, Imperial Ambassador, was tricked into acknowledging Anne Boleyn as Queen. Chapuys had refused the offer of visiting Anne and kissing her hand, but George Boleyn conducted the ambassador to mass and manoeuvred him behind the door through which Anne would enter. As Anne entered with the King, she turned, stopped and bowed to Chapuys. He had no choice, and had to bow and recognise the woman he called "the concubine" as Queen.

1540 – King Henry VIII made Thomas Cromwell Earl of Essex, just three months before he was executed after being found guilty of treason, heresy, corruption and more.

1552 – Death of John Leland, poet and antiquary, in the parish of St Michael le Querne, Cheapside, London. He was buried there. In 1547, Leland "fell besides his wits" and in 1551, his brother was granted custody of him and his possessions. Leland is known for the notebooks of his travels around England and Wales, which were published as "The Itinerary of John Leland the Antiquary" by Thomas Hearne.

1555 – Death of Polydore Virgil, Italian humanist scholar and historian, at Urbino. He was buried in the Chapel of St Andrew in the Duomo in Urbino. Virgil has been called the "Father of English History", and his famous works include *De inventoribus rerum* and the *Anglica Historia*.

1556 – Death of Sir John Gage, military administrator and courtier, at his home, Firle Place, Sussex. He was buried at West Firle church. Gage's offices included Chancellor of the Duchy of Lancaster, Comptroller of the Household, Constable of the Tower and Lord Chamberlain.

1570 – Burial of William Herbert, 1st Earl of Pembroke, at St Paul's, beside his wife. He had died at Hampton Court Palace on 17th March.

19TH APRIL

On 19th April 1587, Sir Francis Drake entered the harbour of Cadiz on the Spanish coast and led a pre-emptive strike on the Spanish fleet, destroying a number of ships (20-30) and their supplies, and causing the planned Spanish attack on England to be postponed for over a year. Drake referred to this successful attack as "Singeing the King of Spain's beard".

———

1558 – Mary, Queen of Scots and Francis, the Dauphin, were formally betrothed at the Louvre.

1568 – Funeral of Sir Ambrose Cave, Knight of the Hospital of St John of Jerusalem and administrator, at the Savoy Chapel. He was buried at Stanford, Northamptonshire. Sir Francis Knollys was his chief mourner.

1601 – Hanging of James Duckett, bookseller and Catholic martyr, at Tyburn, after Roman Catholic books were found in his possession.

1608 – Sudden death of Thomas Sackville, 1st Baron Buckhurst and 1st Earl of Dorset, poet, member of Parliament and administrator, at Whitehall from a stroke suffered at the council table. Sackville's offices in Elizabeth I's reign included ambassador, Chancellor of the University of Oxford and Lord Treasurer. His literary works included the 1561 drama "Gorboduc", written with Thomas Norton, the poem "Complaint of Henry, Duke of Buckingham" and the allegorical poem "Induction".

1615 – Death of Laurence Bodley, Church of England clergyman and brother of Thomas Bodley, founder of the Bodleian Library. He died at the age of sixty-seven and was buried in Exeter Cathedral.

20TH APRIL

On this day in 1534, Elizabeth Barton, known as "the Nun of Kent" or "the Holy Maid of Kent", was hanged at Tyburn with her spiritual adviser, Father Edward Bocking, Richard Risby, Warden of the Observant Friary at Canterbury, and Hugh Rich, Warden of the Observant Friary at Richmond.

Elizabeth Barton went from being an ordinary servant girl to a religious visionary in 1525, at around the age of nineteen. She was working in a household in Aldington, Kent, when she was taken ill and fell into trances where she had visions which were "of marvellous holiness in rebuke of sin and vice".

Richard Master, the local parish priest, was convinced that her visions were genuine, and so reported the matter to William Warham, the Archbishop of Canterbury, who sent a commission consisting of her parish priest, a diocesan official, two Franciscans (Richard Risby and Hugh Rich) and three Canterbury Benedictines (Bocking, Barnes and William Hadleigh). This commission was also convinced of Barton's sincerity and pronounced in her favour. Shortly after Barton was examined, one of her predictions came true – in front of a large crowd, Barton was cured of her illness by the Blessed Virgin. At this time, her visions and prophecies seemed harmless, as they simply encouraged people to live a good Catholic life.

After being cured of her illness, Elizabeth Barton left her job as a servant to become a Benedictine nun near Canterbury. She carried on having visions and became a bit of a celebrity, becoming known as the "Nun of Kent" or the "Holy Maid of Kent". People would undertake pilgrimages to see this nun who was thought to communicate directly with the Virgin Mary. She was humoured by the English government, and even corresponded with people like Sir Thomas More and Bishop John Fisher, and actually met with Cardinal Wolsey, but then she started opposing Henry VIII's plans to annul his marriage to Catherine of Aragon and marry Anne Boleyn. No longer was she a harmless nun. She was a threat to Henry VIII's popularity, and what she was saying could be classed as treason.

According to Nancy Bradley Warren, author of "Women of God and Arms: Female Spirituality and Political Conflict, 1380–1600", in 1532 Elizabeth Barton claimed to have been miraculously and invisibly present when Henry VIII attended Mass in Calais during his visit to see the French King. She reported that an angel denied Henry the consecrated host, removed it from the priest's hands and, instead, offered it to Elizabeth Barton. She said that this was a clear sign that God was displeased with Henry. Barton also prophesied that if Henry proceeded with his divorce and married Anne Boleyn, then he would lose his kingdom within a month and "should die a villain's death". Nancy Bradley Warren writes of how Elizabeth Barton and her prophecies "struck at the heart of Henry VIII's foreign policy and, perhaps even more significantly, at the heart of his representation of the English monarchy".

It was clear that she was now a threat to Henry and his plans, and this threat had to be dealt with. In 1533 Elizabeth Barton was examined by the new Archbishop of Canterbury, Thomas Cranmer. Having had her reputation damaged by rumours of sexual misconduct with priests, it is said that Elizabeth Barton confessed to fabricating her prophesies. She was then imprisoned in the Tower of London, along with her supporters, like Bocking and Hadleigh, and forced to do public penance and make a public confession at St Paul's Cross.

In January 1534, Elizabeth Barton and thirteen of her supporters were accused of treason by a bill of attainder. Those accused included Sir Thomas More and Bishop John Fisher, but More escaped when he produced a letter he had written to Barton in the past, telling her that she should not meddle in state affairs. Bishop Fisher and five of the other sympathisers were condemned to imprisonment and Barton and seven others, including Risby, Rich, Bocking and Masters, were condemned to death. Fisher was later pardoned. Here is what is recorded in the "Letters and Papers" from Henry VIII's reign from 15th January 1534:-

"Names of those implicated with Eliz. Barton:-

Eliz. Berton, nun, Edw. Bokkyng, John Deryng, Ric. Master, Harry Gold, Hugh Ryche and Ric. Rysby. These by the Act shall be attainted of high treason and suffer death.

John bishop of Rochester, Adyson, clerk, his chaplain, Thomas Gold, Thomas Laurens. Edw. Thwaytes, gent., Thomas Abell. To be attainted of misprision. suffer imprisonment at the King's will and lose all their goods." (LP vii 70)

They went to their deaths 20th April 1534.

It is not known whether Elizabeth Barton confessed of her own volition, or whether she was tortured, either physically or psychologically. It is impossible to judge whether Elizabeth was a fraudster, mentally ill or medically ill. She may have suffered from fits, she could have been delusional or perhaps she did have visions or what she believed to be visions. We just can't say.

1483 – Burial of Edward IV in St George's Chapel, Windsor Castle.

1523 – Death of Henry Clifford, 10th Baron Clifford, magnate. At around the age of sixty, Clifford led a force at the *Battle of Flodden* in 1513 against the Scots.

1534 – Prominent citizens of London were required to swear the "Oath of the Act of Succession".

1578 – Death of Lady Mary Keys (née Grey), sister of Lady Jane Grey and wife of Thomas Keys, Sergeant Porter to Elizabeth I. Mary married Keys in secret in 1565, angering Elizabeth I. As a result, Keys was thrown into Fleet Prison and Mary was put into the care of Sir William Hawtrey at Chequers. Mary was later moved to the home of Katherine Willoughby, Duchess of Suffolk and her stepgrandmother, and then on to that of Sir Thomas Gresham. In 1568, Keys was released from prison, but he died in 1571 without ever being reconciled with Mary. Mary stayed with Gresham, voluntarily because she had nowhere else to go, until moving to her stepfather's house in 1573 and setting up her own home in London. She died at her home in London.

1584 – Execution of sixty year-old James Bell, Catholic priest and martyr, at Lancaster. Bell had been found guilty of being a Catholic recusant and celebrating the mass, and sentenced to death for high treason.

1587 – Burial of John Foxe, martyrologist, in St GilesCripplegate. He died 18th April at his home in Grub Street, in the same parish.

21ST APRIL

At 11pm on Saturday 21st April 1509, Henry VII died. He had known that he was dying for some time, and had retired to Richmond at the end of February to spend his last days there.

John Fisher, the bishop Henry's son would end up executing, was the main person helping the King through those last days. However, it wasn't spiritual comfort he offered. According to Henry VII's biographer, Thomas Penn, Fisher "interrogated Henry relentlessly, in the way that priests did in order to bring the dying to a 'wholesome fear and dread' of their sinful condition". Poor Henry promised that there would be a "true reformation of all them that were officers and ministers of his laws" if God spared him. It wasn't to be.

Henry kissed the crucifix, beat it against his chest and then slipped away as he held a taper to light his path. His death was kept secret for two days, being announced to the Knights of the Garter at their *St George's Day* feast 23rd April. It was not announced to the public until 24th April.

It was the end of Henry Tudor, the man who had beaten Richard III at the *Battle of Bosworth Field*, starting a new dynasty. The throne passed successfully (a feat in itself) to his son, also named Henry, who became Henry VIII.

◇◇

1566 (20th or 21st) – Death of Sir John Mason, member of Parliament, diplomat in the reigns of four Tudor monarchs, Privy Councillor in Edward VI's reign and Treasurer of the Chamber in Elizabeth I's reign. He was buried in St Paul's Cathedral, in the north choir.

1566 – Death of Sir Richard Sackville, member of Parliament and administrator, in London. He served Henry VIII as Under-Treasurer of the Exchequer, Chancellor of the Court of Augmentations and Escheator of Surrey and Sussex, Edward VI as Custos Rotulorum of Sussex (a post held until his death) and Lord Lieutenant of Sussex, and Elizabeth I as Privy Councillor and Chancellor of the Exchequer. He was buried at Withyham in Sussex.

1580 – Death of philanthropist William Lambe. He was buried at St Faith under St Paul's. Lambe was a Gentleman of the Royal Chapel in Henry VIII's reign, but is known for his philanthropy in Elizabeth I's reign. For example, he funded the building of almshouses and a grammar school in Sutton Valance, Kent, also the building of Holborn conduit.

1581 – Burial of Thomas Charnock, alchemist, at Otterhampton in Somerset after dying at his home in Combwich. In his "Booke dedicated vnto the queenes maiestie" he offered Elizabeth I the health and wealth that the philosopher's stone could bring if she would finance his work.

22ND APRIL

1520 – Death of Sir John Ernley, lawyer and Attorney-General in the reigns of Henry VII and Henry VIII. He was made Chief

Justice of the Common Pleas in January 1519, and was knighted that year. He was buried at Sidlesham, near Chichester.

1542 – Death of Henry Clifford, 1ˢᵗ Earl of Cumberland. He supported Henry VIII during the *Pilgrimage of Grace*, when he was Warden of the West Marches, by leading a force in Northumberland. His reward for his loyalty was to be elected to the Order of the Garter in 1537. Cumberland was buried at Skipton Parish Church.

1598 – Death of Francis Beaumont, member of Parliament, Serjeant-at-Law and Justice of the Common Pleas in the reign of Elizabeth I. He died from gaol fever at his home in Grace Dieu, Leicestershire and was buried in Belton Church. His colleague Serjeant Drew also died of the fever, which they picked up on the *Lent* circuit in Lancaster.

23RD APRIL

Today is the day that traditionally marks the birth of the Bard, William Shakespeare, the famous Elizabethan playwright and actor, in 1564. It is not known on what date Shakespeare was actually born but he was baptised at Stratford-upon-Avon on 26ᵗʰ April 1564, and baptism usually took place around three days after birth.

William Shakespeare also died on this day in 1616. He was buried at the Holy Trinity Church, Stratford-upon-Avon, in the chancel with the epitaph:-

> "Good frend for Iesvs sake forbeare,
> To digg the dvst encloased heare.
> Bleste be ye man yt spares thes stones,
> And cvrst be he yt moves my bones."

Or, in modern English:-

"Good friend, for Jesus' sake forbear,
To dig the dust enclosed here.
Blessed be the man that spares these stones,
And cursed be he who moves my bones."

William Shakespeare has got to be one of the greatest (if not *the* greatest) writers in the English language. His plays have been performed the world over by some of the greatest actors and actresses. They have been turned into films and have been translated into many different languages. Students study his works and are examined on them. Authors like Robin Maxwell have turned his plays into novels, tourists flock to Stratford-upon-Avon to visit Shakespeare's birthplace, Mary Arden's house and Anne Hathaway's Cottage, and the Royal Shakespeare Company (RSC) still perform his plays to crowds of people in Shakespeare's home town. What a legacy!

St George's Day – The day for announcing new appointments to the Order of the Garter, the highest order of chivalry in England.

1500 – Birth of Alexander Ales (Alesius, Aless), Scottish theologian and reformer, at Edinburgh. His mother was Christina Bigholm, and his actual surname seems to have been Alan or Allane. He changed his name when he went into exile, choosing "Alesius", meaning "bird", or in this case, "exile".

1512 – Birth of Henry Fitzalan, 12th Earl of Arundel, son of William Fitzalan, 11th Earl of Arundel, and Anne (née Percy), daughter of Henry Percy, 4th Earl of Northumberland. At his baptism, Henry VIII stood as his godfather. He served Henry VIII as Deputy of Calais, Privy Councillor and Lord Chamberlain.

1536 – Sir Nicholas Carew was elected to the Order of the Garter at the annual chapter meeting at Greenwich, rather than George Boleyn, brother of Queen Anne Boleyn.

24TH APRIL

On 24th April 1558, Mary, Queen of Scots married Francis, the Dauphin of France, at Notre Dame in Paris. Mary was fifteen, and Francis was fourteen.

Francis became King Consort of Scotland at the marriage and then he became King of France, and Mary Queen Consort of France on the death of his father, Henry II, in July 1559. Unfortunately, Francis's reign only lasted 17 months, because he died in December 1560 from an abscess in the brain caused by an ear infection.

1536 – Commissions of oyer and terminer were set up by Thomas Audley, Lord Chancellor. These particular commissions were for offences committed in the counties of Middlesex and Kent, and covered the crimes of misprision, treason, rebellion, felonies, murder, homicide, rioting, plotting, insurrection, extortion, oppression, contempt, concealment, ignorance, negligence, falsities, deception, conspiracy and being an accessory to these crimes. It is not known whether they were set up specifically to try the men who would later be charged with committing adultery with Queen Anne Boleyn.

1545 – Baptism of Henry Wriothesley, 2nd Earl of Southampton, at St Andrews, Holborn. He was the son of Thomas Wriothesley, 1st Earl of Southampton and 1st Baron Wriothesley, Henry VIII's Lord Chancellor.

1549 – Death of Ralph Neville, 4th Earl of Westmorland, English peer, soldier and Privy Councillor. He was buried at Staindrop in County Durham. Neville was one of the peers who sat in judgement on Anne Boleyn in May 1536 and served Henry VIII as a soldier in the North of England and borders, and Edward VI in Scotland.

1551 – Execution of Dutchman George van Parris, surgeon and religious radical at Smithfield. He was burned at the stake for Arianism (denying the divinity of Christ).

1555 – Burning of George Marsh, Protestant martyr, former curate at All Hallows Church, London and a preacher in Lancashire, at Spital Boughton outside the walls of Chester. He had refused the offer of a royal pardon if he would recant his Protestant faith. His ashes were buried in the St Giles cemetery.

25TH APRIL

On this day in 1557, Thomas Stafford, son of Henry Stafford, 10th Baron Stafford, and Ursula Pole, seized Scarborough Castle, declared himself "The Lord Thomas Stafford, son to the Lord Henry, rightful Duke of Bokingham" then proclaimed himself "Protector of the Realm". He also denounced Mary's marriage to Philip and warned the people that they would be made slaves by the Spaniards, thus inciting rebellion.

His rebellion backfired due to lack of support, and he and his followers were captured by the Earl of Westmorland on 28th April. Stafford was executed for treason on 28th May 1557, at Tyburn.

This wasn't his first brush with trouble. He had been involved in *Wyatt's Rebellion* in 1554, and had been imprisoned in Fleet prison, and then while in exile in France he plotted to murder Sir William Pickering.

His seizing of Scarborough Castle was the catalyst for the English declaration of war on France, because Stafford had been supported by around a hundred Frenchmen. This war resulted in the loss of Calais, something that haunted Mary I for the remaining months of her life.

1509 – Birth of Thomas Vaux, 2nd Baron Vaux, poet associated with Sir Thomas Wyatt and Henry Howard, Earl of Surrey.

1513 – Death of Sir Edward Howard, naval commander, by drowning, in an attack on the French fleet. Edward was the second son of Thomas Howard, 2nd Duke of Norfolk.

1526 – Death of Charles Somerset, 1st Earl of Worcester, illegitimate son of Henry Beaufort, 2nd Duke of Somerset, and his mistress Joan Hill. He was buried in St George's Chapel, Windsor.

1544 – Publication of Queen Catherine Parr's English translation of John Fisher's "Psalms or Prayers". It was published anonymously.

1551 – Death of Alice More, Lady More, second wife of Sir Thomas More. Her exact date of death is not known, but it was around 25th April 1551. She was buried at Chelsea.

1557 – "A Masque of Almains, Pilgrims and Irishmen" was performed in front of Queen Mary I and Philip of Spain.

1599 – Birth of Oliver Cromwell, future Lord Protector of England, Scotland and Ireland.

1603 – Burial of Katherine Howard, Countess of Nottingham, eldest daughter of Henry Carey, 1st Baron Hunsdon, at All Saints, Chelsea. Elizabeth I was said to be very distressed at her friend's death.

26TH APRIL

Around 26th April 1536, Queen Anne Boleyn met with her chaplain, thirty-two year-old Matthew Parker. Parker recorded later that Anne had asked him to watch over her daughter, the two year-old Princess Elizabeth, if anything happened to her.

It is not known what part Parker did play in Elizabeth's upbringing, but she made him her Archbishop of Canterbury in 1559. It was a post which Parker admitted to William Cecil, Lord Burghley, he would not have accepted if he "had not been so much bound to the mother".

<hr>

1540 – Marriage of Francis Knollys and Catherine Carey, daughter of Mary Boleyn and William Carey, or, as some historians believe, Henry VIII.

1546 – Death of Sir Ralph Ellerker, soldier, in a French ambush while serving as Marshal of Boulogne for Henry VIII. He was buried in St Mary's Church in the town.

1564 – Baptism of William Shakespeare at Holy Trinity Church, Stratford-upon-Avon. Shakespeare was the third son of John Shakespeare, a glover and whittawer, and Mary Arden, who lived in Henley Street, Stratford-upon-Avon.

1589 – Death of Andrew Perne, Dean of Ely and Vice-Chancellor of Cambridge University, at Lambeth while visiting his friend, Archbishop John Whitgift. He was buried at Lambeth Parish Church.

1596 – Burial of Henry Hastings, 3rd Earl of Huntingdon, at St Helen's Church, Ashby-de-la-Zouch.

27TH APRIL

On 27th April 1536, writs were issued summoning Parliament, and a letter was sent to Thomas Cranmer, the Archbishop of Canterbury, asking him to attend Parliament. Here is the record from "Letters and Papers":

"Summons to the archbishop of Canterbury to attend the Parliament which is to meet at Westminster, 8 June; and to warn the prior and chapter of his cathedral and the clergy of his province to be present, the former in person and the latter by two proctors. Westm., 27 April 28 Hen. VIII.

ii. Similar writs to the different bishops, abbots, and lords; to the judges, serjeants-at-law, and the King's attorney, to give counsel; to the sheriffs to elect knights of the shires, citizens, and burgesses; also to the chancellor of the county palatine of Lancaster; to the deputy and council of Calais to elect one burgess, and to the mayor and burgesses to elect another."

According to Eustace Chapuys, the Imperial Ambassador recorded that John Stokesley, Bishop of London, was approached on this day in 1536 to see if the King could "abandon" his second wife, Anne Boleyn.

***

1584 – Death of David Lewis, civil lawyer and judge involved in the maritime cases of Elizabeth I's reign. He was buried in St Mary's Church, Abergavenny, in the part of the church now known as the Lewis Chapel.

1609 – Death of Sir Edward Michelborne, member of Parliament, soldier and adventurer, after becoming ill in January that year. In James I's reign, he obtained a royal licence "to discover the countries of Cathay, China, Japan, Corea, and Cambaya, and to trade there", and he set sail on 1st December 1604, returning in July 1606 after time spent plundering Dutch settlements in Indonesia. He was buried in Hackney.

28TH APRIL

On this day in 1603, Elizabeth I's funeral took place in London.

After her death on 24th March 1603, the body of Queen Elizabeth I was placed inside a lead coffin and carried by night in a torchlit barge along the Thames from Richmond Palace to Whitehall. There, the Queen was to lie in state until her funeral, giving time for King James to travel down to London. While the coffin lay in state, a life size effigy of the Queen, dressed in her royal robes, was placed on top of it to act as a symbol of the monarchy while there was no monarch in England.

On 28th April 1603, Elizabeth's coffin was carried from Whitehall to Westminster Abbey on a hearse drawn by horses hung with black velvet. The coffin was covered in a rich purple cloth, topped with the effigy of Elizabeth with a sceptre in her hands and a crown on her head. Above the coffin was a canopy supported by six knights, and behind the hearse was the Queen's Master of the Horse, leading her palfrey. The chief mourner was the Countess of Northampton who led the party of peers of the realm, all dressed in black. Chronicler John Stow wrote:-

"Westminster was surcharged with multitudes of all sorts of people in their streets, houses, windows, leads and gutters, that came out to see the obsequy, and when they beheld her statue lying upon the coffin, there was such a general sighing, groaning and weeping as the like hath not been seen or known in the memory of man."

Elizabeth was then buried at Westminster Abbey in the vault of her grandfather, Henry VII, until she was moved in 1606 to her present resting place, a tomb in the Lady Chapel of Westminster Abbey which she shares with her half-sister Mary I. King James I spent over £11,000 on Elizabeth I's lavish funeral, and he also arranged for this white marble monument to be built. The tomb is inscribed with the words:-

"Consorts both in throne and grave, here we rest two sisters, Elizabeth and Mary, in hope of our resurrection."

1442 – Birth of Edward IV at Rouen, Normandy. Edward was the son of Richard, 3rd Duke of York, and Cecily Neville, and was King of England from 1461 to 1470, until he was overthrown by the Earl of Warwick who restored Henry VI, and then from 1471 to his death in 1483.

1489 – Death of Henry Percy, 4th Earl of Northumberland, magnate. He was killed when he confronted protesters at South Kilvington, near Thirsk, and his retainers failed to defend him. His unpopularity had been caused by his actions, or rather inaction, at the *Battle of Bosworth*, when he chose to keep his retainers out of the battle and Richard III, who his people supported, was defeated and killed.

1533 – Death of Nicholas West, Bishop of Ely, diplomat and former Chaplain to Catherine of Aragon, at his manor in Downham. He was buried in Ely Cathedral, in the chantry chapel that he had built. West got into trouble in 1530, actually being charged with praemunire, for his support of Catherine of Aragon and, therefore, opposition to Henry VIII's policies. He was imprisoned briefly.

1536 – Reports of council meetings and Thomas Cromwell's meeting with Dr Richard Sampson aroused suspicion.

1548 – Death of Sir Anthony Browne, courtier and Keeper of Oatlands Palace, at Byfleet, Surrey. Browne was involved in Anne Boleyn's downfall, reporting that his sister, the Countess of Worcester, had told him that Anne had committed adultery and possible incest. Browne was also the one who informed King Henry VIII that he was dying.

1556 – Execution of Richard Uvedale at Tyburn for his involvement in Henry Dudley's plot against Mary I.

1558 – Execution of eighty-two year old Walter Mylne, priest and Protestant martyr, for heresy at St Andrews, Scotland. So appalled at the planned burning of this aged man were the townsfolk that they refused to provide materials for the burning, and Mylne had to be escorted to the stake by armed guard.

1572 – Burial of William Paulet, 1st Marquis of Winchester, administrator and nobleman. He was buried at Basing. Under Henry VIII he was Lord Great Chamberlain, Great Master of the Household, Lord President of the Privy Council and Lord

Treasurer. He also served Edward VI, Mary I and Elizabeth I as Lord Treasurer.

1580 – Baptism of William Herbert, 3rd Earl of Pembroke, courtier and patron of the Arts, at St Mary's Church, Wilton, Wiltshire. Herbert was Chancellor of Oxford University and Broadgates Hall honoured him for his patronage and financial support by changing its name to Pembroke College.

29TH APRIL

1500 – Birth of William Dacre, 3rd Baron Dacre of Gilsland and 7th Baron Greystoke. He was the eldest son of Thomas Dacre, 2nd Baron of Gilsland, and Elizabeth Greystoke, Baroness Greystoke. He was married twice, to Lady Elizabeth Talbot and then to Anne Hastings. His offices included Captain of Norham Castle, Steward of Penrith, Warden of the West Marches, Governor of Carlisle and Warden of the Middle Marches. He died on 18th November 1563.

1536 – Anne Boleyn argued with Sir Henry Norris, rebuking him with the words "You look for dead men's shoes, for if aught came to the King but good, you would look to have me" and thereby speaking of the King's death, something that amounted to treason. When she realised her mistake, Anne instructed Norris to go to her almoner the next day and take an oath that she "was a good woman".

1579 – Death of Richard Cheyney, Bishop of Gloucester, at The Lodge in Painswick, Gloucestershire, the bishop's manor. He was buried in his cathedral.

1594 – Death of Thomas Cooper, Bishop of Winchester and theologian, at Winchester. He was buried in his cathedral, on the south side. Cooper's works included "Cooper's Chronicle", *Thesaurus Linguae Romanae et Britannicae* and "An Admonition to the People of England", which was directed against Puritans.

1617 – Death of Sir Dru Drury, courtier, member of Parliament, friend of Thomas Howard, 4th Duke of Norfolk, and Lieutenant of the Tower of London (1595-6), at Riddlesworth Hall in Norfolk. In 1586, Drury and Sir Amyas (Amias) Paulet were chosen to supervise Mary, Queen of Scots during her imprisonment. He was buried in Riddlesworth Parish Church.

30TH APRIL

On this day in 1532, James Bainham, lawyer and Protestant martyr, was burned at Smithfield. He had been condemned to death for heresy after denying the doctrines of transubstantiation and purgatory, and rejecting the recantation he made after being tortured and imprisoned in the Tower of London between December 1531 and his release in February 1532. His imprisonment and torture were ordered by Sir Thomas More.

George Stokes wrote of how, as he was being burned, Bainham said, "O ye papists, behold ye look for miracles, and here now you may see a miracle: for in this fire I feel no more pain, than if I were in a bed of down; but it is to me as a bed of roses."

Bainham was married to the widow of reformer Simon Fish, author of "The Supplication of Beggars", a man who had also been charged with heresy.

1536 – Scottish theologian Alexander Alesius witnessed an argument between Queen Anne Boleyn and Henry VIII, and at 11 o'clock that night, the King and Queen's upcoming visit to Calais was cancelled and arrangements made for the King to journey alone a week later. Also 30th April, court musician and member of the Boleyn circle, Mark Smeaton, was taken to Thomas Cromwell's house in Stepney and interrogated. Within twenty-four hours, he had confessed to making love three times to the Queen.

1544 – Death of Thomas Audley, Baron Audley of Walden and Lord Chancellor, at his home in Aldgate, London. Audley was Cromwell's right hand man in 1536, during the fall of Anne Boleyn, and became even more important after Cromwell's fall.

1547 – Sir Anthony Denny was made Henry VIII's Groom of the Stool.

1563 – Death of Henry Stafford, 10th Baron Stafford, at Caus Castle, Shropshire. Stafford was the only legitimate son of Edward Stafford, 3rd Duke of Buckingham, and his wife, Eleanor, daughter of Henry Percy, 4th Earl of Northumberland.

1595 – Death of Thomas Bedwell, mathematician, engineer and keeper of the ordnance store at the Tower of London. He was buried at the Tower, in the Chapel of St Peter ad Vincula. Bedwell's engineering projects included him supervising the building of Dover harbour, giving advice on the fortification of Portsmouth and working on the River Thames' defences at Tilbury and Gravesend in 1588, at the time of the Spanish Armada.

1596 – Death of Sir John Puckering, administrator and Speaker of the House of Commons, from apoplexy. Puckering's other offices included Serjeant-at-Law, Recorder of Warwick, Privy Councillor and Lord Keeper of the Great Seal. In 1587, he was involved in the trial of Elizabeth I's secretary William Davison, appearing for the Crown. He was buried at Westminster Abbey, in St Paul's Chapel.

1596 – Death of Thomas Bickley, Bishop of Chichester, at the bishop's palace in Aldingbourne. He was buried in his cathedral.

HENRY VIII (1491-1547)

1ST MAY

On this day in 1517, *May Day*, a mob of young apprentices and labourers gathered at St Paul's and then went on a rampage through the streets of London, causing damage to property and hurting those who stood in their way.

The rioters of this *Evil May Day Riot* focused particularly on damaging and looting the shops and houses which belonged to foreign traders, such as the shoe shops around Leadenhall and the house of French merchant John Meautys. Chronicler Edward Hall put the trouble down to John Lincoln, a London broker, who wrote a bill that *Easter* encouraging "doctor standyche" to use his *Easter* sermon at St Mary Spital to try and persuade the Mayor and aldermen "to take parte with the comminaltie agaynst the straungiers", the foreigners he felt who were damaging London's economy and taking work away from Englishmen. Standish refused to preach what Lincoln wanted, so he turned to Dr Bell who was to preach on *Easter* Tuesday. Dr Bell listened to Lincoln and preached what he wanted the people to hear. Bell said:

"or so it is that the alyens and strangiers eate the bread from the poore fatherles chyldren, and take the liuynge from all the artificers and the entercourse from all merchauntes, wherby pouertie is so muche encreased that euery man bewaileth the misery of other, for craftes me be brought to beggery and merchauntes to nedyues"

…and called on the people to to act against the foreigners causing their poverty:

"and as byrdes woulde defende their nest, so oughte Englishemen to cherysbe and defende them selfes, and to hurt and greue aliens for the common weak."

Hall believes that it was this sermon, this call to action (or even call to arms), that caused the *Evil May Day Riot*, but historian Graham Noble points out that the sermon actually took place two weeks before the trouble started, and that it's more likely to have been the government's fault for reacting to some "sporadic attacks" two days before the riot by instituting a curfew on *May Day*, a night which was usually one of fun and celebration.

Arrests were made by the Duke of Norfolk and his men. On 4th May, thirteen people were executed, and on 7th May John Lincoln was executed. Others were saved by the intercession of Henry VIII's wife, Catherine of Aragon, and his sisters, Margaret and Mary, who pleaded with him to spare them, although, as Noble points out, this was probably a PR exercise thought up by Henry or Wolsey.

***

1461 – Execution of James Butler, 1st Earl of Wiltshire and 5th Earl of Ormond, at Newcastle after being captured by the Yorkists.

1508 – Birth of Sir William Cavendish, administrator. Cavendish was one of Cromwell's main agents in the dissolution of the monasteries and was appointed Treasurer of the Chamber in February 1546.

1536 – The *May Day* Joust. Henry VIII left abruptly, taking Sir Henry Norris with him and interrogating him about his alleged affair with Queen Anne Boleyn.

1551 – Death of Sir Edmund Knyvet, Norfolk landowner and MP. He helped the Duke of Norfolk suppress the *Pilgrimage of Grace* rebellion in 1536, served as Sheriff of Norfolk and Suffolk in 1539, and went with Norfolk to meet Anne of Cleves in January 1540. He also helped John Dudley, Earl of Warwick, suppress *Kett's Rebellion* in 1549. Knyvet was known for his hot temper and nearly had his his hand cut off after he was charged with hitting Thomas Clere, a servant of Henry Howard, Earl of Surrey, during a game of tennis.

1590 – James VI of Scotland brought Anne of Denmark, his bride, to Scotland. The couple had been married by proxy in Copenhagen in August 1589, but Anne had to abandon her journey to Scotland due to storms. James decided to go and fetch her, and the couple married properly at the Bishop's Palace in Oslo in November 1589.

1621 – Death of Robert Chaloner, Church of England clergyman and educational benefactor, probably at Amersham. He was buried there at St Mary's Church. Chaloner was Canon of Windsor, but is more known for the bequests he left supporting a master at a grammar school and scholars or lecturers at Christ Church, Oxford.

2ND MAY

At dawn on 2nd May 1536, Sir Henry Norris, Henry VIII's Groom of the Stool and great friend, was taken to the Tower of London. Musician Mark Smeaton had also been taken there, and the Imperial Ambassador, Eustace Chapuys, wrote to Charles V on 2nd May telling him that George Boleyn, Lord Rochford and brother of Queen Anne Boleyn, was also in the Tower.

Anne Boleyn was watching a game of real tennis when she was disturbed by a messenger telling her that the King had ordered her to present herself to his Privy Council. Anne left the tennis match and presented herself in the council chamber in front of a royal commission consisting of the Duke of Norfolk (her uncle), Sir William Fitzwilliam and Sir William Paulet. There she was informed that she was being accused of committing adultery with three different men, and that Smeaton and Norris had confessed.

Anne was then taken to her apartments until the tide of the Thames turned and then, at two o'clock in the afternoon, she was escorted by barge to the Tower of London.

1542 – Burial of Henry Clifford, 1st Earl of Cumberland and close friend of Henry VIII, at Skipton Church in Yorkshire. Cumberland served the King as Warden of the West Marches, and was rewarded for his service and loyalty during the *Pilgrimage of Grace* by being elected as a Knight of the Order of the Garter.

1550 – Burning of Joan Bocher, an Anabaptist, at Smithfield. Bocher believed that Christ's flesh was "not incarnate of the Virgin Mary" and was convicted of heresy and condemned to death.

1551 – Birth of William Camden, historian, headmaster and herald, at the Old Bailey, London. Camden is known for his "Britannia", the first chorographical survey of Great Britain and Ireland, and his *Annales Rerum Gestarum Angliae et Hiberniae Regnate Elizabetha*, his history of Elizabeth I's reign, but he also wrote a Greek grammar and "Remaines of a Greater Worke, Concerning Britaine", which was a collection of historical essays.

1568 – Mary, Queen of Scots escaped from Lochleven Castle. As a *May Day* masque took place at the castle, Mary was smuggled out and taken to a waiting boat.

1587 – Burial of Sir Thomas Bromley, Lord Chancellor, in Westminster Abbey.

1620 – Burial of Edward More, poet and grandson of Sir Thomas More. He was buried at Barnborough, Yorkshire.

3RD MAY

On 3rd May 1536, a very shocked Archbishop Thomas Cranmer wrote to King Henry VIII regarding his patron Queen Anne Boleyn's arrest. In his letter, he wrote "I am clean amazed, for I had never better opinion of woman", but tempered this with "but I think your Highness would not have gone so far if she had not been culpable", so as not to offend the King.

He added a postscript after seeing "my lords Chancellor, Oxford, Sussex, and my Lord Chamberlain of your Grace's house" in the Star Chamber and being told of the evidence against Anne:

"I am sorry such faults can be proved against the Queen as they report."

<hr />

1415 – Birth of Cecily Neville, Duchess of York, daughter of Ralph Neville, 1st Earl of Westmorland, and Joan Beaufort. Cecily was the wife of Richard, 3rd Duke of York, and the mother of twelve children, including Richard III, George, Duke of Clarence, and Edward IV.

1446 – Birth of Margaret, Duchess of Burgundy, also known as Margaret of York, third daughter of Cecily Neville (see above) and Richard, 3rd Duke of York. She was married to Charles the Bold, who became Duke of Burgundy, and she was godmother to Emperor Charles V.

1524 – Death of Richard Grey, 3rd Earl of Kent, son of George Grey, 2nd Earl of Kent, and Anne Bourchier (née Woodville).

1568 – Death of Sir Edward Rogers, courtier, member of Parliament and Comptroller and Vice-Chamberlain of the Household to Elizabeth I. Rogers served Henry VIII as Esquire of the Body, Sewer of the Privy Chamber and Carver; Edward VI as a Gentleman of the Privy Chamber and Elizabeth I as Vice-Chamberlain, Captain of the Guard, Privy Councillor and Comptroller. In Mary I's reign, he was imprisoned for a time after being implicated in *Wyatt's Rebellion*.

1580 – Death of Thomas Tusser, poet, farmer and writer on agriculture, at the age of sixty-five. He was buried at Manningtree in Essex. Tusser is known for his "A Hundreth Good Pointes of Husbandrie", a poem recording the country year, and "Five Hundreth Points of Good Husbandry United to as many of Good Huswiferie", an instructional poem on farming.

1610 – Death of Sir William Skipwith, member of Parliament, Sheriff of Leicestershire and poet. In his "Worthies of England", author and historian Thomas Fuller described

Skipwith as "dexterous at the making fit and acute epigrams, poesies, mottoes and devices". He was buried at Prestwold Church in Leicestershire.

4TH MAY

1471 – Death of Edward of Westminster, Prince of Wales and only son of Henry VI, at the *Battle of Tewkesbury*.

1513 – Execution of Edmund de la Pole, 8th Earl of Suffolk and claimant to the English throne. He was executed after his brother, Richard de la Pole, claimed the throne of England in his own right and was recognised as king by Louis XII of France. Edmund and Richard were sons of John de la Pole, 2nd Duke of Suffolk, and his wife, Elizabeth Plantagenet, sister of Edward IV.

1535 – Executions of three Carthusian monks and a Bridgettine monk at Tyburn for rejecting the royal supremacy.

1536 – Arrests of Sir Francis Weston and Sir William Brereton during the fall of Anne Boleyn. They were both taken to the Tower of London.

1608 – Funeral of Elizabeth Talbot (Bess of Hardwick), Countess of Shrewsbury, in All Hallows, Derby. At the time of her death, she was one of the richest people in England.

5TH MAY

On this day in 1542, Agnes Tilney, Dowager Duchess of Norfolk, was pardoned after spending nearly five months imprisoned in the Tower of London. Her home and valuables had been seized but she had kept her head, unlike her step-granddaughter, Queen Catherine Howard.

The Dowager Duchess had been arrested and interrogated in December 1541 regarding the behaviour of Catherine at the Dowager Duchess's home at Lambeth, before Catherine's marriage to Henry VIII. Archbishop Thomas Cranmer had learned that Catherine had had sexual relationships with her music tutor, Henry Manox, and with Francis Dereham. It then came to light that Catherine had also had a relationship with Thomas Culpeper, a gentleman of Henry VIII's Privy Chamber, after her marriage. The revelations led to the executions of Catherine, one of her ladies, Lady Jane Rochford, and Culepeper and Dereham.

On 20th May 1542, some of the Dowager Duchess's manors were restored to her, but not Norfolk Hall. That was granted to the Duke of Norfolk in 1543.

***

1535 – Death of Charles Booth, Bishop of Hereford. He was buried in Hereford Cathedral.

1536 – By the 5th May, the final arrests (Sir Thomas Wyatt and Richard Page) had been made in the fall of Anne Boleyn.

1542 – Birth of Thomas Cecil, 1st Earl of Exeter, courtier and soldier, and the eldest son of William Cecil, 1st Baron Burghley, by his first wife Mary Cheke.

1543 – Execution of George Bucker (aka Adam Damplip), religious radical. He was hanged, drawn and quartered in Calais for treason.

1586 – Death of Sir Henry Sidney, courtier and Lord Deputy of Ireland. His body was buried in the Sidney Chapel at Penshurst and his heart in Ludlow, where he lived as President of the Council in the Marches of Wales.

1623 – Death of Philip Rosseter, lutenist, composer and theatre manager.

1625 – Burial of James I (VI of Scotland) in the Henry VII Chapel of Westminster Abbey. He had been King of England for twenty-two years, and was known for uniting the crowns of England and Scotland.

6TH MAY

On 6th May 1536, it is said that Anne Boleyn wrote a letter to her husband, King Henry VIII, from the Tower of London. It was headed with the words "To the King from the Lady in the Tower", alleged to have been written by Thomas Cromwell.

In this letter, Anne Boleyn emphasised her innocence and asked the King to "let not any light Fancy, or bad Counsel of mine Enemies, withdraw your Princely Favour from me". She asked for a "lawful trial" and put her present predicament down to the King's affection settling on another, i.e. Jane Seymour. Anne also wrote of how she hoped that God would not call the King to account for his "unprincely and cruel usage of me" at judgement. She concluded the letter by begging mercy for "the Innocent Souls of those poor Gentlemen" who were in the Tower for her "sake" and then signed off "Your most Loyal and ever Faithful Wife, Anne Bullen".

There is controversy between historians over the authenticity of this letter, with many being sceptical because of the tone, handwriting and signature.

1471 – Execution of Edmund Beaufort, styled 3rd Duke of Somerset, in Tewkesbury market place. He had headed Margaret of Anjou's troops at the *Battle of Tewkesbury*, and after their defeat had tried to take sanctuary at Tewkesbury Abbey. Edward IV broke into the abbey and captured him.

1502 – Execution of Sir James Tyrell, former royal councillor, for treason after he had spent time with Edmund de la Pole. He is known for a confession which he was alleged to have made after his arrest, confessing to murdering the Princes in the Tower.

1527 – *The Sack of Rome*. Rome was attacked and looted by mutinous Imperial troops. Pope Clement VII managed to escape, but the majority of the Swiss Guard were killed.

1540 – Death of Juan Luis Vives, scholar, at Bruges. Tudor history lovers know him for being a friend and spiritual adviser to Catherine of Aragon and a tutor to Princess Mary. He wrote a treatise, "Education of a Christian Woman", with Catherine's encouragement, and also wrote *Satellitium animi*, or "Escort of the Soul", a plan of study for Mary.

1541 – Henry VIII issued an injunction ordering "the Byble of the largest and greatest volume, to be had in every churche". The Bible referred to was "The Great Bible" or "Coverdale Bible", the first authorised Bible in English. It had been prepared by Miles Coverdale and was based on the work of William Tyndale.

1563 – Burial of Henry Stafford, 10th Baron Stafford, in Worthen Church near Caus Castle in Shropshire.

7TH MAY

On this day in 1535, John Fisher, former Bishop of Rochester, was visited by Thomas Cromwell, Master Secretary, and member of the King's Council. Cromwell read out the "Act of Supremacy" and Fisher refused to acknowledge the King as the supreme head of the Church, saying "The King owre Soveraign Lord is not supreme hedd yn erthe of the Cherche of Englande."

It is alleged that Richard Rich tricked him into saying those words, telling him that the King wished to know his real opinion in secret, but whatever the truth of the matter, Fisher was found guilty of treason and executed on 22nd July 1535.

1536 – Queen Anne Boleyn's chaplain, William Latymer, was searched by the Mayor and jurates of Sandwich on his arrival back in England. He was returning from a business visit to Flanders, a visit he had undertaken on behalf of the Queen. Latymer had often brought Anne religious books back from the Continent, so it was lucky for him that he did not have anything which could have been deemed as heretical in his luggage. Records were made of the books that he was carrying and of those which he was having sent directly to London, but he was allowed to carry on with his journey.

1540 – Death of Sir William Weston, Prior of the Hospital of St John of Jerusalem in England. He died at the priory on the day that the order to dissolve it was passed through the Commons. He was the uncle of Sir Francis Weston, a man executed in 1536 in the coup against Anne Boleyn.

1547 – Death of John Longland, Bishop of Lincoln, at Wooburn. He had requested that his body be buried at Eton College and his heart in the cathedral church at Lincoln.

1560 – English troops charged the wall of Leith at the siege of Leith. They were unsuccessful and suffered heavy losses.

1567 – Divorce of James Hepburn, 4th Earl of Bothwell, and Jean Gordon. The grounds for divorce were her alleged adultery with her servant, but Bothwell married Mary, Queen of Scots, just eight days later.

1592 – Death of Sir Christopher Wray, judge, Chief Justice of the King's Bench and Speaker of the House of Commons. He was buried at St Michael's Church, Glentworth, Lincolnshire.

1594 – Death of Edmund Scambler, Bishop of Peterborough and Norwich, at Norwich. He was buried in the cathedral, but his tomb was destroyed in the Civil War.

1603 – James VI/I arrived in London after travelling from Edinburgh to claim the English throne. His predecessor, Elizabeth I, had died on 24th March.

8TH MAY

1508 – Birth of Charles Wriothesley, herald and chronicler, in London. His chronicle is one of the major primary sources for Henry VIII's reign. Charles came from a family of heralds; he was the younger son of Sir Thomas Wriothesley, Garter King of Arms, grandson of John Writhe, Garther King of Arms, and nephew of William Wriothesley, York Herald. Charles' offices included Rouge Croix Pursuivant and Windsor Herald of Arms in Ordinary, but he did not go as far as his father and grandfather.

1538 – Death of Edward Fox, Bishop of Hereford and diplomat. He was active in trying to secure the annulment of Henry VIII's marriage to Catherine of Aragon, and produced several books and polemics on Henry's "Great Matter", including *Henricus octavus*.

1539 – The troops mustered between Whitechapel and Mile End marched through the City and Westminster to St James's, where Henry VIII reviewed them. This was in response to the war panic caused by Francis I and Charles V signing the *Peace of Toledo*.

1546 – Death of Thomas Knollys, President of Magdalen College, University of Oxford, from 1528 to 1536. In 1536, Knollys became Vicar of South Kirlby and died there in 1546. He was buried at Wakefield.

1559 – The "Act of Uniformity" was signed by Elizabeth I, and the "Act of Supremacy" was given royal assent. The monarch was Head of the Church again, and still is today.

9TH MAY

On this day in 1509, the body of Henry VII was taken to St Paul's. Here's an account by James Peller Malcolm (1767-1815) in *Londinium redivivum*:-

"On the 9th of May, 1509, the body of Henry VII. was placed in a chariot, covered with black cloth of gold, which was drawn by five spirited horses, whose trappings were of black velvet, adorned with quishions of gold. The effigies of his Majesty lay upon the corpse, dressed in his regal habiliments. The carriage had suspended on it banners of arms, titles, and pedigrees. A number of prelates preceded the body, who were followed by the deceased king's servants; after it were nine mourners. Six hundred men bearing torches surrounded the chariot.

The chariot was met in St George's Fields [he died at Windsor] by all the priests and clergy of London and its neighbourhood; and at London Bridge by the Lord Mayor, aldermen, and common council, in black. To render this awful scene sublimely grand, the way was lined with children, who held burning tapers: those, with the flashes of great torches, whose red rays, darting in every direction upon glittering objects, and embroidered copes, showing the solemn pace, uplifted eyes, and mournful countenances, must have formed a noble picture. The slow, monotonous notes of the chaunt, mixed with the sonorous tones of the great bells, were not less grateful to the ear. When the body had arrived at St Paul's, which was superbly illuminated, it was taken from the chariot and carried to the choir, where it was placed beneath a hearse arrayed with all the accompaniments of death. A solemn mass and dirge were then sung, and a sermon preached by the Bishop of Rochester. It rested all night in the church. On the following day the procession recommenced in the same manner, except that Sir Edward Howard rode before, on a fine charger, clothed with drapery on which was the king's arms.

We will now suppose him removed by six lords from his chariot to the hearse prepared for him, formed by nine pillars, set full of burning tapers, enclosed by a double railing; view him placed under it, and his effigies on a rich pall of gold; close to him the nine mourners; near them knights bearing banners of saints, and surrounded by officers of arms. The prelates, abbot, prior, and convent, and priests, in measured paces, silently taking their places; when, breaking through the awful pause, Garter King-at-Arms cried, with an audible voice, 'Pray for the soul of the noble prince, Henry the Seventh, late king of this realm.' A deep peal from the organ and choir answers in a chaunt of placebo and the dirge; the sounds die away, and with them the whole assembly retires."

1538 – Marie de Guise (Mary of Guise) and James V of Scotland were married by proxy at the Château de Châteaudun, with Robert Maxwell, 5th Lord Maxwell, standing in for James.

1558 – Death of Sir Philip Hoby, diplomat and administrator, at his home in Blackfriars, London. He had risen due to his friendship with Cromwell, and in Edward VI's reign, he was resident ambassador to the Emperor and a Privy Councillor.

1597 – Death of Thomas Hide, religious controversialist and writer of "A Consolatorie Epistle to the Afflicted Catholikes". He fled into exile in Louvain in Elizabeth I's reign after he was labelled as a man who favoured the old religion. He then moved to Douai, where he died in 1597.

1657 – Death of William Bradford, founder of the Plymouth Colony, in Plymouth. He is also known for "Of Plimmoth Plantation", his chronicle of the founding of the colony and its early years.

10TH MAY

On 10th May 1536, Giles Heron, foreman of the Grand Jury of Middlesex and son-in-law of the late Sir Thomas More, announced that the jury had decided that there was sufficient evidence to suggest that Anne Boleyn, George Boleyn, Mark Smeaton, Sir Henry Norris, Sir Francis Weston and Sir William Brereton were guilty of the alleged crimes carried out at Hampton Court Palace and Whitehall, and that they should be indicted and sent to trial before a jury.

The language used in the indictment aimed to shock. Anne Boleyn was described as "seduced by evil", as having malice in her heart, and having "frail and carnal appetites". The indictment also went into detail on the incest charge, accusing Anne of seducing her brother George by "alluring him with her tongue".

Five men were named as committing adultery with the Queen – Sir Henry Norris, Mark Smeaton, Sir Francis Weston, Sir William Brereton and George Boleyn, Lord Rochford – and they were also all accused of conspiring to kill the King. The indictment ended with the words "And thus the said Queen and the other traitors aforesaid have committed their treasons in contempt of the Crown, and of the issue and heirs of the said King and Queen".

Also, on this day in 1536, Sir William Kingston, the Constable of the Tower of London, was ordered "to bring up the bodies of Sir Francis Weston, knt. Henry Noreys, esq. William Bryerton, esq. and Mark Smeton, gent. at Westminster, on Friday next after three weeks of Easter", i.e. on 12th May. This would be the day of their trial.

⁕⁕⁕⁕⁕⁕⁕⁕⁕⁕⁕⁕⁕⁕⁕⁕⁕⁕⁕⁕⁕⁕⁕⁕⁕⁕⁕⁕⁕⁕

1509 – Birth of Edward Stanley, 3rd Earl of Derby and Privy Councillor to Mary I and Elizabeth I. He was born in Lancashire and was the eldest surviving son of Thomas Stanley, 2nd Earl of Derby, and his wife, Anne Hastings.

1533 – Opening of special court at Dunstable by Archbishop Cranmer to rule on the validity of the marriage of Henry VIII and Catherine of Aragon. On 23rd May, Cranmer's court ruled that the marriage between Henry VIII and Catherine of Aragon was against the will of God, and declared that the marriage was null and void.

1552 – Suicide of John Clerk, author and secretary to Thomas Howard, 3rd Duke of Norfolk, in the Tower of London. Clerk hanged himself with his girdle after books about necromancy were found in his possession, and he was interrogated regarding "lewd prophecies and slanders".

1553 – The first expedition of the Company of Merchant Adventurers (Mystery and Company of Merchant Adventurers for the Discovery of Regions, Dominions, Islands, and Places unknown), led by Sir Hugh Willoughby, left London in search of a Northeast passage for Asia.

1554 – Death of Thomas Goodrich, Bishop of Ely and Lord Chancellor during the reign of Edward VI. He died at the palace of Somersham, Huntingdonshire, and was buried in Ely Cathedral. His tomb brass shows him in Protestant episcopal dress and with the Bible and Great Seal in his hands.

11TH MAY

On this day in 1537, two Carthusian monks from the London Charterhouse, Blessed John Rochester and Blessed James Walworth, were hanged in chains from the battlements of York. They had been tried in the city for treason for denying the King's supremacy following the *Pilgrimage of Grace* rebellion.

In all, eighteen Cathusian monks were killed between May 1535 and August 1540, all for denying Henry VIII's supremacy as head of the Church in England. Some were hanged, drawn and quartered, some were hanged in chains and others were starved to death. All eighteen have been recognised by the Catholic Church as martyrs.

They were beatified by Pope Leo XIII in the 19th century.

1509 – Henry VII was laid to rest next to his wife, Elizabeth of York, in Westminster Abbey.

1532 – Henry VIII accused the clergy of being "scarce our subjects", and attacked their oath to the Pope.

1536 – Just as the Grand Jury of Middlesex met at Westminster on 10th May 1536, the Grand Jury of Kent met on 11th May in front of Chief Justice John Baldwin and six of his colleagues at Deptford. They met to rule on the alleged crimes committed at Greenwich Palace, East Greenwich, and Eltham Palace by Queen Anne Boleyn, Sir Henry Norris, Sir William Brereton, Sir Francis Weston, George Boleyn (Lord Rochford) and Mark Smeaton. It was ruled that the Queen and the five men would stand trial.

1560 – Death of Thomas Wendy, physician to Henry VIII and Queen Catherine Parr, at Haslingfield. According to martyrologist John Foxe, Wendy helped to save Catherine Parr from a plot against her. He also attended the dying King in January 1547.

1560 – Burial of John Falconer, physician and botanist, at St Stephen's Church, Coleman Street, London. Falconer. He is known as the first English person to have owned a herbarium.

1598 – Death of Edward Drew, lawyer, member of Parliament and Recorder of London, at Broad Clyst in Devon from gaol fever, which he had picked up working on the Northern Circuit. He was buried in Broad Clyst Parish Church.

1607 – Burial of Sir Edward Dyer, courtier and poet, at St Saviours, Southwark. With Philip Sidney and Fulke Greville, Dyer made up the "happy blessed Trinitie" that Sidney wrote of. His known works included the poems "The Songe in the Oke", "The lowest trees have tops" and "He that his mirth hath lost". He also dabbled in alchemy, studying under John Dee.

1610 – Death of Sir Henry Maynard, administrator. He was buried at St Mary the Virgin in Little Easton, Essex. Maynard served William Cecil, Lord Burghley, as his Chief Secretary and then, after Burghley's death, he became Secretary to Lord Admiral Nottingham.

12TH MAY

On 12th May 1536, Mark Smeaton, Sir Henry Norris, Sir Francis Weston and Sir William Brereton were tried at a special commission of oyer and terminer, just a day after the Grand Jury of Kent had assembled, and only eight days after Weston and Brereton had been arrested. The legal machinery had worked incredibly quickly.

The four men were tried separately from Anne Boleyn and George Boleyn, Lord Rochford, who, as members of the aristocracy, were entitled to be tried in the court of the Lord High Steward of England by a jury of their peers. Sir William Kingston, Constable of the Tower of London, escorted the four men by barge along the Thames, and brought them to the bar of the special commission of oyer and terminer at Westminster Hall, where all four were arraigned for high treason.

The jury was a hostile one, being made up of men who were religious conservatives or who were close to Cromwell, and Tudor defendants were at a distinct disadvantage. Defendants did not have counsel, they were not aware of what evidence was being presented against them, and could not prepare their defence case. All they could do was react to what was said in court, and the onus was on them to prove their innocence, rather than the Crown proving their guilt. There was little chance of justice for men. Eustace Chapuys, the Imperial Ambassador, summed it up when he wrote:

"The others were condemned upon presumption and certain indications, without valid proof or confession."

All four men were found guilty on all charges, declared traitors and sentenced to the usual traitor's death, to be hanged, drawn and quartered at Tyburn.

Also on 12th May 1536, the Duke of Norfolk, uncle of Anne and George Boleyn, was appointed Lord High Steward of England in readiness for ruling, as Lord President, over the trials of his niece and nephew.

◇◇◇◇◇◇◇◇◇◇◇◇◇◇◇◇◇◇◇◇◇◇◇◇◇◇◇◇◇◇◇◇◇◇◇◇◇◇◇

1521 – Cardinal Wolsey announced the papal bull against Martin Luther in a ceremony outside St Paul's. Luther's books were then burned.

1537 – John Hussey, Baron Hussey, was charged with treason, for conspiring against Henry VIII and raising a rebellion against the King in Lincoln during the *Pilgrimage of Grace*. Hussey was executed in Lincoln on 29th June 1537.

1538 – John Forest, a Franciscan friar, refused to recant his allegiance to Rome.

13TH MAY

On this day in 1536, Henry Percy, Earl of Northumberland, wrote to Thomas Cromwell regarding the alleged pre-contract which was said to have existed between himself and Anne Boleyn before she married Henry VIII. Percy had already denied the existence of such a pre-contract when interrogated by the Duke of Norfolk and two archbishops in 1532 by swearing an oath on the Blessed Sacrament. However, Cromwell resurrected the issue in May 1536, and put pressure on Percy to admit to a pre-contract. Percy stuck to his guns and Cromwell had to enlist the help of Archbishop Cranmer to find another way to annul the King's marriage to Anne Boleyn.

◇◇◇◇◇◇◇◇◇◇◇◇◇◇◇◇◇◇◇◇◇◇◇◇◇◇◇◇◇◇◇◇◇◇◇◇◇◇◇

1515 – Official marriage of Mary Tudor, Queen of France, and Charles Brandon, Duke of Suffolk, at Greenwich Palace, following their secret marriage in France.

1536 – Queen Anne Boleyn's royal household at Greenwich was broken up, even though she hadn't been tried yet.

1568 – Mary, Queen of Scots's forces were defeated at the *Battle of Langside*.

1619 – Funeral of Anne (Anne of Denmark), consort of James VI and I. She was buried in Henry VII's Chapel in Westminster Abbey.

14TH MAY

1511 – Death of Walter Fitzsimmons, Archbishop of Dublin and Lord Deputy of Ireland, at Finglas, Dublin. He was buried in the nave of St Patrick's Cathedral.

1523 – Death of Nicholas Vaux, 1st Baron Vaux, courtier and soldier, at the Hospital of the Knights of St John of Jerusalem in Clerkenwell.

1571 – Matthew Stewart, Earl of Lennox and regent to James VI, held the "Creeping Parliament".

1595 – Death of Anne Fiennes (née Sackville), Lady Dacre, at Chelsea. She was buried in the More Chapel, Chelsea, next to her husband, Gregory Fiennes, 10th Baron Dacre.

1629 – Death of Jean Gordon, Countess of Bothwell and Sutherland. She is known for having been married, albeit briefly, to James Hepburn, 4th Earl of Bothwell, who went on to marry Mary, Queen of Scots. In 1573 she married Alexander Gordon, 12th Earl of Sutherland, and after his death she married Alexander Ogilvy of Boyne, the man she had been in love with before she married Bothwell.

1635 – Burial of Helena Gorges (née Snakenborg), Lady Gorges, in Salisbury Cathedral. Helena was married twice, firstly to William Parr, Marquis of Northampton (brother of Catherine Parr), and secondly to Sir Thomas Gorges, courtier.

15TH MAY

On the 15th May 1536, Queen Anne Boleyn was tried in the King's Hall of the Tower of London in front of an estimated 2,000 spectators. A great platform had been erected in the hall so that everybody could see.

As Queen, Anne Boleyn was given the privilege of being tried by a jury of her peers, presided over by her uncle, the Duke of Norfolk as Lord High Steward, rather than by the commission of oyer and terminer who sat in judgement on Norris, Weston, Smeaton and Brereton. In reality, this was no privilege. Her trial had already been prejudiced by the guilty verdicts of the four men, and her jury was made up of her enemies.

The chronicler Charles Wriothesley, recorded that after her indictment was read out, Anne "made so wise and discreet aunsweres to all thinges layde against her, excusing herselfe with her wordes so clearlie, as thoughe she had never bene faultie to the same". The Queen defended herself admirably, denying all of these preposterous charges and admitting only to giving money to Sir Francis Weston, just as she gave money to many young gentlemen at court. Notwithstanding, the jury were unanimous in their verdict: "guilty". The Queen was then stripped of her crown and her titles, all except that of "Queen". With tears running down his cheeks, Anne's uncle, the Duke of Norfolk, pronounced the sentence:

"Because thou hast offended against our sovereign the King's Grace in committing treason against his person, and here attainted of the same, the law of the realm is this, that thou hast deserved death, and thy judgment is tis: that thou shalt be burned here within the Tower of London on the Green, else to have thy head smitten off, as the King's pleasure shall be further known of the same."

The Queen kept her composure. Although she did not argue against the sentence, she said that she "believed there was some other reason for which she was condemned than the cause alleged". Anne Boleyn was then escorted out of the court by her gaoler, Sir William Kingston, with the axe turned against her to show that she had been sentenced to death.

While Anne Boleyn was taken back to her lodgings in the Tower of London, her brother, George Boleyn, Lord Rochford, was taken to the King's Hall to stand before the same jury. All witnesses agree that George put up a good fight in the court room that day. In his Chronicle, Charles Wriothesley recorded that after George pleaded not guilty, "he made answer so prudently and wisely to all articles laid against him, that marvel it was to hear, but never would confess anything, but made himself as clear as though he had never offended" and Lancelot de Carles commented on George's good defence and his eloquence, which de Carles likened to that of Sir Thomas More.

George defended himself so well in court "that several of those present wagered 10 to 1 that he would be acquitted", but he was also rather reckless. Perhaps he realised that there was no hope of justice and thought he had nothing to lose, for when he was handed a note regarding the King's impotence, George recklessly read it aloud even though he had been commanded not to. George had allegedly joked or gossiped about the King's sexual problems, his lack of sexual prowess, and he had also joked about Elizabeth not being the King's daughter. This meant that he had unwittingly committed treason because this kind of talk impugned the King's issue. What was worse was that George had disobeyed instructions and read out this note in court, embarrassing the King and not endearing himself to the jury. Unsurprisingly, George was found guilty and sentenced to a full traitor's death. Like his sister before him, George Boleyn was then taken back to his prison in the Tower to prepare himself for death.

1464 – Execution of Henry Beaufort, 2nd Duke of Somerset, immediately after the *Battle of Hexham*. He was buried in Hexham Abbey.

1537 – Thomas Darcy, 1st Baron Darcy de Darcy, and his cousin, John Hussey, 1st Baron Hussey of Sleaford, were tried for treason at Westminster after being implicated in the *Pilgrimage of Grace*. "Letters and Papers" recorded the verdict as guilty and the sentence was "Judgment as usual in cases of high treason. Execution to be at Tyburn." They were actually beheaded.

1555 – Death of Sir Thomas Bromley, judge. Mary I made him her first Chief Justice of the Queen's Bench, but was unhappy when Nicholas Throckmorton was acquitted in 1554.

1556 – John Knox appeared in Edinburgh to face heresy charges.

1567 – The marriage of Mary, Queen of Scots and James Hepburn, 4th Earl of Bothwell, at Holyrood.

16TH MAY

1511 – Burial of Walter Fitzsimons, Archbishop of Dublin and Lord Deputy of Ireland, in the nave of St Patrick's Cathedral.

1532 – Resignation of Sir Thomas More as Chancellor.

1536 – Archbishop Cranmer visited Queen Anne Boleyn at the Tower of London. It is thought that his visit's purpose was to get Anne to confess to an impediment to her marriage and to consent to him dissolving her marriage to Henry VIII. This would disinherit and bastardise her daughter Elizabeth.

1544 – Death of John Skewys, lawyer and chronicler.

1566 – Death of Patrick Ruthven, 3rd Lord Ruthven, a man who was involved in the murder of David Riccio, Mary, Queen of Scots's private secretary.

1567 – Death of Sir Anthony Browne, judge, at his home Weald Hall, South Weald, Essex. He had served Mary I as Chief Justice of the Common Pleas, but was removed from this office by Elizabeth I and made a Puisne Justice of the same court.

1568 – Mary, Queen of Scots landed at Workington after losing at the *Battle of Langside*.

1576 – Burial of Nicholas Bullingham, Bishop of Lincoln and Worcester. His burial was originally registered at Hartlebury (he died at Hartlebury Castle), but his tomb can now be found in the north aisle of Worcester Cathedral.

1579 – Death of George Freville, judge and 2nd Baron of the Exchequer.

1618 – Death of Dorothy Wadham (née Petre), founder of Wadham College, Oxford. She is buried in St Mary's Church, Ilminster.

1620 – Death of William Adams, navigator, in Hirado, Japan. He is thought to be the first Englishman to have reached Japan (arriving there in 1600) and was the inspiration for the character of John Blackthorne in the famous novel Shōgun.

17TH MAY

On 17th May 1536, Sir Henry Norris, Sir Francis Weston, Mark Smeaton, Sir William Brereton and George Boleyn, Lord Rochford, were led out of the Tower of London to a scaffold which had been erected on Tower Hill. I cannot imagine how they felt as they surveyed the scene and realised that death was closing in on them. Their only comfort was that their sentences had been commuted to beheading, a much more merciful death than being hanged, drawn and quartered.

As the highest in rank, Anne Boleyn's brother, George Boleyn, Lord Rochford, was the first to be executed. This at least spared him the ordeal of watching as his friends and colleagues were killed one by one. Before he knelt at the block, he made a speech, but it is hard to know exactly what he said; there are a few different versions of his final speech. Here is "The Chronicle of Calais" version:

"Christen men, I am borne undar the lawe, and judged undar the lawe, and dye undar the lawe, and the lawe hathe condemned me. Mastars all, I am not come hether for to preche, but for to dye, for I have deserved for to dye yf I had xx. lyves, more shamefully than can be devysed, for I am a wreched synnar, and I have synned shamefully, I have knowne no man so evell, and to reherse my synnes openly it were no pleaswre to you to here them, nor yet for me to reherse them, for God knowethe all; therefore, mastars all, I pray yow take hede by me, and especially my lords and gentlemen of the cowrte, the whiche I have bene amonge, take hede by me, and beware of suche a fall, and I pray to God the Fathar, the Sonne, and the Holy Ghoste, thre persons and one God, that my deathe may be an example unto yow all, and beware, trust not in the vanitie of the worlde, and especially in the flateringe of the cowrte.

And I cry God mercy, and aske all the worlde forgevenes, as willingly as I wowld have forgevenes of God; and yf I have offendyd any man that is not here now, eythar in thowght, worde, or dede, and yf ye here any suche, I pray yow hertely in my behalfe, pray them to forgyve me for God's sake. And yet, my mastars all, I have one thinge for to say to yow, men do comon and saye that I have bene a settar forthe of the worde of God, and one that have favored the Ghospell of Christ; and bycawse I would not that God's word shuld be slaundered by me, I say unto yow all, that yf I had followecl God's worde in dede as I dyd rede it and set it forthe to my power, I had not come to this. I dyd red the Ghospell of Christe, but I dyd not follow it; yf I had, I had bene a lyves man amonge yow: therefore I pray yow, mastars all, for God's sake sticke to the trwthe and folowe it, for one good followere is worthe thre redars, as God knowethe."

George followed convention by acknowledging that he had been condemned by the law and confessing that he was a sinner who deserved death. However, although he started by saying that he was not going to preach a sermon, he spoke what historian Eric Ives describes as "the language of Zion", urging those witnessing his death to "stick to the truth and follow it", and not make the mistakes that he had. George then knelt at the block and was beheaded.

As the next in rank, Sir Henry Norris followed George Boleyn onto the scaffold. George Constantine, Norris's manservant and a witness of these bloody events, recorded that the others confessed, "all but Mr. Norice, who sayed allmost nothinge at all". I do not think that Constantine means that the men confessed to sleeping with the Queen, rather that they had confessed to being sinners, as was usual at executions.

Sir Francis Weston was the third of the men to be executed. Before he knelt at the bloody block, he warned people to learn by his example. He then knelt at the bloodsoaked block and his life was taken.

Sir William Brereton was the fourth man to climb the scaffold. According to "The Spanish Chronicle", he simply said, "I have offended God and the King; pray for me", but other reports have him repeating the phrase "I have deserved to dye if it were a thousande deethes. But the cause wherfore I dye, judge not. But yf ye judge, judge the best." He was then beheaded.

Mark Smeaton was the final man to be executed. How awful it must have been to stand by as the four men died such violent deaths in front of him, knowing that he himself had only minutes to live. He was lucky, however. As a man of lower class he could have ended his life in a much more brutal way by being hanged, drawn and quartered. The axe was preferable. He did not take the opportunity to retract his confession on the scaffold and when Anne Boleyn heard of this she said, "Did he not exonerate me…before he died, of the public infamy he laid on me? Alas! I fear his soul will suffer for it."

Because they were commoners, Sir Henry Norris, Mark Smeaton, Sir William Brereton and Sir Francis Weston were buried in the churchyard of the Chapel of St Peter ad Vincula. George Boleyn's head and body were taken inside the Chapel, however, and interred in the chancel area before the high altar.

Also on 17th May 1536, at Lambeth, Archbishop Thomas Cranmer, in the presence of Sir Thomas Audley, the Duke of Suffolk, the Earl of Oxford and others, declared that the marriage between Henry VIII and Anne Boleyn was null and void. This sentence of "nullity" meant that it was as if the marriage had never happened, and automatically rendered the couple's daughter, Elizabeth, illegitimate.

***

1521 – Execution of Edward Stafford, 3rd Duke of Buckingham, for treason. Stafford was the great-grandson of Thomas of Woodstock, Edward III's youngest son, and his Plantagenet blood made him a threat to Henry VIII. In 1520, he was suspected of treason, and so Henry VIII ordered an investigation. Stafford was summoned to Court in April 1521 and arrested. He was imprisoned in the Tower of London and then tried for treason, with the charges including listening to prophesies of the King's death and plotting to kill the King. He was found guilty by a jury of his peers and executed on Tower Hill.

1575 – Death of Matthew Parker, Archbishop of Canterbury, at Lambeth Palace. Parker had also served Queen Anne Boleyn as chaplain, and was known for his patronage of scholars.

1581 – Death of Sir William Cordell, lawyer and Speaker of the House of Commons, at The Rolls in Chancery Lane. He was buried in Long Melford church.

1601 – Burial of Anthony Bacon in St Olave's, London. Bacon was a spy, providing intelligence for William Cecil, Sir Francis Walsingham and Robert Devereux, 2nd Earl of Essex.

1610 – Death of Gervase Babington, theologian and Bishop of Worcester. He was buried in Worcester Cathedral.

18TH MAY

1497 – Death of Katherine Woodville, wife of Henry Stafford, Duke of Buckingham, then Jasper Tudor, Duke of Bedford, and finally Richard Wingfield, whom she married without royal licence. Katherine was the sister of Elizabeth Woodville, wife of Edward IV. Her eldest son was Edward Stafford, 3rd Duke of Buckingham.

1515 – John Stewart, 2nd Duke of Albany, landed in Dumbarton with French soldiers to obtain the regency of Scotland.

1536 – Anne Boleyn's execution was postponed.

1554 – Execution of William Thomas, scholar and administrator. Thomas was hanged, drawn and quartered at Tyburn for his alleged involvement in *Wyatt's Rebellion*.

1581 – Birth of Mary, Lady Vere (née Tracy), gentlewoman and patron of clergymen.

19TH MAY

At dawn on the 19th May 1536, Anne celebrated the Mass for the last time, receiving the Sacrament from her almoner, John Skip. She then ate breakfast at 7am and waited to hear Sir William Kingston's footsteps outside her door. At 8am, the Constable appeared, informing Anne that the hour of her death was near and that she should get herself ready, but Anne was already prepared.

Dressed in a robe of grey or black damask trimmed with ermine, with a crimson kirtle underneath and an English style gable hood, Anne took her final walk out of the Queen's Lodgings, past the Great Hall, through Cole Harbour Gate, along the western side of the White Tower to the black draped scaffold. Kingston helped her up the scaffold steps and Anne stepped forward to address the crowd which included many people she knew – Thomas Cromwell, Charles Brandon, Duke of Suffolk, Henry Fitzroy, Duke of Richmond (Henry VIII's son), and Thomas Audley, the Lord Chancellor. The crowd fell silent as they gazed at their queen, who one witness described as being "never so beautiful". Anne then gave her final speech:-

"Good Christian people, I have not come here to preach a sermon; I have come here to die. For according to the law and by the law I am judged to die, and therefore I will speak nothing against it. I am come hither to accuse no man, nor to speak of that whereof I am accused and condemned to die, but I pray God save the King and send him long to reign over you, for a gentler nor a more merciful prince was there never, and to me he was ever a good, a gentle, and sovereign lord. And if any person will meddle of my cause, I require them to judge the best. And thus I take my leave of the world and of you all, and I heartily desire you all to pray for me."

She did not protest her innocence and preach to the crowd as her brother had. She simply did what was expected of her. Executions were carefully choreographed, and there was a set format for execution speeches. Anne followed it to the letter. There was no way that she would risk her daughter's safety by defying the King and proclaiming her innocence, Elizabeth's safety and her future relationship with her father, the King, were paramount in Anne's mind as she prepared to meet her Maker.

Her ladies then removed Anne's mantle and Anne lifted off her gable hood and tucked her famous dark locks into a cap to keep it out of the way of the sword. Historian Eric Ives writes of how her only show of fear was the way that she kept looking behind her to check that the executioner was not going to strike the fatal blow too soon. Anne paid the executioner, he asked Anne's forgiveness and then Anne knelt upright in the straw, praying all the while "O Lord have mercy on me, to God I commend my soul. To Jesus Christ I commend my soul; Lord Jesu receive my soul." As Anne prayed, the executioner called out to his assistant to pass him his sword and, as Anne moved her head to follow what the assistant was doing, the executioner came up unnoticed behind her and beheaded her with one stroke of his sword.

As the shocked crowd dispersed, Anne's ladies wrapped her head and body in white cloth and took them to the Chapel of St Peter ad Vincula, where she was placed inside an old elm chest which had once contained bow staves. Anne Boleyn, Queen of England and mother of Elizabeth I, was then buried as a traitor in an unmarked grave.

1527 – Death of Henry Algernon Percy, 5th Earl of Northumberland, at Wressle. He was buried in Beverley Minster.

1536 – Archbishop Thomas Cranmer issued a dispensation for Henry VIII to marry Jane Seymour, because they were fifth cousins.

1536 – Chapuys reported that Jane Seymour received a message from the King that morning telling her that "he would send her news at 3 o'clock of the condemnation of the putain."

1554 – The future Elizabeth I was released from the Tower of London and allowed to go to Woodstock under house-arrest. She had been taken to the Tower on 18th March 1554 after her half-sister, Queen Mary I, ordered her arrest for her alleged involvement in *Wyatt's Rebellion*.

1597 – Death of Richard Rogers, Bishop-Suffragan of Dover.

20TH MAY

On 20th May 1536, Eustace Chapuys, the Imperial Ambassador, wrote to Seigneur de Granvelle informing him of the latest developments in London. He informed him that at 9am on 20th May 1536, just a day after Anne Boleyn's execution, Henry VIII and Jane Seymour were betrothed in the King's lodgings.

Chapuys was no friend of Anne Boleyn, and was hopeful that Jane would help to restore the Lady Mary to the succession, but even he found this betrothal distasteful, commenting that, "everybody begins already to murmur by suspicion, and several affirm that long before the death of the other there was some arrangement which sounds ill in the ears of the people; who will certainly be displeased at what has been told me, if it be true".

He also reported that on hearing news of Anne's execution, Henry VIII had immediately gone by barge to see Jane.

Chapuys' report shows that Henry and Jane's relationship was surrounded by gossip. There had already been pamphlets deriding Jane circulating in London, and now the speed of this new relationship caused ill feeling and sympathy for Anne Boleyn, the fallen queen.

1512 – Alain de Chantrezac wrote to M. D'Aumont from Caen regarding a rumour of an English invasion: "Persistent rumour of invasion from England. One who came thence ten days ago says the men are ready but the ships cannot be so till the end of this month. The King will land at Calais, part of his army in Normandy and the rest at Fontarabie. Their 120 or 140 ships seem few for so large an army. The French victory beyond the Mountains and their distrust of Scotland cool the English somewhat; but the young Councillors, by whom the King is ruled, advise this invasion. English ships (15 or 16) have taken a bark of Dieppe and some fishing boats."

1535 – The imprisoned Bishop John Fisher was made a Cardinal by Pope Paul III. It made no difference to his treatment, as he was executed 22nd June 1535.

1573 – Death of Robert Weston, Lord Chancellor of Ireland, in Dublin. He was buried beneath the altar in St Patrick's Cathedral, Dublin.

1579 – Burning of Matthew Hamont, alleged heretic, in the castle ditch at Norwich. He was considered an Arian.

1598 – Death of John Bullingham, Bishop of Gloucester. He died in Kensington and was buried in Gloucester Cathedral.

1620 – Burial of Mary Honywood (née Waters), "sustainer of protestant martyrs". She died at Marks Hall and was buried at Lenham in Kent.

1935 – Cardinal Fisher and Sir Thomas More were canonised by Pope Pius XI.

21ST MAY

On this day in 1471 Henry VI, King of England and Lord of Ireland, Duke of Aquitaine, died at the Tower of London. The chronicle "The Historie of the arrivall of Edward IV" recorded him dying "of pure displeasure and melancholy", but many believe that he was in fact killed on Edward IV's orders.

1508 – Death of Giles Daubenay, 1ˢᵗ Baron Daubeney, administrator, soldier, and diplomat. He was buried in St Paul's Chapel, Westminster Abbey.

1524 – Death of Thomas Howard, 2ⁿᵈ Duke of Norfolk, courtier, magnate and soldier, and grandfather of Anne Boleyn and Catherine Howard. He was created Duke of Norfolk in 1514 as a reward for his part in the English victory at the *Battle of Flodden*.

1527 – Birth of Philip II of Spain, King of Spain and consort of Mary I, at Valladolid, Spain. He was the son of Charles V, Holy Roman Emperor, and Isabella of Portugal.

1535 – The arrest of William Tyndale, Bible translator and religious reformer, in Antwerp, after he was tricked into leaving the English House owned by Thomas Pontz. He was condemned as a heretic and strangled, then burned in October 1536.

1558 – Death of William Glyn, Bishop of Bangor, at Bangor. He was buried in Bangor Cathedral.

1580 – Death of Sir John Thynne, member of Parliament and builder of Longleat. He was buried at Longbridge Deverill, Wiltshire.

22ND MAY

1490 – Death of Edmund Grey, 1st Earl of Kent.

1537 – Edward Seymour, brother of Jane Seymour, was sworn in as a Privy Councillor.

1538 – The burning of John Forest, Franciscan friar and martyr, at Smithfield for heresy, for his allegiance to Rome.

1539 – Probable birthdate of Edward Seymour, 1st Earl of Hertford and son of Edward Seymour, Duke of Somerset (the Edward mentioned above). Hertford was also the husband of Katherine Grey, sister of Lady Jane Grey.

1570 – Death of John Best, Bishop of Carlisle. He was buried in Carlisle Cathedral.

23RD MAY

On this day in history, 23rd May 1533, Archbishop Thomas Cranmer declared that Henry VIII's marriage to Catherine of Aragon had been annulled:

"My lord of Canterbury gave sentence this day at 11 o'clock in the great cause of matrimony; has declared it to be against the law of God, and has divorced the King from the noble lady Katharine. He has used himself in this matter very honorably, and all who have been sent hither on the King's behalf have acted diligently and towardly. Sentence shall be given for the King's second contract of matrimony before the Feast of Pentecost. The process is partly devised. 23 May."

Convocation had already ruled, in March 1533, that the marriage was contrary to God's laws and that the Pope should never have issued a dispensation for it, but, following his consecration as Archbishop, Cranmer had opened a special trial into the annulment proceedings at Dunstable Priory, Bedfordshire. It was on 23rd May 1533 that this court ruled on the marriage and Cranmer could send notification of the sentence to the King.

1547 – Henry Grey, 3rd Marquis of Dorset (future Duke of Suffolk) and father of Lady Jane Grey, was installed as a Knight of the Garter.

1554 – The future Elizabeth I arrived at Woodstock, where she was put under house arrest. She had been released from the Tower of London on 19th May after being examined regarding *Wyatt's Rebellion*.

1572 – Burial of John Carré, entrepreneur and glass manufacturer, at Alford parish church. According to his biographer, Andrew Spicer, Carré "is credited with the re-establishment of window glass production in England and for introducing the manufacture of cristallo tableware".

1576 – Burial of Francis Barnham, alderman and draper, and husband of Alice Barnham, silkwoman and benefactor, at St Clement Eastcheap.

1591 – Death of John Blitheman, composer of organ and vocal sacred music, and tutor of John Bull. He was buried at the parish church of St Nicholas Olave, London.

24TH MAY

Chronicler Raphael Holinshed recorded that on this day in 1562, a monstrous child was born in Chichester, Sussex:

"The foure and twentith of Maie, a manchild was borne at Chichester in Sussex, the head armes, and legs whereof were like to an anatomic, the breast and bellie monstruous big, from the nauill as it were a long string hanging: about the necke a great collar of flesh and skin growing like the ruffe of a shirt or neckercher, comming vp aboue the eares pleited and folded."

1562, according to Holinshed, was a year of "manic monstrous births" with a mare giving birth to a two-headed foal (with a tail growing between the heads) and a sow giving birth to a piglet with legs "like to the armes of a manchild with armes and fingers" in the March, and in the April a pig giving birth to a piglet with "two bodies, eight feet, and but one head". Apparently, deformed calves and lambs were also born, some with collars of skin which looked like ruffs.

1522 – Birth of John Jewel, Bishop of Salisbury and Apologist of the Church of England, in Berrynarbor, North Devon.

1546 – Letters were sent from Privy Council to Anne Askew (future Protestant martyr) and her estranged husband Thomas Kyme, ordering them to appear in front of the council within fourteen days.

1576 – Birth of Elizabeth Chamberlain, Lady Chamberlain, daughter of Sir George Carey, 2nd Baron Hunsdon (grandson of Mary Boleyn), and Elizabeth Spencer. Elizabeth I was Elizabeth's godmother.

1612 – Death of Robert Cecil, 1st Earl of Salisbury, politician, courtier and Elizabeth I's Secretary of State, at Marlborough, Wiltshire. Cecil was the only surviving son of William Cecil, 1st Baron Burghley.

1616 – Death of Margaret Clifford, Countess of Cumberland, at Brougham Castle, Westmorland. She was buried in Appleby Church.

25 MAY

On this day in 1553, a triple wedding took place at Durham House, the London residence of John Dudley, Duke of Northumberland. Lady Jane Grey married Guildford Dudley, one of the Duke's sons, her sister Lady Katherine Grey married Lord Henry Herbert, son of the Earl of Pembroke, and Guildford's sister, twelve year-old Lady Catherine Dudley, married Lord Henry Hastings.

Historian Leanda de Lisle describes how all three of the young couples were dressed in silver and gold, "fabrics forfeited to the King from the Duke of Somerset in 1551 and, figuratively at least, marked with his blood". King Edward VI was too ill to attend the marriage, and was in fact dying, but it was an "extravagant spectacle" attended by most of the English nobility and celebrated with jousting, feasting and masques.

Although John Dudley is often thought to have masterminded Lady Jane Grey's marriage to his son, Guildford, in order to further his control of the country on the death of Edward VI, Leanda de Lisle points out that the marriage was, according to William Cecil, the brainwave of Elizabeth Brooke, second wife of William Parr, Marquis of Northampton. Christine Hartweg, in her wonderful article "John Dudley the Family Man", writes that Dudley and Henry Grey, Jane's father, were second cousins once removed and "more importantly, they were also good friends, and Henry Grey owed both his place on the Privy Council and his dukedom to John Dudley. Thus, a match between their children was not unlikely or inappropriate."

There does not seem to be anything suspicious or underhanded in this marriage match. We can argue until we're blue in the face about whether this marriage was "a plot to snatch the Crown from its rightful heirs", or an example of "routine actions of dynastic politics", but there is no evidence either way. Nobody was to know on that *May Day* in 1553, that the bride and groom had less than nine months of marriage and life ahead of them.

◇◇◇◇◇◇◇◇◇◇◇◇◇◇◇◇◇◇◇◇◇◇◇◇◇◇◇◇◇◇◇◇◇◇◇◇

1524 – Death of Sir Thomas Lovell, administrator and Speaker of the House of Commons, at Elsings in Enfield.

1537 – Hanging of John Pickering, Dominican friar, at Tyburn. Pickering had been found guilty of treason for his part in the *Pilgrimage of Grace* uprising.

1551 – Croydon (London) and its neighbouring villages experienced a shock from an earthquake.

1554 – Edward Courtenay, Earl of Devon, was moved from the Tower of London to Fotheringhay Castle. He had been implicated in *Wyatt's Rebellion*.

1607 – Funeral of John Rainolds (Reynolds), theologian and President of Corpus Christi College, Oxford. He was buried in the college chapel.

1625 – Death of William Barlow, philosopher and Church of England clergyman. He was buried in the chancel of Easton church, the church where he was rector.

1632 – Death of William Knollys, 1st Earl of Banbury and courtier. He was the son of Sir Francis Knollys and Catherine Carey, and grandson of Mary Boleyn. He was buried at Rotherfield Greys.

26TH MAY

On this day in 1536 the Lady Mary, daughter of Henry VIII, wrote to Thomas Cromwell asking him to intercede with her father on her behalf, now that Anne Boleyn was gone:

"Master Secretary, I would have been a suitor to you before this time to have been a mean for me to the King's Grace to have obtained his Grace's blessing and favor; but I perceived that nobody durst speak for me as long as that woman lived, which is now gone; whom I pray our Lord of His great mercy to forgive." Is now the bolder to write, desiring him for the love of God to be a suitor for her to the King, to have his blessing and leave to write to his Grace. Apologises for her evil writing; "for I have not done so much this two year and more, nor could not have found the means to do it at this time but by my lady Kingston's being here. Hunsdon, 26 May."

1520 – Meeting of Henry VIII and Charles V at Dover Castle.

1537 – Executions of Adam Sedbergh, Cistercian monk and Abbot of Jervaulx, and William Wood, Prior of Bridlington, at Tyburn. They were condemned for treason following the *Pilgrimage of Grace.*

1538 – Death of Sir Anthony Fitzherbert, judge and legal writer. He was buried at Norbury, Derbyshire. He is one of the best-known English legal writers of the sixteenth century.

1583 – Death of Esmé Stuart, 1st Duke of Lennox, only child of John Stuart, fifth Seigneur d'Aubigny, and his wife, Anne de La Queulle.

1596 – Burial of Thomas Bickley, Bishop of Chichester, in Chichester Cathedral.

1604 – Death of Godfrey Goldsborough, Bishop of Gloucester. He was buried in the Cathedral.

1621 – Burial of Barbara Sidney (née Gamage), Countess of Leicester, at Penshurst.

1623 – Death of Francis Anthony, alchemist and physician. He was buried in the church of St Bartholomew-the-Great.

27TH MAY

1492 – Birth of Sir Antonio Guidotti, merchant and diplomat, in Florence, Italy. Guidotti brought together England and France in 1549–50 in negotiations for peace and the restoration of Boulogne to France. His rewards from Edward VI included a knighthood.

1536 – Cardinal Reginald Pole sent Henry VIII a copy of *De Unitate* (*Pro Ecclesiasticae Unitatis Defensione*). In it, he criticised the King's divorce and the trouble it had caused.

1537 – Chronicler Edward Hall recorded that "there was a *Te Deum* sung in St Paul's Cathedral for joy at the queen's [Jane Seymour] quickening of her child".

1541 – Execution of Margaret Pole, suo jure (in her own right) Countess of Salisbury. It is recorded that she was beheaded by "a wretched and blundering youth … who literally hacked her head and shoulders to pieces in the most pitiful manner". She was buried in the Chapel of St Peter ad Vincula.

1560 – Burial of Thomas Wendy, royal physician, at Haslingfield, Cambridgeshire.

1601 – Death of Robert Beale, administrator and diplomat, at his home, Barn Elms, Surrey. He served Elizabeth I as a clerk of the Privy Council and as a special ambassador. He was buried in All Hallows, London Wall.

1614 – Death of Peter Turner, physician and MP, in London. He had attended Sir Walter Ralegh in the Tower of London.

28TH MAY

Following on from the decision of the special court held at Dunstable, and Cramner's declaration that Henry VIII's marriage to Catherine of Aragon was invalid and had been annulled, Cranmer proclaimed the validity of Henry's marriage to Anne Boleyn on this day in 1533.

Henry VIII and Anne Boleyn had already been married four months, long before the annulment, but Henry believed that his marriage to Catherine had never been valid because she was his brother's widow. Convocation and the Dunstable court agreed with him, ruling that the Pope had no authority to issue a dispensation for a marriage which was contrary to God's law.

This proclamation came just the day before Anne Boleyn's coronation pageantry began.

1509 – Death of Edward Courtenay, 1st Earl of Devon. He was buried at Tiverton.

1535 – Birth of Sir Thomas North, translator, in London.

1582 – Executions of Roman Catholic priests Thomas Forde, John Shert and Robert Johnson at Tyburn. They were hanged, drawn and quartered.

1611 – Funeral of Thomas Sutton, founder of the London Charterhouse.

29TH MAY

Queen Anne Boleyn's coronation was a four-day affair, beginning on the 29th May and culminating in the coronation ceremony on the 1st June, Whitsun.

The pageantry began at 1pm on Thursday 29th May when the London livery companies' fifty barges set off from

Billingsgate. These sixty to seventy foot long barges, escorted by small boats, were decorated with banners displaying the arms of the companies, streamers, bunting and cloth of gold. Minstrels entertained the fleet with music, and in front of the Mayor's barge was a "foyst", or wherry, bearing a great dragon which was was "continually moving and casting wildfire". This dragon was surrounded by "terrible monsters" and "wild men" also casting fire and making "hideous noises". What a spectacle!

Then came the Mayor's barge and the bachelors' barge, which was full of musicians playing trumpet and other instruments. The bachelors' barge was hung with cloth of gold and silk, and bore two huge banners displaying the arms of the King and Queen, along with streamers and bells. It also bore the arms of the company of "Haberdashers" and "merchant adventurers", and on the starboard gunwale were thirty-six "scochyons", or metal shields, showing the King and Queen's arms impaled (the King's colours on the right and the Queen's colours on the left). These shields were fastened to hangings of cloth of gold and silver.

Another feature of this river procession was a wherry carrying Anne's falcon badge. This crowned, white falcon stood on a gold tree stump surrounded by white and red roses, and "virgins singing and playing sweetly".

The procession arrived at Greenwich Palace at 3pm to pick up the pregnant Queen and take her to the Tower of London. Anne appeared, dressed in cloth of gold, and boarded her barge. Anne's ladies boarded a second barge and the King's guard boarded the King's barge – the King was not part of the procession. These three barges were joined by the barges of bishops and of courtiers. Noblemen in attendance that day included the Duke of Suffolk, the Marquis of Dorset, the Earls of Arundel, Derby, Rutland, Worcester, Huntingdon, Sussex and Oxford, and Anne's father, Thomas Boleyn, Earl of Wiltshire. By this time, there were "some 120 large craft and 200 small ones" on the Thames.

"Letters and Papers" describes how gun salutes heralded the Queen as she made her way along the Thames and that "when she came over against Wapping mills the Tower 'lousyd their ordinaunce' most triumphantly, shooting four guns at once." Anne landed at Tower Wharf and was greeted by dignitaries lined up across the King's bridge to the Tower's private royal entrance, the Court Gate of the Byward Tower. Among the dignitaries were Sir Edward Walsingham, Lieutenant of the Tower, and Sir William Kingston, Constable of the Tower. When Anne entered the Tower, she was received by her husband, the King, "who laid his hands on both her sides, kissing her with great reverence and a joyful countenance", before leading her to her chamber. The King and Queen then supped together.

1500 – Death of Thomas Rotherham, Archbishop of York, at Cawood Castle, Yorkshire. He was buried in York Minster.

1542 – Death of Sir Thomas Neville, lawyer and Speaker of the House of Commons, county commissioner in Kent, Surrey, Sussex, and Middlesex, and Knight of St John. He was the fifth son of George Neville, 2nd Baron Bergavenny. Neville was buried in Mereworth church in Kent.

1546 – Murder of David Beaton, Cardinal and Archbishop of St Andrews, at the castle in St Andrews. He was killed by a small group of Fife lairds. One motive was their outrage at the recent trial and execution of Protestant preacher George Wishart at St Andrews.

1555 – Birth of George Carew, Earl of Totnes, soldier, administrator and Lord President of Munster. He was a member of James I's Privy Council and his Council of War. He was also a friend of Sir Walter Ralegh, and pleaded unsuccessfully for his life.

1593 – Hanging of religious controversialist John Penry at St Thomas-a-Watering in Surrey. Penry had been found guilty of "publishing scandalous writings against the church" after having been linked to the "Marprelate religious tracts."

1623 – Burial of Francis Anthony, alchemist and physician, in the church of St Bartholomew-the-Great.

30TH MAY

On Tuesday 30th May, just eleven days after the execution of his second wife, Anne Boleyn, Henry VIII married Jane Seymour in the Queen's Closet at York Place (Whitehall), the property renovated by himself and Anne.

The King and Jane Seymour had become betrothed on 20th May, a day after Anne's execution, but did not marry immediately because the speed of their relationship sounded "ill in the ears of his people".

Historian David Starkey believes that Jane was probably kept in seclusion at Chelsea between the betrothal and her wedding day, after which she took her place at the King's side as Queen. Sir John Russell wrote to Lord Lisle about Jane's first appearance as Queen:

"On Friday last [2nd June] the Queen sat abroad as Queen, and was served by her own servants, who were sworn that same day. The King came in his great boat to Greenwich that day with his Privy Chamber, and the Queen and the ladies in the great barge."

Jane was officially proclaimed Queen at Greenwich Palace 4th June 1536, Whitsun.

1472 – Death of Jaquetta de Luxembourg, Duchess of Bedford, Countess Rivers and mother of Elizabeth Woodville. Her resting place is not known.

1525 – Wolsey proclaimed the King's pardon for the rebels involved in the *Amicable Grant Rebellion*.

1533 – *Order of the Bath* ceremony during the celebrations for Anne Boleyn's coronation

1555 – Burnings of Protestant martyrs John Cardmaker (clergyman) and John Warne (upholsterer) at Smithfield

1582 – Executions of Jesuit priest Thomas Cottam at Tyburn. He was hanged, drawn and quartered along with priests William Filbie, Luke Kirby, and Laurence Richardson. He refused the offer of a pardon, as it would have involved him acknowledging Queen Elizabeth I as Supreme Head of the Church.

1593 – Death of Christopher Marlowe, playwright and poet. He was stabbed to death at a house in Deptford Strand, near London, in what has been described as a "tavern brawl". However, he was killed in a private room of a house, not a tavern. Some believe that he was assassinated.

1630 – Death of Emanuel Scrope, Earl of Sunderland. He was buried at Langar in Nottinghamshire. Scrope was married to Philadelphia Carey, granddaughter of Mary Boleyn.

1640 – Death of Sir Peter Paul Rubens, painter, in Antwerp. It is thought that he died of complications caused by gout. He was buried in the family vault at St Jacob's Church, Antwerp.

31ST MAY

On this day in 1443, Lady Margaret Beaufort, Countess of Richmond and Derby, and matriarch of the Tudor dynasty, was born at Bletsoe Castle in Bedfordshire. Margaret was the daughter of Margaret Beauchamp of Bletsoe and John Beaufort, 1st Duke of Somerset, grandson of John of Gaunt, 1st Duke of Lancaster, and his mistress (and eventual wife) Katherine Swynford. Margaret was their only child. Although a 1397 act of Parliament legitimized the children of John of

Gaunt and Katherine Swynford, Henry IV declared that they could never inherit the throne.

Margaret was married four times: c.1450 to John de la Pole, a marriage which was dissolved in 1453 (some say that the marriage never happened and was just a betrothal); 1453 to Edmund Tudor, 1st Earl of Richmond, eldest son of Owen Tudor and Catherine of Valois and half-brother of Henry VI; 1462 to Henry Stafford, son of the 1st Duke of Buckingham; and finally in 1472 to Thomas Stanley, 1st Earl of Derby and the Lord High Constable and King of Mann. Margaret had just one child, Henry VII. She gave birth to him at the age of thirteen, and his father was Edmund Tudor.

Margaret was a powerful lady, and was a key figure in the *Wars of the Roses* between the Houses of York and Lancaster. She actively supported her son Henry Tudor's claim to the throne, and was able to persuade her then husband, Thomas Stanley, and his brother to swap sides and support Henry at the *Battle of Bosworth Field*. Henry defeated Richard III and became Henry VII of England. Margaret and Elizabeth Woodville co-plotted the marriage of Henry, Margaret's son, and Elizabeth of York, Elizabeth Woodville's daughter by Edward IV.

Margaret was the Countess of Richmond and Derby but, after her son's victory at Bosworth, was referred to as "My Lady the King's Mother", and refused to accept a lower status than the queen consort, Elizabeth of York.

She took an active interest in education and established the Lady Margaret's Professorship of Divinity at Cambridge University, refounded and added to God's House, Cambridge, turning it into Christ's College, and her estate founded St John's College, Cambridge. The Queen Elizabeth's School, formally Wimborne Grammar School, came about as a result of her intention to build a free school in Wimborne, Dorset.

Lady Margaret Beaufort died 29th June 1509, aged sixty-six, and was buried at Westminster Abbey in London, in the south aisle of Henry VII's Chapel.

***

1516 – Birth of John Harpsfield, religious writer and Catholic priest. He was born in the parish of St Mary Magdalen, Old Fish Street, London. His brother was Nicholas Harpsfield, later Archdeacon of Canterbury. Nine of his sermons were published in Bonner's 1555 "Homilies", and he was a well known spokesman for Catholicism, even preaching before Philip of Spain.

1529 – Opening of the Legatine Court at Blackfriars, presided over by Cardina Campeggio. This court's purpose was to hear the evidence with regards to Henry VIII's demand for an annulment of his marriage to Catherine of Aragon.

1533 – Anne Boleyn's coronation procession through the streets of London, from the Tower of London to Westminster Abbey.

1545 – Burial of Agnes Howard (née Tilney), dowager Duchess of Norfolk, at Thetford Abbey. She was the widow of Thomas Howard, 2nd Duke of Norfolk.

1578 – Sir Martin Frobisher set sail with his fleet from Harwich, England to Frobisher Bay, Canada. By 31st August, he and his men had mined 1370 tons of ore, which was loaded onto the ships to take back to England. Unfortunately, no gold or other precious metal was found in the ore.

1589 – Death of Sir Walter Mildmay, administrator and founder of Emmanuel College, Cambridge, at his home in Smithfield.

1590 – Birth of Frances Howard, Countess of Somerset, daughter of Thomas Howard, 1st Earl of Suffolk, and his second wife, Katherine Knyvett. Frances was married twice, first to Robert Devereux, 3rd Earl of Essex, and then to Robert Carr,

Viscount Rochester and Earl of Somerset. Her first marriage was annulled because Devereux was unable to consummate the marriage.

1596 – Death of John Lesley, Bishop of Ross, historian and conspirator. He was a supporter of Mary, Queen of Scots and published "A defence of the honour of the right high, mightye and noble Princess Marie, queene of Scotland". a treatise defending Mary against charges that she was involved in Lord Darnley's murder.

1601 – Death of Katherine Brettergh (née Bruen), "exemplar of godly life". Her biographer, Steve Hindle, writes of her deathbed crisis of faith "during which she raged against God's unmercifulness and threw her Bible repeatedly to the floor", and how "Her agonies formed the centrepiece of a polemical account of her embattled life appended to the two sermons preached by William Harrison and William Leigh at her funeral", and which were published. Her crisis, they said, was a struggle between God and Satan for her soul.

1ST JUNE

On the 1st June 1533, Whit Sunday, a pregnant Anne Boleyn was crowned Queen at a ceremony at Westminster Abbey. Anne was dressed in ermine-trimmed purple velvet coronation robes, and had a gold coronet on her head as she joined the procession assembled at Westminster Hall just before 9am. How beautiful she must have looked with her dark hair and purple robes as she walked under the golden canopy of the Cinque Ports!

Eric Ives gives a vivid description of her coronation ceremony in his book "The Life and Death of Anne Boleyn". He writes of how the 700 yard route between the dais of the hall and the abbey high altar was carpeted with cloth of blue ray, and how everyone – monks, Lord Mayor, aldermen, judges, staff of the Royal Chapel, bishops, archbishops and abbots – were in their very finest robes.

As Anne processed behind the sceptre of gold, the dove topped rod of ivory and the Lord Great Chamberlain (the Earl of Oxford) who bore the crown of St Edward, she was followed by the bishops of London and Winchester, ladies and gentlewomen all dressed in scarlet, and her train was carried by the Dowager Duchess of Norfolk. This procession was watched secretly by the King, who hid behind a lattice screen in a special stand. How proud he must have been.

After the procession, Anne rested for a moment on the gold-draped St Edward's Chair, situated on a dais covered in tapestries, before she moved on. Anne then prostrated herself (not an easy thing to do when you're pregnant) before the altar, and Archbishop Thomas Cranmer prayed over her and anointed her before she made her way back to St Edward's Chair, where he crowned her with the crown of St Edward, previously used only for crowning the reigning monarch. Cranmer also handed Anne the sceptre and the rod. She was now the crowned Queen of England.

The *Te Deum* was then sung, and Anne was able to swap the heavy St Edward's crown for a lighter one before she took the sacrament and gave the customary offering at the saint's shrine. The service was now over, and Anne was able to get some fresh air and refreshment before processing back into Westminster Hall, via New Palace Yard with its cisterns running with wine. However, this was not the end of the rituals and celebration for an exhausted Anne. She also had to attend her coronation banquet in Westminster Hall.

At the banquet, Anne sat on the King's marble chair set under a cloth of state. She sat next to Thomas Cranmer, Archbishop of Canterbury, and was attended by the Dowager Countess of Oxford and the Countess of Worcester, who stood beside her, and two gentlewomen at her feet. The Earl of Oxford was High Chamberlain, the Earl of Essex was the Carver, the Earl of Sussex the Sewer, the Earl of Derby the Cupbearer, the Earl of Arundel the Chief Butler and Thomas Wyatt the chief Ewer, on behalf of his father. Between Anne and the Archbishop stood the Earl of Oxford, with his white staff of office. When everyone was seated, the Duke of Suffolk and William Howard entered the hall on horseback to announce the first course, which was being carried by the Knights of the Bath. Suffolk is described by Hall as wearing a jacket and doublet "set with orient perle" and a gown of embroidered crimson velvet, sitting on a horse draped with crimson velvet, embroidered with real gold letters, which reached the ground. "Trumpets and hautbois sounded at each course, and heralds cried 'largesse'." Henry VIII did not join the banquet, but watched the proceedings accompanied by the ambassador of France and Venice, from a special "little closet".

The banquet was followed by wafers and hippocras, then the Queen washed and enjoyed "a voyde of spice and comfettes", after over eighty dishes! After that, the Mayor passed her a gold cup, from which she drank before giving it back to him. Anne then retired to her chambers where she had to go through the formalities of thanking everyone before she could rest. At 6pm it was finally over. It had been a long and exhausting day for her.

~~~~~~

1451 or 1452 – Birth of Giles Daubenay, administrator, soldier, and diplomat. He was influential in Henry VII's reign, and Catherine of Aragon wrote that "he was the man who could do most in private with the king".

1563 – Birth of Robert Cecil, 1ˢᵗ Earl of Salisbury, politician and courtier. Cecil was the son of William Cecil, 1st Baron Burghley, and his second wife, Mildred. It was Cecil who proclaimed the accession of King James I after Elizabeth I's death.

1571 – Execution of Catholic martyr and civil lawyer John Story, at Tyburn.

1573 – Birth of explorer James Rosier in Suffolk. Rosier went on the 1605 voyage to explore the fishing grounds off the Maine coast as "cape merchant, observer, and reporter", and recorded the voyage in a journal.

1579 – Death of Robert Horne, Bishop of Winchester, at Winchester Place, Southwark. He was buried at Winchester.

1583 – Death of George Carew, Dean of Exeter and Dean of the Chapel Royal. He was buried at St Giles-in-the-Fields, London.

1593 – Inquest into the death of Christopher Marlowe after he was stabbed on the 30ᵗʰ May. The coroner ruled that Ingram Frizer had killed Marlowe in self-defence after a fight over a bill.

1598 – Death of Thomas Preston, playwright and Master of Trinity Hall, Cambridge. He was buried in Trinity Hall Chapel. He is best known for his play "Cambises".

1616 – Burial of Sir Thomas Parry, MP and administrator, at Westminster Abbey. His father was the Thomas Parry who was Comptroller and Treasurer of Elizabeth I's household.

2ND JUNE

1535 – Death of Sir Humphrey Coningsby, judge.

1536 – Death of John Stewart (Stuart), 2nd Duke of Albany, at his château of Mirefleur in the Auvergne.

1536 – Jane Seymour's first appearance as Queen.

1537 – Executions of rebels Sir Francis Bigod, George Lumley and Sir Thomas Percy after *Bigod's Rebellion* in the aftermath of the *Pilgrimage of Grace*.

1567 – Death of Shane O'Neill, Irish chieftain. He was killed by the Scots who cut his throat.

1572 – Execution of Thomas Howard, 4th Duke of Norfolk. He was buried in the Chapel of St Peter ad Vincula at the Tower of London.

1581 – Execution of James Douglas, 4th Earl of Morton and former regent of Scotland, for treason. He was executed in Edinburgh, at the cross, by the "maiden", a type of guillotine.

1595 – Death of William Wickham, Bishop of Winchester, at Winchester House, Southwark - either this date or 12th June.

1609 – Burial of Elizabeth Russell (née Cooke), Lady Russell, linguist and courtier. She was buried at Bisham Church. She was the daughter of Sir Anthony Cooke and wife of Sir Thomas Hoby and then, after his death, Lord John Russell.

1626 – Death of Sir Edward Bromley, judge.

1636 – Death of Theophilus Field, Bishop of Hereford. He was buried at Hereford Cathedral.

3RD JUNE

On this day in 1535, the King's former Lord Chancellor, Sir Thomas More, was interrogated in the Tower of London by Thomas Boleyn, Thomas Audley, Thomas Cromwell and the Duke of Suffolk regarding the royal supremacy. They tried to make him give them an answer as to whether the statute of supremacy was lawful:

"The said Sir Thomas likewise, when examined at the Tower, 3 June 27 Hen. VIII., maliciously persevered in refusing to give a direct answer, and, imagining to move sedition and hatred against the King, said to the King's councillors, "The law and statute whereby the King is made Supreme Head as is aforesaid be like a sword with two edges; for if a man say that the same laws be good then it is dangerous to the soul, and if he say contrary to the said statute then it is death to the body. Wherefore I will make thereunto none other answer, because I will not be occasion of the shorting of my life"."

He would not give them a straight answer.

⸺

1535 – Thomas Cromwell, Henry VIII's Vicar-General, ordered all bishops to preach in support of the royal supremacy and to remove all references to the Pope from mass books and other church books.

1536 – Richard Sampson was nominated as Bishop of Chichester by Henry VIII. Sampson had acted as the King's proctor in the annulment proceedings of Henry VIII's marriage to Anne Boleyn in May 1536.

1594 – Death of John Aylmer, Bishop of London, at Fulham Palace. He was buried at St Paul's Cathedral.

4TH JUNE

On this day in history, the 4th June 1550 (some sources say the 5th), Robert Dudley married Amy Robsart at the royal palace of Sheen at Richmond, near London. The marriage was attended by the then king, Edward VI.

Both Amy and Dudley were a few days short of their 18th birthdays when they got married, and the marriage was a love-match, or a "carnal marriage" as William Cecil described it, rather than an arranged union. The couple were sweethearts and very much in love, but it was not to be a happy marriage and events conspired against them.

Just three years after their wedding, Dudley was imprisoned in the Tower of London for his involvement in the brief reign of Lady Jane Grey, the wife of his brother Guildford. Amy was allowed to visit him, but he was imprisoned until October 1554, and when he was released, the couple had nothing to live on and had to depend on handouts from their families. The couple were again parted when Dudley went to fight for King Philip II of Spain, Mary I's husband, in 1557 at the *Battle of St Quentin* in France, but there is no evidence at this point that the couple were anything other than happy. In the summer of 1558, they were looking for a home together in Norfolk, although events soon conspired against them again.

In November 1558, Mary I died and Elizabeth I, Dudley's childhood friend, became Queen of England. Elizabeth soon rewarded Dudley for his friendship and support by making him Master of the Horse. This role required him to be away from Amy at court, and to spend most of his time with the Queen. Just five months later, ambassadors and diplomats were repeating the gossip that the Queen was in love with her favourite, Dudley, and that the couple were planning to marry after Amy's death – Amy had some malady in one of her breasts, probably breast cancer.

Although Amy's health had improved enough for her to visit London in May 1559, she never saw her husband again, and died on Sunday 8th September 1560 at Cumnor Place near Abingdon, her rented accommodation. Her death is rather a mystery. Her body was found at the foot of the stairs when her servants returned from their day out at the Abingdon Fair, and although the coroner ruled that Amy, "being alone in a certain chamber … accidentally fell precipitously down", there were rumours and mutterings that Dudley, and even the queen, had been poisoning Amy and had arranged her death. There is still controversy today over whether it was suicide, murder or an accident.

1534 – Death of Sir Edward Guildford at Leeds Castle. Guildford acted as guardian to John Dudley (future Duke of Northumberland) and held the posts of Marshal of Calais, Constable of Dover Castle and Lord Warden of the Cinque Ports.

1536 – Jane Seymour was proclaimed Queen at Greenwich Palace. Charles Wriothesley, the Tudor chronicler, recorded: "Also the 4th daie of June, being Whitsoundaie, the said Jane Seymor was proclaymed Queene at Greenewych, and went in procession, after the King, with a great traine of ladies followinge after her, and also ofred at masse as Queen, and began her howsehold that daie, dyning in her chamber of presence under the cloath of estate."

1561 – The spire of St Paul's Cathedral caught fire after being struck by lightning. The fire melted the Cathedral's bells and lead from the spire "poured down like lava upon the roof".

1573 – Death of Sir Francis Jobson, administrator, at Monkwick, near Colchester. He was buried in St Giles, Colchester. Jobson was a member of Henry VIII's household, was Master of the Jewel House in 1553, escaped trial for supporting John Dudley in July 1553 and was pardoned by Mary I, and served Elizabeth I as Lieutenant of the Tower of London.

1590 – Baptism of William Cecil, 16th Baron Ros, courtier, ambassador. He was baptised at Newark Castle and was the son of the eldest son of William Cecil, 2nd Earl of Exeter, and Lady Elizabeth Manners.

1597 – Death of Sir Thomas Baskerville, soldier, at Picquency, in Picardy. He had served in the Netherlands under Robert Dudley, Earl of Leicester, and Peregrine Bertie, Baron Willoughby de Eresby, and was knighted in 1588 after the capture of Bergen op Zoom. He was buried in St Paul's Cathedral.

1603 – Death of Christopher Goodman, Church of England clergyman and radical Protestant, at Chester.

1626 – Burial of Thomas Howard, 1st Earl of Suffolk, naval officer and administrator, at Charing Cross, London. He was buried in the Howard vault of Saffron Walden church. He captained the *Golden Lion* in the struggle against the *Spanish Armada* in 1588.

5TH JUNE

1516 – Maria de Salinas married William, 10th Lord Willoughby of Eresby. Maria was a good friend of Catherine of Aragon, and she and William were the parents of Katherine Willoughby, who went on to marry Charles Brandon, Duke of Suffolk.

1536 – Edward Seymour was created Viscount Beauchamp of Hache, Somerset, following the wedding of his sister, Jane Seymour, and Henry VIII.

1539 – Death of Brian Hygdon, Dean of York. Hygdon was close to Wolsey and Cromwell, and served on the King's Council in the North. He was buried in York Minster.

1577 – Death of John Rastell, author, Jesuit and Vice-Rector at Ingolstadt. He died in Ingolstadt.

1588 – Death of Anne de Vere (née Cecil), Countess of Oxford, at Greenwich. She was buried at Westminster Abbey.

Anne was the daughter of William Cecil, 1ˢᵗ Baron Burghley, and his second wife, Mildred. She had been contracted to marry Philip Sidney, but married Edward de Vere, 17ᵗʰ Earl of Oxford in 1571. It was not a successful marriage, and the couple separated after Oxford refused to recognise their daughter, Elizabeth, as his.

1597 – Death of Sir John North, soldier, member of Parliament, Justice of the Peace and traveller. He died in the Low Countries.

1600 – Robert Devereux, 2ⁿᵈ Earl of Essex, was charged with insubordination during his time in Ireland at a special hearing at York House. He was ordered to remain under house arrest.

1604 – Death of Thomas Moffet, physician and naturalist, at Wilton, Wiltshire. He is known for his poem, "The Silkewormes and their Flies", which was "the first Virgilian georgic poem in English", and his work on insects, diet and eating habits.

6TH JUNE

1522 – Grand entry of Charles V, Holy Roman Emperor, into London, accompanied by King Henry VIII. There was pageantry and celebration.

1527 – Probable date for burial of Henry Algernon Percy, 5ᵗʰ Earl of Northumberland, in Beverly Minster.

1549 – An army of rebels assembled at Bodmin, Cornwall, and Mayor Bray convened a town meeting where resolutions were put containing the demands of the rebels who were against the introduction of the new "Book of Common Prayer". This led to the *Prayer Book Rebellion*.

1556 – Birth of Edward la Zouche, 11ᵗʰ Baron Zouche, at Harringworth, Northamptonshire. He was the only son of George la Zouche, 10ᵗʰ Baron Zouche of Harringworth, and his wife, Margaret. Zouche was a landowner, diplomat and member of James I's Privy Council.

1563 – Baptism of Robert Cecil, only son of William Cecil, 1st Baron Burghley, and his wife, Mildred, at St Clement Danes, Strand.

1597 – Death of William Hunnis, musician and conspirator. He was Master of the Children of the Chapel (royal) in Elizabeth I's reign. He was imprisoned in 1556 in the Tower of London after being involved in a plot to rob the treasury, and was released when Elizabeth I became Queen.

1605 – Playwright William Haughton made his will and died in the next couple of days. His plays included "Englishmen for my Money, or, A Woman will Have her Will", "Patient Grissil" and "Grim the Collier of Croydon, or, The Devil and his Dame", and he wrote or co-wrote many more.

1618 – Death of Sir James Lancaster, merchant and Director of the East India Company, in London. He was buried in All Hallows, London Wall.

7TH JUNE

This day in history, the 7th June 1520, was the first day of the historic meeting between Henry VIII and Francis I of France between the English stronghold of Guînes and the French town of Ardres, on a piece of land referred to as the *Field of Cloth of Gold*.

Henry VIII and his queen, Catherine of Aragon, were accompanied by over five thousand people, and although the meeting was supposed to solidify the *Treaty of London* between the two countries, historian David Loades points out that "the omens for success were not good" and that the event was really "an exercise in competitive display".

Here are some details about the Field of Cloth of Gold:-

- The English court was housed in "exotic pavilions".
- The King's chamber was a palace made out of wood and canvas.
- Courtiers were dressed in "velvet, satin and cloth of gold".
- Rich furnishings were used for the state apartments.
- 6,000 men were employed in building the English quarters.
- There were two wine fountains flowing with red wine.
- There was plenty of entertainment – jousts, singing from the French and English choirs, banquets, wrestling and archery displays.
- The tents of the English court featured cloth decorated with gold, fringing of the Tudor livery colours, fleurs-de-lis designs on some of the roofs, some with candelabra and friezes bearing the Royal mottoes and others with Tudor roses and "King's beasts", e.g. lions, greyhounds, dragons etc., on tent poles.

1532 – Birth of Amy Robsart (later Lady Dudley) probably at Stanfield Hall, Norfolk. Amy was the daughter of Sir John Robsart of Syderstone, Norfolk, and his wife, Elizabeth. Amy married Robert Dudley, Elizabeth I's favourite, in 1550.

1536 – A water pageant was held in honour of Jane Seymour, the new queen, on the Thames.

1546 – Henry VIII and Francis I signed the *Treaty of Ardres* (also known as the *Treaty of Camp*).

1592 – Death of Peter Osborne, administrator. He was buried at St Faith's under St Paul's. He held offices in the Exchequer during Edward VI's reign and is thought to have supported Lady Jane Grey. Osborne served Elizabeth I as an ecclesiastical commissioner and various other posts.

1594 – Roderigo Lopez, Elizabeth I's physician, was hanged, drawn and quartered at Tyburn after being accused by Robert

Devereux, Earl of Essex, of conspiring with Spanish emissaries to poison the Queen. Lopez maintained his innocence, and the Queen seemed unsure of his guilt. It is thought that the charges were trumped up.

Trivia: Lopez may have been the inspiration for Shakespeare's character, Shylock, in "The Merchant of Venice".

1599 – Death of Henry Porter, playwright, after being mortally wounded in his left breast by a rapier in an assault carried out by John Day, a fellow writer.

1604 – Death of John Ley, explorer, in London. He was buried in the chancel of St Andrew by the Wardrobe. Ley was the first Englishman to enter the Amazon and one of the first to explore the coast of Guiana.

1618 – Death of Thomas West, 3rd Baron De La Warr, colonial governor (of Virginia), at sea, on his way to Virginia.

8TH JUNE

1476 – Death of George Neville, administrator and Archbishop of York, at Blyth in Nottinghamshire. He was buried in York Minster.

1492 – Death of Elizabeth Woodville at Bermondsey Abbey. Elizabeth was the consort of Edward IV and mother of the Princes in the Tower. She was buried beside her husband in St George's Chapel, Windsor Castle.

1533 – Papal authority in England was denied by Parliament.

1536 – Parliament passed the second Act of Succession removing Henry VIII's daughters, Mary and Elizabeth, from the line of succession.

1536 – Henry Fitzroy, Duke of Richmond, made his last public appearance (at Parliament) before his death.

1590 – Death of Thomas Randolph, Elizabethan diplomat, at his home in St Peter's Hill, London. He was buried at St Peter

Paul's Wharf. Randolph acted as a go-between for Elizabeth I and Mary, Queen of Scots, and also served his Queen in Russia and France. He has been described as the first English "career diplomat".

9TH JUNE

1511 – Death of William Courtenay, 1ˢᵗ Earl of Devon, at Greenwich. He died of pleurisy and was buried at Blackfriars, London, with the honours due an earl, even though he hadn't been officially invested yet. Courtenay was Henry VIII's uncle, having married Katherine, daughter of Edward IV and Elizabeth Woodville.

1563 – (or 10ᵗʰ June) Death of William Paget, 1ˢᵗ Baron Paget, diplomat and administrator, probably at his estate of West Drayton in Middlesex. Paget's career included serving as an ambassador to the French court, being a member of Henry VIII's Privy Council, sitting on the commission which tried the Earl of Surrey and serving on Mary I's Privy Council.

1573 – Death of William Maitland of Lethington, Scottish courtier, politician, reformer and diplomat. He died in prison in Leith, in suspicious circumstances, though it was said to be suicide. Maitland supported the restoration of Mary, Queen of Scots, and was imprisoned as a result.

1583 – Death of Thomas Radcliffe, 3ʳᵈ Earl of Sussex, Lord Lieutenant of Ireland and President of the Council of the North, at Bermondsey. His body was buried at Boreham in Essex, but his innards were buried at the church in Bermondsey.

10TH JUNE

At 3pm on 10th June 1540, Thomas Cromwell, 1st Earl of Essex and Henry VIII's right-hand man, was in the council chamber at Westminster when the door swung open and the Captain of the Guard strode into the room with a royal warrant for Cromwell's arrest on a charge of treason.

The French Ambassador, Charles de Marillac, reported Cromwell's arrest in a letter dated 23rd June:-

"As soon as the Captain of the Guard declared his charge to make him prisoner, Cromwell in a rage cast his bonnet on the ground, saying to the duke of Norfolk and others of the Privy Council assembled there that this was the reward of his services, and that he appealed to their consciences as to whether he was a traitor; but since he was treated thus he renounced all pardon, as he had never thought to have offended, and only asked the King not to make him languish long.

Thereupon some said he was a traitor, others that he should be judged according to the laws he had made, which were so sanguinary that often words spoken inadvertently with good intention had been constituted high treason. The duke of Norfolk having reproached him with some "villennyes" done by him, snatched off the order of St George which he bore on his neck, and the Admiral, to show himself as great an enemy in adversity as he had been thought a friend in prosperity, untied the Garter. Then, by a door which opens upon the water, he was put in a boat and taken to the Tower without the people of this town suspecting it until they saw all the King's archers under Mr. Cheyney at the door of the prisoner's house, where they made an inventory of his goods, which were not of such value as people thought, although too much for a "compaignon de telle estoffe." The money was 7,000l. st., equal to 28,000 crs., and the silver plate, including crosses, chalices, and other spoils of the Church might be as much more. These movables were before night taken to the King's treasury—a sign that they will not be restored."

The Spanish Chronicle also reported the arrest:-

"As usual, they all went to the Parliament at Westminster, and when they came out and were going to the palace to dinner, the wind blew off the Secretary's bonnet, and it fell on the ground. The custom of the country is, when a gentleman loses his bonnet, for all those who are with him to doff theirs, but on this occasion, when Cromwell's bonnet blew off, all the other gentlemen kept theirs on their heads, which being noticed by him, he said, "A high wind indeed must it have been to blow my bonnet off and keep all yours on." They pretended not to hear what he said, and Cromwell took it for a bad omen.

They went to the palace and dined, and all the while they were dining the gentlemen did not converse with the Secretary, as they were wont to do, and as soon as they had finished all the gentlemen went to the Council-chamber. It was the Secretary's habit always after dinner to go close up to a window to hear the petitioners; and when the gentlemen had gone to the Council-chamber, the Secretary remained at his window as usual for about an hour, and then joined the other gentlemen; and finding them all seated, he said, "You were in a great hurry, gentlemen, to get seated." The chair where he was in the habit of sitting was vacant, and the gentlemen made no answer to his remark; but just as he was going to sit down the Duke of Norfolk said, "Cromwell, do not sit there; that is no place for thee. Traitors do not sit amongst gentlemen." He answered, "I am not a traitor;" and with that the captain of the guard came in and took him by the arm, and said, "I arrest you." "What for?" said he. "That you will learn elsewhere" answered the captain. He then asked to see the King, as he wished to speak with him; and he was told that it was not the time now, and was reminded that it was he who passed the law. God's judgment! For he was the first to enact that the King should speak to no one who was accused of treason.

Then the Duke of Norfolk rose and said, "Stop, captain; traitors must not wear the Garter," and he took it off of him; and then six halberdiers took him by a back door to a boat which the captain had waiting, and he was carried to the Tower; and the Council sent a gentleman, who was said to be Knyvett, to go to his (Cromwell's) house, with fifty halberdiers, and take an inventory of everything they might find, and hold it for the King."

It had become clear by early June 1540 that Cromwell was not going to help the King set aside Anne of Cleves and replace her with Catherine Howard because he knew that a break with the Lutheran princes and an alliance with the Howards would lead to a collapse of everything he'd been working for with regards to the Reformation in England. However, it had come to the point where Henry had to choose between Anne and Catherine, and thus between Cromwell and the Catholic Conservatives (Stephen Gardiner and the Duke of Norfolk). Henry chose Catherine and Cromwell had to go.

1464 – Birth of John Islip, Abbot of Westminster, probably at Islip, Oxfordshire. Islip became Abbot of Westminster in 1500, and was the last to hold this office by free choice of the community.

1528 – Birth of Thomas Percy, 7th Earl of Northumberland. Percy was a staunch Catholic, and was involved in the failed *Rising of the North* in Elizabeth I's reign. He fled to Scotland, but was captured and taken to York on 22nd August 1572, where he was beheaded in the Pavement, and his head put on display on Micklegate Bar. His body was buried in St Crux Church.

1537 – Deaths of Blessed Thomas Green and Blessed Walter Pierson, Carthusian monks from London Charterhouse, in Newgate Prison, from starvation. They were two out of nine monks who were purposely starved to death for refusing to accept the royal supremacy. Others were hanged, drawn and quartered.

1584 – Death of Francis, Duke of Anjou and Alençon, a suitor whom Elizabeth I dubbed "Frog", in Paris. It is thought that he died of malaria.

1607 – Death of Sir John Popham, lawyer, judge and Speaker of the House of Commons. He was buried in Wellington, Somerset.

1612 – Funeral of Robert Cecil, 1st Earl of Salisbury, at Hatfield.

11TH JUNE

1456 – Birth of Anne Neville, Queen Consort of Richard III, at Warwick Castle. Anne was the daughter of Richard Neville, 16th Earl of Warwick and 6th Earl of Salisbury, known as the Kingmaker, and his wife, Anne Beauchamp.

1488 – Death of James III of Scotland, at Sauchieburn, or "the field of Stirling". It is not known whether he died in battle or after the battle.

1509 – Marriage of Henry VIII and Catherine of Aragon at Greenwich Palace

1540 – Birth of Barnabe Googe, translator and poet. Googe is known as one of the earliest English pastoral poets.

1544 – Bishops ordered by Henry VIII to ensure that the new litany was "in our native englysshe tonge".

1560 – Death of Marie de Guise (Mary of Guise), former consort of James V and regent of Scotland, at Edinburgh Castle. Her body lay in a lead coffin at the castle, in St Margaret's Chapel, until March 1561 when it was taken back to France. Marie was buried in the convent of St Pierre at Rheims.

1576 – Death of Sir Anthony Cooke, humanist and educator. Cooke educated his daughters to a high standard, teaching them Latin and Greek, and probably also modern languages and Hebrew. He was appointed royal tutor to Edward VI, but it is not known whether he actually tutored the King. It may have been more of a guiding role. He was buried at Romford, and his effigy can be seen at St Edward's Church there.

12TH JUNE

On the 12th June 1540, the newly imprisoned Thomas Cromwell wrote to King Henry VIII from the Tower of London, asking for mercy and pleading his innocence. It is an eloquent and rational letter written by a man in fear of his life:

"Prostrate at your Majesty's feet, I have heard your pleasure by your Controller, viz., that I should write such things as I thought meet concerning my most miserable state. And where I have been accused of treason, I never in all my life thought to displease your Majesty; much less to do or say "that thing which of itself is so high and abominable offence." Your Grace knows my accusers, God forgive them. If it were in my power to make you live for ever, God knows I would; or to make you so rich that you should enrich all men, or so powerful that all the world should obey you. For your Majesty has been most bountiful to me, and more like a father than a master. I ask you mercy where I have offended. Never spoke with the Chancellor of the Augmentations and Frogmerton together at a time; but if I did, I never spoke of any such matter. Your Grace knows what manner of man Throgmerton has ever been towards you and your proceedings. What Master Chancellor has been to me, God and he know best; what I have been to him your Majesty knows. If I had obeyed your often most gracious counsels it would not have been with me as now it is. But I have committed my soul to God, my body and goods to your pleasure. As for the Commonwealth, I have done my best, and no one can justly accuse me of having done wrong wilfully. If I heard of any combinations or offenders against the laws, I have for the most part (though not as I should have done) revealed and caused them to be punished. But I have meddled in so many matters, I cannot answer all.

The Controller showed me that you complained that within these 14 days I had revealed a matter of great secrecy. I remember the matter, but I never revealed it. After your Grace had spoken to me in your chamber of the things you misliked in the Queen, I told you she often desired to speak with me, but I durst not, and you thought I might do much good by going to her and telling her my mind. Lacking opportunity I spoke with her lord Chamberlain, for which I ask your mercy, to induce her to behave pleasantly towards you. I repeated the suggestion, when the lord Chamberlain and others of her council came to me at Westminster for licence for the departure of the strange maidens. This was before your Grace committed the secret matter to me, which I never disclosed to any but my lord Admiral, by your commandment on Sunday last; whom I found equally willing to seek a remedy for your comfort, saying he would spend the best blood in his belly for that object.

Was also accused at his examination of retaining contrary to the laws. Denies that he ever retained any except his household servants, but it was against his will. Was so besought by persons who said they were his friends that he received their children and friends—not as retainers, for their fathers and parents did find them; but if he have offended, desires pardon. Acknowledges himself a miserable sinner towards God and the King, but never wilfully. Desires prosperity for the King and Prince. "Written with the quaking hand and most sorrowful heart of your most sorrowful subject, and most humble servant and prisoner, this Saturday at your [Tower] of London.""

1492 – Burial of Elizabeth Woodville, former consort of Edward IV, next to her husband in St George's Chapel, Windsor Castle.

1511 – Burial of William Courtenay, 1st Earl of Devon, at Blackfriars.

1530 – Catherine of Aragon told Henry VIII to abandon his "wicked" life.

1535 – Richard Rich interviewed Sir Thomas More in the Tower of London. He later reported, at More's trial, that More had denied the royal supremacy during this interview.

1553 – Edward VI's council commanded the judges of the King's Bench to turn Edward's "Devise for the succession" into a legal will.

1567 – Death of Richard Rich, 1st Baron Rich and Lord Chancellor, at Rochford. He was buried at Felstead. Richard Rich was Lord Chancellor in Edward VI's reign and went on to serve in Mary I's Privy Council.

1573 – Birth of Robert Radcliffe, 5th Earl of Sussex, courtier and soldier. He was the son of Henry Radcliffe, 4th Earl of Sussex, and his wife, Honor. Radcliffe served Elizabeth I as an ambassador and as Earl Marshal and Colonel General of her army. He was appointed Lord Lieutenant of Essex by James I in 1603.

13TH JUNE

1535 – Death of George Neville, 3rd Baron Bergavenny, on 13th or 14th June at his home in Sussex. He was buried at Birling. Neville was a member of Henry VII's council and a Garter knight, but his career was adversely affected when his father-in-law, Edward Stafford, 3rd Duke of Buckingham, fell in 1521. Neville was imprisoned for a year in the Tower of

London, and although he was pardoned, he lost his offices and was forced to sell his home, Birling, to the King. He bought back his home in 1530, when he had once again risen in favour.

1574 – Baptism of Richard Barnfield, poet, at the parish church of Norbury, Shropshire. Barnfield published various works in the 1590s, including "The Affectionate Shepheard: Containing 'The Complaint of Daphnis for the Love of Ganymede'".

1587 – Death of actor William Knell in a pub brawl in Thame. A coroner's inquest ruled that actor John Towne had drawn his sword and stuck it through Knell's neck in self-defence.

1592 – Death of Henry Scrope, 9th Baron Scrope of Bolton, soldier and Warden of the West Marches, in Carlisle. He was buried in Carlisle Cathedral.

1595 – Burial of William Wickham, Bishop of Winchester, in Southwark Cathedral.

1596 – Death of Hugh Bellot, Bishop of Bangor and Chester, at Ty Bellot, Denbighshire. His funeral was at Chester Cathedral, but he was buried in the parish church at Wrexham.

14TH JUNE

1557 – William Peto was made cardinal and papal legate, replacing Reginald Pole, Archbishop of Canterbury, as legate. During Henry VIII's Great Matter, Peto had been Catherine of Aragon's Confessor and had preached in support of her, comparing the King to Ahab.

1571 – Death of Sir Christopher Danby, a Yorkshire nobleman and Catholic. During the *Pilgrimage of Grace,* he was with the rebels at Pontefract Castle, but escaped punishment. However, his Catholic beliefs did cause him problems in Elizabeth I's reign, and he was brought before the Council of the North for questioning. Again, he escaped being charged.

1572 – Death of Thomas Warton, 2nd Baron Warton, soldier, Justice of the Peace, member of Parliament and a member of Mary I's Privy Council. He died at home, in Cannon Row, Westminster, and was buried in Westminster Abbey.

1598 – Death of Sir Henry Knyvet, MP and soldier, at Charlton in Wiltshire. He was buried in the church at Charlton in July 1598. Knyvet was a Gentleman Pensioner to Elizabeth I, a Justice of the Peace, Sheriff, Deputy Lieutenant, member of Parliament and soldier. He also wrote "Defence of the Realm."

1612 – Death of Giles Tomson, Bishop of Gloucester, at Windsor Castle. He was buried in Bray Chapel at St George's Chapel, Windsor Castle. He had only been Bishop a year and hadn't even visited his diocese.

15TH JUNE

On 15th June 1536, Henry VIII sent members of his council, led by Thomas Howard, 3rd Duke of Norfolk, to visit his daughter, the Lady Mary, and bully her into accepting her father as supreme head of the Church in England, and acknowledging that she was not the legitimate heir to the throne.

Eustace Chapuys, the Imperial Ambassador and a friend of Mary, recorded the visit of these bullies in a letter to the Emperor:

"To induce her to obey his commands and accede to his wishes, the King sent to her a deputation composed of the duke of Norfolk, the earl of Sussex (Robert Ratcliffe), the bishop of Chester (Roland Lee), and several others, whom she literally confounded by her very wise and prudent answers to their intimation. Upon which, finding that they could not persuade her, one of them said that since she was such an unnatural daughter as to disobey completely the King's injunctions, he could hardly believe (said the interlocutor) that she was the King's own bastard daughter. Were she his or any other man's daughter, he would beat her to death, or strike her head against the wall until he made it as soft as a boiled apple; in short that she was a traitress, and would be punished as such. Many other threats of the same sort did the said deputies utter on the occasion, assisted in their task by the Princess' governess, who happens to be the same as before, having then and there received orders not to allow the Princess to speak a word to any one, and to watch over her so that she should never be left alone by night or day."

It must have been a scary encounter, and it is little wonder that Chapuys, who must have been worried about Mary's health and safety, encouraged her to make the "sacrifice" and submit to her father. Mary finally relented on 22nd June 1536, signing her submission:

"The confession of me, the lady Mary, made upon certain points and articles under written, in the which, as I do now plainly and with all mine heart confess and declare mine inward sentence, belief, and judgment, with a due conformity of obedience to the laws of the realm; so minding for ever to persist and continue in this determination, without change, alteration, or variance, I do most humbly beseech the King's Highness, my father, whom I have obstinately and inobediently offended in the denial of the same heretofore, to forgive mine offences therein, and to take me to his most gracious mercy."

She went on to acknowledge the King as her sovereign and as Supreme Head of the Church of England, to repudiate the authority of the Pope and to acknowledge that her parents' marriage had been "by God's law and man's law incestuous and unlawful".

<hr />

1519 – Date traditionally given for the birth of Henry Fitzroy, 1st Duke of Richmond and Somerset, at the priory of St Lawrence in Blackmore, Essex. Fitzroy was the illegitimate son of King Henry VIII by his mistress, Elizabeth (Bessie Blount). Henry VIII recognised Fitzroy as his son and gave him a double dukedom in June 1525, making his son the highest ranking peer in the country. Unfortunately, Fitzroy died young in July 1536.

1547 – Baptism of Peter Bales, calligrapher, schoolmaster and master of micrography, at St Michael Cornhill in London. His micrographical work included a hand-written Bible which could fit into a walnut shell and a ring, which he presented to Elizabeth I, containing a collection of devotional texts. Bales also wrote the copybook "The Writing Schoolemaster".

1559 – Death of William Somer (Sommers), court fool to Henry VIII, Edward VI and Mary I. Somer had had a narrow escape in July 1535 when Henry VIII threatened to kill him because he praised Catherine of Aragon and Mary, but called Anne Boleyn "ribald" and her daughter, Elizabeth, a "bastard". Somer's last public appearance seems to have been Elizabeth I's coronation in January 1559. Somer was buried at St Leonard, Shoreditch, London.

1567 – *Battle of Carberry Hill*, near Edinburgh, between the Protestant nobles and the army of Mary, Queen of Scots and her husband, the Earl of Bothwell. Mary surrendered and was imprisoned. It was the end of her relationship with Bothwell.

1596 – Death of Richard Fletcher, Bishop of London, at his house in Chelsea. He was buried in St Paul's. Fletcher fell out of favour with Elizabeth I and was temporarily suspended of his episcopal duties in 1595 after his marriage, which Elizabeth had warned against.

16TH JUNE

Tudor scholar, humanist and administrator, Sir John Cheke, was born on 16th June 1514 in Cambridge. He was the son of administrator Peter Cheke and his wife Agnes Duffield. Cheke studied at St John's College, Cambridge, where he excelled at Latin and Greek. He was the first Regius Professor of Greek at Cambridge University and worked as tutor to the young Edward VI, and as Secretary of State for Lady Jane Grey during her short reign.

Cheke was imprisoned in the Tower of London by Mary I for his part in Lady Jane Grey's "usurpation" of the throne, but released just over a year later. Cheke then travelled to the continent, but was arrested between Brussels and Antwerp in spring 1556, along with Sir Peter Carew, and taken back to England, where he was once again imprisoned in the Tower. In fear of being burned at the stake for his Protestant beliefs, he agreed to be received into the Catholic Church and was released from prison in October 1556, after making a public recantation in front of Mary I. Afterwards, he was ashamed of himself and regretted his cowardice. He died just over a year later, on 13th September 1557.

1487 – The *Battle of Stoke Field* between Henry VII's forces and the Yorkist forces of Lord Lovell and John de la Pole, Earl of Lincoln, who had had pretender Lambert Simnel crowned King Edward VI in Dublin on 24th May 1487. Henry VII was victorious, Lincoln was killed and Lovell fled to Scotland. Simnel was spared by Henry VII, who put him to work in his kitchens. Simnel later became a falconer.

1614 – Death of Henry Howard, Earl of Northampton, author, courtier and administrator, at his house in Charing Cross. He died of gangrene after an operation on a tumour on his thigh. Northampton is known for his learning and intelligence, but also for his alleged involvement in the Overbury scandal, the plot that led to the poisoning of Thomas Overbury in the Tower of London. Although it is not known whether Northampton was definitely involved, it was something that affected his posthumous reputation. His niece Frances Howard, Countess of Somerset, and her husband were tried after Northampton's death, and the lawyer for the prosecution claimed that Northampton was involved. Of course, he was not there to defend himself.

17TH JUNE

1497 – The *Battle of Blackheath* (also known as the *Battle of Deptford Bridge*) which ended the *Cornish Rebellion*. Henry VII's forces were triumphant against the Cornish rebels.

1551 – Death of Sir George Blage, courtier, poet and friend of Sir Thomas Wyatt the Elder, at Stanmore, Middlesex. His offices included Chief Steward and Bailiff of Maidstone, and Comptroller of the Petty Custom of London. He was a reformer and was arrested in July 1546 after he was heard denouncing the mass. Blage was condemned to death but, fortunately, was pardoned by Henry VIII.

1567 – Mary, Queen of Scots was imprisoned at Loch Leven Castle after her surrender to the Protestant nobles at the *Battle of Carberry Hill* a couple of days earlier. It was there that she is said to have miscarried twins fathered by the Earl of Bothwell. Mary managed to escape in May 1568.

1601 – Death of Gabriel Goodman, Dean of Westminster and founder of Ruthin School, Ruthin, Denbighshire. He was buried in St Benedict's Chapel, Westminster Abbey.

18TH JUNE

1529 – Catherine of Aragon makes her first appearance at the Legatine Court at Blackfriars.

1546 – Anne Askew was arraigned at London's Guildhall for heresy, along with Nicholas Shaxton, Nicholas White and

John Hadlam (Adlams or Adams). She was sentenced to be burned at the stake.

1558 – Proving of the will of Robert Recorde, Welsh mathematician and physician. His date of death is not known, but is thought to have been mid June 1558. He is known for introducing the "equal to" sign, i.e. "=". He published several mathematical works, including "The Grounde of Artes, teachings the Worke and Practise, of Arithmeticke, both in whole numbers and fractions" in 1543, which was the first book on Algebra published in England, and "The Whetstone of Witte, whiche is the seconde parte of Arithmeteke: containing the extraction of rootes; the cossike practise, with the rule of equation; and the workes of Surde Nombers", in which he introduced the "=" sign.

1588 – Death of Robert Crowley, Protestant printer, author, poet and Church of England clergyman. He was buried in the chancel of St Giles Cripplegate under the same stone as his great friend martyrologist, John Foxe.

1592 – Death of Francis Wyndham, judge, at the Committee House, St Peter Mancroft, Norwich. His trials included the treason trials of John Somerville and William Parry in the 1580s, and his legal knowledge led to him being approached for advice on Mary, Queen of Scots.

1616 – Death of Thomas Bilson, Bishop of Winchester, at Westminster. He was buried at Westminster Abbey.

19TH JUNE

On this day in history, 19th June 1535, Sebastian Newdigate, William Exmew and Humphrey Middlemore, monks of the Carthusian Order of London Charterhouse, were hanged, drawn and quartered at Tyburn. Their crime: refusing to accept King Henry VIII as the Supreme Head of the Church.

In "Letters and Papers", there is a report regarding "The Charter House Moncks":-

"In 1535 eighteen of the Charterhouse were condemned for defending the liberty of the Church. Seven of them, viz., John Houghton, Robt. Lawrence, Austen Webster, Humfrey Middellmore, Wm. Exmeu, Sebastian Newdegate, and Wm. Horne, were drawn on hurdles through the city of London to the open place of execution, and there hanged, quartered, &c. Three of them, Humfrey, William, and Sebastian, had stood in prison upright, chained from their necks to their arms, and their legs fettered with locks and chains for 13 days. Their quarters were hanged on the gates and walls of the city and on the gate of the Charterhouse. Two of the eighteen, John Rochester and James Walwercke, remained hanging. The other nine died in prison with stink and miserably smothered, 'the which were these that follow...'"

The London Charterhouse's Cathusian Order was an order known for its sanctity, so their support for the King's supremacy would have been a real coup for Henry VIII and Thomas Cromwell, but, after praying about the matter for three days, the Order's Prior, John Houghton, stated that he could not take the King to be Supreme Head of the Church. This was a huge blow for the King, and their resistance had to be punished as an example to other orders.

Eighteen Cathusian monks in all were killed between May 1535 and August 1540. Some were hanged, drawn and quartered, some were hanged in chains and others were starved to death. All 18 have been recognised by the Catholic Church as martyrs.

One of the men executed in 1535, Sebastian Newdigate, was a close friend of the King and a former Privy Councillor. Newdigate went as far as signing the "Oath of Succession", in June 1534, but would not accept his friend's supremacy. He was arrested on the 25th May 1535 and taken to Marshalsea Prison, where he spent two weeks chained in an upright position to a pillar before appearing before the King's Council, then being taken to the Tower of London. The King visited him at Marshalsea and at the Tower, trying to convince his friend to accept him as Supreme Head of the Church, but Newdigate refused. He was condemned to death at his trial on 11th June 1535, and was executed eight days later.

These were men of God, known for their austerity and sanctity. Executing them had to be one of the most brutal acts of Henry VIII's reign.

1502 – The *Treaty of Antwerp* was signed between Henry VII and Emperor Maximilian I at Antwerp. Henry VII promised a payment of £10,000 for aid against the Turks in exchange for Maximilian's promise to banish Yorkist rebels from his territories.

1566 – Birth of James VI and I, King of Scotland, England and Ireland, at Edinburgh Castle in Scotland. James was the only son of Mary, Queen of Scots, and Henry Stuart (Stewart), Lord Darnley. James became James VI of Scotland when his mother was forced to abdicate 24th July 1567, and he became James I of England on the death of Elizabeth I, 24th March 1603.

1573 – Execution of Thomas Woodhouse, Jesuit priest and martyr, at Tyburn. He was the first priest to be executed in Elizabeth I's reign. Woodhouse was beatified in December 1886 by Pope Leo XIII.

1616 – Death of Henry Robinson, Bishop of Carlisle, at his home, Rose Castle in Carlisle. He died of the plague. Robinson was buried in Carlisle Cathedral.

20TH JUNE

On the 20th June 1567, a few days after Scottish rebels apprehended Mary, Queen of Scots, servants of James Douglas, 4th Earl of Morton, allegedly found a silver casket of eight letters, two marriage contracts (which apparently proved that Mary had agreed to marry Bothwell before his divorce) and twelve sonnets, in the possession of James Hepburn, 4th Earl of Bothwell and third husband of Mary, Queen of Scots.

The eight letters found in the casket were allegedly written by Mary to Bothwell, and one was said to implicate the couple in the murder of Mary's second husband, Henry Stuart, Lord Darnley, who had been murdered in February 1567. Elizabeth I ordered a commission to investigate the matter of Mary's involvement in Darnley's murder and, on 14th December 1568, the letters were produced at the Royal Commission as proof against Mary.

In his excellent book on Mary, Queen of Scots, "My Heart is My Own", historian John Guy explains that the *Casket Letters* were the only evidence that Mary was part of the murder plot. The letters no longer exist, so cannot be examined today, but we still have the transcripts and translations, complete with William Cecil's notes. It is these notes which Guy says give us a "glimpse" into Cecil's thoughts as he read letters that were "dynamite", in that if they were indeed genuine, then "an anointed Queen could justifiably be deposed from her throne, Elizabeth's 'safety' would be guaranteed, and the threat of an international Guise conspiracy ended for ever". However, if they were forgeries, then Mary would have to be released because it could not be proved that she was complicit in Darnley's murder.

The letters consisted of:

- The Sonnets – Said to be proof of Mary's adultery with Bothwell and her passion for him.

- Two marriage contracts – A written promise by Mary to marry Bothwell before his divorce and a contract, thought to be a forgery, of their marriage on 5th April 1567, a month before their actual marriage.

- Letters – Letters 1 and 2, the Glasgow letters, were proof that Mary was Bothwell's lover, and that she was involved in the plot to kill her husband, Lord Darnley. However, they're only proof if they were actually genuine.

The controversy and debate over these letters still continues today. Unfortunately, without the original letters to examine, we will never know the truth about Mary's alleged involvement in the plot to murder Darnley.

※◇◇◇◇◇◇◇◇◇◇◇◇◇◇◇◇◇◇◇◇◇◇◇◇◇◇◇◇◇◇◇◇◇◇◇◇◇◇

1540 – Anne of Cleves complained to her brother's ambassador, Karl Harst, about Henry VIII's attraction to Catherine Howard.

1560 – Death of Francis Hastings, 2nd Earl of Huntingdon, at Ashby-de-la-Zouch. Francis was married to Katherine Pole, daughter of Henry Pole, Baron Montagu, but was fortunate to survive the fall of the Poles in 1538. His son, Henry, was educated with Henry VIII's son, the future Edward VI, who made Hastings a member of his Privy Council in 1550. Hastings and his son were imprisoned in the Tower by Mary I for their support of Lady Jane Grey in 1553, but were pardoned a few months later. He served Edward VI, Mary I and Elizabeth I as Lord Lieutenant of Leicestershire.

1565 – Margaret Douglas was sent to the Tower of London by Elizabeth I after the announcement of the betrothal of Mary, Queen of Scots and Lord Darnley, Margaret's son. She was released after Darnley's murder in February 1567.

1568 – Death of Armagil Waad (Wade), Chief Clerk of the Privy Council and member of Parliament during Edward VI's reign, at Belsize Park, Hampstead. He was buried in Hampstead Church. Waad lost his office and his seat in Parliament in Mary I's reign.

1584 – Hanging of Dermot O'Hurley, Catholic Archbishop of Carshel and martyr, at Hoggen's Green, just outside Dublin. He had been linked with the Roman Inquisition and was tortured by having his feet out in tin boots and then put in front of a fire. He was beatified 27th September 1992.

1585 – Death of Henry Percy, 8th Earl of Northumberland, on the night of the 20th/21st June in the Tower of London. Northumberland had, allegedly, shot himself through the heart, although it was rumoured that he was murdered by Sir Christopher Hatton on the orders of Elizabeth I's government. Northumberland had been imprisoned in the Tower in January 1584 for his Catholic beliefs and his involvement in plots to do with Mary, Queen of Scots. He was laid to rest in the chapel of St Peter ad Vincula at the Tower.

1595 – Burning of Walter Marsh, spy and Protestant martyr, in Rome's Campo dei Fiori. Before he was burned, he had his hands and tongue cut off. He had been accused of spying on Catholics for Elizabeth I, and of committing offences against Catholics.

21ST JUNE

On the 21st June 1529, Henry VIII and his first wife, Catherine of Aragon, appeared in front of Cardinal Wolsey and Cardinal Campeggio at the Legatine Court at Blackfriars.

The purpose of this court was to listen to the testimonies of the King and Queen regarding the validity of their marriage and to rule on the marriage, which Henry VIII wanted annulled so that he could marry Anne Boleyn.

Henry VIII addressed the court speaking of his love for Catherine, but also of his troubled conscience regarding the fact that he had acted contrary to God's law in marrying his brother's widow. Henry, as always, would have been eloquent and persuasive, but it was Catherine who stole the show that day. She sank to her knees in front of her husband and gave the speech of her life:

"Sir, I beseech you for all the love that hath been between us, and for the love of God, let me have justice. Take of me some pity and compassion, for I am a poor woman, and a stranger born out of your dominion. I have here no assured friends, and much less impartial counsel…

Alas! Sir, wherein have I offended you, or what occasion of displeasure have I deserved?…I have been to you a true, humble and obedient wife, ever comfortable to your will and pleasure, that never said or did any thing to the contrary thereof, being always well pleased and contented with all things wherein you had any delight or dalliance, whether it were in little or much. I never grudged in word or countenance, or showed a visage or spark of discontent. I loved all those whom ye loved, only for your sake, whether I had cause or no, and whether they were my friends or enemies. This twenty years or more I have been your true wife and by me ye have had divers children, although it hath pleased God to call them out of this world, which hath been no default in me…

When ye had me at first, I take God to my judge, I was a true maid, without touch of man. And whether it be true or no, I put it to your conscience. If there be any just cause by the law that ye can allege against me either of dishonesty or any other impediment to banish and put me from you, I am well content to depart to my great shame and dishonour. And if there be none, then here, I most lowly beseech you, let me remain in my former estate… Therefore, I most humbly require you, in the way of charity and for the love of God – who is the just judge – to spare me the extremity of this new court, until I may be advised what way and order my friends in Spain will advise me to take. And if ye will not extend to me so much impartial favour, your pleasure then be fulfilled, and to God I commit my cause!"

After her speech, Catherine got up, curtseyed to her husband and walked out of the court, ignoring those who tried to make her return to her seat and saying, "On, on, it makes no matter, for it is no impartial court for me, therefore I will not tarry. Go on."

1494 – Birth of George Cavendish, Cardinal Wolsey's Gentleman Usher. Cavendish wrote a biography of Wolsey, "The Life and Death of Cardinal Wolsey", and a collection of tragic poems, "Metrical Visions". His poetry and biography are widely used by Tudor historians as primary sources.

1509 - Henry VIII travelled from Greenwich to the Tower of London in readiness for his and Catherine of Aragon's coronation procession on 23rd June. He was accompanied by "many a well appareled gentleman", including the Duke of Buckingham who "had a gowne all of goldsmithes work".

1529 – Death of John Skelton, poet, clergyman and former tutor to Henry VIII when he was prince, at Westminster. He was buried in St Margaret's, Westminster. His works included "Garlande of Laurell" and "The Boke of Phyllyp Sparowe".

1553 – Letters patent issued changing Edward VI's heir from his half-sister, Mary, to Lady Jane Grey: The following is taken from "The chronicle of Queen Jane, and of two years of Queen Mary, and especially of the rebellion of Sir Thomas Wyat written by a resident in the Tower", edited by John Gough Nichols:

"Letters Patent for the Limitation of the Crown.

From the transcript of Ralph Starkey in the MS. Harl. 35, f. 364, which is preceded by this title:

"A true coppi of the counterfet wille supposed to be the laste wille and testament of kinge Edwarde the Sixt, forged and published under the Great Scale of Englande by the confederacie of the dukes of Suffolke and Northumberlande, on the behalfe of the Lady Jane, eldest daughter to the said duke of Suffolke, and testefied with the handes of 101 of the cheife of the nobilliti and princepall men of note of this kingdome; dated the 21 day of June an . 1553; " and followed by this memorandum: " This is a true coppie of Edward the Sixte his will, taken out of the originall under the Greate Scale, which sir Robart Cotton delyvered to the kinges majestic the xij th of Apprill 1611, at Roystorne, to be canseled."'"

1596 – Death of Sir John Wingfield, soldier. He was shot in the head after being wounded in the thigh, and being unable to walk, in the attack on Cadiz. He was buried in the Cathedral at Cadiz.

1612 – Death of James Elphinstone, 1st Lord Balmerino, administrator and judge, at Balmerino. Elphinstone was James VI's Secretary of State, but was attainted as a traitor and sentenced to death in 1609 after he tricked the King into signing a letter to the Pope. He escaped death, but was imprisoned until 1609.

22ND JUNE

On this day in history, 22nd June 1535, John Fisher, Bishop of Rochester, was beheaded. He was beatified in 1886 by Pope Leo XIII and then canonised in 1935 by Pope Pius XI. His feast day is celebrated today, the 22nd June, a feast day which he shares with his friend Thomas More. He is seen as a Catholic martyr because he died for his beliefs.

He was one of the many victims of Henry VIII and was executed for treason, for refusing to take the "Oath of Succession" and accept Henry as the Supreme Head of the Church of England. He was arrested on 26th April 1534, and his words to Richard Rich, Cromwell's right hand man, were used as evidence against him. He said "that the King was not, nor could be, by the Law of God, Supreme Head in earth of the Church of England". The Pope tried to save Fisher by making him Cardinal-Priest of San Vitale (a member of the College of Cardinals), but this simply provoked the King. Richard Rex, in his book "Henry VIII", writes of how Henry joked that Fisher would have to wear the Cardinal's red hat on his shoulders, i.e. he would have no head on which to place it.

What is so chilling about the imprisonment and execution of John Fisher is that he was once a good friend of the King, and it was he who at the King's command preached a sermon against Luther at St Paul's Cross on 11th February 1526. His undoing was his support of Catherine of Aragon during the *Great Matter*. He appeared on Catherine's behalf in the Legatine Court and spoke out against the King and the divorce, comparing himself to St John the Baptist, saying that he "regarded it as impossible for him to die more gloriously than in the cause of marriage". Henry could not tolerate opposition, particularly when it came from someone he had once counted as a friend and adviser. He could not and would not forgive Fisher.

John Fisher was kept in the Tower of London from April 1534 until his death in June 1535, and during that time he was denied a priest, and had to rely on friends and servants to bring him food. On 22nd December 1534, Fisher wrote a letter to Thomas Cromwell, and this is how it is recorded in the "Letters and Papers" of Henry VIII's reign:-

"John [Fisher] Bishop of Rochester to [Cromwell].

Does not wish to displease the King. When last before him and the other commissioners he swore to the part concerning the succession for the reason he then gave, but refused to swear to some other parts, because his conscience would not allow him to do so. "I beseech you to be good master unto me in my necessity, for I have neither shirt nor sheet nor yet other clothes that are necessary for me to wear, but that be ragged and rent too shamefully. Notwithstanding, I might easily suffer that if they would keep my body warm. But my diet also God knows how slender it is at many times. And now in mine age my stomach may not away but with a few kind of meats, which if I want I decay forthwith, and fall into coughs and diseases of my body, and cannot keep myself in health." His brother provides for him out of his own purse, to his great hindrance. Beseeches him to pity him, and move the King to take him into favor and release him from this cold and painful imprisonment. Desires to have a priest within the Tower to hear his confession "against this holy time;" and some books to stir his devotion more effectually. Wishes him a merry Christmas. At the Tower, 22 Dec."

This once great man had no bedding or clothes, did not have enough food and was in ill health, and was being denied spiritual guidance from a priest.

His suffering came to an end on the 22nd June 1535, over a year after he was arrested and taken to the Tower. Although he had been condemned to be hanged, drawn and quartered at Tyburn, the King, in his mercy, commuted his sentence to beheading. Henry VIII was worried that the people were comparing the bishop to St John the Baptist, a man who had challenged King Herod's marriage, and he was keen for Fisher to die before the 24th June, the feast day of St John the Baptist. Fisher was beheaded on Tower Hill and his body left on the scaffold for hours before it was thrown into a grave in the nearby church of All Hallows. Fisher's body was eventually buried at the Chapel of St Peter ad Vincula, with his friend Thomas More who died 6th July, but his head was stuck on a pole on London Bridge as an example to the people of London of what happened to traitors.

***

1477 – Birth of Thomas Grey, 2nd Marquis of Dorset, courtier and Constable of Warwick Castle and of Kenilworth Castle. He was the third son and heir of Thomas Grey, first Marquis of Dorset, and his wife, Cicely.

1509 - Henry VIII created twenty-four Knights of the Bath.

1528 – Death of William Carey, courtier, distant cousin of Henry VIII and husband of Mary Boleyn. He died of sweating sickness, leaving behind his wife and two children, Catherine and Henry.

1536 - Henry VIII's eldest daughter, Mary, finally submitted to her father and accepted her father as Supreme Head of the Church in England and the invalidity of her parents' marriage.

1547 – Death of George Lokert (or Lockhart), Dean of Glasgow, logician and theologian. Lokert studied at the University of Paris and was prior of the Collège de Sorbonne.

1557 – Death of Richard Woodman, Protestant martyr. He was burnt at Lewes, in Sussex, with nine other martyrs after he refused to recant.

1599 – Death of Sir William Fitzwilliam, Lord Deputy of Ireland in Elizabeth I's reign, at Milton, Northamptonshire, after a long illness. He was buried at the church of Marham, Norfolk.

23RD JUNE

1556 – Baptism of Thomas Hood, mathematician and physician, at St Leonard Eastcheap. His works included the 1590 "The Use of the Celestial Globe in Plano, Set Foorth in Two Hemispheres", the 1592 "The Use of Both the Globes Celestiall and Terrestriall", the 1596 "Two Mathematicall Instruments, the Crosse-Staffe and the Jacobs Staffe" and the 1598 "The Making and Use of the Geometricall Instrument called a Sector".

1559 – Death of Thomas Dockray (Docwra), ecclesiastical lawyer and Master of the Stationers' Company. He was buried in the church of St Faith's under St Paul's. Dockray acted as a lawyer for the defence at the trial of Stephen Gardiner, Bishop of Winchester.

1576 – Death of Levina Teerlinc, painter and miniaturist, at Stepney. Originally from Bruges, Teerlinc, who was the daughter of Simon Benninck, a master illuminator, travelled to England in the 1540s. Teerlinc was court painter to Edward VI, Mary I and Elizabeth I, and produced many paintings and miniatures.

1586 – Death of Henry Cheke, translator and son of Sir John Cheke. He died in York and was buried in York Minster.

Cheke's works included "A Certayne Tragedie Entituled Freewyl" and his translation of *Tragedia del libero arbitrio.*

1600 – Death of Richard Howland, Bishop of Peterborough, in his palace at Castor. He was buried in Peterborough Cathedral. Howland presided over the burial of Mary, Queen of Scots in 1587.

24TH JUNE

Henry VIII became King on the 21st April 1509, on the death of his father, Henry VII, but he was not crowned until 24th June 1509, thirteen days after his marriage to Catherine of Aragon, daughter of Isabella I of Castile and Ferdinand II of Aragon.

Henry decided that he and his Queen would have a joint coronation, and that this was to be their big event, rather than their wedding, which was a rather low key and private affair at Greenwich Palace. There is no denying that their coronation was a lavish and very public event.

Celebrations began on the on 21st June when Henry rode from Greenwich to the Tower of London to spend the time before his coronation in the Royal Palace there, as was customary for monarchs. There, on the night of 22nd June, various royal favourites were created Knights of the Bath at a special ceremony.

On Saturday 23rd June, the eve of the coronation, Henry and his new queen, Catherine of Aragon, processed through London, from the Tower to Westminster. The procession started at 4pm, and consisted of the Knights of the Bath dressed in splendid blue gowns followed by Edward Stafford, Duke of Buckingham, who had been made Constable of England for the day, was richly dressed and carrying a silver baton to denote his special office, followed by the King.

The Chronicler Edward Hall describes how the streets were hung with tapestries and arras, "and the greate parte, of the South side of Chepe, with clothe of gold, and some parte of

Cornehill also." The young King wore a robe of crimson velvet, trimmed with ermine, a jacket of cloth of gold decorated with diamonds, rubies, emeralds, pearls and other precious stones. His horse was dressed with ermine and cloth-of-gold, and the canopy held over him by the four barons of the Cinque Ports was also made of cloth-of-gold. Following Henry came his master of the horse, Sir Thomas Brandon, brother of Charles Brandon, who led the King's charger, and then came the Queen's procession led by the Queen herself, reclining in a litter covered by a decorative canopy.

Catherine of Aragon wore her auburn hair loose down her back, as was customary at coronations, and Edward Hall describes it as "of a very great length, bewtefull and goodly to behold." She was "richely appareled in Tissues, clothe of Golde, Siluer, Tynsels, And Velvetes Embroudered" with a coronet "set with many riche orient stones." Her litter was borne by two white palfreys "trapped in White clothe of Gold". Behind the Queen, processed a train which included her husband's former wet-nurse, Anne Luke. Giles Tremlett writes that "even the draught harnesses were speckled with ermine and cloth of gold".

At 8am on the 24th June, Henry and Catherine, under canopies carried by the barons of the Cinque Ports, processed behind twenty-eight bishops from the Palace of Westminster to the Abbey for the coronation ceremony. They walked on a carpet of striped cloth which was immediately torn to bits by the excited crowd who wanted a souvenir of that special day.

In the Abbey, the Archbishop of Canterbury, William Warham, presented Henry to his people who acclaimed him by calling out "Vivat, vivat rex!", or "Long Live the King!", four times. When asked if they would "receive, obey and take" Henry as their King, the crowd in the Abbey all cried "Yeh! Yeh!" Henry then swore the nine oaths of kingship before Warham anointed him with holy oils and crowned him. Catherine was then crowned Queen of England, and the royal party processed back to Westminster Hall for a celebration banquet. The banquet was opened by a fanfare of trumpets and special procession of dishes, led by the Duke of Buckingham and the Lord Steward, both on horseback.

The celebrations did not end with the banquet. There was a special tournament that night and then two days of jousting and feasting. It was the end of an era and the beginning of a new one, a new age, the reign of King Henry VIII who was to become one of England's most infamous monarchs. In his "Coronation Ode of King Henry VIII", Thomas More wrote "This day is the end of our slavery, the fount of our liberty; the end of sadness, the beginning of joy... Such a King will wipe the tears from every eye and put joy in the place of our long distress".

1513 – Death of Sir Edmund Carew, administrator and soldier. Carew was killed at Thérouanne in Artois when the town was under siege by English troops. He was there as Master of the Ordnance. He was buried in the church of St Nicholas at Calais two days later.

1532 or 1533 – Birth of Robert Dudley, Earl of Leicester and favourite of Elizabeth I. Dudley was the fifth son of John Dudley, Duke of Northumberland, and his wife, Jane. Dudley served Elizabeth I as Privy Councillor and Governor-General of the Netherlands. There is some controversy over his birthday, with some of his contemporaries believing that he was born on exactly the same day as Elizabeth I (7th September 1533). However, it is now believed that he was born 24th June 1532 or 1533, most likely 1532, making him just over a year older than his Queen and great friend.

1604 – Death of Edward de Vere, 17th Earl of Oxford, courtier and poet. He was buried in the graveyard of the church of St Augustine, Hackney. Oxfordians believe that de Vere was actually the author of Shakespeare's works, and some people go as far as saying that de Vere was the son of Elizabeth I by Thomas Seymour.

25TH JUNE

1503 – Catherine of Aragon was formally betrothed to Prince Henry, the future Henry VIII, and second son of Henry VII. She had been married to Arthur, Prince of Wales, Henry VII's eldest son, but he died in 1501 after only six months of marriage.

1533 – Death of Mary Tudor, Queen of France, the thirty-seven year-old sister of Henry VIII and wife of his friend Charles Brandon, Duke of Suffolk. She died at her home, Westhorpe Hall in Suffolk, and was buried at the local abbey in Bury St Edmunds, Suffolk. When the abbey was dissolved, however, her remains were moved to St Mary's Church, Bury St Edmunds.

1539 – Baptism of courtier Gregory Fiennes, 10th Baron Dacre, the younger son of Thomas Fiennes, 9th Baron Dacre, and Mary, the daughter of George Neville, Baron Bergavenny.

1601 – Death of Peregrine Bertie, 13th Baron Willoughby, Beck and Eresby, at Berwick upon Tweed. He died of a fever. Bertie was the only son of Richard Bertie and Katherine, Duchess of Suffolk, 12th Baroness Willoughby de Eresby and the well known Protestant patron. Bertie was a soldier, nobleman, ambassador, Governor of Berwick upon Tweed and Warden of the East March.

26TH JUNE

On 26th June 1535, a new commission of oyer and terminer was appointed for the county of Middlesex. The commission ordered the Sheriff of Middlesex to gather the Grand Jury on the 28th June at Westminster Hall. This was to try Sir Thomas More who, according to the indictment, had been "traitorously attempting to deprive the King of his title of Supreme Head of the Church". The indictment went on to give details of how, when More was examined by the King's councillors, on 7th May, regarding whether he would accept Henry VIII as supreme head, he "refused to give a direct answer, saying "I will not meddle with any such matters, for I am fully determined to serve God, and to think upon His Passion and my passage out of this world."

When he was examined again on 3rd June, he "maliciously persevered in refusing to give a direct answer, and, imagining to move sedition and hatred against the King, said to the King's councillors, "The law and statute whereby the King is made Supreme Head as is aforesaid be like a sword with two edges; for if a man say that the same laws be good then it is dangerous to the soul, and if he say contrary to the said statute then it is death to the body. Wherefore I will make thereunto none other answer, because I will not be occasion of the shorting of my life"." On 12th June, Richard Rich visited More "and charitably moved him to comply with the Acts", but More allegedly told him that subjects could not be forced by an act of Parliament to recognise the King as Supreme Head:

"...a King can be made by Parliament, and deprived by Parliament; to which Act every subject being at the Parliament may give his assent; but as to the primacy, a subject cannot be bound, because he cannot give his consent to that in Parliament; and although the King is so accepted in England, yet many foreign countries do not affirm the same."

The trial was set for 1st July 1535 with "Sir Thos. Audeley, chancellor; Thos. duke of Norfolk; Charles duke of Suffolk; Hen. earl of Cumberland; Thos. earl of Wiltshire; Geo. earl of Huntingdon; Hen. lord Montague; Geo. lord Rocheford; Andrew lord Windsor; Thos. Crumwell, secretary; Sir Will. Fitzwilliam; Sir Will. Paulet; Sir John Fitzjames; Sir John Baldewyn; Sir Ric. Lister; Sir John Porte; Sir John Spelman; Sir Walter Luke; and Sir Ant. Fitzherbert" all chosen to sit on the special commission of oyer and terminer.

1513 – Burial of Sir Edmund Carew, landowner, administrator and soldier, in the church of St Nicholas, Calais, after he was shot dead during the siege of Thérouanne in Artois.

1568 – Death of Thomas Young, Archbishop of York, at Sheffield. He was buried in York Minster.

1576 – Death of Edward Dering, scholar, Church of England clergyman and controversial evangelical preacher, from tuberculosis at Thobie Priory in Essex. A collection of his works, which included sermons, lectures, prayers and letters, was first published in 1590.

1596 – Burial of Sir John Wingfield in the cathedral at Cadiz, Spain. He was shot in the head in the attack on Cadiz on 21st June. At Wingfield's funeral, "the generalls threw their handkerchiefs wet from their eyes into the grave" (Stow, 775) and the poet John Donne, who was a member of the expedition, composed an epigram as a tribute to Wingfield: "Farther then Wingefield, no man dares to go".

27TH JUNE

1497 – The executions of Thomas Flamank and Michael Joseph (known as Michael an Gof, or Michael the blacksmith), two of the chief commanders of the Cornish rebels, at Tyburn. They were hanged, drawn and quartered. In 1997 the London Cornish Association and the Cornish Gorsedd erected a plaque on the north side of Blackheath common in memory of the two men. It reads:

"In memory of Michael Joseph the Smith and
Thomas Flamank
Leaders of the Cornish who marched to
London. They were defeated here and suffered
execution at Tyburn 27ᵗʰ June 1497.
They shall have a name perpetual and fame
permanent and immortal."

1505 – Prince Henry (future Henry VIII) renounced his betrothal to Catherine of Aragon, his brother's widow, claiming that it had been contracted without his consent. It was the day before his 14ᵗʰ birthday, the day on which the marriage was due to be solemnised.

1578 – Death of William Bradbridge, Bishop of Exeter, in poverty at Newton Ferrers. He was buried on the north side of Exeter Cathedral choir. His poverty was due to the deception of his sub-collector of taxes, Henry Borough, who embezzled taxes rather than paying them to the Exchequer.

28TH JUNE

On this day in history, the 28ᵗʰ June 1491, King Henry VIII was born at Greenwich Palace. He was Henry VII's and Elizabeth of York's third child and second son, the "spare" they needed in reserve in case anything happened to his older brother, Prince Arthur. On 2ⁿᵈ April, Prince Arthur the Prince of Wales died at the age of fifteen, just a few months after his marriage to Catherine of Aragon. Not only did Henry inherit Arthur's position, Prince of Wales, he also inherited his wife.

This second son of Henry VII became King of England on 21ˢᵗ April 1509 and married his brother's widow, Catherine of Aragon, on the 11ᵗʰ June of the same year. He ruled for over thirty-seven years, and today, over five hundred years since his accession to the throne, he is still discussed, debated and is the subject of countless movies, TV shows and documentaries.

1461 – Coronation of Edward IV at Westminster Abbey.

1497 – Execution of Sir James Tuchet, 7th Baron Audley, by beheading at Tower Hill. Like Flamank and Joseph, who were executed the previous day, he was one of the chief commanders of the Cornish rebels in the 1497 *Cornish rebellion*. The three commanders were captured after the rebels were beaten at the *Battle of Blackheath* in London.

1516 – Birth of Charles Blount, 5th Baron Mountjoy, courtier and educational patron. He was born in Tournai to William Blount, 4th Baron Mountjoy, and his third wife, Alice Brown, while his father was governor of Tournai. Mountjoy received an excellent humanist education and was tutored by the likes of Jan van der Cruyce, a friend of Erasmus, and Petrus Vulcanius of Bruges. Scholars such as Erasmus, Juan Luis Vives and John Leland dedicated works to Mountjoy.

1536 – Death of Richard Pace, diplomat, humanist, administrator and Dean of St Paul's, Exeter and Salisbury. He was buried in the church of St Dunstan in Stepney. Pace served Cardinal Wolsey as his Secretary, and was appointed Henry VIII's Personal Secretary in 1516. He was imprisoned for some time in 1528 and 1529 after being critical of the King's desire for an annulment. Pace suffered with ill health from 1522 onwards, which included fits, gastric problems and possible bipolar disorder.

1541 – Execution of Leonard Grey, Viscount Graney and Lord Deputy of Ireland, on Tower Hill. He was executed for treason after being accused of abusing his authority, encouraging attacks on the King's subjects and having Geraldine sympathies.

1557 – Birth of Philip Howard, 13th Earl of Arundel, at Arundel House, the Strand, London. Arundel was the only child of Thomas Howard, 4th Duke of Norfolk, and his first wife, Mary Fitzalan. Howard was married to Anne Dacre, daughter of Thomas Dacre, 4th Lord Dacre of Gilsland, who converted to Catholicism in the 1580s. Her conversion affected her husband, who was imprisoned and fined in 1586 for his faith, among other things. He was tried, attainted and condemned to death in April 1589, but he remained imprisoned in the Tower and died there 15th October 1589, allegedly after being poisoned by his cook.

1558 – Death of Thomas Darcy, 1st Baron Darcy of Chiche, courtier, soldier and administrator, at Wivenhoe. He was buried at St Osyph's Priory. Darcy served as Captain of the Gentlemen Pensioners in the Scottish campaign of 1547, was a member of the Privy Council in 1550 and served as Lord Chamberlain of the Household. He was arrested after he supported Northumberland's bid to put Lady Jane Grey on the throne, but was pardoned in November 1553.

1598 – Death of Abraham Ortelius, map maker, at Antwerp. He was buried in Antwerp's church of St Michael. Ortelius is known as the creator of the first modern atlas, the *Theatrum Orbis Terrarum* (Theatre of the World), which was published in 1570.

1603 – Death of Sampson Erdeswick, Catholic recusant and antiquary, at Sandon in Staffordshire. He was buried in the local church. Erdeswick claimed to be the real author of "The True Use of Armorie", which had been published in 1592 under the name of William Wyrley, his assistant. His "A Survey of Staffordshire" was published after his death.

1621 – Death of Sir Richard Bulkeley, landowner and courtier, at Hen Blas, Beaumaris, Anglesey. He was buried at Beaumaris Church. Bulkeley owned lands in Anglesey and Cheshire.

29TH JUNE

Lady Margaret Beaufort, grandmother of Henry VIII and the matriarch of the Tudor dynasty, died on this day in 1509 at Cheyneygates, the Abbot's house at Westminster.

Henry Parker, Lord Morley, described how she "took her infirmity with eating of a cygnet" at Henry VIII's coronation banquet on 24th June. Her good friend John Fisher, Bishop of Rochester, performed the last rites, and Margaret died as he elevated the host. She was buried in the south aisle of Henry VII's Chapel in Westminster Abbey, and her tomb features an effigy sculpted by Pietro Torrigiano. It shows Margaret dressed in traditional widow's dress, her head resting on two pillows decorated with the Tudor badge, her hands raised in prayer and the Beaufort family crest at her feet. The Latin inscription, written by Erasmus, translates as "Margaret of Richmond, mother of Henry VII, grandmother of Henry VIII, who gave a salary to three monks of this convent and founded a grammar school at Wimborne, and to a preacher throughout England, and to two interpreters of Scripture, one at Oxford, the other at Cambridge, where she likewise founded two colleges, one to Christ, and the other to St John, his disciple. Died A.D.1509, III Kalends of July [29 June]".

1536 – Thomas Boleyn, Earl of Wiltshire, was stripped of his office of Lord Privy Seal. Cromwell succeeded him and was formally appointed 2nd July 1536. Wiltshire had held the office since January 1530.

1537 – Death of Henry Algernon Percy, 6th Earl of Northumberland. He was buried at Hackney parish church, and his will appointed the King as Supervisor and Edward Fox, Bishop of Hereford, and Thomas Cromwell as executors. Percy is known for his romance with Anne Boleyn when he was part of Cardinal Wolsey's household and she was serving Catherine of Aragon. The romance was broken up by Wolsey and Percy's father, and he was forced to marry Mary Talbot. Percy served Henry VIII as Warden of the East and Middle Marches, and was one of the peers appointed to judge George and Anne Boleyn in May 1536. He collapsed after Anne's death sentence was pronounced, and his illness prevented him from taking an active role on the *Pilgrimage of Grace*, which may have been fortunate, since his brothers, Thomas and Ingram, were arrested for their involvement, and Thomas was executed.

1537 – Execution of John Hussey, Baron Hussey and Chief Butler of England, by beheading at Lincoln after he was accused of conspiring with Lord Darcy during the *Pilgrimage of Grace*.

1540 – Bill of attainder passed against Thomas Cromwell for the crimes of corruption, heresy and treason, stripping him of his honours and condemning him to death.

1541 – Hanging of Thomas Fiennes, 9th Baron Dacre, at Tyburn. He was hanged after he and his companions murdered a servant of Nicholas Pelham while poaching on Pelham's estate in April 1541. He was buried in the church of St Selpulchre.

1552 – Birth of Elizabeth Carew (née Spencer), Lady Hunsdon, literary patron, at Althorp, Northamptonshire. Elizabeth was the sixth child of Sir John Spencer of Wormleighton and Althorp, and his wife, Katherine. Elizabeth was married first to Sir George Carey, 2nd Baron Hunsdon and grandson of Mary Boleyn, and then, after his death, to Ralph Eure, 3rd Baron Eure. Edmund Spenser's "The Faerie Queene" was addressed to "the most vertuous, and beautifull Lady, the Lady Carew" and men such as Thomas Churchyard, Thomas Nashe, Abraham Fleming, Thomas Playfere, Henry Lok and John Dowland also dedicated works to her.

1613 – The Globe Theatre burned to the ground after catching fire during a performance of Shakespeare's "Henry VIII". Sparks from a cannon fired during the play ignited the thatched roof.

30TH JUNE

On this day in 1541, Henry VIII and his fifth wife, Catherine Howard, set off on their royal progress to the

North, the aim being to meet Henry's nephew, King James V of Scotland, at York in September and also "to emphasise the extent of his defeat of the Pilgrims [from the Pilgrimage of Grace] and the Percy interest, and to humiliate utterly all but the most clearly loyal elements".

The progress was successful in showing the people of Yorkshire that Henry VIII was their King and their master, but the Scottish King stood Henry up, and it was on this progress that Catherine Howard decided to amuse herself by having secret assignations with a member of her husband's Privy Chamber, Thomas Culpeper. Julia Fox, author of "Jane Boleyn: The Infamous Lady Rochford", writes of how the lovers were able to meet at night in Lincoln, Pontefract and York, and how they were nearly discovered when Anthony Denny arrived at Catherine's room to fetch her to the King but found her door locked – Catherine was otherwise engaged with a certain Master Culpeper.

It was Catherine's alleged infidelity with Culpeper which sealed her fate after the King found out about her colourful past, her escapades with Henry Manox and Francis Dereham at Lambeth. Perhaps the King could have forgiven her past, but he could not forgive her for cuckolding him and making a fool of him. Catherine was executed on 13th February 1542 at the Tower of London.

1537 – Execution of Thomas Darcy, Baron Darcy of Darcy. He was beheaded on Tower Hill after being found guilty of treason for his part in the *Pilgrimage of Grace* and *Bigod's Revolt*.

1559 – Henry II of France suffered a mortal head wound while jousting at the Place Royale at the Hôtel des Tournelles against Gabriel Montgomery, Captain of the King's Scottish Guard. The joust was held to celebrate the *Peace of Cateau-Cambrésis*. The King died 10th July and was succeeded by Francis II.

1567 – Death of Thomas Becon, clergyman, reformer and theologian. Becon acted as chaplain to Edward Seymour, Lord Protector, and Archbishop Thomas Cranmer, and was appointed by Cranmer as one of the six preachers at Canterbury. Becon was imprisoned in the Tower of London from August 1553 to March 1554, during Mary I's reign, due to his religious beliefs, and on release went into exile in Strasbourg, Frankfurt and Marburg. He returned to England on Elizabeth I's accession. Becon wrote many theological works, which, in time, changed from Lutheran to Zwinglian in their theology. It is thought that he was buried somewhere in Canterbury.

1590 – Death of Sir Roger Townshend, member of Parliament and courtier in Elizabeth I's reign, at Stoke Newington in Middlesex. He was buried at St Giles Cripplegate. Townshend began his career serving the Howard family and was knighted by Charles Howard, Baron Howard of Effingham and the Lord Admiral, at sea for his part in defeating the *Spanish Armada* in 1588.

1ST JULY

On this day in 1543, the *Treaties of Greenwich* were signed. In these treaties between England and Scotland, it was agreed that Prince Edward, the future Edward VI, would marry Mary, Queen of Scots. The second treaty said:

"That Prince Edward, eldest son and heir apparent of Henry VIII., now in his sixth year, shall marry Mary queen of Scotland, now in her first year. (2) Upon the consummation of the marriage, if the King is still alive, he shall assign to the said Mary, as dower, lands in England to the annual value of 2,000l.; to be increased upon his death to 4,000l. (3) Until, by force of this treaty, the said Mary is brought into England she shall remain in custody of the barons appointed thereto by the Three Estates of Scotland; and yet, for her better education and care, the King may send, at his expense, an English nobleman or gentleman, with his wife or other lady or ladies and their attendants, not exceeding 20 in all, to reside with her. (4) Within a month after she completes her tenth year she shall be delivered to commissioners of England at the bounds of Berwick, provided that before her departure from Scotland the contract of marriage has been duly made by proxy. (5) Within two months after the date of this treaty shall be delivered into England six noblemen of Scotland, two of whom, at the least, shall be earls or next heirs of earls and the rest barons or their next heirs, as hostages for the observance on the part of Scotland of these three conditions, viz., the first and fourth articles of this treaty and the condition that if any of these hostages die he shall be replaced within two months by another of equal quality; Scotland, however, is to have power to change the hostages every six months for others of equal quality. (6) Scotland shall continue to be called the kingdom of Scotland and retain its ancient laws and liberties. (7) If after the marriage the Prince should die without issue the said Princess shall be at liberty to return into Scotland unmarried and free of impediment. (8) Upon her going into England, James earl of Arran, governor of Scotland, who meanwhile shall receive the fruits of that realm, shall receive an acquittance thereof from the King and Prince Edward, a convenient portion for her honourable entry into England reserved. (9) This treaty to be ratified within two months."

1511 – Birth of Hadrianus Junius (Adriaen de Jonghe), physician, scholar, poet and historian, at Hoorn in the Netherlands. His contemporaries dubbed him as a "second Erasmus" and his works included "Philippeis" (1554), a poem celebrating the marriage of Mary I and Philip II of Spain, and "The Batavia", which was the first history of Holland.

1535 – The trial of Sir Thomas More began. He was tried by a special commission of oyer and terminer, and found guilty under the 1534 Treason Act for "traitorously attempting to deprive the King of his title of Supreme Head of the Church". He was condemned to death, to be executed at Tyburn, though his sentence was commuted to beheading. More was beheaded on 6th July 1535, on Tower Hill.

1536 – Parliament declared that Henry VIII's two daughters, Mary and Elizabeth, were illegitimate. This meant that the King had no legitimate children, just three bastards, so the pressure was now on the King's new wife, his third wife Jane Seymour, to provide a legitimate heir, and preferably a male one.

1555 – Execution of John Bradford, evangelical preacher and martyr, at Smithfield. Bradford was burned at the stake after being condemned as a heretic. He was influenced by his friend, Martin Bucer.

1572 – Death of John Clement, physician, in exile in Louvain. He was buried near the high altar of the cathedral church of St Rumbold. Clement started his career as tutor to Thomas More's children before moving into the service of Cardinal Wolsey, who sent him to be educated at Corpus Christi College, Oxford. He also studied medicine at Louvain and in Italy. On his return to England, he joined More's household and married More's adopted daughter, Margaret Giggs, before becoming a Court Physician. Clement was imprisoned in the Tower of London in 1535, along with More, for refusing to take the "Oath of Supremacy". He was eventually released, and in 1544 became President of the College of Physicians. Clement was forced into exile in the reign of the Protestant Edward VI and Elizabeth I.

1582 – Death of John Harington, courtier, scholar and poet, at Stepney, London. He was buried beside his second wife, Isabell, in the church of St Gregory by Paul, London. Some of his poems can be found in the 1557 "Tottel's Songes and Sonettes". Harington served Henry VIII and Sir Thomas Seymour, and was close enough to Elizabeth I for her to stand as godmother to his son, John, in 1560.

1591 – Execution of Catholic priest and martyr George Beesley in Fleet Street London. He was hanged, drawn and quartered with Montford Scott, another Catholic priest. He was condemned to death by the statute which made being a Catholic missionary priest treason in the reign of Elizabeth I. While he was imprisoned in the Martin Tower at the Tower of London, Beesley carved his name on the wall of his cell, an inscription which can still be seen today.

1614 – Death of Isaac Casaubon, classical scholar and ecclesiastical historian, in Drury Lane, London. He was buried in Westminster Abbey. His first major work was a commentary on the work of Strabo, the Greek geographer.

1622 – Death of William Parker, 13th Baron Morley and the man who discovered the *Gunpowder Plot*. He died in his Essex home at Great Hallingbury.

2ND JULY

On this day in 1489, Archbishop Thomas Cranmer was born in Aslockton, Nottinghamshire, England. He was the son of Thomas Cranmer, and his wife Agnes (nee Hatfield). Cranmer was educated at Jesus College, Cambridge, the college where he was also elected as Fellow. He took holy orders in 1520 and obtained his Doctorate of Divinity in 1526.

From 1527, as a reputable university scholar, Thomas Cranmer was involved in assisting with the proceedings to get Henry VIII's first marriage to Catherine of Aragon annulled, and it was he who suggested to Edward Foxe and Stephen Gardiner, in 1529, that they should canvass the opinions of university theologians throughout Europe, rather than just relying on a legal case in Rome. The King liked the plan and Cranmer was chosen as a member of the team to gather these opinions. Under Edward Foxe, the team at Rome produced the *Collectanea Satis Copiosa* ("The Sufficiently Abundant Collections") and "The Determinations", which supported, both historically and theologically, the idea that Henry VIII as king exercised supreme jurisdiction within his realm.

In 1532, Thomas Cranmer was appointed as ambassador at the court of Charles V, Holy Roman Emperor, and it was in this role that he saw the effects of the *Reformation* in cities like Nuremberg, and met his wife, Marguerite. He was, however, unable to persuade Charles V to support Henry VIII's annulment from Catherine of Aragon, the Emperor's aunt. In the autumn of 1532, while in Italy, Thomas Cranmer received a letter dated 1st October 1532, informing him that he was the new Archbishop of Canterbury, due to the death of William Warham, the former archbishop. Cranmer was ordered home to England to take up his new position, one which had been arranged by Anne Boleyn and her family. Cranmer arrived back in England in January 1533, and was consecrated as Archbishop of Canterbury on 30th

March 1533, after the arrival of papal bulls which were needed for his promotion from priest to Archbishop.

The new archbishop worked closely with his King on the annulment proceedings. Anne Boleyn was already pregnant and the couple had secretly married in January 1533, so the annulment was now considered urgent. On the 10th May 1533, Archbishop Cranmer opened court for the annulment proceedings. Catherine of Aragon did not attend, and the King was represented by Stephen Gardiner. On 23rd May, Cranmer ruled that the marriage between Henry VIII and Catherine of Aragon was against the will of God, and the marriage was declared null and void. Five days later, on 28th May, Cranmer declared the marriage between Henry VIII and Anne Boleyn valid, and on 1st June he crowned Anne Boleyn Queen of England. In September 1533, he had the pleasure of baptising the couple's daughter, Elizabeth, and becoming her godfather. Anne Boleyn fell from power and was executed in May 1536, but Cranmer fortunately survived the fall of his patron and friend.

In the summer of 1536, Archbishop Cranmer's "Ten Articles" were finally published, after much debate between the conservatives and reformers. These "Ten Articles" defined the beliefs of the new Church of England, the Henrician Church, which had been established after the break with Rome. The first five articles explained that the new church recognised only three sacraments, those of baptism, the Eucharist and penance, and the second five articles were concerned with the roles of purgatory, saints, rites and images, and were more conservative in flavour to balance out the reformist first five articles. It was these articles that caused the Northern uprising known as *The Pilgrimage of Grace*.

In 1537, Cranmer headed a team of forty-six divines in writing "The Bishops' Book", or "The Institution of the Christian Man", which aimed to rectify the inadequacies of the earlier "Ten Articles". It set out the religious reforms of Henry VIII and established the new *Ecclesia Anglicana*, the Church of England. The 1539 Act of the "Six Articles" reversed some of the reforms and reaffirmed traditional Catholic doctrine on transubstantiation, the withholding of the communion cup from the laity, clerical celibacy, vows of chastity, permission for private masses and the importance of auricular confession. As a result of this Act, Cranmer was forced to send his wife and children abroad for safety.

In June 1541, Henry VIII left Cranmer, Thomas Audley and Edward Seymour in charge as a council while he went on a royal progress with his fifth wife, Catherine Howard, to the north of England. It was during the King's absence that the council became aware of Catherine's colourful past and possible extramarital affairs. Audley and Seymour chose Cranmer to be the one to tell the King, and Cranmer did so by giving the King a letter during mass. Catherine Howard was executed in February 1542.

Cranmer survived a plot by clergymen in 1543, and the King gave him his full support. When Cranmer was arrested in the November, he was supported by the King, and two of the ringleaders of the plot were sent to prison. Stephen Gardiner's nephew, Germain Gardiner, who had been heavily involved, was executed. In 1544, on 27th May, Cranmer's "Exhortation and Litany" was published, the first officially authorised liturgy in English, which is still part of the "Book of Common Prayer" today.

On the 28th January 1547, Henry VIII died. While he was dying, Archbishop Thomas Cranmer held his hand and gave the King a reformed statement of faith instead of the usual last rites. Cranmer showed his grief for his master, the King, by growing a beard, which was also a symbol of his rejection of the old church and its ideas. Cranmer was one of the executors of Henry VIII's will, and so was an important of the Lord Protector's (Edward Seymour's) administration. In August 1547, each parish was instructed to obtain a copy of "The Homilies", a book of twelve homilies, four of which were written by Cranmer. The 1549 "Act of Uniformity" established "The Book of Common Prayer", which set out the new legal form of worship in England. It was made compulsory in June 1549, which led to the *Prayer Book Rebellion*, a series of revolts in the southwest of England which then spread into the east of England. The rebels called for the rebuilding of abbeys, the restoration of the "Six Articles", the restoration of prayers for souls in purgatory, the policy of only the bread being given to the laity, and the use of Latin for the mass. On 21st July, Cranmer preached a sermon at St Paul's Cathedral, defending the church line and the "Book of Common Prayer".

Although the *Prayer Book of Rebellion* was squashed, it did have a negative effect on the Lord Protector's administration, and in October 1549, despite Cranmer supporting Seymour, John Dudley took over Seymour's role. Cranmer was unaffected by this change in government, and he continued to work with his friend Martin Bucer on the Ordinal, the liturgy for the ordination of priests, which was published in 1550. Cranmer also went on to publish "The Defence of the True and Catholic Doctrine of the Sacrament of the Body and Blood of Christ" in 1550 and in 1552, despite a breach between Cranmer and Dudley caused by the execution of Edward Seymour. Cranmer worked on revising the Prayer Book and canon law, and forming a statement of doctrine. His canon law bill came to nothing, but the 1552 "Act of Uniformity" replaced the "Book of Common Prayer" with a more Protestant "Book of Common Prayer", and "The Forty-Two Articles" were issued on 19th June 1553. However, the "Forty-Two Articles" were never properly authorised, as some bishops opposed them. Cranmer was working on getting bishops to subscribe to them when King Edward VI died and scuppered all of these plans.

On 6th July 1553 Edward VI died, leaving his throne to Lady Jane Grey, whom he had appointed his successor in his "Device for the Succession", which also excluded his half-sisters Mary and Elizabeth as heirs to the throne. Thomas Cranmer had opposed the documents, but reluctantly signed them when Edward had asked him to respect his will. Lady Jane Grey was proclaimed Queen after Edward's death, but her throne was seized by Mary I in mid July. Although John Dudley and other members of council were imprisoned, Cranmer was not, and on 8th August 1553, he performed the Protestant funeral rites as Edward VI was buried in the Henry VII Chapel at Westminster Abbey. While other reformed clergy fled the country, now that the Catholic Mary I was in control, Cranmer chose to stay, but after proclaiming that "all the doctrine and religion, by our said sovereign lord King Edward VI is more pure and according to God's word, than any that hath been used in England these thousand years", he was ordered to stand before the Queen's Council on 14th September in the Star Chamber. He was sent to the Tower of London and eventually executed for heresy on 21st March 1556.

1497 – Death of Sir William Haute, composer and cousin of Elizabeth Woodville. Haute was Sheriff of Kent at various times, as well as a Justice of the Peace and Commissioner. According to his biographer, Peter Fleming, he was also a patron of musicians, and a composer, composing carols and "polyphonic settings of the *Benedicamus domino*".

1536 – Thomas Cromwell formally appointed Lord Privy Seal in Thomas Boleyn's place.

1540 – Henry Fitzalan, the future 12th Earl of Arundel, appointed Deputy of Calais, replacing Arthur Plantagenet, Viscount Lisle.

1557 – Baptism of Philip Howard, 13th Earl of Arundel, son of Thomas Howard, 4th Duke of Norfolk, and his wife Mary (née Fitzalan). He was baptised in the Chapel Royal at Whitehall Palace with Philip of Spain and Nicholas Heath, Archbishop of York, standing as godfathers and Elizabeth Howard, dowager Duchess of Norfolk, standing as godmother.

1594 – Burial of Robert Scarlett (Old Scarlett), sexton at Peterborough Cathedral. A verse accompanying his portrait in the cathedral states that he buried Catherine of Aragon and Mary, Queen of Scots at the cathedral, but it is not known whether this is true.

1610 – Burial of Richard Knolles, historian and translator, at St Mary's Church, Sandwich. His works include "The Generall Historie of the Turkes" (1603), The "Six Bookes of a Commonweale" (1606), which was a translation of Jean Bodin's "La république", and a translation of Camden's "Britannia", which was not published.

3RD JULY

On this day in 1533, William Blount, 4th Baron Mountjoy, Catherine of Aragon's Chamberlain, was ordered to inform Catherine again that she must recognise her new title of "Princess Dowager" and not use the title of "Queen". Catherine refused, and whenever she saw her new title written in letters, she crossed it out with a pen.

Mountjoy reported back:

"To the effect that on Thursday, 3 July, they found her lying on a pallet, as she had pricked her foot with a pin, and could not stand, and was also sore annoyed with a cough. On our declaring that our instructions were to her as Princess Dowager, she took exception to the name, persisting that she was the King's true wife, and her children were legitimate, which she would claim to be true during her life. To our assertion that the marriage with Anne Boleyn had been adjudged lawful by the universities, the Lords and Commons, she said the King might do in his realm by his royal power what he would; that the cause was not theirs but the Pope's to judge, as she had already answered the duke of Norfolk. To other arguments, that she might damage her daughter and servants, she replied she would not damn her own soul on any consideration, or for any promises the King might make her. She did not defend her cause upon obstinacy, nor to create any dissension in the realm, but to save her own rights; and as for the withdrawing of the King's affection from her, she would daily pray for the preservation of his estate; but as she sues by his licence, she trusts in so doing to lose no part of his favor. In fine, she will not abandon the title till such time as a sentence is given to the contrary by the Pope. She asked for a copy of these instructions, which she would translate into Spanish, and send to Rome. [The expression "Princess Dowager" in the first clause is obliterated by Katharine herself.]"

1495 – The pretender Perkin Warbeck landed at Deal in Kent with men and ships. Around 150 of his men were killed and over 160 captured by Henry VII's troops. Warbeck escaped, fleeing to Ireland. Warbeck claimed to be Richard, Duke of York, the younger of the Princes in the Tower.

1541 – Death of Girolamo Ghinucci, Italian Papal administrator, Bishop of Worcester, Papal Nuncio and ambassador. He died in Rome and was buried in the church of San Clemente.

1557 – Mary I bid farewell to her husband, Philip of Spain, at Dover as he set off for war with France.

1579 – Death of Sir Edward Fitton, administrator and Vice-Treasurer for Elizabeth I in Ireland. His death was recorded as being 'from the disease of the country', which he had apparently caught on an expedition to Longford. He was buried in St Patrick's Cathedral, Dublin, beside his wife, Anne.

1594 (3rd or 4th) – Executions of Catholic priest John Cornelius, Thomas Bosgrave (a relation of Sir John Arundell) and two servants of the Arundell family at Dorchester. They had been arrested when Cornelius was found hiding in a priest hole at Chideock Castle on 14th April 1594.

4TH JULY

1533 – Burning of John Frith, reformer, theologian and martyr, at Smithfield for heresy. Frith was charged with heresy because of his religious views, which included his belief that Christ's words about the sacrament, "This is my body", were not to be taken literally. Frith was given the chance to recant, but he refused. He was burned with Andrew Hewet, a young tailor's apprentice.

1550 – Appointment of Dr Robert Huick (Hewicke) as Physician Extraordinary to Edward VI by letters patent. His annual stipend was £50. Huick had served Edward's father, Henry VIII, during his final illness, and he also went on to serve Elizabeth I.

1597 – Executions of Catholic priest and martyr William Anlaby with Thomas Warcop, who had been charged with harbouring him, and layman Edward Fulthrop. They were executed at Knavesmire, York. Anlaby was beatified in 1929 by Pope Pius XI.

1623 – Death of William Byrd, the famous Elizabethan English composer. He was buried next to his wife in the parish of Stondon Massey in Essex. His biographer, Craig Monson, writes that "Byrd was the first Englishman to master fully the quintessential feature of continental Renaissance music, systematic but flexible imitative textures" and he started his career as a pupil of Thomas Tallis. Byrd's works include "Cantiones sacrae" (1575), "Psalmes, Sonets, & Songs of Sadness and Pietie" (1588), "Songs of Sundrie Natures" (1589) and "Gradualia" (1605-1607).

5TH JULY

On the 5th July 1535, Sir Thomas More, who was imprisoned in the Tower of London and awaiting execution, wrote his final letter. It was to his beloved daughter, Margaret Roper, and it was written in coal. Here it is:

"Our Lord bless you good daughter and your good husband and your little boy and all yours and all my children and all my godchildren and all our friends. Recommend me when you may to my good daughter Cecilye, whom I beseech our Lord to comfort, and I send her my blessing and to all her children and pray her to pray for me. I send her an handekercher and God comfort my good son her husband. My good daughter Daunce hath the picture in parchment that you delivered me from my Lady Coniers; her name is on the back side. Show her that I heartily pray her that you may send it in my name again for a token from me to pray for me.

I like special well Dorothy Coly, I pray you be good unto her. I would wit whether this be she that you wrote me of. If not I pray you be good to the other as you may in her affliction and to my good daughter Joan Aleyn to give her I pray you some kind answer, for she sued hither to me this day to pray you be good to her.

I cumber you good Margaret much, but I would be sorry, if it should be any longer than tomorrow, for it is Saint Thomas even, and the Vtas of Saint Peter and therefore tomorrow long I to go to God, it were a day very meet and convenient for me. I never liked your manner toward me better than when you kissed me last for I love when daughterly love and dear charity hath no leisure to look to worldly courtesy.

Fare well my dear child and pray for me, and I shall for you and all your friends that we may merrily meet in heaven. I thank you for your great cost.

I send now unto my good daughter Clement her algorism stone and I send her and my good son and all hers God's blessing and mine.

I pray you at time convenient recommend me to my good son John More. I liked well his natural fashion. Our Lord bless him and his good wife my loving daughter, to whom I pray him be good, as he hath great cause, and that if the land of mine come to his hand, he break not my will concerning his sister Daunce. And our Lord bless Thomas and Austen and all that they shall have."

More was executed the following day.

∞∞∞∞∞∞∞∞∞∞∞∞∞∞∞∞∞∞∞∞∞∞∞∞∞∞∞∞∞∞∞∞∞

1583 – Execution of John Copping, shoemaker and religious radical, for 'dispersing' books by Robert Browne and Richard Harrison, which were viewed as "sundry seditious, schismatical and erroneous printed books". Copping had been arrested with his friend Elias Thacker, a tailor, and Thacker was executed the day before. Books were burned at each of their executions.

1589 – Executions of Catholic priests and martyrs George Nichols and Richard Yaxley, along with Catholics Thomas Belson and Humphrey Prichard. Nichols and Yaxley were hanged, drawn and quartered, and Belson and Prichard were hanged.

1589 – Hanging of Joan Cunny (Cony), one of the 'Essex Witches', at Chelmsford. Cunny had been accused of killing her neighbours and causing a great storm. Cunny had told of how she knelt in a circle and prayed to Satan to conjure her familiar and spirits. The pre-trial examinations of Cunny, Joan Prentice and Joan Upney were published in 1589 as "The Apprehension and Confession of Three Notorious Witches". Joan Prentice, who had a ferret-shaped familiar named Satan who had killed a child, was also hanged on 5th July, as was Joan Upney.

1591 – Burial of Humfrey (Humfray) Cole, goldsmith, engraver, mathematical instrument maker and die sinker, at St Gregory by St Paul's, London. Cole was a die sinker at the Tower of London mint. His mathematical instruments included an armillary sphere, astrolabe and instruments needed for Martin Frobisher's 1576 voyage. Twenty-six of his instruments still survive today.

1600 – Execution of Jean Livingston (Lady Warriston) at the Girth Cross in Edinburgh. She was beheaded by the "Maiden", a type of guillotine, for murder. Livingston was unhappily married to John Kincaid of Warriston when her nurse, Janet Murdo, came up with the idea of murdering him to release Livingston from her torment. Livingston asked a servant, Robert Weir, to do the deed, which he did on the night of 1st July 1600. Murdo was burned at the stake on Castle Hill and Weir, who had fled after the murder, was arrested in 1604 and 'broken on the wheel' at Edinburgh.

6TH JULY

Between 8 and 9pm on 6th July 1553 King Edward VI lay dying at Greenwich Palace. He prayed:

"Lord God, deliver me out of this miserable and wretched life, and take me among thy chosen: howbeit not my will, but thy will be done. Lord I commit my spirit to thee. O Lord! Thou knowest how happy it were for me to be with thee: yet, for thy chosen's sake, send me life and health, that I may truly serve thee. O my Lord God, bless thy people, and save thine inheritance! O Lord God save thy chosen people of England! O my Lord God. defend this realm from papistry, and maintain thy true religion; that I and my people may praise thy holy name, for thy Son Jesus Christ's sake!"

Then, Sir Henry Sidney, one of the Chief Gentlemen of his Privy Chamber, took the dying King in his arms and Edward said "I am faint; Lord have mercy upon me, and take my spirit", as indeed, his spirit was taken by his Father in Heaven.

Edward VI's death was not a shock to those around him; he had been ill for some time. It had started with a cough in early January 1553, and when his half-sister, Mary, visited him on the 10th February, she found him bedridden. Although he had rallied at various points, by the 20th May, the Imperial Ambassador, Jehan Scheyfve, described Edward's condition as "desperate", and on the 30th May he wrote:

"The King of England is wasting away daily, and there is no sign or likelihood of any improvement. Some are of opinion that he may last two months more, but he cannot possibly live beyond that time. He cannot rest except by means of medicines and external applications; and his body has begun to swell, especially his head and feet. His hair is to be shaved off and plasters are going to be put on his head. The illness is judged to be the same as that which killed the late Earl of Richmond."

It was while he was confined and wasting away that Edward VI wrote his "Devise for the Succession", his plan to disinherit his illegitimate half-sisters and "to create a new dynasty, one founded upon the true faith". The original draft stipulated that the Crown would descend through the male heirs of Frances, Duchess of Suffolk, and the male heirs of her children, if Edward died childless. The problem was that there were no male heirs yet, so when Edward made a turn for the worse, he decided to change the Device to read: "To the Lady Fraunceses heirs males, if she have any such issue before my death to the Lady Jane and her heirs males." Edward had decided on Lady Jane Grey as his heir if she or her mother did not produce a male heir in time.

On 11th June, Scheyfve reported that "The King's indisposition is becoming graver and graver", and on 12th June the judges of the King's Bench were shown the King's Devise and ordered to turn it into a legal will. The judges refused, as they were worried that overturning the succession would be considered treason, but Edward explained the reasons behind his decision:-

"For indeed my sister Mary was the daughter of the king by Katherine the Spaniard, who before she was married to my worthy father had been espoused to Arthur, my father's elder brother, and was therefore for this reason alone divorced by my father. But it was the fate of Elizabeth, my other sister, to have Anne Boleyn for a mother; this woman was indeed not only cast off by my father because she was more inclined to couple with a number of courtiers rather than reverencing her husband, so mighty a king, but also paid the penalty with her head – a greater proof of her guilt. Thus in our judgement they will be undeservedly considered as being numbered among the heirs of the king our beloved father."

He then demanded that the judges should accept his wishes and legalise his "Devise", and the judges were told that to refuse the King's command would be seen as treason. Edward got his wish, and the letters patent were drawn up there and then.

Edward was well enough to receive visitors and to continue with his studies with Sir John Cheke in early June, but Scheyfve reported to the Emperor on 15th June, that Edward was attacked by a violent hot fever on 11th June and by an even more violent one on the 14th, continuing:

"Since the 11th, he has been unable to keep anything in his stomach, so he lives entirely on restoratives and obtains hardly any repose. His legs are swelling, and he has to lie flat on his back, whereas he was up a good deal of the time (i.e. before the violent attack of the 11th). They say it is hardly to be believed how much the King has changed since the 11th."

On 19th June, Scheyfve reported to the Emperor:

"The King of England has sunk so rapidly since my last letter of the 15th, that the physicians no longer dare to answer for it that he will last one day more. His state is such that the King himself has given up hope, and says he feels so weak that he can resist no longer, and that he is done for (qu'il est faict de luy)."

And then on the 24th, he wrote of how the King was so ill "that he cannot last three days", and that a prayer had been printed and posted up in London. On 27th June Scheyfve reported that the King had been so ill on the 25th that it was thought that he was going to die, but that there had been a change, "and no one knows what the hour may bring forth." On the 4th July, Scheyfve wrote of how Edward had appeared at a window at Greenwich some days before to prove to everyone that he was still alive, but that he was "so thin and wasted that all men said he was doomed" and that as Sheyfve was writing the King was seriously ill and could not last long. Scheyfve was right, the next document in the "Calendar of State Papers, Spain", is a letter from Scheyfve and the other three ambassadors to the Emperor reporting on the King's death between 8 and 9 o'clock on the evening of 6th July.

King Edward VI was no more, and Lady Jane Grey was now queen, although it was to be a rather short-lived reign.

1535 – Execution of Sir Thomas More, Henry VIII's former friend and Lord Chancellor, for high treason for denying the King's supremacy. Tudor chronicler Edward Hall wrote of Thomas More's execution:

"When he came to the Scaffold, it seemed ready to fall, whereupon he said merrily to the Lieutenant, Pray, Sir, see me safe up; and as to my coming down, let me shift for myself. Being about to speak to the People, he was interrupted by the Sheriff, and thereupon he only desired the People to pray for him, and bear Witness he died in the Faith of the Catholic Church, a faithful Servant both to God and the King. Then kneeling, he repeated the Miserere Psalm with much Devotion; and, rising up the Executioner asked him Forgiveness. He kissed him, and said, Pick up thy Spirits, Man, and be not afraid to do thine Office; my Neck is very short, take heed therefore thou strike not awry for having thine Honesty. Laying his Head upon the Block, he bid the Executioner stay till he had put his Beard aside, for that had committed no Treason. Thus he suffered with much Cheerfulness; his Head was taken off at one Blow, and was placed upon London-Bridge, where, having continued for some Months, and being about to be thrown into the Thames to make room for others, his Daughter Margaret bought it, in closed it in a Leaden Box, and kept it for a Relique."

1537 – Execution of Sir Robert Constable at Beverley's Gate in Hull. Constable had been an active participant in the *Pilgrimage of Grace Rebellion* in 1536, but had received a royal pardon and had gone on to try and suppress *Bigod's Revolt* in 1537. However, he was summoned to London in 1537, and subsequently tried and condemned to death. He was hanged in chains.

1560 – Signing of *Treaty of Edinburgh* (Treaty of Leith) between representatives of Elizabeth I and Francis II of France, husband of Mary, Queen of Scots. The terms were that French and English troops were to withdraw from Scotland and that Francis and Mary should stop using the title and arms of the monarch of England and Ireland, which belonged to Elizabeth I.

1570 – Death of Margaret Clement (née Giggs), wife of John Clement and adopted daughter of Sir Thomas More, in Mechelen where she and her husband had gone into exile. Margaret was buried in the Cathedral of St Rumbald.

Trivia: In 1537, Margaret bribed the gaoler at Newgate Prison to let her feed the Carthusian priests who were starving there.

1583 – Death of Edmund Grindal, Elizabeth I's Archbishop of York and of Canterbury, at Croydon.

1585 – Executions of Thomas Alfield, Catholic priest, and Thomas Webley, a dyer, at Tyburn. They had been tried and condemned under statute 23 Eliz. c.2 s.2, which made the publication of any book attacking the queen a felony punishable by death. The book in question was Dr William Allen's book, "Modest Defence of the English Catholiques", which Alfield and Webley had helped to distribute.

1614 – Death of Sir Anthony Cope, 1ˢᵗ Baronet, politician and Puritan. He was buried at Hanwell, Oxfordshire.

1618 – Death of John Davies of Hereford, poet and writing master. He was buried in the church of St Dunstan-in-the-West, London. His works included "The Scourge of Folly", "Writing Schoolmaster", or, "The Anatomy of Fair Writing" and "Mirum in modum: a Glimpse of Gods Glorie and the Soules Shape".

7TH JULY

1537 – Death of Madeleine de Valois, also known as Madeleine of France, first wife of King James V of Scotland. Madeleine died in her husband's arms at Edinburgh just six months after their wedding and less than two months after her arrival in Scotland. She was buried in Holyrood Abbey.

1540 – Anthony St Leger was appointed Lord Deputy of Ireland.

1545 – Death of William Crane, merchant, musician and Master of the Choristers of the Chapel Royal. He was buried in St Helen's Church, Bishopsgate, before the high altar.

1548 – *Treaty of Haddington* between France and Scotland. By the terms of this treaty, the Scots and French agreed to the marriage of Mary, Queen of Scots, and Francis, the Dauphin.

1553 – Goldsmith Robert Reyns informed Mary (future Mary I) of Edward VI's death. Mary was staying with Lady Burgh at Euston Hall, near Thetford, and Reyns had rushed from London to give her the news.

1556 (or 8th July) – Executions of Henry Peckham and John Danyell, conspirators. They were hanged, drawn and quartered after being found guilty of treason for their involvement in the *Dudley Conspiracy*.

1568 – Death of William Turner, naturalist, herbalist, ornithologist, reformer, physician and the man referred to as "the father of English botany and of ornithology". He died at his home in Crutched Friars, London, and was buried in St Olave's Church, Hart Street.

1585 – Birth of Thomas Howard, 14th Earl of Arundel, 4th Earl of Surrey, and 1st Earl of Norfolk, politician and art collector, at Finchingfield, Essex. He was the only son of Philip Howard, 13th Earl of Arundel, and his wife, Anne Dacre.

1607 – Death of Penelope Rich (née Devereux), Lady Rich, at Westminster. Penelope was the sister of Robert Devereux, 2nd Earl of Essex, and is thought to have inspired poet Philip Sidney's "Astrophel and Stella". She married Robert Rich, Lord Rich, in 1581, but was having a love affair with Charles Blount, Baron Mountjoy, by 1595. Penelope married Blount, who was now Earl of Devonshire, in a private ceremony in 1605 after her divorce. The marriage led to the couple's banishment from court. Devonshire died in 1606.

8TH JULY

On Saturday 8th July 1553 at Kenninghall, Norfolk, Mary Tudor declared herself Queen. She had been informed of her half-brother Edward VI's death by goldsmith Robert Reyns the previous day, when she was staying with Lady Burgh at Euston Hall, near Thetford, and the news had been confirmed by Thomas Hughes, her physician.

Mary gathered together her loyal household at Kenninghall and informed them of Edward VI's death, stating that "the right to the crown of England had therefore descended to her by divine and by human law". The news was greeted by cheering and the household proclaiming her Queen. Mary then wrote a letter to the Privy Council telling them in no uncertain terms that they were to recognise her as Queen: to "cause our right and title to the crown and government of this realm to be proclaimed in our city of London and other places as your wisdom shall seem good." However, Edward VI's 'devise for the succession' had named Lady Jane Grey as his successor, so trouble was brewing.

***

1503 – Margaret Tudor said farewell to her father, Henry VII, and set off to Edinburgh to marry James IV. Anne Boleyn's father, Thomas Boleyn, was one of the men who accompanied her.

1536 – Death of William Wyggeston, merchant and benefactor, at Leicester. He was buried in the collegiate church of St Mary in the Newarke, Leicester, which was destroyed around 1548.

1540 – Abolition, by Henry VIII, of all heretical books and those containing errors.

1549 – The beginning of *Kett's Rebellion*. Robert Kett, a Norfolk farmer, agreed to lead a group of protesters who were angry with the enclosure of common land. The protesters marched on Norwich, and by the time they reached the city walls, it is said that they numbered around 16,000.

9TH JULY

On the 9th July 1540, just over six months after their wedding, it was declared that the marriage of King Henry VIII and Anne of Cleves was null and void, and that both parties were free to marry again.

The process of "nullity of the marriage" is recorded in "Letters and Papers". It records how convocation met on 7th July, in the chapter house of St Peter's, Westminster, and that it opened with Richard Gwent presenting "the King's letters of commission under the Great Seal addressed to the archbishops and clergy, which were then read by Ant. Husey, notary public, in presence of Thos.

Argall, notary public". It was then agreed that the commission could go ahead, and Stephen Gardiner, Bishop of Winchester, "explained the causes of the nullity of the marriage of the King and lady Anne of Cleves in a lucid speech".

The clergy of the lower house left the proceedings after it was decreed that "the two Archbishops, the bps. of London, Durham, Winchester, and Worcester, and Ric. Gwent, Thos. Thirleby, Thos. Incent, Edw. Leighton, and Thos. Robertson, Ric. Layton, and Wm. Ryvett, doctors of Theology and Law, and Thos. Magnus, archd. of the East Riding, should receive and weigh all the evidences in the case and explain them to the Convocation". Depositions were then taken from " Thos. lord Audeley, Chancellor, Thos. duke of Norfolk, Charles duke of Suffolk, Wm. earl of Southampton, Privy Seal, John lord Russell, Great Admiral, Sir Ant. Browne, master of the Horse, knights of the Garter; and of George lord Cobham, Sir Thos. Henneage, Sir Thos. Wryothesley, King's secretary, Ant. Denny, and Wm. Butt, M.D" as witnesses, and on the 8th July convocation reassembled to hear the evidence. It was agreed that Henry VIII and Anne of Cleves "were nowise bound by the marriage solemnised between them", and on 9th July, letters were drawn up containing convocation's judgement:

"The clergy of both provinces have received the King's commission (recited), dated Westm., 6 July 32 Hen. VIII. After mature deliberation, they have found the marriage null by reason of a precontract between lady Anne and the marquis of Lorraine, that it was unwillingly entered into and never consummated, and that the King is at liberty to marry another woman, and likewise the lady Anne free to marry. Westm., 9 July 1540."

The King's fourth marriage was over and he was free to marry again. Henry VIII married his fifth wife, Catherine Howard, 28th July 1540.

1539 – Execution of Sir Adrian Fortescue, courtier and landowner, on Tower Hill. He was condemned for treason by act of attainder, but it is not known what he had done to deserve this. He was beatified in 1895 as a martyr, but historian Richard Rex points out that he is unlikely to have opposed Henry VIII's supremacy because he was a cousin of Anne Boleyn.

1553 – Nicholas Ridley, Bishop of London, preached at St Paul's Cross denouncing Henry VIII's daughters, Mary and Elizabeth, as bastards. The congregation were "sore annoyed with his words".

1553 – The Duke of Northumberland officially informed Lady Jane Grey of Edward VI's death in front of the Council and nobles, going on to explain the terms of Edward's will which named Lady Jane Grey as the heir to the throne. Lady Jane Grey accepted that she was Queen.

1553 – Mary (future Mary I) wrote to the Privy Council stating her claim to the throne and demanding their allegiance. While Mary was writing this letter, John Dudley, Duke of Northumberland, was informing his daughter-in-law, Lady Jane Grey, of Edward VI's death and informing her that the King had nominated her as his successor. Jane collapsed weeping and declared "The crown is not my right and pleases me not. The Lady Mary is the rightful heir." Northumberland and Jane's parents then explained Edward's wishes to the distressed Jane, and she accepted the crown as her duty.

1575 (9th-27th) – Elizabeth I was entertained at Kenilworth Castle by Robert Dudley, Earl of Leicester. It was a special visit in that it lasted nineteen days and was the longest stay at a courtier's house in any of her royal progresses. We know a substantial amount about Elizabeth's visit to Kenilworth because it was recorded in a letter by Robert Langham, a member of Dudley's household, and in an account by poet and actor George Gascoigne, a man hired by Robert

Dudley to provide entertainment during the royal visit. Many see Elizabeth's final visit to Kenilworth in 1575 as Dudley's last chance to impress the Queen and win her hand in marriage. Dudley went to extraordinary lengths to impress his Queen – a new gatehouse, new luxury apartments fit for a Queen, new gardens, firework displays, hunting, a masque and other lavish entertainment. Unfortunately, the plan did not work. Dudley ended up marrying Lettice Knollys and Elizabeth never returned to Kenilworth.

1586 – Death of Edward Sutton, 4th Baron Dudley, soldier and landowner, at Westminster. He was buried in St Margaret's, Westminster. Sutton served as a soldier in Henry VIII's reign in Ireland and Boulogne, and in Edward VI's reign against the Scots. He was made a Knight of the Bath at Mary I's coronation, and then given Lordship of Dudley Castle, where he entertained Elizabeth I in 1575.

10TH JULY

On the afternoon of Monday 10th July 1553, Lady Jane Grey, her husband, Guildford Dudley, her parents and Guildford's mother arrived by barge at the Tower of London, having travelled from Syon. They were greeted there by Guildford's father, John Dudley, Duke of Northumberland, and other councillors, before they made their way through the Tower gates, Jane and Guildford walking under the canopy of state.

As the procession reached the Tower, there was a gun salute and trumpets blasted to silence the crowd. Two heralds then proclaimed that Lady Jane Grey was now Queen of England before they moved on to proclaim their message in Cheapside and Fleet Street. At Cheapside, a boy declared that it was Mary who was the rightful queen, and he was punished the next morning by having his ears cut off.

On this very same day, a letter arrived from Mary informing the council that she was the rightful heir to the throne, not Jane, and demanding their support. As Jane was proclaimed Queen in London, Mary was gathering support for her cause in East Anglia. Jane was going to have a fight on her hands. Death of Henry Redman, Master Mason of Westminster Abbey, Chief Mason of Windsor Castle and the King's Chief Mason. He was buried in the chapel of St Lawrence, Brentford, Middlesex.

1559 – Death of Henry II of France. He had been injured in a joust on 30th June when he was hit in the face by a lance. It is thought that a splinter entered his eye and went into his brain. He was buried in the Saint Denis Basilica.

1559 – Accession of Francis II and Mary, Queen of Scots as King and Queen of France.

1561 – Elizabeth I visited the Tower of London mint to check on the progress of her new coins. Her recoinage, which restored the silver content of coins following the debasements in her father and half-brother's reigns, restored the reputation of English coins.

1584 – Assassination of William of Orange, also known as William the Silent or William I, Prince of Orange. He was shot in the chest at his home in Delft by Balthasar Gérard, a Catholic Frenchman. A reward of 25,000 crowns had been offered by Philip II of Spain for the assassination of William, who was the main leader of the Dutch Protestant revolt against Spanish forces in the Netherlands. William was buried in the New Church in Delft. Gérard was captured and was tortured for days before being executed on 14th July 1584.

1584 – Execution of Francis Throckmorton, Catholic conspirator, at Tyburn for high treason after he was found guilty of conspiring to remove Elizabeth I from the throne and to replace her with Mary, Queen of Scots. It appears that

Throckmorton was acting as an intermediary between Mary, Queen of Scots and Mendoza, the Spanish ambassador.

1588 – Death of Edwin Sandys, Archbishop of York. He was buried in Southwell Minster.

11TH JULY

1533 – Pope Clement VII ordered Henry VIII to abandon Anne Boleyn and drew up a papal bull excommunicating Henry VIII. He held off issuing it in the hope that Henry would abandon Anne, and in the end the bull was not issued until 1538.

1536 – Death of Desiderius Erasmus, the famous Humanist scholar, from dysentery at Basel during the night of the 11th/12th July. He was buried in the cathedral at Basel on 18th July. His works included *Novum Instrumentum omne* (a Latin translation of the epistles and gospel), "The Praise of Folly," "De Copia", "Adagia" and "The Education of a Christian Prince".

1558 – Baptism of Robert Greene, writer and playwright, at St George's Church, Tombland, Norwich. His works included the plays "The Scottish History of James IV" and "Friar Bacon and Friar Bungay", and the romance "Mamillia".

1564 – The plague hit Stratford-upon-Avon in Warwickshire. The epidemic lasted six months and killed over 200 people, around a fifth of the population. William Shakespeare was born in April of that year, and his family were fortunate in escaping the plague.

12TH JULY

On this day in 1543, King Henry VIII married his sixth and final wife, Catherine Parr, in the Queen's Closet at Hampton Court Palace. Catherine Parr, or Lady Latimer as she was known, was also not new to marriage, having been married and widowed twice before, firstly to Edward Burgh (or Borough), son of Sir Thomas Burgh and grandson of Edward, 2ⁿᵈ Baron Burgh, and secondly to John Neville, 3ʳᵈ Baron Latimer of Snape in Yorkshire.

The marriage of Henry VIII and Catherine Parr was a private ceremony attended by around twenty courtiers and friends of the couple. Catherine's supporters at the ceremony included her sister, Anne Herbert; Henry VIII's daughter's, Mary and Elizabeth; his niece, Lady Margaret Douglas; Anne Stanhope, the Countess of Hertford; Catherine Willoughby, the Duchess of Suffolk; and Jane Dudley, Viscountess Lisle and wife of John Dudley. The men included Catherine's brother-in-law, William Herbert; Anthony Denny; Sir Thomas Speke; Sir Edward Baynton; Sir Richard Long; Sir Thomas Darcy; Sir Henry Knyvet; Sir Thomas Heneage; Edward Seymour, Earl of Hertford; John, Lord Russell, the Lord Privy Seal, and Sir Anthony Browne, Captain of the King's Pensioners.

Although Thomas Cranmer had issued the licence for the marriage on the 10ᵗʰ July, it was the Bishop of Winchester, Stephen Gardiner, who performed the ceremony. The notarial attestation in "Letters and Papers," by Richard Watkins, gives details of the ceremony:-

"The King and lady Katharine Latymer alias Parr being met there for the purpose of solemnising matrimony between them, Stephen bp. of Winchester proclaimed in English (speech given in Latin) that they were met to join in marriage the said King and Lady Katharine, and if anyone knew any impediment thereto he should declare it. The licence for the marriage without publication of banns, sealed by Thos. abp. of Canterbury and dated 10 July 1543, being then brought in, and none opposing but all applauding the marriage, the said bp. of Winchester put the questions (recited) to which the King, hilari vultu, replied "Yea" and the lady Katharine also replied that it was her wish; and then the King taking her right hand, repeated after the Bishop the words, "I, Henry, take thee,

Katharine, to my wedded wife, to have and to hold from this day forward, for better for worse, for richer for poorer, in sickness and in health, till death us depart, and thereto I plight thee my troth." Then, releasing and again clasping hands, the lady Katharine likewise said "I, Katharine, take thee Henry to my wedded husband, to have and to hold from this day forward, for better for worse, for richer for poorer, in sickness and in health, to be bonayr and buxome in bed and at board, till death us depart, and thereto I plight unto thee my troth." The putting on of the wedding ring and proffer of gold and silver (described) followed; and the Bishop, after prayer, pronounced a benediction. The King then commanded the prothonotary to make a public instrument of the premises."

The wedding was followed by a celebration breakfast and a proclamation that Catherine was now Queen.

<hr>

1537 – Execution of Robert Aske, lawyer and rebel. He was hanged in chains outside Clifford's Tower, the keep of York Castle. Aske was one of the leaders of the rebels in the 1536 northern uprising known as the *Pilgrimage of Grace*.

1549 – The rebels of *Kett's Rebellion* set up camp on Mousehold Heath, overlooking Norwich.

1555 – Burnings of preachers John Bland and John Frankesh, rector Nicholas Sheterden and Vicar Humphrey Middleton at Canterbury. They were all Protestants burned for heresy.

1581 – Death of Maurice Chauncy, martyrologist, Carthusian monk and prior of Sheen Anglorum Charterhouse at Nieuwpoort in Flanders. He died in the Paris Charterhouse on his way back to Flanders from Spain, where he had been trying to get funding for the Charterhouse.

1584 – Death of Stephen Borough, navigator and naval administrator, at Chatham in Kent. He was buried in St Mary's Church, Chatham. His memorial brass paid tribute to his career: "He in his lifetime discovered Moscovia, by the northern sea pasage to St Nicholas, in the yere 1553. At his setting forth of England he was accompanied in his ship by Sir Hugh Willoughbie, being Admirell of the fleete, who, with all the company of the said two shippes, were frozen to death in Lappia the same winter. After his discoverie of Roosia and the costes adjoyning to wit Lappia, Nova Zembla, and the cuntry of Samoyeda etc: he frequented the trade to St Nicholas yearlie, as chief pilot for the voyages, until he was chosen one of the four principal Masters in ordinarie of the Queen's Majesties royall Navy, where in he continued in charge of sundrie sea services till time of his death."

1598 – Execution of John Jones, Franciscan friar, at St Thomas's Waterings, Southwark. He was hanged, drawn and quartered for being a Catholic priest.

13TH JULY

On this day in 1527, John Dee, astrologer, mathematician, alchemist, antiquary, spy, philosopher, geographer and adviser to Elizabeth I and various influential statesmen during her reign, was born in London. He was the son of Rowland Dee, a gentleman server at the court of Henry VIII, and was educated at St John's College, Cambridge, and Louvain. In the early 1550s, he returned to England with various navigational instruments and began work under the patronage of the Earl of Pembroke, the Duke of Northumberland and the Grey family. He also acted as tutor to Robert Dudley, Earl of Leicester, and Edward VI.

Dee's career highlights include:

- Drawing up an electional chart to determine the most auspicious date for Elizabeth I's coronation.
- Undertaking secret foreign missions for Elizabeth I and William Cecil, Lord Burghley.
- Presenting his mathematical and astronomical work, *Propaedeumata Aphoristica*, to the Queen.

- Being consulted by famous explorers and navigators.
- Working with Edward Kelley and communicating with angels.

He was one of the most learned men of the Elizabethan age, and was known for his huge library. He died in 1609.

◇◇◇◇◇◇◇◇◇◇◇◇◇◇◇◇◇◇◇◇◇◇◇◇◇◇◇◇◇◇◇◇◇◇◇◇

1551 – Death of Sir John Wallop, soldier and diplomat, at Guînes from sweating sickness. His body was buried at Guînes, but then moved to the parish church at Farleigh Wallop, his home town.

1566 – Death of Sir Thomas Hoby, diplomat, courtier and translator, at Paris. He was buried in Bisham parish church. His translations included "The Gratulation of M. Martin Bucer unto the Church of England" (1549) and Castiglione's "Il cortegiano" (1561).

1612 – Death of Edward Seymour, Viscount Beauchamp, eldest son of Edward Seymour, 1st Earl of Hertford, and Lady Katherine Grey, at Wick in Wiltshire. He was buried first at Bedwyn Magna and then in Salisbury Cathedral.

1626 – Death of Robert Sidney, 1st Earl of Leicester, poet and courtier, at Penshurst Place. He was buried at Penshurst on the 16th July. His notebook, which still survives today, holds a collection of poems and sonnets, and also shows the revisions he made to them.

14TH JULY

1486 – Death of Margaret of Denmark, Queen of Scots and consort of James III, at Stirling Castle. She was buried in Cambuskenneth Abbey. False rumours spread that she had been murdered by poison by John Ramsay, 1st Lord Bothwell, but there was no evidence of this.

1514 – Death of Cardinal Christopher Bainbridge, also Ambassador and Archbishop of York, in Rome. His death was controversial, in that his servant, Raimondo da Modena, confessed to poisoning him on the orders of Silvestro Gigli, Bishop of Worcester, and the English ambassador at Rome. He was buried in chapel of the English Hospice (now the English College) in Rome.

1544 – Henry VIII landed at Calais in preparation for the *Siege of Boulogne*, which began five days later.

1551 – Deaths of Henry Brandon and Charles Brandon, sons of the late Charles Brandon, Duke of Suffolk, and Catherine Brandon (née Willoughby), Duchess of Suffolk, from sweating sickness in Buckden, Huntingdonshire. They were buried at Buckden. Charles survived his brother by just half an hour.

1575 – Death of Richard Taverner, evangelical reformer and translator, at Woodeaton in Oxfordshire. Taverner is known for his Bible translation known as "Taverner's Bible", or, to give it its full name, "The Most Sacred Bible whiche is the holy scripture, conteyning the old and new testament, translated into English, and newly recognized with great diligence after most faythful exemplars by Rychard Taverner". He was buried in the parish church at Woodeaton.

1599 – Death of Sir Robert Salesbury, member of Parliament, Justice of the Peace and Deputy Lieutenant of Denbighshire.

1621 – Death of Edmund Hooper, composer and organist of Westminster Abbey and the Chapel Royal, in London. He was buried in the cloisters of Westminster Abbey.

15TH JULY

1497 – Birth of William Neville, poet. He was the son of Richard Neville, 2nd Baron Latimer, and his wife, Anne (née

Stafford). Neville was the author of the allegorical 'The Castell of Pleasure'.

1553 – The royal ships guarding the Eastern coast for 'Queen Jane' swapped their allegiance to 'Queen Mary'. Their crews had not been paid, and they received a visit from Sir Henry Jerningham asking them to support Mary instead, so it was an easy decision.

1556 – Beginning of the trial of Julins Palmer, John Gwyn and Thomas Robyns, now known as the *Newbury Martyrs*. They were tried for sedition and heresy at St Nicholas Church, Newbury.

1561 – Death of William Bill, Dean of Westminster, at Westminster. He was buried in St Benedict's chapel, Westminster Abbey. Bill's other offices included Master of St Johns College, Cambridge, Vice-Chancellor of the University of Cambridge, Master of Trinity College, Cambridge, and Provost of Eton College.

1573 – Birth of Inigo Jones, architect and theatre designer, in London. Jones is known for his design of the Banqueting House, the Queen's House at Greenwich and his stage design work, in collaboration with Ben Jonson.

1597 – Death of Sir Robert Dillon, lawyer, judge, Privy Councillor and Chief Justice of Common Pleas, at Riverston, County Meath, Ireland. He was buried in the church at Tara.

16TH JULY

On this day in 1546 the Protestant martyrs Anne Askew, John Lascelles, John Adams and Nicholas Belenian were burned at the stake at Smithfield in London for heresy.

Anne had been illegally racked while imprisoned in the Tower of London by Thomas Wriothesley and Richard Rich in an attempt to make her implicate Queen Catherine Parr or influential people like Anne Seymour (née Stanhope) and her husband, Edward Seymour. Anne refused, even though the men racked her "till her bones and joints were almost plucked asunder, in such sort as she was carried away in a chair". So badly was this young woman racked that a few weeks later, on the day of her execution, she had to be carried to the stake on a chair and "was tied by the middle with a chain, that held up her body".

The famous martyrologist, John Foxe, recorded the burning of Anne Askew and the men in his book "Actes and Monuments", also known as "Foxe's Book of Martyrs". Here is what he says of Anne's death:-

"Hitherto we have entreated of this good woman: now it remaineth that we touch somewhat as touching her end and martyrdom. She being born of such stock and kindred that she might have lived in great wealth and prosperity, if she would rather have followed the world than Christ, but now she was so tormented, that she could neither live long in so great distress, neither yet by the adversaries be suffered to die in secret. Wherefore the day of her execution was appointed, and she brought into Smithfield in a chair, because she could not go on her feet, by means of her great torments. When she was brought unto the stake she was tied by the middle with a chain that held up her body. When all things were thus prepared to the fire, Dr Shaxton, who was then appointed to preach, began his sermon. Anne Askew, hearing and answering again unto him, where he said well, confirmed the same; where he said amiss, "There," said she, "he misseth, and speaketh without the book."

The sermon being finished, the martyrs standing there tied at three several stakes ready to their martyrdom, began their prayers. The multitude and concourse of people was exceeding; the place where they stood being railed about to keep out the press. Upon the bench under St Bartholomew's Church sat Wriothesley, chancellor of England; the old Duke of Norfolk, the old earl of Bedford, the lord mayor, with divers others. Before the fire should be set unto them, one of the bench, hearing that they had gunpowder about them, and being alarmed lest the faggots, by strength of the gunpowder, would come flying about their ears, began to be afraid: but the earl of Bedford, declaring unto him how the gunpowder was not laid under the faggots, but only about their bodies, to rid them out of their pain; which having vent, there was no danger to them of the faggots, so diminished that fear.

Then Wriothesley, lord chancellor, sent to Anne Askew letters offering to her the King's pardon if she would recant; who. refusing once to look upon them, made this answer again, that she came not thither to deny her Lord and Master. Then were the letters like-wise offered unto the others, who, in like manner, following the constancy of the woman, denied not only to receive them, but also to look upon them. Whereupon the lord mayor, commanding fire to be put unto them, cried with a loud voice, "*Fiat justicia*."

And thus the good Anne Askew, with these blessed martyrs being troubled so many manner of ways, and having passed through so many torments, having now ended the long course of her agonies, being compassed in with flames of fire, as a blessed sacrifice unto God, she slept in the Lord A.D. 1546, leaving behind her a singular example of christian constancy for all men to follow."

1517 – Birth of Frances Grey (née Brandon), Duchess of Suffolk, at Hatfield. She was born on St Francis's Day and was the eldest daughter of Charles Brandon, Duke of Suffolk, and Mary Tudor, widow of Louis XII and sister of Henry VIII.

1556 – Burnings of Julins Palmer, John Gwyn, and Thomas Robyns [some sources say Askew or Askin] in the old sandpits in Enborne Road, Newbury, after they were found guilty of sedition and heresy. They are known as the *Newbury Martyrs*.

1557 – Death of Anne of Cleves, fourth wife of Henry VIII, at Chelsea Old Manor after a few months of illness. On the same day, her body was embalmed and placed in a coffin covered with a cloth bearing her arms. Tapers were lit around her coffin and prayers said on a daily basis. She was buried in Westminster Abbey on 4th August.

1574 – Death of John Hart, scholar, phonetician and Chester Herald, in London.

1600 – Death of George Cranmer, scholar, administrator and nephew of Thomas Cranmer, the late Archbishop of Canterbury, in a skirmish with Irish rebels at Carlingford. He was in Ireland serving Charles Blount, Lord Mountjoy, as Secretary during a military campaign.

17TH JULY

On this day in 1555, Protestant martyrs Christopher Wade (Waid) of Dartford, linen-weaver, and Margaret Polley of Tunbridge, were burned for heresy. Margaret Polley was described by martyrologist John Foxe as "in the prime of her life, pious, charitable, humane, learned in the Scriptures, and beloved by all who knew her" and "the first female martyr in England", although surely that title actually belongs to Anne Askew.

When she was interrogated, Polley affirmed her denial of transubstantiation, saying that Christ's body could not be in the sacrament when he had ascended into heaven at his crucifixion. She believed that the bread and wine were "symbols and representatives of the body and blood of Christ, but not as his body really and substantially". While she was imprisoned at Rochester, she refused various offers to recant her beliefs and so was condemned to death. John Foxe wrote of her end:

"She was conducted from the prison at Rochester to Tunbridge, where she was burned, sealing the truth of what she had testified with her blood, and showing that the God of all grace, out of the weakest vessel can give strength, and cause the meanest instruments to magnify the glories of his redeeming love."

1497 – Death of Sir James Ormond (Butler), administrator and illegitimate son of John Butler, 6th Earl of Ormond, in a duel with Sir Piers Butler, near Kilkenny. The Butlers of Ormond were related to Thomas Boleyn, Queen Anne Boleyn's father.

1537 – Burning of Janet Douglas, Lady Glamis, on the castle hill at Edinburgh after being found guilty of two counts of treason. She had been charged with plotting the King's death (by poison) and assisting and corresponding with her brothers, Sir George Douglas and Archibald Douglas, 6th Earl of Angus.

1555 – Birth of Richard Carew, antiquary, bee-keeper, translator and poet, at Antony House, Torpoint, Cornwall. Carew was the eldest son of Thomas Carew and his wife Elizabeth (née Edgcumbe). Carew was a member of the Elizabethan Society of Antiquaries, and his works included his "Survey of Cornwall", a county history.

1565 – Death of Sir Thomas Dacre of Lanercost, illegitimate son of Thomas Dacre, 2nd Baron Dacre. He died while holding the office of Sheriff of Cumberland.

1601 – Death of Richard Latewar, poet, theologian, Vice-President of St John's College, Oxford, and chaplain to Charles Blount, 8th Baron Mountjoy. He died from a gunshot wound sustained in a skirmish at Bennurb, in Ireland, while on a campaign there with Mountjoy. Latewar was buried at Armagh Cathedral, and a monument was erected to him in the chapel of St John's in Oxford.

18TH JULY

1509 – Edmund Dudley, administrator, President of the King's Council (Henry VII) and Speaker of the House of Commons, was convicted of treason after being blamed for the oppression of Henry VII's reign. He was charged with conspiring to "hold, guide and govern the King and his Council" and ordering his men to assemble in London during the final days of Henry VII's life. Dudley was executed on 17th August 1510.

1530 – Death of William Bonde, author and Bridgettine monk, at Syon Abbey. Bonde wrote two religious works, "The Pylgrimage of Perfection" (1526) and "The Directory of Conscience" (1527). He was buried at Syon Abbey and bequeathed twenty-nine works to the Abbey's library.

1536 – Burial of Desiderius Erasmus in Basel Cathedral.

1553 – While John Dudley, Duke of Northumberland, and his forces made their way from Cambridge to Bury St Edmunds to stand against Mary's men, the Earls of Pembroke and Arundel called a council meeting and betrayed Northumberland and Queen Jane. They persuaded many council members that Mary's claim to the throne was legitimate.

1565 – Death of Katherine Ashley (née Champernowne), also known as Astley, in London. Kat was Chief Gentlewoman of the Privy Chamber during the reign of Elizabeth I, and had served as Elizabeth's governess during the latter's teenage years.

19TH JULY

On 19th July 1553, thirteen days after the death of her half-brother, Edward VI, Mary was proclaimed Queen in place of Queen Jane.

The Earls of Pembroke and Arundel had called a council meeting the previous day to convince council members that Mary's claim to the throne was legitimate, but it was on this day in 1553 that they managed to convince the remaining Privy Councillors to switch sides from Jane to Mary. Their strategy was not just gentle persuasion, Pembroke actually drew his sword and cried, "If the arguments of my lord Arundel do not persuade you, this sword shall make Mary queen, or I will die in her quarrel." Of course, everyone agreed with his arguments.

Pembroke announced Mary's accession to the people of London that afternoon:

"the xix. day of the same monyth, [which] was sent Margarettes evyne, at iiij. of clocke at after-none was proclamyd lady Ma[ry to] be qwene of Ynglond at the crose in Cheppe with the erle of Shrewsbery, the earle [of Arundel], the erle of Pembroke, with the mayer of London, and dyvers other lordes, and many of the ald[dermen] and the kynges schrffe master Garrand, with dyvers haroldes and trompettes. And from thens cam to Powlles alle, and there the qwere sange Te Deum with the organs goynge, with the belles ryngynge, the most parte alle [London], and that same nyght had the [most] parte of London Te Deum, with bone-fyers in every strete in London, with good chere at every bone [fyer], the belles ryngynge in every parych cherch, and for the most parte alle nyght tyll the nexte daye to none."

It seems that London was happy with the news.

Back at the Tower of London, Lady Jane Grey's father, the Duke of Suffolk, interrupted his daughter's evening meal to inform her that she was no longer Queen. Her canopy of state was taken down and Lady Jane Grey turned from Queen to prisoner, Queen to traitor. Her reign was over, and she would go down in history as "the Nine Day Queen", although officially she reigned for thirteen days.

Mary didn't actually know that she had been proclaimed Queen at this point. She found out the next day when William Paget and the Earl of Arundel arrived at Framlingham with the news.

───────────────

1543 – Death of Mary Stafford (née Boleyn), other married name Carey. It is not known where she was buried and there is also controversy regarding her date of death.

1545 – Henry VIII's flagship, the *Mary Rose*, sank right in front of his eyes in the *Battle of the Solent* between the English and French fleets. It is not known for sure why the *Mary Rose* sank. All we know for certain is that the English fleet moved out to attack the French fleet in the late afternoon of the 19th as "a fitful wit sprang up" and that something went wrong as the ship carried out a turning manoeuvre. The *Mary Rose* sank and along with her the majority of her crew, including Sir George Carew, the Captain.

1551 – Marriage treaty between King Edward VI and Elizabeth, daughter of Henry II, King of France.

1584 – Death of three year-old Robert Dudley, Baron Denbigh, son of Robert Dudley, Earl of Leicester, and his wife, Lettice, at Wanstead. He was laid to rest in the Beauchamp Chapel of St Mary's Church, Warwick, and his tomb pays tribute to "the noble imp".

1596 – Death of Sir Francis Knollys, courtier, politician, Privy Councillor and Treasurer of the Household in Elizabeth I's reign. He was buried at Rotherfield Greys, Oxfordshire. Knollys was married to Catherine Carey, daughter of William Carey and Mary Boleyn.

20TH JULY

On this day in 1554 John Knox, a leader of the Protestant Reformation in Scotland, published "A Faithful Admonition to the Professors of God's Truth in England".

In this pamphlet, Knox attacked Mary I, the "incestuous bastard", for turning England away from the Protestant faith. He wrote of her being worse than Jezebel, saying that Jezebel "never erected half so many gallows in all Israel, as mischievous Mary has done within London alone". He also attacked her "pestilent council" and her bishops for helping her in her cruelty against Protestants.

As for Mary's impending marriage, Knox wrote:

"But, O England, England! if you obstinately will return into Egypt: that is, if you contract marriage, confederacy, or league, with such princes as maintain and advance idolatry (such as the emperor, who is no less enemy unto Christ than ever was Nero): if for the pleasure and friendship (I say) of such princes, you return to your old abominations, before used under the Papistry, then assuredly, O England! you shall be plagued and brought to desolation, by means of those whose favours you seek, and by whom you are procured to fall from Christ, and to serve Antichrist."

1524 – Death of Queen Claude of France, consort of Francis I, at the age of just twenty-four. She died at Blois and was temporarily laid to rest in the chapel there, but then moved to the royal abbey of St Denis just outside Paris in 1527. Brantôme declared that Claude's husband, Francis I, gave her "a disease that shortened her days", meaning syphilis, but it is not known for certain what she died of.

1547 – Death of Beatus Rhenanus (or Beatus Bild), humanist, classical scholar and friend of Erasmus, in Strasbourg. His works included a biograpy of priest and preacher Johann Geiler von Kaisersberg, a nine volume work on Erasmus, the *Rerum Germanicarum Libri III* and his editions of the work of Roman historian Velleius.

1554 – Philip of Spain arrived in England, at Southampton, in readiness for his marriage to Mary I.

21ST JULY

In 1545, during the *Italian Wars*, French forces landed at Whitecliff Bay and Bonchurch on the Isle of Wight. François van der Delft, the Imperial Ambassador, wrote to his master Charles V:

"On Tuesday [21st] the French landed in the Isle of Wight and burnt 10 or 12 small houses; but they were ultimately driven to take refuge in a small earthwork fort, and a large force, 8,000, is now opposed to them. Yesterday, Wednesday, and the previous night, nothing could be heard but artillery firing, and it was rumored that the French would land elsewhere."

...and added a postscript saying that he'd just heard that the English forces had sunk a French galley, and that the Chevalier D'Aux of Provence had been killed.

The French were not successful in taking the island, and a plaque at Seaview commemorates the repulsion of the forces: "During the last invasion of this country hundreds of French troops landed on the foreshore nearby. This armed invasion was bloodily defeated and repulsed by local militia 21st July 1545".

1553 – Arrest of John Dudley, Duke of Northumberland for his part in placing his daughter-in-law, Lady Jane Grey, on the throne.

1586 – Explorer Thomas Cavendish set sail from Plymouth on his South Sea voyage.

1601 – Burial of Peregrine Bertie, 13th Baron Willoughby of Willoughby, Beck and Eresby, at Spilsby Church. Bertie was the son of Katherine Willoughby (married names Brandon and Bertie), Duchess of Suffolk, who married his father, Richard Bertie, as her second husband.

22ND JULY

Henry VIII's illegitimate son, seventeen year-old Henry Fitzroy, Duke of Richmond and Somerset, died at St James's Palace on this day in 1536, probably of tuberculosis. He was just seventeen years of age. His death was a huge blow for Henry VIII, not only because he loved his son deeply, but because he was left without an heir. Henry had made both his daughters illegitimate, and now he couldn't even legitimize his bastard son.

Burial arrangements were left to Thomas Howard, 3rd Duke of Norfolk, who arranged for Fitzroy to be buried at Thetford Priory in Norfolk. He was later moved to St Michael's Church, Framlingham, Suffolk, due to the dissolution of the priory, and joined there by his wife, Mary Howard, after her death in 1557. St Michael's Church is also home to the tombs of Thomas Howard, 3rd Duke of Norfolk, and Henry Howard, Earl of Surrey.

<hr />

1437/8 – Birth of John Scrope, 5th Baron Scrope of Bolton, soldier and a Councillor of Richard III. He was imprisoned after supporting pretender Lambert Simnel in 1487, but was pardoned in 1488.

1549 – Robert Kett and protesters stormed Norwich and took the city, during *Kett's Rebellion*.

1576 – Baptism of playwright and pamphleteer, Edward Sharpham, at Colehanger, East Allington, in Devon. He is thought to have written the plays "The Fleire" and "Cupid's Whirligig".

1581 – Death of Richard Cox, Bishop of Ely, at Downham in Cambridgeshire. He was buried in Ely Cathedral.

23RD JULY

Henry Carey, 1st Baron Hunsdon, Privy Councillor and Lord Chamberlain, died on 23rd July 1596 at Somerset House. It is said that on his deathbed, Elizabeth I offered to give him the title Earl of Wiltshire, a title once held by his grandfather, Thomas Boleyn, but Henry refused Elizabeth's offer, saying "Madam, as you did not count me worthy of this honour in life, then I shall account myself not worthy of it in death." He was buried at Westminster Abbey on 12th August 1596 in St John the Baptist's Chapel, at Elizabeth I's expense. His tomb is the tallest in the Abbey.

Hunsdon was the son of William Carey and his wife, Mary Boleyn, sister of Anne Boleyn. Mary was mistress to Henry VIII at some point in the 1520s, and some people believe it is possible that Hunsdon was actually fathered by the King.

1543 – Mary of Guise and her daughter, Mary, Queen of Scots, escaped from Linlithgow Palace, where they were being watched, to Stirling Castle. They were helped by Cardinal Beaton.

1563 – Death of Cuthbert Vaughan, soldier and Muster-Master and Comptroller of the English garrison at Newhaven (actually Le Havre), from the plague.

1584 – Death of John Day, Protestant printer, bookseller and publisher of John Foxe's "Actes and Monuments" ("Book of Martyrs"), at Walden in Essex. He was buried at Little Bradley parish church in Suffolk.

24TH JULY

On this day in 1567, Mary, Queen of Scots was forced to abdicate. Her one year old-son, James, became King James VI of Scotland with his uncle, Mary's illegitimate half brother, James Stewart, Earl of Moray, acting as regent.

Mary was unable to fight for her throne, being imprisoned in Lochleven Castle and being ill in bed after recently miscarrying twins:

"On the afternoon of the 24th day of July 1567, the Lords Lyndsay and Ruthven, accompanied by two notaries and the said Melvil, came into the Queen's chamber. She was lying on her bed, in a state of extreme weakness, partly because of the great trouble she was suffering, partly in consequence of a great flux (the result of an abortion of two children, her issue by Bothwell), so that she could move only with great difficulty."

Lyndsay and Ruthven brought Mary the deeds of abdication, and allegedly told her that she would be killed if she didn't sign them.

Mary signed the deeds, in the hope that they would be found invalid because they were signed under duress, but it was the end of her reign, and her son was crowned on 29th July at the Church of the Holy Rude, Stirling.

1534 – Jacques Cartier, the French explorer, landed in Canada, at Gaspé Bay in Quebec, and claimed it for France by placing a cross there.

1553 – Birth of Richard Hesketh, merchant and conspirator, in Lancashire. In 1593, Hesketh urged Ferdinando Stanley, 5th Earl of Derby, to lead a rebellion to claim the throne of England, through his descent from Mary Tudor, Queen of France. Stanley turned Hesketh in, and the latter was executed on 29th November 1593.

1594 – John Boste, Roman Catholic priest and martyr, was hanged, drawn and quartered in Durham after being accused of leaving and re-entering England without permission. He was canonized in 1970 by Pope Paul VI.

25TH JULY

On this day in 1554, the feast day of St James, Mary I married Philip of Spain, son of Charles V, the Holy Roman Emperor, in Winchester Cathedral.

Stephen Gardiner, Bishop of Winchester and Mary's Chancellor, performed the ceremony, which was a public spectacle and a state occasion. The twenty-seven year-old groom wore a white doublet and breeches topped with a mantle of cloth of gold decorated with precious stones, a present from his bride, and the collar of the Order of the Garter. The thirty-eight year-old bride, who had chosen the fashionable French style, wore a gown of "rich tissue with a border and wide sleeves, embroidered upon purple satin, set with pearls of our store, lined with purple taffeta". The dress also had a partlet, a high collar, a kirtle of white satin, embroidered with silver, and a train.

Gardiner began the ceremony by making a speech regarding the marriage treaty, and then announced that Charles V had settled the kingdom of Naples on his son, the groom. He then went on to the marriage ceremony itself, pronouncing it in both English and Latin, and mass.

After the marriage ceremony and mass were completed, heralds announced the titles of the Mary and her new husband:-

"Philip and Mary, by the grace of God king and queen of England, France, Naples, Jerusalem and Ireland, defenders of the faith, princes of Spain and Sicily, archdukes of Austria, dukes of Milan, Burgundy and Brabant, counts of Habsburg, Flanders and Tyrol."

⸺⸺⸺⸺⸺⸺⸺⸺⸺⸺⸺⸺

1538 – Death of John Barnewall, 3rd Baron Trimleston and Lord Chancellor of Ireland.

1539 – Death of Cardinal Lorenzo Campeggio, diplomat, Bishop of Salisbury, Cardinal-Protector and Papal Legate. Campeggio was buried in Santa Maria in Trastevere, but in 1571 his remains were moved to the church of Santi Marta e Bernardino, the church he had built in Bologna.

1556 – Baptism of George Peele, poet and playwright, in St James Garlickhythe, London. Peele's works included the pastoral comedy "The Arraignment of Paris", "The Battle of

Alcazar" and "The Love of King David and fair Bethsabe: with the Tragedie of Absalon".

1577 – Death of Nicholas Barham, Sergeant-at-Law and Queen's Sergeant, at Oxford. He was a victim of the Black Assize (gaol fever), a fever which killed around 300 people associated with the trial of Roland Jenkes, a recusant bookseller.

1602 – Burial of Salomon Pavy, actor, at the church of St Mary Somerset, near Blackfriars Theatre. Pavy was just thirteen years old, and is thought to have been abducted to serve as an actor in the Children of Paul's. He later joined the Children of the Queen's Revels at the Blackfriars Theatre and had parts in Ben Jonson's "Cynthia's Revels" and "The Poetaster".

1603 – Coronation of James I at Westminster Abbey. As Westminster Abbey points out "he was the first Scottish King to be crowned sitting on the Stone of Scone (contained in the Coronation Chair) for over 300 years".

26TH JULY

On this day in1588, 4,000 men assembled at Tilbury Fort, the fort built on the Thames estuary in Essex by Elizabeth's father, Henry VIII.

The Armada had first been spotted off English shores on 19th July, off The Lizard, the time when, according to legend, Sir Francis Drake insisted on finishing his game of bowls on Plymouth Hoe before leaving to vanquish the Spanish threat. On the 19th July, Lord Howard of Effingham and Sir Francis Drake set sail from Plymouth with 55 ships in pursuit of the Spanish Armada. Two days later, there was a skirmish off Eddystone, followed by a more serious engagement two days later off the Isle of Portland, where two Spanish ships, *The Rosario* and the *San Salvador*, were abandoned after being damaged. On the 25th July, two more Spanish ships were wrecked off the Isle of Wight.

By the 22nd July, news of the Spanish threat had reached Elizabeth I at Richmond, by a system of beacons, but the Queen did not panic, and impressed her council with her calm reaction. She knew that her navy, with its smaller, lighter and faster ships, was, in the words of Effingham, "the strongest that any prince in Christendom hath." She composed a prayer of intercession which was read out in England's churches and then Queen, Council and country waited for Spain's next move.

Meanwhile, Robert Dudley, Earl of Leicester, who had been appointed Lieutenant and Captain General of the Queen's Armies and Companies, was gathering troops at Tilbury Fort in anticipation of a Spanish attack. He had also created a blockade of boats across the Thames. England was prepared.

1538 – Death of George Talbot, 4th Earl of Shrewsbury and 4th Earl of Waterford, at South Wingfield Manor, Derbyshire. He was buried at St Peter's Church, Sheffield.

1614 – Death of Henry Grey, 1st Baron Grey of Groby, at Bradgate Park. He was buried in the family chapel.

27TH JULY

1534 – Murder of John Alen, Archbishop of Dublin, in Artane. Alen, his chaplains and servants, were murdered by the men of Thomas Fitzgerald, Baron Offaly, after their ship ran aground near Clontarf and they were taken prisoner. He was buried in a pauper's grave.

1550 – Baptism of George Whetstone, writer, at St Lawrence, Old Jewry. His works included "The Rocke of Regarde", "The Honorable Reputation of a Soldier", "Heptameron of Civill Discourses" and the two-part play " Promos and Cassandra", which was a source for Shakespeare's "Measure to Measure".

1553 – Edward VI's former tutor and principal secretary, Sir John Cheke, was sent to the Tower for his part in putting Lady Jane Grey on the throne. He was released in spring 1554.

1578 – Death of Jane Lumley (née Fitzalan), Lady Lumley, translator, at Arundel Place in London. She was buried at St Clement Danes, the Strand, but later moved to a tomb in Cheam, Surrey. Jane is known as the first person to translate Euripides's "Iphigeneia at Aulis" into English, and she also translated various orations of Isocrates from Greek to Latin. Her work can be found in the British Library.

1593 – Execution of William Davies, Roman Catholic priest and martyr, at Beaumaris Castle on the Island of Anglesey. He was hanged, drawn and quartered. Davies was beatified in 1987 by Pope John Paul II.

1622 – Death of Thomas Knyvett, Baron Knyvett and Gentleman of the Bedchamber to Queen Elizabeth I and James I, at his home in King Street, Westminster. He was buried in Stanwell Church in Middlesex.

28TH JULY

On this day in 1540, Thomas Cromwell, Earl of Essex, was executed by being beheaded on Tower Hill. Cromwell had been arrested on 10th June 1540 at a council meeting, and a bill of attainder was passed against him on 29th June 1540 for the crimes of corruption, heresy and treason.

He climbed the scaffold on Tower Hill and addressed the gathered crowd. He opened by saying "I am come hither to die and not to purge myself, as some think peradventure that I will", and then went on to acknowledge that he had offended God and the King and asked for their forgiveness. He then declared "I die in the Catholic faith, not doubting in any article of my faith... nor in any sacrament of the church". However, Cromwell was using gallows humour and irony here, and did not mean that he was dying a true Catholic. Cromwell was referring to the New Testament "Holy Catholic and Apostolic Church", the one of the Nicene Creed and not the Church of Rome.

Cromwell continued his speech by denying the charges that had been laid against him and saying: "Many have slandered me, and reported that I have been a bearer of such as I have maintained evil opinions; which is untrue: but I confess, that like as God, by His Holy Spirit, doth instruct us in the truth, so the devil is ready to seduce us; and I have been seduced."

He then committed his soul to his Saviour, Jesus Christ, calling on his mercy and stating his faith in the resurrection and justification by faith alone, a reformed idea:-

"I see and acknowledge that there is in myself no hope of salvation, but all my confidence, hope and trust is in thy most merciful goodness. I have no merits or good works which I may allege before thee."

Here, Thomas Cromwell was making it clear that he held Lutheran beliefs, and was indeed what many would call a heretic. He then knelt at the block and was beheaded "by a ragged and Boocherly miser, whiche very ungodly perfourmed the office" – a botched execution in other words.

◇◇◇

1488 – Death of Sir Edward Woodville, courtier and soldier, at the *Battle of St Aubin du Cormier*. Woodville was the brother of Elizabeth Woodville, consort of Edward IV.

1508 – Death of Robert Blackadder, Archbishop of Glasgow and administrator in the governments of James III and James IV. He died at sea, between Venice and Jaffa, while travelling on a pilgrimage to Jerusalem.

1540 – Marriage of Henry VIII and Catherine Howard at Oatlands Palace. Henry's marriage to his fourth wife, Anne of Cleves, had been annulled just a few days before, so the wedding was a low key affair.

1540 – Execution of Walter Hungerford, Baron Hungerford of Heytesbury for treason. He was beheaded on Tower Hill and the charges included buggery and having dealings with witches.

1543 – Burnings of the Windsor Martyrs - Robert Testwood, Anthony Pearson and Henry Filmer – for heresy in Windsor, on waste-ground just north of the castle.

1563 – Ambrose Dudley, Earl of Warwick, surrendered Le Havre to the French after a siege which had lasted since 22nd May.

1585 – Death of Francis Russell, 2nd Earl of Bedford, Privy Councillor and diplomat, at his home in Russell Street, the Strand. He was buried at the chapel of Chenies, his seat in Buckinghamshire.

1588 – Five hell-burners were ordered to be sent amongst the galleons of the *Spanish Armada* at Calais. The high winds at Calais caused an inferno which resulted in complete chaos, and the Armada's crescent formation was wrecked as galleons scattered in panic.

1591 – Execution of William Hacket, puritan and alleged prophet, at Cheapside Cross for treason after he had pierced a portrait of Elizabeth I "in the very place, representing her royall heart", and defaced her coat of arms.

29TH JULY

In 1588, the day after the English had wrecked the crescent formation of the *Spanish Armada* and caused havoc, they attacked the Spanish fleet. This battle is known as the *Battle of Gravelines* because it took place just off the port of Gravelines, a Spanish stronghold in Flanders. The Duke of Medina Sedonia had been unable to reform the Spanish fleet at Calais, due to a south-easterly wind, and was forced to regroup at Gravelines.

The English had learned from previous encounters with the Spanish fleet, and so used new and more successful tactics.

They had learned from capturing *The Rosario* in the Channel that the Spaniards could not easily reload their guns, so with their smaller and lighter ships, the English were able to provoke the Spaniards into firing, but keep out of range, and then close in for the kill. As the Spaniards tried frantically to reload, the English ships took advantage of the situation by getting close to their enemy and firing repeatedly. The Spanish fleet were also adversely affected by the wind, which kept driving them into shallow water.

By around 4pm, both sides had run out of ammunition, although the English had been loading objects like chains into their cannons so that they could continue inflicting damage on the Spanish Armada. Spain was defeated, losing at least five ships and having several others severely damaged. Spain lost around 2,000 men compared to England's 50.

1504 – Death of Thomas Stanley, 1st Earl of Derby, husband of Lady Margaret Beaufort, and stepfather of Henry VII, at Lathom. He was buried at Burscough Priory. It is thought that it was Stanley who placed Richard III's crown on his stepson's head at Bosworth.

1509 – Birth of George Neville, son of Richard Neville, 2nd Baron Latimer, and his wife, Anne Stafford. Neville was Archdeacon of Carlisle and Rector of Salkeld, Spofforth and Morland.

1565 – Marriage of Mary, Queen of Scots, and Henry Stuart, Lord Darnley, at Holyrood Palace (the Palace of Holyroodhouse), Edinburgh.

1573 – Death of John Caius, scholar, Physician to Edward VI, Mary I and Elizabeth I, and founder of Gonville and Caius College, Cambridge, at his home near St Bartholomew's Hospital.

1589 – Hanging of Agnes Waterhouse, one of the Essex Witches, at Chelmsford in Essex.

1591 – Death of Edmund Coppinger, puritan and alleged prophet, after a 7-8 day hunger strike. Coppinger was an associate of William Hacket, who had been executed the day before.

30TH JULY

On this day in 1553, Princess Elizabeth left her new home, Somerset House, to ride to Wanstead and greet her half-sister, Mary, England's new queen.

Princess Elizabeth had moved into Somerset House, a house just off The Strand, on the north bank of the River Thames, just the previous day. Mary had been proclaimed Queen Mary I on 19th July in London and Elizabeth, who had been at Hatfield when she heard the news, rode to London, entering the city on 29th July through Fleet Street and on to her new townhouse, or rather palace, Somerset House.

Somerset House was the former home of Edward Seymour, the 1st Duke of Somerset and former Lord Protector. After Somerset's fall and subsequent execution in 1552, John Dudley, the Earl of Northumberland and new leader of Edward VI's Regency Council, offered Somerset House to Elizabeth in return for her acquiescence to him taking Durham Place, Elizabeth's townhouse.

Somerset House was built by Edward Seymour, Protector Somerset, between 1547-1550, using stone scavenged from the charnel house of St Paul's Cathedral. It had cost him £10,000 to build, and was built in a Renaissance style.

Even though the house had only been completed in 1550, and Somerset had not exactly used it much, historian David Starkey writes that £900 was spent on preparing the house for its new royal mistress in 1553. Starkey also points out that the keeper of the house was no other than Robert Dudley, Northumberland's son and Elizabeth's childhood friend.

1540 – Executions of Catholic martyrs Thomas Abell, Edward Powell and Richard Fetherston for refusing to acknowledge the royal supremacy. They were hanged, drawn and quartered at Smithfield.

1540 – Burnings of religious reformers Robert Barnes, William Jerome and Thomas Garrard at Smithfield for heresy.

1550 – Death of Thomas Wriothesley, 1st Earl of Southampton, at Lincoln House in Holborn. He was buried in St Andrew's Church, Holborn, but then moved later to Titchfield. Wriothesley served Henry VIII as Lord Privy Seal and Lord Chancellor.

1563 – Birth of Robert Parry, writer and diarist, at Tywysog in Debighshire, North Wales. His works included "Moderatus: the most Delectable and Famous Historie of the Black Knight".

1570 – Burial of Sir William Godolphin, soldier, at Breage.

31ST JULY

In 1544, the future Elizabeth I wrote her earliest surviving letter to her stepmother, Catherine Parr. It was written in Italian and in a beautiful italic hand:

"Inimical fortune, envious of all good and ever revolving human affairs, has deprived me for a whole year of your most illustrious presence, and, not thus content, has yet again robbed me of the same good; which thing would be intolerable to me, did I not hope to enjoy it very soon. And in this my exile I well know that the clemency of your highness has had as much care and solicitude for my health as the king's majesty himself. By which thing I am not only bound to serve you, but also to revere you with filial love, since I understand that your most illustrious highness has not forgotten me every time you requested from you. For heretofore I have not dared to write to him. Wherefore I now humbly pray your most excellent highness, that, when you write to his majesty, you will condescend to recommend me to him, praying ever for his sweet benediction, and similarly entreating our Lord God to send him best success, and the obtaining of victory over his enemies, so that your highness and I may, as soon as possible, rejoice together with him on his happy return. No less pray I God, that He would preserve your most illustrious highness; to Whose grace, humbly kissing your hands, I offer and recommend myself.

From St James's this 31st July.

Your most obedient daughter, and most faithful servant, Elizabeth"

1549 – Death of Edmund Sheffield, 1st Baron Sheffield, in Norwich. It is said that he was killed by a butcher called Fulke, while serving in the royal army against the rebels of *Kett's Rebellion*. Apparently he stumbled into a ditch and then was killed by a blow from Fulke. Sheffield was buried in St Martin's at the Palace, Norwich.

1574 – Death of John Douglas, Archbishop of St Andrews and educational reformer, in St Andrews. He was buried in the public cemetery. It is said that he died in the pulpit.

LADY JANE GREY (1537-1554)

1ST AUGUST

Apothecary, alchemist and medium Sir Edward Kelley was born on this day in 1555 in Worcester. In 1582, Kelley impressed astrologer and mathematician Dr John Dee with his abilities as a medium, after Dee had been unsuccessful in making contact with angels. He worked closely with Dee for seven years, taking part in seances and allegedly communicating with angels in a special angelic language. Their work was recorded in Dee's "Book of Enoch".

Kelley also claimed to be an alchemist. He possessed a red powder which, with the help of the alchemical book "The Book of Dunstan", he claimed he could make into a red tincture to transmute base metals into gold. Although he has been viewed as a charlatan, it is clear that he took his work very seriously, as did Dee.

1534 – Germain Gardiner wrote a tract against reformer and martyr John Frith entitled "A letter of a yonge gentylman named mayster German Gardynare, wherein men may se the demeanour and heresy of John Fryth late burned".

1545 – Birth of Andrew Melville, Scottish theologian and Principal of St Mary's College, St Andrews University, at Baldovy, Angus.

1556 – Burning of Joan Waste, a blind woman, in Derby for heresy after she refused to recant her Protestant faith.

1596 – Death of John Astley (Ashley), courtier, probably at Maidstone in Kent. He was buried there at All Saints' Church. Astley served Elizabeth I as a Gentleman of the Privy Chamber, Master of the Jewel House and Treasurer of the Queen's Jewels and Plate. He was also married to Katherine Astley (née Champernowne), Elizabeth I's former governess and Chief Gentlewoman of the Privy Chamber.

1605 – Death of Sir Edmund Anderson, judge and Chief Justice in Elizabeth I's reign, in London. He was buried in the parish church at Eyworth.

2ND AUGUST

1514 – Edward Stafford, Duke of Buckingham, was granted a licence to found a college at Thornbury.

1521 – Cardinal Wolsey arrived in Calais to act as peacemaker and preside over a conference aiming to put an end to the fighting between France and the Empire.

1553 – Elizabeth greeted her half-sister, the newly proclaimed Queen Mary I, in London.

1555 – Burning of James Abbes, Protestant martyr, in Bury for heresy.

1556 – Death of George Day, Bishop of Chichester. He was buried in Chichester Cathedral.

1581 – Burning of Richard Atkins, Protestant martyr, before St Peter's in Rome. It is said that as he was taken to St Peter's, his back and breast were burned by men holding torches, and that his right hand was then cut off and his legs burned first to prolong his suffering.

1589 – Death of Henry III of France after being stabbed in the abdomen by Jacques Clément, a fanatical Dominican friar, the day before. He was buried at the Basilica of Saint-Denis.

1595 – *The Battle of Cornwall.* Spanish forces landed at Mount's Bay and the English militia fled, allowing the Spanish troops to move on and burn Penzance, Mousehole, Paul and Newlyn.

1596 – Burial of Thomas Whithorne, composer and autobiographer, at St Mary Abchurch, London. Whithorne was Chapel Master to Archbishop Matthew Parker.

1601 – Death of George Eyste, author, town lecturer, preacher and Vicar. He died in Bury St Edmunds, Suffolk, and was buried in his church, the Church of St Mary.

1605 – Death of Vice Admiral Sir Richard Leveson in the Strand, London. He was buried in St Peter's Church, Wolverhampton.

3RD AUGUST

On this day in 1553, Mary, who had just been proclaimed Queen Mary I, rode with her half-sister, Elizabeth, from Wanstead to Aldgate to be greeted by the city as its new Queen. Wriothesley's Chronicle describes Mary's appearance that day:-

"Her gowne of purple velvet French fashion, with sleues of the same, hir kirtle purple satten all thicke sett with gouldsmithes work and great pearle, with her foresleues of the same set with rich stones, with a rich bowdricke of goulde, pearle, and stones about her necke, and a riche billement of stones and great pearle on her hoode, her pallfray that she rode on richly trapped with gould embrodred to the horse feete."

Mary was then welcomed by the Lord Mayor of London, who presented her "with the scepter perteyninge to the office". After thanking the Lord Mayor and the aldermen for their "gentlenes", Mary handed the sceptre back to him and entered the city followed by Sir Anthony Browne, "the Lady Elizabethes Grace, hir sister", the Duchess of Norfolk, the Marquis of Exeter and various ladies. In front of the Queen processed the Lord Mayor with the sceptre and the Earl of Arundel bearing the sword.

The royal party passed St Buttolphes Church (St Botolph's), where she was greeted by the children of Christ's Hospital, through Aldgate, which was decorated with arras and streamers, past Leadenhall, down Gracechurch Street, up Fenchurch Street, down Mark Lane and to the Tower of London. There Mary was met by Sir John Gage, the Constable of the Tower, and Thomas Bruges, who welcomed her to the Tower. After entering the Tower, Mary encountered the Duke of Norfolk, Bishop Gardiner and Edward Courtenay, who knelt and asked for her to pardon them. She saluted them "biddinge them ryse up."

Wriothesley's Chronicle goes on to describe the city of London as it celebrated the accession of its new Catholic Queen, the daughter of their beloved Bluff King Hal:-

"All the streates in London, from Algate up to Leadenhall, and so the Tower, were richly hanged with clothes of arras and silke, the streates gravelled all the way, and the citizens standinge at rayles with theyr streamers and banners of eury Company or occupation standinge at theyr rayles, eury Company in their best liueryes with theyr hoodes. Allso there were iiii great stages between Algate and the Tower where clarkes and musicians stoode playinge and singinge goodly ballets which reioysed the Quene's highnes greatly. Allso there was such a terrible and great shott of guns shot within the Tower and all about the Tower wharf that the lyke hath not bene hard, for they neuer ceased shootinge from the tyme her highnes entred in at Algate til she came to Marke Lane ende, which was like great thunder, so that yt had bene lyke to an earthquake. And all the streets by the way as her highnes rode standing so full of people shoutinge and cryinge Jesus saue her Grace, with weepinge teares for ioy, that the lyke was neuer seen before."

It is obvious that the people were happy to see their new queen, and nobody seems to have given a thought to the fate of Lady Jane Grey, the young woman who was Queen from the 6th July to the 19th July after being named Edward VI's heir in his "Devise for the Succession".

***

1528 – Death of Hugh Inge, Archbishop of Dublin and Lord Chancellor of Ireland, from sweating sickness in Dublin. He was buried in St Patrick's Cathedral, Dublin.

1548 – Birth of Sir Robert Houghton, judge, Treasurer (1599) and Sergeant-at-Law (1603), in Gunthorpe, Norfolk.

1549 – Lord Russell marched his 1000 men from Honiton to Woodbury and set up camp for the night. He was heading towards Clyst St Mary and the rebels of the *Prayer Book Rebellion*.

1558 – Burial of Thomas Alleyne, clergyman and benefactor, at St Nicholas Parish Church, Stevenage. Alleyne was known for his support of education, through his financing of schoolmasters and the free tuition he arranged for boys.

1562 – Death of John de Vere, 16th Earl of Oxford, leading magnate in Essex and notorious rake, at Hedingham Castle in Essex.

4TH AUGUST

On this day in history, 4th August 1540, Brother William Horne, laybrother of the London Charterhouse was hanged, disembowelled and quartered at Tyburn. He was the last of the Carthusian martyrs to be killed after eighteen members of the Carthusian order of monks based at the London Charterhouse were condemned to death in 1535 for refusing to accept King Henry VIII as the Supreme Head of the Church.

Horne was executed at Tyburn with Edmund Brindholme, an English Catholic priest and chaplain to Lord Lisle in Calais, and Clement Philpot, a servant of Lord Lisle. Brindholme and Philpot had both been attainted for betraying England by offering assistance to Cardinal Reginald Pole.

According to the Chronicler Raphael Holinshed, at Tyburn on 4th August, "six persons were there hanged and quartered, and had beene atteinted of treason by parlement" including "Giles Heron gentleman", and adds that a gentleman named Charles Carew was also hanged that day "for robbing of the ladie Carew". Holinshed also writes:-

"The fourth of August, Thomas Empson sometime a moonke of Westminster, which had beene in prison for treason in Newgate now for the space of three yeares and more, came before the justices of gaole deliuerie at Newgate, and for that he would not aske the king's pardon, nor be sworne to be true to him, his moonks garment was plucked from his backe, and he repriued, till the king were informed of his malicious obstinacie: and this was the last moonke that was seene in his clothing in England till queene Maries daies."

1549 – The *Battle of Woodbury Common*, part of the *Prayer Book Rebellion*. The battle took place at 4am and happened when the rebels, who had been defending Clyst St Mary, marched to Woodbury Mill where Lord Russell and his troops had camped for the night. The rebels were defeated.

1557 – Burial of Anne of Cleves, fourth wife of Henry VIII, at Westminster Abbey.

1560 – Baptism of Sir John Harington, courtier, translator and author, in the church of All Hallows, London Wall. His godparents were Elizabeth I and William Herbert, 2nd Earl of Pembroke. In his "New Discourse of a Stale Subject, called the Metamorphosis of Ajax" (1596), Harington outlined his design for a flush toilet – a privy with a cistern and flush valve. The Ajax, as it was called, was eventually installed at Richmond Palace.

1566 – Death of Sir Martin Bowes, goldsmith, politician, Lord Mayor of London and Under-Treasurer of the Royal Mint in the Tower of London. He was buried at St Mary Woolnoth, Lombard Street, London.

1578 – Death of soldier Thomas Stucley at the *Battle of Alcazar*. Stucley was fighting against the Moors, with King Sebastian of Portugal, when his legs were blown off by a cannon shot.

1598 – William Cecil, 1ˢᵗ Baron Burghley, died at his home in London aged seventy-six. He was laid to rest at St Martin's Church, Stamford, in his home county of Lincolnshire.

1612 – Death of Hugh Broughton, scholar, theologian and Hebraist, in Cheapside, London. He was buried at St Antholin's Church. Broughton spent the last twenty years of his life petitioning for a new translation of the Bible. His works included "A Concent of Scripture" (1588), "An Epistle to the learned Nobilitie of England, touching translating the Bible from the Original" (1597) and "An Advertisement of Corruption in our Handling of Religion" (1604).

5TH AUGUST

1503 – Death of Sir Reynold (Reginald) Bray, administrator in the reign of Henry VII. He served the King as Chancellor of the Duchy of Lancaster, Treasurer of England and Treasurer for War. Some say that he was an architect and designed Henry VII's Chapel in Westminster Abbey, St George's Chapel in Windsor Castle, where he is buried, and Great Malvern Priory. He definitely funded their building.

1532 – Death of Sir Nicholas Harvey, diplomat, at Ampthill, Bedfordshire. He was buried in Ampthill Church where his memorial brass can still be seen.

1549 – The *Battle of Clyst St Mary* during the *Prayer Book Rebellion*. The Devonian and Cornish rebels were defeated by Lord Russell's troops, and around 900 prisoners were massacred later that day on Clyst Heath.

1551(5th or 6th) – Death of Henry Holbeach, Bishop of Lincoln, at Nettleham.

1600 – Deaths of John Ruthven, 3ʳᵈ Earl of Gowrie, and his brother, Alexander Ruthven, Master of Ruthven, at Gowrie House near Perth. The brothers were killed as they tried to kidnap James VI. They were posthumously found guilty of treason on 15th November 1600 and their bodies hanged, drawn and quartered in Edinburgh.

1601 – Burial of Henry Norris, 1st Baron Norris of Rycote, courtier, diplomat and son of Sir Henry Norris, one of the men executed for alleged adultery with Queen Anne Boleyn. Norris was buried at the chapel at Rycote in Oxfordshire.

6TH AUGUST

1504 – Birth of Matthew Parker, Archbishop of Canterbury, in the parish of St Saviour, Norwich. Parker was the son of worsted weaver William Parker and his wife Alice Monings [Monins] from Kent.

1514 – Marriage of Margaret Tudor, sister of Henry VIII and widow of James IV of Scotland, and Archibald Douglas, 6th Earl of Angus, at Kinnoull in Perthshire.

1549 – *Battle of Clyst Heath* during the *Prayer Book Rebellion*. Upon hearing of the news of the massacre at Clyst St Mary, Two thousand rebels made their way to Clyst Heath where Lords Russell and Grey were camped, and opened fire. The battle lasted all day, but the rebels were defeated in the end. The 18th century historian, John Hooker, wrote of the battle: "Great was the slaughter, and cruel was the fight; and such was the valour of these men, that the Lord Grey declared that he never, in all the wars that he had been, knew the like." Russell marched on to Exeter to relieve the city, which had been under siege for five weeks.

1623 – Death of Anne Hathaway, wife of William Shakespeare. Anne was buried next to her husband in the Church of the Holy Trinity, Stratford-upon-Avon.

7TH AUGUST

Sir Robert Dudley, mariner, cartographer and landowner, was born on this day in 1574 at Sheen House, Richmond. He was the illegitimate son of Robert Dudley, Earl of Leicester and favourite of Elizabeth I, and his lover Lady Douglas Sheffield, daughter of William Howard, 1st Baron Howard of Effingham, and widow of John Sheffield, 2nd Baron Sheffield.

Dudley matriculated from Christ Church, Oxford, in 1588 and inherited the lordships of Denbigh, Chirk and Kenilworth on the death of his uncle, Ambrose Dudley, Earl of Warwick, in 1590.

Dudley is known for his 1594 expedition to the West Indies, and for his publication of the maritime encyclopaedia "Dell'Arcano del Mare", a six part work containing a maritime atlas of the whole world and covering navigation, shipbuilding and fortifications, and astronomy.

1514 – Peace treaty signed between England and France, arranging the marriage of the widowed fifty-two year old Louis XII of France and the eighteen year-old Princess Mary Tudor, sister of Henry VIII.

1541 – Death of Sir Richard Weston, courtier and father of Sir Francis Weston who was executed in 1536 for alleged adultery with Queen Anne Boleyn. Richard served Henry VII as Groom of the Chamber and Henry VIII as an Esquire of the Body, Governor of Guernsey and Treasurer of Calais. He was buried in Holy Trinity Church, Guildford.

1549 – The five year-old Mary, Queen of Scots set sail from Dumbarton, Scotland, for France. A marriage had been agreed between Mary and Francis, the Dauphin, so Mary was going to be brought up at the French court. Mary arrived at Saint-Pol-de-Léon, near Roscoff in Brittany, just over a week later.

1600 – Burial of Sir Thomas Lucy in the parish church at Charlecote, Warwickshire. Lucy was a magistrate and member of Parliament, but is best known for his links with William Shakespeare. Tradition has it that Shakespeare wrote a satirical ballad about Lucy, or he made a caricature of him in the character of Judge Shallow, as revenge after he was judged too harshly for poaching on Lucy's estate, Charlecote Park. There is no evidence to support this story.

1613 – Death of Sir Thomas Fleming, Solicitor-General to Elizabeth I and James I, at Stoneham Park. He also served James I as Chief Justice of the King's Bench. He was buried at North Stoneham Church.

8TH AUGUST

On the 8th August 1588, Elizabeth I decided to accept the Earl of Leicester's invitation, and set out to visit the troops he had gathered near Tilbury Fort, to bring comfort to them. Leicester had written a letter of invitation to the Queen on 27th July in an attempt to stop her recklessly riding to the South Coast to meet Parma's troops. Against the advice of her Council, who wanted her to remain in the safety of London, Elizabeth travelled from St James's Palace to Tilbury by state barge.

On her arrival at Tilbury, the Queen reviewed the 8,000 men Leicester had assembled and then spent the night at Saffron Garden, in Edward Ritchie's manor house. Leicester must have been exhausted; not only had he assembled these men, but he had also organised a boom across the Thames and, as he complained to Sir Francis Walsingham, "he was having to do everything – to be cook, caterer and huntsman".

1503 – The formal wedding of Margaret Tudor and James IV of Scotland in the chapel of Holyroodhouse. The couple had been married by proxy on 15th January 1503 with Patrick Hepburn, the Earl of Bothwell and Lord High Admiral of Scotland, standing in for James. Bothwell was the great-grandfather of James Hepburn, 4th Earl of Bothwell, husband of Mary, Queen of Scots.

1553 – Burial of Edward VI in a white marble vault beneath the altar of Henry VII's Lady Chapel in Westminster Abbey. His grave was unmarked until a memorial stone was placed in front of the altar in 1966. The funeral service was performed by Thomas Cranmer, in keeping with Edward VI's Protestant faith, so Mary I attended a private mass for her half-brother's soul in the Tower of London.

1558 – Birth of George Clifford, 3rd Earl of Cumberland, courtier and privateer, at Brougham Castle, Westmorland. Elizabeth I nicknamed Cumberland her "rogue", and he was her Champion from 1590 until her death.

1560 – Death of William May, Archbishop-elect of York, in London. He died on the day that he was elected Archbishop.

1570 – Execution of John Felton, Roman Catholic martyr, at St Paul's Churchyard. He was hanged, drawn and quartered.

1573 – Death of Simon Renard, Imperial Ambassador, in Madrid, Spain.

1586 or 1587 – Execution of John Finglow, Roman Catholic priest and martyr, at York. He also was hanged, drawn and quartered.

9TH AUGUST

On this day in 1561, from Ipswich, Elizabeth I issued a royal mandate "that no manner of person, being either the head or member of any college or cathedral church within this realm, shall, from the time of notification hereof in the same college, have, or be permitted to have, within the precinct of any such college, his wife, or other woman, to abide and dwell in the same, or to frequent and haunt any lodging within the same college, upon pain that whoever shall do to the contrary shall forfeit all ecclesiastical promotions in any cathedral or collegiate church within the realm".

William Cecil, Lord Burghley, sent the mandate to Archbishop Parker, commenting that "Her Majesty continueth very evil affected to the state of matrimony in the clergy. And if I were not therein very stiff, Her Majesty would utterly and openly condemn and forbid it." The news must have worried the archbishop, who had been married since 1547, and Richard Cox, Bishop of Ely, wrote to Parker concerning the edict, saying "if their wives be driven out, I suppose ye shall seldom find in most of the churches either Dean or Prebendary resiant [resident] there... Now if there families be hurled out suddenly, it seemeth a poor reward for their preaching and godly travail hitherto. There is but one Prebendary continually dwelling with his family in Ely church. Turn him out, daws [doves] and owls may dwell there for any continual house-keeping."

***

1556 – Funeral of Sir William Laxton, Lord Mayor of London (1544-5) and one of the wealthiest London merchants, at the parish church in St Mary Aldermary. The funeral was followed by a banquet hosted by the Grocers' Company of London and a mass led by John Harpsfield, Archdeacon of London.

1557 – Burial of the composer Nicholas Ludford in St Margaret's Church, Westminster. Ludford is known for his festal masses, which can be found in the Caius and Lambeth choirbooks (1521-27) and the Peterhouse partbooks (1539-40), and has been described as "one of the last unsung geniuses of Tudor polyphony" (David Skinner).

1588 – Elizabeth I appeared before her troops at Tilbury and gave her "Tilbury Speech".

1611 – Death of John Blagrave, mathematician and land surveyor. He was buried in St Lawrence's Church, Reading. Blagrave's works included "The Mathematical Jewel" (1585), *Astrolabium Uranicum generale* (1596) and "The Art of Dyalling" (1609). He also designed and made instruments, including sundials and astrolabes.

10TH AUGUST

1512 – *The Battle of Saint-Mathieu* between the English and Franco-Breton fleets off the coast of Brest. Henry VIII's largest ship, *The Regent*, sank as did the Breton ship *The Marie La Cordelière*.

1512 – Death of Sir Thomas Knyvet, courtier and Captain of the Regent. According to one report, he died before the ship sank, being killed by gunfire.

1518 – Death of Sir Robert Sheffield, lawyer and Speaker of the House of Commons. He was imprisoned in the Tower of London after making an enemy of Cardinal Wolsey, being accused of negligence as a Justice of the Peace and of harbouring a killer. It is not clear whether he was still in the Tower at his death, but he was buried in the nearby church of the Austin friars.

1520 – Birth of Madeleine de Valois, consort of James V of Scotland, at St Germain-en-Laye. She was the fourth child of Francis I of France and his wife, Queen Claude.

1532 – Birth of Thomas Jones, known as Twm Siôn Cati, the Welsh-language poet and genealogist. It is unclear whether he was born on *Lammas Day* (1st August) or *St Lawrence's Day* (10th August). Few of his poems have survived, and Welsh folklore has turned him into a "Welsh Robin Hood".

1553 – Mary I held an obsequy or requiem mass for the soul of her late half-brother, Edward VI. While she allowed him to have a Protestant burial on the 8th August, she ordered three days of Catholic requiem masses for him.

1621 – Death of Grey Brydges, 5th Baron Chandos, courtier and magnate. He died in Spa, Belgium, where he had travelled for his health. He was buried in the family chapel at Sudeley.

11TH AUGUST

On this day in 1534, or shortly before, the friars observant were expelled from their houses due to their support of Catherine of Aragon and their refusal to accept the King's supremacy. Some were sent to houses of the Grey Friars where, according to Eustace Chapuys, the Imperial ambassador, "they were locked up in chains and treated worse than they could be in prison". Others were imprisoned in London and a few fled abroad.

Those who remained in England were treated abominably, and we know from "Letters and Papers" that out of the one hundred and forty friars who were expelled in August 1534, at least thirty-one died soon after:

"John Spens died at London; also Thos. Artte, Thos. Kellam, Jeremy Manson, John Kinge, John Kyxe and Nic. Harfforthe. Judocus Asterdam died at Canterbury; Andrew Danolde at Greenwich; John Scryvner at Reading; also Ant. Lenes. Alex. Hyll died in patria; Theodoric Barkham at Greenwich; James Wylyamson at Colchester; Cornelius Symondys in patria; also Edw. Pope and John Biltone. Wm. Ellell at Dancaster. Gerard Dyryson in patria. John Martyne at Newcastle. Rob. Bynkys at Reading. Fras. Caro at Bristol. Hen. Heltryne in patria; also Adrian Dehohe, Thos. Danyell and Fras. Carre. Lewis Wylkynson at Canterbury. Bryan Fysshborne at Yarmouth. Wm. Hasarde at Dunwyche. John Wells at Ipswich. Robt. Bakare at Doncaster."

Thomas Bourchier, a friar in Mary I's reign, wrote of further deaths. He mentioned Anthony Brockby, who was strangled with his own cord after being imprisoned and tortured so badly that "for twenty-five days he could not turn in bed or lift his hands to his mouth"; Thomas Cortt, who died in Newgate prison and Thomas Belchiam, who died of starvation in the same prison.

1556 – Death of Sir John Kingsmill, politician and a man who had been close to Thomas Cromwell and Thomas Wriothesley. He served as Sheriff in the reign of Henry VIII and as a Commissioner for the Dissolution of Chantries in 1548 to Edward VI.

1575 – Death of Alexander Home, 5th Lord Home, in Friar Wynd, Scotland. Home was imprisoned after the 1573 fall of Edinburgh Castle and the garrison loyal to Mary, Queen of Scots.

1581 – Death of Sir Maurice Berkeley, Gentleman Usher of Henry VIII's Privy Chamber. Berkeley served Edward VI as a Gentleman of the Privy Chamber, and was the man who arrested the rebel Thomas Wyatt the Younger in Mary I's reign.

12TH AUGUST

On this day in 1560, the translator, lawyer, physician and paediatrician Thomas Phaer made his will after suffering an accident which made his right hand completely useless. His date of death is unknown, but he died at his Cilgerran estate in Pembrokeshire, Wales, within weeks of his will being drawn up.

Phaer started out his working life as a lawyer and published two legal handbooks, *Natura brevium* (c1530-1535) and "A Newe Book of Presidentes" (1543), but changed direction in the early 1540s to become a physician and medical writer. His medical works include "The Boke of Chyldren" (1545), the first book on paediatrics written in English, "A Goodly Bryefe Treatise of the Pestylence and A Declaration of the Veynes". He has become known as the "Father of English Paediatrics".

Phaer was a renowned translator and had completed translations of nine books of Virgil's *Aeneid* before his death. He was also a writer and contributed verses to "Preceptes of Warre" (1544) and "A Mirror for Magistrates" (1578).

Phaer was laid to rest in Cilgerran Church where a memorial table laid in 1986 reads:

> "Thomas Phaer M.D. Of Cilgerran 1510-1560
> Author of the first work in English on child care
> 'To do them good that have most need,
> that is to say children:
> and to shew the remedies
> that God hath created for the use of man'
> The Book of Children"

1557 – Death of Sir John Pollard, judge, Speaker of the House of Commons (1553 and 1555) and Second Justice of Chester. He was buried in London.

1570 – Death of Lady Ursula Stafford (née Pole), daughter of Margaret Pole, Countess of Salisbury, and wife of Henry Stafford, 10th Baron Stafford.

1573 – Death of nobleman and rebel Leonard Dacre from a fever while in exile in Brussels. He was buried in St Nicolas Church in the city. Dacre is known for his participation in the 1569 *Rising of the North*, a rebellion seeking to remove Elizabeth I and to replace her with Mary, Queen of Scots.

1577 – Death of Sir Thomas Smith, humanist scholar and diplomat, at Hill Hall in Essex. He was buried in St Michael's Church, Theydon Mount. Smith served Elizabeth I as Chancellor of the Order of the Garter and as Secretary of State, but is known for his political books "The Discourse of the Commonweal" and "De Republica Anglorum; the Manner of Government or Policie of the Realme of England".

1596 – Burial of Henry Carey, 1ˢᵗ Baron Hunsdon, in Westminster Abbey at the expense of his cousin Elizabeth I.

13TH AUGUST

On this day in 1514, Princess Mary Tudor, sister of Henry VIII, married King Louis XII by proxy at Greenwich Palace. Mary was present at the ceremony, but the Duke of Longueville stood in for the groom. Records show that the ceremony was attended by Henry VIII and his wife Catherine of Aragon, the Archbishop of Canterbury (William Warham), the Archbishop of York (Thomas Wolsey), the Dukes of Buckingham, Norfolk and Suffolk, the Bishops of Winchester and Durham, the Marquis of Dorset, the Earls of Shrewsbury, Surrey, Essex and Worcester, and French diplomats John de Selva and Thomas Bohier.

Speeches were made by the Archbishop of Canterbury and John de Selva, and then Louis XII's letters patent were read by Thomas Ruthall, the Bishop of Durham, and then the Duke of Longueville and the Princess Mary read their parts of the contract and signed them. The ceremony finished with the Duke giving Mary a gold ring, which she placed on the fourth finger of her right hand.

✧✧✧✧✧✧✧✧✧✧✧✧✧✧✧✧✧✧✧✧✧✧✧✧✧✧✧✧✧✧✧✧

1566 – Death of Sir Humphrey Radcliffe, member of Parliament, at his manor of Elstow. He was buried in Elstow Church. Radcliffe served as a member of Parliament during the reigns of Mary I and Elizabeth I, and then as a Justice of the Peace and Sheriff in Elizabeth I's reign.

1568 – Death of William Barlow, Bishop of Chichester. He was buried in Chichester Cathedral.

1579 – Executions of Roman Catholic martyrs Friar Conn O'Rourke and Patrick O'Healy, Bishop of Mayo. They were hanged just outside Kilmallock, co. Limerick. O'Healy was tortured before his death, by having spikes driven through his hands, in the hope that he would give Sir William Drury, Lord President of Munster, details on James fitz Maurice Fitzgerald's plans to lead a Catholic crusade to Ireland. He would not talk. O'Healy was beatified in 1992.

14TH AUGUST

On the 14th August 1513, William Parr, Marquis of Northampton and brother of Queen Catherine Parr, was born. He was the son of Sir Thomas Parr of Kendal and his wife, Maud (née Green).

At the age of eleven, Parr joined the household of Henry VIII's illegitimate son, Henry Fitzroy, Duke of Richmond and Somerset, at Sheriff Hutton, and in 1527 he married Lady Anne Bourchier, the ten year-old daughter of Henry Bourchier, Earl of Essex. Parr was knighted in 1538 and created Baron Parr of Kendal in 1539, but failed to secure the title of Earl of Essex when his father-in-law died because Thomas Cromwell took it. His marriage to Anne Bourchier was unhappy, with Anne eloping and giving birth to an illegitimate child in 1543. The couple legally separated, but Parr was unable to marry his new love, Elizabeth Brooke, daughter of Baron Cobham, because he was not granted a divorce.

Parr was finally made Earl of Essex in December 1543, due to the influence of his sister, the Queen, and went on to become Captain of the Gentlemen Pensioners and a member of Henry VIII's Privy Council. In 1547, Parr was made Marquis of Northampton after supporting Edward Seymour in his bid to become Lord Protector and Duke of Somerset. A commission ruled in favour of his divorce shortly after he married Elizabeth Brooke in 1547, but Somerset punished Parr for his marriage by removing him from the Privy Council and ordering him to leave Elizabeth. The divorce was finally granted in 1551, and his marriage to Elizabeth was made legal. Their happiness was short-lived, because Parr was imprisoned in the Tower in July 1553 for his part in helping to put Lady Jane Grey on the throne. His divorce was rescinded, and he was stripped of his honours. Parr was lucky to escape with his life, and was released in March 1554.

Parr was restored in favour in Elizabeth I's reign, serving on her Privy Council and being restored as Marquis of Northampton. His divorce was recognised once again, but Elizabeth died in April 1565. Parr married his third wife, Helena Snakenborg, the daughter of a Swedish nobleman, in May 1571, but he died on 28th October that same year.

1473 – Birth of Margaret Pole, Countess of Salisbury, the daughter of George, Duke of Clarence, brother of Edward IV, and his wife Isabel Neville. Margaret was born at Farley Castle, near Bath.

1479 – Date given as the birthdate of Katherine of York (Katherine, Countess of Devon), at Eltham Palace. Katherine was the daughter of Edward IV and Elizabeth Woodville, and she married Sir William Courtenay, the future Earl of Devon, in 1495.

1539 – Death of Sir Peter Edgcumbe. Edgcumbe served as Sheriff of Devon and Cornwall at various times between 1494 and 1534, was at the 1513 *Battle of the Spurs* and was present at the Field of Cloth of Gold in 1520.

1620 – Burial of Katherine Hastings (née Dudley), Countess of Huntingdon, in Chelsea Old Church. Katherine was the daughter of John Dudley, Duke of Northumberland, and his wife Jane, and was married to Henry Hastings, 3rd Earl of Huntingdon. Katherine was buried in her mother's tomb.

15TH AUGUST

On this day in 1588, Catholics Robert Wilcox, Edward Campion, Christopher Buxton and Robert Widmerpool were examined. Campion, Wilcox and Buxton were found guilty of being Roman Catholic priests and Widmerpole was charged with giving aid to a priest. They were executed by being hanged, drawn and quartered at Oaten Hill in Canterbury on 1st October 1588. Buxton was allegedly offered his life if he recanted his Catholic faith, but he refused, saying "I would not purchase a corruptible life at such a rate, and, if I had one hundred lives, I would willingly lay them all down in defence of my faith." The men became known as the *Oaten Hill Martyrs*, and all four were beatified in 1929 by Pope Pius XI.

1544 – Birth of Sir Peter Young, Scottish diplomat and tutor to the young James VI of Scotland, at Dundee.

1551 – Robert Dudley, the future Earl of Leicester, and his friend Barnaby Fitzpatrick, 2nd Baron Upper Ossory, were appointed as Gentlemen of Edward VI's Privy Chamber.

1552 – Death of Sir Anthony Wingfield, soldier and administrator, in Bethnal Green. He was buried at Stepney. Henry VIII named Wingfield as an assistant counsellor of his will and Wingfield served Henry's son, Edward VI, as Vice-Chamberlain of the Household, Comptroller of the Household and Exchequer Chamberlain.

1563 – Death of Thomas Argall, administrator in the reigns of Henry VIII, Edward VI, Mary I and Elizabeth I, at his house in Ivy Lane, London. He was buried in St Faith's under St Paul's. Argall is described by his biographer J.D. Alsop as being "one of the most prominent royal administrators of clerical revenue and accounts" between 1540 and his death in 1563.

1594 – Burial of Thomas Kyd, playwright, at St Mary Colechurch in London. Kyd is known for his play "The Spanish Tragedy" (c1537), and some scholars believe that he wrote a "Hamlet" play before that of William Shakespeare.

1603 – Burial of Lady Mary Scudamore (née Shelton), a member of Elizabeth I's Privy Chamber and one of her favourite sleeping companions, at Home Lacy in Herefordshire. In 1584, Mary, Queen of Scots, accused Elizabeth I of breaking one of Mary Scudamore's fingers in a fit of temper after finding out about Mary's marriage to Sir John Scudamore.

1610 – Death of Peter Lowe, surgeon and founder of the Royal College of Physicians and Surgeons of Glasgow, as it is now known, in Glasgow. He was buried at Glasgow Cathedral.

1612 – Death of administrator Sir Michael Hickes at Ruckholt in Essex from a "burning ague". He was buried at Leyton Church in Essex. Hickes served William Cecil, Lord Burghley, as one of his principal secretaries and was close friends with Burghley's son, Robert Cecil.

16TH AUGUST

On this day in history, 16th August 1513, the *Battle of Spurs* took place at Guinegate (Enguinegatte) in France. It was a battle between the English, backed by Imperial troops, and the French, and is called the *Battle of the Spurs* because the French knights, taken by surprise and realising that they were outnumbered and outmanoeuvred, fled on horseback, their spurs glinting in the sunlight.

In a letter to Margaret of Savoy, written on 17th August 1513, Henry VIII reported that:

"Yesterday morning, after he and the Emperor had crossed the Lys, which passes before Terouenne, towards Guinegate, news came that all the French horse at Blangy were moving, some toward Guinegate, the others to the place where Lord Talbot was stationed before Terouenne to cut off supplies. A skirmish took place and there were taken on his side 44 men and 22 wounded. The French, thinking that the English were still beyond the Lys, considered they would not be in time to prevent them revictualling the town. The English horse however passed by Guinegate and confronted the French, who were three times their number. Several encounters took place and men were wounded on both sides. After this, in the Emperor's company, advanced straight against the French, causing the artillery to be fired at them, whereupon they immediately began to retire, and were pursued for 10 leagues without great loss to the English. Nine or ten standards were taken and many prisoners, among whom are the Duke of Longueville, Marquis of Rothelin, Count de Dunois, Messire René de Clermont, Viceadmiral of France, and others whose names are enclosed. It is said that Lord Fiennes is killed, for his horse is in the English camp. The standard bearer of the "grand escuyer de France," Count Galeace de St. Severin, is also taken. De La Palice is said to be either wounded or killed. The Emperor has been as kind to him as if he were his real father."

<hr />

1533 (16th or 17th) – Death of Thomas Skevington, Abbot of Beaulieu and Bishop of Bangor, at Beaulieu. His body was buried at Beaulieu and his heart buried on the north wall of Bangor Cathedral, before the picture of St Deiniol.

1549 – Death of Sir Christopher More, landowner and administrator. He was buried in St Nicholas's Church, Guildford, in the Loseley Chapel. More was a Justice of the Peace and Sheriff during the reign of Henry VIII and was appointed, in 1539, to the guard of honour prepared for Anne of Cleves in late 1539.

17TH AUGUST

On the 17th August 1510, Henry VII's chief administrators, Sir Edmund Dudley and Sir Richard Empson, were beheaded on Tower Hill after being found guilty of treason.

Dudley had served the late King as Privy Councillor, Speaker of the House of Commons and President of the King's Council, and Empson had served as Speaker of the House of Commons and Chancellor of the Duchy of Lancaster. Both men were arrested shortly after Henry VII's death and accused of plotting to "hold, guide and govern the King and his Council" by assembling men to undertake a coup d'état. This is unlikely to have been true, and historians believe that the men were actually made scapegoats for Henry VII's unpopular financial measures.

Dudley wrote the allegorical treatise "The Tree of Commonwealth" while in prison, in the hope of gaining favour with the new king, Henry VIII. In it, the tree of polity, or government, was supported by its roots which were the virtues of godliness, justice, truth, concord, and peace. It was advice for the new king, but may never have been read by him.

Empson and Dudley were buried in the London Whitefriars.

∞∞∞∞∞∞∞∞∞∞∞∞∞∞∞∞∞∞∞∞∞∞∞∞∞∞∞∞∞∞∞∞∞∞∞∞∞∞∞

1498 – Death of John Scrope, 5th Baron Scrope of Bolton. It is likely that the Yorkist Scrope fought on Richard III's side at the *Battle of Bosworth* in 1485, but escaped punishment by the victor, Henry VII. He was imprisoned in 1487 after supporting the pretender Lambert Simnel, but was released, and by 1492 was loyal to Henry VII.

1517 – Death of Andreas Ammonius (also known as Andrea Ammonio and Andrea della Rena), the Italian humanist scholar, cleric and poet, from sweating sickness during the night of the 17th/18th. He died in London and was buried at St Stephen's,

Westminster. He served Henry VIII as Latin Secretary and received various church offices, including the Canonry and Prebendary of St Stephen's, Westminster. Ammonius also served the papacy as sub-collector of taxes in England.

1545 – Death of Thomas Poynings, 1st Baron Poynings, of dysentery while serving Henry VIII as Lieutenant of Boulogne.

18TH AUGUST

On this day in 1587, the first European Christian was born in the New World. Virginia Dare was the daughter of Ananias Dare and his wife, Eleanor, daughter of Governor John White. She was born in the Roanoke colony, in what is now North Carolina, just days after the arrival of the colonists on Roanoke Island. Virginia was baptised the following Sunday.

It is not known what happened to Virginia or the other colonists. Her grandfather, John White, returned to England for supplies at the end of 1587, and did not return to the colony until August 1590. He found no sign of his family or the other colonists; the colony was deserted. The only clue to their fate was a word carved into a post. White had instructed the colonists to leave a message if they had to leave the colony or were attacked. If they moved to a new place, they were to carve the location on a tree or post, and if they were attacked then they were to try and leave the Maltese cross symbol. There was no cross, just the word "Croatoan", which White took to mean that they had moved to Croatoan Island. He was unable to search for them due to bad weather and he returned to England in October 1590. The colony became known as "the lost colony", and their fate is still a mystery.

1536 – Baptism of William Borough, explorer and naval officer, at St Mary's in Northam, Devon. Borough served Elizabeth I as Comptroller of the Queen's Ships.

1562 – Death of John Mordaunt, 1ˢᵗ Baron Mordaunt of Turvey, politician, peer and member of Henry VIII's Council. He died at his home at Turvey, in Bedfordshire, and was buried in the church there.

1572 – Marriage of Henry III, King of Navarre (future Henry IV of France), and Margaret of Valois at Notre Dame Cathedral in Paris. The aim of the marriage was to unite the Bourbon and Valois families, and also to bring peace between the Catholics and Huguenots. *The St Bartholomew's Day Massacre* of the Huguenots took place just six days after the wedding.

19TH AUGUST

On this day in 1561, at six o'clock in the morning, Mary, Queen of Scots landed at Leith harbour, in Scotland, the country of her birth. The reason for her return to her homeland was the death of her husband, Francis II, King of France. He died in December 1560, and was succeeded by his brother, Charles IX, with his mother, Catherine de' Medici acting as regent for the ten year-old boy. Mary knew that there was no sense in her staying in France. There was no place for her there, so she handed her jewels in to Catherine and set about planning her return to Scotland and making a fresh start.

While she was planning her return, she received a visit from Sir Nicholas Throckmorton and the Earl of Bedford, who had been sent by Elizabeth I to get Mary to ratify the *Treaty of Edinburgh*. Mary refused, pointing out that she was "without counsel". William Cecil, Elizabeth I's primary adviser, saw Mary's refusal as a hostile act and a refusal to accept Elizabeth as England's rightful ruler. It seemed to him that Mary was going to cause trouble.

Scotland, too, was wary of Mary's planned return. There had been a revolt in 1559-60 against the regency of Mary's mother, Mary of Guise, which resulted in her deposition. Mary was briefed on this by Henri Cleutin, Seigneur d'Oysel, her mother's former chief lieutenant, and advised to give her support to Lord James Stuart, her illegitimate half brother. D'Oysel knew that he was the only one who could hold the Scottish Lords together.

Mary, Queen of Scots left the port of Calais on 14th August, and as her galley left the harbour, a ship collided with another vessel and sank, drowning all of its crew. Mary worried that this was a bad omen. She broke down and burst into tears as the French coast disappeared from view, saying "Adieu France. It's all over now. Adieu France. I think I'll never see your shores again."

1531 – Burning of Thomas Bilney, Protestant martyr, at Lollard's Pit, just outside Bishopsgate. Although he was burned as a heretic, he actually denied his reformist views and affirmed his Catholic faith at his execution.

1578 – Death of John Harpsfield, humanist, scholar and Roman Catholic priest, in London. He was buried in St Sepulchre Church, London. Harpsfield is known for his leading role in the Marian persecutions of Protestants and his nine sermons, which appear in Edmund Bonner's 1555 "Homilies".

1591 – Death of Welsh clergyman and Bible translator Thomas Huet at Ty Mawr, Llysdinam, Brecknockshire. He was buried in the chancel of Llanafan Fawr church. Huet helped Richard Davies and William Salesbury translate the "New Testament" into Welsh in 1567.

1601 – Death of William Lambarde, writer, antiquary and lawyer, at Westcombe in East Greenwich. He was buried in St Alphege Church, East Greenwich, but in 1710 his monument was moved to the Lambarde chapel in St Nicholas's Church, Sevenoaks. Lambarde's works included his 1570 "Perambulation of Kent", the 1581 "Eirenarcha: or of the Office of the Justices of Peace" and the 1591 "Archeion, or, A Discourse Upon the High Courts of Justice in England".

20TH AUGUST

On this day in 1588, a thanksgiving service was held at St Paul's in London to give thanks to God for England's victory over the Spaniards. The *Spanish Armada* had been defeated, obliterated in fact, yet the English fleet was left intact, and only around 100 English men were lost in the skirmishes.

Although Sir Francis Drake and Lord Howard of Effingham should be given credit for the English fleet's successful tactics, much of England's victory was down to the weather, the "Protestant Wind" which scattered the Spanish fleet and caused damage to their ships. King Philip II of Spain commented on the defeat of his fleet - "I sent you out to war with men, not with the wind and waves", recognising that it was the weather and not any shortcomings of his commanders who were to blame for England's victory.

Elizabeth I also recognised that England's victory was down to the weather, but she believed that it was because God was on England's side, and had a special medal struck to commemorate England's victory. The medal was inscribed with the words *"Flavit Jehovah et Dissipati Sunt"* – "God blew and they were scattered". The defeat of the *Spanish Armada* was a divine victory, or so the English people believed.

1509 – Birth of Sir William Stanford (Staunford), judge and legal writer. Stanford served Mary I as one of her queen's Sergeants, and is known for his legal books, "Les plees del coron" (1557), on criminal law, and "Exposicion of the Kinges Prerogative" (1567)

1580 – Death of Sir George Bowes, soldier and administrator, at Streatlam, county Durham. He was buried in the family vault at Barnard Castle Church. Bowes served Elizabeth I as a member of the Council of the North and the Ecclesiastical High Commission for York, a Justice of the Peace and Sheriff, and as the Earl of Sussex's Deputy in co. Durham and Richmondshire, and Provost Marshal. Bowes was also chosen to escort Mary, Queen of Scots from Carlisle to Bolton Castle in 1568.

1589 – Marriage of James VI of Scotland and Anne of Denmark, second daughter of King Frederick II of Denmark, by proxy at Kronborg Castle, Helsingør, Denmark. James was represented by his ambassador at the Danish court, George Keith, 5th Earl Marischal.

1599 – Death of Sir Thomas Norris, soldier and Lord President of Munster, at his house at Mallow, County Cork, Ireland. Norris died from an injury to his jaw sustained in a skirmish with Thomas Burke and his troops in May1599.

1610 – Death of courtier Edmund Tilney, censor of plays and Master of the Revels. He was buried in St. Leonard's Church, Streatham, London.

1648 (or 5th August) – Death of Edward Herbert, 1st Baron Herbert of Cherbury and 1st Baron Herbert of Castle Island, diplomat, philosopher and the author of "The Life and Raigne of King Henry the Eighth". He was buried at St Giles-in-the-Fields, London.

21ST AUGUST

On this day in 1535, King Henry VIII and his wife, Queen Anne Boleyn, visited Sir Nicholas Poyntz at his home, Acton Court, in South Gloucestershire as part of their progress to the south-west.

This summer progress, as well as getting the royal couple out of smelly London with its risk of plague, was a chance for Henry to display Anne publicly as Queen, and for the couple to promote the Reformation, and visit the households of people seen as "pro-Reform". It was a political and social progress, and far more than a chance for the couple to get away and have a break.

In preparation for the royal visit, Poyntz had added an entire new wing to Acton Court, just for the royal couple. He decked it out with the latest luxury items, such as Venetian glass, and continental furnishings, and modelled the rooms on Hampton Court. The wing was built so quickly that it didn't have any foundations! Poyntz was obviously in a rush to prepare his house for the very special visit.

1536 – Death of Robert Sherborn (Sherborne), former Bishop of Chichester, at Chichester. He was buried in the cathedral there. The elderly and conservative bishop was forced to resign his see in June 1536 after being examined by Dr Richard Layton.

1551 – Death of Sir John Packington, judge. He was buried at Hampton Lovett in Worcestershire, where he had settled in 1528. Packington was an active member of the Council of the Marches, a justice for North Wales, Recorder of Worcester, a judge on the Brecon circuit in Wales, and Recorder of Ludlow.

1553 – Death of Sir Thomas Heneage, courtier. Heneage served Henry VIII as Groom of the Stool and Chief Gentleman of the Privy Chamber, and served Edward VI as a Gentleman of the Privy Chamber. He was buried in the chancel of the parish church at Hainton, Lincolnshire.

1568 – Death of Humphrey Llwyd, antiquary, translator and cartographer from a fever. He was buried in the north aisle of St Marcella's (Llanfarchell) Church, which is also known as Whitchurch or Eglwys Wen. Llwyd is known for producing the first ever printed map of Wales.

22ND AUGUST

On this day in history, the 22nd August 1485, in rural Leicestershire near Market Bosworth, the armies of King Richard III and Henry Tudor faced each other in a battle that would see the death of the King and the beginning of a new dynasty: the Tudor dynasty.

When Henry Tudor challenged the King on that August day, Richard III had been King for just over two years. He had gone from being Lord Protector to the young King Edward V, the twelve year-old son of Richard's brother Edward IV, to being King after Edward IV's sons were declared illegitimate. His challenger, Henry Tudor, was the son of Edmund Tudor, 1st Earl of Richmond, and Lady Margaret Beaufort, a woman descended from John of Gaunt, third son of Edward III. As a Lancastrian, Henry had fled to Brittany in France, after Edward IV successfully regained the throne from Henry VI in 1471. He returned to England after his mother had conspired with Elizabeth Woodville, Edward IV's widow, to arrange a marriage between Elizabeth's daughter, Elizabeth of York, and Henry, and to promote Henry as an alternative to Richard III.

In the summer of 1485, Henry made his move. With the support of the French and some English exiles, he sailed from France to Milford Haven on the Welsh coast to declare war on the King. His Welsh heritage enabled Henry to gain more support there and add to his army, and when he finally met Richard at *Bosworth*, it is estimated that he had around 5000 men. Henry requested the support of his stepfather, Lord Thomas Stanley, and his step-uncle, Sir William Stanley, who were both wealthy men and could raise large armies to support Henry. The Stanleys, although linked to Henry through Thomas's marriage to Margaret Beaufort, were actually supporters of the King, so it was not known who they would support on the battlefield. Richard, on hearing of Henry's landing in Wales, took Thomas Stanley's eldest son, Lord Strange, hostage in an attempt to ensure that the Stanleys would stay true.

Although Henry had managed to build an army of around 5000 men, Richard's men, who were marching out from Leicester in an attempt to cut Henry off as he marched from Wales to London, are thought to have numbered around 12000. Richard must have felt confident that he could squash Henry, particularly when they finally met, and Henry's men were struggling to negotiate marshland while Richard's men were on higher ground. Richard and his army certainly had the advantage, particularly as Henry had no battle experience whatsoever.

Richard took the initiative and sent the Duke of Norfolk and some men out to attack Henry's men who had become strung out in a line below them after being forced to circle around the marsh. Fortunately for Henry, he had the Earl of Oxford, an experienced soldier on his side, who knew just what to do. Oxford quickly created a wedge of men between two banners and, in the fighting that followed, the Duke of Norfolk was killed – a blow for the King, but he still had a huge army at his disposal. Things looked good for the King until the Stanleys, who had been watching events unfold, but had not committed their armies to any particular side, made a decision. As Richard III's cavalry clashed with Henry and his men, who had been on their way to appeal to the Stanleys, William Stanley ordered his men to attack the King and his cavalry. Before the Stanleys and their men reached Henry and Richard, Richard's men managed to kill Henry's standard bearer, Sir William Brandon (father of Charles Brandon, Duke of Suffolk), and unhorse Sir John Cheyne, but the tide turned when Stanley's men reached the spot. King Richard III was killed and Henry Tudor was crowned King Henry VII later that day when Richard's crown was recovered.

Richard III's body was recovered from the battlefield and taken to Leicester, where it was displayed for several days before being buried.

The new king, Henry VII, secured his claim to the throne by marrying Elizabeth of York on the 18th January 1486, thus uniting the Houses of York and Lancaster and starting a new dynasty: The House of Tudor. The emblem of the Tudor Rose symbolised this union by combining the white rose of York and the red rose of Lancaster. This was the start of a new era, the reign of the Tudors, that iconic family who reigned over England for just 118 years, but who have captured the hearts and minds of many people all over the world.

◇◇◇◇◇◇◇◇◇◇◇◇◇◇◇◇◇◇◇◇◇◇◇◇◇◇◇◇◇◇◇◇◇◇◇◇◇◇◇

1532 – Death of William Warham, Archbishop of Canterbury and administrator to Henry VIII, in Hackington, Kent. Warham served Henry VIII as Keeper of the Great Seal, and Lord Chancellor. Warham was buried in Canterbury Cathedral, having left instructions to be buried near the spot where Thomas Becket was killed.

1545 – Death of Charles Brandon, Duke of Suffolk, magnate, courtier, soldier and close friend of Henry VIII, at Guildford, while making preparations to lead an army to Boulogne. He was laid to rest in St George's Chapel, Windsor Castle.

1552 – Edward VI visited Christchurch on his royal progress.

1553 – Execution of John Dudley, Earl of Warwick and Duke of Northumberland, on Tower Hill for his part in putting his daughter-in-law, Lady Jane Grey, on the throne in place of Mary

I. He was buried in the Chapel of St Peter ad Vincula, at the Tower of London, and is thought to lie under the Chancel floor next to Edward Seymour, Duke of Somerset, and between Anne Boleyn and Catherine Howard. Northumberland's friends, Sir John Gates and Sir Thomas Palmer, were also executed on this day in 1553 for supporting Northumberland.

1572 – Execution of Thomas Percy, 7th Earl of Northumberland, in the Pavement at York. He was executed for treason after leading the *Rising of the North* against Elizabeth I. His body was buried in St Crux Church, York.

1583 – Death of Sir Henry Bedingfeld of Oxburgh Hall, administrator. He was buried at Oxborough parish church in Norfolk. Bedingfeld's career included him serving Edward VI and Mary I as a Privy Councillor, and Mary I as Lieutenant of the Tower of London, Captain of the Guard and Vice-Chamberlain of the Household. He was Constable of the Tower of London during the imprisonment of Mary I's half-sister, Elizabeth (the future Elizabeth I).

23RD AUGUST

On 23rd August 1548, Francis Talbot, 5th Earl of Shrewsbury, arrived at the *Siege of Haddington*, in East Lothian, Scotland, with a large army.

The siege was actually part of a series of sieges at Haddington, which were all part of the Anglo-Scottish war known as the *War of the Rough Wooing*, so named because it was had been started in 1543 by Henry VIII in a bid to secure a marriage agreement between England and Scotland, between Prince Edward and Mary, Queen of Scots.

James Hamilton, 2nd Earl of Arran and Regent of Scotland, had taken Haddington in September 1547, with the help of the French, but English troops led by William Grey, 13th Baron Grey de Wilton, and Sir Thomas Palmer took Haddington in

February1548, and set about fortifying it. It came under heavy attack from French and Scots troops in July 1548, so English reinforcements became necessary. Shrewsbury's arrival led to the French and Scottish armies abandoning the siege and moving to Edinburgh and Leith.

The English troops eventually withdrew in September 1549. They had used up their supplies and suffered heavy losses from the plague, and from attacks by the Scots.

1524 – Death of Edmund Audley, Bishop of Salisbury, at Ramsbury. He was buried in Salisbury Cathedral, on the north side of the presbytery.

1535 – Anne Boleyn and Henry VIII visited the Walsh family at Little Sodbury Manor in the village of Little Sodbury, South Gloucestershire, while on their progress to the southwest. The Walsh family were reformers, and had even once hired William Tyndale, a leading figure in the Reformation, a Bible translator and the author of "The Obedience of a Christen [Christian] Man", as a tutor for their children.

1553 – Stephen Gardiner, Bishop of Winchester, was made Lord Chancellor by Mary I.

1568 – Death of Thomas Wharton, 1st Baron Wharton, who was rewarded with a barony after his victory at the *Battle of Solway Moss* in 1542. He died at Healaugh, in the West Riding of Yorkshire, and was buried there.

1613 – Death of John Harington, 1st Baron Harington of Exton, courtier, from a fever at Worms. His body was sent back to England for burial at Exton. In Elizabeth I's reign, Harington served as a member of Parliament, Justice of the Peace, Sheriff and Deputy Lieutenant of Rutland and Warwickshire.

24TH AUGUST

On this day in 1572, the *St Bartholmew's Day Massacre* took place. An estimated 3,000 French Protestants (Huguenots) were massacred in Paris, and a further estimated 7,000 in the provinces. According to tradition, Catherine de' Medici persuaded her son, King Charles IX of France, to order the assassination of key Huguenot leaders who had gathered in Paris for the wedding of their leader, Henry of Navarre, to Margaret of Valois, the King's sister.

The wedding had taken place six days earlier, on 18th August, but the Huguenots were still in the city to discuss grievances regarding the 1570 *Peace of Saint-Germain-en-Laye*, the peace treaty which had ended the third *French War of Religion*. On the 22nd August, Admiral Gaspard de Coligny, the leader of the Huguenots, was shot and seriously wounded. It is not known who ordered the attempt on his life, but there are three main suspects: the Guises (leaders of the Catholic party), the Duke of Alba (the man governing the Netherlands) and Catherine de' Medici. Whatever the truth behind the assassination attempt, the shooting triggered trouble. The Huguenots were angry and demanded an investigation into the shooting, which the King agreed to do, but on 23rd August the King and his mother agreed that the Huguenots were a threat that needed dealing with, and made the decision to order the murders of the Huguenot leaders.

Just before dawn on 24th August 1572, Admiral Coligny was stabbed to death by Besme, one of the Duke of Guise's men, and thrown out of his bedroom window. This killing sparked off city-wide violence with Parisians turning on Huguenot men, women and children, killing them and throwing their bodies into the River Seine. The violence in Paris lasted three days, but news of the Paris trouble sparked off massacres in Toulouse, Bordeaux, Lyon, Bourges, Rouen, Orléans, Meaux,

Angers, La Charité, Saumur, Gaillac and Troyes, and the violence lasted until well into October in some cases.

We do not know exactly how many people died in these horrific massacres. The Huguenot Maximilien de Béthune, duc de Sully, who escaped the massacre in Paris by carrying a "Book of Hours" under his arm, reported that 70,000 Huguenots were murdered, whereas modern historians, Ranke and Henri Martin, estimate the number of victims in Paris at 2000. Philip Benedict, in his article "The Saint Bartholomew's Massacres in the Provinces", puts the death toll at 2,000 in Paris and 3,000 in the provinces, compared to a total of 30,000 quoted by historians F. Fernández-Armesto and D. Wilson in "Reformation: Christianity and the World 1500 – 2000". Whatever the true figure, it was an horrific event.

1507 – Death of Cecily, Viscountess Welles, third daughter of Edward IV and Elizabeth Woodville, at Hatfield, Hertfordshire. She was buried at "the friars", but it is not known what religious house the record was referring to.

1549 – Death of Sir Wymond Carew, administrator. Carew served Henry VIII as Deputy Receiver-General of the Duchy of Cornwall, as Receiver-General to Queens Jane Seymour and Anne of Cleves, as Treasurer to Queen Catherine Parr, and as Treasurer of the Court of First Fruits and Tenths.

1561 – Birth of Thomas Howard, 1st Earl of Suffolk, naval officer and administrator. Howard was the eldest son of Thomas Howard, 4th Duke of Norfolk, and Margaret Dudley. Howard served Elizabeth I as Vice-Admiral in the 1596 Cadiz expedition and the 1597 voyage to the Azores, and as Constable of the Tower of London. He went on to have a distinguished career under James I until his fall in 1619.

1587 – Death of Richard Barnes, Bishop of Durham. He was buried at Durham Cathedral, in the choir.

1595 – Death of Thomas Digges, mathematician, astronomer, soldier and member of Parliament. Digges is known as the first man to expound the Copernican system in English, and one of the first to put forward the idea of an infinite universe with an infinite number of stars.

25TH AUGUST

Mildred Cecil, Lady Burghley, was born on 25th August 1526 as Mildred Cooke. She was the daughter of Sir Anthony Cooke, a scholar and the man who became Edward VI's tutor, and his wife, Anne Fitzwilliam. Cooke educated his daughter himself, at home, providing her with the classical education usually reserved for boys.

Mildred is known not only for being the second wife of William Cecil, 1st Baron Burghley and Elizabeth I's trusted minister, but for her humanist education, intelligence and fluency in Greek and Latin. Mildred also translated several works, including a Greek sermon by Basil the Great. Her huge library contained works in Latin, Greek, French and English, covering the subjects of religion, literature, history and medicine. At her death in 1589, on her instruction, many of her books were given to educational institutions, and seventeen of her books are housed today at Hatfield House.

Mildred was an influential woman, and used her position to help charity and to listen to petitioners before presenting their cases to her husband. Her husband's devotion to her is shown in his eulogy on her monument, in which he describes her as "dearest above all" and "far beyond the race of womankind".

1538 – Death of Thomas Starkey, humanist and political theorist. He was buried in the chancel of St Mary's, North Petherton, Somerset. Starkey is known for his works, "Dialogue between Pole and Lupset" and "An Exhortation to the People Instructing them to Unity and Obedience".

1540 – Date traditionally given for the birth of Lady Katherine Grey, daughter of Henry Grey, 1st Duke of Suffolk, and his wife, Frances (née Brandon), at Bradgate Park. Katherine was one of the sisters of Lady Jane Grey.

1549 – Robert Kett, leader of the rebels in *Kett's Rebellion*, launched an attack on the south side of Norwich and burned a number of buildings.

1554 – Death of Thomas Howard, 3rd Duke of Norfolk, at Kenninghall.

1557 – Death of Mary Howard (née Fitzalan), Duchess of Norfolk, at Arundel House, London. It is thought that she died of complications after childbirth. Mary was buried in St Clements without Temple Bar.

1558 – Death of John Robins, clergyman, mathematician and astrologer, at Windsor. He was buried in St George's Chapel, Windsor Castle. It is thought that Robins tutored Henry VIII in the subjects of mathematics and astronomy.

1559 – Death of Sir Thomas Cawarden, courtier and Master of Revels to Henry VIII, Edward VI and Mary I, at Horsley. He was buried in Bletchingley church.

26TH AUGUST

On this day in 1533, the ceremony of the Queen's "taking her chamber" took place at Greenwich Palace.

A heavily pregnant Queen Anne Boleyn attended a special mass at the Chapel Royal of Greenwich Palace and then processed, with her ladies, to the Queen's great chamber. There, the group enjoyed wine and spices before Anne's lord chamberlain prayed that God would give the Queen a safe delivery. After the prayer, Anne and her ladies retired to her chamber, which, from that moment on, would be a male-free zone.

The room would have been rather dark and claustrophobic. The walls and ceiling would have been hung with tapestries, the floor covered with rugs, and any windows also covered. The canopied bed was accompanied by a pallet on which the Queen would give birth, and an altar was set up with crucifixes and candles.

The birthing chamber, which sounds as if it would have been rather stifling in a hot August, was to be Anne Boleyn's home until she was churched thirty days after the birth. Fortunately for Anne, her baby came sooner than expected and she gave birth to a girl, the future Elizabeth I, on 7th September 1533.

1539 – Death of Piers Butler, 1st Earl of Ossory and 8th Earl of Ormond, Lord Deputy of Ireland and a man known as "Red Piers". He died at Kilkenny Castle and was laid to rest in the chancel of St Canice's Cathedral, Kilkenny.

1549 – The Earl of Warwick received 1,000 mercenaries as reinforcements to fight the rebels of *Kett's Rebellion*.

1552 – Death of Sir Clement Smith, administrator, brother-in-law of Jane Seymour and Lord Treasurer's Remembrancer from 1539 until his death. He died at Little Baddow in Essex.

1555 – Mary I and her husband, Philip of Spain, departed from Whitehall in preparation for Philip's return to the Low Countries.

1570 – Death of Thomas Thirlby, Bishop of Westminster and of Ely, at Lambeth Palace. He was deprived of his sees in 1559 due to his Catholic sympathies, and then imprisoned in the Tower in 1560. He was eventually released into house arrest at Lambeth, where he spent his last years. Thirlby was buried in the parish church at Lambeth.

1613 – Death of George Owen of Henllys, Welsh antiquary, author, naturalist, Deputy Lieutenant of Pembrokeshire and

High Sheriff of Pembrokeshire, in Haverfordwest. He was buried at Nevern church. His works include "The Description of Penbrokshire".

27TH AUGUST

On this day in 1549, the *Battle of Dussindale* took place, ending *Kett's Rebellion* in Norfolk. The mercenaries John Dudley, Earl of Warwick, had received the day before forced Kett and his rebels to move from Mousehold to the valley of Dussindale by cutting off their supply lines. It was in this valley – the actual location is not known – that a bloody battle took place on 27th August. There were heavy losses on both sides, with reports ranging from 1,000 to 10,000 rebels being killed. Warwick was victorious, and the rebellion was over.

Robert Kett fled the battle scene, but was captured the following day at the nearby village of Swannington. He and his brother, William, were imprisoned in the Tower of London and then tried for treason. They were both found guilty and were hanged on 7th December 1549; Robert at Norwich Castle and William at Wymondham Abbey.

On 28th August 1549, rebels who had been captured during the battle were hanged at the Oak of Reformation, the tree where the rebels had previously gathered for prayer, and outside the Magdalen Gate, Norwich.

***

1557 – The storming of St Quentin by English and Imperial forces. Admiral de Coligny and his French troops, numbering only a thousand, were overcome by around 60,000 soldiers, and St Quentin fell. Henry Dudley, the youngest son of the late John Dudley, Duke of Northumberland, was killed by a cannonball during the storming.

1590 – Death of Pope Sixtus V at Rome.

1610 – Funeral of Lady Anne Bacon (née Cooke), mother of Sir Francis Bacon, at St Michael's Church, near St Albans. Anne was the daughter of Sir Anthony Cooke, and was known for her translation of John Jewel's "Apologie of the Church of England".

28TH AUGUST

On this day in 1551, Lord Chancellor Richard Rich, Sir Anthony Wingfield and Sir William Petre went to Copthall in Essex to see Edward VI's half-sister Mary. The purpose of their visit was to deliver the King's order that Mary and her household should desist from celebrating the Catholic mass, and that Wingfield should replace Robert Rochester, whom Edward's council had removed, as Mary's comptroller.

Mary was furious with the men. She replied that she was her brother's "most humble and obedient subject", but that "she would lay her head on a block" before using "any other service than was used at the death of the late king, her father". Mary rebuked the men for trying to appoint her servants, telling them that she would appoint her own. She continued, saying, "I am sickly, and yet I will not die willingly, but will do the best I can to preserve my life: but if I shall chance to die, I will protest openly, that you of the council be the causes of my death. You give me fair words, but your deeds be always ill towards me."

Mary refused to obey them and they were forced to leave, having failed their mission.

1550 – Death of Thomas Magnus, administrator, Archdeacon of the East Riding of Yorkshire, member of the King's Council and diplomat, at Sessay in the North Riding of Yorkshire. He was also buried there.

1553 – Death of Sir John Harington, administrator, in Bishopsgate, London. He was buried in Exton. Harington served Henry VIII as Esquire of the Body, Treasurer of War (1542 and 1543), Vice-Treasurer of the army for the 1544 French campaign and Treasurer of the expedition to France (1546).

1583 – Burial of William Latymer, Chaplain to Queen Anne Boleyn, Dean of Peterborough, chaplain to Elizabeth I and author of the "Cronickille of Anne Bulleyne", a biography of Anne Boleyn. He was buried in Peterborough Cathedral.

1588 – Execution of William Dean, Roman Catholic priest and martyr, by hanging at Mile End Green, Middlesex. He was found guilty of high treason for being a Catholic priest.

1588 – Execution of Franciscan friar and martyr, Thomas Felton, near Brentford, Middlesex. He was hanged, drawn and quartered for his beliefs, and for proclaiming that he could not accept a woman as supreme head of the Church.

1588 – An ill Robert Dudley, Earl of Leicester, wrote his final letter to his queen and childhood friend, Elizabeth I. It was a letter she kept beside her bed for the rest of her life. Leicester wrote the letter from the home of Lady Norreys at Rycote, where he was staying on his way to Buxton, to take the waters there.

1609 – Death of Sir Francis Vere (de Vere), soldier. He served in the English army in the Low Countries, and also in the 1596 Cadiz expedition. He was buried in Westminster Abbey.

29TH AUGUST

1503 – Death of Oliver King, Bishop of Bath and Wells, diplomat, former Secretary to Edward V and Registrar of the Order of the Garter.

1538 – Arrest of Geoffrey Pole on suspicion of being in contact with his brother, Cardinal Reginald Pole, who had denounced the King and his policies in his treatise, *Pro ecclesiasticae unitatis defensione.*

1582 – Death of Sir Thomas Offley, Mayor of London, in London. He was buried in the church of St Andrew Undershaft.

1583 – Death of Maurice Browne, courtier, adventurer and mariner. Browne captained *The Swallow* and then *The Delight* on a venture to colonize North America in 1583. The venture failed and Browne, and the voyage leader, Sir Humphrey Gilbert, both died.

1584 – Death of Lucas de Heere, the Flemish painter and poet, probably in Paris. His works included "Solomon and Sheba" (1559) in which de Heere gave Solomon the face of Philip II of Spain.

1599 – Death of Henry Charteris, Scottish printer and bookseller.

30TH AUGUST

On this day in 1548, Mary Seymour, daughter and only child of Catherine Parr, Queen Dowager, and Thomas Seymour, Baron Seymour of Sudeley, was born at Sudeley Castle in Gloucestershire.

Catherine Parr died of puerperal fever on 5th September 1548, just six days after the birth of Mary, and Thomas Seymour was executed as a traitor on 17th March 1549, leaving Mary orphaned at the age of just seven months. We know that Catherine Parr's friend, Katherine Brandon (née Willoughby), the Duchess of Suffolk, was appointed as Mary's guardian, because she appealed to William Cecil to talk to the Duke of Somerset about helping her with the upkeep of Mary's household, which was the household of a Queen's daughter and therefore very expensive to run. The Duchess must have been very relieved in January 1550 when an act of Parliament allowed Mary to inherit her father's property – money would be forthcoming at last.

But that is the last we hear of little Mary Seymour, who would have been around sixteen months old when she was allowed to inherit Thomas Seymour's remaining property. She just disappears from the records, and never claimed her inheritance.

What happened to the little girl has always been a mystery, but historian Linda Porter writes of a poem that might just tell us the fate of Catherine Parr's daughter. The poem, from a Latin book of poem and epitaphs written by Catherine Parr's chaplain, John Parkhurst, in 1573, reads as follows:-

> "I whom at the cost
> Of her own life
> My queenly mother
> Bore with the pangs of labour
> Sleep under this marble
> An unfit traveller.
> If Death had given me to live longer
> That virtue, that modesty,
> That obedience of my excellent Mother
> That Heavenly courageous nature
> Would have lived again in me.
> Now, whoever
> You are, fare thee well
> Because I cannot speak any more, this stone
> Is a memorial to my brief life."

Linda Porter is of the opinion that, although no name is given, it must be the epitaph of Mary Seymour and that she did, indeed, die young. Porter ponders whether she may have been buried at the Lincolnshire estate of the Duchess of Suffolk, near Grimsthorpe. We just don't know.

1501 – Death of Thomas Grey, 1ˢᵗ Marquis of Dorset, courtier and son of Elizabeth Woodville by her first husband, Sir John Grey of Groby. Dorset was buried in the collegiate church of Astley in Warwickshire.

1525 – The *Treaty of the More*, negotiated by Cardinal Thomas Wolsey, was agreed by Henry VIII and Louise of Savoy, who was acting as regent while Francis I was imprisoned by Imperial forces. He had been captured at the *Battle of Pavia*. It was an about-face for Wolsey as he had, in the recent past, been allying England with the Empire, rather than France. By the terms of the treaty, Henry VIII agreed to help secure Francis I's release, and to give up claims to several French territories. In return, France was to award England with a pension of £20,000 per year. The treaty was known as the *Treaty of the More* because negotiations took place at Wolsey's property in Hertfordshire, "The More".

1534 – Death of Thomas Belchiam, Observant Franciscan friar and Catholic martyr. The twenty-eight year-old friar was starved to death at Newgate Prison. Belchiam had allegedly called the King a heretic. It is also alleged that there was an earthquake at the time of his death.

1582 – Death of Richard Curteys, Bishop of Chichester. He was buried at Chichester Cathedral. In 1600, a collection of ten of his sermons on Psalm 25 was published as "The Care of a Christian Conscience".

1595 – Death of William Vaux, 3ʳᵈ Baron Vaux, English peer and Catholic recusant. He was imprisoned in Elizabeth I's reign for his Catholic faith and for harbouring Edmund Campion, a Jesuit priest.

1596 – Death of George Gower, English portrait painter and Sergeant Painter to Elizabeth I, in the parish of St Clement Danes in London. He was buried at the church there.

31ST AUGUST

On this day in 1555, Robert Samuel, former minister of East Bergholt Church in Suffolk, was burned at the stake in Ipswich, probably at the Cornhill. He was one of the *Ipswich Martyrs*, Protestants who were executed in Ipswich during the reign of the Catholic queen, Mary I.

While he was imprisoned in Norwich Castle, Samuel was tortured by being kept "chained bolt upright to a greate post, in such sort, that standing only on tiptoe, he was faine to stay up the whole paise or waight of his bodye thereby". Martyrologist John Foxe goes on to describe how he was starved, only being allowed "2. or 3. mouthfuls of bread, and 3. sponefuls of water" a day.

A few days before his burning, Samuel fell unconscious and had a dream or vision in which an angel appeared to him and said "Samuel, Samuel! be of good cheer, and take a good heart unto thee, for after this day shalt thou never be either hungry or thirsty." He didn't suffer from hunger or thirst again and went to his execution feeling comforted by Christ. According to Foxe, witnesses to his burning told of how "his body in burning did shine as bright and white as new tried silver".

1545 – A contagious disease known as the 'Bloody flux' hit Portsmouth, killing many men serving on the ships stationed there.

1580 – Death of Wiliam Llyn, the Welsh language poet and elegist, at Oswestry.

1613 – Death of Matthew Baker, shipwright and first man to record ship designs on paper. His papers were catalogued by Samuel Pepys as "Fragments of ancient English shipwrightry".

HENRY VII (1457-1509)

1ST SEPTEMBER

On 1ˢᵗ September 1532, Henry VIII made Anne Boleyn Marquis of Pembroke, a title in her own right, to "fit" her for the European stage and in readiness for the couple's upcoming meeting with King Francis I of France. *The Great Matter* was still not resolved and Anne was not yet Henry's wife and Queen, so she required some status befitting of England's future Queen.

The ceremony took place at Windsor Castle and Anne, loose haired and dressed in jewels and ermine trimmed velvet, must have looked like a queen. Accompanied by her cousin, Mary Howard, and the Countesses of Derby and Rutland, Anne was taken into Henry VIII's presence by the Garter King-at-arms. She knelt in front of the King and the Dukes of Norfolk and Suffolk, and listened as Stephen Gardiner read out the patent which gave her the title of Marquis of Pembroke, a title that would pass on to her offspring. After this patent was read, the King crowned her with the gold coronet of a marquis and placed on her a crimson velvet mantle. Anne received not only the patent but also her own lands, which were worth over £1000 per year. The lavish ceremony was followed by a sumptuous banquet.

1566 – Birth of Edward Alleyn, actor, theatre entrepreneur and founder of Dulwich College and Alleyn's School, in the parish of St Botolph without Bishopsgate, London. Alleyn was a major figure in the Elizabethan theatre, being a member of the Earl of Worcester's Players, Lord Strange's Men and then leading the Admiral's Men. In the 1590s, he played title roles in "Doctor Faustus", "Tamburlaine", and "The Jew of Malta" by Christopher Marlowe. The business side of his career saw him partnering with Philip Henslowe and becoming part owner of the Rose Theatre, the Paris Garden and the Fortune Theatre.

1599 – Death of Dorcas Martin (née Eccleston), Lady Martin, translator, bookseller and Puritan. She was buried at All Hallows, Tottenham. Dorcas was married to Sir Richard Martin, Master of the Mint and Lord Mayor of London, and is known for her translations of prayers, psalms and catechisms.

1615 – Death of Sir Richard Knightley, member of Parliament, Sheriff of Northamptonshire and patron of Puritans, at Fawsley in Northamptonshire. Knightley was present at the executions of Anthony Babington and Mary, Queen of Scots, and was involved in the publication of the "Marprelate tracts".

2ND SEPTEMBER

On this day in 1591, naval commander and explorer Sir Richard Grenville died at sea from injuries sustained while commanding his ship, *The Revenge*, in the *Battle of Flores* in the Azores.

Grenville had been made Vice-Admiral of the fleet, under Lord Thomas Howard, and put in charge of the 500 ton galleon, *The Revenge*, for a mission in the Azores to intercept Spanish ships carrying treasure from America. On 31st August 1591, just off the island of Flores, Howard received news that a fleet of fifty Spanish ships had been sent to protect a cargo of silver. Howard's fleet numbered only sixteen, so he made the decision to retreat. It is not known exactly what happened, but it appears that Grenville ignored Howard's orders and, instead chose to sail through the enemy's fleet. In the long battle which ensued, Grenville was fatally wounded, most of his crew were killed and *The Revenge* was destroyed.

Alfred, Lord Tennyson, wrote about the battle and the loss of *The Revenge* in his "The Revenge: A Ballad of the Fleet", including an account of Grenville ordering his men to sink the ship rather than let the Spanish fleet capture it:

"But Sir Richard cried in his English pride:
'We have fought such a fight for a day and a night
As may never be fought again!
We have won great glory my men!
And a day less or more
At sea or ashore,
We die - does it matter when?
Sink me the ship, Master Gunner - sink her, split her
in twain!
Fall into the hands of God, not into the hands of
Spain!'"

1507 (2nd or 3rd) – Death of Thomas Savage, diplomat, Henry VII's Lieutenant and High Commissioner in York, and also Archbishop of York, at Cawood Castle. His body was buried at York Minster, but his heart was buried at Macclesfield, in one of the chapels at St Michael's Church.

1534 – Death of Gerald Fitzgerald, 9th Earl of Kildare and Lord Deputy of Ireland, in the Tower of London. An already ill Kildare had been arrested on 29th June 1534, accused of corruption and causing rebellion in Ireland. He was buried in the Chapel of St Peter ad Vincula at the Tower.

1554 – Anthony Browne, son of Sir Anthony Browne, was created 1st Viscount Montagu as part of the celebrations for Mary I's marriage to Philip of Spain.

3RD SEPTEMBER

Diarist Henry Machyn, who described himself as a "citizen and merchant-taylor of London" recorded on 3rd September 1557:
"The sam day at nyght cam commendement that evere chyrche in London, and oder contrey and shyre, to syng and make bonfeyrs for the wynnynge of Sant Qwynten; and ther

was slayn my lord Hare Dudley the yonger sone of the duke of Northumberland that was he[aded,] with mony mo, at the wynnyng of yt."

News had reached London that the English and Imperial troops had been successful in storming St Quentin, and there were widespread celebrations; bonfires were lit, bells were rung and there was singing. The good news was marred, however, by news of the death of Henry Dudley.

1553 – Edward Courtenay was created Earl of Devon. He had been imprisoned in 1538, at the age of twelve, due to his family's links with the Poles and Nevilles, but was released shortly after the accession of Mary I.

1588 (3rd or 5th) – Death of Richard Tarlton, actor and famous clown, in Shoreditch. He was buried in St Leonard's Church, Shoreditch. Tarlton was a member of the Queen's Men, but is famed for his post-play jigs as a clown.

1592 – Death of writer and playwright Robert Greene in Dowgate. He died from a fever and was buried in a churchyard near Bedlam. Greene was a prolific writer, writing autobiographical works, plays and romances, but is best known for his pamphlet "Greene's Groats-worth of Wit bought with a Million of Repentance", which is the first contemporary reference to William Shakespeare. It was actually an attack on Shakespeare, whom Greene accused of plagiarism, and of being uneducated.

1597 – Death of Sir John Norreys (Norris), military commander, at his brother Thomas's home, Norris Castle in Mallow, co. Cork. He died in his brother's arms, and it is thought that his death was due to trouble from old wounds, perhaps gangrene. Norris served as a soldier in France, the Low Countries and Ireland.

4TH SEPTEMBER

On the 4th September 1588, Robert Dudley, Earl of Leicester died at his lodge at Cornbury, near Woodstock in Oxfordshire.

He had been ill for some time with a recurring stomach ailment, and so had decided to travel to Buxton to take the waters. His journey had started on 26th August and on 28th August, at the home of Lady Norreys at Rycote, he wrote his final letter to his queen and childhood friend, Elizabeth I; a letter she kept beside her bed for the rest of her life:-

"I most humbly beseech your Majesty to pardon your poor old servant to be thus bold in sending to know how my gracious lady doth, and what ease of her late pains she finds, being the chiefest thing in this world I do pray for, for her to have good health and long life. For my own poor case, I continue still your medicine and find that (it) amends much better than with any other thing that hath been given me. Thus hoping to find perfect cure at the bath, with the continuance of my wonted prayer for your Majesty's most happy preservation, I humbly kiss your foot. From your old lodging at Rycote, this Thursday morning, ready to take on my Journey, by your Majesty's most faithful and obedient servant,

R. Leicester

Even as I had writ thus much, I received Your Majesty's token by Young Tracey."

Elizabeth I was devastated by the death of the man she referred to as her "Eyes", or as "Sweet Robin". It was reported that she shut herself in her chamber for days and refused to speak to anyone. It got so bad that her councillors had to have her doors broken down.

1504 – Birth of Antoine de Noailles, soldier and French diplomat at the English court in Mary I's reign, at Château de la Fage.

1539 – William, Duke of Cleves, signed the marriage treaty promising his sister, Anne of Cleves, in marriage to King Henry VIII. The Duke then sent the treaty to England, where it was ratified and concluded by early October.

1550 – Death of Sir Thomas Paston, Gentleman of the Privy Chamber in the reigns of Henry VIII and Edward VI.

1590 – Death of Sir James Croft, Lord Deputy of Ireland, member of Parliament and conspirator. Croft was one of the leaders of *Wyatt's Rebellion* in 1554, but although he was sentenced to death for treason, he was eventually released and pardoned. He served Elizabeth I as Comptroller of the Household, but was imprisoned briefly in her reign for negotiating with the Duke of Parma without permission. Croft was buried at Westminster Abbey, in the Chapel of St John the Evangelist.

5TH SEPTEMBER

Early on the morning of 5th September 1548, Catherine Parr, Queen Dowager, wife of Thomas Seymour and widow of Henry VIII, died aged around 36 at Sudeley Castle. She had given birth to her first child, a daughter Mary, on 30th August, but within a few days of the birth, she had contracted puerperal fever.

Her body was wrapped in cere cloth and waxed cloth, then encased in a lead envelope for burial. Her funeral service reflected Catherine's reformed beliefs and the sermon was preached by Miles Coverdale, the famous Bible translator. Lady Jane Grey acted as the chief mourner.

In the spring of 1782, some ladies visiting Sudeley Castle decided to investigate the remains of the chapel there. They found a large block of alabaster on the north wall and concluded that it might be part of a monument that had once stood there. They decided to open up the ground in that area and not far from the surface they discovered a lead envelope coffin inscribed with the following:-

"KP
Here lyeth Queen Katheryne Wife to Kinge
Henry the VIII and
The wife of Thomas
Lord of Sudely high
Admy... of Englond
And ynkle to Kyng
Edward VI"

They cut holes in the coffin and unwrapped the corpse to discover that Catherine had been completely preserved. However, in their excitement at their discovery, they did not seal the coffin properly and Catherine's remains had decayed by the time the coffin was investigated again.

◇◇◇◇◇◇◇◇◇◇◇◇◇◇◇◇◇◇◇◇◇◇◇◇◇◇◇◇◇◇◇◇◇◇◇◇

1558 (5th or 6th) – Death of Sir Robert Broke, judge, legal writer and Speaker of the House of Commons, at a friend's house in Patshull, Staffordshire. He was buried in Claverley Church, Shropshire. Broke also served as Deputy Chief Steward for the Duchy of Lancaster, Serjeant-at-Law and Chief Justice of the Common Pleas.

1569 – Death of Edmund Bonner, Bishop of London and a man nicknamed "Bloody Bonner", in Marshalsea Prison. He was buried at St George's, Southwark, but it is thought that his remains were later moved to Copford, near Colchester, a manor held by Bonner as Bishop of London. In Mary I's reign, he was in charge of burning reformers in London, hence his nickname

"Bloody Bonner". Bonner was imprisoned in Elizabeth I's reign for refusing to follow the "Book of Common Prayer" in his services, and for refusing to take the "Oath of Supremacy".

6TH SEPTEMBER

On this day in 1520, reformer Martin Luther sent his pamphlet "On the Freedom of a Christian" (also known as "A Treatise on Christian Liberty") to Pope Leo X. The pamphlet opened with the following dedicatory address to the Pope:

"AMONG those monstrous evils of this age with which I have now for three years been waging war, I am sometimes compelled to look to you and to call you to mind, most blessed father Leo. In truth, since you alone are everywhere considered as being the cause of my engaging in war, I cannot at any time fail to remember you; and although I have been compelled by the causeless raging of your impious flatterers against me to appeal from your seat to a future council—fearless of the futile decrees of your predecessors Pius and Julius, who in their foolish tyranny prohibited such an action—yet I have never been so alienated in feeling from your Blessedness as not to have sought with all my might, in diligent prayer and crying to God, all the best gifts for you and for your see. But those who have hitherto endeavoured to terrify me with the majesty of your name and authority, I have begun quite to despise and triumph over. One thing I see remaining which I cannot despise, and this has been the reason of my writing anew to your Blessedness: namely, that I find that blame is cast on me, and that it is imputed to me as a great offence, that in my rashness I am judged to have spared not even your person."

In his pamphlet, Luther emphasised the "two-fold nature" of Christians as saints and sinners, flesh and spirit. He examined the paradox of a Christian's life - his freedom, due to God's forgiveness, but also his duty to serve God and his neighbours; and his sinful nature which caused him to be deserving of death, but his freedom of sin and his redemption because of his rebirth in faith. Luther believed that a Christian became free from the bondage of sin by faith rather than good works. This was his doctrine of justification by faith alone.

∞∞∞∞∞∞∞∞∞∞∞∞∞∞∞∞∞∞∞∞∞∞∞∞∞∞∞∞∞∞∞∞

1506 – Death of Sir Richard Guildford, courtier and administrator in the reign of Henry VII, in Jerusalem on pilgrimage. He was buried on Mount Syon. Guildford's offices included Master of the Ordnance and Armoury in the Tower of London, Master of the Horse and Privy Councillor.

1572 – Death of Sir Henry Jerningham at his manor of Costessey in Norfolk. He was buried in the parish church there. Jerningham served Henry VIII, Edward VI, Mary I and Elizabeth I, and his offices in Mary's reign included Privy Councillor, Vice-Chamberlain of the Household, and Captain of the Yeomen of the Guard.

1578 – Sir Francis Drake and his ship, the *Golden Hind* (or *Pelican* as it was called then), entered the Pacific Ocean on its circumnavigation of the globe.

1615 – Burial of Timothy Bright, physician, clergyman and inventor of modern shorthand, at St Mary's Church, Shrewsbury. Bright is known for two works, his "A Treatise of Melancholie" (1586) and his "Characterie: an Arte of Shorte, Swifte, and Secrete Writing by Character" (1588).

7TH SEPTEMBER

On this day in history, 7th September 1533, at 3 o'clock in the afternoon and less than two weeks after having gone into confinement at Greenwich Palace, Queen Anne Boleyn gave birth to a little girl who, although a disappointment at her birth,

418

would become one of the greatest monarchs in English history: Elizabeth I the Virgin Queen, Gloriana, Good Queen Bess.

Astrologers had predicted that Anne Boleyn's baby would be a boy, and the couple were so confident that God would bless their marriage in this way that Anne had a letter written in advance of the birth giving thanks to God for sending her "good speed, in the deliverance and bringing forth of a prince". An 's' was added to this letter and a celebratory joust was cancelled, for the "prince" was actually a lowly girl and Henry had one of those already. There were celebrations though: a herald proclaimed the good news, the Chapel Royal choristers sang a *Te Deum* and preparations began in earnest to a lavish christening.

1500 – Birth of Sebastian Newdigate, member of Henry VIII's Privy Chamber, Carthusian monk and Roman Catholic martyr, at Harefield in Middlesex.

1523 – Birth of Alice Barnham (née Bradbridge), silkwoman and benefactor, at Chichester. Alice is known for being one of the subjects of one of the earliest English family group portraits: "Alice Barnham and her Sons Martin and Steven" (once entitled "Lady Ingram and her Two Boys Martin and Steven" in error) from 1557.

1571 – Arrest of Thomas Howard, 4th Duke of Norfolk, for his part in the *Ridolfi Plot* to assassinate Elizabeth I and to replace her with Mary, Queen of Scots. Howard confessed to corresponding with Mary's supporters and was taken to the Tower of London. He was executed on 2nd June 1572 after being found guilty of high treason.

1587 – Burial of Richard Barnes, Bishop of Durham during Elizabeth I's reign, in the choir of Durham Cathedral.

8TH SEPTEMBER

On this day in history, 8th September, 1560, Amy Dudley (née Robsart), wife of Robert Dudley, Earl of Leicester, died at her home, Cumnor Place in Oxfordshire. Her servants found her body at the bottom of the stairs when they returned from "Our Lady's Fair" at Abingdon, and it appeared that she had fallen down the stairs.

At the inquest into Amy's death, the coroner ruled that her death was the result of "misfortune", an accident, but there is still controversy today over Amy's death. The theories include:

- Accident – Professor Ian Aird (1956) suggests that Amy's death could have been an accident caused by a spontaneous fracture of the vertebrae as she walked down the stairs. Professor Aird based this theory on the fact that breast cancer, which sources suggest Amy was suffering from, can cause a weakening of the bones.

- Suicide – On the day of her death, Amy ordered all of her servants out of the house, giving them permission to go to the fair for the day. When some of them protested that it was not "fitting" to go to a fair on a Sunday, Amy was said to have been quite sharp with them, asking them to obey her orders. A Mrs Odingsells refused to go, much to Amy's displeasure, but Mrs Odingsells did eventually retire to her room, leaving Amy alone. Did Amy arrange to be alone so that she could commit suicide? After all, she was said to be very depressed. Amy's maid said that she wondered if Amy "might have an evil toy in her mind", in other words, suicide.

- Murder – Some sources believe that Amy's husband, Robert Dudley, arranged her murder so that he could be free to marry Elizabeth I, and others believe that William Cecil orchestrated the murder to blacken Dudley's name and to prevent him from marrying Elizabeth.

- An aortic aneurism – A modern theory that Amy was killed by the terminal enlargement of one of the arteries from the heart. Symptoms of this include depression, fits of anger, mental aberrations and pain and swelling in the chest.
- We will never know the truth of the matter.

Amy was buried at St Mary's, Oxford, but the exact location of her tomb is unknown.

1462 – Birth of Henry Medwall, the playwright known as England's first vernacular dramatist. His 1497 play "Fulgens and Lucres" is the first known secular play written in English. He also wrote a play entitled "Nature".

1475 – Birth of John Stokesley, Bishop of London and ambassador, at Collyweston, Northamptonshire. Stokesley supported Henry VIII's quest for an annulment of his marriage to Catherine of Aragon, and carried out diplomatic missions for the cause.

1495 – Death of Sir William Hussey, Chief Justice of the King's Bench in Edward IV's reign.

1601 – Burial of John Shakespeare, father of playwright William Shakespeare, at Stratford-upon-Avon.

1603 – Death of George Carey, 2nd Baron Hunsdon, courtier, son of Henry Carey, 1st Baron Hundson, and grandson of Mary Carey (née Boleyn). Carey served Elizabeth I as Marshal of the Household, Justice of the Peace, Lord Lieutenant of Hertfordshire, Captain of the Isle of Wight, member of Parliament, Captain of the Gentlemen Pensioners, Lord Chamberlain and Privy Councillor.

9TH SEPTEMBER

On the 9th September 1513, while Henry VIII was away, busy campaigning against the French, James IV and his Scottish troops crossed the border and challenged the English force, which was headed by Thomas Howard, the Earl of Surrey, at Flodden in Northumberland.

Before leaving for France, Henry VIII had left his wife, Catherine of Aragon in charge of England as Governor of the Realm and Captain General of the Forces. She was Regent and was to manage the kingdom, with the help of a council, while Henry was fighting France, with the help of Imperial forces. Flodden was a victory for Catherine. After about three hours of fighting, the English army had defeated the Scots, killing most of the Scottish aristocracy, including two abbots, two bishops, twelve earls and King James IV himself. The English army lost around 1,500 men, whereas the Scottish army lost 5,000 – 17,000, depending on which source you believe.

Catherine of Aragon wrote to Henry VIII of the victory:-

"This battle hath been to your grace and all your realm the greatest honour that could be, and more than ye should win all the crown of France. Your grace shall see how I can keep my promise, sending you for your banners a king's coat."

At least she only sent him James IV's coat. She had originally wanted to send the King of Scotland's body.

The battle was also a victory for the Earl of Surrey, and his reward was being restored as the Duke of Norfolk.

1543 – The infant Mary, Queen of Scots, daughter of James V, King of Scotland, was crowned queen at Stirling Castle.

1583 – Death of Sir Humphrey Gilbert, explorer, soldier, member of Parliament and half-brother of Sir Walter Ralegh, on board *The Squirrel* after a storm off the Azores. The crew of the *Golden Hind* heard Gilbert shout "We are as near to heaven, by sea as by land" as *The Squirrel* sank.

10TH SEPTEMBER

On Wednesday 10th September 1533, Princess Elizabeth, daughter of Henry VIII and Anne Boleyn, was christened at the Church of Observant Friars in Greenwich.

Elizabeth was just three days old, having been born on the 7th September, when she was processed along a carpet of green rushes from the Great Hall at Greenwich to the church. The "Letters and Papers, Foreign and Domestic, Henry VIII", contain a record of Elizabeth's christening:-

"The mayor, Sir Stephen Pecock, with his brethren and 40 of the chief citizens, were ordered to be at the christening on the Wednesday following; on which day the mayor and council, in scarlet, with their collars, rowed to Greenwich, and the citizens went in another barge.

All the walls between the King's place and the Friars were hanged with arras, and the way strewed with rushes. The Friars' church was also hanged with arras. The font, of silver, stood in the midst of the church three steps high, covered with a fine cloth, and surrounded by gentlewomen with aprons and towels about their necks, that no filth should come into it. Over it hung a crimson satin canopy fringed with gold, and round it was a rail covered with red say.

Between the choir and the body of the church was a close place with a pan of fire, to make the child ready in. When the child was brought to the hall, every man set forward. The citizens of London, two and two; then gentlemen, squires, and chaplains, the aldermen, the mayor alone, the King's council, his chapel, in copes; barons, bishops, earls; the earl of Essex bearing the covered gilt basons; the marquis of Exeter with a taper of virgin wax. The marquis of Dorset bare the salt. The lady Mary of Norfolk bare the chrisom, of pearl and stone. The officers of arms. The old duchess of Norfolk bare the child in a mantle of purple velvet, with a long train held by the earl of Wiltshire, the countess of Kent, and the earl of Derby. The dukes of Suffolk and Norfolk were on each side of the Duchess. A canopy was borne over the child by lord Rochford, lord Hussy, lord William Howard, and lord Thomas Howard the elder. Then ladies and gentlewomen.

The bishop of London and other bishops and abbots met the child at the church door, and christened it. The archbishop of Canterbury was godfather, and the old duchess of Norfolk and the old marchioness of Dorset godmothers. This done, Garter, with a loud voice, bid God send her long life. The archbishop of Canterbury then confirmed her, the marchioness of Exeter being godmother. Then the trumpets blew, and the gifts were given; after which wafers, comfits, and hypocras were brought in. In going out the gifts were borne before the child, to the Queen's chamber, by Sir John Dudley, lord Thos. Howard, the younger, lord Fitzwater, and the earl of Worcester. One side was full of the Guard and King's servants holding 500 staff torches, and many other torches were borne beside the child by gentlemen. The mayor and aldermen were thanked in the King's name by the dukes of Norfolk and Suffolk, and after drinking in the cellar went to their barge."

In his "Chronicle of England", Charles Wriothesley writes that "and the morrowe after their was fiers[bonfires] made in London, and at everie fire a vessell of wyne[wine] for people to drinke for the said solempnitie." but the Imperial Ambassador, Eustace Chapuys, contradicts this in his report to Charles V on the 15th September, saying "the christening has been like her mother's coronation, very cold and disagreeable, both to the Court and to the city, and there has been no thought of having the bonfires and rejoicings usual in such cases." However, Anne Boleyn's coronation was a lavish affair.

1515 – Thomas Wolsey was made Cardinal.

1543 – Death of Sir Edward Chamberlayne, Oxfordshire gentleman and soldier. He was buried at Woodstock.

1547 – The *Battle of Pinkie Cleugh*, part of the *War of the Rough Wooing* between England and Scotland. It took place near Musselburgh, in Scotland, on the banks of the River Esk. The English forces, led by Edward Seymour, Duke of Somerset, defeated the Scots, killing thousands.

1549 – Death of Sir Anthony Denny, Henry VIII's great friend and Groom of the Stool, at Cheshunt. He was buried in St Mary's Church, Cheshunt.

1557 – Execution of Joyce Lewis (née Curson and other married name Appleby, Lady Appleby), Protestant martyr, at Lichfield. She was burned at the stake for her Protestant beliefs.

1569 – Death of Gilbert Bourne, Bishop of Bath and Wells, at Silverton in Devon. Bourne was deprived of his see in Elizabeth I's reign after refusing to take the "Oath of Supremacy". He was buried in Silverton Church.

1604 – Death of William Morgan, Bishop of St Asaph and Bible translator, at the Bishop's Palace at St Asaph. He was buried there in the cathedral church.

11TH SEPTEMBER

Pope Gregory XIII ordered a joint commemoration on 11th September 1572 for the defeat of the Ottoman troops by the Holy League at the *Battle of Lepanto* on 7th October 1571, and for the *St Bartholomew's Day Massacre* of the Huguenots in France, in August 1572.

It seems distasteful of the Pope to be ordering celebrations for the massacre of thousands of Huguenots, but he viewed it as divine retribution on heretics. When Pope Gregory had heard news of the massacre, he ordered the singing of a *Te Deum* and ordered a commemorative medal to be struck. This medal depicted the Pope's head on one side and an image of an angel, holding a sword and a cross, standing over the fallen Huguenots with the motto *UGONOTTORUM STRAGES* or "Huguenot Bloodbath".

1540 – Death of Thomas Kytson (Kitson) the Elder, merchant, Sheriff of London and builder of Hengrave Hall in Suffolk. He died at Hengrave and was buried in the church there.

1561 – Mary, Queen of Scots began her first royal progress, visiting Holyrood Palace, Edinburgh Castle, Linlithgow Palace, Stirling Castle, Kincardine Castle, Leslie Castle, Perth, Dundee, St Andrews, Cupar, Falkland Palace and Edinburgh, between the 11th and 29th September.

1581 – Death of Barnaby Fitzpatrick, 2nd Baron of Upper Ossory, at Dublin, in the home of a surgeon, William Kelly. In his youth, Fitzpatrick had been friends with Prince Edward (future Edward VI) and had been educated with him. He went on to serve his friend, when he became king, as a Gentleman of the Privy Chamber.

1605 – Death of Sir Thomas Tresham the Younger, Catholic recusant politician, at his home, Rushton Hall, in Northamptonshire. He was buried at St Peter's Church, Rushton.

1613 – Death of Sir John Brograve, lawyer. He was buried at St Mary's Church, Braughing, Hertfordshire in the Brograve Chapel. Brograve was one of the leading lawyers in the House of Commons in Elizabeth I's reign.

1614 – Death of Sir Edward Phelips, Elizabeth I's Sergeant-at-Law and Speaker of the House of Commons in James I's reign. He died at Rolls House, London, and was buried at St Catherine's Church, Montacute, Somerset.

12TH SEPTEMBER

On Thursday 12th September 1555, the trial of Archbishop Cranmer began in the University Church of St Mary the Virgin at Oxford. He was accused of two offences, or doctrinal errors: repudiating papal authority and denying transubstantiation.

A ten foot high scaffold, decorated with cloth of state, had been erected in the eastern end of the church in front of the high altar, and it was on this scaffold that James Brooks, the Bishop of Gloucester and representative of the Pope, sat. Below him sat Dr Martin and Dr Storey, Queen Mary I's commissioners (or proctors) and doctors of the law.

Archbishop Thomas Cranmer was brought into the court. John Foxe describes him as "clothed in a fair black gown, with his hood on both shoulders, such as doctors of divinity in the university use to wear, and in his hand a white staff", and goes on to say that he would not doff his cap to any of the commissioners. One of the commissioners called him forward, saying, "Thomas archbishop of Canterbury! Appear here, and make answer to that shall be laid to thy charge; that is to say, for blasphemy, incontinency, and heresy; and make answer here to the bishop of Gloucester, representing the pope's person!", and Cranmer was brought up to the scaffold. Cranmer then doffed his cap and bowed to the Queen's proctors, but did not bow or doff his cap to Brooks. An offended Brooks asked Cranmer why he did not show him respect, and Cranmer replied "that he had once taken a solemn oath, never to consent to the admitting of the bishop of Rome's authority into this realm of England again; that he had done it advisedly, and meant by God's grace to keep it; and therefore would commit nothing either by sign or token which might argue his consent to the receiving of the same; and so he desired the said bishop to judge of him."

After Brooks and Martin had given their 'orations', Cranmer replied that he did not recognise or acknowledge this court:-

427

"My lord, I do not acknowledge this session of yours, nor yet you, my mislawful judge; neither would I have appeared this day before you, but that I was brought hither as a prisoner. And therefore I openly here renounce you as my judge, protesting that my meaning is not to make any answer, as in a lawful judgment, (for then would I be silent,) but only for that I am bound in conscience to answer every man of that hope which I have in Jesus Christ, by the counsel of St. Peter; and lest by my silence many of those who are weak, here present, might be offended. And so I desire that my answers may be accepted as extra judicialia."

Then he knelt, "both knees towards the west", and recited the Lord's Prayer, and then rose and recited the Creed. According to John Foxe, Martin asked Cranmer who he thought was "supreme head of the church of England", to which Cranmer replied, "Christ is head of this member, as he is of the whole body of the universal church". When Martin pushed him further, asking why he had then made Henry VIII the supreme head, Cranmer stated, "Yea, of all the people of England, as well ecclesiastical as temporal" and went on to say, "for Christ only is the head of his church, and of the faith and religion of the same. The king is head and governor of his people, which are the visible church." He explained that "there was never other thing meant" by the King's title.

After the commission had heard from Cranmer, they ordered him to appear at Rome "within fourscore days" to answer to the Pope. Cranmer agreed to do this and was then taken back to his prison. Cranmer was never taken to Rome, but his fate was decided there on the 4th December 1555. The Pope stripped him of his office of Archbishop and gave the secular authorities permission to sentence him. He was burned at the stake on 21st March 1556.

1542 – Death of Sir Edmund Knightley, lawyer and Sergeant-at-Law. He was buried at Letheringham in Suffolk.

1544 – Baptism of Richard Bancroft, Archbishop of Canterbury in the reign of James I, at Prescot, near Farnworth, in Lancashire.

1559 – Death of Marten Micron (Martin Micronius), Dutch theologian and Protestant minister in the strangers' churches of London, from the plague at Norden in Lower Saxony, Germany.

1573 – Sudden death of Archibald Campbell, 5th Earl of Argyll, Protestant reformer and a leading politician in the reign of Mary, Queen of Scots, at Barbreck. He had got married six weeks earlier and had shown no signs of illness before retiring to bed. He was laid to rest in the family mausoleum at Kilmun Church on the Holy Loch.

13TH SEPTEMBER

William Cecil, 1st Baron Burghley and Elizabeth I's chief advisor, was born on this day in 1520 at Bourne in Lincolnshire. He was the son of Richard Cecil, former Groom of the Robes, Constable of Warwick Castle and High Sheriff of Rutland, and his wife Jane Heckington. His grandfather, David Cecil, had been one of Henry VIII's favourites, and was High Sheriff of Nottingham.

Cecil was educated at The King's School Grantham and then Stamford School. At the age of fourteen, he started at St John's College, Cambridge, where he met men like John Cheke and Roger Ascham. It was at Cambridge that Cecil met Mary Cheke, John Cheke's sister, and fell in love. This relationship led to Cecil's father removing him from Cambridge to Gray's Inn before Cecil had obtained his degree. The couple married in 1541, but Mary died in February 1543, and Cecil went on to marry Mildred Cooke, daughter of Sir Anthony, the eminent humanist and scholar, in December 1546. According to Cecil's friend, Roger Ascham, Mildred was on a par with Lady Jane Grey as far as intellect was concerned, being one of the two most learned young women in England.

Cecil started his career by serving Edward Seymour, the Duke of Somerset and Lord Protector from 1547 – 1549. He became Somerset's Master of Requests in 1548 and acted as his secretary. Fortunately for Cecil, he managed to escape harm when Somerset fell from power in late 1549, but he was imprisoned in the Tower of London for a few months. In September 1550, Cecil was made a Secretary of State in Edward VI's government, under the new "rule" of John Dudley, Earl of Warwick, and became Chancellor of the Order of the Garter in April 1551.

In June 1553, Cecil was commanded by Edward VI to sign his "Devise for the Succession" naming Lady Jane Grey as heir, although he tried to resist signing it, knowing it put him in danger. When Lady Jane Grey fell from power, Cecil once more escaped from harm, and although he was a Protestant, he conformed to the Catholic regime of the new queen, Mary I. It was not until 1558 when Mary I died and Elizabeth I became Queen that Cecil once again became important in government. He had always been close to Elizabeth and she trusted him, making him her Secretary of State and chief adviser. She nicknamed him her "spirit" and relied on his wisdom and intelligence. William Cecil was responsible for creating the intelligence service headed up by Sir Francis Walsingham.

His titles and offices in Elizabeth I's reign included Secretary of State (1558), member of Parliament for Lincolnshire (1559) and Northamptonshire (1563), Master of the Court of Wards and Liveries (1561), Chancellor of Cambridge University (1559), Chancellor of Trinity College, Dublin (1592), Baron Burghley or Burleigh (1571) and Lord High Treasurer (1572). He really was Elizabeth I's right hand man.

Cecil died on 4th August 1598.

◊◊◊

c.1503 – Birth of John Leland, poet and antiquary. Leland is known for his Latin poems and his antiquarian writings which included *Assertio inclytissimi Arturii regis Britanniae*, which he presented to Henry VIII, his "New Year's Gift" to Henry VIII, *Antiquitates Britanniae, De uiris illustribus*, his travel notes and his defence of the legends of King Arthur.

1544 – Death of Edward Lee, Archbishop of York. He was buried at York Minster, in the south choir aisle. Lee served Henry VIII as his almoner and a diplomat, as well as being an archbishop.

1557 – Death of Sir John Cheke, Tudor scholar, one time tutor to Edward VI, Secretary of State for Lady Jane Grey and the first Regius Professor of Greek at Cambridge University. He died at the home of his friend, Peter Osborne, in Wood Street, London, probably from influenza, and was buried nearby at the church of St Alban, Wood Street, in the north chapel of the chancel.

1596 – Death of Sir Francis Englefield, courtier, politician and pro-Spanish Catholic exile, at St Alban's College in Valladolid, Spain. He was buried in the college chapel.

1598 – Death of Philip II of Spain at El Escorial, near Madrid. He was buried there the next day. It is thought that he died of cancer, and he had been ill for fifty-two days.

14TH SEPTEMBER

On this day in 1540, Sir William Kingston, Constable of the Tower of London, Knight of the Garter and comptroller of the King's household, died at Painswick in Gloucestershire. He was buried at Painswick.

Kingston was appointed Constable of the Tower of London in May 1524, and is known for his role in the imprisonment of Anne Boleyn and the reports he sent to Thomas Cromwell of Anne's behaviour and conversations in the Tower. Other high profile prisoners he was in charge of include Cardinal Wolsey, whom he was ordered to escort from Yorkshire to London in November 1529, and Thomas Cromwell at his fall in 1540.

Kingston seems to have treated Anne Boleyn with respect and sympathy while she was imprisoned in the Tower. When Anne was upset about the postponement of her execution, saying that she thought to be past her pain by that time, Kingston comforted her saying that the blow of the sword would be "so subtle". He was also concerned about Anne's brother George's peace of mind, while he was awaiting execution. George was fretting that his debtors would not be paid after his death and that they would end up getting into trouble if they had to pay the King instead. Kingston wrote to Thomas Cromwell twice about George, begging him to "help my lord of Rochford's conscience".

Kingston benefited from the dissolution of the monasteries when he was awarded the land and possessions associated with the abbey of Flaxley in Gloucestershire in 1537. After Cromwell's execution in July 1540, he was able to buy Cromwell's property in Gloucestershire, the manor of Painswick and Morton Valence. He died at Painswick, in Gloucestershire, on 14th September 1540.

◇◇

1514 – Second proxy marriage of King Louis XII of France and Mary Tudor, sister of Henry VIII.

1523 – Death of Pope Adrian VI in Rome. He was buried in Rome's Santa Maria dell'Anima church. Adrian had only been Pope since January 1522.

1538 – The Destruction of the Shrine of Our Lady of Caversham, near Reading, by Dr John London, on the orders of Henry VIII. The shrine had been established in 1106.

1585 – Sir Francis Drake set sail from England on a mission to raid Spanish ports. He had been given royal approval for these raids, and raids in the West Indies at the end of 1584.

15TH SEPTEMBER

On this day in 1589, the *Battle of Arques* began. The battle, which was part of the final war of the *French Wars of Religion* (1562-1598), was between the troops of Henry IV of France and those of the Catholic League led by Charles of Lorraine, Duke of Mayenne. It was a bloody battle, and it was not looking good for the French king until he was rescued by troops sent by Elizabeth I. On the 23rd September, around 4,000 soldiers arrived from England to reinforce the King's troops. Seeing these troops arrive, the Duke of Mayenne had no choice but to retreat, conceding the victory to Henry IV.

1500 – Death of John Morton, Archbishop of Canterbury and Chancellor to Henry VII, at Knole from the plague.

1514 – Thomas Wolsey was appointed Archbishop of York after having been elected in the August. He had already been appointed Bishop of Lincoln in February of that year, and in 1515 he would be elevated to the office of Cardinal.

1556 – Charles V departed from Vlissingen in Zeeland bound for Spain following his voluntary abdication of his titles in October 1555. He spent his retirement in the monastery of Yuste in Extremadura.

1564 – The final day of Mary, Queen of Scots' fourth progress. The progress had begun on 22nd July 1564, and had included stops at Edinburgh, Linlithgow Palace, Stirling Castle, Kincardine Castle, Perth, Blair Atholl, Glen Tilt, Inverness, Beauly Priory, Redcastle, Dingwall, Gartly Castle, Aberdeen, Dunnotar Castle, Dundee and St Andrews.

16TH SEPTEMBER

On this day in 1541, King Henry VIII entered the city of York through Walmgate Bar, and was met by the city's officials at Fulford Cross.

The mayor and the aldermen of the city then begged forgiveness from the King for the North's rebellion during the *Pilgrimage of Grace*, and gave the King and his wife, Queen Catherine Howard, a gold cup each full of gold coins.

Henry VIII's 1541 progress to the North was not only the King's way of emphasising his power over the North, but was also a diplomatic journey, with the King planning to meet the Scottish king, James V, at York. Henry VIII spent nine days in York waiting for James, but unfortunately he was stood up.

***

1519 – Death of John Colet, scholar, humanist, theologian, Dean of St Paul's and founder of St Paul's School, after suffering three attacks of sweating sickness between 1517 and 1519. He was buried in St Paul's Cathedral. Humanists such as Erasmus were influenced by Colet's work.

1539 – Birth of Walter Devereux, 1st Earl of Essex, nobleman, soldier and adventurer, at Chartley in Staffordshire. Devereux was the eldest son of Sir Richard Devereux and Dorothy Hastings, and was the father of Robert Devereux, 2nd Earl of Essex and a favourite of Elizabeth I.

1574 – Death of Sir Robert Catlin, judge and Lord Chief Justice of the Queen's Bench, at Newnham, near Bedford. He was buried at Sutton in Bedfordshire. Catlin was Chief Justice during the *Ridolfi Plot* and attended the trial of Thomas Howard, 4th Duke of Norfolk, in 1571.

17TH SEPTEMBER

1558 – Death of Walter Devereux, 1ˢᵗ Viscount Hereford, at the Devereux seat at Chartley in Staffordshire. He was buried in Stowe church. Devereux served Henry VIII as joint Constable of Warwick Castle, as a member of the jury at the trial of Edward Stafford, Duke of Buckingham, in 1521, in the government of the Welsh Marches, as Steward in Princess Mary's household at Ludlow and Chamberlain of the Court of General Surveyors. He also served Edward VI as a Privy Councillor.

1563 – Death of Henry Manners, 2ⁿᵈ Earl of Rutland, courtier and soldier, during an outbreak of the plague. He was buried at Bottesford parish church in Leicestershire. Manners served Edward VI as Warden of the East and Middle Marches on the Scottish borders, joint Lord Lieutenant of Lincolnshire and Nottinghamshire, and Lord Lieutenant of Nottinghamshire. He was imprisoned when Mary I came to the throne for his support of John Dudley, Duke of Northumberland, but was released into house arrest and then pardoned. He served Mary I as Captain-General of Horsemen and Lieutenant and Captain-General in Calais. During Elizabeth I's reign, he served as Lord Lieutenant of Nottinghamshire and Rutland, and President of the Council of the North.

1575 – Death of Heinrich (Henry) Bullinger, the Swiss reformer and theologian, in Zurich. Bullinger succeeded Huldrych Zwingli as pastor at Grossmünster and head of the church in Zurich. His main work was "The Decades", a theological work, but his sermons were also translated and published, and he wrote historical works.

1577 – The *Edict of Poitiers* ratified the *Treaty of Bergerac*, which had been signed between Henry III of France and the Huguenot princes.

18TH SEPTEMBER

1501 – Birth of Henry Stafford, 10th Baron Stafford, at Penshurst in Kent. He was the son of Edward Stafford, 3rd Duke of Buckingham, and his wife Eleanor (née Percy), daughter of Henry Percy, 4th Earl of Northumberland. Henry married Ursula Pole, daughter of Sir Richard Pole and Margaret Pole, Countess of Salisbury, in 1519, and the couple had around fourteen children. Stafford served Mary I as a Chamberlain of the Exchequer and Elizabeth I as a Lord Lieutenant of Staffordshire.

1535 – Birth of Henry Brandon, son of Charles Brandon, Duke of Suffolk, and his wife Katherine (née Willoughby). Henry Brandon died on 14th July 1551, at the age of fifteen, from sweating sickness. His younger brother, Charles, survived him by just half an hour.

1544 – Henry VIII rode triumphantly through the streets of Boulogne after the French surrendered, ending the *Siege of Boulogne*.

1556 – Death of Edward Courtenay, 1st Earl of Devon, from a fever at Padua in Italy. He was buried there in the church of Sant'Antonio. Courtenay had been sent overseas after he was implicated in *Wyatt's Rebellion* as a future husband and consort of Mary I's half-sister, Elizabeth.

1559 – The fifteen year-old Francis II was crowned King of France at Rheims by the Cardinal of Lorraine, following the death of his father Henry II in July 1559 after a jousting accident. Mary, Queen of Scots was Francis' consort.

19TH SEPTEMBER

On the 19th September 1580, Katherine Bertie (née Willoughby and previous married name Brandon) died after a long illness. She was buried in Spilsby church, Lincolnshire.

Katherine was the daughter of William Willoughby, 11th Baron Willoughby de Eresby, and his wife, Lady Maria de Salinas, who had travelled to England from Spain in Catherine of Aragon's entourage. In 1529, three years after her father's death, Katherine was made a ward of Charles Brandon, Duke of Suffolk, and in 1533, at the age of fourteen, Katherine became Brandon's fourth wife. The marriage resulted in two sons, Henry and Charles, who unfortunately died of sweating sickness in their teens in 1551. Katherine was widowed in August 1545, and went on to remarry, probably in 1552, her gentleman usher, Richard Bertie. The couple had two children, Peregrine, 13th Baron Willoughby de Eresby, and Susan.

Katherine was known for her firm faith and her outspoken defence of reform. She was part of the circle of reformist women who were friends with Queen Catherine Parr, and had many humanist and reformist books dedicated to her. She was a known Protestant patron, helping clergyman of a reformist persuasion attain livings in Lincolnshire, inviting Hugh Latimer to preach at her home, Grimsthorpe, and hiring Miles Coverdale to teach her children.

Katherine, Bertie and their household went into exile at the beginning of 1555 when it became apparent that Katherine could not support the Catholic Mary I. They returned to England in 1559, following Elizabeth I's accession.

Visitors to Spilsby Church can see a huge monument to Katherine and her husband, Richard Bertie, who died two years later.

1551 – Birth of Henry III of France. He was born at the Château de Fontainebleau, and was the fourth son of King Henry II and Catherine de' Medici. He was King of France from 1574 to 1589, succeeding his brother, Charles IX.

1555 – Burnings of Protestant martyrs, Robert Glover and Cornelius Bungey, at Coventry. John Foxe gives the date of their burnings as "about the 20th day" in his "Actes and Monuments" (1563), but Rev. Thomas Brice gives the date as the 19th in his "A Compendious Regester" of 1559. Foxe actually used Brice's "Regester" as a source.

1560 – Baptism of Thomas Cavendish, explorer, navigator and privateer, at St Martin's Church, Trimley St Martin, Suffolk. Cavendish is known for his imitation of Sir Francis Drake's circumnavigation of the globe, which he undertook in 1586, and for being the first Englishman to explore the island of St Helena, in the mid-Atlantic.

20TH SEPTEMBER

On this day in history, 20th September 1486 (some say the 19th), "afore one o'clock after midnight", Arthur, Prince of Wales, was born at Winchester, just eight months after his parents' marriage.

Arthur's mother, Elizabeth of York, daughter of Edward IV, got pregnant straight after her marriage to Henry VII, and the news of her pregnancy was celebrated throughout England. His father, Henry VII, was ecstatic at the news and decided that the birth of his first-born would take place at Winchester, the place believed to have been the capital of the legendary Camelot, and the site of King Arthur's castle, and that the child would be called Arthur. Henry was convinced that Arthur's birth would bring about a new golden age.

The court arrived at Winchester in early September, and historian David Starkey believed the long and arduous journey on bad roads may have caused the Queen to go into labour about a month early. Despite being premature, little Arthur was healthy. His mother did go on to suffer with some type of fever, but fortunately survived. The birth of the heir to the throne was celebrated with bonfires in the streets and the singing of the *Te Deum* at Winchester Cathedral.

1554 – Death of Sir William Paston, courtier and landowner, at Paston. He was buried there. Paston served Henry VIII as a Sheriff and Commissioner, and was also chosen to welcome Anne of Cleves to court in January 1540.

1586 – Executions of Anthony Babington, John Ballard, John Savage, Chidiock Tichborne and three other conspirators near St Giles-in-the-Fields in London. They were hanged, drawn and quartered for plotting to assassinate Queen Elizabeth I in the famous *Babington Plot* in support of Mary, Queen of Scots. A further seven were executed the following day.

1596 – Death of William Day, Bishop of Winchester.

21ST SEPTEMBER

On the morning of Sunday 21st September 1578, between seven and eight o'clock, Robert Dudley, Earl of Leicester, married Lettice Devereux (née Knollys), widow of Walter Devereux, Earl of Essex, at his house in Wanstead, Essex.

Leicester's chaplain, Humphrey Tindall officiated, and the guests at this secret and private ceremony included Sir Francis Knollys, father of the bride; Richard Knollys, the bride's brother; Ambrose Dudley, Earl of Warwick and brother of Leicester; and Leicester's friends, the Earl of Pembroke and Lord North. Tindall described Lettice as wearing a "loose gown", which has led to people thinking that the marriage was a shot-gun wedding, but there is no evidence that Lettice was pregnant. She did not give birth to their first and only child, Robert, Lord Denbigh, until June 1581. The marriage was low-key because Leicester had not told Elizabeth I of his relationship with Lettice, whom Elizabeth dubbed "the she-wolf". Elizabeth never forgave Lettice.

○○

1550 – Death of William Rugg (Repps), Bishop of Norwich. He was buried at the cathedral there. Rugg supported Henry VIII's quest for an annulment of his marriage to Catherine of Aragon and his subsequent supremacy, but his conservativism in other areas caused conflict between him, Thomas Cromwell and Thomas Cranmer. Rugg resigned his episcopate in January 1550 in return for pardons for his alleged support of the rebels in *Kett's Rebellion*.

1557 – Burial of Henry Pendleton, theologian, chaplain and friend of Bishop Bonner, at St Stephen Walbrook, London. Pendleton is known for his changing religious beliefs: he was against Lutheranism in Henry VIII's reign, supported Protestantism in Edward VI's reign and then converted back to Catholicism in Mary I's reign.

1558 – Death of Charles V, former Holy Roman Emperor, from malaria at the monastery of Yuste in the Extremadura region of Spain. He had previously been suffering from debilitating attacks of gout which had necessitated him being carried around in a chair. Charles was buried at the monastery church, but later moved to the Royal Pantheon of El Escorial, the Royal Palace at San Lorenzo de El Escorial near Madrid.

1579 – Burial of Sir Edward Fitton, President of Connacht and Thomond, Vice-Treasurer and Treasurer-at-Wars during Elizabeth I's reign. He was buried beside his wife, Anne, at St Patrick's Cathedral in Dublin, Ireland.

22ND SEPTEMBER

On this day in history, the 22nd September 1515, Anna von Jülich-Kleve-Berg, or Anne of Cleves, was born near Düsseldorf. She was the second daughter of John III, Duke of Jülich, Cleves and Berg, an important German ruler, and Maria of Jülich-Berg. Anne had royal blood; not only was she descended from Edward I, she was also, on her father's side, closely related to Louis XII of France and the Duke of Burgundy.

In 1526 Anne's elder sister, Sybille, married John Frederick I, Elector of Saxony and Head of the Protestant Confederation of Germany, and in 1527, Anne's father arranged for Anne to marry Francis, the heir of the Duke of Lorraine. This betrothal was broken when Anne's brother, who became Duke of Jülich-Cleves-Berg on the death of his father in 1538, refused to give up the territory of Guelders to the Duke of Lorraine in 1539.

The *Schmalkaldic League*, an alliance of Lutheran Princes established by Anne's brother-in-law, John Frederick I, Elector of Saxony, had been trying to establish a relationship with England in the late 1520s, and in 1531 sent ambassadors to Henry VIII. The Duke of Cleves, Anne's father, had also been involved with marriage negotiations with England in 1530, although Henry had chosen to marry Anne Boleyn. These marriage negotiations were resurrected in January 1539 when Henry was looking for a fourth wife, following the death of Jane Seymour (1537). Henry's chief advisor, Thomas Cromwell, was keen to build links with the *Schmalkaldic League*, and when Henry saw that Francis I of France and Charles V, Holy Roman Emperor, were becoming friendly, he too looked towards Germany for support.

By the end of September 1539, a marriage treaty between England and Cleves had been agreed upon, and preparations were made for Anne to travel to Calais and then on to

England. Anne arrived in England on the 27th December 1539, and the royal couple were married on the 6th January 1540, at Greenwich Palace. It was not to be a happy marriage, and just over 6 months later the marriage was annulled, and Henry VIII married his fifth wife, Catherine Howard. Anne became known as the King's sister, and was rewarded for her acquiescence with £4000 per year and houses at Richmond, Bletchingley and Lewes. She was also given Hever Castle, jewels, plate, hangings and furniture. She kept her head and became a wealthy woman.

Anne of Cleves outlived Henry VIII and all of his other wives, dying on 15th July 1557, aged 41.

1544 – Death of James Nedeham, architect, while accompanying King Henry VIII to Boulogne. He was buried in Boulogne at the church of Our Lady, and a monument was erected to him at the church in Little Wymondley, Hertfordshire. Nedeham worked for Cardinal Wolsey on York Place, and then for the King on Hampton Court Palace, the Jewel House at the Tower of London and St Augustine's in Canterbury.

1557 – Death of Robert Steward, Prior and Dean of Ely, at Ely. He was buried in Ely Cathedral.

1557 – Death of Robert Warton, Bishop of Hereford. He was buried in Hereford Cathedral, in the north-east transept.

1560 – Burial of Amy Dudley (née Robsart), wife of Robert Dudley, Earl of Leicester, at St Mary's, Oxford.

1610 – Burial of Puritan politician and author Sir Francis Hastings at North Cadbury Church in Somerset, next to his wife. Hastings was a member of Parliament and Sheriff in Leicestershire during Elizabeth I's reign, and is known for his Puritan pamphlets, which included "A Watch-Word to All Religious, and True Hearted English-Men".

23RD SEPTEMBER

On this day in history, 23rd September 1571, the forty-nine year-old Bishop of Salisbury, Bishop John Jewel, died at Monkton Farleigh Manor after being taken ill while preaching a sermon in Lacock.

Jewel had started his career in 1552 when he became Vicar of Sunningwell in Berkshire, and also acted as a public orator at Oxford University. It was in his job as orator to compose an epistle to congratulate Mary I on her accession in 1553. Mary I's accession brought to an end the Protestant reforms of Edward VI's reign, and brought trouble for Jewel. His college expelled him for not attending the Mass, for preaching heresy and for his friendship with Peter Martyr (Pietro Martire Vermigli), whom Jewel considered a father figure. In 1554, he acted a notary at the disputation of Thomas Cranmer and Nicholas Ridley, but then, fearing for his life, went on to sign a series of Catholic articles. However, he was still living under suspicion, and so fled to Frankfurt, on the continent.

In Frankfurt, Jewel did not exactly receive a warm welcome from John Knox and William Whittingham. After all, he had signed those Catholic articles. He also sided with Richard Cox and the "Coxians" against Knox and Whittingham. Cox stood up for the "Prayer Book of 1552" service and the teachings of Cranmer, whereas Knox and Whittingham wanted a far more puritanical service and followed the doctrines of Calvin. Jewel then made a public confession to atone for his previous weakness in signing the Catholic articles, but the growing divisions between the Coxians and Knoxians led to him leaving Frankfurt and joining his good friend, Peter Martyr in Strasbourg. The two men then travelled to Zurich and also Padua.

In November 1558, the Catholic Mary I died and Elizabeth I became Queen of England. All of the Protestant exiles knew that it was now safe to return to England, and Jewel returned home. In 1559, he confuted the Catholics at the conference held at Westminster after Easter, and preached a rousing sermon at St Paul's Cross in November 1559. In this sermon, he outlined 27 doctrines held by the Catholic Church and offered to return to the Catholic Church if anyone could prove the practice of these doctrines in the first 600 years after Christ's death. When he repeated this challenge in 1560, it was taken up by Henry Cole, former Provost of Eton College, and this resulted in Cole being imprisoned in the Tower and Jewel writing his *Apologia ecclesiae Anglicanae* ("Apology of the Church of England"), which was published in 1562, and which is "considered by some to form the groundwork for all subsequent controversy the Church of England would have with the Church of Rome."

On the 21st January 1560, Jewel was consecrated as Bishop of Salisbury, a diocese which was impoverished as a result of Jewel's predecessor, John Capon (or Salcot), abusing his role. Jewel set about turning things around, and encouraged men who showed promise to teach in the church.

In the 1560s, a literary and theological battle sprang up between Jewel and Thomas Harding, a man Jewel had known at Oxford and a man he had also ejected from his post in Salisbury Cathedral. In 1564, Harding published his "Answer", which was followed in 1565 by Jewel's "Reply", then Harding's 1566 "Confutation" and Jewel's 1567 "Defence of the Apology".

In 1571, John Jewel was taken ill while preaching a sermon in Lacock and Wiltshire, and died on 23rd September at Monkton Farleigh Manor. He was laid to rest in Salisbury Cathedral.

<hr />

1568 – *Battle of San Juan de Ulúa*, near present day Veracruz, Mexico, between Spanish forces and English privateers led by John Hawkins. The Spanish forces were victorious.

1605 – Burial of William Averell, pamphleteer, at St Peter's Cornhill. Averill's works included the romantic "An excellent historie, both pithy and pleasant, on the life and death of Charles and Julia, two Brittish, or rather Welsh lovers" (1581), the Protestant "A wonderfull and straunge newes, which happened in the county of Suffolke, and Essex, the first of February, being Friday, where in rayned wheat, the space of vi or vii miles compass" (1583), a collection of moral narrative "A Dyall for Dainty Darlings" (1584) and "A Mervalious Combat of Contrarieties" (1588).

24TH SEPTEMBER

On this day in 1486, Arthur, Prince of Wales and son of Henry VII, was christened at a lavish ceremony at Winchester Cathedral.

Arthur had been born on the 20th September, but was not baptised straightaway because his intended godfather, John de Vere, 13th Earl of Oxford, needed time to travel from Suffolk to Winchester. On the day, those taking part gathered in Queen Elizabeth of York's apartments, while Arthur's grandmother, Elizabeth Woodville, who was standing as his godmother, waited at the cathedral. After three hours, the Earl of Oxford still hadn't arrived, so the King ordered Thomas Stanley, the Earl of Derby and the baby's stepgrandfather, to stand in for Oxford. Shortly after the baby had been baptised and named, Oxford arrived and was able to present Arthur for his confirmation. The party then processed to the shrine of St Swithun, the cathedral's saint, where hymns were sung, and then they enjoyed the traditional spices, hypocras and wine. The baby, held by his Aunt Cecily, was processed past burning torches back to his nursery and to his mother.

1516 – Birth of Richard Pate, lawyer, member of Parliament and refounder of Cheltenham Grammar School, now known as Pate's Grammar School.

1526 – Sometime before 24th September 1526, Marmaduke Huby, Abbot of Fountains since 1495, died at around the age of 87. It is thought that he was buried under the floor of the chapter house.

1561 – Birth of Edward Seymour, Viscount Beauchamp, son of Katherine Grey (sister of Lady Jane Grey) and Edward Seymour, 1st Earl of Hertford, in the Tower of London. He was born in the Tower because his parents had been imprisoned for marrying without the Queen's permission.

1589 – Executions of William Spenser, Roman Catholic priest and martyr, and layman Robert Hardesty at York. Spenser was executed for being a priest, and Hardesty for sheltering Spenser.

25 SEPTEMBER

On this day in 1525, the explorer, navigator and naval administrator Stephen Borough (Burrough) was born at Borough House, Northam Burrows, Northam in Devon, to Walter Borough and his wife Mary Dough.

In his childhood, Borough was influenced by his uncle, the seaman John Borough, and probably helped him with his first measured coastal surveys of south Devon and Cornwall in 1538. His uncle taught him navigational skills, sailing skills, Spanish and Portuguese.

In 1553, Borough served as master of the *Edward Bonaventure*, in a fleet of three ships, on a voyage to look for a northern passage to Cathay and India. Bad weather meant that only Borough's ship got through to St Nicholas (Archangel). Borough undertook a second voyage in 1556 in *The Serchthrift* and discovered Novaya Zemlya and the Viagatz Strait, which was named the Burrough Strait until the late 1800s.

In 1558, Borough travelled to Seville to trade his knowledge of the Arctic for navigational training from Spanish pilots. On his return to England, Borough had Martin Cortés' manual "Breve compendio del arte de navegar" translated by Richard Eden and published for use by English seamen.

In the early 1560s, Borough traded in the Arctic as chief pilot of *The Swallow*, but in 1564 became one of four keepers of Elizabeth I's ships on the Medway and settled at Chatham. He was made Master of Trinity House in 1572 and died at Chatham in 1584.

1513 – Vasco Núñez de Balboa, the Spanish explorer, reached the Pacific Ocean. He was the first European to have discovered the Pacific Ocean from the New World.

1534 – Death of Pope Clement VII in Rome from eating a death cap mushroom. He was laid to rest in Santa Maria sopra Minerva.

1554 – Death of Richard Sampson, Bishop of Coventry and Lichfield, and former President of the Council of the Welsh Marches, at Eccleshall in Staffordshire. He was buried in the parish church at Eccleshall. Sampson had acted as the King's Proctor at the fall of Anne Boleyn in 1536.

1555 – The *Peace of Augsburg*, or *Augsburg Settlement*, was signed by Charles V, Holy Roman Emperor, and the princes of the *Schmalkaldic League* at Augsburg.

1558 – Gertrude Courtenay, Marchioness of Exeter, made her will. She died soon after and was buried in Wimborne Minster, Dorset. Gertrude was the mother of Edward Courtenay, 1st Earl of Devon, who was imprisoned for his part in *Wyatt's Rebellion* in 1554. Gertude, herself, was imprisoned in 1538, and her husband was executed for treason.

1584 – Death of Thomas Copley, Roman Catholic, in exile near Antwerp. He had served Elizabeth I as Commissioner of the Peace for Surrey, and she was godmother to his son, Henry, but he lost royal favour when he converted to Catholicism in 1563. He left England in 1570, being unable to accept royal supremacy and Elizabeth I's religious measures.

1586 – Mary, Queen of Scots was moved to Fotheringhay Castle in Northamptonshire, and Elizabeth finally backed down and agreed to the appointing of 36 commissioners to act as judges in her trial.

1594 – Death of Gregory Fiennes, 10th Baron Dacre, at Chelsea. He was buried in Chelsea Old Church.

1602 – Death of William Redman, Bishop of Norwich, at the Episcopal Palace. He was buried in the cathedral choir.

26TH SEPTEMBER

On 26th September 1580, Sir Francis Drake arrived at the port of Plymouth in the *Golden Hind*, which was laden with treasure and spices after his three year voyage around the world.

Drake had successfully circumnavigated the globe in his ship, the *Pelican*, which had been renamed the *Golden Hind* in October 1578 when it reached the Pacific Ocean safely. Drake came back from his voyage with a beautiful jewel for the Queen from Mexico. It consisted of a ship with an ebony hull, an African diamond and enamelled gold. In return, Elizabeth gave him a jewel, now known as the "Drake Jewel". It had a sardonyx double cameo portrait of an African male and a European regal figure on one side and a locket containing a miniature of her by Nicholas Hilliard on the other.

Drake was the first Englishman to circumnavigate the globe, and was rewarded by Queen Elizabeth I with a knighthood on 4th April 1581, aboard the *Golden Hind* at Deptford.

1533 – Death of William Benet, diplomat, at Susa in Italy. He had been appointed Henry VIII's Resident Ambassador to Rome in 1529 and remained in that position until the break with Rome. He was on his way home from Rome when he died.

1555 – Death of Thomas Berthelet, printer, in London. Berthelet had been Henry VIII's printer from 1530 until the King's death in 1547.

1588 – Death of Sir Amias (Amyas) Paulet, administrator, diplomat, Governor of Jersey and gaoler of Mary, Queen of Scots. He was buried in St Martin-in-the-Fields, Westminster. Paulet served Elizabeth I as her resident ambassador in France and a Privy Councillor, and was present at the execution of Mary, Queen of Scots. When he was acting as Mary's gaoler, Elizabeth I had suggested that it would be easier if Paulet quietly murdered her. He refused.

1592 – Burial of Thomas Watson, poet and translator, at St Bartholomew-the-Less. Watson is known for his unusual eighteen line sonnets and his Latin works.

1595 – Burial of Sir Owen Hopton, administrator and politician, at St Dunstan's Church, Stepney. Hopton served Elizabeth I as Lieutenant of the Tower of London from 1570-1590, as a member of Parliament and a Sheriff.

27TH SEPTEMBER

On this day in history, 27th September 1501, at 5 o'clock in the afternoon, the fifteen year-old Catherine of Aragon left the port of Laredo in Spain bound for England to marry Arthur, Prince of Wales. It was her second attempt at sailing from Spain to England. Her first attempt, on 17th August, from A Coruña, had been a failure: strong storms in the notoriously rough Bay of Biscay had forced Catherine's fleet to land at Laredo, near Bilbao.

Catherine had left her home, the Alhambra Palace in Granada, on 21st May 1501 to travel over 500 miles on horseback to the northern coast of Spain. This journey today takes over ten hours by car, so it was a long and arduous journey on horseback in the heat of the summer.

Catherine finally arrived at Plymouth, on the southwestern coast of England, on the 2nd October. She must have been exhausted.

1442 – Birth of John de la Pole, 2nd Duke of Suffolk, to William de la Pole, 1st Duke of Suffolk, and his wife Alice (née Chaucer). Suffolk married the six year-old Margaret Beaufort, future mother of Henry VII, in 1449, but the marriage was annulled by Henry VI in 1453, and he went on to marry Elizabeth, daughter of Richard of York and sister of Edward IV.

1488 – Death of William Hobbes, physician and surgeon. He was buried in Holy Trinity Priory, Aldgate, London. Hobbes served Richard, Duke of York, and Edward IV, and was Royal Physician to Richard III. He became Master of St Mary of Bethlehem Hospital (Bedlam) in 1479.

1540 – Birth of Michael Heneage, politician and antiquary. Heneage was a member of Parliament, a Keeper of the Records in the Tower of London, and a member of the Society of Antiquaries.

1571 – Death of Sir William Garrard, merchant, in London. He was buried in the church of of St Magnus the Martyr near London Bridge. Garrard was Mayor of London in 1555, and a member of Parliament during Mary I's reign. He also went on voyages to Guinea in the 1550s and 1560s, and became a consul of the Russia Company in 1553.

28TH SEPTEMBER

On this day in 1553, Mary I travelled in a decorated barge to the Tower of London to prepare for her coronation. She was accompanied by her half-sister, Elizabeth, and as they pulled up to Tower Wharf, they were greeted by music and cannons firing.

It was traditional for monarchs to go to the Tower before their coronations and process from there to Westminster, and it was also traditional for Knights of the Bath to be created before a monarch's coronation. Mary created fifteen Knights of the Bath on 29th September, and these knights included Thomas Howard, Earl of Surrey; William Courtenay, Earl of Devon, and William Dormer. As the ceremony consisted of the monarch dubbing the Knights when they were naked, in their baths, the Earl of Arundel had to stand in for Mary.

Mary left the Tower on her coronation procession on the 30th September 1553.

***

1502 – Death of Robert Willoughby, 1st Baron Willoughby de Broke, at Callington, Cornwall. He was buried at Callington Church. Willoughby had been in exile in Brittany with Henry Tudor and fought with him at the *Battle of Bosworth*. He served Henry VII as Lord Steward and was made a Knight of the Garter in 1489.

1558 (28th or 29th) – Death of Sir Robert Acton, Royal Saddler and member of Parliament. He was buried in Elmley Lovett church. Acton also served as a Justice of the Peace and Sheriff during Henry VIII's reign, as well as being on the council in the Marches of Wales. As Royal Saddler, he went with the King to Boulogne in 1544.

1560 – Death of Francis Talbot, 5th Earl of Shrewsbury, at Sheffield. He was buried at St Peter's Church, Sheffield, which is now the cathedral.

1582 – Death of George Buchanan, Scottish historian, humanist scholar and poet. He was buried in Greyfriars churchyard in Edinburgh. His works included his 1579 "History of Scotland" *(Rerum Scoticarum Historia),* the 1579 treatise *De Jure Regni apud Scotos,* his satire "Chamaeleon" and his poems.

1594 – Death of John Piers, Archbishop of York, at his home, Bishopthorpe. He was aged seventy-one. Piers was buried at York Minster.

1599 – Robert Devereux, 2nd Earl of Essex, strode into Elizabeth I's bedchamber unannounced and saw the Queen without her makeup or wig, without her "mask of youth".

29TH SEPTEMBER

On this day in history, 29th September 1564, Robert Dudley was made Earl of Leicester, an earldom which had been planned earlier in the year to make him more acceptable as a bridegroom to Mary, Queen of Scots. This earldom was an important one, having previously been held by royal princes like John of Gaunt and Henry of Bolingbroke (Henry IV). Although Dudley behaved impeccably at the ceremony, the Queen did not. As she put the chain of earldom around Dudley's neck, she "could not refrain from putting her hand in his neck to kittle him smilingly." A loving gesture and perhaps one that was meant to reassure Dudley that he was still hers.

When Elizabeth first spoke to William Maitland of Lethington, the Scottish Ambassador, about the potential marriage match, he laughed it off and then asked why Elizabeth herself did not marry Dudley; that way she could leave both her husband and kingdom to Mary, Queen of Scots!

Elizabeth's chief advisor, William Cecil, supported the plan. After all, it killed two birds with one stone: it got rid of the troublesome Dudley and it formed an alliance with Scotland. Cecil wrote to Maitland in praise of Dudley but Maitland did not pass on the proposal to his queen because Dudley was not even a peer. He was a nobody. This was something that Elizabeth said that she would rectify by giving Dudley an earldom. However, although Elizabeth's ambassador to Scotland, Thomas Randolph, was ordered to keep on urging the Scottish queen to marry Dudley, neither Mary, Queen of Scots or Robert Dudley were keen on the idea.

In the spring of 1564, when Randolph spoke to Mary of the idea, she was flabbergasted. She had been married to the King of France, and here was Elizabeth trying to marry her off to a nobody. She did not say an outright "no", and demanded that if she were to marry Dudley then she should be named Elizabeth's heir, but this was something that Elizabeth would never consider.

The marriage never took place, and it is hard to know how serious Elizabeth was in her offer of Dudley, her favourite, to her nemesis, Mary, Queen of Scots.

***

1528 – The papal legate, Cardinal Lorenzo Campeggio, landed at Dover on the Kent coast. He had arrived in preparation for hearing the case for the annulment of the marriage of Henry VIII and Catherine of Aragon at a special legatine court.

1558 – Death of George Brooke, 9th Baron Cobham, soldier and landowner. He was buried at Cobham Church. Cobham acted as Lieutenant-General in spring 1544 when English forces invaded Scotland, and was made Deputy of Calais in June 1544. He was created a Knight of the Garter in 1549, and was on Edward VI's Privy Council. He was imprisoned in the Tower of London temporarily in 1554 after being implicated in *Wyatt's Rebellion*, but was released and fined.

30TH SEPTEMBER

On Saturday 30th September 1553, at 3 o'clock in the afternoon, Mary I left the Tower of London to the sound of guns firing and church bells ringing. This was her coronation procession, and the next day she would be crowned Queen of England.

The procession leaving the Tower consisted of the Queen's messengers, trumpeters, Esquires of the Body, the Knights of the Bath (including 15 young noblemen who had been knighted that morning), heralds, bannerets, the council, the clergy, the Garter Knights, the nobility, foreign ambassadors, merchants, soldiers, Knights and then the Queen's entourage. In Mary's personal entourage were the Earl of Sussex, acting as Mary's Chief Server; two knights with powdered heads and old-fashioned hats, representing the dukes of Normandy and Guienne; Stephen Gardiner and William Paulet carrying the seal and mace; the Lord Mayor of London carrying the gold sceptre; the Sergeant at Arms and the Earl of Arundel carrying the Queen's sword.

After this huge procession came the Queen herself, in an open litter pulled by six horses in white trappings. She was dressed in a a mantle and kirtle of sumptuous cloth of gold, with a gold tinsel cloth and a jewelled crown on her head. Mary was dressed as a queen consort, but then England had never had a queen regnant.

Mary was escorted by the wives of the Duke of Norfolk, Earl of Arundel and Sir William Paulet, as well as the mother of Edward Courtenay, on horseback. Behind her was a carriage bearing her sister, Elizabeth, and Anne of Cleves, Henry VIII's fourth wife, followed by noblewomen and then royal henchmen robed in green and white, the Tudor colours. This mile and a half procession must have been quite an exciting spectacle for the people of London.

The pageants and displays on Mary's route from the Tower to Whitehall included a triumphal arch decorated with verses praising her accession, created by the Genoese merchants; an image of Judith, the Israelite heroine, at Cornhill, created by the Florentines; conduits running with wine at Cornhill and Cheap, and the singing of verses in praise of the Queen at Cornhill and Cheap. At St Paul's, the Queen was addressed by the Recorder of London and presented with a purse containing 1000 marks of gold by the Chamberlain. John Heywood, the playwright, delivered an oration in Latin and English at the school in St Paul's Churchyard, and then at St Paul's Gate choristers held burning perfumed tapers.

Finally, Mary I reached Whitehall and retired for the day to prepare herself for her coronation at Westminster Abbey.

1515 – Margaret Tudor, sister of Henry VIII and former Queen Consort of James IV, fled to England. Margaret was pregnant with the child of her new husband, Archibald Douglas, 6th Earl of Angus. John Stewart, 2nd Earl of Albany, was acting as Regent for Margaret's son, the young James V, and had custody of the boy and his brother, Alexander.

1544 – Henry VIII returned to England after his victory in Boulogne. The French forces had surrendered on 13th September after a siege which lasted from 19th July.

1546 – Death of Sir Richard Long, member of Parliament and Gentleman of Henry VIII's Privy Chamber.

1585 – Philip Howard, Earl of Arundel and son of Thomas Howard, 4th Duke of Norfolk, was received into the Catholic Church by Jesuit William Weston at Arundel Castle.

1ST OCTOBER

On Sunday 1st October 1553, Mary I was crowned Queen at Westminster Abbey by Stephen Gardiner, the Bishop of Winchester.

At 11am, Mary processed into the Abbey, dressed traditionally, as a male monarch would be, in the usual state robes of crimson velvet. Before her processed the Bishop of Winchester, gentlemen, knights and councillors, the Earl of Arundel carrying the ball and sceptre, the Marquis of Winchester carrying the orb and the Duke of Norfolk carrying the crown. A canopy carried by the barons of the Cinque Ports was carried over the Queen as she processed along a raised walkway to the coronation chair.

Gardiner opened the ceremony with the following address:-

"Sirs, Here present is Mary, rightful and undoubted inheritrix by the Laws of God and man to the Crown and Royal Dignity of this realm of England, France and Ireland, whereupon you shall understand that this day is appointed by all the peers of this land for the consecration, injunction and coronation of the said most excellent Princess Mary; will you serve at the time and give your wills and assent to the same consecration, unction and coronation?"

To which the congregation replied: "Yea, yea, yeah! God save Queen Mary!"

As was usual for the monarch, Mary then prostrated herself before the altar on a velvet cushion while prayers were said over her. Afterwards, the Bishop of Chichester, George Day, preached a sermon on the obedience owed to a monarch, and Mary made her oaths before lying prostrate once again in front of the high altar while the Abbey choir sang *Veni Creator Spiritus*. Accompanied by her ladies, Mary then went to change in preparation for her anointing. Dressed in a petticoat of purple velvet, she lay in front of the altar and was anointed with holy oil on her shoulders, breast, forehead and temples by Gardiner. Once again dressed in her robes of state, Mary then received the sword, the sceptre and orbs, and was crowned with the crown of Edward the Confessor, the Imperial Crown and then a specially custom-made crown. The ermine-furred crimson mantle was then put about her shoulders, and she sat in the coronation chair as nobles paid homage to their new queen.

Finally at 4pm, Mary walked out of Westminster Abbey, processing to Westminster Hall for the coronation banquet, where she was joined by her half-sister, Elizabeth, and her former step-mother, Anne of Cleves. There was much to celebrate. Mary was now the recognised queen of the realm, the first crowned queen regnant of England – Mary, Queen Mary I.

***

1500 – Death of John Alcock, Bishop of Ely, scholar and Royal Tutor, at Wisbech Castle. He was buried at Ely Cathedral, in the chantry chapel he had designed. Alcock had acted as tutor to Prince Edward, son of Edward IV, and had also been president of the Prince's Council at Ludlow. He was also Henry VII's first Chancellor and opened his first Parliament.

1505 – Death of Sir Henry Colet, merchant and Lord Mayor of London, at Stepney. He was buried there.

1526 – Birth of Dorothy Stafford, Lady Stafford, daughter of Henry Stafford, 10th Baron Stafford, and his wife, Ursula (née Pole). Dorothy married Sir William Stafford, widower of Mary Boleyn, in 1545. She served Elizabeth I as a gentlewoman of the Privy Chamber.

2ND OCTOBER

On this day in 1452, Richard III, the last Plantagenet king, was born at Fotheringhay Castle, Northamptonshire.

Richard was the youngest surviving child of Richard, 3rd Duke of York, and Cecily Neville. Richard claimed the English throne in June 1483, claiming that his brother Edward IV's sons were illegitimate because Edward had been pre-contracted to another woman when he married Elizabeth Woodville. Richard III was killed at the *Battle of Bosworth* on 22nd August 1485, and Henry Tudor claimed the throne as Henry VII.

1501 – Catherine of Aragon arrived in England, landing at Plymouth in Devon. She had come to England to marry Prince Arthur, the heir to the throne of England.

1514 – Mary Tudor, sister of Henry VIII, set off from Dover to sail to France to marry King Louis XII. She was eighteen and he was fifty-two, and not in the best of health. They married on 9th October 1514, but the marriage was short-lived as Louis died in January 1515. Mary went on to marry Charles Brandon, the Duke of Suffolk, on the 3rd March 1515.

1518 – *Treaty of London* – Cardinal Wolsey's treaty of "Universal" peace between France and England was signed.

1521 – Pope Leo X was given Henry VIII's *Assertio septem sacramentorum* or "Defence of the Seven Sacraments" in Rome. This work led to Henry VIII being proclaimed *Fidei Defensor* or "Defender of the Faith".

1528 – Publication of William Tyndale's "The Obedience of the Christian Man and How Christian Rulers Ought to Govern" published by William Tyndale. This book said that rulers were accountable to God, not the Pope. Anne Boleyn owned a copy of this book, as well as Tyndale's "New Testament", and it is this book which she intended to show Henry VIII, marking key passages for his attention. The book got into his hands when it was confiscated from George Zouche, suitor of Anne Gainsford who had borrowed it from her mistress, Anne Boleyn. Henry VIII read it and declared "This book is for me and all kings to read."

1536 – Start of the *Lincolnshire Rising*, the beginning of the *Pilgrimage of Grace*. It was sparked off by a sermon at evensong on the 1st October at St James's Church, Louth, and by a visitation from a registrar on 2nd October. Mary Polito, author of "Governmental Arts in Tudor England" describes how Nicholas Melton, a local shoemaker who came to be known as "Captain Cobbler", seized the registrar, burned his papers and then forced him and the priests to swear an oath of loyalty to the rebel cause. The rebels then marched to the nunnery at Legbourne where they took the royal commissioners hostage. The nunnery had been formally suppressed a few weeks earlier.

3RD OCTOBER

On this day in 1518, Cardinal Wolsey sang a mass to Henry VIII and the French ambassadors at St Paul's Cathedral in celebration of the treaty agreed between the two countries the previous day. The King and ambassadors also took oaths to the treaty.

In the evening, there was a sumptuous banquet followed by a mummery featuring the King and his sister, Mary. Jousting and pageants were also part of the celebrations of this treaty.

1559 – Death of Sir William Fitzwilliam, Gentleman of Edward VI's Privy Chamber. He was buried in St George's Chapel, Windsor Castle.

1584 – Death of Sir Gilbert Dethick, herald, Garter Principal King of Arms and diplomat, in London. He was laid to rest in the church of St Benet Paul's Wharf. Dethick's offices included Hampnes Pursuivant of Arms Extraordinary (1536), Rouge Croix Pursuivant of Arms in Ordinary (1540), Richmond Herald of Arms in Ordinary (1540), Norroy King of Arms (1547) and Garter Principal King of Arms (1550).

4TH OCTOBER

On Wednesday 4th October 1536, there was trouble in Horncastle, Lincolnshire. This was part of what we know as the *Lincolnshire Rising* which, in turn, was part of the *Pilgrimage of Grace* rebellion.

Dr Raynes, the chancellor of the Bishop of Lincoln, who was staying nearby at Bolingbroke, after having held a session of the commissionary's court there, was dragged from his sickbed and taken to Horncastle. Francis Aidan Gasquet, the 19th century Benedictine monk and historical scholar, describes what happened next in his book "Henry VIII and the English Monasteries":-

"As the chancellor rode into the field with his captors the passions of the mob were stirred, and there occurred one of the two acts of violence, which alone in this or the subsequent Yorkshire rising, disgraced the movement! "At his coming into the field," declares Brian Staines, "the rebels, whereof were many parsons and vicars, cried out with a loud voice, ' Kill him, kill him.' And upon that one William Hutchinson, of Horncastle, and William Balderstone, by the procurement of the said parsons and vicars, pulled him violently off his horse, kneeling upon his knees, and with their staves they slew him. And being dead, this deponent saith the priests continually crying, 'Kill him, kill him,' he also struck the said chancellor upon the arm with a staff."

There was also a second murder that day, that of Thomas Wulcey (or Wolsey), one of Cromwell's men, who was hanged by the mob. It was also on this day that Robert Aske made his decision to become one of the rebels.

Gasquet writes of how the rebels at Horncastle "devised certain articles of grievance which were to be forwarded to the king". These articles of complaint were drawn up by the gentry, Sheriff Dymmoke and his brother, and then presented to the crowd who held up their hands and said "We like them very well." The rebels' complaints included the dissolution of the monasteries, the grant to the king of the tenths and first-fruits of spiritual benefices, the promotion of Thomas Cromwell and Richard Rich to the King's Council, and the promotion of the archbishops of Canterbury and Dublin, the bishops of Rochester and St. David's, and others, who, in their opinion, had clearly 'subverted the faith of Christ'.

These articles were dispatched immediately to the King, and on the 11th October the King's herald arrived at Lincoln with the King's reply:-

"Concerning choosing of counsellors," the king wrote, "I never have read, heard nor known, that princes' counsellors and prelates should be appointed by rude and ignorant common people; nor that they were persons meet or of ability to discern and choose meet and sufficient counsellors for a prince. How presumptuous then are ye, the rude commons of one shire, and that one of the most brute and beastly of the whole realm and of least experience, to find fault with your prince for the electing of his counsellors and prelates, and to take upon you, contrary to God's law and man's law, to rule your prince whom ye are bound to obey and serve with both your lives, lands, and goods, and for no worldly cause to withstand.

As to the suppression of houses and monasteries, they were granted to us by the parliament and not set forth by any counsellor or counsellors upon their mere will and fantasy, as you, full falsely, would persuade our realm to believe. And where ye alledge that the service of God is much thereby diminished, the truth thereof is contrary; for there are no houses suppressed where God was well served, but where most vice, mischief, and abomination of living was used: and that doth well appear by their confessions, subscribed with their own hands, in the time of our visitations. And yet were suffered a great many of them, more than we by the act needed, to stand; wherein if they amend not their living, we fear we have more to answer for than for the suppression of all the rest. And as for their hospitality, for the relief of poor people, we wonder ye be not ashamed to affirm, that they have been a great relief to our people, when a great many, or the most part, hath not past 4 or 5 religious persons in them and divers but one, which spent the substance of the goods of their house in nourishing vice and abominable living. Now, what unkindness and unnaturality may we impute to you and all our subjects that be of that mind that had rather such an unthrifty sort of vicious persons should enjoy such possessions, profits and emoluments as grow of the said houses to the maintenance of their unthrifty life than we, your natural prince, sovereign lord and king, who doth and hath spent more in your defences of his own than six times they be worth."

Henry was not giving in to their demands, and concluded his message with a warning:-

"We charge you, eftsoon, upon the foresaid bonds and pains, that ye withdraw yourselves to your own houses, every man; and no more to assemble, contrary to the laws and your allegiances; and to cause the provokers of you to this mischief to be delivered to our lieutenant's hands or ours and you yourselves to submit to such condign punishment as we and our nobles shall think you worthy."

1507 – Birth of Sir Francis Bigod, leader of *Bigod's Rebellion*, at Seaton, Hinderwell, Yorkshire. Bigod led an uprising in Beverley, Yorkshire, in January 1537, following the *Pilgrimage of Grace*, and was executed in June 1537.

1531 – Baptism of Henry Stanley, 4th Earl of Derby, at Lathom House, Lancashire. He was the eldest son of Edward Stanley, 3rd Earl of Derby, and his wife, Dorothy (née Howard). Derby served Elizabeth I as an Ambassador, Privy Councillor and Lord High Steward at the trial of Philip Howard, Earl of Arundel and Surrey.

1539 – Signing of the marriage treaty between Henry VIII and Anne of Cleves.

1556 – John Cheke made a public recantation of his Protestant faith in front of Queen Mary I.

1581 – Death of Henry Wriothesley, 2nd Earl of Southampton, at Itchel in Hampshire. He was buried at Titchfield.

5TH OCTOBER

1518 – Formal betrothal of Princess Mary, daughter of Henry VIII and Catherine of Aragon, and the Dauphin of France.

1528 – Death of Richard Foxe, Bishop of Winchester, founder of Corpus Christi College, Oxford, and Lord Privy Seal in the reign of Henry VII and at the beginning of Henry VIII's.

1549 – Edward Seymour, Protector Somerset, ordered a gathering of men at Hampton Court Palace, where he was lodged with the young Edward VI due to tensions mounting between Somerset and John Dudley, Earl of Warwick.

1553 – Parliament met in Mary I's reign – It repealed the "treason act" of Edward VI's reign, passed an act declaring the legitimacy of Mary I, reinstated the Mass in Latin, celibacy of the clergy and ritual worship. It was as if the reformation of Edward's reign had never happened.

1555 – Death of Edward Wotton, physician and naturalist. He was buried in St Alban Church, Cheapside, London. Wotton is known for starting the study of zoology and his works included *De differentiis animalium libri decem* which he dedicated to Edward VI.

1598 – Burial of Thomas Crooke, Church of England clergyman, at St Mary Woolchurch in the chancel.

1605 – Death of Sir Edward Lewkenor, politician and Puritan patron, at Denham Hall from smallpox. He was laid to rest at Denham church.

6TH OCTOBER

The 6th October 1536 is the traditional date given to the execution of reformer, scholar and Bible translator, William Tyndale. Tyndale, whose works include "The Obedience of a Christian Man" (a book Anne Boleyn shared with Henry VIII), had incurred the wrath of Henry VIII after the publication of his "The Practyse of Prelates", in which he opposed Henry VIII's planned annulment from Catherine of Aragon.

Henry VIII was determined to get the man he viewed as a traitor and heretic apprehended, and in 1535 Tyndale was betrayed by an Englishman, Henry Philips, and arrested in Antwerp.

According to the martyrologist John Foxe, Tyndale was then taken to the "castle of Filford" (Vilvoorde), eighteen miles from Antwerp, and imprisoned there for a year and a half. Tyndale was then tried and "condemned by virtue of the emperor's decree". The exact date of his execution is not known, but it is traditionally commemorated on the 6th October. Foxe wrote of his execution:-

"He was tied to the stake, and then strangled first by the hangman, and afterwards consumed with fire in the town of Filford, A.D. 1536; crying thus at the stake with a fervent zeal, and a loud voice, "Lord, open the King of England's eyes.""

Foxe went on to say of Tyndale:-

"Such was the power of the doctrine, and sincerity of life of this amiable man, and glorious martyr, that during his imprisonment, he converted the keeper, his daughter and others of his household. Also all that were conversant with him in the castle, acknowledged, that "if he were not a good Christian, they could not tell whom to trust.".... Suffice it to say, that he was one of those who by his works shone as a sun of light amidst a dark world, and gave evidence that he was a faithful servant of his master and Savior, Jesus Christ."

1510 – Birth of John Caius, theological scholar, Royal Physician and founder of Gonville and Caius College, Cambridge, at Norwich. He was the son of Robert Caius and his wife, Alice (née Wode). Caius studied medicine at Padua and was physician to Edward VI, Mary I and Elizabeth I.

1557 – Death of John Capon (also known as John Salcot), former Benedictine monk and Bishop of Salisbury, probably from influenza. He was buried in the choir at Salisbury Cathedral. He appeared to have reformist leanings in the reigns of Henry VIII and Edward VI, but became a conservative Catholic again in Mary I's reign, and was involved in the examination of those deemed to be heretics.

7TH OCTOBER

1506 – Death of Sir Thomas Frowyk, judge and Chief Justice of the Common Pleas. He was buried with his first wife, Joan, at Finchley Parish Church in Middlesex, on the north side of the chancel.

1533 – Death of Sir John Scott, soldier. Scott served as a Senior Captain in the army sent to the Low Countries in 1511 to support Margaret of Austria, and was rewarded for his service by a knighthood. He also served in France in 1514 and 1523.

1577 – Death of George Gascoigne, author, poet, courtier and soldier, in Stamford, Lincolnshire. He was buried there, at St Mary's parish church. He is listed as one of the most important Tudor poets, along with the likes of Sir Thomas Wyatt, Henry Howard, Earl of Surrey, and Philip Sidney. His works included "A Discourse of the Adventures of Master FJ", "The Supposes", "A Hundredth Sundry Flowres..." and "The Posies of George Gascoigne, Esquire".

1589 – Death of William Hawkins, merchant and sea captain, at Deptford. He was buried at St Nicholas's Church. In 1580, Hawkins led an expedition to the Caribbean, returning to England with treasure and sugar. In 1588, he was involved in leading seven ships from Plymouth against the *Spanish Armada*.

8TH OCTOBER

Lady Margaret Douglas, Countess of Lennox, was born on this day in 1515. Margaret was the daughter of Margaret Tudor, Queen Dowager of Scotland and sister of Henry VIII, and Archibald Douglas, 6th Earl of Angus. She was born at Harbottle Castle in Northumberland, home of Thomas, 2nd Lord Dacre, because her mother went into labour as she fled Scotland to go to Henry VIII's court in London. Margaret was baptised on 9th October, but her mother was ill after the birth and wasn't well enough to travel onward to London until spring 1516. Mother and baby stayed in England until June 1517, when Henry VIII sent his sister and niece back to Scotland.

Margaret became the focus of a custody battle when her parents argued over Archibald keeping a mistress. Archibald took custody of Margaret for many years, but in 1530 she joined the household of Henry VIII's daughter, Mary, at Beaulieu. The two, being close in age, became close friends, and the friendship stayed strong even when Margaret became Henry VIII's heir presumptive, when he made his daughters, Mary and Elizabeth, illegitimate.

Margaret was said to be a beauty, and when she was acting as lady-in-waiting to Queen Anne Boleyn, she fell in love with Lord Thomas Howard, son of Thomas Howard, 2nd Duke of Norfolk. The couple became secretly betrothed, but were split up by a furious Henry VIII, who threw them both in the Tower. Margaret was released when she became ill, but was sent to Syon Abbey and kept there under house arrest. She was released on 29th October 1537, but her beloved died in the Tower on 31st October.

Margaret went on to serve as a lady to Anne of Cleves and Catherine Howard, but was sent back to Syon for a while when she fell in love with Catherine Howard's brother. She acted as a bridesmaid at the marriage of Henry VIII and Catherine Parr in July 1543 and then, in 1544 she married Matthew Stewart, 13th or 4th Earl of Lennox, a descendant of James I of Scotland and an influential man. The couple's first child, Henry, Lord Darnley, died in infancy in 1545, but his namesake, Henry Stuart (Stewart), Lord Darnley, who was born just a week after his brother's death, survived and is known for his marriage to Mary, Queen of Scots and his murder in 1567. In total, the couple had eight children.

Margaret was cut out of Henry VIII's will after an argument, and kept to herself during the Protestant Edward VI's reign. However, she was treated well during the Catholic Mary I's reign, and attended Mary's marriage to Philip of Spain as Mary's chief lady. Margaret viewed Elizabeth I as illegitimate and supported Mary, Queen of Scot's claim to the throne, so was ecstatic when her son became betrothed to Mary. Elizabeth was not happy, and as she could not get at Darnley to punish him, she threw his mother into the Tower. On 19th February 1567, the imprisoned Margaret was told that her husband and son had been killed. It was actually a mistake. Her son had been killed, but Lennox was still alive. Margaret was in such a state that a royal physician had to be fetched, and she was released to Sheen. Lennox joined her there after the acquittal of James Hepburn, 4th Earl of Bothwell, for their son's murder. They then moved to Coldharbour, a property given to them by Elizabeth.

Lennox was killed on 4th September 1571, when he was shot at Stirling Castle, and in 1574 Margaret was allowed to visit Scotland accompanied by her only living child, Charles. On the way, Charles met and fell in love with Elizabeth Cavendish, daughter of Lady Shrewsbury (Bess of Hardwick).

The couple married and had a daughter, Arabella, in 1575. On hearing of the news of the marriage match, Elizabeth I had thrown Bess and Margaret into the Tower, but Margaret was released in autumn 1574, and went to live with her son and his new wife in Stepney. Unfortunately, Charles died of tuberculosis in 1576, and his mother was griefstricken. She died on 9th March 1578, after being taken ill at a dinner party attended by Robert Dudley, Earl of Leicester. Margaret was buried in Westminster Abbey, in the Henry VII Chapel.

***

1536 – The commons, i.e. the people, approved the petition of grievances drawn up by the rebels of Horncastle, Lincolnshire.

1549 – Edward Seymour, Duke of Somerset and Lord Protector, was proclaimed a traitor by the King's Privy Council.

1561 – Baptism of Edward Wright, mathematician and cartographer, at Garveston in Norfolk. Wright is known for his treatise "Certaine Errors in Navigation" (1599), his work on Mercator's map projection and his translation of John Napier's 1614 *Mirifici logarithmorum canonis descriptio* into English.

1594 – Death of Ellis Price (Prys), scholar and administrator. Price served Henry VIII as a monastic visitor in Wales 1535, Commissary-General and Chancellor of the diocese of St Asaph, and as an administrator in Wales after the "Acts of Union". He also later served as Sheriff of Merioneth, Anglesey, Caernarfon, and Denbigh, and a member of the council in the Marches of Wales.

9TH OCTOBER

On this day in history, 9th October 1514, the eighteen year-old Mary Tudor, sister of Henry VIII, married the fifty-two year-old King Louis XII of France at Abbeville.

In a letter to Antonio Triulzi, Bishop of Asti, dated the 10th October 1514, the Venetian ambassador described Mary Tudor's arrival in Abbeville and the wedding:

"Then followed the Queen, under a white canopy, above and around which were the roses, supported by two porcupines. She was alone beneath it, and Monseigneur [d'Angoulême] on her left hand, but outside. She rode a white palfrey, with rich trappings, and was herself clad in very handsome stiff brocade.

Next came her litter, very beautiful, adorned with lilies; then five of the principal English ladies, very well dressed; then a carriage of brocade, on which were four ladies, followed by a second carriage with as many more ladies. Next came six ladies on horseback; and then a third carriage, of purple and crimson velvet (veluto paonazo cremesin), with four ladies; after which a crowd of ladies, some twenty in number; then 150 archers in three liveries. In this order they went to the Queen's house, which was near that of the King. It was a sumptuous entry, and these noblemen of England have very large chains, and are otherwise in good array.

Before the entry there was a heavy shower, which drenched them all, especially the ladies. The Queen was dressed in the English fashion. In the evening, "Madame," the King's daughter, wife of Monseigneur d'Angoulême, went to visit her, and they gave a ball. This morning the King had preparation made for the mass in his own hall (salla), whither the Queen came, preceded by 73 (sic) English barons and gentlemen; the King doffed his bonnet, and the Queen curtseyed to the ground, whereupon his Majesty kissed her. The treasurer Robertet then presented to the King a necklace, in which were set two beautiful jewels, and his Majesty placed it round the Queen's neck; after which mass was performed.

The two candles were held, the one by Monseigneur de Vendôme and the other by the Prince de Vendôme. After the King had kissed the "1 pax" at the mass, he kissed the Queen.

At the offertory Monseigneur [d'Angoulême?] gave the money to the King, and Madame to the Queen.

The mass by the Cardinal de Bayeux being ended, he gave the consecrated wafer, one half to the King and the other to the Queen, who kissed and then swallowed it; and after making a graceful curtsey she departed, the King and Queen going each to their own apartments to dine. In the evening the Queen arrayed herself in the French fashion, and there was dancing; the whole Court banqueting, dancing, and making good cheer; and thus, at the eighth hour before midnight, the Queen was taken away from the entertainment by Madame to go and sleep with the King.

I promise you that she is very handsome, and of sufficiently tall stature (de statura honestamente granda). She appears to me rather pale, though this I believe proceeds from the tossing of the sea and from her fright. She does not seem a whit more than 16 years old, and looks very well in the French costume. She is extremely courteous and well mannered, and has come in very sumptuous array…"

There is another account in the same archives ("Calendar of State Papers Relating to English Affairs in the Archives of Venice, Volume 2": 1509-1519) of Mary Tudor's entrance to Abbeville and the wedding, in which Mary is described:-

"She is generally considered handsome and well favoured, were not her eyes and eyebrows too light; for the rest it appears to me that nature optime suplevit: she is slight, rather than defective from corpulence, and conducts herself with so much grace, and has such good manners, that for her age of 18 years—and she does not look more—she is a paradise."

1529 – A writ of praemunire was filed against Cardinal Thomas Wolsey in the court of King's Bench.

1536 – *Pilgrimage of Grace*: The rebels of Horncastle, Lincoln, dispatched their petition of grievances to the King and also north into Yorkshire.

1547 – Baptism of Miguel de Cervantes, author of Don Quixote, in Alcalá de Henares, Spain. His actual birthdate is unknown.

1573 – Death of Sir Thomas Wroth, courtier, politician and landowner. Wroth served Edward VI as a Gentleman of the Privy Chamber and was with him when he died.

1604 – Death of Sir William Peryam, judge, at Little Fulford, near Credington in Devon. He was laid to rest at Holy Cross Church. Peryam was on the commissions at the trials of Mary, Queen of Scots, the Earl of Arundel, the Earl of Essex and Sir John Perrot, and served as Chief Baron of the Exchequer from 1593 until his death.

10TH OCTOBER

On this day in 1562, the twenty-nine year-old Queen Elizabeth I was taken ill at Hampton Court Palace, with what was thought to be a bad cold. However, the cold developed into a violent fever, and it became clear that the young queen actually had smallpox. Just seven days later, it was feared that the Queen would die. Fortunately, Elizabeth survived the disease and was not too badly scarred, although her friend Lady Mary Sidney, who nursed Elizabeth through the illness, was terribly disfigured by the disease. In his "Memoir of Services", Mary's husband, Henry Sidney, recorded the effect nursing Elizabeth had on his wife:

"When I went to Newhaven [Le Havre] I lefte her a full faire Ladye in myne eye at least the fayerest, and when I retorned I found her as fowle a ladie as the smale pox could make her, which she did take by contynuall attendance of her majesties most precious person (sicke of the same disease) the skarres of which (to her resolute discomforte) ever syns hath don and doth remayne in her face, so as she lyveth solitairilie sicut Nicticorax in domicilio suo [like a night-raven in the house] more to my charge then if we had boorded together as we did before that evill accident happened."

It was while Elizabeth was recovering from the illness that she ordered her council to make Robert Dudley protector of the kingdom, and she made it clear that "as God was her witness nothing improper had ever passed between them."

1505 (10th or 11th) – Death of William Barons (Barnes), Bishop of London and former Master of the Rolls. He was buried at St Paul's Cathedral.

1530 – Death of Thomas Grey, 2nd Marquis of Dorset, magnate, soldier and courtier. He was buried at Astley Collegiate Church in Warwickshire. Grey's offices included Constable of Warwick Castle and of Kenilworth Castle, and he also acted as Chief Answerer at the marriage of Prince Arthur and Catherine of Aragon. Grey was also the grandfather of Lady Jane Grey.

1549 – Edward Seymour, Duke of Somerset and Lord Protector, was ordered to leave Windsor Castle and to give himself up. He had moved there with the young Edward VI on the 6th October, from Hampton Court Palace, after learning that his protectorship was in danger.

1588 – Funeral of Robert Dudley, Earl of Leicester. He was buried in the Beauchamp Chapel of the Collegiate Church of St Mary, Warwick.

11TH OCTOBER

On this day in 1542, Sir Thomas Wyatt the Elder, poet and diplomat, died at Sherborne in Dorset. He had been complaining of severe headaches since 1539. Wyatt was just thirty-nine years old at his death, but his poetry, and that of his friend, Henry Howard, Earl of Surrey, is still enjoyed the world over, although the majority of his work was not published in his lifetime. Literary critic, and author of two books on Wyatt, Patricia Thompson, calls Thomas Wyatt "the Father of English Poetry" and Wyatt is known for introducing the sonnet into English.

He was laid to rest at Sherborne Abbey. His plain tomb can be found in the Wykenham Chapel of the Abbey.

Wyatt's poetry can still be enjoyed today in books such as R A Rebbholz's "Sir Thomas Wyatt, The Complete Poems". Here is one of his poems, which is said to be about Anne Boleyn:

Whoso list to hunt

Whoso list to hunt, I know where is an hind,
But as for me, hélas, I may no more.
The vain travail hath wearied me so sore,
I am of them that farthest cometh behind.
Yet may I by no means my wearied mind
Draw from the deer, but as she fleeth afore
Fainting I follow. I leave off therefore,
Sithens in a net I seek to hold the wind.
Who list her hunt, I put him out of doubt,
As well as I may spend his time in vain.
And graven with diamonds in letters plain
There is written, her fair neck round about:
Noli me tangere, for Caesar's I am,
And wild for to hold, though I seem tame.

As well as being a poet, Wyatt was an important courtier and diplomat. Career highlights include serving as a Sewer-Extraordinary at Princes Mary's Christening in 1516, serving Henry VIII as Clerk of the King's Jewels (1524) and Esquire of the King's Body (1525), undertaking embassies to France (1526), Rome (1527) and the court of Charles V (1537 and 1539), serving as High Marshall of Calais (1529-30), and serving as a Sewer-Extraordinary at Anne Boleyn's coronation (1533).

Wyatt was one of the men imprisoned in May 1536 when Anne Boleyn fell from power, but his father's friendship with Thomas Cromwell appears to have saved him. He was imprisoned again in 1541, after Cromwell's fall, accused of communicating with Cardinal Pole, but was released after Queen Catherine Howard interceded on his behalf. He quickly worked his way back up in royal favour and was awarded various grants and offices in 1541 and 1542.

1521 – The title of Fidei Defensor, "Defender of the Faith", was conferred by Pope Leo X on Henry VIII. This was a reward for Henry VIII writing his pamphlet *Assertio septem sacramentorum adversus Martinum Lutherum* ("Declaration of the Seven Sacraments Against Martin Luther"), defending the Catholic Church against the works of Martin Luther.

1531 – *The Battle of Kappel* and the death of Huldrych Zwingli, the Swiss Reformer, at the battle.

1532 – Henry VIII and Anne Boleyn left England for Calais, where Anne was treated as Henry VIII's Queen and consort.

1537 – Solemn procession at St Paul's to pray for the Queen, Jane Seymour, who was in labour, a labour which lasted over 30 hours. Charles Wriothesley wrote of how the procession was made up of "all the orders of friars, preistes, and clarkes... the major and aldermen, with all the craftes of the citie" and that it was "donne to pray for the Queene that was then in laboure of chielde."

1537 – Traditional date given to the birth of Lady Jane Grey. It is now thought that she was born in spring 1537, "before the end of May" (Leanda de Lisle).

1549 – Arrest of Edward Seymour, the Duke of Somerset, Lord Protector of the Realm and Governor of the King's Person.

He was brought in front of Edward VI, who summarised his charges as "ambition, vainglory, entering into rash wars in mine youth, negligent looking on Newhaven, enriching himself of my treasure, following his own opinion, and doing all by his own authority, etc."

1551 – John Dudley, Earl of Warwick, became the Duke of Northumberland and Henry Grey, father of Lady Jane Grey, became the Duke of Suffolk.

1558 – Death of Paul Bush, Bishop of Bristol, at Winterbourne. He was buried in Bristol Cathedral.

1982 – The raising of the *Mary Rose*, Henry VIII's ship, from the seabed just off the coast off Portsmouth where she had lain since she sank on 19th July 1545.

12TH OCTOBER

At two o'clock in the morning on Friday 12th October 1537, St Edward's Day, Jane Seymour finally gave birth to the future King Edward VI after a long and tiring 30 hour labour. Henry VIII had a legitimate son and heir at long last!

Church bells around London pealed in celebration, parish churches around the country sang the Te Deum, bonfires were lit, the city merchants gave out fruit and wine, German merchants gave wine and beer to the poor, and the happiest of days was ended by two thousand rounds being fired into the sky from the Tower of London. It was a day of celebration, not only for Henry and Jane, but also for the country.

Although the Queen seemed to be recovering well from her ordeal at first, she was seriously ill by the 18th. Jane had developed puerperal fever, and by the 23rd, she was delirious, and septicaemia had set in. Jane, the Queen who had given Henry the longed for son and heir, died on the night of the 24th of October.

Edward VI was Henry VIII's third child, following on from Mary, who was born in 1516 to Catherine of Aragon, and Elizabeth who was born in 1533 to Anne Boleyn. He was Henry VIII's only legitimate surviving son – Henry and Catherine's son, Henry, had only lived a few days, Anne Boleyn had miscarried a son and Henry VIII's only other son, Henry Fitzroy, was the result of an extramarital affair with Elizabeth Blount, one of Catherine of Aragon's ladies.

As a baby, Edward was cared for by Lady Margaret Bryan, who had also cared for his half-sisters, Mary and Elizabeth, and then Blanche Herbert, Lady Troy. When he reached the age of six, the young prince started his formal education and enjoyed the tutelage of scholars such as John Cheke, Richard Cox, Roger Ascham and Jean Belmain. It seems that he was an intelligent child, and by the age of twelve he was undertaking work on religious issues and controversies, and had written a treatise about the Pope being the Antichrist.

Edward's father, King Henry VIII, died on 28th January 1547, making Edward King Edward VI of England.

1555 – Birth of Peregrine Bertie, 13th Baron Willoughby of Willoughby, Beck, and Eresby, at Wesel in Cleves. Bertie was the son of Richard Bertie and his wife, Katherine (née Willoughby), Duchess of Suffolk and widow of Charles Brandon, Duke of Suffolk. Bertie was born while his Protestant parents were in exile during Mary I's reign.

1555 – Assassination of Lewis Owen, member of Parliament and administrator in Wales, on Dugoed Mawddwy, a mountain pass. He had become unpopular after supporting new legislation in Wales, and his assassination is viewed as revenge for his campaign, with John Wyn ap Meredydd of Gwydir, against outlaws. It had resulted in around eighty hangings.

1598 – Death of Thomas Stapleton, Roman Catholic theologian, at Louvain. He was buried there, at St Peter's Church. Stapleton's works included translations, commentaries on parts of the Bible and anti-Calvinist treatises such as *Antidota*.

1616 – Death of Henry Cavendish, soldier and son of Sir William Cavendish and his third wife Elizabeth (Bess of Hardwick). He was buried at Edensor in Derbyshire.

13TH OCTOBER

Queen Claude of France, wife of Francis I, was born on this day in 1499 in Romorantin-Lanthenay.

Claude was the eldest daughter of Louis XII of France and Anne of Brittany, whom Pierre de Bourdeille, Seigneur de Brantôme, described as "the most worthy and honourable queen that has ever been since Queen Blanche, mother of the King Saint-Louis, and very sage and virtuous".

Claude was the heiress of the Duchy of Brittany and also to the throne, but Salic Law prevented her becoming the Queen of France when her father died. She actually became queen by marrying Francis, Duke of Angoulême, who became Francis I of France.

Millicent Garrett Fawcett writes of how Claude "was from her birth delicate, plain and lame", and it is said that she was slightly hunch-backed, being a sufferer of scoliosis. Brantôme describes Queen Claude of France as charitable and gentle, and it is clear that she followed her mother's example by running a virtuous and learned court.

Claude's husband, Francis I, was brought up at the Royal Château Amboise, and he was often there during his reign (as well as Fontainebleau and the Louvre), living a life full of banquets, balls and tournaments, but Queen Claude preferred a quieter life at Château Blois, which Francis had renovated for her.

Claude had seven children, including Henry II, King of France, but died in 1524 at the tender age of twenty-four. Brantôme declared that Claude's husband, Francis I, gave her "a disease that shortened her days", meaning syphilis, but it is not known for certain, although it was rumoured that the King's death in 1547 was due to syphilis. It seems that after it had lost its pious queen, the French court slid into debauchery.

1534 – Alessandro Farnese became Pope Paul III.

1549 – The Council abolished Edward Seymour, Duke of Somerset's Protectorate, and his membership of the Council.

1579 – Death of Sir William Drury, soldier and Lord Justice of Ireland, at Waterford, during *Desmond's Rebellion*. He was buried in Dublin, at St Patrick's Cathedral.

1591 – Death of Sir Edward Waterhouse, administrator, at his estate of Woodchurch in Kent. Waterhouse served Elizabeth as Chancellor of the Exchequer and of the Green Wax in Ireland from October 1586 to October 1589.

14TH OCTOBER

On this day in history, 14th October 1586, the trial of Mary, Queen of Scots began at Fotheringhay Castle in Northamptonshire.

Mary, Queen of Scots had, at first, refused to appear before Elizabeth I's commission, but had been told by William Cecil that the trial would take place with or without her. She appeared in front of the commission at 9am, dressed in a black velvet gown and a white cambric cap and veil. Mary then protested against the commission, arguing that the court was not legitimate, and arguing against the fact that she was not allowed legal defence and was not able to call any witnesses. Mary was also not permitted to examine any of the documents being used against her. Her protests were in vain, and the prosecution went ahead and opened the trial with an account of the *Babington Plot*, arguing that Mary knew of the plot, had given it her approval, agreed with it and had promised to help. Mary protested her innocence, declaring that she did not know Babington. Unfortunately for Mary, Elizabeth's spymaster, Sir Francis Walsingham, had collected a great deal of evidence:

- A confession made by Sir Anthony Babington who had also pleaded guilty at his own trial.
- A deciphered transcript in English of Mary's reply to Babington.
- A reciphered copy of Mary's original letter to Babington which looked exactly like the original.
- Confessions from Mary's secretaries.

When the prosecution produced all of this evidence, Mary burst into tears, but still denied her involvement, claiming that the documents were counterfeit. Walsingham proclaimed his innocence, stating that the documents were real. A distraught Mary proclaimed that "I would never make shipwreck of my soul by conspiring the destruction of my dearest sister." The court was then adjourned for lunch.

After lunch, the secretaries' confessions were read out, much to Mary's shock and horror. Mary argued that her letters must have been tampered with after she had seen them, and then argued:-

"The majesty and safety of all princes falleth to the ground if they depend upon the writings and testimony of their secretaries… I am not to be convicted except by mine own word or writing."

The trial continued the next day with the prosecution accusing Mary of consenting to Elizabeth's assassination in her reply to Babington. Mary tried to argue that although she had written "then shall it be time to set the gentlemen to work taking order upon the accomplishing of their design", she had not specified what the "work" was. However, as the prosecution pointed out, Mary had also appealed for foreign help, and although she argued that an act of war, even if it resulted in Elizabeth's death, was legitimate if it allowed her, a queen, to be free at last, the commission saw her actions as an act of treason.

As the trial closed, Mary demanded that she should be heard in front of Parliament or the Queen, but she was fighting a losing battle. Sentence was delayed as long as possible, by order of Elizabeth, but on the 25th October the commission reconvened and found Mary guilty.

On the 8th February 1587 Mary, Queen of Scots was executed at Fotheringhay Castle.

1536 – *Pilgrimage of Grace*. By 14th October the uprising in the north had turned into a proper rebellion. On 13th October, Lord Darcy had reported to Henry VIII that the East Riding, West Riding, North Riding and "all the commons of Yorkshire" were "up" in rebellion, and on 14th October William Haryngton, Mayor of York, and Sir George Lawson, wrote to the King asking for aid because "the commons... have rebelliously assembled to take York".

1559 – Death of John Williams, Baron Williams and Lord President of the Council in the Marches of Wales, at Ludlow Castle. He was buried in Thame Church.

1565 – Statesman and poet, Thomas Chaloner, died at his home in Clerkenwell, London. During the reign of Elizabeth I he acted as the English ambassador to Ferdinand I, Holy Roman Emperor, in 1558, and then ambassador to Philip II in the Low Countries, and then Spain between 1559 and 1561. Chaloner was a great friend of William Cecil, Lord Burghley.

In 1564, his health began to fail, and he was allowed to return home. He died there on the 14th October 1565, aged forty-four.

1593 – Death of Arthur Grey, 14th Baron Grey of Wilton, soldier and Lord Deputy of Ireland, at his home of Whaddon in Buckinghamshire. He was buried there. Grey had a reputation for radical Protestantism.

1596 – Death of John Coldwell, Bishop of Salisbury, at Salisbury. He was buried in the cathedral, in the grave of Bishop Wyvil due to his state of poverty.

15TH OCTOBER

On this day in 1537, three days after his birth, Henry VIII's son, the future Edward VI, was christened in the Chapel Royal at Hampton Court in a lavish ceremony.

The day started with a procession from the Queen's apartments to the chapel where Archbishop Thomas Cranmer performed the baptismal rites in front of three to four hundred people. Edward's half-sister Mary stood as godmother, while his other half-sister, the four year-old Elizabeth, bore the chrisom cloth, helped by Edward's uncle, Edward Seymour. Thomas Howard, the Duke of Norfolk, Charles Brandon, the Duke of Suffolk, and Archbishop Cranmer stood as godfathers.

A report of Edward's christening in "Letters and Papers, Foreign and Domestic", Henry VIII, tells of how Sir John Russell, Sir Francis Bryan, Sir Nicholas Carew and Sir Anthony Browne surrounded the font, equipped with aprons and towels while a procession of gentleman carrying torches, children and ministers of the King's chapel (with the Dean), gentlemen esquires and knights, chaplains, abbots and bishops, King's councillors and lords, the comptroller and treasurer, ambassadors, lord chamberlains, Lord Cromwell, the Duke of Norfolk and the Archbishop all processed, two by two, into the Chapel. The Earl of Sussex, supported by Lord Montague, carried a pair of covered basins, Thomas Boleyn, the Earl of Wiltshire, bore a "taper of virgin wax", and a salt of Gold was carried by the Earl of Essex (Cromwell). Behind these gentlemen came little Elizabeth with "the crysome richly garnished", supported by Edward Seymour, Viscount Beauchamp.

The baby prince was carried under a canopy by the Lady Marquis of Exeter, Gertrude Blount, supported by the Duke of Suffolk and her husband. The Earl of Arundel carried the train of the Prince's robe, helped by Lord William Howard, and the canopy above them was supported by Sir Edward Nevyll, Sir John Wallop, Richard Long, Thomas Seymour, Henry Knyvett and Mr Ratclif, all of the King's Privy Chamber. The Prince's wetnurse and midwife walked alongside the bearers of the train, and torchbearers surrounded the canopy. After the canopy processed the Lady Mary, with Lady Kingston carrying her train, followed by the other ladies of the court.

After Archbishop Cranmer had performed the rites of baptism, all of the torches were lit, and the Garter King of Arms proclaimed the Prince's name and titles, Prince Edward, Duke of Cornwall and Earl of Chester. The *Te Deum* was then sung, spice, hippocras, bread and sweet wine were served, and then the torchlit procession made its way out of the Chapel, and the little prince was taken back to his mother and father, King Henry VIII and Queen Jane Seymour.

Christening gifts included a gold cup from the Lady Mary, three bowls and two pots of silver and gilt from the Archbishop, and the same from the Duke of Norfolk, and two flagons and two pots of silver and gilt from the Duke of Suffolk.

1536 – Henry VIII wrote to the Earl of Shrewsbury, the Duke of Suffolk "and others" with instructions on handling the rebellion which we now know as the *Pilgrimage of Grace*. The King also wrote to the rebels in Lincolnshire promising "to show them mercy if they leave all their harness and weapons in the market-place of Lincoln".

1542 – Death of William Fitzwilliam, Earl of Southampton, courtier, diplomat and naval commander, in Newcastle-upon-Tyne. It is thought that he was buried in Newcastle. Southampton's offices included Vice Admiral, Treasurer of the Household and Lord Privy Seal. He died while leading troops to Scotland under the command of Thomas Howard, 3rd Duke of Norfolk.

1582 – The first day of the Gregorian calendar following the last day of the Julian calendar, 4th October 1582, meaning that the 5th-14th October did not exist in the year 1582. Many countries ignored Pope Gregory XIII's papal bull and carried on using the Julian Calendar. England, for example, did not introduce the Gregorian calendar until 1752.

1584 – Execution of Richard Gwyn (White), martyr, schoolteacher and Welsh language poet, at Wrexham in Wales. He was hanged, drawn and quartered for high treason because of his Catholic faith.

1590 – Death of William Bleddyn (Blethin), Bishop of Llandaff. He was buried in Matharn Church, in the chancel.

1595 – Death of Philip Howard, 13th Earl of Arundel, in the Tower of London. It was rumoured that his cook had poisoned him. Arundel had been imprisoned for high treason, because of his Catholic faith and for fleeing England without Elizabeth I's permission. He was buried in the Tower chapel, St Peter ad Vincula.

16TH OCTOBER

The burnings of two of the Oxford martyrs: Hugh Latimer, Bishop of Worcester, and Nicholas Ridley, Bishop of London took place on this day in 1555, in the reign of the Catholic Mary

I. The two men, along with Thomas Cranmer, who was burnt at the stake on the 21st March 1556, are known as the Oxford Martyrs and their lives and deaths are commemorated in Oxford by Martyr's Memorial, a stone monument just outside Balliol College and near to the execution site, which was completed in 1843.

Hugh Latimer was appointed Bishop of Worcester in 1535 but was forced to resign his bishopric in 1539 when he opposed Henry VIII's Six Articles. He went on to become the Court Preacher during the reign of Edward VI and was chaplain to Katherine Brandon (née Willoughby), Duchess of Suffolk. His Protestant beliefs led to him being tried and imprisoned during the Catholic Mary I's reign and subsequently burnt at the stake.

Nicholas Ridley became one of Archbishop Thomas Cranmer's chaplains in 1537 and became Vicar of Herne, Kent, in 1538. He served as one of the King's Chaplains in 1540-41 and was made Master of Pembroke College. He was accused of heresy in 1543 but managed to escape punishment and was made Bishop of Rochester in 1547 and then Bishop of London in 1550. He helped his good friend, Cranmer, with the Book of Common Prayer in 1548 and was also a member of the commission who tried Stephen Gardiner and Edmund Bonner in 1549. Ridley is known for his clashes with John Hooper, a reformer who had lived in Zurich in exile during Henry VIII's reign. In July 1553, after the death of Edward VI, Ridley signed letters patent confirming that Lady Jane Grey was Queen and went on to preach a sermon at St Paul's Cross on the 9th July 1553 proclaiming that Mary and Elizabeth were bastards. He was imprisoned when Mary I proclaimed herself Queen and was tried for heresy and burnt at the stake.

Martyrologist John Foxe recorded that as the fire was started at Ridley's feet, Latimer said to him "Be of good comfort, Mr Ridley, and play the man: we shall this day light such a candle by God's grace in England, as I trust never shall be put out." Ridley then cried out "Into thy hands, O Lord, I commend my spirit… Lord, Lord, receive my spirit" and Latimer cried out, "O father of heaven, receive my soul." Latimer "soon died, seemingly with very little pain", but Ridley suffered longer due to "the fagots being green, and piled too high". Foxe wrote of their deaths:-

"Thus did these two pious divines and stedfast believers, testify with their blood the truth of the everlasting gospel, upon which depends all the sinners' hopes of salvation; to suffer for which was the joy, the glory of many eminent Christians, who having followed their dear Lord and Master though much tribulation in this vale of tears, will be glorified for ever with him, in the kingdom of his father and our father, of his God and our God."

1573 – Death of Thomas Davies, Bishop of St Asaph, at Abergele in Denighshire.

1594 – Death of Cardinal William Allen at his home in the via Monserrato, Rome, while in exile. He was buried in Rome, in the English College's Church.

17TH OCTOBER

On this day in history, 17th October 1586, the poet, courtier and soldier, Sir Philip Sidney, died as a result of an injury inflicted by the Spanish forces at the *Battle of Zutphen* in the Netherlands. His body was returned to England and laid to rest on the 16th February 1587 in St Paul's Cathedral.

Philip Sidney was born on the 30th November 1554 at Penshurst Place, Kent. He was the eldest son of Sir Henry Dudley and Lady Mary Dudley, sister of Elizabeth's favourite, Robert Dudley, Earl of Leicester, and daughter of John Dudley, the Duke of Northumberland. Sidney was educated at Shrewsbury School, where he met Fulke Greville, and Christchurch, Oxford, and in 1572 he was chosen by Elizabeth I to undertake an embassy to France to negotiate a marriage between the Queen and the Duke of Alençon.

After a few years of travelling around Europe, Sidney returned to England in 1575, where he met the inspiration for his famous work "Astrophel and Stella", the fourteen year-old Lady Penelope Devereux. Although the couple were due to marry, after the death of her father Penelope's guardian, Henry Hastings, 3rd Earl of Huntingdon, married her off to Robert Rich, 3rd Baron Rich.

Sidney famously challenged Edward de Vere, Earl of Oxford, to a duel after an argument, probably over Sidney's opposition to the French marriage plans, which also led to him falling out with Elizabeth and retiring from court. Retirement from court, at the home of his sister, the literary patron Mary Herbert, Countess of Pembroke, gave Sidney the time to focus on his artistic side, and it was then that he wrote "The Arcadia" (a pastoral romance) and "A Defense of Poetry" (or Poesy). He also spent his time with poets such as Edmund Spenser, Gabriel Harvey, Edward Dyer and Fulke Greville.

In 1581, Sidney returned to court, and in 1583 he married the fourteen year-old Frances Walsingham, daughter of Sir Francis Walsingham. After Sidney's death in 1586, Frances went on to marry Robert Devereux, 2nd Earl of Essex, and a favourite of the Queen.

Philip Sidney was a staunch Protestant. He was in Paris at the time of the *St Bartholomew's Day massacre*, but took refuge in Sir Francis Walsingham's house. His religious views led to him being anti-Spanish and being vocal in his support of the Protestants in the Netherlands. He even argued for an assault on Spain in the 1580s, something which never happened, but when he was Governor of Flushing in 1586, he led a successful raid on Spanish troops in Axel. On the 22nd September 1586, Sidney was shot in the thigh at the *Battle of Zupthen*. According to legend, as he lay wounded, Sidney offered his water bottle to a wounded comrade, saying, "Thy necessity is yet greater than mine". Sir Philip Sidney died twenty-six days later.

⬦⬦⬦⬦⬦⬦⬦⬦⬦⬦⬦⬦⬦⬦⬦⬦⬦⬦⬦⬦⬦⬦⬦⬦⬦⬦⬦⬦⬦

1560 – Baptism of Walter Marsh, spy and Protestant martyr, at St Stephen's Church, Coleman Street, London. Marsh was burned to death in Rome's Campo dei Fiori after having his tongue and hands cut off. He had been accused of being paid by Elizabeth I to spy on Catholics and showing contempt for the Eucharist.

1592 – Death of Frances Brooke, Lady Cobham, wife of William Brooke, 10th Baron Cobham. She was buried at Cobham. Lady Cobham is known for being featured in the famous Elizabethan family portrait, The Cobham Family (1567). She served Elizabeth I as Mistress of the Robes and Lady of the Bedchamber.

1595 – Death of Sir Thomas Heneage, courtier and politician, at the Savoy. He was buried at St Paul's Cathedral, in the Lady Chapel. Heneage served Elizabeth I as a member of Parliament, gentleman of the Privy Chamber, Vice-Chamberlain of the Household, Privy Councillor and Chancellor of the Duchy of Lancaster.

18TH OCTOBER

On this day in 1541, Margaret Tudor died of a stroke at Methven Castle, Perthshire, Scotland. She was laid to rest at the Carthusian Priory of St John in Perth, which was later destroyed.

Margaret Tudor was born on the 28th November 1489. She was the eldest surviving daughter of Henry VII and Elizabeth of York, and was the sister of Henry VIII. After lengthy negotiations, Margaret was promised in marriage to James IV of Scotland in the *Treaty of Perpetual Peace* between England and Scotland on the 24th January 1502. The couple were married by proxy, and in 1503 Margaret travelled to

Scotland, stopping at various places, including York, on the way. James and Margaret married properly at Holyrood Abbey, Edinburgh, on the 8th August, and poet William Dunbar wrote of the occasion in his poem "The Thistle and the Rose".

James IV and Margaret Tudor went on to have six children, including the future James V of Scotland, father of Mary, Queen of Scots. James died at the *Battle of Flodden* in 1513, a battle between Scotland and Margaret's brother's forces. For a time, Margaret acted as Regent and although she had opposition, being the enemy's sister, she managed to reconcile Scotland and England.

On the 6th August 1514, Margaret secretly married Archibald Douglas, 6th Earl of Angus, a member of the powerful Scottish House of Douglas. When news of the marriage got out, it was opposed by the nobles, and in September 1514 the Privy Council ruled that she had acted against the terms of James IV's will and could no longer act as Regent. She was replaced by John Stewart, 2nd Duke of Albany, who took custody of her sons, James and Alexander.

In 1515, Margaret and her husband fled across the border, and were taken to Harbottle Castle by Lord Dacre, Warden of the Marches. There, on 8th October 1515, Margaret gave birth to a daughter, Lady Margaret Douglas, the future mother of Henry Stuart, Lord Darnley. A couple of months later, Margaret received news that her son, Alexander, had died at Stirling Castle. It was also around this time that Margaret's husband, Angus, abandoned his wife to return to Scotland and make peace with Albany, and escape a charge of treason. Margaret, on the other hand, continued her journey on to London where her brother, Henry VIII, arranged lodgings for her at Scotland Yard in Whitehall.

After a treaty was negotiated between Albany, Cardinal Wolsey and Henry VIII, Margaret returned to Scotland in 1517, only to find out that her husband had been living with Lady Jane Stewart in her absence. Margaret decided that she wanted a divorce, and sought her brother's help. However, Henry VIII did not believe in divorce (at this time anyway!) and was also unwilling to make an enemy of his brother-in-law. Margaret carried on fighting for her divorce, even enlisting the help of Albany, who even spread rumours that he and Margaret were lovers. In March 1527, Albany finally convinced Pope Clement VII to grant Margaret's petition, and Margaret went on to marry Henry Stewart, 1st Lord Methven, on 3rd March 1528. However, the marriage was not happy for long. Margaret had managed to pick another unfaithful husband, so she again fought for a divorce, although this was not supported by her son, King James V. Margaret was later able to reconcile with Methven.

On the 12th June 1538, Margaret's son, James V, married Mary of Guise by proxy, and when Mary arrived in Scotland she became good friends with her mother-in-law. Margaret died on the 18th October 1541, and it was to her great-grandson, King James VI of Scotland, that the Tudor crown passed on the death of her niece, Elizabeth I, in 1603. On the 24th March 1603, James VI became King James I, uniting Scotland and England and beginning a new dynasty, the House of Stuart.

***

1529 – Cardinal Thomas Wolsey surrendered the Great Seal following the writ of praemunire being filed against him on the 9th October.

1536 – Birth of William Lambarde, antiquary and lawyer, in London. Lambarde is known for his "Perambulation of Kent" (1570) and "Eirenarcha: or of the Office of the Justices of Peace" (1581).

1538 – Baptism of Francis Kinwelmersh (Kindlemarsh), poet, at All Hallows Church, Bread Street, London. Kinwelmersh is known for his collaboration with George Gascoigne on "Jocasta" (1566) and his contributions to "The Paradyse of Dainty Devises" (1576).

1555 – Elizabeth Tudor, the future Elizabeth I, was finally given permission to leave court and travel to her own estate at Hatfield, rather than return to house arrest at Woodstock.

19TH OCTOBER

On the 19th October 1536, Henry VIII got tough on the *Pilgrimage of Grace* rebels. In a letter to Charles Brandon, Duke of Suffolk, Henry wrote:-

"You are to use all dexterity in getting the harness and weapons of the said rebels brought in to Lincoln or other sure places, and cause all the boats on the Humber or means of passage into Yorkshire to be taken up. After this, if it appear to you by due proof that the rebels have since their retires from Lincoln attempted any new rebellion, you shall, with your forces run upon them and with all extremity 'destroy, burn, and kill man, woman, and child the terrible example of all others, and specially the town of Louth because to this rebellion took his beginning in the same.' We have sent you this day a good sum of money, and will send more as required."

And in a letter to the Earl of Derby:-

"We lately commanded you to make ready your forces and go to the earl of Shrewsbury, our lieutenant to suppress the rebellion in the North; but having since heard of an insurrection attempted about the abbey of Salley in Lancashire, where the abbot and monks have been restored by the traitors, we now desire you immediately to repress it, to apprehend the captains and either have them immediately executed as traitors or sent up to us. We leave it, however, to your discretion to go elsewhere in case of greater emergency. You are to take the said abbot and monks forth with violence and have them hanged without delay in their monks' apparel, and see that no town or village begin to assemble."

1469 – Marriage of Ferdinand of Aragon and Isabella of Castile, the famous 'Reyes Católicos' and the parents of Catherine of Aragon, in the Palacio de los Vivero, Valladolid, Spain. Isabella became Queen Isabella I of Castile in 1474 and Ferdinand became King Ferdinand II of Aragon in 1479, so their marriage united the powerful kingdoms of Aragon and Castile, a vast territory which comprised most of what is modern-day Spain.

1512 – Reformer Martin Luther was awarded his Doctorate of Theology from the University of Wittenberg.

1592 – Death of Anthony Browne, 1st Viscount Montagu, courtier and member of Parliament, at his manor of West Horsley, Surrey, He was buried at Midhurst. Montagu served Mary I as an ambassador and Privy Councillor, and Elizabeth I as Lord Lieutenant of Sussex.

20TH OCTOBER

On the night of the 19th October 1536, Thomas Maunsell, Robert Aske and the rebels of the *Pilgrimage of Grace* threatened an assault on Pontefract Castle and its owner, Lord Darcy. By 8 o'clock on the morning of the 20th October, the castle had surrendered to the rebels and its inhabitants – which included the likes of Lord Darcy, Sir William Gascoigne, Sir Robert Constable, Edmund Lee, Archbishop of York, and Thomas Magnus, Archdeacon of the East Riding – had sworn the rebel oath.

No force had been necessary. Their leader, Robert Aske, had written down the grievances of the common people in a letter, on the 19th, asking the lords in the castle to intercede with the King on their behalf. He then visited the castle on the 20th and rebuked the lords for failing in their duty to their people by allowing heresy in their territory, and by not making the King aware of 'the poverty of his realm and that part specially'. Lord Darcy replied that they would submit to him on the 21st, but Aske insisted on it happening that day, threatening action against the castle otherwise. Darcy surrendered.

Darcy had little choice when there were only around 300 men in the castle, and the rebels numbered in the tens of thousands, but historian M.L. Bush makes the point that the castle inmates could have tried to crush the rebels ten days earlier when the rebellion was in its infancy and its numbers much, much smaller. Bush explains that the elderly Lord Darcy actually sympathised with the rebel cause, because of his reservations about the dissolution of the monasteries and the power of Thomas Cromwell, whom he would have viewed as a heretic and an "upstart". The grievances of the rebels were justified in Darcy's opinion, but he did not want to raise a revolt himself, or take an active part in one, so he fled to Pontefract Castle and hoped that he would not need to get involved.

◇◇

1549 – Death of John Uvedale, administrator. Uvedale served Henry VIII as Secretary to the Duke of Richmond's Council in the North, Secretary to Queen Anne Boleyn (1533-1536), Commissioner in the Dissolution of the Monasteries and Paymaster to the forces in the East and Middle Marches. In Edward VI's reign, he was Under-Treasurer for the Scottish war.

1557 (20th or 21st) – Death of Mary Arundell, (other names Mary Radcliffe, Countess of Sussex and Mary Fitzalan, Countess of Arundel), at Bath Place, London. She was originally buried at St Clement Danes' Church, but now rests in the Fitzalan Chapel at Arundel Castle. Mary was the daughter of Sir John Arundell of Lanherne in Cornwall and was married twice, first to Robert Radcliffe, Earl of Sussex, and second to Henry Fitzalan, Earl of Arundel.

1573 – Death of Thomas Smith, colonial adventurer, at Comber in the Ards, co. Down, Ireland, after being shot by one of his Irish employees. Smith had been attempting to colonise that part of Ireland and had become unpopular with the locals.

1581 – Death of James Blount, 6th Baron Mountjoy, at Hooke in Dorset. Blount was made a Knight of the Bath at Mary I's coronation, served as a Justice of the Peace, and experimented with alchemy.

21ST OCTOBER

On 21st October 1536, during the *Pilgrimage of Grace rebellion*, Lancaster Herald, on nearing Pontefract Castle, encountered a group of armed peasants. The peasants explained that they were armed "to prevent the 'comontte' and Church being destroye; for, they said no man should bury, christen, wed, or have beasts unmarked without paying a tax and forfeiting the beast unmarked to the King's use."

On this same day, rebel leader Robert Aske met with Lancaster Herald at Pontefract Castle. Aske refused to let the Herald read out the proclamation which told of how the Lincolnshire rebels had submitted, and declared that he and his people were intent on staying true to their cause and would be marching on London "on pilgrimage to the King to have all vile blood put from his Council and noble blood set up again; to have the faith of Christ and God's laws kept, and restitution for wrongs done to the Church, and the "comonte" used as they should be". Lancaster Herald asked for this in writing and so Aske "called for the oath he gave his people and said the articles were in it, and delivered it to me, offering to put his hand to it." When asked to put his hand to it, Aske "did so, saying with a proud voice "This is mine act who so ever say to the contrary." Lancaster Herald reiterated that he was required to read his proclamation to the people, but Aske would not let him and instead offered him safe conduct out of the castle and town.

∞∞∞∞∞∞∞∞∞∞∞∞∞∞∞∞∞∞∞∞∞∞∞∞∞∞∞∞

1449 – Birth of George, Duke of Clarence, son of Richard, Duke of York, and brother of Edward IV and Richard III, at Dublin. He was born in Ireland because his father was serving there as Lord Lieutenant of Ireland. Clarence was also the father of Margaret Pole, Countess of Salisbury.

1532 – Henry VIII left Anne Boleyn in Calais to spend four days with Francis I, "his beloved brother", at the French court in Bolougne. He returned with Francis on the 25th October.

1542 – "The 21st day of October in the xxxiiij year of the reign of our Sovereign lord King Henry the viijth., the duke of Norfolk's grace, lieutenant to the King's Highness, removed and camped in the borders of Barwicke". Records show that Norfolk and his men went on to burn and pillage a number of towns in the Scottish borderlands.

1554 – Death of John Dudley, 2nd Earl of Warwick and son of John Dudley, Duke of Northumberland, at Penshurst, the house of his brother-in-law Henry Sidney, in Kent. Dudley and his brothers, Robert and Henry, had just been released from the Tower of London after the fall of their father, brother Guildford and sister-in-law, Lady Jane Grey.

22ND OCTOBER

1521 – Death of Sir Edward Poynings, soldier, administrator and diplomat at his manor of Westenhanger in Kent. Poynings served Henry VII as Lord Deputy of Ireland and Henry VIII as an ambassador, Lord Warden of the Cinque Ports and Chancellor of the Order of the Garter,

1554 (22nd or 23rd) – Death of John Veysey (born John Harman), Bishop of Exeter, at Moor Hall, Sutton Coldfield, Warwickshire.

1577 – Death of Henry Parker, 11th Baron Morley and Roman Catholic exile, in Paris. Morley had fled abroad after refusing to subscribe to Elizabeth I's "Act of Uniformity" and after being implicated in the 1569 *Rising of the North*.

23RD OCTOBER

1545 – Death of Sir Humphrey Wingfield, lawyer, Speaker of the House of Commons (1533-36) and patron of humanist education, at Ipswich.

1556 – Death of Sir John Gresham, brother of Sir Richard Gresham and Lord Mayor of London (1547). He was buried in the church of St Michael Bassishaw.

1570 – Burial of John Hopkins, poet, psalmodist and Church of England clergyman, at Great Waldingfield. Churchman and historian John Bale described Hopkins as "not the least significant of British poets of our time". Hopkins' psalms were included in the 1562 "The whole booke of Psalmes, collected into Englysh metre by T. Starnhold, J. Hopkins & others".

24TH OCTOBER

On the night of the 24th October 1537, just twelve days after giving birth to the future King Edward VI, Henry VIII's third wife and queen, Jane Seymour, died of suspected puerperal fever (childbed fever) at Hampton Court Palace.

Jane had initially recovered well from her long and arduous labour, but started to go downhill in the days following Edward's christening, suffering with a fever and delirium.

On 17th October, her fever reached crisis point, and it looked like Jane would recover, but then it struck again. On the 24th October her condition worsened, and she died that night.

Jane was buried in St George's Chapel, Windsor Castle, on the 13th November, although legend has it that her heart was buried in the Chapel Royal of Hampton Court Palace. Henry VIII chose to be buried beside the woman he regarded as his true wife, and he was laid to rest beside her after his death in January 1547.

1521 – Death of Robert Fayrfax (Fairfax), church musician and composer, in St Albans. He was buried in the abbey there. Fayrfax was a Gentleman of the Chapel of the households of both Henry VII and Henry VIII, and attended the 1521 *Field of Cloth of Gold*. His works included the *Magnificat Regale*, *Salve regina*, six masses and English part-songs.

1525 – Death of Thomas Dacre, 2nd Baron Dacre of Gilsland, from a fall from his horse in the English borders. He was buried at Lanercost Priory, in the Dacre family mausoleum. Dacre fought at the *Battle of Bosworth* on the side of Richard III, but was able to earn Henry VII's trust and favour afterwards. Henry VII put Dacre in charge of the English west march and he was active in the borders, until he was imprisoned in early 1525 after trouble in the borders. He was fined and released in September 1525.

1545 – Death of Sir John Baldwin, judge and Chief Justice of the Common Pleas. He was buried at Aylesbury.

1572 – Death of Edward Stanley, 3rd Earl of Derby and Privy Councillor during the reigns of Mary I and Elizabeth I, at Lathom House in Lancashire. He was buried at the parish church in Ormskirk.

1589 – Death of Christopher St Lawrence, 7th Baron Howth and an active participant in Irish politics. He was buried in Howth Abbey in Dublin.

1590 – John White, governor of the Roanoke Colony, returned to England after failing to find the lost colonists, which included his daughter, Ellinor (Elenora), and his granddaughter, Virginia Dare. Virginia was the first child born to English parents in the Americas. Nobody ever found out what had happened to the colony.

25TH OCTOBER

On 25th October 1529, Sir Thomas More became Henry VIII's Lord Chancellor.

Cardinal Wolsey had been forced to surrender the Great Seal to the Dukes of Norfolk and Suffolk at his house in Westminster, in front of Sir William Fitzwilliam, John Tayler and Stephen Gardiner on the 17th October. The seal was then delivered by Tayler to the King at Windsor on the 20th October. According to "Letters and Papers", the seal delivered to Sir Thomas More by the King himself on the 25th, and Sir Thomas More took the oath of Chancellorship the following day:-

"On the 25th Oct. the seal was delivered by the King at East Greenwich to Sir Thos. More, in the presence of Hen. Norres and Chr. Hales, Attorney General, in the King's Privy Chamber; and on the next day, Tuesday, 26 Oct., More took his oath as Chancellor in the Great Hall at Westminster, in presence of the dukes of Norfolk and Suffolk, Th. marquis of Dorset, Hen. marquis of Exeter, John earl of Oxford, Hen. earl of Northumberland, Geo. earl of Shrewsbury, Ralph earl of Westmoreland, John bishop of Lincoln, Cuthbert bishop of London, John bishop of Bath and Wells, Sir Rob. Radclyf, viscount Fitzwater, Sir Tho. Boleyn, viscount Rocheforde, Sir Wm. Sandys, Lord and others."

Eustace Chapuys, the Imperial Ambassador reported this event to his master, Charles V, saying:-

"The Chancellor's seal has remained in the hands of the duke of Norfolk till this morning, when it was transferred to

Sir Thomas More. Every one is delighted at his promotion, because he is an upright and learned man, and a good servant of the Queen. He was chancellor of Lancaster, an office now conferred on the Sieur Villeury (Fitzwilliam). Richard Pace, a faithful servant of your Majesty, whom the Cardinal had kept in prison for two years, as well in the Tower of London as in a monastery (Syon House), is set at liberty. Unless his mind should again become unsettled, it is thought he will rise in higher favour at Court than ever."

Although Wolsey was stripped of his office and his home, York Place, he was able to carry on as Archbishop of York, until he was again accused of treason in 1530. On the 29th November 1530, Cardinal Wolsey died on his way to London to answer charges of treason.

***

1532 – Henry VIII arrived back at Calais with Francis I to a 3,000 gun salute. Francis I sent Anne Boleyn a diamond via the Provost of Paris, but she was nowhere to be seen. She was waiting to make a dramatic entrance on the 27th.

1532 – Dukes of Norfolk and Suffolk received the collar of the Order of Saint-Michel from Francis I in a ceremony in Boulogne before leaving for Calais.

1536 – Four Chaplains of Poverty were appointed by the *Pilgrimage of Grace* rebels: Barnard Townley (Chancellor to the Bishop of Carlisle and Rector of Caldbeck), Christopher Blenkow (Vicar of Edenhall), Christopher Slee (Vicar of Castle Sowerby) and pluralist Roland Threlkeld. The rebels threatened them with execution if they failed in their duty, which was "to instruct the commons 'concerning faith'". Also on this day in 1536, and the following day, a special mass, called the Captains' Mass was performed at Penrith Church.

1555 – A worn out Charles V abdicated a number of his titles, giving his son Philip control of the Low Countries.

1557 – Death of Sir William Cavendish, courtier, Privy Councillor and administrator. Cavendish served Henry VIII as a Visitor of the Monasteries, in the Exchequer and as Treasurer of the Chamber, a post which he also held in Edward VI's reign. Cavendish married Bess of Hardwick in 1547.

1558 – Death of John Bird, Bishop of Chester, at Great Dunmow, Essex. He was buried there, in his own church. Bird was deprived of his see when Mary I came to the throne, due to his marriage, but was able to become Vicar of Great Dunmow after setting aside his wife.

26TH OCTOBER

1529 – Thomas More took his oath as Chancellor.

1536 – The rebels of the *Pilgrimage of Grace* halted at Scawsby Leys near Doncaster, where they met troops captained by the Duke of Norfolk. The rebels were said to number around 30,000 and Norfolk's army only a fifth of the size, but Robert Aske chose to negotiate, and a deal was eventually struck, with Norfolk giving promises from Henry VIII that their demands would be met and that they would be pardoned. Aske then dismissed his troops. Unfortunately, Henry VIII later broke his promises to the rebels.

1538 – Geoffrey Pole, brother of Cardinal Reginald Pole and son of Margaret Pole, Countess of Salisbury, was interrogated in his prison at the Tower of London regarding letters he and his family had received from his brother, and words which he had uttered showing his support for the Cardinal, who had denounced the King and his policies in his treatise, *Pro ecclesiasticae unitatis defensione*.

1559 – Death of Sir Robert Southwell, lawyer and member of Parliament. It is thought that he was buried in Kent, probably near his seat of Mereworth. Southwell's offices included High Sheriff of Kent and Master of the Rolls. As High Sheriff of

Kent in Mary I's reign, Southwell was active in putting down *Wyatt's Rebellion* of 1554.

27TH OCTOBER

On Sunday 27th October 1532, Anne Boleyn made a dramatic entrance to the great banquet held by Henry VIII in Calais for Francis I.

The chronicler Edward Hall writes of how the room was lavishly decorated with cloth of tissue, cloth of silver, gold wreaths decorated with stones and pearls, and candelabra. It also had a cupboard stacked high with gold plate. He then describes the entrance of Anne Boleyn and her masked ladies:-

"After supper came in the Marchiones of Penbroke, with. vii. ladies in Maskyng apparel, of straunge fashion, made of clothe of gold, compassed with Crimosyn Tinsell Satin, owned with Clothe of Siluer, liyng lose[loose] and knit with laces of Gold: these ladies were brought into the chamber, with foure damoselles appareled in Crimosin satlyn[satin], with Tabardes of fine Cipres[cypress lawn]: the lady Marques tooke the Frenche Kyng, and the Countes of Darby, toke the Kyng of Nauerr, and euery Lady toke a lorde, and in daunsyng[dancing] the kyng of Englande, toke awaie the ladies visers, so that there the ladies beauties were shewed."

The French King then spoke a while with Anne Boleyn, before being escorted by Henry VIII to his lodgings.

c.1467 – Desiderius Erasmus, humanist, Catholic priest, classical scholar and theologian, was born on the night of the 27th/28th October in Rotterdam. His works included *Enchiridion militis Christiani*, or the "Handbook of the Christian Soldier" (1503), "The Praise of Folly" (1511), *Institutio principis Christiani* (1516) and *Sileni Alcibiadis* (1515).

1526 – Bishop Cuthbert Tunstall presided over the burning of Lutheran books, such as William Tyndale's New Testament, at St Paul's. He had issued an edict commanding that copies of the English New Testament should be found and delivered to him because members of Luther's sect had "translated the new Testament into our English tongue, entermedling there with many heretical articles and erroneous opinions… seducing the simple people."

1538 – Baptism of Sir John Brograve, lawyer and member of Parliament, at St Mildred Poultry, London.

1561 – Birth of Mary Herbert (née Sidney), Countess of Pembroke, writer and literary patron, at Tickenhall, near Bewdley in Worcestershire. She was the daughter of Sir Henry Sidney and his wife, Mary (née Dudley), daughter of John Dudley, Duke of Northumberland, and sister of the poet Sir Philip Sidney. She married Henry Herbert, 2nd Earl of Pembroke, in 1577. Her known works include her "Psalmes", her translations "A Discourse of Life and Death" and "Antonius", and "A dialogue between two shepherds, Thenot and Piers, in praise of Astrea", which was a pastoral dialogue written in praise of Elizabeth I.

28TH OCTOBER

1479 – Birth of Sir John Gage, courtier, at Burstow in Surrey. Gage served Henry VIII, Edward VI and Mary I, and his offices included Privy Councillor, Comptroller of Calais, Chancellor of the Duchy of Lancaster, Comptroller of the Household, Constable of the Tower and Lord Chamberlain.

1532 – The last full day of Henry VIII and Anne Boleyn's time with Francis I in Calais. This included a chapter of the Order of the Garter and a wrestling match, which saw the English Cornish wrestlers beat the French side. This time, Henry VIII refrained from challenging the French king to a wrestling match, something he had done at the 1521 *Field of Cloth of Gold.*

1561 – Death of Sir Rowland Hill, merchant and Lord Mayor of London. He was buried in the church of St Stephen Walbrook.

1570 – Death of Thomas Causton, composer, in London. It is thought that he was a chorister in Cardinal Wolsey's household and a Gentleman of the Royal Household Chapel from 1550. His works included some metrical psalms which were published by John Day in 1563 in "Whole Psalmes in Foure Partes", and also in "Certaine Notes".

1571 – Death of William Parr, Marquis of Northampton and brother of Queen Catherine Parr, at Thomas Fisher's house in Warwick. He had suffered from severe gout. Parr was laid to rest on 5th December in St Mary's Church, Warwick.

29TH OCTOBER

On this day in 1618, Sir Walter Ralegh, courtier, explorer, author and soldier, was executed at Westminster. Ralegh had originally been found guilty of treason and sentenced to death in 1603, after being implicated in the Main Plot against James I, but the King spared his life.

Ralegh was released from the Tower of London in 1616 to undertake a voyage in search of El Dorado, but the voyage was a failure and incurred the wrath of Spain when the English stormed and occupied the Spanish settlement of San Thomé, killing the Spanish governor. He was arrested on his return to England and imprisoned once again in the Tower of London.

Ralegh was tried on 28th October 1618 in front of Sir Henry Montagu, Lord Chief Justice, and the 1603 death sentence was reinstated. At his execution the following day, Ralegh made a forty-five minute speech and then joked with his executioner, commenting, as he touched the blade of the axe,

"This is a sharp medicine, but it is a physician for all diseases and miseries". After his execution, Ralegh's wife, Elizabeth (née Throckmorton), took his head and kept it at her side in a red leather bag until her death. His body was laid to rest at St Margaret's, Westminster.

Trivia: Although Sir Walter Ralegh is often credited with introducing the potato and tobacco into England, the potato had already spread around Europe after being brought back from Peru to Seville sometime before 1570. Ralegh definitely played a role in making the smoking of tobacco fashionable in England, but it was already being smoked by 1573.

⸏⸏⸏⸏⸏⸏⸏⸏⸏⸏⸏⸏⸏⸏⸏⸏⸏⸏⸏⸏⸏⸏⸏⸏⸏⸏

1532 – Henry VIII accompanied Francis I to the border between English Calais and France to bid farewell to him.

1586 – Four days after a commission had found Mary Queen of Scots guilty of conspiring to assassinate Elizabeth I, Parliament met to discuss Mary's fate. They decided that they should petition the Queen for Mary's execution.

1605 – Death of George Clifford, 3rd Earl of Cumberland, courtier and naval commander, at the duchy house, near the Savoy in London. He was buried in the family vault in Holy Trinity Church, Skipton, near Skipton Castle. Clifford was Elizabeth I's second champion. He commanded a ship in the Anglo-Spanish War and is known for capturing Fort San Felipe del Morro in San Juan, Puerto Rico, in 1598. Elizabeth I nicknamed him her "rogue".

30TH OCTOBER

On this day in 1485, the founder of the Tudor dynasty, Henry Tudor, was crowned King Henry VII at Westminster Abbey. The Tudor chronicler, Raphael Holinshed, recorded:

"...with great pompe he rowed unto Westminster, & there the thirtith daie of October he was with all ceremonies accustomed, anointed, & crowned king, by the whole assent as well of the commons as of the nobilitie, & called Henrie the seaventh of that name..."

His biographer, Thomas Penn, describes how this was the occasion that Henry was united with his mother, Lady Margaret Beaufort, whom he'd not seen for fourteen years. Margaret was said to have "wept marvellously".

Henry Tudor had claimed the crown of England after defeating Richard III at the *Battle of Bosworth Field* on the 22nd August 1485, and had actually been unofficially crowned with Richard's crown on the battlefield that day.

31ST OCTOBER

1491 – Henry VII's son, Henry (the future Henry VIII), was created Duke of York.

1517 – Martin Luther wrote to Albert, Archbishop of Mainz, and the Bishop of Brandenburg protesting against the sale of indulgences and sending them a copy of "The Ninety-Five Theses" (proper title: "Disputation of Martin Luther on the Power and Efficacy of Indulgences").

According to Philipp Melancthon, "Luther, burning with passion and just devoutness, posted the Ninety-Five Theses at the Castle Church in Wittenberg, Germany at All Saints Eve, October 31", rather than sending them in a letter, but no other contemporary source supports this.

1537 – Death of Lord Thomas Howard, second son of Thomas Howard, 2nd Duke of Norfolk, and his second wife, Agnes Tilney, in the Tower of London. He was buried at Thetford Abbey. Howard had been imprisoned in 1536 after becoming betrothed to Lady Margaret Douglas, the King's niece, without the King's permission.

1557 – Death of Sir Nicholas Hare, lawyer, Speaker of the House of Commons and Master of the Rolls. He was buried in Temple Church, London. Hare is known for presiding over the trial of Sir Nicholas Throckmorton for high treason, after *Wyatt's Rebellion*, and actually arguing with the accused. Throckmorton stated that it was Hare who had influenced his dislike of the proposed marriage between Mary I and Philip of Spain, and Hare reacted by refusing to examine one of the witnesses. Throckmorton was acquitted.

1612 – Death of Sir Christopher Yelverton, judge and Speaker of the House of Commons, at the age of seventy-five. He was buried at Easton Maudit Church.

ELIZABETH I (1533-1603)

1st November

On this day in 1456, Edmund Tudor, 1st Earl of Richmond, died from the plague at Carmarthen Castle.

Edmund was the son of Owen Tudor and Catherine of Valois (widow of Henry V and mother of Henry VI). He was made Earl of Richmond by his step-brother, Henry VI, in 1452 and married his twelve year-old ward, Margaret Beaufort, the daughter and heir of John Beaufort, Duke of Somerset, around November 1455. Margaret was actually six months pregnant with their son, the future Henry VII, when Edmund died at around the age of twenty-six.

Edmund was buried at the monastery of Greyfriars in Carmarthen, but was moved to St Davids Cathedral on the orders of his grandson, Henry VIII, after the dissolution of the monastery. His elaborate tomb can still be seen today in the middle of the high altar, although his effigy and other decorations were removed during the Civil War in the 17th century. His elegy was written by Lewys Glyn Cothi, the Welsh poet.

1527 – Birth of William Brooke, 10th Baron Cobham, courtier and diplomat. He was the son of George Brooke, 9th Baron Cobham, and his wife, Anne (née Bray). Cobham was a close friend of William Cecil, and so became powerful in Elizabeth I's reign. He served as Lord Warden of the Cinque Ports, Privy Councillor and Lord Chamberlain. Cobham also undertook diplomatic missions.

1530 – Henry VIII sent Sir Walter Walsh (some say William Walsh) with Henry Percy, Earl of Northumberland, to Cawood Castle to arrest Cardinal Thomas Wolsey for high treason. They arrived on 4th November and took him into custody.

1558 – Death of Michael Throckmorton, agent for Cardinal Reginald Pole, probably at Mantua in Italy. He studied law in

Italy, in Padua, in 1533 before becoming Pole's secretary. It is thought that he may well have been the agent who took Pole's *Pro ecclesiasticae unitatis defensione* to Henry VIII in 1536.

2ND NOVEMBER

On this day in 1541, Archbishop Thomas Cranmer left a letter for Henry VIII in the Holy Day Closet at Hampton Court Palace detailing Catherine Howard's colourful past, and how she had "lived most corruptly and sensually". Cranmer had been persuaded by Chancellor Audley and the Earl of Hertford to relate the story told by Mary Hall to her brother, John Lassells. Hall, who knew Catherine from her time in the Dowager Duchess of Norfolk's household, had told Lassells:-

"There is one Francis Derrham, who was servant also in my lady of Norfolk's house, which hath lien in bed with her [Catherine] in his doublet and hose between the sheets an hundred nights. And there hath been such puffing and blowing between them, that once in the house a maid which lay in the house with her, said to me, she would lie no longer with her, because she knew not what matrimony meant."

Hall also went on to say that Catherine's music tutor, Henry Manox, "knew a privy mark on her body".

Cranmer consulted Audley and Hertford, and it was decided that the King really needed to know about the allegations concerning his fifth wife, the woman he called his "rose without a thorn". Cranmer decided the best course of action was to tell the King by letter and the note was left for the King to find when he went to mass. Henry VIII "conceived such a constant opinion of her honesty, that he supposed it rather to be a forged matter, than of truth", and ordered an investigation to clear it up. Of course, the investigation was to show the King that the Queen's past indiscretions were the least of his worries, and that there was more bad news to come.

1470 – Birth of Edward V, son of Edward IV and Elizabeth Woodville, in Westminster Abbey sanctuary during his father's exile. He was baptised there. In June 1471, his father made him Prince of Wales and Earl of Chester. His father died in April 1483, making Edward King Edward V, but his uncle, Richard, Duke of Gloucester, claimed the throne as Richard III. Edward and his brother, Richard, Duke of York, disappeared and their fate is unknown. They became known as the Princes in the Tower, and there is still controversy today over whether they were murdered on the orders of Richard III.

1581 – Death of Gilbert Berkeley, Bishop of Bath and Wells, at Wells. He was buried at the cathedral and his tomb chest can still be seen today, in the aisle of the north chancel.

3RD NOVEMBER

On this day in 1592, Sir John Perrot, Privy Councillor and former Lord Deputy of Ireland, died at the Tower of London. He was buried in the Chapel of St Peter ad Vincula at the Tower.

John Perrot was born between 1527 and 1530 in Pembrokeshire, and was the son of Mary and Sir Thomas Perrot, or was he? Historian Philippa Jones writes of how it was widely believed that he was actually the illegitimate son of Henry VIII.

John's mother, the pretty Mary Berkeley, had served Henry VIII's first wife, Catherine of Aragon. The King was a friend of her husband, Sir Thomas Perrot, a keen huntsman, and Jones believes that Henry VIII began an affair with Mary after noticing her when he came to visit and hunt. Jones writes of how Mary's son, John, was said to resemble the King, being tall and auburn haired, and when the King found John fighting with two of his Yeoman of the Guard he chose to give him a Promise of Preferment instead of sending him to jail. Was it because he was his son? Jones seems to think so.

John later became friends with Henry VIII's legitimate son, Edward VI, and was made a Knight of the Bath at his coronation. In Mary I's reign, although John was a Protestant and was reported for hiding heretics in his house, he managed to escape serious punishment and was just imprisoned for a short time. At Elizabeth I's coronation in 1559, he was one of the men chosen to bear her canopy of state, and in 1562 was made Vice-Admiral of the South Wales coast and Keeper of the Jail at Haverfordwest. In 1570 he became Mayor of Haverfordwest, and in 1571 was involved in suppressing a rebellion in Ireland, ordering the hanging of around 800 rebels. He was rewarded for his work in Ireland by Elizabeth, who gave him Carew Castle in Milford Haven and land.

Sir John Perrot later joined the Council in the Marches of Wales, working hard to stop piracy along the Welsh coast. In 1584, after his "Discourse" of 1581, giving the Queen advice on the governing of Ireland, he was appointed Lord Deputy of Ireland and spent four years there, although it was a troubled time and Perrot was stuck between a rock and a hard place, trying to reward the English and keep the Irish people happy. All the while, his enemies at the English Court were ganging up on him.

In July 1588, Perrot returned to England where he faced many questions about the situation in Ireland, and accusations that he had made decisions against orders. He was able to rebut these charges and was made a member of the Queen's Privy Chamber in 1589. However, trouble seemed to follow him, and in 1590, new accusations of treason were made against him. Perrot was accused of offering to help Philip of Spain conquer England and Ireland in return for Perrot being given Wales. The letters produced by Sir Dennis O'Rowghan were forgeries, and O'Rowghan was condemned for counterfeiting Perrot's writing and signature. Although O'Rowghan had been dealt with, Perrot's enemies kept up the pressure, and he was accused of speaking rudely of the Council, King James VI and Elizabeth I. Perrot was arrested, kept under house arrest at Lord Burghley's house and then sent to the Tower of London. Just over a year later, in April 1592, he was tried for treason, found guilty and returned to the Tower. As he was led to his prison, it is said that he exclaimed "God's death! Will the Queen suffer her brother to be offered up a sacrifice to the envy of his frisking adversary". Perrot was later sentenced to death, but he died in the Tower of London in September 1592 from illness. He died a destitute, convicted traitor, but the Queen did allow his estate, which had been seized by the Crown, to pass on to his eldest son, Thomas.

Historian Roger Turvey believes that the story that Perrot was Henry VIII's son is just a myth, and that it is attributed to the work of Sir Robert Naunton, who others point out never knew Perrot or his family. There is no evidence that Perrot's mother was ever the King's mistress.

1568 – Death of Nicholas Carr, physician, classical scholar and Regius Professor of Greek at Cambridge. He was laid to rest in St Michael's Church, Cambridge, and a monument was erected in his memory at St Giles's Church. His works included *De Scriptorum Britannicorum Paucitate et Studiorum Impedimentis Oratio, Epistola de morte Buceri ad Johannem Checum, Eusebii Pamphili de vita Constantini* and *Demosthenis Graecorum Oratorum Principis Olynthiacae orationes tres, et Philippicae quatuor, e Greco in Latinum conversae.*

4TH NOVEMBER

On 4th November 1538, Henry Pole, 1st Baron Montagu, was arrested for treason along with his brother-in-law, Sir Edward Neville; Henry Courtenay, Marquis of Exeter, and Courtenay's family (wife Gertrude Blount and son Edward

Courtenay). The three men were accused of conspiring against the King, seeking to deprive the King of his title of supreme head of the church and plotting with Cardinal Reginald Pole, the exiled brother of Montagu. Montagu's brother, Geoffrey Pole, had been imprisoned in the Tower of London at the end of August 1539 and had implicated Henry Pole during his interrogation on the 26th October.

Margaret Pole, Countess of Salisbury and mother of Reginald, Henry and Geoffrey, was interrogated on the 12th November by William Fitzwilliam, Earl of Southampton, and Thomas Goodrich, Bishop of Ely.

What happened to these prisoners in the end?

Neville was beheaded on the 9th December 1538. Geoffrey Pole was pardoned on the 2nd January 1539, after having attempted suicide several times. Montagu and Exeter were beheaded on Tower Hill on the 9th January 1539, and Margaret Pole was eventually executed on the 27th May 1541. Exeter's wife was released in 1540, and his son in 1553. Cardinal Pole escaped the wrath of Henry VIII as he was in exile. He was attainted for treason in 1539 'in absentia' but this was reversed by Mary I in 1554, and he became her Archbishop of Canterbury, serving in that office until his death in 1558.

1501 – Catherine of Aragon met Arthur, Prince of Wales, for the first time at Dogmersfield in Hampshire. They married ten days later at St Paul's.

1530 – William (some say Walter) Walsh and Henry Percy, Earl of Northumberland, arrived at Cawood Castle and arrested Cardinal Thomas Wolsey for high treason.

1551 – Date given in the epitaph of John Redman, theologian and first Master of Trinity College, Cambridge. He died of consumption and was buried at Westminster Abbey, in the north transept. Redman's works included *De justificatione*, which he presented to Henry VIII in 1543, and "A Necessary Doctrine and Erudition for any Christian Man".

5TH NOVEMBER

On the night of 4th/5th November 1605, Guy Fawkes was caught with thirty-six barrels of gunpowder in the cellars beneath Westminster. The idea was to blow up the House of Lords at the opening of Parliament on the 5th November, and to assassinate King James I.

Although the plot happened in the Stuart period, in the reign of King James I, it actually had its origins in Elizabeth's reign. Elizabeth had continued the work of Henry VIII, and Edward VI and made England a Protestant country. By the end of her reign, England was a dangerous place for Catholics, with the threat of persecution and even death hanging over them. As Elizabeth's health deteriorated, the Catholics pinned their hopes on James VI of Scotland, who was married to a Catholic, and who was the son of the late Catholic queen, Mary, Queen of Scots. Although he himself was a Protestant, the Catholics felt sure that he would be sympathetic to their cause.

James VI of Scotland became James I of England in 1603, on Elizabeth's death, and although his reign started well for the Catholics, with James limiting the restrictions on Catholics, things took a turn for the worse when, after opposition from Protestants, James reversed his policy less than a year after implementing it. The Catholics' hopes were dashed and they felt betrayed. One party of young Catholics, headed by Robert Catesby, a popular and rebellious young man at court, decided to seek revenge through rebellion. They met in London in May 1604 and hatched a plan to blow up the Palace of Westminster on the opening session of Parliament, thus killing the King, the Royal family, members of Parliament (MPs), the Lords and the leading bishops. This would be the first step in their rebellion which sought to replace James I with his daughter, nine year-old Princess Elizabeth, as a Catholic queen.

One of the plotters, Thomas Percy, a member of the King's Bodyguard, was able to lease lodgings that were situated adjacent to the House of Lords, and the idea was that the plotters would dig down underneath the foundations of the House of Lords and place gunpowder there. Guy Fawkes (also known as Guido Fawkes), a man who had been fighting for the Spanish in the Low Countries, was the man chosen to put the plan into operation by preparing the gunpowder and lighting the fuse, and he posed as Percy's servant, calling himself John Johnson so that he could stay in the property.

The *Black Plague* of summer 1604 meant that the plan had to be changed due to the opening of Parliament being delayed. However, this delay worked in the mens' favour because during this time, they learned of a vacant ground-floor undercroft directly under the House of Lords Chamber. Thomas Percy was able to secure the lease of this undercroft. Guy Fawkes and other members of the group set about filling this space with 36 barrels of gunpowder, which had the potential to completely level the Palace of Westminster.

Everything seemed fine, and the plot looked as if it would be successful, until Lord Monteagle received an anonymous tip-off just over a week before the state opening of Parliament was due to take place. The letter, thought to be from Lord Monteagle's brother-in-law, Sir Francis Tresham, who had recently become a member of the plot, gave enough details for Lord Monteagle to go to Robert Cecil. Cecil took the news to the King, who ordered the cellars beneath Westminster to be searched. It was on the night of the 4th/5th November that Guy Fawkes was found red-handed with the evidence – 36 barrels of gunpowder!

Guy Fawkes was arrested and tortured for information, but despite this failure, Catesby still attempted to incite armed rebellion in the Midland. It, too, was a failure and Catesby, along with a few of his co-conspirators, was killed in a shoot-out on 8th November. Those who weren't killed were arrested, tried and then hanged, drawn and quartered in January 1606.

On 5th November 1605, Londoners were encouraged to celebrate the King's narrow escape by lighting bonfires around the city, and it is that celebration that is remembered in the UK every year on 5th November, along with the fireworks which have their origins in Guy Fawkes' gunpowder. In fact, this celebration to give thanks for the deliverance of the King was made compulsory in the United Kingdom until 1859.

The traditional rhyme which is said on Guy Fawkes Night is:-

> Remember, remember the Fifth of November,
> The Gunpowder Treason and Plot,
> I know of no reason
> Why the Gunpowder Treason
> Should ever be forgot.
> Guy Fawkes, Guy Fawkes, t'was his intent
> To blow up the King and Parli'ment.
> Three-score barrels of powder below
> To prove old England's overthrow;
> By God's providence he was catch'd
> With a dark lantern and burning match.
> Holloa boys, holloa boys, let the bells ring.
> Holloa boys, holloa boys, God save the King!

The UK has a Queen on the throne at present, so the last part of the last line is changed to "God save the Queen".

⸻

1514 – Mary Tudor, sister of Henry VIII, was crowned Queen of France. She had married King Louis XII at Abbeville on the 9th October 1514. The marriage was rather short-lived, as Louis died on the 1st January 1515, and Mary went on to marry Charles Brandon, Duke of Suffolk.

1520 – Death of Sir Robert Poyntz, courtier, landowner and Vice-Chamberlain and Chancellor of the Household to Queen Catherine of Aragon. He was around seventy when he died.

1530 – Death of Sir John More, lawyer, judge and father of Sir Thomas More. More served as Serjeant-at-Law, Justice of Assize, Justice of the Common Pleas, and also served on the King's Bench from 1520 until his death.

6TH NOVEMBER

On this day in 1514, Mary Tudor, Queen of France, processed into Paris following her coronation the day before at St Denis.

It was a lavish occasion and must have been an incredible sight. According to Pierre Grigore, the pageants of Mary's triumphant entry into the city included:

- A fountain with three jets watering a lily and red rose, representing France and England, and three ladies dressed as the Graces – Beauty, Mirth and Prosperity – who were uniting the lily and the rose.

- Mary as the Queen of Sheba bringing her gift of peace to her husband, Louis XII, whose wisdom was renowned, just like that of Solomon.

- A pageant showing God the Father in a cloud "holding in his right hand a large heart surrounded with the King's order, and in the other a lily and rose intertwined. Underneath were a King and Queen, in their triumph and magnificence, and at the foot was written, "*Cor regis in manu Domini est, quocunque voluerit inclinabit illud*" (Prov. XXII), and under the King and Queen "Veni amica mea, veni, coronaberis" (*Canticorum* 4). Below stood five ladies, viz., France and England seated in chairs at the two ends of the scaffold, and between them standing Peace, Amity, and Confederation."

- The throne of honour – Mary was taken to the Church of the Holy Innocents where there was a scaffold with a tent called the throne of honour. "Within was planted a lily in an orchard called the orchard of France, surrounded by four Virtues – Pity and Truth on the right, and Fortitude and Mercy on the left…On the large scaffold below was an enclosure like the wall of a town, with towers and a gate. In the centre a rosebush, with "*Plantatio rose in Jherico*" written thereon. From the bush a stalk with a bud on it rose up towards the throne, and the lily descended and met it half way. They then rose together to the throne where the bud opened, disclosing within a maiden richly dressed" who gave an oration.

- A pageant at the Chastellet of Paris showing Justice descending from a cloud with his sword and Truth rising up. "Below the scaffold stood Phœbus, Diana, Minerva, Stella Maris and Bonaccord. Stella Maris signifies the Queen."

- A scaffold at the Palais Royal showing the Garden of France, the King and Queen with Justice holding a sword, and Truth holding a peace.

- Orations praising Mary were also said at each pageant.

It ended with Mary's entry into the church of Notre Dame, where she was welcomed by Cardinals, Archbishops and other members of the clergy. After a service there, she ended the day with a banquet at the Palais Royal.

⬦⬦⬦⬦⬦⬦⬦⬦⬦⬦⬦⬦⬦⬦⬦⬦⬦⬦⬦⬦⬦⬦⬦⬦⬦⬦⬦⬦

1541 – Henry VIII abandoned Catherine Howard, his fifth wife, at Hampton Court Palace. The investigation into John Lassell's claims that Catherine had two sexual relationships during her time in the Dowager Duchess of Norfolk's household had proved them true.

1558 – Baptism of Thomas Kyd, translator and playwright, at St Mary Woolnoth in London. Kyd is known for his play "The Spanish Tragedy".

1612 – Death of Nicholas Fitzherbert, author and former secretary of Cardinal William Allen, near Florence in Italy. Fitzherbert drowned while trying to ford a stream en route to Rome. Fitzherbert left England in the 1570s because of his Catholic faith and to study law at Bologna. In 1580, while he was in Italy, he was attainted of treason back in England due to his Catholic faith. He was buried at Florence, in the Benedictine abbey.

1617 – Death of William Harborne, merchant and diplomat, at Mundham in Norfolk, Harborne served Elizabeth I as the English ambassador to the Ottoman Empire in Constantinople. He was buried at Mundham.

7TH NOVEMBER

On this day in 1541, Archbishop Thomas Cranmer and the Duke of Norfolk went to Hampton Court Palace to interrogate Queen Catherine Howard, and to arrange that she should be confined to her chambers there.

They did not confiscate Catherine's keys to her apartments, so she could move between her chambers, but her jewels were seized. It was clear that he was in terrible trouble, and Catherine burst into tears and became hysterical. It was impossible to interrogate her while she was in such a state, so Cranmer decided to come back the following day.

1485 – Richard III and his supporters were attainted at Henry VII's first Parliament.

1557 – Death of Sir John Arundell of Lanherne. He was buried at St Mawgan Church. Arundell served Henry VIII as Sheriff of Cornwall and Commander of troops against the rebels during the *Pilgrimage of Grace*. He also served in France in 1544. During Edward VI's reign, in 1549, he was imprisoned after John, Baron Russell, accused him of refusing to raise troops and of ordering the mass to be performed. He was released in June 1552.

1565 – Death of Sir Edward Warner, soldier, member of Parliament and Lieutenant of the Tower of London during the reigns of Edward VI and Elizabeth I. He was the gaoler of Katherine Seymour (née Grey), Countess of Hertford, who had been imprisoned for secretly marrying Edward Seymour, Earl of Hertford. Warner died in Norfolk and was buried at Little Plumstead Church in the county.

1568 – Baptism of Dunstan Gale, poet and author of "Pyramus and Thisbe", at St Giles Cripplegate, London.

1581 – Death of Richard Davies, scholar and Bishop of St David's, in Abergwili, Camarthenshire, in the bishop's palace. He was a friend of Matthew Parker, Archbishop of Canterbury, and undertook translations of parts of the Bible.

1603 – Burial of Robert Allot, literary compiler, bookseller, poet and editor of the 1599 "Wits Theater" and the 1600 "Englands Parnassus", at St Ann Blackfriars.

8TH NOVEMBER

On the 8th November 1541, Archbishop Thomas Cranmer returned to Hampton Court Palace to interrogate Catherine Howard, Henry VIII's fifth wife and queen.

Cranmer reported to the King that he had intended to question her severely, "first, to exaggerate the grievousness of her demerits; then to declare unto her the justice of your grace's laws, and what she ought to suffer by the same", but that she was in such a state that "the recital of your grace's laws, with the aggravation of her offences, might peradventure have driven her unto some dangerous ecstasy, and else into a very frenzy." He therefore changed tactics and treated her more gently.

Cranmer reported that after Catherine had recovered from a sobbing fit, she told him:-

"Alas, my lord, that I am alive! the fear of death grieved me not so much before, as doth now the remembrance of the king s goodness: for when I remember how gracious and loving a prince I had, I cannot but sorrow; but this sudden mercy, and more than I could have looked for, shewed unto me, so unworthy, at this time, maketh mine offences to appear before mine eyes much more heinous than they did before: and the more I consider the greatness of his mercy, the more I do sorrow in my heart that I should so misorder myself against his majesty."

She went on to make a written confession, a copy of which can be found in Volume IV of "The History of the Reformation of the Church of England" by Gilbert Burnet. Here is a snippet concerning Francis Dereham:-

"Examined whether I called him Husband, and he me Wife.— I do Answer, that there was Communication in the House that we Two should Marry together; and some of his Enemies had Envy thereat, wherefore he desired me to give him Leave to call me Wife, and that I would call him Husband. And I said I was content. And so after that, commonly he called me Wife, and many times I called him Husband. And he used many Times to Kiss me, and so he did to many other commonly in the House...

As for Carnall Knowledge, I confess as I did before, that diverse Times he hath lyen with me, sometimes in his Doublet and Hose, and Two or Thre Times naked: But not so naked that he had nothing upon him, for he had al wayes at the least his Doublet, and as I do think, his Hose also, but I mean naked when his Hose were putt down. And diverse Times he would bring Wine, Strawberryes, Apples, and other Things to make good Chear, after my lady was gone to Bed."

At the end of this confession, she also mentioned Culpeper:-

"As for the Communication after his coming out of Ireland, is untrue. But as far as I remember, he then asked me, if I should be Married to Mr. Culpepper, for so he said he heard reported. Then I made Answer, What should you trouble me therewith, for you know I will not have you; and if you heard such Report, you heard more than I do know."

Catherine also wrote a letter of confession to her husband the King which can be read in "The Calendar of the Manuscripts of the Marquis of Bath Preserved at Longleat, Wiltshire Volume II" on pages 8 and 9:-

"I your grace's most sorrowful subject and most vyle wretche in the world not worthy to make any recomendacions unto your moste excellent majestye do oonely make my most humble submyssion and confession of my fawtz. And where no cawse of mercye is gyven uppon my partie yet of your most accustomed mercy extended unto all other men undeserved most humbly of my haundes and kneez do desire oon sparcle therof to be extended unto me although of all other creaturez most unwourthy eyther to be called your wyfe or subject. My sorowe I can by no wrytyng expresse neverthelesse I trust your most benygn nature will have some respect unto my youthe my ignorans my fraylnez my humble confession of my fawte and playne declaracion of the same referryng me holly mito your graces pitie and mercy. Fyrste at the flateryng and feire perswacions of Mannoke beyng bat a yong gyrle suffred hym at soundry tymez to handle and towche the secrett partz of my body whiche neyther became me with honesty to permytt nor hym to requyre. Also Frauncez Derame by many persuasions procured me to his vicious purpose and obteyned first to lye uppon my bedde with his doblett and hose and after within the bedde and fynally he lay with me nakyd and used me in suche sorte as a man doith his wyfe many and sondry tymez but howe often I knowe not and our, company ended almost a yere before the Kynges majestye was maried to my lady Anne of Cleve and contynued not past oon quarter of a yere or litle above. Nowe the holl trouythe beyng declared unto your majestye I most humble beseche the same to considre the subtyll persuasions of young men and the ignorans and fraylnez of young women. I was so desierous to be taken unto your gracez favor and so blynded with the desier of wordly glorie that I cowde not nor had grace to considre how grett a fawte it was to conceyle my former fawtz from your majestic consideryng that I entended ever duryng my lyfe to be feithful and true unto your majestie after, and neverthlesse the sorowe of my oflensez was ever before myn eyez consideryng the infynyte goodnez of your majestye towardes me from tyme to tyme ever encressyng and not dymynysshyng. Nowe I referre the judgement of all myn offensez with my lyff and dethe holly unto your most benygne and mercjrfull grace to be considered by no justice of your majestiez lawez but onely by your infynyte goodnez pytie compassion and mercye without the whiche I knowledge myseliff worthy of most extreme punnysshement. —

Kateryn Howard"

Tip: Read it aloud and you'll understand the old English.

1528 – Henry VIII made a public oration to "the nobility, judges and councillors and divers other persons" at Bridewell Palace to explain his troubled conscience regarding the lawfulness of his marriage to Catherine of Aragon. In this speech, the King explained that due to his worry that Mary was not his lawful daughter and that Catherine was not his lawful wife, he had sent for a legate "to know the truth and to settle my conscience." He went on to say "if it be adiudged by the law of God that she is my lawfull wife, there was neuer thyng more pleasaunt nor more acceptable to me in my lifebothe for the discharge & cleryng of my conscience & also for the good qualities and condicions the which I know to be in her" and "if I were to mary againe if the mariage might be good I would surely chose her aboue all other women".

1534 – Death of William Blount, 4th Baron Mountjoy, courtier, scholar and literary patron, at Sutton on the Hill in Derbyshire.

He was buried at Barton Blount. Mountjoy was a pupil of the great humanist scholar, Erasmus, and served Henry VIII as Master of the Mint and Chamberlain to Catherine of Aragon. It was Mountjoy who had to tell Catherine of her demotion to Princess Dowager in July 1533.

1543 – Birth of Lettice Knollys, daughter of Sir Francis Knollys and Catherine Carey, granddaughter of Mary Boleyn and wife of Walter Devereux, 1st Earl of Essex; Robert Dudley, 1st Earl of Leicester; and Sir Christopher Blount. Lettice was also mother to Robert Devereux, 2nd Earl of Essex; Penelope Rich, Lady Rich; and Dorothy Percy, Countess of Northumberland.

1602 – The opening of the Bodleian Library (Bodley's Library), Oxford, to the public.

1605 – Deaths of *Gunpowder Plot* conspirators Robert Catesby and Thomas Percy at Holbeche House on the Staffordshire border. It is thought that they were both shot by a single bullet fired from the gun of John Street of Worcester. Their heads were displayed on London Bridge.

9TH NOVEMBER

On the night of the 9th November 1518, Queen Catherine of Aragon gave birth to a daughter. We don't know the full details of what happened, but either the baby was stillborn, or did not survive very long. Sebastian Giustinian, the Venetian ambassador reported the birth in a letter dated 10th November 1518:-

"In the past night the Queen had been delivered of a daughter, to the vexation of everybody. Never had the kingdom so anxiously desired anything as it did a prince."

And this is followed by a later report in the Venetian archives:-

"The Queen bad been delivered in her eighth month of a stillborn daughter, to the great sorrow of the nation at large."

It was a huge disappointment for Catherine and Henry VIII, and it was to be Catherine's last pregnancy.

‹‹‹‹‹‹‹‹‹‹‹‹‹‹‹‹‹‹‹‹‹‹‹‹‹‹‹‹‹‹‹‹‹‹‹‹‹‹‹›

1569 – The *Northern Rebellion* or *Rising of the North*. In November 1569, an uprising led by Charles Neville, 6th Earl of Westmorland and Thomas Percy, 7th Earl of Northumberland, sought to depose Elizabeth I, replace her with Mary, Queen of Scots (who would marry the Duke of Norfolk) and restore the Catholic faith as the faith of England. Although the rebels were successful in occupying Durham, where they took mass in the cathedral, Staindrop, Darlington, Richmond, Ripon and also Barnard Castle, they were finally forced to retreat north. Northumberland and Westmorland fled to Scotland. Their rebellion had been a failure.

1593 – Death of William Harris, historian and topographer, at St George's Chapel, Windsor. He was buried in the chapel. Harris's works included "Historicall Description of the Island of Britain" and "The Great English Chronology".

1596 – Burial of George Peele, poet and playwright, at St James's Clerkenwell. His plays included "The Arraignment of Paris", "Edward I", "The Battle of Alcazar", "The Old Wives' Tale" and "The Love of King David and fair Bethsabe".

1623 – Death of William Camden, Richmond Herald, antiquary, historian, topographer and officer of arms, at Chislehurst in Kent. He was aged seventy-three. He was buried in the south aisle of Westminster Abbey. Camden is known for his "Britannia", which was the first chorographical survey of Great Britain and Ireland, and his *Annales Rerum Gestarum Angliae et Hiberniae Regnate Elizabetha*, his history of Elizabeth I's reign.

10TH NOVEMBER

Robert Devereux, 2nd Earl of Essex, was born on this day in 1565 at Netherwood, Herefordshire. Devereux was the eldest son of Walter Devereux, 1st Earl of Essex, and Lettice Knollys, granddaughter of Mary Boleyn, and was a favourite of Elizabeth I.

After his father's death in 1576, William Cecil, Lord Burghley, was made his guardian, and in 1578 his mother married his godfather, Robert Dudley, Earl of Leicester.

Essex first caught the Queen's attention in 1584 when his stepfather, Leicester, brought him to court, and he was appointed Master of the Horse on his return to court after successful military service in the Netherlands with his stepfather. He was just twenty-one, and the Queen was fifty-three.

Although Robert Devereux is often described as "the darling of Elizabeth's old age", having replaced his stepfather in Elizabeth's affections after Dudley's death in 1588, Alison Plowden says that "it would probably be more accurate to describe him as one of its greatest headaches". Although Essex was dashing and charming, he was rash, ambitious, arrogant, headstrong and used to getting his own way. Unlike Dudley, Essex did not know Elizabeth as only a childhood friend or sweetheart can, and he constantly underestimated her and attempted to bully her into submission.

After a successful raid on Cadiz in 1596 during the war with Spain, Essex returned to England as a hero. His return to court caused the forming of two factions: the Devereux faction, who were seeking military profit and glory, and the opposing faction headed by Lord Burghley and his son, Robert Cecil, who were on the side of peace. Although Elizabeth loved flirting with the handsome Essex and doted on him, she sought to keep a balance between the factions, and would not always give her favourite what he wanted. This led to Essex sulking like a spoiled child, and to stormy rows between him and the Queen. Essex ignored the advice of friends like Francis Bacon, who warned him not to offend Elizabeth by seeking to be overly powerful, because he did not want to settle for "just" being a servant like his stepfather. He wanted more. Wise counsel fell on deaf ears, and Elizabeth's attempts to tame wild-child Essex failed.

Ultimately, it was his pride and his need for recognition and power that led to his undoing. In 1599, Essex became Lord Lieutenant of Ireland, but his campaign against the Irish was unsuccessful. Essex constantly ignored the Queen's orders, acted contrary to her wishes and constantly worried about what the Cecil faction were getting up to back at court. His obsession with power led to him giving up on the Irish situation, making a truce with the Irish rebel leader (against the Queen's wishes) and returning to England without the Queen's permission. This amounted to desertion and disobedience, something which Elizabeth could not and would not tolerate. The situation was made worse on the 28th September 1599, by Essex striding into Elizabeth's bedchamber unannounced and seeing the Queen without her makeup or wig, without her "mask of youth".

On the 29th September, Essex was interrogated before the Queen's Council for around 5 hours, and the Council concluded that his truce with the Irish rebels was indefensible, and that his return to England was a desertion of duty. Essex was then put under house arrest. In June 1600, Essex appeared before a special court and was punished by being deprived of his public office and being confined to his home. However, in August, he was granted his freedom, although his sweet wines monopoly, his one source of income, was not renewed.

He may well have wormed his way back into the Queen's affections if he had apologised and appealed to the Queen for mercy - after all, she had a soft spot for him and was used to his impulsive behaviour - but Essex made the fatal mistake of trying to enlist the support of the Scottish king, James VI, against Cecil's faction at court, and planning a coup for March 1601 to force Elizabeth to summon Parliament and deal with Cecil and his faction. When, on the 7th February, Essex received a message from the Queen that he was to present himself before Council, he decided to move things forward and summoned three hundred followers, telling them that Cecil and Ralegh were planning to assassinate him, and that the rising should therefore take place the next day, instead of in March.

On the 8th February 1601, Essex, his supporters and two hundred soldiers gathered at Essex House. Essex then marched into the city crying "For the Queen! For the Queen! The crown of England is sold to the Spaniard! A plot is laid for my life!" but London's citizens remained indoors instead of joining him on his march. As his supporters deserted him, Essex was forced to give up and return home, where he surrendered after Lord Admiral Nottingham threatened to blow up his house if he did not give himself up.

On the 9th February, Elizabeth I told the French ambassador that the "shameless ingrate, had at last revealed what had long been in his mind". Her patience had been stretched beyond breaking point and she could no longer excuse her past favourite's behaviour. On the 13th February the full details of the coup planned by Essex were made public, and on the 17th February indictments were laid against Essex and his key supporters, including Henry Wriothesley, 4th Earl of Southampton. Two days later, on the 19th February, Robert Devereux, Earl of Essex, and his friend, Southampton, were tried at Westminster Hall by a jury of their peers. Both men were accused of high treason, found guilty and sentenced to death. Elizabeth I, in her mercy, commuted Southampton's sentence to life in prison and Essex's sentence of a traitor's death to death by beheading. On the 20th February, the Queen signed his death warrant.

Essex was executed on Tower Green on the 25th February 1601.

1536 – Death of Sir Henry Wyatt, politician, courtier, Privy Councillor and father of Sir Thomas Wyatt. He was buried at Milton in Kent. He acted as an executor of Henry VII's will, and his offices during Henry VIII's reign included Privy Councillor, Joint Captain of Norwich Castle, Knight-Banneret, Master of the Jewels and Treasurer of the King's Chamber.

1542 – Death of Sir Richard Pollard, law reporter, member of Parliament and King's Remembrancer of the Exchequer.

1556 – Death of Richard Chancellor, English explorer and navigator. Chancellor was drowned after saving the Russian ambassador, Osip Napeya, when their ship, *The Edward Bonaventure*, was wrecked in Pitsligo Bay, just off the Aberdeenshire coast. Chancellor is known as being the first foreigner to enter the White Sea and establish relations with Russia. He met Ivan the Terrible, the Russian Tsar, in the winter of 1553/4.

1597 – Death of Peter Wentworth, member of Parliament, in the Tower of London. He had been imprisoned in 1593 after drafting the treatise "A Pithie Exhortation to her Majestie for Establishing her Successor to the Crowne" on the royal succession.

1610 – Death of Sir Thomas Wilford, member of Parliament and soldier, at his home in Hedding, Kent. He served as a soldier in Ireland, the Low Countries and France. His offices included Deputy Lieutenant of Kent and Governor of Camber Castle.

11TH NOVEMBER

On 11th November 1534, Philippe de Chabot, Seigneur De Brion and Admiral of France, landed on English soil. As the French ambassador to England, his visit was apparently intended to renew relations between England and France, so it was an important one.

George Boleyn, Lord Rochford and brother of Queen Anne Boleyn, was chosen to meet the Admiral and escort him from Dover to London. This was no easy task, when, according to Eustace Chapuys, the Imperial Ambassador, the Admiral had a huge train consisting of over 350 horses.

"Letters and Papers" includes letters from George Boleyn at this time, showing just what an administrative nightmare this visit was. First, George writes to Lord Lisle in Calais:

"I have sent the bearer, the King's servant, only to bring me sure word in what sort the Admiral will cross the sea, and whether he will send his train before him or come first himself. I beg you to inquire and send word by the bearer, and that he may have the first passage after the Admiral has arrived at Calais. Vaghan, the bailly of Dover, whom you have required to come to Calais as one of the retinue there, cannot be spared, as the Admiral is lodged in his house. Commend me to my lady. Dover, 6 Nov."

We can see George's concern over the travel arrangements of the Admiral and his train.

Then, on the 11th November 1534, we have a letter from George to his uncle, the Duke of Norfolk, who was also involved in the Admiral's travel arrangements:

"The Admiral arrived this day at 10 o'clock. I and such as were commanded to attend met him at his landing, and brought him to Dover. Next day he goes to Canterbury, where he wishes to stop all day, that his train may meet him. I have sent the King the names of all of them. You shall be sure to hear from me from Canterbury. Dover, 11 Nov."

The Admiral had landed, but he obviously wanted to wait for his train. Then, on the 14th November, George wrote to Henry VIII explaining the delay:-

"The admiral of France has remained here since Thursday night. His whole train is not yet disembarked. Will convey him to Sittingbourn on Monday, there to stay the night, and to Rochester on Tuesday, on Wednesday to Dartford, and on Thursday by 12 noon to Blackheath, where Norfolk is appointed to meet him. Canterbury. Saturday, 14 Nov."

According to Chapuys's reports to Charles V, the Admiral finally arrived in London on the 17th November. Chapuys explained that he was held up because he had to wait for his train to cross the Channel, and also "to give leisure to those here to make the necessary preparations for his reception". Chapuys also reported on what the Admiral discussed with the King, and it was not good news for the Queen and the Boleyn faction. Although the King's Council had "made propositions for the marriage of the King's second daughter", i.e. Anne's daughter, Elizabeth, Chapuys wrote of how "opinions" had been collected in France, Italy and other parts of Europe, and that it was generally thought "that even if the King's first marriage were invalid, the Princess was still legitimate, and the succession belonged to her". Europe still saw Mary as legitimate and above Elizabeth in the line of succession.

On his visit to England, the Admiral upset Anne Boleyn in two ways. He snubbed her and then put forward the idea of a marriage alliance between Mary and the dauphin, rather than Princess Elizabeth and the Dauphin. The French tried to justify this by explaining that "there never had been any talk about marrying the Dauphin to the Infants", but it was still a snub to Anne and Elizabeth as it showed that Francis I viewed Mary's claim to the throne as better than Elizabeth's. Henry replied to Francis with a counter offer, a marriage between Elizabeth and the Duke of Angoulême, Francis I's third son, but that wasn't the same as marrying the Dauphin.

The Admiral's visit hadn't gone to plan for Anne, but she held a lavish banquet toward the end of his visit to try and improve relations.

1491 – Birth of Martin Bucer, theologian and leading reformer, at Sélestat in Alsace. Bucer was the leading reformer of Strasbourg and was influenced by Martin Luther. His works included *Defensio adversus axioma Catholicum,* "Von der Waren Seelsorge" ("Concerning true pastoral care"), *Gratulatio ad ecclesiam Anglicanam* ("Congratulation to the English church"), "Bestendige Antworten ("Steadfast response") and *De ordinatione legitima* ("On restoring lawful ordination"). While in exile in England in 1549, Bucer was commissioned to review the "Book of Common Prayer".

1508 – Death of Sir Edward Brampton, soldier and merchant, at Lisbon in Portugal. He had been given a licence to settle in Portugal in 1487, and was known there as Duarte Brandão.

1541 – Catherine Howard, fifth wife of Henry VIII, was moved from Hampton Court Palace to Syon House where she was "examined touching Culpeper", i.e. her alleged relationship with Thomas Culpeper, a member of her husband's Privy Chamber.

1546 – Birth of Richard Madox, diarist and Church of England clergyman, in Shropshire. He is known for the diary he kept of Captain Edward Fenton's voyage to the Moluccas, while he was serving as Fenton's Chaplain and Secretary. Madox died during the voyage.

1563 – Burial of chronicler Henry Machyn (Machin) in London. He died after contracting the plague. Machyn is known for his chronicle "The Diary of Henry Machyn, Citizen and Merchant-Taylor of London, from A.D. 1550 to A.D. 1563".

1593 – Death of Christopher Carleill, soldier and naval commander, in London. Carleill's naval and military career saw him serving in the Low Countries, France and Ireland. He also commanded the land force on Sir Francis Drake's expedition to Santo Domingo. Carleill was also known for his knowledge of mathematics, languages and his skill at poetry.

12TH NOVEMBER

On this day in 1555, Stephen Gardiner, Bishop of Winchester and Mary I's Lord Chancellor, died. He was laid to rest at Winchester Cathedral in what is now known as the Bishop Gardiner Chantry Chapel.

Stephen Gardiner's date of birth is not known, with some saying 1483 and others saying 1493 or 1497, but he was born in Bury St Edmunds in Suffolk. His father was William Gardiner (some say John Gardiner), a cloth merchant and a mercenary hired during the *War of the Roses*. According to Welsh accounts of the 1485 *Battle of Bosworth*, it was "Wyllyam Gardynyr" who killed King Richard III with a poleaxe. Sir William Gardiner later married Helen Tudor, a woman said to have been the illegitimate daughter of Jasper Tudor, uncle of King Henry VII.

As a young man, Gardiner met the famous humanist scholar, Desiderius Erasmus, in Paris and he studied at Trinity Hall, Cambridge. He received the degree of Doctor of Civil Law in 1520 and of Canon Law in 1521, and went on to work for Cardinal Thomas Wolsey as secretary. He met Henry VIII for the first time in 1525 at The More in Hertfordshire for the signing of the *Treaty of the More* between the King and Francis I of France. Two years later, in 1527, Gardiner and Sir Thomas More worked as commissioners in arranging, with the French ambassadors, a treaty to obtain support for an army against the Holy Roman Emperor, Charles V, in Italy.

In 1527, Gardiner accompanied his master, Wolsey, on a diplomatic mission to France to gain the French King's support for "the King's Great Matter" (or "secret matter"), his wish to divorce Catherine of Aragon. A year later, Gardiner was sent to Italy with Edward Foxe, the provost of King's College, Cambridge, to secure a decretal commission from the Pope which would allow Cardinal Wolsey to rule on the validity of the King's marriage without appeal to Rome. Although

Gardiner was an expert on canon law, and so was at a great advantage, Pope Clement VII had recently been imprisoned by Charles V's troops, and was wary of offending the Emperor who was Catherine of Aragon's nephew, and so refused to grant the decretal commission and instead granted a general commission to allow Cardinal Wolsey to try the case in England with the Papal Legate, Cardinal Campeggio. You can read more about the Legatine Court in Cardinal Campeggio and the Legatine Court.

In 1526, Gardiner was appointed Archdeacon of Taunton and then in 1529 Archdeacon of Norfolk, a post from which he resigned from in 1531 when he became Archdeacon of Leicester. In November 1531, he was appointed Bishop of Winchester after successfully procuring a decision from the University of Cambridge on the unlawfulness of a man marrying his dead brother's wife. However, he offended the King a year later when he was involved in preparing the "Answer of the Ordinaries", a reply to the "Supplication Against the Ordinaries".

In May 1533, Gardiner assisted the Archbishop of Canterbury, Thomas Cranmer, in pronouncing the marriage between Henry VIII and Catherine of Aragon null and void, and in 1535 he was one of the bishops asked to vindicate Henry VIII's new title "Supreme Head of the Church of England", something which he did by writing his treatise *De vera obedientia*, in which he argued that rulers were entitled to supremacy in their own country's churches, and that the pope had no legitimate power over other churches.

Between 1535 and 1539, Gardiner was mostly abroad on diplomatic missions, but in 1539 he helped to prepare "The Six Articles", which reaffirmed the traditional Catholic doctrine on transubstantiation, clerical celibacy, the vow of chastity, the withholding of the cup from the laity at communion, private masses and auricular confession. In 1543, Gardiner was involved in the *Prebendaries' Plot* against Cranmer, along with his nephew, Germain Gardiner. The plot failed when the

King supported Cranmer, but Gardiner survived, although his nephew, the scapegoat, was executed for treason. In 1546, Gardiner, along with Lord Chancellor Wriothesley, attempted to turn the King against his sixth wife, the Reformist Catherine Parr. The plot failed when Catherine managed to reconcile with the King.

On the 28th January 1547, King Henry VIII died, and although Gardiner had been one of his trusted advisers, he was not named as an executor in the King's will. During the Protestant reign of Edward VI, Gardiner was imprisoned, first in Fleet and then in the Tower of London, for his opposition to the religious changes being made. However, he was released at the accession of Mary I in 1553, restored to his bishopric and made the Queen's Lord Chancellor. He crowned Mary I Queen of England at her coronation at Westminster Abbey on the 1st October 1553, and helped Mary to restore Catholicism and, ironically, overturn the annulment of her parents' marriage, making her legitimate. He was also instrumental in the marriage negotiations between Mary and Philip II of Spain, and married the couple at Winchester Cathedral on the 25th July 1554.

It is not clear what Gardiner's role was in the Marian persecutions, but it appears that he preferred to try and persuade people to save themselves by recanting and reconciling themselves to the church. It has been pointed out that in his own diocese, nobody was persecuted until after Gardiner's death.

In May 1555, Gardiner carried out his last diplomatic mission to France, to promote peace, a mission that was not successful, and in October 1555 he opened Parliament. On the 12th November 1555, after being taken ill at the end of October, the famous Tudor statesman and lawyer, Stephen Gardiner, Bishop of Winchester and Lord Chancellor of England, died. It is thought that he was in his sixties, and that he had been suffering from jaundice and dropsy. It is said that as he lay dying, the story of the Passion was read to him, and that his dying words, after hearing of the denial of Peter, were *"Erravi cum Petro, sed non flevi cum Petro"*, "Like Peter I have erred, unlike Peter I have not wept", an allusion to his weakness during the reign of Henry VIII.

~~~~~~

1532 – Henry VIII and Anne Boleyn finally left Calais after being delayed by a Channel fog. They landed at Dover on Thursday 14th November. They had been visiting Calais to meet with the French king, Francis I.

1537 – Jane Seymour's body was taken by chariot from Hampton Court Palace to Windsor Castle. The chariot was followed by a procession led by the Duke of Suffolk and the Marquis of Dorset. Jane's stepdaughter, the Lady Mary, acted as chief mourner in the procession and the service, which was held at St George's Chapel on arrival at Windsor. A solemn watch was kept that night, and then Jane was buried on the morning of the 13th November.

1554 – The opening of Mary I's third Parliament. At this Parliament, a bill was passed allowing the exiled Cardinal Reginald Pole to return to England as papal legate.

1555 – Mary I's Parliament re-established Catholicism in England.

1576 – Death of Sir Edward Saunders, judge. He was buried at Weston under Wetherley, Warwickshire. Saunders' offices included Serjeant-at-Law, Recorder of Coventry, Chief Justice of the King's Bench and Chief Baron of the Exchequer.

1586 – A delegation of forty members of Parliament and twenty peers presented Elizabeth I with a petition demanding that "a just sentence might be followed by as just an execution" in the case of Mary, Queen of Scots.

1595 – Death of Sir John Hawkins, merchant, shipbuilder, navigator, explorer, slave trader and naval commander, at Puerto Rico on a voyage, with Sir Francis Drake, which aimed to capture Panama. He was buried at sea. Hawkins is known for being the chief architect of Elizabeth I's navy, and he was knighted for gallantry after serving as Vice-Admiral during the *Spanish Armada*.

13 NOVEMBER

On 13th November 1553, Lady Jane Grey, her husband Guildford Dudley, his brothers Ambrose and Henry, and Archbishop Thomas Cranmer were tried for treason at a public trial at London's Guildhall. They were led from the Tower of London, through the streets on foot, in a procession led by a man carrying an axe turned away from the prisoners, to show that they had not yet been found guilty of a capital crime: treason.

The trial opened with a Catholic liturgy and the commission chosen to try Jane and the men was headed by Sir Thomas White, the Lord Mayor, and also the Duke of Norfolk, both staunch Catholics. Jane, Guildford, Ambrose, Henry and Cranmer were all charged with high treason. Jane and Guildford were charged with treason for taking possession of the Tower of London and proclaiming Jane as queen, Cranmer was charged with proclaiming Jane as queen and sending forces to Cambridge, and Jane was charged with 'signing various writings' as queen.

Cranmer, at first, pleaded 'not guilty', but after the case had been presented, and before the jury delivered their verdict, he changed his plea to 'guilty', like the others. They were all found guilty as charged, with the men being sentenced to being hanged, drawn and quartered, and Jane to be burned alive, or beheaded. Michel Angelo Florio recorded that Jane remained cool and calm during the proceedings, and did not react at all to the sentence.

Lady Jane Grey and Guildford Dudley were executed on 12th February 1554.

1536 – Murder of Robert Pakington, mercer and member of Parliament, at Cheapside, while making his way to mass at St Thomas of Acre Chapel. He was shot dead by an unknown assailant. Theories regarding his murder included that it was ordered by conservative bishops, or John Stokesley, Bishop of London, or John Incent, Dean of St Paul's. He was definitely interested in reform and Rose Hickman, a Protestant, recalled how he "used to bring English bybles from beyond sea".

1537 – Burial of Jane Seymour, Henry VIII's third wife, at St George's Chapel, Windsor Castle. Henry VIII's daughter, Mary, acted as chief mourner.

1601 – Burial of Lady Mary Ramsey (née Dale), famous philanthropist, at Christ Church in London.

1612 – Death of Sir George Carew, administrator, member of Parliament and diplomat, from typhus at his home in Tothill Street, Westminster, London. He was buried at St Margaret's Church, Westminster. Carew's served as secretary to Lord Chancellor Hatton and served Elizabeth I and James I as an ambassador.

14TH NOVEMBER

On this day in 1501, Catherine of Aragon married Arthur, Prince of Wales at St Paul's Cathedral. A huge wooden stage, measuring 12 feet by 350 feet, had been erected in the cathedral. It stood on four-foot struts, and its railings were decorated with "say", a fine wool or silk twill cloth. The stone walls of the cathedral were covered with tapestries, and there was a red carpeted raised circular dais.

Catherine, dressed in a white satin wedding dress was escorted from the Bishop's Palace to the cathedral door by the ten year-old Prince Henry, who would later become her second husband, and Lady Cecily of York carried her train.

Catherine's dress was Spanish in style with a farthingale and "many pleats", and her face was covered with a white silk veil decorated with a border of gold, pearls and gemstones. Her bridegroom, Prince Arthur, was also dressed in white satin.

The marriage agreements were read out, Catherine's dowry was announced and the bride was also given letters patent detailing her endowment and surety. After that, it was time for the religious part of the ceremony: the vows and mass. Catherine was escorted out of the cathedral to the sound of trumpets by the young Henry, while Arthur got himself ready to welcome her at the door of her chamber.

While the people of London enjoyed a pageant with a fountain running with wine, Catherine and Arthur enjoyed a sumptuous wedding banquet. Historian Giles Tremlett writes of how this was only the start of the celebrations and that the partying went on for a fortnight, consisting of jousts, masques and banquets.

After the feasting, it was, of course, time for the wedding night, the consummation of their marriage. The question of whether this marriage was ever actually consummated is still debated today. When Henry VIII was trying to annul his marriage to Catherine in the late 1520 and early 1530s, Catherine vowed that she had never slept with Arthur, and this is backed up by evidence heard in Zaragoza, Spain, in 1531. There, Juan de Gamarra, who had been a boy in Catherine's service at the time of her wedding, told of how the Prince had got up early the morning after and that when he, Gamarra, had entered Catherine's rooms her ladies were concerned for Catherine and disappointed with the Prince. Gamarra stated:-

"Francisca de Cáceres, who was in charge of dressing and undressing the queen and whom she liked and confided in a lot, was looking sad and telling the other ladies that nothing had passed between Prince Arthur and his wife, which surprised everyone and made them laugh at him."

English witnesses, however, tell of Arthur demanding ale the next morning "for I have been this night in the midst of Spain!"

We just don't know for sure what happened that night and during their short marriage.

◇◇

1531 – Birth of Richard Topcliffe, member of Parliament, priest-hunter, interrogator and torturer, in Lincolnshire. During the reign of Elizabeth I, Topcliffe was issued with warrants allowing him to use torture when examining imprisoned Catholic recusants and priests. His famous victims included Robert Southwell, John Gerard and Henry Garnet.

1532 – On this day in 1532, according to the chronicler Edward Hall, Henry VIII and Anne Boleyn secretly married: "The kyng, after his returne [from Calais] maried priuily[privily] the lady Anne Bulleyn on sainet Erkenwaldes daie, whiche mariage was kept so secrete, that very fewe knewe it, til she was greate with child, at Easter after."

As Hall says, the couple had just landed at Dover after a successful trip to Calais to meet Francis I, the French King, a trip on which Anne had played the part of Queen Consort to Henry. Hall is not the only person to give this date as their wedding date, Nicholas Sander, a Catholic recusant writing in Elizabeth I's reign, also gave it as their wedding date in his book "The Rise of the English Schism":-

"The king, now impatient of further delay, though everything had not yet been duly prepared, determined to marry Anne Boleyn secretly on the 14th of the following November. He must marry her, for in no other way could he accomplish his will; and the marriage must be secret, because he and Catherine had not been separated by any judicial decision."

1539 – Hanging of Hugh Cook (Faringdon), Abbot of Reading, for treason, for upholding papal supremacy. He was born Hugh Cook, but took the name Faringdon when he took Benedictine orders.

1541 – An inventory was taken "of the goods and chattels, lands and fees of Thos. Culpeper, the younger", the alleged lover of Queen Catherine Howard.

1559 – Death of Thomas Brydges, landowner, member of Parliament and administrator. He was buried at Chadlington in Oxfordshire. Brydges had been present at the execution of Lady Jane Grey while serving as Deputy Lieutenant of the Tower of London.

1581 – Death of Richard Bristow, Roman Catholic priest and scholar, while in prison for his faith. He died of consumption. Bristow is known for being one of the men responsible for the translation of the Douay-Rheims Bible.

15TH NOVEMBER

1527 – Death of Katherine, Countess of Devon (also known as Katherine of York) at Tiverton Castle, She was aged forty-nine. She was buried at St Peter's Church, Tiverton, in funeral ceremonies on 2nd and 3rd December. Katherine had taken a vow of chastity after the death of her husband William Courtenay, Earl of Devon, in 1511. Katherine was the sixth daughter and ninth child of King Edward IV and Elizabeth Woodville. Her sister, Elizabeth of York, had married Henry VII, so Katherine was aunt to Henry VIII.

1555 – Death of Robert Holgate, former Bishop of Llandaff and then Archbishop of York, in London. He was buried at St Sepulchre. Holgate was imprisoned for a time during the reign of Mary I for being married, but was released when he renounced his marriage in his "Apology".

1592 – Burial of Sir Thomas Cokayne, soldier, huntsman and author of "A Short Treatise of Hunting" (1591), at Ashbourne church in Derbyshire. Cokayne attended Mary, Queen of Scots on her journey to Fotheringhay in 1587, and helped found Ashbourne Grammar School.

1597 – Death of Robert Bowes, member of Parliament and Elizabeth I's English ambassador in Scotland, at Berwick. He was buried at Berwick on the 16th November.

16TH NOVEMBER

1531 – Death of John Batmanson, Prior of the London Charterhouse, at the Charterhouse. He was buried in the cemetery there. Batmanson is said to have written treatises against the works of Martin Luther and Jacques Lefèvre d'Étaples, and he also criticised Erasmus.

1585 – Death of Gerald Fitzgerald, 11th Earl of Kildare and an Irish peer, in London. His body was taken to Kildare and buried there in February 1586. Fitzgerald was created Earl of Kildare and Baron of Offaly after helping put down *Wyatt's Rebellion* in 1554. He was imprisoned in the Tower of London twice for treason (1575 and 1582), but was cleared both times.

1596 – Death of Sir Francis Willoughby, industrialist and coalowner, in London. He was buried at St Giles Cripplegate. Willoughby is known for building Wollaton Hall in Nottinghamshire, developing coal mines on the estate, growing and processing woad there and in Ireland, and establishing two blast furnaces, for iron, at Middleton and Oakamoor, in Staffordshire, and buying one at Codnor in Derbyshire.

1601 – Death of Charles Neville, 6th Earl of Westmorland, nobleman and rebel, at Nieuwpoort in Flanders, while in exile. With the Percy family, the Nevilles had led the *Rising of the North*, a plot to release Mary, Queen of Scots and overthrow Elizabeth I. When the plot failed, Neville fled to Scotland and then on to Flanders. He was also involved in the *Ridolfi Plot* against Elizabeth.

1612 – Death of William Stafford, conspirator. Stafford was the son of William Stafford, widower of Mary Boleyn, and his second wife, Dorothy. Stafford was imprisoned in the Tower of London after being implicated in the plot of Baron de Châteauneuf, the French ambassador, to kill Elizabeth I. It is speculated that the plot was actually orchestrated by Walsingham and Cecil to show Elizabeth I that her life was in danger, and to persuade her to act against Mary, Queen of Scots. No charges were brought against Stafford, and he was released in 1588.

17TH NOVEMBER

On 17th November 1558, Henry VIII's eldest child, Queen Mary I, died. She was just forty-two years old.

After Easter 1558, Mary I made her will because she believed that she was pregnant. The birth should have been imminent because Philip departed in July 1557, yet there is no mention in the records of preparations being made such as nursery staff being appointed, remarks on her changing body shape, preparations for confinement etc. The pregnancy was all in Mary's mind.

Mary's health began to decline from that point on, although nobody seems to have been unduly worried at the time. In August 1558, Mary contracted a fever, and although she was able to fight that off, she was reported to be suffering from a "dropsy" at the end of September. At the end of October she made an addition to her will, and although she did not name Elizabeth, her half-sister, she did confirm that the throne would go to the next lawful heir, and that was Elizabeth. The Duke of Feria arrived at the English court on the 9th November and reported to his master, Mary's husband Philip II of Spain, on the 14th November:-

"there is… no hope of her life, but on the contrary each hour I think that they will come to inform me of her death, so rapidly does her condition deteriorate from one day to the next."

In her last days, Mary spoke of visions of angels, and of how the word "Calais" would be found written across her heart after her death. She received the 'viaticum', the special holy communion for the dying, on the 17th November, and was able to make the appropriate responses before she lapsed into unconsciousness, never to wake again. The exact time of her death is not recorded as it was not noticed, and she slipped peacefully away.

On Mary's death, her twenty-five year-old half-sister, Elizabeth, became Queen.

Elizabeth I was proclaimed Queen at around noon at Whitehall by the Houses of Lords and Commons who had been in session that morning. In the meantime, Sir Nicholas Throckmorton rode from London to Hatfield, carrying Mary's ring to Elizabeth as proof that Mary was dead. Members of Mary's council also made their way to Hatfield to see Elizabeth.

According to tradition, Elizabeth was sitting under an old oak tree in the parkland around the palace of Hatfield, reading a book, when lords of the council disturbed her to give her the news. Overcome with emotion, she sank to her knees and said in Latin "This is the Lord's doing: it is marvellous in our eyes", from Psalm 118. Another story, told by Elizabeth's godson, Sir John Harington, has Elizabeth making the following speech:

"My lords, the law of nature moveth me to sorrow for my sister; the burden that is fallen upon me maketh me amazed; and yet, considering I am God's creature, ordained to obey His appointment, I will thereto yield, desiring from the bottom of my heart that I may have assistance of His grace to be the minister of His heavenly will in this office now committed to me. And as I am but one body naturally considered, though by His permission a body politic to govern, so I shall desire you all, my lords (chiefly you of the nobility, everyone in his degree and power), to be assistant to me, that I with my ruling and you with your service may make a good account to almighty God and leave some comfort to our posterity in earth. I mean to direct all my actions by good advice and counsel. And therefore, considering that divers of you be of the ancient nobility, having your beginnings and estates of my progenitors, kings of this realm, and thereby ought in honour to have the more natural care for maintaining of my estate and this commonwealth; some others have been of long experience in governance and enabled by my father of noble memory, my brother, and my late sister to bear office; the rest of you being upon special trust lately called to her service only and trust, for your service considered and rewarded; my meaning is to require of you all nothing more but faithful hearts in such service as from time to time shall be in your powers towards the preservation of me and this commonwealth. And for council and advice I shall accept you of my nobility, and such others of you the rest as in consultation I shall think meet and shortly appoint, to the which also, with their advice, I will join to their aid, and for ease of their burden, others meet for my service. And they which I shall not appoint, let them not think the same for any disability in them, but for that I do consider a multitude doth make rather discord and confusion than good counsel. And of my goodwill you shall not doubt, using yourselves as appertaineth to good and loving subjects."

1493 – Birth of John Neville, 3rd Baron Latimer. He was the eldest son of Richard Neville, 2nd Baron Latimer, and his wife, Anne (née Stafford), and he was the brother of the poet William Neville. Latimer was married three times: Dorothy de Vere, sister of John de Vere, 14th Earl of Oxford; Elizabeth Musgrave, daughter of Sir Edward Musgrave; and Catherine Parr (the future Queen Catherine Parr), daughter of Sir Thomas Parr of Kendal and the widow of Edward Borough.

Latimer died in March 1543 and his widow, Catherine Parr, married Henry VIII in July 1543.

1525 – Death of Sir John Fyneux, judge and Chief Justice of the King's Bench. He was appointed Chief Justice in 1495, and was also an executor of Henry VII's will.

1551 – Death of Richard Fermor, wool merchant, at Easton Neston. He was buried at the parish church there. Fermor was one of the jurors at the trial of Sir Richard Empson, and purchased the manor of Easton Neston from Empson's family. He was imprisoned at Marshalsea prison in May 1540 for misprision of treason, for supporting his Catholic chaplain who was vocal in his support of the Pope as head of the Church, but was released in August 1540 and pardoned in 1541.

1558 – Death of Cardinal Reginald Pole, Mary I's Archbishop of Canterbury, at Lambeth Palace in London. He had been ill since September 1558 and died after hearing news of Mary I's death. He lay in state at the palace for forty days before being buried at Becket's Corona in Canterbury Cathedral.

1571 – Death of Sir Thomas Leigh, Lord Mayor of London. He was buried in the Mercer's Chapel. As Lord Mayor at the time of Elizabeth I's accession and coronation, he led Elizabeth's coronation procession.

1584 – Death of William Ayloffe, Justice of the Queen's Bench.

1589 – Death of Valentine Dale, member of Parliament, civil lawyer and diplomat, in the parish of St Gregory by Paul's in London. He was buried in the parish church there. Dale was sent on embassies to Flanders in 1563 and to Alexander Farnese, Duke of Parma, in 1588. He was on the commission which indicted Anthony Babington, and was also present at the trial of Mary, Queen of Scots. After Mary's trial, he wrote a memorandum justifying Mary's execution, at the behest of William Cecil, Lord Burghley.

18TH NOVEMBER

On this day in 1559, eighty-five year-old Cuthbert Tunstall, Bishop of Durham, died in prison at Lambeth Palace. He had had an amazing career, which spanned the reigns of Henry VIII, Edward VI and Mary I, but fell from grace in Elizabeth I's reign after he refused to take the Oath of Supremacy and refused to participate in the consecration of Matthew Parker as Archbishop of Canterbury.

Cuthbert Tunstall was born in 1474 in Hackforth, Yorskshire. He was the illegitimate son of Thomas Tunstall of Thurland Castle, Lancashire. He was educated at Oxford and Cambridge, and then spent six years at the University of Padua in Italy. He studied mathematics, law and theology, and he was awarded a doctorate in law.

In Henry VIII's reign, Tunstall was Bishop of London and then Bishop of Durham, served as Lord Keeper of the Privy Seal, acted as a diplomat and negotiated with Charles V after the *Battle of Pavia*. He was also involved in negotiating the *Peace of Cambrai*, acted as one of Catherine of Aragon's counsel during the *Great Matter*, and served as President of the Council of the North.

In Edward VI's reign, Tunstall fell from favour due to his Catholic faith, and the fact that he voted against the "Act of Uniformity". He was confined to house arrest, then imprisoned in the Tower of London and deprived of his bishopric. He wrote his treatise on the Eucharist, *De Veritate Corporis et Sanguinis Domini nostri Jesu Christi in Eucharistia*, while imprisoned.

He was released from the Tower after the accession of the Catholic Mary I, and his bishopric was re-established. His treatise was also published in Paris. Unfortunately for Tunstall, Mary I's reign was short, and he was imprisoned again in Elizabeth I's reign. He died in prison at the age of eighty-five.

1531 – Birth of Roberto di Ridolfi, merchant, banker and conspirator, in Florence, Italy. In the 1570s, Ridolfi, who was a papal agent, acted as a go-between for the Spanish and the Duke of Norfolk, and was the man responsible for funding the rebellion which aimed to have a Northern Catholic rebellion and an invasion by Spanish forces under Philip of Spain. The plot became known as the *Ridolfi Plot*, and was uncovered before it was put into action.

1559 – Death of Ralph Baynes, Bishop of Coventry and Lichfield, during his imprisonment at the London home of Edmund Grindal, Bishop of London. He was buried in the church of St Dunstan-in-the-West, London. Baynes had been deprived of his bishopric and put into the care of Grindal in June 1559, due to his opposition to Elizabeth I's religious legislation.

1600 – Death of William Hughes, Bishop of St Asaph and former chaplain to Thomas Howard, 4th Duke of Norfolk, at Diserth. He was buried in the cathedral choir. Hughes acted as patron to the Welsh poets William Cynwal, William Ll█n, and Siôn Tudur.

19TH NOVEMBER

On this day in 1563, Robert Sidney, 1st Earl of Leicester, courtier, patron of the arts and poet, was born at Penshurst in Kent. Sidney was the second son of Sir Henry Sidney and his wife, Mary (née Dudley), daughter of John Dudley, Duke of Northumberland. It was discovered that Robert was a poet, like his more famous brother Philip, when his notebook came to light in the library of Warwick Castle in the 1960s. The notebook contained a collection of over sixty sonnets, pastorals, songs and shorter pieces written in the 1590s. It can now be found in the British Library.

Sonnet 31 by Robert Sidney, Earl of Leicester, reads:

"Forsaken woods, trees with sharpe storms opprest
whose leaves once hidd, the sun, now strew the grownd
once bred delight, now scorn, late usde to sownd
of sweetest birds, now of hoars crowes the nest

Gardens which once in thowsand coulers drest
shewed natures pryde: now in dead sticks abownd
in whome prowd summers treasure late was fownd
now but the rags, of winters torn coate rest

Medows whose sydes, late fayre brookes kist now slyme
embraced holds: feelds whose youth green and brave
promist long lyfe, now frosts lay in the grave

Say all and I with them: what doth not tyme!
But they who knew tyme, tyme will finde again
I that fayre tymes lost, on tyme call in vaine."

⬦⬦⬦⬦⬦⬦⬦⬦⬦⬦⬦⬦⬦⬦⬦⬦⬦⬦⬦⬦⬦⬦⬦⬦⬦⬦⬦⬦

1564 – Death of Lord John Grey, youngest son of Thomas Grey, 2nd Marquis of Dorset and courtier. Grey was arrested with his brothers, Thomas and Henry (Duke of Suffolk and father of Lady Jane Grey), in 1554 for their involvement in *Wyatt's Rebellion*. Thomas and Henry were executed, and although John was condemned to death, he was released and pardoned due to the intercession of his wife, Mary, sister of Anthony Browne, Viscount Montagu.

1566 – Death of Reynold Corbet, member of Parliament and judge. He was buried at Stoke upon Tern in Shropshire. Corbet's offices included recorder of Shrewsbury, Justice of the Peace for Shropshire, a member of the Council in the Marches and Puisne Justice of the Queen's Bench.

1584 – Death of William Bendlowes, member of Parliament, Serjeant-at-Law and law reporter. He was buried at Great Bardfield in Essex, where his monumental brass can still be seen today. Bendlowes reported on court cases from the period 1534-1579.

1587 – Death of Henry Vaux, poet, Catholic recusant and priest harbourer, of consumption at Great Ashby, the home of his sister, Eleanor Brooksby. Vaux was sent to Marshalsea prison after being arrested in November 1586 for offering accommodation and assistance to Catholic priests. He was released in May 1587 due to ill health.

1590 – Death of Thomas Godwin, physician and Bishop of Bath and Wells, at Wokingham in Berkshire, his birthplace. He had retired there due to ill health, and was buried in the local church. Elizabeth I chose Godwin as one of her Lent preachers, and he served in that post for eighteen years.

1604 – Death of Richard Edes, Dean of Worcester, royal chaplain and court preacher, at Worcester. He was buried in Worcester Cathedral. Edes was a royal chaplain to Elizabeth I and James I, and had just been appointed to work on a new version of the English Bible when he died.

20TH NOVEMBER

On this day in 1591, Sir Christopher Hatton, Elizabeth I's Lord Chancellor and favourite, died aged fifty-one.

Sir Christopher Hatton, the man Elizabeth I nicknamed her "mouton" (sheep), was born in 1540. He was the son of William Hatton of Holdenby, Northamptonshire, and his wife, Alice Saunders, and was educated at St Mary Hall, Oxford.

As one of Elizabeth I's favourites, he had an amazing career. Offices included Captain of the Queen's bodyguard (1572), Vice-Chamberlain of the Royal Household and member of the Privy Council (1578), Queen's Spokesman in the House of Commons (1578), Lord Chancellor (1587), Chancellor of the University of Oxford (1588) and High Steward, Salisbury (1590).

Between 1564 and 1587 he was such a favourite that he saw the Queen most days, and the longest he was ever away from court was one week. This led to Mary, Queen of Scots claiming that he was Elizabeth's secret lover. He was a member of the commission that found Mary guilty of treason in 1586, and was one of the councillors who urged William Davison, Elizabeth I's private secretary, to send Mary, Queen of Scots' death warrant to Fotheringhay.

Sir Christopher Hatton died on the 20th November 1591 at Ely Palace in London. He had been ill for some time and Elizabeth I had visited him on the 11th November. He was given a state funeral on 16th December at the old St Paul's Cathedral, and a monument was erected at the high altar. The old St Paul's Cathedral was destroyed in the *Great Fire of London* in 1666.

1515 – Birth of Mary of Guise (Marie de Guise), Queen of Scots, consort of James V, regent of Scotland and mother of Mary, Queen of Scots, at the castle of Bar-le-Duc in Lorraine. She was the eldest daughter of Claude of Lorraine, Duke of Guise, and Antoinette de Bourbon, daughter of Francis, Count of Vendome, and Marie de Luxembourg. Mary was Queen Consort of Scotland from 1538-1542, and regent from 1554 until her death in 1560.

1518 – Death of Sir Marmaduke Constable, soldier and administrator. He served in France with Edward IV and Henry VII, and although he fought on the side of Richard III at the *Battle of Bosworth*, he managed to gain Henry's trust. He commanded the left wing of the forces under Thomas Howard, Earl of Surrey, at the 1513 *Battle of Flodden*, and this service led to him receiving a letter of thanks from King Henry VIII.

1556 – Death of Sir John Godsalve, member of Parliament, landowner and administrator, at Norwich. He was buried in St Stephen's Church, Norwich, in the Lady Chapel. Godsalve's offices included Constable of Norwich Castle, Keeper of the Gaol there, commissioner for chantries in Norfolk and Suffolk, Justice of the Peace for Norfolk and Comptroller of the Tower of London Mint.

1558 – Death of Maurice Griffin, Bishop of Rochester, probably at the Bishop's Palace in Southwark. He was buried at the church of St Magnus the Martyr, London Bridge. Griffin was Welsh and he left provision in his will for the setting up of Friars School in Bangor, with the support of William Glyn, Bishop of Bangor, and Jeffrey Glyn.

1600 – Burial of Robert Wilson, actor and playwright, at St Giles Cripplegate in London. Wilson acted in the companies Leicester's Men and the Queen's Men, and is known for his plays which include "The Three Ladies of London" (1581), "The Three Lords and Three Ladies of London" (1590), "The Cobbler's Prophecy" (1594) and "The Pedlar's Prophecy" (1595). He was also one of Philip Henslowe's writers, writing plays for the Rose Theatre.

1612 – Death of Sir John Harington, courtier, author and inventor of the flush toilet. He was buried at the family estate of Kelston, near Bath.

21ST NOVEMBER

On this day in 1559, Frances Brandon, Duchess of Suffolk, died at Richmond. She was buried in St Edmund's Chapel, Westminster Abbey, on the orders of her cousin, Queen Elizabeth I, and her second husband, Adrian Stokes, erected a tomb in her memory.

Frances was born on the 16th July 1517, St Francis's Day, at Hatfield. She was the eldest daughter of Charles Brandon, Duke of Suffolk, and his third wife Mary Tudor, Queen of France, sister of Henry VIII. "Lady Boleyn and Lady Elizabeth Grey" acted as proxies for Catherine of Aragon and Princess

Mary at Frances's christening at Hatfield on the 18th July. Some believe the mystery "Lady Boleyn" to be Anne Boleyn's aunt, also named Anne Boleyn, and others believe it to be Elizabeth Boleyn, mother of the future Queen Anne Boleyn.

Frances married Henry Grey, Marquis of Dorset, at Suffolk House, Southwark, around May 1533. Her mother, Mary, died in June 1533, and Frances acted as chief mourner at her funeral. Just three months later, her father, Charles Brandon, married his ward, Katherine Willoughby de Eresby. Frances became the Duchess of Suffolk in 1551 when her husband was made Duke of Suffolk on 11th October following the deaths of Frances's half-brothers that summer.

Frances's first two children, a son and a daughter, died in infancy, but she had three surviving daughters with her first husband, Henry Grey: Lady Jane Grey, Lady Katherine Grey and Lady Mary Grey. Her daughter, Jane, became Thomas Seymour's ward and lived with him and his wife, Catherine Parr for a time. Frances has often been portrayed as an overly harsh mother after John Aylmer wrote of how Lady Jane Grey had complained of her parents' treatment of her and their correction of her with "pinches, nips and bobs", but there is no other evidence of this. Jane married the Duke of Northumberland's son, Guildford Dudley, in May 1553, and was proclaimed queen on 6th July 1553, after being named Edward VI's heir in his "Devise for the Succession". Jane, Frances and her husband, Guidford Dudley, his father and brothers, were imprisoned in the Tower of London following Mary I's overthrowing of Jane's short reign, but Frances and Suffolk were released on 31st July 1553.

Following Suffolk's involvement in *Wyatt's Rebellion*, his and Frances's daughter, Lady Jane Grey, was executed on the 12th February 1554, and Suffolk was executed on the 23rd February. Frances went on to marry the Master of her Horse, Adrian Stokes, and Mary I allowed them to reside at

Richmond. Frances gave birth to a daughter, Elizabeth, who died in infancy.

Frances was ill enough on 7th November 1559 to draw up her will. She was forty-two year-old at her death on 21st November 1559. The Latin transcription on the monument erected at Westminster Abbey by Adrian Stokes for his wife reads, when translated:

"Dirge for the most noble Lady Frances, onetime Duchess of Suffolk: naught avails glory or splendour, naught avail titles of kings; naught profits a magnificent abode, resplendent with wealth. All, all are passed away: the glory of virtue alone remained, impervious to the funeral pyres of Tartarus [part of Hades or the Underworld]. She was married first to the Duke, and after was wife to Mr Stock, Esq. Now, in death, may you fare well, united to God."

<hr />

1495 – Birth of John Bale, churchman, Protestant playwright, historian and Bishop of Ossory, at Cove, near Dunwich, in Suffolk. Bale wrote twenty-four plays, including "Three Laws of Nature, Moses and Christ, corrupted by the Sodomytes, Pharisees and Papystes most wicked", "A Tragedye; or enterlude manifesting the chief promyses of God unto Man", "The Temptacyon of our Lorde", "A brefe Comedy or Enterlude of Johan Baptystes preachynge in the Wyldernesse, etc" and " Kynge Johan". His most famous work is his *Illustrium majoris Britanniae scriptorum, hoc est, Angliae, Cambriae, ac Scotiae Summarium...* ("A Summary of the Famous Writers of Great Britain, that is, of England, Wales and Scotland"), which was his effort to record every work by a British author.

1558 – Death of James Bassett, courtier and stepson of Arthur Plantagenet, Viscount Lisle. Bassett was a member of Philip of Spain's Privy Chamber and private Secretary to Mary I. He was buried at Blackfriars, London.

1579 – Death of Sir Thomas Gresham, merchant and founder of the Royal Exchange and Gresham College, at Gresham House in Bishopsgate, London. He was buried at St Helen's Church, Bishopsgate.

1613 – Death of Rose Throckmorton (née Lok), businesswoman and Protestant exile, at the age of eighty-six. Rose was the daughter of Sir William Lok, mercer and Gentleman Usher of the Chamber to Henry VIII, and in her memoirs she claimed that her father had been responsible for supplying Queen Anne Boleyn with religious books from the Continent.

22ND NOVEMBER

On 22nd November 1545, Henry VIII's trusted physician, Sir William Butts, died at Fulham Manor, Middlesex, after suffering from a "dooble febre quartanz".

Sir William Butts acted as a Royal Physician at the court of Henry VIII from 1528 until his death. His patients included the King himself, queens Anne Boleyn and Jane Seymour, the Lady Mary (Mary I), Henry Fitzroy the Duke of Richmond, George Boleyn, Cardinal Wolsey and the Duke of Norfolk. He treated Anne Boleyn when she had sweating sickness in June 1528, and acted as her "talent spotter" when she was queen, helping her find and employ reformist scholars as her chaplains. He also helped advance men like Hugh Latimer and Sir John Cheke.

Henry VIII discussed his difficulties in consummating his marriage to Anne of Cleves with Butts and Dr John Chamber, explaining that "he found her body in such sort disordered and indisposed to excite and provoke any lust in him". The marriage was later annulled due partly to this lack of consummation.

Butts was buried in a tomb against the south wall of All Saints Church, Fulham, but his tomb and brass were later destroyed. In 1627, his epitaph (a slab with verses by Sir John Cheke) was restored by Leonard Butts of Norfolk.

∞∞∞∞∞∞∞∞∞∞∞∞∞∞∞∞∞∞∞∞∞∞∞∞∞∞∞∞∞∞∞

1538 – Burning of John Lambert, Protestant martyr, at Smithfield in London. He was accused of heresy for denying the real presence of Christ in the Eucharist. As he burned at the stake he cried out "None but Christ, none but Christ!"

1559 – Proving of the will of Sir Andrew Dudley, second son of Edmund Dudley and brother of John Dudley, Duke of Northumberland. Dudley served Edward VI as a Gentleman of the Privy Chamber, Joint Keeper of the Palace of Westminster, keeper of the king's jewels and robes, and captain of Guînes. In 1553, he was sentenced to death for helping to put Lady Jane Grey on the throne, but was released in April 1555. His date of death is not known.

1594 – Death of Sir Martin Frobisher, naval commander, privateer and explorer, at Plymouth from gangrene. He had been shot in the thigh during hand-to-hand combat during the Siege of Fort Crozon. His entrails were buried at St Andrews, Plymouth, and his body was taken to London and buried at St Giles Cripplegate. Frobisher is known for the three voyages he made to the New World in search of the Northwest Passage, and his service during the *Spanish Armada*, for which he was knighted. After the Armada, he became one of Elizabeth I's most trusted officers and commanders.

23RD NOVEMBER

On Wednesday 23rd November 1558, the new queen, Elizabeth I, left Hatfield and processed to London. The procession consisted of over a thousand people, and as it travelled through the counties of Hertfordshire and Middlesex, Elizabeth was cheered by crowds of people lining the streets.

Elizabeth was met at Barnet by the Sheriffs of London, who rode with her to the gates of the Charterhouse, a new house built by Lord North on the site of the old Carthusian monastery. Elizabeth was to stay at the Charterhouse until the following Monday, the 28th, the day on which she actually entered the City as Queen.

◇◇

1499 – The hanging of the pretender Perkin Warbeck at Tyburn. Warbeck had claimed to be one of the Princes in the Tower - Richard of Shrewsbury, Duke of York - and had challenged Henry VII's claim to the throne by raising a rebellion in Cornwall after he was declared Richard IV on Bodmin. The rebellion was squashed and Warbeck was captured and imprisoned.

1503 – Death of Margaret, Duchess of Burgundy (Margaret of York), daughter of Richard, 3rd Duke of York, and sister of Edward IV and Richard III. She died at Mechelen in the Low Countries. Margaret was buried in the house of the Recollects, or the Observant Franciscans.

1583 – Death of Richard Whalley, member of Parliament and administrator, at the age of eighty-four. He was buried at Screveton church in Nottinghamshire. Whalley served Edward Seymour, Protector Somerset, and so was imprisoned after Somerset's fall. He was released after Mary I's accession.

1585 – Death of Thomas Tallis, musician and composer at his home in Greenwich. He was buried in St Alfege's Church, Greenwich, in the chancel. Tallis is known as one of England's greatest early composers, and his works include *Gaude gloriosa Dei mater, Puer natus est nobis, Audivi vocem, In pace in idipsum, Videte miraculum, Loquebantur variis linguis* and *In ieiunio et fletu.*

1598 – Execution of Edward Squire, scrivener and sailor. He was hanged, drawn and quartered at Tyburn for treason after being accused of plotting in Seville to poison Elizabeth I and the Earl of Essex.

24TH NOVEMBER

On 24th November 1572, the Scottish clergyman, famous Reformer and founder of Presbyterianism, John Knox, died at his home in Edinburgh as his wife read aloud from Paul's First Letter to the Corinthians. He was buried in the cemetery of St Giles' Cathedral, Edinburgh, where he had served as minister. Knox is known for bringing the Protestant reformation to the church in Scotland.

It is not known when Knox became a Protestant, but he was good friends with George Wishart, who was burned at the stake for his Protestant faith in 1546, and was influenced by Heinrich Bullinger and John Calvin, whom he met while in exile in Geneva during Mary I's reign.

Knox's works include "A Faithful Admonition unto the Professors of God's Truth in England" (1555), which was an attack on the Catholic Mary I and her regime, and his famous "The First Blast of the Trumpet Against the Monstrous Regimen of Women" (1558), in which he attacked women rulers such as Mary I and Mary of Guise.

In early August 1560, Knox was involved in drawing up the Scots Confession, which was approved by Parliament who also abolished the jurisdiction of the Pope in Scotland, forbade the celebration of mass, condemned doctrine and practice which did not adhere to the reformed faith, and asked Knox and other Reformist ministers to organise the new Scottish Kirk (church). Knox and his fellow ministers drew up the "Book of Discipline", but Parliament delayed over ruling on it because Mary, Queen of Scots was due to come back to Scotland. Over the next three years, Knox was summoned into Mary's presence five times, accused of inciting rebellion and speaking against her. He was lucky to escape charges of treason.

After Lord Darnley's Protestant supporters murdered Mary's secretary, David Rizzio, in March 1566, Knox fled to Kyle in Ayrshire where he worked on his "History of the Reformation in Scotland". Darnley's subsequent murder and Mary's marriage to Bothwell, the chief suspect in Darnley's murder, led to divisions in the Protestant nobles as they tried to figure out what to do. Mary was eventually forced to abdicate and was imprisoned in Loch Leven Castle, while James Stewart acted as regent for Mary's infant son, James VI. On 29th July 1567, John Knox preached in Stirling at the coronation of James VI, and started preaching against Mary, even pushing for her execution. On 23rd January 1570, James Stewart was assassinated, and his successor, Matthew Stewart, 4th Earl of Lennox, was shot dead a year later. On 30th April 1571, all enemies of the Queen were ordered by the controller of Edinburgh to leave the city. However, Knox knew the controller, and so was offered the option of staying in Edinburgh as a captive in the castle. Knox refused this offer and left the city on the 5th May to travel to St Andrews. After the truce of July 1572, he was able to return to Edinburgh and he preached there, at St Giles, until his death.

1534 – Death of Sir Thomas Wriothesley, herald and father of the Tudor chronicler Charles Wriothesley. It is thought that he was buried at the family church, St Giles Cripplegate, in London.

1542 – The *Battle of Solway Moss* between England and Scotland. The battle took place on Solway Moss, a moss or peat bog in Cumbria near the Scottish border. The Scottish troops were led by Robert, Lord Maxwell, and the English troops by Sir Thomas Warton. The Scots were forced to surrender after they found themselves trapped between the River Ersk and the moss. Many drowned.

1550 – Burial of Sir James Wilford, soldier and commander at Haddington during the *War of the Rough Wooing*, at St Bartholomew by the Exchange. Bible translator Miles Coverdale preached at the service.

1559 – Death of Thomas Raynold, Dean of Exeter and nominee for the bishopric of Hereford. Mary I's death and the accession of Elizabeth I put a stop to him being consecrated as bishop, and he died in Marshalsea prison after refusing the "Oath of Supremacy". He was buried in St Margaret's Church, Westminster.

1587 – Death of Sir William Pelham, soldier and Lord Justice of Ireland, shortly after landing at Flushing in the Netherlands with reinforcements. He had been shot in the stomach in August 1586 at Doesburg while shielding Robert Dudley, Earl of Leicester and his commander in chief, and returned to England in April 1587 to take the waters at Bath. He felt well enough to return to the Netherlands in November 1587, but it was too much for him.

1598 – Death of William Paulet, 3rd Marquis of Winchester, nobleman and author, at Basing in Hampshire. He was buried there. Paulet was made a Knight of the Bath at Mary I's coronation in 1553, and his offices during the reigns of Mary I and Elizabeth included High Sheriff of Hampshire, Commissioner for Musters, Joint Lord Lieutenant of Hampshire, Lord Lieutenant of Dorset and a commissioner at the trial of Mary, Queen of Scots. He was also the author of the 1586 "The Lord Marques Idlenes", which was dedicated to Elizabeth I, and was described as "containing manifold matters of acceptable advice; as sage sentences, prudent precepts, morall examples, sweete similitudes, proper comparisons, and other remembrances of speciall choice".

25TH NOVEMBER

1467 – Birth of Thomas Dacre, 2nd Baron of Gilsland, magnate and soldier, in Cumberland. He was the son of Humphrey Dacre, 1st Baron Dacre, and Mabel (née Parr), great-aunt of Queen Catherine Parr. Dacre eloped with Elizabeth Greystoke, 6th Baroness Greystoke, around 1488, and the couple had seven children. Dacre served under Thomas Howard, Earl of Surrey, at the 1513 *Battle of Flodden.*

1545 – Death of Sir Thomas Legh, lawyer, member of Parliament, diplomat and ecclesiastical administrator. He was buried at St Leonard's Church, Shoreditch. Legh served Henry VIII as ambassador to Denmark. He interrogated Bishop John Fisher before his trial in 1535, was a Commissioner in the Visitations of the Monasteries in 1535-36, and examined prisoners involved in the 1536 *Pilgrimage of Grace* rebellion.

1605 – Death of George Withers, Church of England clergyman and Archdeacon of Colchester, at Danbury in Essex, where he was Rector. Withers was the author of the 1579 "Certaine godly instructions, verie necessarie to be learned of the younger sorte before they be admitted to be partakers of the holie communion" and the 1585 "An ABC for Laymen, otherwise called the Laymans Letters". He also compiled "A view of the marginal notes of the popish testament, translated into English by the English fugitive papists at Rhemes in France", which he dedicated to Archbishop John Whitgift.

1626 – Death of Edward Alleyn, Elizabethan actor, patron, theatre builder and founder of Dulwich College and Alleyn's School. He was buried in the chapel of Dulwich College.

26TH NOVEMBER

On the 26th November 1533, Henry Fitzroy, the Duke of Richmond and Somerset, married Lady Mary Howard at Hampton Court Palace.

Henry Fitzroy was the illegitimate son of Henry VIII by his mistress Elizabeth (Bessie Blount), and the King openly acknowledged that he was his father and was proud of the boy. He was enobled at the age of 6 in 1525. He was given the title Earl of Nottingham first, and then made the Duke of Richmond and Somerset. By giving him a double dukedom, Henry VIII was making his son the highest ranking peer in the country.

When Henry Fitzroy was aged six, Henry VIII considered marrying the boy off to his half-sister Mary in order to legitimize his claim to the throne. Henry was desperate at this time, because it was evident that Catherine was no longer fertile, and he had no male heir. The marriage never took place, and instead, Henry pinned his hopes on marrying Anne Boleyn and having a legitimate son by her. Ten months after his father's marriage to Anne Boleyn, the fourteen year-old Richmond married Lady Mary Howard, daughter of Thomas Howard, the 3rd Duke of Norfolk, and the cousin of Anne Boleyn. It may well have been Anne Boleyn who arranged this marriage.

Henry VIII ordered the couple not to consummate their union, because he believed that too much sexual activity at a young age may have killed off his brother, Arthur, and the couple were both fourteen. Unfortunately, Richmond died in July 1536, and it is thought that his and Mary's marriage was never consummated. Mary never remarried, but from 1548 she took responsibility for the upbringing of her brother's children, following his execution in 1547. Mary died in 1555 and was laid to rest beside her husband in St Michael's Church, Framlingham.

1542 (26th or 27th) – Death of Robert Radcliffe, 1st Earl of Sussex, courtier, soldier and Lord Great Chamberlain of England. He was buried at St Laurence Pountney Church in London, but then moved to Boreham in Essex. Radcliffe was made Lord Great Chamberlain of England for life on 3rd May 1540 for his loyal service to Henry VIII.

1546 – Baptism of Sir Giles Fletcher the Elder, diplomat, member of Parliament and author, in Watford, Hertfordshire. Fletcher was the son of Richard Fletcher, Church of England clergyman, and his wife, Joan. Fletcher is known for his poetical work, "Licia" (1593), but his other works included the Latin pastorals *Poemata varii argumenti*, the poem *De literis antiquae Britanniae* and the account of his travels as diplomat, "Of the Russe Common Wealth. Or, Maner of gouernement of the Russe emperour, (commonly called the Emperour of Moskouia) with the manners, and fashions of the people of that countrey". He was the father of the poet Sir Giles Fletcher the Younger.

1585 – Executions of Hugh Taylor, Catholic priest, and his friend Marmaduke Bowes at York. They were both hanged, and were the first men executed under the 1585 statute which made it treason to be a Jesuit or seminary priest in England, or to harbour such a priest. Both men were beatified in 1987.

1612 – Death of Sir Thomas Walmsley, judge and Justice of the Common Pleas, at his home at Dunkenhalgh in Lancashire. He was buried at Blackburn.

27TH NOVEMBER

On this day in 1582, the eighteen year-old William Shakespeare married the twenty-six year-old Anne (also known as Agnes) Hathaway, who was pregnant at the time of the ceremony at Temple Grafton near Stratford-upon-Avon in Warwickshire. Vicar John Frith officiated at the ceremony.

Controversy surrounds this marriage, because on that same day a marriage licence was issued for a marriage between "Wm Shaxpere et Annam Whateley[Anne Whateley] de Temple Grafton". Some have claimed that Shakespeare had intended to marry Anne Whateley but was forced to marry Anne Hathaway because of her pregnancy. Others have argued that Anne Hathaway and Anne Whateley were actually the same person, and that there was either a mix-up with the names or Anne had been widowed and that was her other name.

Anne Hathaway was the eldest child of Richard Hathaway, yeoman farmer of Hewland Farm, Shottery, who evidently knew

John Shakespeare, Shakespeare's father, because John had acted as surety for him and helped him pay his debts. Her pregnancy caused the hasty marriage, and on 28th November 1582 a bond was issued binding Fulke Sandells and John Richardson for the sum of £40 as surety for the marriage in case of lawful impediment, by pre-contract or consanguinity, to the marriage. This was because the ceremony was performed after only one reading of the banns and Shakespeare was a minor, being under the age of twenty-one. The couple lived with Shakespeare's father in Henley Street in Stratford-upon-Avon.

In May 1583, Anne gave birth to a daughter, Susannah, who was baptised on 26th May at Stratford-upon-Avon parish church. The couple went on to have twins, Hamnet and Judith, in February 1585.

◇◇

1531 (some say 4th December) – Burning of Richard Bayfield, Benedictine monk and reformist, at Smithfield for heresy. Sir Thomas More caught Bayfield importing Lutheran books into England, and he was tried by John Stokesley, Bishop of London, at St Paul's on 10th November 1531, and convicted.

1544 – Death of Sir Edward Baynton, soldier, courtier and Vice-Chamberlain to five of Henry VIII's wives, in France. His cause of death is unknown, but he may have been wounded while serving as a soldier in France. Baynton had arranged to be buried at Bromham, but it appears that he was buried in France.

1556 – Death of Henry Parker, 10th Baron Morley, nobleman, diplomat, translator and father of Jane Boleyn (wife of George Boleyn), at his home, Hallingbury Place, Great Hallingbury, Essex. He was in his late seventies at the time of his death. He was buried at St Giles's Church, Great Hallingbury. Morley grew up in the household of Lady Margaret Beaufort, mother of Henry VII, and although he was a prominent courtier, he is remembered more for his literary translations from Latin and Italian, which he gave to Henry VIII and Mary I as New

Year's gifts. His translations include Petrarch's "Trionfi", the "Life of Thesius" and the "Lyfe of Paulus Emelius".

1556 (27th or 28th) – Death of Sir Nicholas Poyntz, soldier, courtier and landowner. Poyntz was a reformer and was visited at his home at Iron Acton, in Gloucestershire, in 1535 by King Henry VIII and Anne Boleyn. He actually built a whole new wing to impress the royal couple.

1575 – Death of Sir Peter Carew, soldier, adventurer and conspirator, at Ross in County Waterford, Ireland. He was buried at Waterford Church, beside the altar. Carew had gone to Ireland in 1568 to lay claim to lands there, and this had put him at loggerheads with the powerful Butler family. Carew had been involved in plotting with the leaders of *Wyatt's Rebellion*, but had deserted and fled to France in disguise when Mary I's Privy Council got wind of the rebellion.

28TH NOVEMBER

1489 – Birth of Margaret Tudor, Queen of Scotland and consort of James IV, at Westminster Palace. Margaret was the eldest daughter of Henry VII and his wife, Elizabeth of York, and the sister of Henry VII. She spent her childhood at Sheen and at Eltham Palace, but was sent to Scotland at the age of thirteen to marry James IV.

1499 – Execution of Edward Plantagenet, styled Earl of Warwick, on Tower Hill. Edward was the son of George, Duke of Clarence, brother of Edward IV and Richard III, and so was a potential claimant to the throne. He was imprisoned in the Tower of London after Henry VII's accession, and was executed for treason after the pretender Perkin Warbeck had allegedly plotted to free himself and Edward. He was buried at Bisham Abbey.

1557 – Death of Sir Robert Rochester, administrator. He was buried at the Charterhouse at Sheen. Rochester served Mary

I as Comptroller of the Royal Household, Privy Councillor, Chancellor of the Duchy of Lancaster, Keeper of the Privy Seal and a member of Parliament.

1565 – Francis Yaxley, member of Parliament and political agent, set sail from Antwerp, and drowned when his ship foundered off the coast of Northumberland. Yaxley worked for Mary, Queen of Scots, was Secretary to her husband, Lord Darnley, and acted as Mary's envoy to the Spanish court. He was returning to Scotland from a mission to ask Philip of Spain to intercede with Elizabeth I to secure the release of Darnley's mother and to stop helping Mary's enemies, when he died. Although Philip declined to talk to Elizabeth on Mary's behalf, he did give Yaxley 20,000 crowns to give Mary. This gold, and Yaxley's body, were seized by the English when they washed up on Holy Island.

1584 – Sir Christopher Hatton, as government spokesman, spoke to Parliament on the dangers of Spain, in a speech lasting 'above two hours'.

1609 – Death of Sir Thomas Smith, Chief Secretary to Robert Devereux, 2nd Earl of Essex, at his home at Parson's Green in Fulham, London. He was buried at Fulham Church.

29TH NOVEMBER

At around 8am on the 29th November 1530, Cardinal Thomas Wolsey died at Leicester Abbey. He had left his home of Cawood Castle on the 6th November after the Earl of Northumberland, and William Walsh had taken him into custody on the 4th November for high treason.

Wolsey travelled from Cawood to Pontefract and Doncaster, and then to Sheffield Park, home of the Earl of Shrewsbury, on the 8th. Wolsey's journey was delayed due to the onset of dysentery, and he did not leave Sheffield until the 24th, two days after the arrival of Sir William Kingston, Constable of the Tower of London, who had been sent to escort Wolsey to the Tower.

On the 24th November, Wolsey was well enough to travel from Sheffield to Hardwick Hall, and then on to Nottingham on the 25th. However, by the 26th, he had obviously gone down hill again, and George Cavendish, his gentleman usher, records how on arrival at Leicester Abbey Wolsey said "Father abbott I ame come hether to leave my bones among you". Wolsey never left Leicester. On the morning of the 29th November 1530, after making his last confession, he said his famous words:-

"I se the matter ayenst me howe it is framed, But if I had served god as dylygently as I have don the kyng he wold not have geven me over in my grey heares". He then told Kingston to advise the King to act against the new Lutheran heresy before it took hold in England. Wolsey lapsed into unconsciousness, and the abbot performed the last rites. He died at around 8am, and his body was laid out in his pontifical robes for people to see before he was buried at the Abbey, where he still rests today.

Historian J.J. Scarisbrick writes of how Wolsey's death en route to the Tower of London had "cheated his master of the final reckoning" and that is very true. Wolsey cheated the axeman, the King and the men who had conspired against him and, instead, died a peaceful death in a house of God. He was denied the black marble sarcophagus he'd commissioned from Benedetto da Rovezzano. This was taken by the King but never actually used, and it is actually Lord Nelson who was laid to rest in that tomb in St Paul's Cathedral after his death in the *Battle of Trafalgar*, in 1805.

1528 – Birth of Anthony Browne, 1st Viscount Montagu, nobleman and courtier. Montagu was the eldest son of Sir Anthony Browne of Cowdray Park, Sussex, and his first wife, Alice, daughter of Sir John Gage. Montagu's offices in Mary I's reign included Master of the Horse to Philip of Spain, Lord Lieutenant of Sussex and Privy Councillor.

1593 – Execution of Richard Hesketh, merchant, at St Albans for treason. Hesketh had incited Ferdinando Stanley, the new 5ᵗʰ Earl of Derby, to lead a rebellion to claim the throne by right of his descent from Mary Tudor, sister of Henry VIII.

30TH NOVEMBER

On St Andrews Day 1529, Catherine of Aragon confronted her husband, Henry VIII, about his treatment of her.

Eustace Chapuys gave a full report of the meeting between Catherine and Henry in a letter to Charles V, writing that Catherine said "that she had long been suffering the pains of Purgatory on earth, and that she was very badly treated by his refusing to dine with and visit her in her apartments." The King replied that she had no right to complain, "for she was mistress in her own household, where she could do what she pleased" and explained that he had not dined with her because he had been busy with "affairs of government".

He then went on to address her complaint about not visiting her apartments, saying that "she ought to know that he was not her legitimate husband, as innumerable doctors and canonists, all men of honour and probity, and even his own almoner, Doctor Lee, who had once known her in Spain, were ready to maintain" and that "should not the Pope, in conformity with the above opinions so expressed, declare their marriage null and void, then in that case he (the King) would denounce the Pope as a heretic, and marry whom he pleased."

According to Chapuys:-

"The Queen replied that he himself, without the help of doctors, knew perfectly well that the principal cause alleged for the divorce did not really exist, "cart yl l'avoit trouvé pucelle," as he himself had owned upon more than one occasion. "As to your almoner's opinion in this matter," she continued, "I care not a straw; he is not my judge in the present case; it is for the Pope, not for him, to decide. Respecting those of other doctors, whether Parisian or from other universities, you know very well that the principal and best lawyers in England have written in my favour. Indeed, if you give me permission to procure counsel's opinion in this matter, I do not hesitate to say that for each doctor or lawyer who might decide in your favour and against me, I shall find 1,000 to declare that the marriage is good and indissoluble."

After further words on the matter, the King then "left the room suddenly" and Chapuys describes him as "very disconcerted and downcast". Unfortunately, worse was to come as the King was then reproached by Anne Boleyn, who said:-

"Did I not tell you that whenever you disputed with the Queen she was sure to have the upper hand? I see that some fine morning you will succumb to her reasoning, and that you will cast me off. I have been waiting long, and might in the meanwhile have contracted some advantageous marriage, out of which I might have had issue, which is the greatest consolation in this world; but alas! farewell to my time and youth spent to no purpose at all."

1554 – Both Houses of Parliament presented a petition to Mary I and her husband Philip to intercede with Cardinal Reginald Pole, the papal legate, for absolution for the years of separation from Rome and for reconciliation with Rome. Pole then absolved England and restored it to the Catholic fold, pronouncing "Our Lord Jesus Christ, which with his precious blood has redeemed us, and purified all our sins and pollutions, in order to make himself a glorious bride without stains and without wrinkle, whom the Father made chief over the church, he through his mercy absolves you."

1554 – Birth of Philip Sidney, the poet, courtier and soldier, at Penshurst Place in Kent. Sidney is known for his famous work "Astrophel and Stella".

1558 – Death of Elizabeth Howard (née Stafford), Duchess of Norfolk, eldest daughter of Edward Stafford, 3ʳᵈ Duke of Buckingham, and wife of Thomas Howard, 3ʳᵈ Duke of Norfolk. Her marriage to Norfolk broke down after he took Elizabeth (Bess) Holland as a mistress in 1527. She gave evidence against her husband when he was accused of treason in 1546, and she bore Mary I's train at her coronation in 1553. Elizabeth was buried in the Howard Chapel at St Mary's Church, Lambeth, now a garden museum.

1577 – Execution of Cuthbert Mayne, Roman Catholic priest, at Launceston in Cornwall after refusing to accept Elizabeth I as supreme head of the church in England. He was hanged, drawn and quartered, and his head was put on display on the gate of Launceston Castle and his quarters sent to Bodmin, Barnstaple, Tregony and Wadebridge as a warning to others.

1601 – Elizabeth delivered her famous *Golden Speech* to the House of Commons, to address their concerns over England's economic state of affairs. It was the last speech that she gave to Parliament, and in it she spoke of her position as Queen and her love and respect for her realm and for her members of Parliament.

1ST DECEMBER

Today marks the feast day of St Alexander Briant, the Roman Catholic priest, who was hanged, drawn and quartered on this day in 1581 at Tyburn.

Briant studied at Hart Hall and Balliol College, Oxford, where his tutors included Richard Holtby and Robert Persons, who later became Jesuits. Their influence led to him abandoning his studies and joining the seminary at Douai. On 29th March 1578, he was ordained as a priest and in August 1579, he was sent on a mission to England.

In March 1581, men with a warrant for Father Persons, Briant's former tutor and now his friend, arrested Briant at a London bookseller's. He was taken to the Tower of London and subjected to torture to try and get him to talk about Persons and the mission he had been sent on. In a confession made on 6th May 1581, Briant affirmed that Elizabeth I was the queen, but that he could not "affirm that she is so lawfully".

In November 1581, Briant, along with some other Roman Catholic priests, was arraigned for high treason and condemned to death for plotting against the queen. Briant was executed on 1st December 1581 along with Ralph Sherwin and Edmund Campion. All three men were canonised in 1970 by Pope Paul VI.

1530 – Death of Margaret of Austria at Mechelen. She was buried alongside her second husband, Philibert II, Duke of Savoy, in their mausoleum at Bourg-en-Bresse.

1539 – Execution of Thomas Marshall, Abbot of Colchester, at Colchester. Marshall was hanged, drawn and quartered for treason for his opposition to the dissolution of the monasteries, his refusal to accept Henry VIII as the Supreme Head of the Church in England and his belief that those carrying out the

King's wishes regarding religion and the monasteries were heretics.

1541 – Trial of Francis Dereham and Thomas Culpeper at Guildhall. They were both found guilty of treason and were condemned to death.

2ND DECEMBER

On 2nd December 1546, Henry Howard, Earl of Surrey, eldest son of Thomas Howard, 3rd Duke of Norfolk, and the renowned Tudor poet, was arrested after Richard Southwell gave evidence against him. He was charged with improper heraldry after using the arms of his ancestor Edward the Confessor, something which only the King was entitled to do. Surrey was held at Ely Place, then led on foot on the 12th December to the Tower, where he was joined by his father.

Antonia Fraser points out Surrey's real mistake was in having quarrelled with the Earl of Hertford, who took over Surrey's command in France. Surrey was jealous of Hertford and his achievements, so the improper use of the royal arms "could be construed by his rivals as a deliberate advancement of the superior Howard claims to the regency."

Surrey was executed on the 19th January 1547. His father was lucky because King Henry VIII died before he was due to be executed. Norfolk was kept in the Tower during Edward VI's reign, but released in 1553 when Mary I pardoned him.

1560 – Death of Charles de Marillac, French diplomat and Archbishop of Vienne, at Melun in France. Marillac was a resident ambassador at the court of Henry VIII from 1538 to 1543 and described Henry VIII as having three vices, which he described as "plagues": "the first is that he is so covetous that all the riches of the world would not satisfy him. Thence proceeds the second, distrust and fear. This King, knowing how many changes he has made, and what tragedies and scandals he has created, would fain keep in favour with everybody, but does not trust a single man, expecting to see them all offended, and he will not cease to dip his hand in blood as long as he doubts his people. The third vice lightness and inconstancy." Marillac was banished from the French court in 1560 after opposing the policies put forward by the Guises at the Assembly of Notables at Fontainebleau.

1586 – Parliament met on the 2nd December following their request for Elizabeth I to sanction the execution of Mary, Queen of Scots, and the commissioners' meeting in the Star Chamber where they condemned her to death. A draft proclamation of sentence, written by Elizabeth and William Cecil, Lord Burghley, was published at the Parliament, and this was followed by the drafting of an execution warrant by Sir Francis Walsingham.

1615 – Burial of Edward Wright, mathematician and cartographer, at St Dionis Backchurch, London. He died in late November 1615, while working on his book "A Description of the Admirable Table of Logarithmes". Wright is known for his work on the mathematics of navigation and his 1599 treatise "Certaine Errors of Navigation", which explained and developed the Mercator projection.

3RD DECEMBER

On this day in 1536, a proclamation was made to the rebels of the *Pilgrimage of Grace* offering them a pardon. It read:

"Proclamation of the King's pardon to the rebels of the different districts, viz.: That those of Yorkshire, with the city of York, Kingston upon Hull, Marshland, Holdenshire, Hexham, Beverley, Holderness, &c., on their submission to Charles duke of Suffolk, president of the council and lieutenant general in Lincolnshire, at Lincoln or elsewhere that he may appoint, shall have free pardons granted to them under the Great Seal without further bill or warrant or paying anything for the Great Seal. Richmond, 3 Dec., 28 Henry VIII."

The same proclamation was also made in "Northumberland, Cumberland, Westmoreland, York, city of York, bishopric of Durham, &c., and in the parts north of Lancaster, on their submission to Henry earl of Cumberland".

Henry VIII had also consented to the rebels' demand for a free Parliament to be held at York. The rebellion dispersed, but was followed by another rebellion, *Bigod's Rebellion*, in early 1537.

◇◇

1577 – Death or burial of William Downham, Bishop of Chester and former chaplain of Elizabeth I before her accession. He was buried in the choir of Chester Cathedral.

1600 – Death of Roger North, 2nd Baron North, peer and politician in Elizabeth I's reign, at his London home in Charterhouse Square. He was given a funeral service at St Paul's, followed by a burial at Kirtling in Cambridgeshire. North was a friend of Robert Dudley, Earl of Leicester, and served Elizabeth I as Privy Councillor and Treasurer of the Household.

4TH DECEMBER

On this day in history, 4th December 1555, the Papal sentence was passed on Thomas Cranmer in Rome, depriving him of his archbishopric "and of all ecclesiastical dignities". Permission was also given for the secular authorities to decide on his fate. Although Cranmer recanted his Protestant faith five times, which should have resulted in absolution, his execution date was set for the 21st March 1556. He was ordered to make a final public recantation before his execution but, instead, he renounced his previous recantations and spoke of the Pope as "Christ's enemy and antichrist". He was burned at the stake, a martyr to his faith.

∽∽∽∽∽∽∽∽∽∽∽∽∽∽∽∽∽∽∽∽∽∽∽∽∽∽∽∽∽∽∽

1506 – Birth of Thomas Darcy, 1ˢᵗ Baron Darcy of Chiche, courtier and administrator. He was the son of Roger Darcy, Esquire of the Body to Henry VII, and his wife, Elizabeth (née Wentworth). Darcy served as a Privy Councillor in Edward VI's reign, and also Captain of the Yeoman of the Guard and Lord Chamberlain of the Household. He was arrested for supporting the Duke of Northumberland's bid to place Lady Jane Grey on the throne, but was pardoned in November 1553.

1514 – Death of Richard Hunne, merchant tailor and leading member of the Lollard community in London. He had been arrested for heresy, and imprisoned in "Lollards' Tower" in St Paul's Cathedral on 14ᵗʰ October after the discovery of a Wycliffite Bible at his home, and his body was discovered hanging in his cell from a silk girdle. It was claimed that he had committed suicide, but a coroner's jury ruled that the hanging had been faked, and that he had been murdered.

1531 – Execution of Rhys ap Gruffudd for treason. He was beheaded after being accused of plotting against the King, although his biographer, R.A. Griffiths, points out that his trial was a "show trial" consisting of contrived testimonies and coached witnesses.

1557 – Death of Robert King, Abbot of Thame and Bishop of Oxford. He was buried in Oxford Cathedral. King was one of the judges who sat in judgement at the trial of Thomas Cranmer in 1555.

1585 – Death of John Willock, physician and Scottish reformer, at Loughborough in Leicestershire. He was buried at his church, All Saints, in Loughborough. Willock became the Chaplain of Henry Grey, Marquis of Dorset, and father of Lady Jane Grey, in the 1540s.

1595 – Death of William Whitaker, theologian and Master of St John's College, Cambridge, at the master's lodge after going to bed with a hot "ague". He was buried at St John's. His works included *Liber precum publicarum* (1569), *Ad rationes decem Edmundi Campiani jesuitæ responsio* (1581), responses to Nicholas Sander and Edmund Campion, *Disputatio ad sacra scriptura* and *Adversus Thomae Stapletoni* (1594).

1609 – Death of Alexander Hume, Scottish poet and writer. He is known for his 1599 "Hymnes, or Sacred Songs", which includes his great poem "Of the Day Estivall" which describes a summer's day, from dawn until dusk.

5TH DECEMBER

1556 – Birth of Anne de Vere (née Cecil), Countess of Oxford, daughter of William Cecil, 1st Baron Burghley, and his second wife, Mildred (née Cooke), and wife of Edward de Vere, 17th Earl of Oxford. The marriage was not the happiest of matches, with de Vere refusing to acknowledge their daughter Elizabeth as his. The couple were eventually reconciled.

1558 – Death of Gabriel Dunne (Donne), Abbot of Buckfast and 'keeper of the spiritualities', in the diocese of London. He was buried at St Paul's, before the high altar.

1560 – Death of King Francis II of France and King Consort of Scotland as husband of Mary, Queen of Scots. Francis was aged just fifteen when he died from some type of ear infection. He was succeeded as King of France by his brother, Charles, who became Charles IX. Francis was buried at the Cathedral Basilica of Saint-Denis on 23rd December.

1562 – Death of Sir Humphrey Browne, judge. He was buried at St Martin Orgar. London. Browne had served Henry VIII as a Sergeant-at-Law, but lost the office when he was imprisoned for hunting in Waltham Forest and for, allegedly, advising criminals on how to avoid having their possessions forfeited.

1593 – Death of Sir Rowland Hayward (Heyward), merchant adventurer, President of St Bartholomew's Hospital and member of Parliament, in London. He was buried at St Alfege, London Wall.

6TH DECEMBER

On the 6th December (the feast of St Nicholas), Tudor people would often celebrate the Boy Bishop, a tradition which had been going on since the 10th century. This tradition would usually consist of a boy from the choir being chosen on St Nicholas's Day to lead the community, and do everything apart from leading the mass from Vespers on the 27th December until the 28th December (Holy Innocents' Day). Historian Alison Sim writes of how Boy Bishops would lead processions around their communities, collecting money for the church and parish funds, and that the Boy Bishop of St Paul's Cathedral would lead a procession through the city of London to bless the city.

In an article on the topic, Salisbury Cathedral explain how the tradition was a reminder of Christ "calling to him a child, put him in the midst of the disciples" and was a lesson about humility and belonging to God's Kingdom.

The tradition of the Boy Bishop went on until 1541, when King Henry VIII banned it, perhaps because he felt that it was mocking Church authorities and himself as head of the Church. Although the tradition made a brief return in Mary I's Catholic reign, it disappeared again in Elizabeth I's reign.

The Cathedrals of Hereford and Salisbury actually still continue the tradition of Boy Bishop today.

1549 – Death of John Wakeman (born Wiche), Abbot of Tewkesbury and Bishop of Gloucester, in Forthampton, Gloucestershire. He took the name Wakeman when he surrendered his monastery to the commissioners in 1540.

1555 – Death of Thomas Cottisford, clergyman, translator and reformer, at Frankfurt while in exile in Mary I's reign. In Edward VI's reign, Cottisford published a translation of Zwingli's confession of faith.

1573 – Death of Sir Hugh Paulet, soldier and administrator, at Hinton St George in Somerset. He was buried in the parish church there. Paulet was one of Henry VIII's executors and served Edward VI as Captain of Jersey and Governor of Mont Orgueil Castle. In Mary I's reign, he was made Vice-President of the Welsh Marches, and in Elizabeth I's reign he served as a special adviser to Ambrose Dudley, Earl of Warwick, at Le Havre.

7TH DECEMBER

Traditional date given for the birth of Henry Stewart (Stuart), Duke of Albany and Lord Darnley, in 1545. Darnley was the son of Matthew Stewart, 13th or 4th Earl of Lennox, and Lady Margaret Douglas, and the grandson of Margaret Tudor and her second husband Archibald Douglas, 6th Earl of Angus. He was born at Temple Newsam, Yorkshire, not long after the death of his older brother, also called Henry. Darnley is known for being the second husband of Mary, Queen of Scots and for being murdered on 10th February1567.

Here is some trivia about Darnley:

- He had claims to both the Scottish and English thrones, being descended from James II of Scotland and Henry VII of England.

- His grandmother, Margaret Tudor, was Henry VII's eldest daughter.

- His father was declared a traitor after he had taken part in the *War of the Rough Wooing* between England and Scotland.

- Darnley suffered with an attack of measles in April 1565.

- He was created Knight of Tarbolton, Lord Ardmannoch, and Earl of Ross in May 1565, and swore his allegiance to Mary, Queen of Scots.

- On the 22nd July 1565, he was made Duke of Albany in anticipation of his marriage to Mary.

- Darnley married Mary, Queen of Scots on 29th July 1565, and was proclaimed "King Henry" the following day, although Mary refused to grant him the crown matrimonial.

- It was not a happy marriage, and the couple were estranged by Christmas 1565, even though Mary was pregnant by then.

- Mary's private secretary David Rizzio (Riccio) was stabbed to death by a gang of assassins, who Darnley let into the Palace of Holyroodhouse.

- His son, the future James VI and I, was born on 19th June 1566.

1549 – Hanging of Robert Kett, leader of *Kett's Rebellion* in Norfolk. Kett was hanged from the walls of Norwich Castle after being found guilty of treason by a commission of oyer and terminer. He had been captured the day after the *Battle of Dussindale*, which ended the rebellion. His brother, William, was also hanged on the same day, but at Wymondham Abbey.

1573 – Death of John Thorne, Master of the Choristers and Organist of York Minster, composer and poet, in York. He was buried in York Minster.

1613 – Death of Thomas Hesketh, botanist and physician, at Clitheroe Castle. John Gerard used Hesketh as a source for his "Herball" and was known for supplying gardens and nurseries with seeds and plants, including wild flowers.

1626 – Death of Sir John Davies, lawyer, politician, Attorney-General for Ireland and poet. Davies was found dead on the morning of the 8ᵗʰ December, the day that he was going to be installed as Chief Justice of the King's Bench. He was buried at St Martin-in-the-Fields, Westminster, and John Donne preached at his funeral service. Davies sat in the House of Commons in the reigns of Elizabeth I and James I, and was a favourite of Elizabeth I. His work included the 1599 "Hymns of Astraea", which he addressed to the queen, and "Orchestra" (1595).

8TH DECEMBER

On 8ᵗʰ December 1542, Mary Stewart (Stuart), or Mary, Queen of Scots, was born at Linlithgow Palace in Scotland.

Mary, Queen of Scots was the daughter of James V of Scotland and his second wife, Mary of Guise, and the granddaughter of Margaret Tudor (Henry VIII's sister) and James IV of Scotland. On the 14ᵗʰ December, when she was just six days old, Mary became Queen of Scotland after her father died of a fever. She was crowned Queen on 9ᵗʰ September 1543 at Stirling Castle. As Mary was a baby, James Hamilton, 2ⁿᵈ Earl of Arran, acted as regent until 1554 when he surrendered the regency to Mary's mother, Mary of Guise, who acted as regent until her death in 1560.

At the age of five, Mary was sent to France after the marriage between her and François, the French Dauphin, had been agreed in a treaty in 1548. As the future queen consort of France, she received an excellent education and showed herself to be an excellent linguist. She married Francis (François) on the 24th April 1558 at Notre Dame Cathedral in Paris. She was 15 and her husband was 14. Henry II of France died in July 1559, and Mary's husband became Francis II of France. The couple already believed that they were King and Queen of England, Henry II having proclaimed them so after Mary I's death in 1558. Although Elizabeth I was Queen of England, having been named as next in the succession after Mary I in her father's will, many Catholics did not accept Elizabeth as Queen, because they believed her to be illegitimate, and believed that Mary Stuart was the true queen.

Francis II died on 5th December 1560, and Mary returned in August 1561 to her homeland of Scotland, a country divided by religious conflict. Although she was a staunch Catholic, she tolerated Protestants and had many Protestants on her Privy Council.

On the 29th July 1565, Mary married her second husband, Henry Stuart, Lord Darnley, at Holyrood Palace. The marriage broke down when Darnley was involved in the murder of Mary's secretary, David Rizzio, who was actually murdered in front of a pregnant Mary. The couple's son, James, the future James VI (James I), was born on 19th June 1566, and was just eight months old when his father, Darnley, was killed in an explosion at Kirk o' Field in February 1567. Mary went on to marry James Hepburn, 4th Earl of Bothwell, a man implicated in Darnley's murder, after allegedly being abducted and raped by him in April 1567. The couple married at Holyrood on the 15th May 1567. The Scottish nobility did not approve of the match, and raised an army against Bothwell and Mary. Mary was imprisoned in Loch Leven Castle where, in July 1567, she miscarried twins. On the 24th July 1567 she was forced to abdicate, and her son became James VI of Scotland with

Mary's illegitimate half brother, James Stewart, Earl of Moray, acting as Regent.

Mary managed to escape from Loch Leven on the 2nd May 1568, and fled to England where she was placed in protective custody in Carlisle Castle under the orders of Elizabeth I. She was to spend the rest of her life as a prisoner, being moved from Carlisle to Bolton Castle in July 1568, from Bolton to Tutbury Castle in January 1569, from Tutbury to Wingfield Manor, Chatsworth and Sheffield Castle and then back to Tutbury, from Tutbury to Chartley in December 1585, and finally to Fotheringhay Castle in 1586.

On her arrival in England in 1568, Mary had expected Elizabeth to support her in her endeavour to win back the throne of Scotland, but Elizabeth was unwilling to help a woman who was implicated in the murder of her second husband, Lord Darnley, and who refused to ratify the *Treaty of Edinburgh*. Mary was a threat to Elizabeth, as was shown by the *Ridolfi Plot* of 1570, a plot to assassinate Elizabeth and replace her with Mary. Mary denied any involvement in the plot, but was implicated in the *Babington Plot* of 1586 after Sir Francis Walsingham intercepted letters in which Mary gave her support for an attempt on Elizabeth I's life. Mary was tried for treason in October 1586 and found guilty. Parliament and Elizabeth's Privy Council put pressure on Elizabeth to execute Mary, but Elizabeth was unwilling to sign the death warrant of a fellow sovereign, who she believed to be appointed by God, and also a woman with Tudor blood. Elizabeth finally signed Mary's death warrant on the 1st February 1587 and it was delivered, without the Queen's knowledge to Fotheringhay, where the sentence was carried out on the 8th February 1587.

1538 – Death of Sir William Coffin, courtier and Master of the Horse to Queens Anne Boleyn and Jane Seymour, at Standon in Hertfordshire. It is thought that he died of the plague because his wife, Margaret, wrote to Cromwell saying that Coffin had "died of the great sickness, full of God's marks all over his body". He was buried at the parish church in Standon.

1558 – Death of Hugh Weston, Dean of Windsor, at William Wynter's house in Fleet Street, London. He was buried at the Savoy. Weston had just been released from imprisonment in the Tower of London due to his ill health. He had been deprived of his deanery for alleged indecency in August 1557, and was arrested at Gravesend while he was on his way to Rome to appeal against his deprivation.

9TH DECEMBER

On 9th December 1538, Sir Edward Neville, courtier, Gentleman of the Privy Chamber and son of George Neville, 2nd Baron Bergavenny, was beheaded on Tower Hill.

Neville had been arrested for treason along with his brother-in-law, Henry Pole, 1st Baron Montagu, Henry Courtenay, Marquis of Exeter, and Courtenay's wife and son in November 1538. They were all accused of plotting with Cardinal Reginald Pole and, according to his indictment, Neville was accused of openly saying "The King is a beast and worse than a beast...I trust knaves shall be put down and lords reign one day, and that the world will amend one day." He protested his innocence, but was attainted of high treason and condemned to death.

Neville was buried at the Tower's Chapel Royal, St Peter ad Vincula.

1522 – Death of Hugh Ashton, Archdeacon of York and former Comptroller of Lady Margaret Beaufort's household. He died at York was was buried at York Minster. Ashton helped Lady Margaret with the arrangements involved in founding Christ's

College and St John's at Cambridge and, as an executor of her will, supervised the building of St John's.

1541 – Agnes Tilney, the Dowager Duchess of Norfolk and step-grandmother of Catherine Howard, who had been detained at the Lord Chancellor's home after Catherine's fall, was questioned regarding the location of her money and jewels.

1591 – Death of Robert Balthrop, Sergeant-Surgeon to Elizabeth I. Balthrop was buried at St Bartholomew-the-Less Church, in the grounds of St Bartholomew's Hospital.

10TH DECEMBER

On 10th December 1541, Thomas Culpeper, Gentleman of the Privy Chamber, and Francis Dereham, secretary to Queen Catherine Howard, were executed at Tyburn.

In his Chronicle, Charles Wriothesley writes:-

"Culpeper and Dereham were drawn from the Tower of London to Tyburn, and there Culpeper, after an exhortation made to the people to pray for him, he standing on the ground by the gallows, kneeled down and had his head stricken off; and then Dereham was hanged, membered, bowelled, headed, and quartered [and both] their heads set on London Bridge."

Dereham had been arrested after Archbishop Thomas Cranmer was made aware of Catherine Howard's premarital sexual behaviour with her music tutor, Henry Manox, and Dereham. Under interrogation, Catherine had confessed to a past sexual relationship with Dereham, and he confessed that he "had known her carnally many times, both in his doublet and hose between the sheets and in naked bed". Catherine also said that she and Dereham had referred to each other as husband and wife, although she denied that they were in any way pre-contracted. Both Dereham and Catherine affirmed that the relationship had taken place long before she was married to the King.

It was Dereham who first mentioned Thomas Culpeper. During an interrogation, he stated "that Culpeper had succeeded him in the Queen's affections" and when Catherine was questioned about Culpeper she admitted to secret assignations on the back stairs, to calling him her "little sweet fool" and giving him a cap and a ring; however, she denied a sexual relationship. It was Culpeper who sealed his fate by admitting that "he intended and meant to do ill with the Queen and that in like wise the Queen so minded to do with him".

Culpeper and Dereham were tried on 1st December 1541 at the Guildhall, and convicted of treason. Both were executed on 10th December 1541, but Culpeper was beheaded while Dereham had to face the brutal traitor's death of being hanged, drawn and quartered. Culpeper was buried at St Sepulchre Holborn.

1472 - Birth of Anne of Mowbray, Duchess of York and Norfolk, child bride of Richard of Shrewsbury, 1st Duke of York and one of the Princes in the Tower.

1591 – Executions of Edmund Gennings, Roman Catholic priest, and Swithin Wells, Roman Catholic, on a scaffold set up outside Wells' house at Holborn. They were hanged, drawn and quartered for treason due to their Catholic faith and for celebrating the mass.

11TH DECEMBER

1577 – Burial of Benjamin Gonson, Treasurer of the Navy and son of William Gonson, Vice-Admiral of Norfolk and Suffolk from 1536 until 1543. Gonson was buried at St Dunstan's Church.

1589 – Death of Patrick Lindsay, 6th Lord Lindsay of the Byres, at Struthers Castle in Fife, Scotland. Lindsay was a supporter of the Protestant Reformation, and one of the lords of the congregation. He was one of Mary, Queen of Scots' guardians when she was imprisoned at Lochleven and was a Privy Councillor after she was deposed as queen.

1607 – Death of Roger Manners, member of Parliament and Constable of Nottingham Castle. He was buried at Uffington Church in Rutland.

1608 – Burial of Douglas Sheffield (née Howard), Lady Sheffield, at St Margaret's Church, Westminster. Douglas was the eldest daughter of William Howard, 1st Baron Howard of Effingham, and the wife of John Sheffield, 2nd Baron Sheffield. Before her marriage, she served as a Maid of Honour to Elizabeth I. After her husband's death, she had an affair with Robert Dudley, 1st Earl of Leicester, which resulted in the birth of a son, Sir Robert Dudley, the explorer and cartographer, born in 1574. Douglas claimed that she and Dudley had married in secret when she was pregnant in late 1573, but she could not provide any evidence to support this when her son sought to claim his father's and uncle's titles after Elizabeth I's death. Douglas went on to marry Sir Edward Stafford in 1579.

12TH DECEMBER

On 12th December 1546, Henry Howard, Earl of Surrey was led through the streets of London from Ely Place, where he had been held since the 2nd December, to the Tower of London. There, he was joined by his father, Thomas Howard, 3rd Duke of Norfolk, who was taken to the Tower by barge along the Thames. In desperation, Norfolk wrote to the King the next day, proclaiming his innocence, confirming his loyalty and offering the King his lands:-

"Begs for grace. Some great enemy has informed the King untruly; for God knows, he never thought one untrue thought against the King or his succession, and can no more guess the charge against him than the child born this night. Desires that his accusers and he may appear before the King, or else the Council. Knows not that lie has offended any man, or that any are offended with him, "unless it were such as are angry with me for being quick against such as have been accused for Sacramentaries." As for religion I have told your Majesty and many others that knowing your virtue and knowledge I shall stick to whatsoever laws you make; and for this cause divers have borne me ill will, "as doth appear by casting libels abroad against me." Begs that he may recover the King's favour, the King taking all his lands and goods; and that he may know what is laid to his charge and have some word of comfort from his Majesty."

Unfortunately for Howard, the King ignored him.

◇◇

1574 – Birth of Anne of Denmark, Queen of England, Scotland, and Ireland as consort of James I, at Skanderborg Castle, Jutland, Denmark. Anne was the second daughter of Frederick II, King of Denmark and Norway, and his wife, Sophia. She married James I, when he was James VI of Scotland, by proxy on 20th August 1589, and in a proper church ceremony on 23rd November 1589. The couple's children included the future Charles I and Elizabeth Stuart, Queen of Bohemia. Anne died on 2nd March 1619 of consumption and dropsy, and was buried in Henry VII's Chapel, Westminster Abbey.

1595 – Death of Sir Roger Williams, Protestant Welsh soldier and author, from a fever with his patron, Robert Devereux, Earl of Essex, at his side. He was buried at St Paul's Cathedral.

William served as a soldier in the Low Countries and France, and was second in command to Essex of the cavalry gathered at Tilbury in 1588. He wrote the 1590 "A Briefe Discourse of Warre".

13TH DECEMBER

On 13th December 1577, Sir Francis Drake finally left Plymouth with his fleet of five ships on a journey which would see him circumnavigating the Globe. Storm damage to two of his ships had scuppered earlier plans.

The purpose of this journey was to sail into the Pacific and raid the Spanish colonies there. It was a secret mission authorised by Queen Elizabeth I and investors of Drake's mission included the Queen, Sir Francis Walsingham, William and George Wynter, Christopher Hatton and John Hawkins.

Only one ship, the *Pelican*, made it safely to the Pacific, arriving there in October 1578. As a tribute to its success it was renamed the *Golden Hind*, after Sir Christopher Hatton's coat of arms. Drake sailed along South America's Pacific coast, plundering towns and Spanish ports, and capturing Spanish ships laden with gold, silver and jewels. In June 1579, Drake landed just north of Point Loma (present day San Diego, California), which was Spain's northernmost holding in the Americas. He claimed it for England in the name of the Holy Trinity and called it Nova Albion, "New Britain". He then turned south and made his way back home, arriving in England in September 1580. He was the first Englishman to circumnavigate the Globe.

1558 – Death of William Clyffe, civil lawyer and one of the authors of the 1537 "Bishops' Book" or "The Godly and Pious Institution of a Christian Man". Clyffe's expertise on marriage and divorce law led to convocation seeking his advice regarding Henry VIII's Great Matter.

1561 – Death of Lawrence Dalton, Richmond Herald, Rouge Croix Pursuivant and Norroy King of Arms. He was buried at St Dunstan-in-the-West, London.

14TH DECEMBER

On this day in 1542, James V died at Falkland Palace in Falkland, Fife, Scotland, after being taken ill following the Scots' defeat at the *Battle of Solway Moss* on 24th November. It is not known what killed him – some argue that it was a nervous collapse, and others that it was a virus.

While James was on his deathbed, his consort, Mary of Guise, gave birth to a daughter, and it was the six day-old baby who became Mary, Queen of Scots on her father's death. John Knox and the chronicler Robert Lindsay of Pitscottie both recorded that James uttered the words "it came wi a lass, it'll gang wi a lass" ("it came with a lass, it will end with a lass") as he lay dying, referring to how the Stuart dynasty began with a girl, through Marjorie Bruce, Robert the Bruce's daughter, and how he feared it would now end with his daughter, Mary. However, the Stuart dynasty actually ended with another girl, Queen Anne, in 1714, and it is not known that James actually ever said these words.

James was buried at Holyrood Abbey on 8th January 1543.

1558 – Burial of Queen Mary I at Westminster Abbey in the Henry VII chapel with only stones marking her grave. In 1606, forty-eight years after her death, the stones were cleared, Elizabeth I's coffin was added to the vault, and James I commissioned a monument to Elizabeth I.

1562 – Death of William Grey, 13th Baron Grey of Wilton and military commander, during the night of 14th/15th December at the home of his son-in-law, Henry Denny, at Cheshunt in Hertfordshire. Grey served as a commander in the expedition to France in 1544, as Field-Marshal and Captain-General of Horse in Scotland in 1547, as a soldier in France in 1557, and as Warden of the Eastern and Middle Marches in 1559.

1563 – Baptism of Thomas Belson, Roman Catholic martyr, at Aston Rowant Church in Oxfordshire. He was hanged on 5th July 1589 for assisting the Catholic priests, George Nichols and Richard Yaxley, who were hanged, drawn and quartered on that day.

1563 – Burial of William Dacre, 3rd Baron Dacre of Gilsland and 7th Baron Greystoke, at Carlisle Cathedral.

1585 – Burial of Thomas Bentley, editor of "The Monument of Matrones: Conteining Seven Severall Lamps of Virginitie, or Distinct Treatises; Whereof the First Five Concerne Praier and Meditation: the Other Two Last, Precepts and Examples" (1582), a collection of prayers and meditations for and by women. It is said to be the first published anthology of English women's writing. Bentley was buried at St Andrew's, Holborn.

1592 – Death of Sir Roger Manwood, judge, member of Parliament and Elizabeth I's Lord Chief Baron of the Exchequer, in St Stephen's Parish, Hackington, near Canterbury.

1593 – Death of Henry Radcliffe, 4th Earl of Sussex, soldier, member of the Irish Privy Council, member of Parliament and patron of the Earl of Sussex's men. He was buried at Borham in Essex.

1595 – Death of Henry Hastings, 3rd Earl of Huntingdon, administrator, diplomat, and military commander, at York. He was buried at St Helen's Church, Ashby-de-la-Zouch. Huntingdon was educated with the young Edward VI, and served in the household of Cardinal Reginald Pole, his great-uncle. He served Elizabeth I as President of the Council of the

North, and was one of the peers at the trial of Mary, Queen of Scots in 1586.

1624 – Death of Charles Howard, 2nd Baron Howard of Effingham and 1st Earl of Nottingham, at Haling in Surrey. He was buried at Reigate Church in the family vault. Nottingham served Elizabeth I and James I as Lord High Admiral, and commanded the English forces against the *Spanish Armada* in 1588.

15TH DECEMBER

1558 – Death of James Fleming, 4th Lord Fleming and Lord Chamberlain of Scotland, at Paris. He had been in France as a commissioner representing Scotland at the wedding of Mary, Queen of Scots, and Francis, the Dauphin, and was taken ill with other commissioners after they had told the French that they had no authority to grant Francis the crown matrimonial. Fleming and three other commissioners died, and it was suspected that they had been poisoned.

1558 – Funeral of Reginald Pole, Cardinal Pole and Mary I's Archbishop of Canterbury, at Canterbury Cathedral.

1560 – Death of Thomas Parry, Comptroller of the Household to Elizabeth I and Lord Lieutenant of Berkshire. He was buried at Westminster Abbey.

1605 – Death of Sir Francis Gawdy, judge and Chief Justice of the Common Pleas, of apoplexy at Sergeant's Inn. He had only been Chief Justice for four months. As Queen's Sergeant in 1586, Gawdy had opened the trial against Mary, Queen of Scots. He was buried at Rungton, near Wallington in Norfolk.

16TH DECEMBER

During the night of 15ᵗʰ/16ᵗʰ December 1485, Catherine of Aragon was born at the recently reformed fortified palace at Alcalá de Henares, a town just east of Madrid. Pregnancy had not stopped Catherine's mother, Isabella I of Castile, from waging war on the Moors, and she had spent the summer of 1485 moving around Andalucia, following her troops' campaign. Isabella and her troops finished warring for the year in September, and the Royal Court travelled from Andalucia to Alcalá for the winter, and for the impending birth.

Catherine of Aragon, Catalina de Aragón, was the last of Ferdinand II of Aragon and Isabella I's children, and was named after her maternal great-grandmother, Catalina of Castile or Catherine of Lancaster. Giles Tremlett, in his biography of Catherine, writes of how we know various details about Catherine's childhood because it was recorded by Gonzalo de Baeza, Isabella's treasurer. For example, we know that she was baptised by the Bishop of Palencia and wore a a white brocade gown which was trimmed with gold lace and lined with green velvet, and that Dutch olanda linen was used to make her sheets, pillowcases, nightshirts and bibs. We also know that scarlet Florentine cloth was ordered to make clothes, fresh cotton was used to stuff her crib mattress, a brass basin was used for washing her, and that she owned a perfume sprinkler - interesting little insights into the life of a newborn Spanish princess.

When Catherine was just three years old, it was agreed that she should be betrothed to the heir to the English throne, Prince Arthur. The English ambassadors, Richard Nanfan and Thomas Savage, visited Medina del Campo, in Spain, in March 1489 to meet Ferdinand and Isabella, and to discuss the matter. They saw little Catherine and were obviously happy with what they saw as the *Treaty of Medina del Campo*, a marriage alliance between England and Spain, was agreed and signed. Catherine was destined to be Queen of England, but not with Arthur at her side – he was to die just a few months after their marriage – but with King Henry VIII, a man known for his six wives and his tyranny.

◇◇◇◇◇◇◇◇◇◇◇◇◇◇◇◇◇◇◇◇◇◇◇◇◇◇◇◇◇◇◇◇◇◇◇◇◇◇

1503 (16th or 18th) – Death of George Grey, 2nd Earl of Kent, at Ampthill, Bedfordshire. He was buried at Warden Abbey, Bedfordshire, where his first wife, Anne Woodville (sister of Elizabeth Woodville), had been laid to rest in 1489. Grey's second wife, Catherine Herbert, daughter of William Herbert, 1st Earl of Pembroke, was also buried there after her death in 1504. Grey was on Henry VII's council, was Constable of Northampton Castle and was a judge at the trial of Edward, Earl of Warwick in 1499.

1558 – Death of Sir Thomas Cheyne (Cheney), diplomat, administrator and Lord Warden of the Cinque Ports, from the "new ague". He was buried at St John-at-Minster in the Isle of Sheppey.

1570 – Death of Francis Mallett, Dean of Lincoln, at Normanton, Yorkshire. During Edward VI's reign, Mallett was the principal chaplain and almoner of Princess Mary, the future Mary I, and was imprisoned in the Tower of London for celebrating mass at Beaulieu before Mary arrived there. He was made Dean of Lincoln by Mary I, who also made him Lord High Almoner.

1591 – Burial of Sir Christopher Hatton, courtier, politician and favourite of Elizabeth I, at St Paul's Cathedral.

17TH DECEMBER

1538 – Pope Paul III announced the excommunication of Henry VIII.

1550 – Birth of Henry Cavendish, soldier, traveller and son of Bess of Hardwick and Sir William Cavendish. He was married to Grace Talbot, daughter of George Talbot, 6th Earl of Shrewsbury. This match was arranged by his mother who had married the Earl of Shrewsbury.

1559 – Matthew Parker was consecrated as Elizabeth I's Archbishop of Canterbury. According to "The Correspondence of Matthew Parker", Anne Boleyn charged him with the care of Elizabeth when she saw him in April 1536, "not six days before her apprehension". Historian Eric Ives writes that this was a request that Parker never forgot, and something which stayed with him for ever. Parker obviously came to be important to Elizabeth, because she made him her Archbishop of Canterbury in 1559. It was a post which Parker admitted to Lord Burghley, he would not have accepted if he "had not been so much bound to the mother". Parker was Archbishop until his death in 1575.

18TH DECEMBER

On this day in 1575, Nicholas Harpsfield, historian, Catholic apologist, priest and former Archdeacon of Canterbury, died in London. He had been released from Fleet prison four months earlier due to ill health. He and his brother, John, had been imprisoned since the early 1560s for refusing to swear the Oath of Supremacy. In Mary I's reign, he had been involved in the persecutions of Protestants, and martyrologist John Foxe described him as "the sorest and of leaste compassion" of all the archdeacons involved.

Harpsfield's works included "The life and death of Sr Thomas Moore, knight, sometymes Lord high Chancellor of England", "Cranmer's Recantacyons", "Treatise on the Pretended Divorce", *Dialogi sex contra summi pontificatus, monasticae vitae, sanctorum, sacrarum imaginum oppugnatores, et pseudomartyres* and *Historia Anglicana ecclesiastica*.

<hr/>

1555 – Burning of John Philpott, former Archdeacon of Winchester and Protestant martyr, at Smithfield. He had been imprisoned in London's coalhouse prison after writing letters to fellow Protestants to encourage them to stay strong in their faith. He was moved to the tower of St Paul's Cathedral, where he was put into solitary confinement before being condemned for heresy by Bishop Bonner.

19TH DECEMBER

On this day in 1576, Katherine Palmer, Abbess of Syon, died in Mechelen during exile in Elizabeth I's reign. Just over a month earlier, on 8th November, her convent had been broken into by a mob of Calvinists, and it is thought that confronting the mob had been too traumatic for her. She was laid to rest at Mechelen in the Church of the Augustinians.

The order later settled in Lisbon, Portugal, but returned to England in 1861. They can now be found in South Brent, Devon, and are the only surviving pre-Reformation religious community in England.

<hr/>

1562 – The *Battle of Dreux* between Catholics, led by Anne de Montmorency, and Huguenots, led by Louis I, Prince of Condé, during the first war of the *French Wars of Religion*. The Catholics were victorious, but both commanders were taken prisoner.

1578 (19th or 26th) – Executions of Egremont Radcliffe and a man called Gray at Namur in Belgium. They were beheaded in the marketplace after being suspected of poisoning Don John of Austria.

1583 – John Somerville, convicted conspirator, was found dead in his cell at Newgate Prison. Death was by strangulation, and it was said that his death was suicide. His body was buried in Moorfields, and his head was put on display on London Bridge. Somerville had been convicted of high treason for intending to shoot and kill Elizabeth I.

1587 – Death of Thomas Seckford, lawyer and administrator, at Clerkenwell in Middlesex. He was buried at Clerkenwell, but then moved to the family vault at Woodbridge in Suffolk. Seckford served Mary I as Deputy Chief Steward of the Duchy of Lancaster and Elizabeth I as Master of Requests and Steward of the Marshalsea court.

20TH DECEMBER

1541 – A "very sickly" Agnes Tilney, Dowager Duchess of Norfolk, who was imprisoned in the Tower of London after the fall of her granddaughter, Catherine Howard, begged Henry VIII for forgiveness. She also confessed to having another £800 hidden at Norfolk House.

1558 – Death of John Holyman, Bishop of Bristol and Rector of Hanborough in Oxfordshire. He was buried at Hanborough Church, in the chancel.

1559 – Burial of John Bekinsau (Beckinsau), scholar and theologian, at Sherborne St John in Hampshire. Bekinsau was the author of the 1546 tract *De supremo et absoluto regis imperio* in support of Henry VIII's supremacy.

1562 – Death of Margaret Kitson (other married name Bourchier and née Donnington), Countess of Bath. She was buried at the church in Hengrave, near Bury St Edmunds in Suffolk, which was near Hengrave Hall, the Kitson family seat. Margaret was the second wife of merchant adventurer Sir Thomas Kitson.

1571 – Death of Richard Butler, 1ˢᵗ Viscount Mountgarret and son of Piers Butler, 1ˢᵗ Earl of Ossory and 8ᵗʰ Earl of Ormond. He was buried in St Canice's Cathedral, Kilkenny city.

1583 – Execution of Edward Arden, conspirator, at Smithfield. He was hanged, drawn and quartered after being convicted of high treason for plotting with John Somerville to kill Elizabeth I. Like Somerville, his body was buried at Moorfields and his head displayed on London Bridge.

1606 – Death of Richard Reynolds (Rainolde), clergyman and author, in Essex. His work included the 1563 " A booke called the foundacion of rhetorike, because all other partes of rhetorike are grounded thereupon" and " A chronicle of all the noble emperours of the Romaines ... setting forth the great power, and devine providence of almighty God, in preserving the godly princes and common wealthes" (1571).

21ST DECEMBER

On this day in 1549, Marguerite of Navarre (also known as Margaret of Navarre, Marguerite of Angoulême and Marguerite de France) died in Odos in France at the age of fifty-seven.

Marguerite was the daughter of Louise of Savoy and Charles of Orléans, Count of Angoulême. Her mother, Louise, brought up her two children, Marguerite and her younger brother Francis, together, giving both of them an excellent Renaissance education, but, according to Millicent Garrett Fawcett, Marguerite soon outstripped her brother "in her knowledge of Greek, Latin and Hebrew, and in her easy grasp of modern languages." But it wasn't just education that Marguerite was passionate about. She also had "genuine religious fervour" and was passionate about the New Religion. As well as being known for her patronage of the arts, Marguerite is also known for her work "Le miroir l'âme pécheresse", the same poem which Anne Boleyn's daughter, Elizabeth, later translated as a gift for her stepmother, Catherine Parr. This wonderful literary work is a mystical poem which combines evangelical protestant ideas with Marguerite's idea of her relationship with God as a very personal and familial one. In her poem, Marguerite sees God as her brother, father or lover.

Although Marguerite's work was condemned as heresy, Margaret never left the Catholic Church. She had a true faith, was an advocate "new learning" and was passionate about reform, but within the church.

***

1495 – Death of Jasper Tudor, 1st Duke of Bedford and 1st Earl of Pembroke, at Thornbury. He was laid to rest at Keynsham Abbey, near Bristol. Jasper was the second son of Owen Tudor and Catherine of Valois, half-brother of Henry VI and uncle of Henry VII. It was alleged that he had an illegitimate daughter, Helen or Ellen, who was the mother of Stephen Gardiner, Bishop of Winchester.

1505 – Birth of Thomas Wriothesley, 1st Earl of Southampton, Lord Privy Seal and Lord Chancellor to Henry VIII. He was the eldest son of William Wriothesley, York herald, and his wife, Agnes, and cousin of Charles Wriothesley, the Tudor chronicler.

1539 – Death of Sir John Shelton, uncle (by marriage) of Queen Anne Boleyn and Controller of the Joint Household of Mary and Elizabeth, Henry VIII's daughters from July 1536. He was buried at Shelton Church in Norfolk, in the chancel.

1540 (or 1542) – Birth of Thomas Allen, mathematician, astrologer and antiquary, at Uttoxeter in Staffordshire. Allen is known for his knowledge of mathematics, history and antiquity, astronomy and astrology, and philosophy. He served as Robert Dudley, Earl of Leicester's astrologer and the horoscope he cast for poet Philip Sidney can be found in the Bodleian Library's Ashmole manuscripts. His links with John

Dee, Thomas Harriot and other mathematicians, combined with his knowledge of astrology, led to him being labelled a necromancer or magician.

1584 – Probable date for the death of John Herd, physician, author and Rector of Waddington. He was buried at Waddington. Herd had acted as Physician to Archbishop Thomas Cranmer from c.1551 until August 1555. Herd wrote a verse history of England, covering the period 1461-1509, and was also said to have written a catechism of Christian doctrine for the young.

1598 – Death of Thomas Owen, judge and member of Parliament. He was buried at Westminster Abbey. Owen served Elizabeth I as Serjeant-at-Law, Queen's Serjeant and Judge of the Court of Common Pleas.

1608 – Death of William Davison, diplomat and administrator, at Stepney. He was buried there, in St Dunstan's Church. Davison served Elizabeth I as a diplomat, carrying out embassies to the Netherlands and Scotland, and as secretary. He is mainly known for his role in the execution of Mary, Queen of Scots. Davison claimed that Elizabeth I signed Mary's death warrant and told him that she wished the execution to take place in the Great Hall of Fotheringhay Castle without delay. As instructed, Davison asked Sir Christopher Hatton, the acting Lord Chancellor, to seal the warrant with the Great Seal of England to validate it. Elizabeth, on the other hand, claimed that she had signed the warrant and then asked Davison not to disclose this fact to anyone. When she learned that it had been sealed with the Great Seal, she then asked Davison to swear on his life that he would not let the warrant out of his hands unless he had permission from her. After Mary's execution, the poor Davison was arrested, tried and sentenced to imprisonment in the Tower, and heavily fined.

22ND DECEMBER

On this day in 1541, members of the Howard and Tilney family, plus their staff, were indicted for misprision of treason for covering up the "unlawful, carnal, voluptuous, and licentious life" of Queen Catherine Howard while she lived with the Dowager Duchess of Norfolk at Lambeth.

The people listed in the trial documents in the "Baga de Secretis" included Lord William Howard and his wife, Margaret; Katherine Tilney, Alice Restwold, Joan Bulmer, Anne Howard, Robert Damporte, Malena Tilney, Margaret Benett, Edward Waldegrave and William Ashby. They were all found guilty and sentenced to "perpetual imprisonment and loss of goods". The ill and aged Dowager Duchess was named, but not tried.

1480 – Baptism of Sir Edward Chamberlayne, soldier, a leading member of Oxfordshire gentry and Commissioner of the Peace for Oxfordshire (1506-1539) at Weston in Northamptonshire.

1534 – An imprisoned John Fisher, Bishop of Rochester, wrote to Thomas Cromwell beseeching him to provide him with a shirt and sheet, neither of which he had, some food, some books "to stir his devotion more effectually" and a priest to hear his confession. He also asked Cromwell to intercede with the King and to "move" him to release Fisher from "this cold and painful imprisonment". Fisher had been imprisoned for denying the King's supremacy.

1545 – Birth of George Bannatyne, compiler of the "Bannatyne Manuscript", at Edinburgh. The "Bannatyne Manuscript" is an anthology of Scots literature and included poems by Bannatyne, Alexander Montgomerie, Alexander Scott, David Lyndsay, William Dunbar, Robert Henryson and King James I.

1557 – Burnings of John Rough and Margaret Mearing, Protestant martyrs, at Smithfield for heresy.

1558 (22nd or 28th) – Death of John Christopherson, Bishop of Chichester. He was buried at Christchurch, Newgate Street. He had been put under house arrest following his definition of Protestantism as "a new invention of new men and heresies" on 27th November 1558, preached in response to a sermon at Paul's Cross.

23RD DECEMBER

1513 – Birth of Sir Thomas Smith, scholar, humanist, colonialist diplomat (in Ireland) and political theorist, at Saffron Walden, Essex. He was the second son of sheep farmer, John Smith, and studied at Cambridge University and also in France and Italy. He served Edward VI as a Secretary of State, and was one of Elizabeth I's most trusted counsellors. He served her as a diplomat, Secretary of State and Chancellor of the Order of the Garter. Smith was the author of "De Republica Anglorum; the Manner of Government or Policie of the Realme of England" and "The Discourse of the Commonweal".

1556 – Burial of Nicholas Udall (Yevedale), schoolmaster, cleric, humanist and playwright, at St Margaret's, Westminster. His play "Ralph Roister Doister", which combined Latin comedy and English tradition, is regarded as the first English language comedy. He played a part in Anne Boleyn's coronation in 1533, composing verses for the pageant, and in 1534 he published his Latin text book, "Floures for Latine Spekynge". In 1541, Udall was imprisoned for a few months at Marshalsea after committing buggery with his pupil Thomas Cheney, but he was back in favour enough the next year to be leading a group of scholars in translating "The Paraphrase of Erasmus upon the New Testament" for Queen Catherine Parr.

Udall's other works included translations of Erasmus's "Apophthegms", Pietro Martire's "Discourse on the Eucharist" and Thomas Gemini's "Anatomia", and the play "Respublica".

1558 – Queen Elizabeth I moved from Somerset House to Whitehall Palace, which became her principal residence.

1558 – Death of Sir John Baker, administrator, Speaker of the House of Commons, Chancellor of the Exchequer and Under-Treasurer of England, in London. He was buried in Cranbrook Church in Kent.

1559 – Death of Henry Morgan, Bishop of St David's, at Wolvercote in Oxfordshire. He had been deprived of his bishopric after Elizabeth I's accession because of his refusal to accept the religious changes of her reign. He was buried at Wolvercote.

1568 – Roger Ascham, scholar and royal tutor, was taken ill, probably with malaria. He died on 30th December.

1588 – The assassination of Henri de Lorraine, 3rd Duke of Guise and founder of the Catholic League, at the Château de Blois. He was killed by King Henry III's bodyguards, "the Forty-five", in front of the King. His brother, Louis II, Cardinal of Guise, was assassinated the following day. The League had been controlling France, and the King was forced to act against it.

1599 – Burial of Thomas Byng, civil lawyer, Regius Professor of the Civil Law at Cambridge and Master of Clare College, Cambridge. He was buried in Hackney Church, Middlesex.

1607 – Death of Sir John Fortescue, Chancellor of the Exchequer and Chancellor of the Duchy of Lancaster in Elizabeth I's reign.

24TH DECEMBER

On 24th December 1545, King Henry VIII made his final speech to Parliament. Historian Robert Hutchinson describes it as "both measured and compelling", and writes of how Henry wanted "to impart a stern message" to all of his subjects.

In this speech, Henry VIII chastised the Lords and the Commons for the divisions regarding religion, saying:

"Yet, although I with you, and you with me, be in this perfect love and concord, this friendly amity cannot continue, except you, my lords temporal, and you my lords spiritual, and you my loving subjects, study and take pains to amend one thing, which is surely amiss, and far out of order, to the which I most heartily require you; which is, that charity and concord is not among you, but discord and dissension beareth rule, in every place. St Paul saith to the Corinthians, in the thirteenth chapter, charity is gentle, charity is not envious, charity is not proud, and so forth, in the said chapter. Behold then what love and charity is amongst you, when the one calleth the other heretic and anabaptist, and he calleth him again, papist, hypocrite, and pharisee. Be these tokens of charity amongst you? Are these the signs of fraternal love between you? No, no. I assure you, that this lack of charity amongst yourselves will be the hindrance and assuaging of the fervent love between us, as I said before, except this wound be salved, and clearly made whole."

He then moved on to addressing the clergy:

"I must needs judge the fault and occasion of this discord to be partly by the negligence of you, the fathers, and preachers of the spirituality... I see and hear daily, that you of the clergy preach one against another, teach, one contrary to another, inveigh one against another, without charity or discretion. Some be too stiff in their old mumpsimus, other be too busy and curious in their new sumpsimus. Thus, all men almost be in variety and discord, and few or none do preach, truly and sincerely, the word of God, according as they ought to do. Shall I now judge you charitable persons doing this? No, no; I cannot so do. Alas! How can the poor souls live in concord, when you, preachers, sow amongst them, in your sermons, debate and discord? Of you they look for light, and you bring them to darkness. Amend these crimes, I exhort you, and set forth God's word, both by true preaching, and good example-giving, or else I, whom God hath appointed his vicar, and high minister here, will see these divisions extinct, and these enormities corrected, according to my very duty, or else I am an unprofitable servant, and an untrue officer."

He concluded by imploring them all to remember the true meaning of God's word and to treat each other like brothers, putting their differences to one side:

"I am very sorry to know and hear how unreverently that most precious jewel, the word of God, is disputed, rhymed, sung, and jangled in every alehouse and tavern, contrary to the true meaning and doctrine of the same; and yet I am even as much sorry that the readers of the same follow it, in doing, so faintly and coldly. For of this I am sure, that charity was never so faint amongst you, and virtuous and godly living was never less used, nor was God himself, amongst christians, never less reverenced, honoured, or served. Therefore, as I said before, be in charity one with another, like brother and brother; love, dread, and serve God (to the which I, as your supreme head, and sovereign lord, exhort and require you); and then I doubt not, but that love and league, which I spoke of in the beginning, shall never be dissolved or broken between us. And, as touching the laws which be now made and concluded, I exhort you, the makers, to be as diligent in putting them into execution, as you were in making and furthering the same, or else your labour shall be in vain, and your commonwealth nothing relieved."

1604 – Death of Sir Thomas Cornwallis, Comptroller of the household of Mary I and member of Parliament, at the age of eighty-six. He was buried at Brome in Suffolk. Cornwallis was active in putting down *Kett's Rebellion* in 1549 and in 1553, after originally proclaiming Lady Jane Grey as Queen in Ipswich, he swapped sides and swore allegiance to Mary I.

25TH DECEMBER

Christmas Day in Tudor times was an end to the fasting of Advent, the four weeks leading up to Christmas, a time when Tudor people were not allowed to eat eggs, cheese or meat. On Christmas Day, the festive celebrations began early with a mass before dawn and then two further masses later in the day. Church congregations held lighted tapers as the genealogy of Christ was sung, and then they went home to enjoy a well-deserved Christmas Day feast.

Henry VIII was one of the first people to have turkey as part of his Christmas feast, after the bird was introduced into Britain in the 1520s. It soon became a popular meat, but such feasting was only enjoyed by those of high society, and not by the masses. The famous Tudor Christmas Pie was a coffin shaped pie crust containing a turkey stuffed with a goose, which was stuffed with a chicken, which was stuffed with a partridge, which was stuffed with a pigeon. If that's not enough, the pie was often served with hare, game birds and wild fowl.

The Lord of Misrule was a popular part of Tudor Christmas traditions and involved a commoner playing the "Lord of Misrule" and supervising entertainments, drinking and revelry, and, in general, causing chaos.

Henry VII loved the tradition and had a Lord of Misrule and an Abbot of Unreason, and it seems that his son, Henry VIII, enjoyed the tradition too, because not only did he appoint a Lord of Misrule for his own court, but also for Princess Mary's household in 1525. During Edward VI's reign, the Duke of Northumberland is known to have spent a huge amount of money on the tradition, but neither Mary I or Elizabeth I kept it.

∞∞∞∞∞∞∞∞∞∞∞∞∞∞∞∞∞∞∞∞∞∞∞∞∞∞∞∞

1549 – Death of Stephen Vaughan, merchant, merchant adventurer, diplomat and administrator, in London. He was buried at London's St Mary-le-Bow. Vaughan served Sir Thomas Cromwell as a diplomat between 1524 and 1539, and moved into Henry VIII's service on Cromwell's fall. He acted as the King's Chief Financial Agent in the Netherlands from 1544 to 1546, and became Under-Treasurer of the Tower of London Mint in 1544.

1553 – Birth of Thomas Thomas, Puritan printer and lexicographer, in London. He became the printer of Cambridge University in 1583, and concentrated on printing Protestant theology and education works. He is known for his Latin dictionary.

1569 (25th or 26th) – Killing of Sir John Borthwick, soldier, diplomat and Protestant, near Bewcastle in Cumberland. He was killed by the Forster family as he was fighting on the side of James Stewart, 1ˢᵗ Earl of Moray and the Regent, against Mary, Queen of Scots's forces. Borthwick had served Edward VI as a diplomat, Elizabeth I as a military commander and Mary, Queen of Scots as a diplomat.

1587 – Death of Brian Darcy, magistrate, Sheriff of Essex, witch-hunter and contributor to the 1582 "A true and just recorde of the information, examination and confession of all the witches, taken at S. Oses". "A true and just recorde" argued for harsher punishments for those found guilty of witchcraft.

1596 – Death of Sir Henry Curwen, member of Parliament, Justice of the Peace and Sheriff. He served Edward VI, Mary I and Elizabeth I loyally.

1634 – Death of Lettice Blount (née Knollys, other married names: Devereux and Dudley) at the age of ninety-one. Lettice died at her home at Drayton Bassett and was buried beside her second husband, Sir Robert Dudley, Earl of Leicester, in the Beauchamp Chapel of St Mary's Church, Warwick.

26TH DECEMBER

On this day in 1546, Henry VIII made some changes to his will, a document which had been prepared two years earlier. These changes were made to ensure successful transfer of royal authority to his son, the future Edward VI, and to prepare for Edward reigning during his minority.

The changes included:

- Changes to proposed titles and grants – For example, Edward Seymour was originally meant to be Duke of Hertford and his son Earl of Wiltshire, but Paget changed it to "duke of Somerset or Exeter or Hertford and his soonne erle of Wiltshire if he be duke of Hertford." There were also cancelled earldoms which affected John, Lord Russell, and William Paulet, and a cancelled barony for Sir Thomas Arundel.

- Confirmation of those men who would form a council to advise his son Edward during his minority.

- The addition of the Suffolk line, the offspring of Henry VIII's sister, Mary Tudor, as heirs after Henry's own children.

These changes were made by William Paget, on Henry's behalf, and then Henry signed the will on 30th December 1546.

1526 – Birth of Rose Throckmorton (née Lok, other married name: Hickman), Protestant and businesswoman, in London. She was the third child of Sir William Lok, a mercer who had also served Henry VIII as a gentleman usher. Rose was married twice: to merchant Anthony Hickman and to Simon Throckmorton of Brampton.

1545 – Death of Sir George Bowes, soldier, rebel and Captain of Norham Castle. He was buried at Alnwick. Bowes was a member of the rebel army during the 1536 *Pilgrimage of Grace*, but the patronage of his uncle, Sir Robert Bowes, protected him. He fought in the 1542 *Anglo-Scottish War* and in the 1544 expedition. He was granted the Barony of Coldingham as a reward for seizing Coldingham Priory on November 1544, but was then taken prisoner in January 1545 and lost the barony.

TWELVE DAYS OF CHRISTMAS

During the Twelve Days of Christmas, which started on Christmas Day, work for those who worked on the land would stop and spinners were banned from spinning. Work would not start again until Plough Monday, the first Monday after Twelfth Night. The Twelve Days of Christmas were a time for communities to come together and celebrate. People would visit their neighbours and friends and enjoy the Christmas "minced pye" which would contain thirteen ingredients, to symbolise Jesus and his apostles.

The mince pie would be rectangular, or crib shaped, rather than our present day round ones, and would be a minced meat pie rather than containing just dried fruit and suet. A cookbook dating back to around 1545 gave the following instructions:-

"To make Pyes – Pyes of mutton or beif must be fyne mynced and ceasoned wyth pepper and salte, and a lyttle saffron to coloure it, suet or marrow a good quantite, a lyttle vyneger, prumes, greate raysins and dates, take thefattest of the broathe of powdred beyfe, and yf you wyll have paest royall, take butter and yolkes of egges and so tempre the flowre to make the paeste".

The mutton in the pie symbolised the shepherds to whom the Angel Gabriel appeared.

On Christmas Eve, a log known as the Yule log was brought into the home. It was decorated with ribbons and then lit and kept burning through the twelve days of Christmas. It is thought that this tradition had its roots in the midwinter rituals of the early Vikings who built huge bonfires for their festival of light. People thought it was lucky to keep some charred remains of the Yule log to light the next year's Yule log.

The chocolate Yule Logs that we see in the shops at Christmas time are a reminder of this old tradition.

27TH DECEMBER

On 27th December 1539, Anne of Cleves landed at Deal in Kent. Anne was to be Henry VIII's fourth wife and their marriage was agreed upon by a treaty in September 1539. Henry had never laid eyes on Anne but instead, had commissioned his court artist, Hans Holbein, to paint her. The portrait was described as a good likeness of Anne and Henry was happy to commit to the marriage, which would see England forming an alliance with the *Schmalkaldic League*.

When Anne of Cleves landed at Deal at 5pm on 27th December 1539, she was met by Sir Thomas Cheyne and taken to Deal Castle to rest after her long journey. There, she was visited by the Duke of Suffolk and his wife, Catherine

Willoughby, the Bishop of Chichester and various knights and ladies. She was informed that she would be meeting the King, her future husband, at Greenwich Palace at a formal reception in a few days time, but she was to be taken by surprise.

On New Year's Day 1540, while Anne was resting at Rochester before travelling on to London, an excited Henry VIII turned up. Henry, the impatient and hopeless romantic, just couldn't wait for his bride to arrive in London and was desperate to see the woman from the portrait, so he decided to follow the chivalric tradition of meeting his future bride in disguise. Tradition said that the love between them would be so strong that Anne would see through his disguise and recognise her future husband. However, as historian Elizabeth Norton points out, Henry should have learned from the disastrous meeting between his great-uncle, Henry VI, and his bride, Margaret of Anjou.

Henry VIII arrived at Rochester on 1st January 1540 and sent his attendant, Sir Anthony Browne, ahead of him to tell Anne that he had been sent by the King with a New Year's gift for her. Browne told Anne and then Henry, in disguise as a lowly servant, entered the room. Anne was not paying much attention to this servant, as she was watching bull-baiting out of the window, so Henry pulled her towards him in an embrace and tried to kiss her. Anne was obviously shocked at such behaviour from a servant, so obviously did not respond to his advances and Henry's dreams of her seeing through his disguise and falling into his arms lay shattered. The meeting was a complete disaster and the King was humiliated. It was not a good start, and Henry decided he did not want to marry this woman. Unfortunately, there was nothing that could be done without offending Anne's brother, the Duke of Cleves, so the marriage went ahead, but only lasted until July 1540, just 6 months. Anne of Cleves was lucky. She kept her head, was given a generous settlement and was allowed to continue seeing Henry's children. She became known as "The King's Sister".

1583 – Death of Katherine Killigrew (née Cooke), scholar and Puritan, after giving birth to a stillborn child. She was buried at St Thomas the Apostle Church in London. Katherine was the daughter of scholar and royal tutor Sir Anthony Cooke, and the wife of diplomat Sir Henry Killigrew. She was known for her ability at writing poetry and her knowledge of languages, including Hebrew, Latin and Greek.

1530 – Death of Thomas Lupset, clergyman and humanist scholar, at Bisham from tuberculosis. He was buried in St Alfege Church, Cripplegate. Lupset joined the household of John Colet in his youth and was taught by William Lilye before attending Pembroke Hall, Cambridge, where he worked with Erasmus on the "New Testament". Lupset tutored Cardinal Wolsey's son, Thomas Wynter, and was friends with Thomas More, Reginald Pole and John Leland. His works included "Exhortacion to Young Men", "A Treatise of Charitie" and "Dieyng Well".

1603 – Death of Thomas Cartwright, theologian, Puritan and Master of the Earl of Leicester's Hospital in Warwick. He spent his last days in Warwick and was buried there. Cartwright is known for the struggle between him and John Whitgift, the man who deprived Cartwright of his position as Lady Margaret's Professor of Divinity at Cambridge. Cartwright supported the attack on the Elizabethan church in the form of "An Admonition to the Parliament" by preachers John Field and Thomas Wilcox. Whitgift answered with "Answere to a Certan Libel Intituled, 'An Admonition'", Cartwright replied with "Replye", Whitgift answered again with "The Defense of the Aunswere to the 'Admonition', Against the 'Replie'" and Cartwright responded with "The Second Replie" and "The Rest of the Second Replie".

1615 – Death of John Fenn, Roman Catholic priest and translator. He was buried in the cloister of St Monica's English Augustinian monastery in Louvain, where he was chaplain. Fenn had settled in Louvain while in exile during Elizabeth I's reign. His works included an English translation of Bishop Osorius's treatise against Walter Haddon: "A Learned and Very Eloquent Treatie, Written in Latin", translations of works by John Fisher, Bishop of Rochester, and the Council of Trent's catechism, and *Concertatio ecclesiae catholicae in Anglia*, which he co-edited with John Gibbons, a Jesuit.

28TH DECEMBER

The 28th December was Holy Innocents' Day or *Childermas*. This feast day commemorated the massacre of baby boys which King Herod ordered in Bethlehem, in an attempt to kill the infant Jesus Christ. The innocent babies were seen by the Catholic Church as the very first martyrs.

1510 – Birth of Sir Nicholas Bacon, lawyer, administrator and Lord Keeper of the Great Seal in Elizabeth I's reign. He was the second son of Robert Bacon, yeoman and sheep-reeve (chief shepherd), and his wife Isabel Cage, and he was the father of the famous philosopher, statesman, scientist and author, Sir Francis Bacon.

1572 – Death of John Hales, member of Parliament, writer and administrator. He was buried in St Peter-le-Poer Church, Broad Street, London. Hales served as Clerk of the Hanaper, a Justice of the Peace and member of Parliament.

1582 – Burial of goldsmith John Mabb at St Matthew Church, Friday Street, off Cheapside in London. Mabb was also Chamberlain of the City of London.

1603 – Death of John Joscelin (Joscelyn), clergyman, antiquary and Old English scholar, at High Roding. He was buried at All Saints' Church, High Roding. Joscelin was Latin secretary to Matthew Parker, Archbishop of Canterbury, and is known for his Old English-Latin dictionary and the work he did for Parker in discovering and publishing lost manuscripts.

29TH DECEMBER

1494 – Death of William Selling (Celling), Prior of Christ Church, Canterbury, diplomat and humanist scholar. He was buried at Canterbury Cathedral, in the martyrium of Thomas Becket.

1605 – Burial of George Clifford, 3rd Earl of Cumberland, courtier, naval commander and Elizabeth I's champion, at Holy Trinity Church, Skipton, Yorkshire.

1605 – Death of Arthur Hall, member of Parliament, courtier and translator. He was buried at Grantham in Lincolnshire. Hall is known for his 1581 "Ten Books of Homer's Iliades, translated out of French", the first English translation of Homer's Iliad. Hall was imprisoned at various times on account of debt and works he published, which were either libellous or offensive. He may even have been in prison for debt at his death.

1606 (29th or 30th) – Death of John Davis (Davys), navigator and explorer, near Bintang, off the coast of Borneo. His ship, *The Tiger*, was attacked by Japanese pirates who killed Davis in hand-to-hand combat. Davis was one of the main Elizabethan navigators and explorers, and the Davis Strait in the Northwest Passage is named after him. He is also known for being the first Englishman to document a sighting of the Falkland Islands. Davis also wrote the 1594 "The Seaman's Secrets" and "The World's Hydrographical Description" (1595).

30TH DECEMBER

On this day in 1568, scholar and royal tutor, Roger Ascham, died after being taken ill on 23rd December. Ascham had suffered from ill health throughout his life, and this was probably down to him contracting malaria. He was buried on 4th January 1569 on the north side of St Sepulchre without Newgate, London, in the St Stephen's chapel.

In 1548, Princess Elizabeth, daughter of Henry VIII, insisted that Ascham become her tutor after the death of William Grindal from the plague. According to his biographer Rosemary O'Day, Ascham "contrived a classical and Christian curriculum for the princess that was designed to equip her for a leading role in the state", and used his pioneering language teaching method on her, double translation. He wrote about this method in "The Scholemaster", his famous and influential treatise on education. He carried on tutoring Princess Elizabeth during Mary I's reign, and was impressed by the Princess' intelligence, her language skills and her "political understanding".

In 1550, Ascham served as secretary to Sir Richard Morison, ambassador to the Imperial court, and travelled to Germany. While travelling on the continent, he was appointed as Edward VI's Latin secretary, a post which he was also given during Mary I's reign after his return to England, and also in Elizabeth I's reign.

In "The Scholemaster", he wrote of visiting Lady Jane Grey at her home, Bradgate. He found her in her room reading Plato while the rest of the family were hunting, and she allegedly told him of the ill treatment she suffered from her parents: "For when I am in presence either of father or mother, whether I spekee, kepe silence, sit, stand, or go, eate, drinke, be merie, or sad, be sowying, plaiying, dauncing, or doing anything els: I must do it, as it were, in soch weight, measure, and number, even as perfectlie as God made the world; or els I am so sharplie taunted, so cruellie threatened, yea presentlie some tymes with pinches, nippes and bobbes, and other waies I will not name for the honour I beare them, so without measure misordered, that I thinke myself in hell, till tyme cum that I must go to Mister Elmer, who teacheth me so jentlie, so pleasantlie, with soch faire allurements to lerning, that I think all the tyme nothing, whiles I am with him." These words have been used by authors and historians to brand the Greys as abusive parents, and Lady Jane Grey as a misunderstood intellectual and victim.

Ascham is also known for his book *Toxophilus*, the first English book on archery, which he dedicated to Henry VIII, a keen archer.

<hr>

1494 – Death of John Russell, Bishop of Lincoln, Keeper of the Privy Seal, Lord Chancellor under Edward IV and Richard III, and Chancellor of Oxford University. He died at his episcopal manor in Nettleham, Lincolnshire, and was buried in Lincoln Cathedral.

1546 – Henry VIII signed his last will and testament, authorising the changes which he had ordered to be made by William Paget on 26th December.

1552 – Death of Francisco de Enzinas (humanist name Francis Dryander), Spanish humanist scholar, translator, author and Protestant apologist, at Strasbourg from the plague. He was buried there the next day. He had been a member of the household of Katherine Brandon, Duchess of Suffolk, for a time, possibly teaching her son Charles, and Archbishop Cranmer paid him as a Greek Reader. While he was at Cambridge, in the late 1540s, Enzinas translated various ancient texts into Spanish before travelling to the Continent in 1549 to set up a publishing house in Strasbourg. There, he published at least nine classical and Biblical translations.

1553 – Death of Roger Barlow, Vice-Admiral of the Pembrokeshire coast and brother of William Barlow, Bishop of Chichester, at Slebech.

1594 – Death of Sir Thomas Scott, member of Parliament and Deputy Lieutenant of Kent. He was buried at Brabourne Church in Kent, but moved to the chapel of Scot's Hall, the family home in Smeeth, after the Civil War. Scott was also a Justice of the Peace, Commissioner of Piracy, Commissioner of Coastal Defence, Commissioner of Grain and Colonel-General of his county's forces during the *Spanish Armada*. He was also a keen horse breeder.

1600 – Death of Michael Heneage, member of Parliament, devout Protestant, archivist and antiquary, at Hoxton in Essex. He and his brother Thomas served as Joint Keepers of the Records in the Tower of London from 1576, and he also helped Robert Hare, Compiler of Cambridge University's records. Heneage delivered two papers, "of the Antiquity of Arms in England" and "of Sterling Money", while he was a member of the Society of Antiquaries, and he also compiled "Collections out of various Charters, &c., relating to the Noble Families in England".

31ST DECEMBER

1535 – Death of Sir William Skeffington, known as "the Gunner", Lord Deputy of Ireland, at Kilmainham in Dublin. He was buried at St Patrick's Cathedral in the city. His nickname, "the Gunner", came from his use of heavy artillery while taking Maynooth Castle in County Kildare. He killed, or had executed, the whole garrison there.

1559 – Death of Owen Oglethorpe, Bishop of Carlisle, while under house arrest in London. He was buried at St Dunstan-in-the-West. He had been deprived of his bishopric due to his

Catholic faith, and had angered Elizabeth I by elevating the host on Christmas Day 1558.

1564 – Death of Edward North, 1st Baron North, administrator, at the London Charterhouse, which he had acquired in 1545. North served Henry VIII as Treasurer of the Court of Augmentations, Chancellor of the reformed Court of Augmentations and executor of his will. In Edward VI's reign, he was a Privy Councillor but lost this position in Mary I's reign. His Charterhouse was used as lodgings for Elizabeth I and her court for a few days following her accession, and she appointed him Lord Lieutenant of Cambridgeshire. North was buried at Kirtling, in the family vault.

1600 – The East India Company, or "Company of Merchants of London trading into the East Indies", was chartered, i.e. given royal approval, by Queen Elizabeth I.

The Gift of a Review

I hope that you enjoyed **On This Day in Tudor History** as much as I enjoyed researching and putting it together.

Now you've finished the book, the best thing you can do to help others to discover more about the Tudors is to add a review with the book store where you bought the book.

Thank you so much for sharing in my passion for Tudor history, and thank you for the gift of your review.

Claire Ridgway.

ABOUT THE AUTHOR

Claire Ridgway is the author of many best-selling Tudor history books *The Fall of Anne Boleyn: A Countdown*, *The Anne Boleyn Collection I*, *The Anne Boleyn Collection II*, *Tudor Places of Great Britain,* and *Illustrated Kings and Queens of Great Britain*

Claire worked in education and freelance writing before creating The Anne Boleyn Files history website and becoming a full-time history researcher, blogger and author. The Anne Boleyn Files is known for its historical accuracy and Claire's mission to get to the truth behind Anne Boleyn's story. Her writing is easy-to-read and conversational, and readers often comment on how reading Claire's books is like having a coffee with her and chatting about history.

Claire loves connecting with Tudor history fans and can be contacted via the contact form or by email at claire@theanneboleynfiles.com

To find her on the web, please visit:
www.theanneboleynfiles.com
Twitter – @anneboleynfiles
Facebook – theanneboleynfiles

BIBLIOGRAPHY

Ashton, John. A history of English lotteries Now for the first time written By John Ashton. The Leadenhall Press, 1893.

Baldwin Smith, Lacey. Catherine Howard: The Queen Whose Adulteries Made a Fool of Henry VIII. Amberley Publishing, 2009.

Bayntun History website - http://bitly.com/Yknzlo

Bell, Doyne C. Notices of the Historic Persons Buried in the Chapel of St Peter Ad Vincula in the Tower of London, 1877.

Bernard, G. W. The King's Reformation: Henry VIII and the Remaking of the English Church. Yale University Press, 2007.

Bruce, J, and T. T. Perowne (ed.) Correspondence of Matthew Parker. Parker Society, 1853.

Bullein, William. A dialogue against the fever pestilence. 1573

Burnet, Gilbert. The History of the Reformation of the Church of England. 7 vols. Clarendon Press,

Burton, Alfred. Rush-bearing: an account of the old custom of strewing rushes; carrying rushes to church; the rush-cart; garlands in churches; morris-dancers; the wakes; the rush (1891).

Bush, M. L. The Pilgrimage of Grace: A Study of the Rebel Armies of October 1536. Manchester University Press, 1996.

Calendar of State Papers Foreign, Elizabeth.

Calendar of State Papers, Spain.

Calendar of the Manuscripts of the Marquis of Bath Preserved at Longleat, Wiltshire Volume II

Childs, Jessie. Henry VIII's Last Victim: The Life and Times of Henry Howard, Earl of Surrey. Jonathan Cape, 2006.

Cornwall Information - http://bitly.com/bOAucc

Cox, Rev. John Edmund (ed.) Miscellaneous writings and letters of Thomas Cranmer.

Cressy, David. Travesties and transgressions in Tudor and Stuart England: Tales of Discord. Oxford University Press, 2000.

Devon Perspectives - http://bit.ly/TlON5V

Dodd, Charles. Dodd's Church History of England from the Commencement of the Sixteenth Century to the Revolution in 1688 (Volume I) 1839.

Doran, Susan. Henry VIII: Man and Monarch. British Library, 2009.

Elizabeth I, Queen of England and Ireland, 1533-1603 (Ipswich, Suffolk, England) to unknown addressee, Bodleian Library, University of Oxford, MS Smith 69 fols. 109-110. 9 Aug 1561.

Exeter Memories - http://bit.ly/Rrrviw

Fox (Foxe), John. Fox's Book of Martyrs: Acts and Monuments of the Church in Three Volumes. Vol. II. London: George Virtue, 1851.

Fox, Julia. Jane Boleyn: The Infamous Lady Rochford. Phoenix, 2008

'Friaries: The observant friars of Greenwich', A History of the County of Kent: Volume 2 (1926), pp. 194-198. http://bit.ly/Svl4uG

Guy, John. My Heart is My Own: The Life of Mary Queen of Scots. Harper Perennial, 2004.

Hall, Edward. Hall's Chronicle. London: J Johnson, 1809.

Harpsfield, Nicholas. A Treatise on the Pretended Divorce between Henry VIII and Catharine of Aragon.

Hartweg, Christine. "John Dudley the Family Man" http://bit.ly/TlOVlI

Herbert, Edward. The Life and Raigne of King Henry the Eighth. London, 1649.

Howell, T.B. A Complete Collection of State Trials and Proceedings for High Treason and Other Crimes and Misdemeanors. Forgotten Books, 2012.

Hoyle, R W. "The Origins of the Dissolution of the Monasteries." Historical Journal 38 (1995): 275–305.

Hume, Martin Andrew Sharp. Chronicle of King Henry VIII. of England: Being a Contemporary Record of Some of the Principal Events of the Reigns of Henry VIII. and Edward VI. Written in Spanish by an Unknown Hand. G. Bell and sons, 1889. (Spanish Chronicle)

Hutchinson, Robert. The Last Days of Henry VIII. Phoenix, 2006.

Hutchinson, Robert. Thomas Cromwell: The Rise and Fall of Henry VIII's Most Notorious Minister. Weidenfeld & Nicolson, 2007.

Ives, Eric. Lady Jane Grey: A Tudor Mystery. Wiley Blackwell, 2009

Ives, Eric. The Life and Death of Anne Boleyn. New ed. Wiley-Blackwell, 2005.

Jenkyns, ed. Rev. Henry. The Remains of Thomas Cranmer. Vol. I. Oxford University Press, 1833.

Jones, Philippa. The Other Tudors: Henry VIII's Mistresses and Bastards. New Holland Publishers Ltd, 2009.

Knox, John. Selected Writings of John Knox: Public Epistles, Treatises, and Expositions to the Year 1559

Letters and Papers, Foreign and Domestic, Henry VIII.

Lewycky, Nadine. The City of York in the Time of Henry VIII - http://bit.ly/UeJnuh

Lipscomb, Suzannah. Henry VIII: The Year that Changed Henry VIII. Lion UK, 2009.

de Lisle, Leanda. The Sisters Who Would Be Queen. Ballantine Books, 2009.

Lisle Letters, The. Edited by Muriel St. Clare Byrne. University of Chicago Press, 1981

Loades, David. Mary Tudor. Amberley Publishing, 2011.

MacCulloch, Diarmaid. Thomas Cranmer: A Life. Yale University Press, 1998.

Magee, John and Angela. Bishop John Jewel (1522-1571) – An article by John and Angela Magee from the Emmanuel Church Salisbury website.

Marie Stuart website - http://bit.ly/Q4SXnI

Miscarriage at Lochleven, History Scotland.

Nichols, John Gough (ed.). Narratives of the Days of the Reformation, Chiefly from the Manuscripts of John Foxe the Martyrologist; with Two Contemporary Biographies of Archbishop Cranmer. Camden Society, 1859.

Noble, Graham. 'Evil May Day': Re-examining the Race Riot of 1517, History Today

Norton, Elizabeth. Anne of Cleves: Henry VIII's Discarded Bride. Amberley Publishing, 2009.

Norton, Elizabeth. Margaret Beaufort: Mother of the Tudor Dynasty. Amberley Publishing, 2011.

Oxford Dictionary of National Biography. Oxford University Press, 2004.

Penn, Thomas. Winter King: The Dawn of Tudor England. Penguin Books, 2012.

Plowden, Alison. Elizabeth I (Elizabethan Quartet Complete). The History Press, 2004.

Polito, Mary. Governmental Arts In Early Tudor England. Ashgate Pub Ltd, 2005.

Porter, Linda. Katherine the Queen: The Remarkable Life of Katherine Parr. Macmillan, 2010.

Porter, Linda. Mary Tudor: The First Queen. Piatkus, 2007.

Rex, Richard. The Tudors. Amberley Publishing, 2009.

Ridgway, Claire. The Anne Boleyn Files http://bit.ly/LcHYV

Ridgway, Claire. The Elizabeth Files http://bit.ly/Q4T4Qd

Ridgway, Claire. The Fall of Anne Boleyn, MadeGlobal Publishing 2012

Scarisbrick, J. J. Henry VIII. Methuen, 1976.

Sim, Alison. Pleasures and Pastimes in Tudor England. History Press, 2009.

Skidmore, Chris. Edward VI: The Lost King of England. Phoenix, 2007.

Starkey, David. Elizabeth: Apprenticeship. Vintage Books, 2001.

Starkey, David. Henry: Virtuous Prince. Harper Press, 2008.

Starkey, David. Six Wives: The Queens of Henry VIII. Vintage, 2004.

Stokes, George. A Brief History of the British Reformation: From the Rise of the Lollards to the Death of Queen Mary. (1799)

Stow, John. Annals of England to 1603, 1603.

Strype, John. Ecclesiastical Memorials Relating Chiefly to Religion, and the Reformation of It, and the Emergencies of the Church of England, Under King Henry VIII, King Edward VI, and Queen Mary I. Clarendon Press, Oxford, 1822.

Strype, John. The Life and Acts of Matthew Parker.

Tadghighi, Nasim on Twitter - http://bit.ly/RrrKKz

The Elizabethan Calendar - http://bit.ly/XUVZfa

The Oaten Hill Martyrs - http://bit.ly/SaTeRQ

Thomas More Studies - http://bit.ly/Ro7fLa

Thompson, Patricia. Thomas Wyatt: The Critical Heritage. Routledge, 1995.

Tremlett, Giles. Catherine of Aragon: Henry's Spanish Queen. Faber and Faber, 2010.

Warren, Nancy Bradley. Women of God and Arms: Female Spirituality and Political Conflict, 1380–1600, University of Pennsylvania Press, 2005.

Watt, Robert. Bibliotheca Britannica: Or, A General Index to British and Foreign Literature, Volume I. Archibald Constable and Company, Edinburgh, 1824.

Weir, Alison. The Lady in the Tower. Jonathan Cape, 2009

Whitelock, Anna. Mary Tudor: Princess, Bastard, Queen. Random House, 2009.

Wiltshire, Paul on Twitter - http://bit.ly/TlP7S7

Wriothesley, Charles. A Chronicle of England During the Reigns of the Tudors, from A.D. 1485 to 1559. 1875th ed. Camden Society

Visit Cumbria website - http://bit.ly/NPsaKn

ILLUSTRATIONS

Edward VI – Vintage engraving by H.T. Ryall (1811-1867), published in 1854, based on the portrait by Hans Holbein the Younger. Colour work by D. Walker.

Mary I – Vintage engraving by Henry Thomas Ryall (1811-1867), published in 1835.

Henry VIII – Vintage engraving by W.T. Fry (1789-1843) from Lodge's Portraits (1835). Photo and toning by D. Walker.

Lady Jane Grey – Vintage engraving published in an 1835 collection of portraits of famous people in English history, by Edmund Lodge (1756-1839). Digital restoration by Steven Wynn Photography.

Henry VII – Vintage engraving from 1830. Published in London by Thomas Kelly.

Elizabeth I - Vintage engraving by W. T. Fry (1789-1843), published in 1835, based on the famous Rainbow portrait by Isaac Oliver. Colour work by by D Walker.

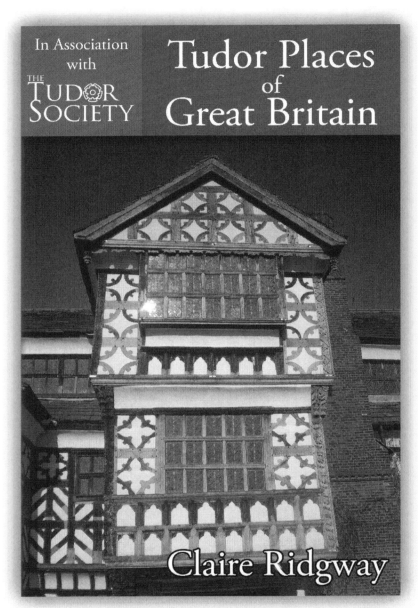

In Association with

THE TUDOR SOCIETY

Tudor Places of Great Britain

Claire Ridgway

Discover more than 170 amazing Tudor properties and castles around Great Britain. With so many stunning historic attractions to visit, you're sure to find many fascinating days out in this detailed guide.

ILLUSTRATED
KINGS AND QUEENS OF ENGLAND

CLAIRE RIDGWAY, TIMOTHY RIDGWAY, VERITY RIDGWAY

With stunning illustrations of the 59 English kings and queens from Alfred the Great to Elizabeth II, "**Illustrated Kings and Queens of England**" is packed with interesting facts about the wonderful English monarchy.

MadeGlobal Publishing

Non-Fiction History

- Jasper Tudor - **Debra Bayani**
- Tudor Places of Great Britain - **Claire Ridgway**
- Illustrated Kings and Queens of England - **Claire Ridgway**
- A History of the English Monarchy - **Gareth Russell**
- The Fall of Anne Boleyn - **Claire Ridgway**
- George Boleyn: Tudor Poet, Courtier & Diplomat - **Ridgway & Cherry**
- The Anne Boleyn Collection - **Claire Ridgway**
- The Anne Boleyn Collection II - **Claire Ridgway**
- Two Gentleman Poets at the Court of Henry VIII - **Edmond Bapst**
- A Mountain Road - **Douglas Weddell Thompson**

"History in a Nutshell Series"

- Sweating Sickness in a Nutshell - **Claire Ridgway**
- Mary Boleyn in a Nutshell - **Sarah Bryson**
- Thomas Cranmer in a Nutshell - **Beth von Staats**
- Henry VIII's Health in a Nutshell - **Kyra Kramer**
- Catherine Carey in a Nutshell - **Adrienne Dillard**

Historical Fiction

- Between Two Kings: A Novel of Anne Boleyn - **Olga Lyakina**
- Phoenix Rising - **Hunter S. Jones**
- Cor Rotto - **Adrienne Dillard**
- The Claimant - **Simon Anderson**
- The Truth of the Line - **Melanie V. Taylor**

Please Leave a Review

If you enjoyed this book, *please* leave a review at the book seller where you purchased it. There is no better way to thank the author and it really does make a huge difference! *Thank you in advance.*

Printed in Great Britain
by Amazon

66638384R10385